Air Traffic Controller

Air Traffic Controller

James W. Morrison, FAA Consultant

ARCO PUBLISHING, INC.
219 PARK AVENUE SOUTH, NEW YORK, N.Y. 10003

Photos courtesy of
Sperry Univac, a Division of Sperry Rand Corporation
Department of Transportation Federal Aviation Administration

First Edition, Second Printing, 1980
Published by Arco Publishing, Inc.
219 Park Avenue South, New York, N.Y. 10003

Library of Congress Cataloging in Publication Data

Morrison, James Warner, 1940-
Air traffic controller.

1. Air traffic control—Examinations, questions, etc. I. Title.

TL725.3.T7M674 629.136'6 78-23357
ISBN 0-668-04593-0

Printed in the United States of America

CONTENTS

Air Traffic Controller

Part I

Background To Air Traffic Control

THE FEDERAL AVIATION ADMINISTRATION

This section provides the atmosphere, gives you the surroundings of your work. The language used may be unfamiliar to you now. But if you read carefully and try to understand the context you'll get with it. And the examiners just might use this kind of language on your test. We can't be sure, but they have in the past drawn upon just such sources as these in writing up their test questions. In any case, you will be taking a long step toward those test jitters that so frequently contribute to low scores.

CREATION AND AUTHORITY. The Federal Aviation Administration, formerly the Federal Aviation Agency, became a part of the Department of Transportation in 1967 as a result of the Department of Transportation Act (80 Stat. 932).

MISSION. The Federal Aviation Administration is charged with: regulating air commerce to promote its safety and development; achieving the efficient use of the navigable airspace of the United States; promoting, encouraging, and developing civil aviation; developing and operating a common system of air traffic control and air navigation for both civilian and military aircraft; and promoting the development of a national system of airports.

ORGANIZATION. The Federal Aviation Administration functions as a single, decentralized organization. The headquarters offices conduct activities which can best be performed centrally including agencywide program planning, direction, control, and evaluation. The eight regional offices and the area offices reporting to them direct field operations within their geographic boundaries. The Aeronautical Center, Oklahoma City, Okla., and the National Aviation Facilities Experimental Center, Atlantic City, N.J., have special program responsibilities.

SAFETY REGULATION. The Administrator issues and enforces rules, regulations, and minimum standards relating to the manufacture, operation, and maintenance of aircraft as well as the rating and certification (including medical) of airmen. The agency performs flight inspection of air navigation facilities in the United States and, as required, abroad.

REGISTRATION AND RECORDATION. The agency provides a system for the registration of an aircraft's nationality, its engines, propellers, and appliances as well as a system for recording aircraft ownership.

RESEARCH AND DEVELOPMENT. The research and development activities of the agency are directed toward providing the systems, procedures, facilities, and devices needed for a safe and efficient system of air navigation and air traffic control to meet the needs of civil aviation and the air defense system. The agency is also involved in developing and testing improved aircraft, engines, propellers, and appliances.

AIR NAVIGATION FACILITIES. The agency is responsible for the location, construction or installation, maintenance, and operation of Federal visual and electronic aids to air navigation. It operates and maintains communications equipment, radio teletype circuits and equipment, and equipment at air traffic control towers and centers.

AIRSPACE AND AIR TRAFFIC MANAGEMENT. The safe and efficient utilization of the navigable airspace is a primary objective of the Federal Aviation Administration. To meet this objective, the agency operates a network of airport traffic control towers, air route traffic control centers, and flight service stations. It develops air traffic rules and regulations and allocates the use of the airspace. It also provides for the security control of air traffic to meet national defense requirements.

CIVIL AVIATION ABROAD. Under the Federal Aviation Act and the International Aviation Facilities Act of 1948, the agency promotes civil aviation abroad by the assignment of technical groups, the training of foreign nationals, and the exchange of information with foreign governments. It provides technical representation at international conferences, including participation in the International Civil Aviation Organization and other international organizations.

OTHER PROGRAMS. The FAA administers the aviation war risk insurance and aircraft loan quarantee programs. It is an allotting agency under the Defense Materials System with respect to priorities and allocation for civil aircraft and civil aviation operations. The agency develops specifications for the preparation of aeronautical charts. It publishes current information on airways and airport service and issues technical publications for the improvement of safety in flight, airport planning and design, and other aeronautical activities.

AIRPORT PLANNING AND DEVELOPMENT PROGRAMS. The Administrator administers programs to identify the type and cost of development of public airports required for a national airport system and to provide grants of funds to assist public agencies in airport system planning, airport master planning, and public airport development.

MAJOR FIELD ORGANIZATIONS—FEDERAL AVIATION ADMINISTRATION

EASTERN REGION: Delaware, District of Columbia, Maryland, New Jersey, Pennsylvania, Virginia, West Virginia.	JFK International Airport, Jamaica, N. Y. 11430.
CENTRAL REGION: Iowa, Kansas, Missouri, Nebraska	601 E. 12th St., Kansas City, Mo. 64106.
GREAT LAKES REGION: Illinois, Indiana, Minnesota, Michigan, Ohio, Wisconsin.	3166 Des Plaines Ave., Des Plaines, Ill. 60018.
NEW ENGLAND REGION: Connecticut, Maine, Massachusetts, New Hampshire, Rhode Island, Vermont.	154 Middlesex St., Burlington, Mass. 01803.
NORTHWEST REGION: Idaho, Oregon, Washington	FAA Bldg. Boeing, Seattle, Wash. 98108.
ROCKY MOUNTAIN REGION: Colorado, Montana, North Dakota, South Dakota, Utah, Wyoming.	10255 E. 25th Ave., Aurora, Colo. 80010.
SOUTHERN REGION: Alabama, Florida, Georgia, Kentucky, Mississippi, North Carolina, South Carolina, Tennessee.	P.O. Box 20636, Atlanta, Ga. 30320.
SOUTHWEST REGION: Arkansas, Louisiana, New Mexico, Oklahoma, Texas.	P.O. Box 1689, Fort Worth, Tex. 76101,
WESTERN REGION: Arizona, California, Nevada	P.O. Box 92007, Worldway Postal Center, Los Angeles, Calif. 90009.
ALASKAN REGION: ALASKA	632 Sixth Ave., Anchorage, Alaska 99501.
PACIFIC REGION: Hawaii, Pacific Ocean area west of continental United States and east of East Pakistan and India, including all free nations south and east of China.	P.O. Box 4009, Honolulu, Hawaii 96813.
EUROPE-AFRICA-MIDDLE EAST REGION: Europe-Africa, the Middle East, including all the free nations west of Burma, Iceland, Greenland, Bermuda, and the Azores.	1 Place Madou, Brussels, Belgium.
AERONAUTICAL CENTER:	P.O. Box 25082, Oklahoma City, Okla. 73125.
NATIONAL AVIATION FACILITIES EXPERIMENTAL CENTER.	Atlantic City, N.J. 08405.

[1] Certain international operating responsibilities cross regional boundaries.
[2] Assistant Administrator.

THE KIND OF WORK YOU MAY BE DOING

To make the most out of this book you should know what good your study will do you. By reading all about the field in which you will be working, you will be absorbing some of the language the examiners might use in their questions.

CIVIL AVIATION OCCUPATIONS

The rapid development of air transportation in the past two decades has increased greatly the mobility of the population and has created many thousands of job opportunities in the civil aviation industry.

Nature and Location of Civil Aviation Activities. Civil aviation activities also include the regulatory and accident investigation functions of the Federal Aviation Administration (FAA), the Civil Aeronautics Board (CAB), and the National Transportation Safety Board (NTSB)--all part of the Federal Government. The FAA develops air safety regulations, inspects and tests aircraft and airline facilities, provides ground electronic guidance equipment, and gives tests for licenses to personnel such as pilots, copilots, flight engineers, dispatchers, and aircraft mechanics. The CAB establishes policy concerning matters such as airline rates and routes. The NTSB investigates all airlines accidents and aircraft accidents involving fatalities.

The FAA employed about 65,000 people in 1978. The largest group of FAA employees worked mainly in occupations relating to the direction of airtraffic and the installation and maintenance of mechanical and electronic equipment used to control traffic. CAB workers were employed mainly in administrative and clerical jobs concerned with the economic regulation of the airlines, supervision of international air transportation matters, promotion of air safety, and investigation of accidents.

AIR TRAFFIC CONTROLLERS

Nature of the Work. Air traffic controllers are the guardians of the airways. These employees of the Federal Aviation Administration (FAA) give instructions, advice, and information to pilots by radio to avoid collisions and minimize delays as aircraft fly between airports or in the vicinity of airports. When directing aircraft, traffic controllers must consider many factors, including weather, geography, the amount of traffic, and the size, speed, and other operating characteristics of aircraft. The men who control traffic in the areas around airports are known as airport traffic controllers; those who guide aircraft between airports are called enroute traffic controllers.

Airport traffic controllers are stationed at airport control towers to give all pilots within the vicinity of the airport weather information and take-off and landing instructions such as which approach and airfield runway to use and when to change altitude. They must control simultaneously several aircraft which appear as tiny bars on a radar scope. They talk on the radio first to one and then to another of the pilots of these planes, remembering their numbers and their positions in the air, and give each of them different instructions. These workers also keep records of all messages received from aircraft and operate runway lights and other airfield electronic equipment. They also may send and receive information to and from enroute traffic control centers about flights made over the airport.

Enroute traffic controllers are stationed at air traffic control centers to coordinate the movements of aircraft which are being flown "on instruments." They use the written flight plans which are filed by pilots and dispatchers before aircraft leave the airport. To make sure that aircraft remain on course, they check the progress of flights, using radar and other electronic equipment and information received from the aircraft, other control centers and towers, and information from FAA or airline communications stations.

Training, Other Qualifications, and Advancement. Applicants for positions or airport traffic controller must be able to speak clearly and precisely. They enter the field through the competitive Federal Civil Service system after passing a rigid physical examination, which they must pass every year. Applicants must pass a written test designed to measure their ability to learn, perform the duties of air traffic controller, and meet certain experience, training, and related requirements.

Successful applicants for traffic controller jobs are given approximately 9 weeks of formal training to learn the fundamentals of the airway system, Federal Aviation Regulations, and radar and aircraft performance characteristics. After completing this training, controllers qualify for a basic air traffic control certificate. At an FAA control tower or center, they receive additional classroom instruction and on-the-job training to become familiar with specific traffic problems. Only after he has demonstrated his ability to apply procedures, and to use available equipment under pressure and stress, may he work as a controller. This usually takes about 3 years.

Controllers can advance to the job of chief controller. After this promotion, they may advance to more responsible management jobs in air traffic control and to a few top administrative jobs in the FAA.

Employment Outlook. Total employment of air traffic controllers is expected to increase moderately through the 1980's. The number of air traffic controllers is expected to increase despite the greater use of automated equipment.

Additional air traffic controllers will be needed because of the anticipated growth in the number of airport towers that will be built to reduce the burden on existing facilities and to handle increasing airline traffic. More airport controllers also will be needed to provide services to the growing number of pilots outside of the airlines, such as those employed by companies to fly executives.

A number of additional enroute traffic controllers will be needed during the next few years to handle increases in air traffic. However, with the expected introduction of an automatic air traffic control system and a further decline in the number of control centers, employment of enroute traffic controllers is expected to moderate in the long run.

A few hundred openings will occur each year for controller jobs because of the need to replace those workers who leave for other work, retire, or die.

FAA controllers work a basic 40-hour week; however, they may work overtime, for which they receive equivalent time off or additional pay. Because control towers and centers must be operated 24 hours a day, 7 days a week, controllers are periodically assigned to night shifts on a rotating basis. However, an additional 10 percent is paid for work between 9 p.m. and 6 a.m.

Because of the congestion in air traffic, a controller works under great stress. He is responsible for directing as many as 10 to 20 aircraft or more at the same time. He must check simultaneously flights already under his control, know the flight schedules of aircraft approaching his area, and coordinate these patterns with other controllers as each flight passes from his control area to another.

THE AIR TRAFFIC CONTROLLER

AIR TRAFFIC CONTROL

"Flight 123 now arriving at Gate 4" is a typical announcement that comes booming over airport loudspeaker systems thousands of times each day all over our country. Behind this matter-of-fact announcement lies a vast complex of men and equipment making up the air traffic control system that has made air travel in the United States the safest and most convenient in the world.

The responsibility for providing a safe and orderly flow of civil and military air traffic rests with the Federal Aviation Agency. It takes about 40 per cent of the FAA's 53,000 employees to do this job.

In the hands of over 20,000 air traffic specialists and some 7,000 electronic maintenance technicians, working in shifts around the clock, lies the safety of many thousands of aircraft making some 12,500 flights daily. It has been estimated that on the average, throughout the air traffic control system, an aircraft takes off or lands every second, 24 hours a day, 365 days a year.

Depending on weather conditions, all aircraft fly by one of two sets of FAA rules --either instrument flight rules (IFR) or visual flight rules (VFR). When the weather is clear, most pilots fly VFR; when it is bad, flights normally are conducted under IFR procedures. Under VFR, the pilot flies by visual reference to the ground and he is solely responsible for avoiding other aircraft. His obligation is more than "see and be seen"--it is to "see and avoid."

But, when weather and visibility are poor and IFR weather conditions prevail, the responsibility for keeping aircraft separated falls to the air traffic controller of the Federal Aviation Agency. Even in good weather many pilots, especially those flying high-speed aircraft, elect to fly under IFR in order to take advantage of the separation and the greater protection afforded by FAA's air traffic specialists. All major scheduled airline flights follow this procedure. When a pilot flies IFR in good weather, however, he must still assume responsibility for seeing and avoiding other traffic, whether it is operating under the "see and avoid" concept or under IFR procedures.

Airport Traffic Control Towers

To a pilot taking off from or landing at an airport, the control tower is an information and guide service combined. A busy airport could not operate efficiently without a tower to supervise and direct the heavy air traffic. Usually operated around the clock every day in the year, FAA's 300-odd control towers provide pilots with vital takeoff and landing services.

FAA tower service begins when the pilot, operating under VFR, first calls by radio from about 15 or 20 miles away. If he is flying under IFR, and therefore under the control of an FAA air route traffic control center, the first call is made when the center controller transfers control to an approach controller in the tower. After the tower controller establishes contact with the aircraft, he provides the pilot with certain essential information--principally the "active" runway (the one to use based on wind), wind direction and velocity, and the altimeter setting (barometric pressure). The pilot is then given a landing sequence. The tower also assists the pilot in locating and identifying any other aircraft that he is to follow in the landing sequence. After landing, he is given taxiing information.

Generally, VFR towers control air traffic within a five-mile radius of the airport. In the case of approach control towers, the area is usually an irregular shape of greater dimensions and is normally limited to 5,000 feet or less above the ground.

Staffing of towers depends mainly on the volume of air traffic being served. Most VFR towers average 10 controllers, while the approach control towers may have 25 or more on duty. These men handle approach control, departure control, local control, ground control and coordination with the air route traffic control centers. Most of the controllers are qualified to work any of the control positions and they rotate through all these control positions to maintain proficiency.

Equipment found in towers includes extensive radio gear for direct communications with the pilot; radar, used to locate, identify, and direct aircraft as far as 60 miles away; and a complex land communications system made up of extensive radio and telephone equipment.

Air Route Traffic Control Centers

Picture the airspace above the 48 contiguous states divided into 21 irregularly shaped areas, each one, for air traffic purposes, under the jurisdiction of an FAA air route traffic control center. The controllers in these centers are responsible for maintaining separation between en route IFR aircraft. They do this by providing each aircraft with a block of moving airspace of its own, using prescribed distance and time separations.

After an aircraft has taken off, the tower controller transfers control to an en route controller in the center. The plane remains the responsibility of the center until it leaves its jurisdiction--as much as 300 to 500 miles. Then the control of the plan is transferred to the next center, and so on.

At designated points along the route, the pilot reports his position to the controller who enters this information, as well as an estimated time over the next reporting point, on a flight progress strip that represents this particular flight. These progress strips are kept on a sloping board in front of the controller.

In areas having radar coverage, the controller "sees" the aircraft he is controlling on a radar screen which has a range of approximately 200 miles.

Pilot and controller communicate by voice radio. When the aircraft is from 20 to 30 miles from its destination, the center controller transfers control to the approach controller in the tower. Not all towers have approach control--only those having a specified amount if IFR traffic provide this service.

The importance of FAA's centers to aviation can be seen in just one figure--centers control more than 12 million IFR aircraft annually.

Flight Service Stations

The motorist has a variety of services to assist him--road signs, service stations, information centers. He may use these as he needs them and in an emergency he can always pull over to the side of the road. Because the pilot cannot "pull over to the side of the road," FAA provides more than 300 flight service stations, each covering an area with a radius of 100 to 200 miles.

Specialists at the stations, with expert aviation knowledge of the area within 400 miles of their station, provide preflight and inflight briefings which include pertinent information about weather, airports, altitudes, routes and other flight-planning data. They also initiate search and rescue service when needed. These services are furnished for more than 300,000 nonairline pilots who constitute more than 95 per cent of all active civil pilots.

This large general aviation fleet--business, private, recreational--comprises more than 88,000 aircraft, compared with about 2,000 for the airlines. General aviation pilots now fly more than 15 million miles a year.

Linking together the highly skilled controllers and specialists in towers, centers and flight service stations are about 950,000 miles of communications lines. Together, man and equipment epitomize the goal of the Federal Aviation Agency--to a chieve the highest possible degree of safety in the air, as well as to maintain world leadership for the United States in the field of civil aviation.

A FLIGHT THROUGH THE ATC SYSTEM

A Boeing 727 stretched jet, packed with 120 Chicago-bound passengers, is waiting on the holding apron at the north end of Runway 18 at Washington National Airport, just across the Potomac River from the Nation's Capital. In a matter of moments it will be airborne, soaring across the Virginia countryside, on the start of a flight that will involve it in a unique partnership with the Federal Aviation Administration of the U. S. Department of Transportation, which operates and maintains the air traffic control/air navigation system in the United States.

The 727 Captain, who already has received a thorough briefing on weather conditions, preferential routings, and other factors that will affect his flight, rechecks his approved flight plan to Chicago's O'Hare International Airport and glances through the cockpit window to the control tower a half mile away. Then he nods to the co-pilot, who presses his microphone button and says:

"Tower, Trans Continental Flight 483 ready for takeoff Runway 18."

"Roger Trans Continental 483," is the reply from the FAA controller in the glass-walled tower cab across the field. "Taxi into position and hold."

The three-engine turns onto the runway and then receives another transmission from the tower: "Trans Continental 483, cleared for take off."

The pilot advances the throttles and the aircraft begins rolling down the 6800-foot runway, gathering speed as it goes. About two-thirds of the way down, the pilot pulls back on his yoke and the aircraft breaks ground and begins climbing out over the waters of the Potomac.

"Trans Continental 483 contact Departure Control," the controller in the tower cab says. The co-pilot's hand moves to the dial that changes one of the cockpit radio frequencies to 118.1 MHz and he says: "Washington Departure Control, Trans Continental 483's with you."

Following departure instructions, the pilot stays aligned with the runway until Departure Control issues a clearance six miles south of the airport: "Trans Continental 483 turn right direct Casanova, climb and maintain flight level two three zero." Then he banks the aircraft right toward the Casanova VORTAC, a radio navigation aid that provides pilots with precise position information.

Progress of the flight is closely monitored by the radar departure controller at National to ensure that the aircraft remains safely separated from all other air traffic within the terminal control area. Trans Continental 483 stands out clearly on the radar scope because the aircraft carries automatic altitude and identity reporting equipment and National is equipped with a computer-based system which takes this information and displays it on the controller's radar next to the appropriate aircraft target or "blip."

The "050" in the second line of the data tag indicates the actual altitude of 4,000 feet and the "250" represents the ground speed. Controllers have the option of erasing all or part of this information when not required.

As the flight approaches the boundary of the National Airport approach control area (approximately 30 miles), the departure controller prepares to hand off control of the flight to the Washington air route traffic control center. When ready, he says: "Trans Continental 483, three miles east of the hand off point, climbing through 10,000."

Washington center replies: "Radar contact." Flight 483 then is instructed to contact the Washington center.

Approximately 40 miles west of Washington, near the town of Leesburg, Va., is one of 20 en route centers run by FAA in the continental U. S. to control aircraft operating under instrument flight rules (IFR) between airports. Known as the Washington center, it is responsible for 140,000 square miles of airspace and 20,000 miles of airways over all or parts of six Eastern states. On any given day, it will handle more than 3,500 flights.

During peak periods, as many as 150 air traffic controllers will be on duty in the huge control room staffing the center's 34 radar sectors. Each of these sectors represents a specific block of airspace over a particular geographic area. There are both high and low altitude sectors so any point on the ground may have two, three, or even four airspace sectors layered over it.

At least two and as many as four controllers work at each sector position. The voice the pilot hears belongs to the radar controller, who monitors the scope to keep traffic safely separated. Next to him sits the handoff controller who handles the transfer of flights between sectors or between facilities. When traffic is light, only these two may be needed to staff a sector. When it's heavy, a manual and assistant controller may be added to handle clerical and other duties.

The handoff of Trans Continental Flight 483 from Washington National departure control to the Washington center requires a minimum of voice communication since both facilities are equipped with computer-based systems for displaying aircraft identity and altitude. Still, the controller at the Washington center will ask Flight 483 to "Ident," or identify itself, using a piece of equipment known as a transponder. This device sends out a coded signal which causes the radar target to enlarge and brighten, thus permitting the controller to make a positive identification. This is generally acknowledged with a cryptic "Radar contact." The new automated equipment now in operation in all 20 centers, also obviates the need for routine position reports and other non-essential conversation between pilots and controllers. This leaves the radio channels free for more urgent communications.

Ten miles west of the Casanova VORTAC the co-pilot of Trans Continental 483 observes an ominous row of thunderheads some distance ahead. A brief discussion with the pilot follows: Can we steer around them? Is there turbulence inside the towering cumulus clouds? Does the small weather radar unit in the aircraft show a comfortable detour? The consensus is no, so the co-pilot calls the center:

"Washington center, 483."

"Center, go ahead."

"We see some thunderheads up front. Request to detour south."

The controller scans the traffic situation south of Flight 483 and responds: "Deviation approved. Report back on the airway."

As Trans Continental turns south, its flight crew can rest assured that the aircraft is being watched on radar and controllers will issue appropriate instructions should a possible traffic conflict arise. The detour takes 15 minutes and generates another radio transmission when completed. "Trans Continental 483 turning back to J149," says the co-pilot using the shorthand for Jet Route 149. "Roger," the center responds, "Washington center requests a PIREP."

"Sure Washington," says the co-pilot responding to the call for a pilot's inflight report on weather conditions. "We got some light rime ice and moderate turbulence inside the clouds but we were in and out in 10 seconds. 483."

PIREPS are an important adjunct to gathering aviation weather information. In this case, the data obtained from Flight 483 is flashed to FAA flight service stations and other facilities coping with the line of thunderstorms for use in briefing other pilots operating in the area. Information on actual icing conditions is especially valuable.

From Washington center, Trans Continental 483--now at Flight Level 350 (35,000 feet)--is handed off first to the Indianapolis center and then to the Chicago center. In each case, the procedure is virtually identical to that employed in the original transfer of the flight from Washington National departure control to the Washington center.

Like all airline aircraft, TCA 483 operates under instrument flight rules (IFR), meaning it must have an approved flight plan and follow instructions from FAA air traffic control facilities which assume responsibility for keeping all IFR aircraft separated from one another. Many general aviation (nonairline) aircraft also fly IFR but most operate under visual flight rules when weather conditions permit. VFR means the aircraft are essentially outside the air traffic control system except in terminal areas and depend upon their own capabilities to see and avoid other air traffic.

As Flight 483 nears Chicago O'Hare, the Captain tunes in the O'Hare Automatic Terminal Information Service (ATIS). This information provides the pilot with a continuous broadcast of recorded airport weather and landing information.

The pilot receives the following O'Hare weather--"O'Hare International Airport information BRAVO measured ceiling two thousand overcast, visibility three, blowing snow. Temperature three zero. Wind three four zero degrees at two five. Altimeter two niner niner eight. ILS runway 32L approach in use. Advise you have BRAVO."

But despite the blowing snow, the ceiling and visibility at O'Hare are well within limits for an instrument approach on Runway 32L. Now the flight is handed off for the last time.

"Trans Continental 483," says the controller at the Chicago center, "descend and maintain five thousand report leaving eight thousand."

A crisp acknowledgement follows and Flight 483 begins its descent. Although 483's data tag on both the center and approach control radar ticks off its altitude in one hundred foot increments like the odometer in an automobile, the co-pilot provides back-up communications designed to ensure flight safety.

In a matter of minutes, the aircraft is on the ground, having "coasted" down the radio beam of the instrument landing system (ILS) that defines the descent path to Runway 32L. Now the ground controller in the tower cab, which soars 200 feet above the world's busiest airport, takes command guiding the aircraft along the taxiways to the terminal.

The flight has been deceptively routine and most of the 120 passengers on board are unaware that they have been guided from boarding gate to boarding gate by a highly trained and skilled team of air traffic controllers. Had the Boeing 727 been a business jet, a private aircraft, or a military transport, it could have availed itself of the same services offered Trans Continental 483. The air traffic control system is a common system which can be used by everyone who flies.

THE ATC SYSTEM

The air traffic control/air navigation system in the United States is a vast network of facilities located in all 50 States and in such far away places as Guam, American Samoa, Panama, and Puerto Rico.

Included are 25 air route traffic control centers, some 400 airport control towers, over 300 flight service stations, more than 1,000 radio navigation aids, nearly 500 instrument landing systems, and some 250 long-range and terminal radar systems. Moreover, nearly half the agency's total complement of 50,000 plus people are engaged in some phase of air traffic control. An additional 10,000 technicians and engineers are involved in the installation and maintenance of this system.

Air route traffic control centers handle enroute aircraft operating under instrument flight rules (IFR) between airport terminal areas. Together the 25 centers log more than 23 million flights a year with 13 centers recording in excess of one million operations each. The total is expected to reach almost 30 million by the end of the decade.

The typical center has responsibility for more than 100,000 square miles of airspace generally extending over a number of states. To keep track of aircraft in its area, a center may use as many as six or seven long-range radars and 10 to 20 remote air-ground communication sites. Each radar covers an area 200 miles in radius.

The controller staff can range from 300 to 700, with more than 150 on duty during peak periods at the busier facilities. In addition, each facility has its own airways facilities sector which may include as many as 125 engineers and technicians.

Airport traffic control towers direct the movement of aircraft on and in the vicinity of an airport. In addition to directing actual takeoffs and landings, approximately 150 of the 400 FAA-run towers also provide radar approach and departure control services to IFR aircraft using the primary airport as well as many secondary airports in the terminal approach control area.

Tower facilities can range from the familiar glass-walled cupola on top an airport terminal building to freestanding structures soaring more than 200 feet in the air. Similarly, staffing can range from a three or four man operation which keeps the tower open 10-12 hours a day to a controller workforce of more than 150 working shifts around the clock. Together the 400 FAA-staffed control towers direct more than 55 million operations annually, and this is forecast to pass the 75 million mark by 1980.

Flight service stations are the direct descendants of the airways communications stations established in the 1920s to provide weather data and other assistance to the early air mail pilots.

FAA presently operates more than 300 of these facilities at airports around the country and they remain a vital link in the air-ground communications system. Although general aviation pilots are the principal users of these facilities, they also serve the military and the air carriers.

Like air traffic control towers, the size, staffing and hours of operation for flight service stations vary from location to location. Busier facilities operate around the clock and may have a total compliment of 50 specialists who brief pilots on weather, airport conditions, winds aloft, preferred routes, and other flight planning data. Many flight service stations also are equipped with direction-finding equipment that enables them to guide lost pilots to safety.

In order to keep pace with the rapid growth of aviation, FAA has implemented a computer-based semiautomated air traffic control system at all of the enroute centers serving the contiguous 48 states and at all major terminal facilities. The system tracks controlled flights automatically and tags each target with a small block of information written electronically on the radar scopes used by controllers. The data block includes both aircraft identity and altitude.

Automated radar systems, tailored to the varied traffic demands of terminal locations, already have been installed and are operational at more than 60 large and medium hub airports. Another 69 systems have been purchased by the agency and will be installed at airports in the small hub category by the end of 1978.

FAA Plans call for the enroute and terminal systems to be tied together nationwide in a common network for the exchange of data between facilities. The capabilities of the automated system also are being continually upgraded to include additional air traffic management functions such as predicting traffic conflicts and suggesting ways of resolving them, provide flow control in congested terminal situations, and preplan and sequence airport arrivals. Further down the line are the use of aeronautical satellites to enhance aircraft communications and surveillance on over-ocean routes, development of a new microwave landing system for more precise airport approaches in all weather conditions, and development of data link systems for automatic air-ground communications.

THE AIR TRAFFIC CONTROLLER JOB

In the past two decades, tremendous technological gains have been made in the FAA air traffic control system. There has been an almost continual process of improvement, expansion, and development. The 1950's saw the advent of radar and improved navigational equipment. The 1960's brought the first widespread implementation of automation techniques. In the 1970's, FAA opened a new central flow control facility which gives us for the first time a total nationwide air traffic picture. FAA is moving ahead rapidly with our automation program, with additional progress daily.

In considering milestones of our development in this area, the thing that has made the whole process possible was the passage by the last Congress of the Airport and Airway Development Act of 1970. That act, of course, provided the financial support to purchase the badly needed facility and hardware items that make the system a much more tractable easy system for our controllers to operate.

Despite the technological gains that have been made in the last several years, and despite the very large advances that we expect to be made over the coming decade, the system still remains and will always remain a system that requires strong input and control from the personnel involved.

The system is a people system. There are nearly 25,000 controllers in our towers and centers, and it is likely that even with a high level of automation in the future there will remain a similar number, and even an expanded number in the next decade.

The duties and responsibilities of an individual involved in the career of an air traffic controller are truly unique. The career represents an exciting challenge, it represents involvement in a very dynamic and forward looking industry. Of course the big part of that challenge and the pressure that is involved stems from the responsibility for safeguarding the air traveler as he moves through the air traffic system. In the discharge of those responsibilities of course there is no tolerance for error.

As the growth of aviation continues to place increasing demand on that system, the demands on the controller will accordingly increase and become more complex.

The job of an air traffic controller is a uniquely demanding one that requires a special kind of person. Essentially, a controller's business is to keep aircraft traffic flowing orderly and efficiently, yet properly separated to avoid accidents. A controller can be assigned to an airport tower or to an en route center which directs traffic between airport terminal areas. Another possibility is a flight service station, which provides pilots with information on weather, air navigation, and airport conditions. There are some 400 airport towers, 25 enroute centers, and more than 300 flight service stations operated by FAA in the United States and its possessions. More than 25,000 controllers work in these facilities.

To be eligible for a controller's job, one must show through previous job experience a potential for learning the controller's work. Graduation from a 4-year college or university, or a combination of experience and education, also can satisfy eligibility requirements. Others can make themselves eligible by demonstrating successful specialized experience, such as in a military or civilian air traffic facility or comparable situation. All applicants must take a written test and show in an interview that he or she possesses the personal characteristics required of a controller. Before appointment, a candidate must also undergo a rigorous physical examination administered by FAA.

All qualified applicants who have not yet reached their 31st birthday will receive consideration for appointment to towers or centers (no maximum entry age for flight service station) without regard to race, religion, color, national origin, or sex. At present, career opportunities are limited, so check with your local Civil Service Commission or Federal Aviation Administration office to see if they are accepting applications.

AIR TRAFFIC CONTROL—ENTRY LEVEL

How Does the FAA Employee Prepare Himself to Meet the Technical Requirements of his Vocation?

A. Air Traffic Control:

Applicants for all grades will be rated on a scale of 200 and must obtain a rating of at least 70 to be eligible.

For GS-5, ratings will be based on the written test score.

For GS-7, ratings will be based on the written test and the kind and quality of experience, education, and training in relation to the requirements of the position.

For GS-9, ratings will be based on an evaluation of the kind, amount and pertinence of qualifying air traffic control experience, education and training.

In addition to meeting the above requirements, applicants must demonstrate in a pre-employment interview that they possess the personal characteristics necessary for successful performance as Air Traffic Control Specialists.

The applicant must also be able to pass an FAA Second Class Medical Examination.

Once an applicant has been selected he will then enter an extensive training program.

An air traffic controller is an extensively trained, highly skilled individual, responsible for the safe, orderly, and expeditious flow of all air traffic. New hires, Grade GS-5 and GS-7 applicants must pass a written test. This test requires about 2 1/2 hours to complete and the results of the test determine the applicant's eligibility for employment.

GS-5	Pass Written Test	Plus	3 yrs. General Experience or 4 yrs. college or combination of both
GS-7	Pass Written Test	Plus	3 yrs. General Experience or 4 yrs. college or combination of both and 1 yr. of specialized experience or 1 yr. graduate work or superior academic achievement
	or		
	Pass Written Test with very high score	Plus	3 yrs. General Experience or 4 yrs. of college or combination of both
	or		
	Pass Written Test	Plus	One of the following certificated: Air Traffic Controller, Air Carrier Dispatcher, Instrument Flight Rating, Navigator (FAA) Pilot --350 hours, Aerospace Intercept Director

GS-9	No Written Test	3 yrs. General Experience or 4 yrs. College and 2 yrs. Specialized Experience or 1 yr. Specialized Experience with 1 yr. Graduate Work

General Experience

Progressively responsible experience in administrative, technical, or other work which demonstrated potential for learning and performing air traffic control work. Graduation from a four-year college or university satisfies the general experience requirements for all grades.

Specialized Experience

Experience in a military or civilian air traffic facility of comparable experience which demonstrated possession of the knowledges, skills and abilities required to perform the level of work for which the application is made, such as:

Flight Service Station

This is experience in providing information to pilots on such matters as weather, air routes, navigation aids, and airport conditions before and during flight. In addition to a comprehensive knowledge of such matters, this specialization requires:

the judgment to select only essential and pertinent information from a great mass of data;

the skill to present essential information to pilots clearly, concisely, and quickly either before or during flight; and

the ability to act decisively in emergency situations.

ATC TOWER: This is experience in issuing control instructions and advice to pilots in the vicinity of airports to assure proper separation of aircraft and to expedite their safe and efficient movement. In addition to a comprehensive knowledge of air traffic control laws, rules, and regulations, positions in this specialization require:

the ability to act decisively under stressful situations and to maintain alertness over sustained periods of pressure;

the skill to coordinate plans and actions with pilots and other controllers;

the judgment to select and take the safest and most effective course of action from among several available choices.

AIR ROUTE TRAFFIC CONTROL CENTER: This is experience in controlling aircraft operating enroute along the airways for the purpose of assuring proper separation and the safe and expeditious movement of such aircraft. In addition to a comprehensive knowledge of the laws, rules and regulations governing air traffic control, positions in this specialization require:

the ability to control aircraft operating at very high speeds over great distances: the skill to arrange air traffic in patterns that assure maximum safely and minimum delay at points where such aircraft are "handed off" or transferred to other facilities or other sectors within the center;

the judgment to estimate when and where traffic congestion will build to a point that necessitates changing patterns and to plan accordingly.

Qualifying specialized experience must have provided candidates with the ability to:

arrive quickly at well-reasoned solutions to complex problems;

adjust quickly to different assignments, changing conditions, and workload fluctuations;

remain calm and controlled during and after long periods of tension and fatigue; and

speak rapidly, clearly, and distinctly.

EDUCATIONAL SUBSTITUTIONS FOR EXPERIENCE

FOR ALL GRADES: Successful completion of a four-year college course leading to a bachelor's degree may be substituted in full for the required three years of general experience.

GS-5: Successful completion of a 4-year college course leading to a bachelor's degree may be substituted in full for the experience required at GS-5.

GS-7: Successful completion of 1 year of graduate study leading to a master's degree may be substituted in full for the experience required at GS-7.

GS-7: Applicants who have passed the written test and completed all requirements for a bachelor's degree from an accredited college or university may be rated eligible for grade GS-7 if they meet one of the following requirements:

standing in the upper third of their class in the college or university or major subdivision;

an average of 2.90 or better on a 4.0 scale (or equivalent) for all courses completed: (1) up to the time of application; or (2) during the last 2 years of the undergraduate curriculum;

election to membership in one of the national honorary societies (other than freshman societies) which meet the minimum requirements of the Association of College Honor Societies;

a score of 600 or better in a Area Test or an Advanced Test of the Graduate Record Examination.

GS-9: A maximum of 1 year of graduate study leading to a master's degree may be substituted for the required specialized experience on the basis of 1 year of study for 1 year of experience.

OTHER SUBSTITUTIONS

GS-7: Applicants who have passed the written test qualify in full for the general and specialized experience requirements for grade GS-7 if they meet one of the following:

hold or have held an appropriate facility rating and have actively controlled air traffic in civilian or military air traffic control terminals or centers;

hold or have held an FAA certificate as a dispatcher for an air carrier;

hold or have held an instrument flight rating;

hold or have an FAA certificate as a navigator or have been fully qualified as a Navigator/Bombardier in the Armed Forces;

have 350 hours of flight time as a co-pilot or higher and hold or have held a private certificate or equivalent Armed Forces rating;

hold or have held a rating as an Aerospace Defense Command Intercept Director;

meet the requirements for GS-5 and in addition pass the written test with a very high score.

These substitutions are applicable for grade GS-7 only and may not be used to satisfy in part the required experience for GS-9.

IS AIR TRAFFIC CONTROL FOR YOU?

If you're interested in air traffic control, but have no previous experience, it's important that you visit an air traffic facility near you--more than one, if possible. Because there's a wide variety in work loads; what is a brisk afternoon at one tower, for example, might be a snail's pace at another.

Investigate the three options, too. The tower, the flight service station and the center have their own individual environments, advantages, and disadvantages. Try to get a realistic picture of what the work involves, in time and temperament.

Virtually all controller jobs involve shift work because most facilities operate on a 24-hour basis. The exact rotation of the shift is usually determined by the individual facility, but it could be that you might work several weeks from midnight to 8 a.m. followed by several weeks working from 4 p.m. until midnight. Your days off might not fall on weekends. So if you're a nine-to-five type, you probably aren't suited for air traffic control.

Some air traffic controllers talk about what they do: In his novel, AIRPORT, Arthur Hailey describes air traffic controllers as "practical men with an exacting job." And that, when you have stripped away the glamour of the out-of-the ordinary situation, is a pretty good description. But doing that exacting job, day after day, demands practical men--and women--with special characteristics. Here's how some controllers describe their work and the qualities they feel you should have to do it.

"It's like weaving a rug in the sky...threading planes at different altitudes, different speeds and traveling in different directions into a pattern."

"It's like a three-dimensional chess game--with speed the third dimension."

"You work with sharp people."

"It's like a fire station; it can be fairly routine until an emergency comes along, and you have to be geared for that emergency."

"It's stimulating; something's happening every minute."

"You've got to be ready for pressure."

"If you're good at contract bridge or poker, you could be a good air traffic controller. You have to be able to carry mental pictures, and constantly adjusting the pictures in your head."

"You have to be a little crazy to go into air traffic control."

Talking with controllers, you get the impression that these are a special breed--tough-minded, alert, not-quite-ordinary people. Which figures. It's not an ordinary job. It might be the job for you.

Flight Service Stations

338 flight service stations are maintained by the Federal Aviation Administration to provide assistance to the more than 700,000 licensed pilots who fly civilian aircraft in this country. These general aviation planes, as well as military flights, use flight service stations to obtain information on the station's particular area, including terrain, weather peculiarities, preflight and inflight weather information, suggested routes, altitudes, indications of turbulence, icing and any other information important to the safety of a flight. This is one air traffic control job where you meet pilots face to face. Approximately 4000 controllers work in flight service stations.

Towers

In 328 operating towers, air traffic controllers control flights within the three to thirty mile radius each serves, under visual flight rules (VFR) or instrument flight rules (IFR). Tower controllers may work either in the glass-walled room at the top of the tower, or in the radar room below it, but their jobs have the same aim--the safe separation and movement of planes within their area in taking off, landing and maneuvering. Tower assignments vary widely, from the relatively quiet Amarillo, Texas, to the rapid paced complex formed by Kennedy, LaGuardia and Newark Airports--from an isolated desert landing strip to the panorama of Washington, D. C. strung out along the Potomac River site of National Airport. Nearly 8,000 controllers work in towers.

Enroute Centers

Controllers who work in centers control traffic operating along established airways across the country between tower jurisdictions. There are presently 27 such centers, where controllers maintain a progressive check on aircraft, issuing instructions, clearances, and advice, as well as initiating search and rescue operations to locate overdue airplanes. Over 9,000 controllers work in centers. In AIRPORT, the Washington Air Route Center at Leesburg, Virginia, was described as follows: "The entire control area--larger than a football field--was, as always, dimly lighted to allow proper view of several dozen radar screens, arranged in tiers and rows under overhanging canopies.... The machinery and human voices merged, producing a constant noise level which was all-pervading, yet strangely muted by acoustic, sound-absorbent walls and ceiling. The control room activity looked not unlike that of a stock exchange."

Projection

By 1980, one million people will board U. S. airliners every day. The number of privately owned planes (now 114,000) will double. The annual air cargo ton miles will be 20 times greater. The flight operations at tower-equipped airports will triple.

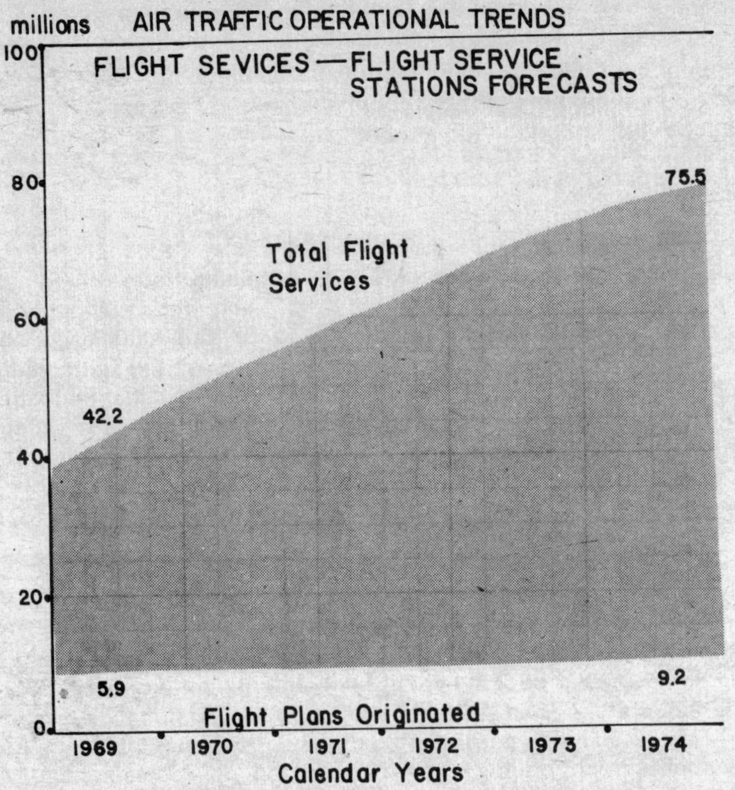
millions
AIR TRAFFIC OPERATIONAL TRENDS
FLIGHT SEVICES — FLIGHT SERVICE STATIONS FORECASTS
100
80
60
40
20
0
75.5
Total Flight Services
42.2
5.9
9.2
Flight Plans Originated
1969
1970
1971
1972
1973
1974
Calendar Years

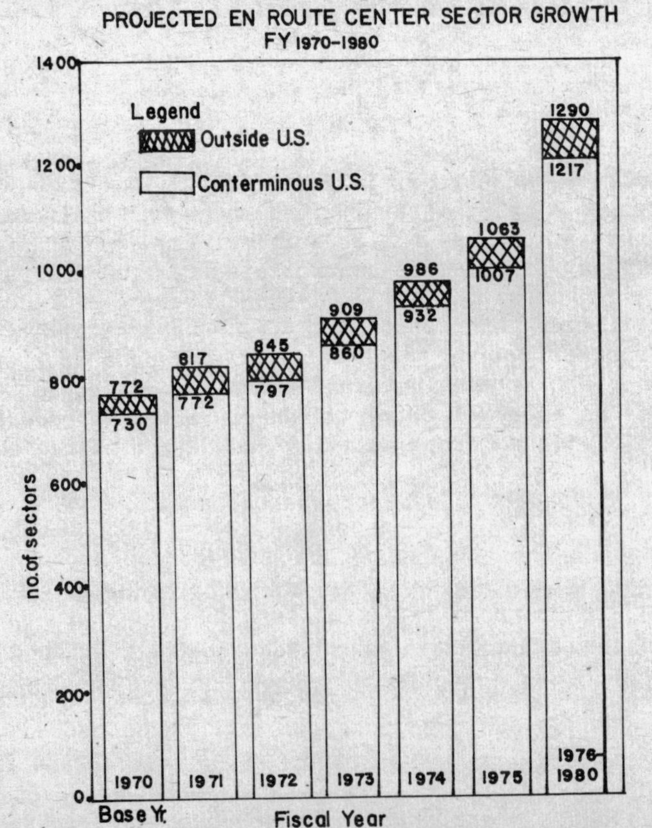
PROJECTED EN ROUTE CENTER SECTOR GROWTH
FY 1970–1980
Legend
Outside U.S.
Conterminous U.S.
no. of sectors
1400
1200
1000
800
600
400
200
0
772
730
817
772
845
797
909
860
986
932
1063
1007
1290
1217
1970
1971
1972
1973
1974
1975
1976–1980
Base Yr.
Fiscal Year

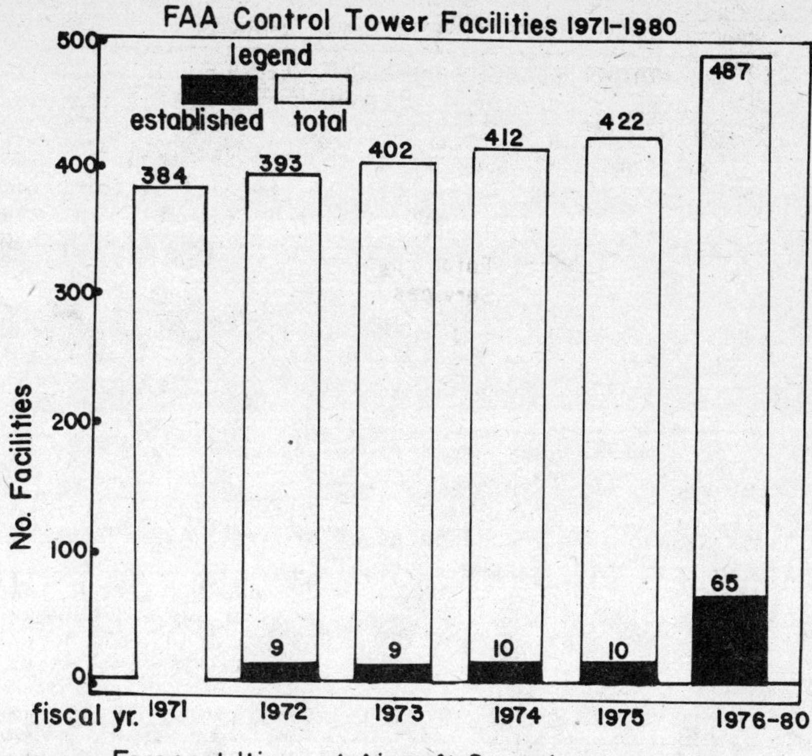

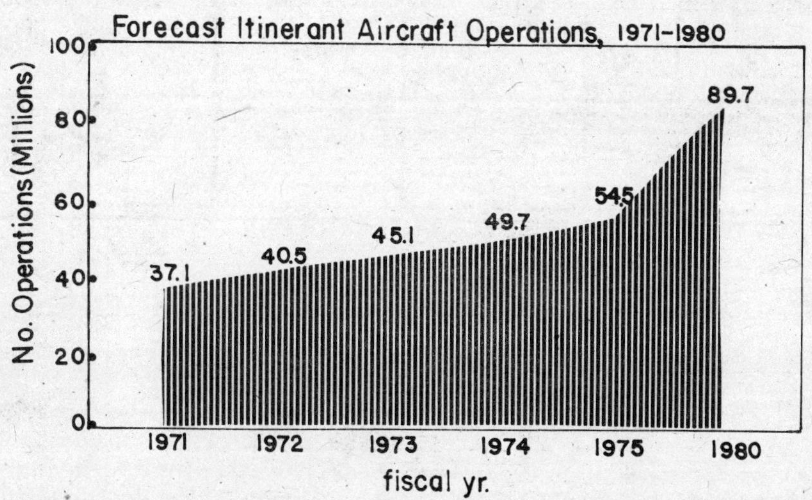

Expanding Opportunities in the FAA

	1971	1972	1973	1974	1975	1980
Air traffic control	27,976	30,300	31,550	32,750	34,200	46,400
(1) En route	11,981	12,300	12,650	12,950	13,300	16,300
(2) Terminal	10,493	10,950	11,500	12,000	12,550	17,700
(3) Flight service stations	4,566	5,700	6,000	6,350	6,800	10,600
(4) Other	936	1,350	1,400	1,450	1,550	1,800

If you measure up to the demands of the job, now is the time when opportunities are greater than at any time in recent years to be selected to train and serve as an air traffic controller.

FAA Training

Because people entering Government service as Air Traffic Control Specialists do so at such varied levels of experience--from having none at all to being fully qualified military Air Traffic Controllers--it is difficult to make any hard and fast statements about training patterns. Generally though, the training combines study at the FAA Academy in Oklahoma City, Oklahoma with training at the facility where the recruit is assigned, although the order of sessions is flexible. Facility training varies somewhat, but is a combination of on-the-job training and classroom time which continues until the controller reaches the journeyman level for his assigned spot.

Journeyman level may vary from facility to facility, depending on the location of the assignment, but at towers and centers it is generally considered to be GS-12 or GS-13.

Air Traffic Control Specialists who fail to maintain the standards during the training periods may be dropped from the program.

The chart below illustrates the patterns of promotions for centers and towers which may be expected to develop on the basis of the grade level at which you enter on duty. Promotions are not automatic, however; they depend on developing proficiency within prescribed time periods.

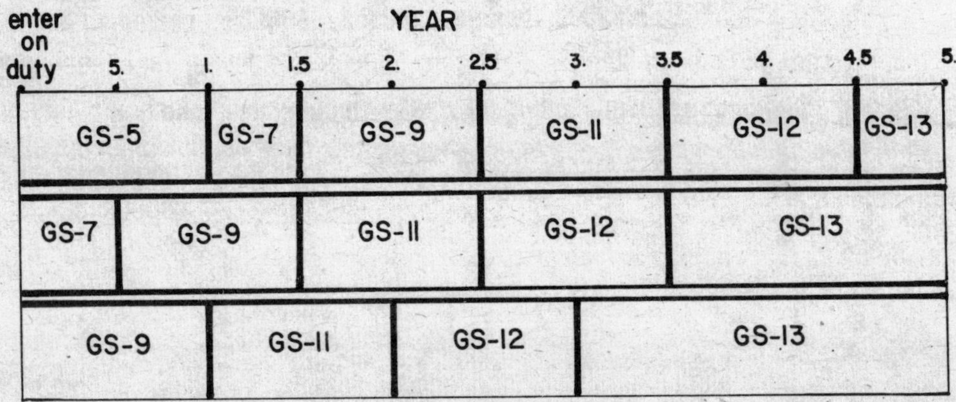

Maintaining Standards and Growing with the Job

All air traffic controllers are required to meet qualification requirements and semiannual proficiency checks. A controller who transfers from one facility to another with a higher density of traffic must meet the check-out standards of the new facility. Controllers who remain in one facility must demonstrate their continued ability to handle the assignment. Failure to do so may result in demotion, separation, or assignment to another facility where the load is lighter.

If all this seems tough, it's because the job is tough. And human lives can depend on the controller's ability to come up with the right decisions quickly every day that he works.

U.S. Civil Service Commission

Air Traffic Controller

Opportunities
in the Federal
Government

Announcement
No. 418
May, 1975

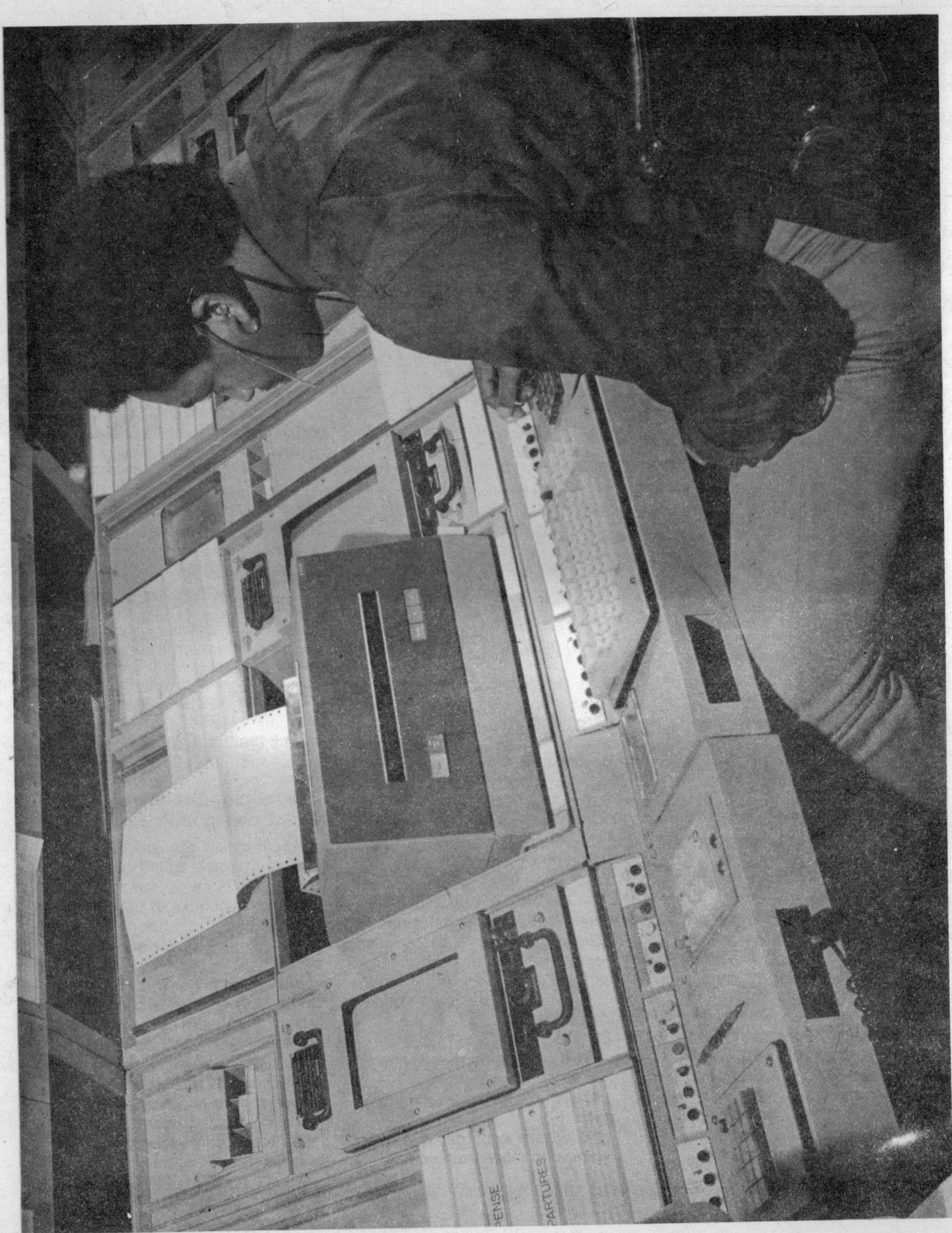

Air Traffic Controllers Work In Three Basic Specialties

Towers

In operating towers, air traffic controllers control flights within the three to thirty mile radius each serves, under visual flight rules (VFR) or instrument flight rules (IFR). Tower controllers may work either in the glass-walled room at the top of the tower, or in the radar room below it, but their jobs have the same aim—the safe separation and movement of planes within their area, in taking off, landing and maneuvering. Tower assignments vary widely, from the relatively quiet Amarillo, Texas, to the rapid paced complex formed by Kennedy, LaGuardia and Newark Airports—from an isolated desert landing strip to the panorama of Washington, D.C. strung out along the Potomac River site of National Airport.

En Route Centers

Controllers who work in centers control traffic operating along established airways across the country between tower jurisdictions. They maintain a progressive check on aircraft, issuing instructions, clearances, and advice, as well as initiating search and rescue operations to locate overdue airplanes. In Arthur Hailey's novel *Airport*, the Washington Air Route Center at Leesburg, Virginia, was described as follows: "The entire control area—larger than a football field— was, as always, dimly lighted to allow proper view of several dozen radar screens, arranged in tiers and rows under overhanging canopies. . . . The machinery and human voices merged, producing a constant noise level which was all-pervading, yet strangely muted by acoustic, sound-absorbent walls and ceiling. . . . The control room activity looked, . . . not unlike that of a stock exchange."

Flight Service Stations

Flight service stations are maintained by the Federal Aviation Administration to provide assistance to the pilots who must obtain information on the station's particular area, including terrain, weather peculiarities, preflight and inflight weather information, suggested routes, altitudes, indications of turbulence, icing and any other information important to the safety of a flight. Only a very few flight service station positions are filled each year.

The Mind's Eye . . .

In the cool dark of the radar room, a controller watches the radar beam swing its way around the radius of the screen's circle. Within the circle, green blips—some moving, some stationary; some single, some double; some important, some irrelevant—compose a pale green galaxy. This pattern, made up of light and the beam's regular rhythm, could lull an unknowing eye to restfulness.

But in the mind's eye of the controller, the blips compose a constantly changing three-dimensional picture of the planes moving through his area, at different altitudes, speeds and directions. The ability to carry mental pictures is vital in air traffic control.

And there's another critical factor: coping with stress. This often means working under extreme pressure without relief up to four hours at a stretch, and measuring up where nothing less than perfection will do.

"You have to be able to think abstractly, especially in the center."

"You have to do first things first, establish priorities."

"You have to have automatic recall."

"You have to be capable of listening to more than one conversation at a time and acknowledging them."

"You have to look at errors objectively and reconstruct situations."

"You have to accept the responsibility of the job."

Training

Generally, the training combines study at the FAA Academy in Oklahoma City, Oklahoma with training at the facility where the recruit is assigned, although the order of sessions is flexible. Facility training varies somewhat, but is a combination of on-the-job training and classroom time which continues until the controller reaches the journeyman level for his or her assigned spot.

Journeyman level may vary from facility to facility, depending on the location of the assignment, but at towers and centers it is generally considered to be GS-12 or GS-13. Although promotions are not automatic and depend on developing proficiency within prescribed time periods, most controllers reach journeyman level in four or five years.

Air Traffic Control Specialists who fail to maintain the standards during the training periods may be dropped from the program.

Maintaining Standards and Growing With the Job . . .

All air traffic controllers are required to meet qualification requirements and semiannual proficiency checks. A controller who transfers from one facility to another with a higher density of traffic must meet the checkout standards of the new facility. Controllers who remain in one facility must demonstrate their continued ability to handle the assignment. Failure to do so may result in demotion, separation, or assignment to another facility where the load is lighter.

If all this seems tough, it's because the job is tough. And

human lives can depend on the controller's ability to come up with the right decisions quickly every day.

Is Air Traffic Control for You?

If you're interested in air traffic control, but have no previous experience, it's important that you visit an air traffic facility near you—more than one, if possible. Because there's a wide variety in work loads; what is a brisk afternoon at one tower, for example, might be a snail's pace at another.

Virtually all controller jobs involve shift work because most facilities operate on a 24-hour basis. The exact rotation of the shift is usually determined by the individual facility, but it could be that you might work several weeks from midnight to 8 a.m. followed by several weeks working from 4 p.m. until midnight. Your days off might not fall on weekends. So if you're a nine-to-five type, you probably aren't suited for air traffic control.

Pages 5 through 8 contain some sample questions of the type you will find on the written test for air traffic control. They may be helpful in determining whether the types of problems involved in the job are in tune with your interests and abilities.

Requirements for education and working experience are on pages 2 and 3. Finally there's a How to Apply section on page 4.

Measuring Yourself Against the Job

Written Test. You will be required to pass a written test which takes about 2½ hours.

Rating. Your qualifications for the job will be rated on the basis of 100, with a minimum score of 70 necessary for you to be rated eligible.

For GS-5, rating will be based on the written test score.

For GS-7, rating will be based on the written test and your experience, education and training in relation to the requirements of the job.

A Chart Showing How You Qualify For Grades Is On The Next Page

General Experience is progressively responsible work which demonstrates your potential for learning and performing Air Traffic Control work. The work could be administrative, technical or other types of employment. You may substitute education for experience, up to four years of college for up to three years of experience.

Specialized Experience is experience in military or civilian Air Traffic Control or comparable experience (for example, military activities involving direct control of aircraft and missiles) which shows that you have the knowledge, skills and abilities required to perform Air Traffic Control work.

Interview. As is the case with any employment, you will be asked to report for an interview. This is critically important in the hiring process.

Age. Under provisions of Public Law 92-297, a maximum entry age for certain air traffic control positions was established. On the basis of extensive studies and experience, it was determined that those unique skills and abilities necessary for the control of air traffic begin to decline at a relatively early age. As a result, a maximum age limit of 30 at the time of initial appointment for all candidates has been established for Air Traffic Controller positions at towers and centers in the FAA. Applications will not be accepted for these positions from candidates who have reached their 31st birthday. Applicants who haven't been appointed before reaching 31 will only be eligible for Flight Service Station positions and positions with the Department of Defense. Because so few of these are filled, chances for appointment are very slim. (DOD plans to hire only 30 Air Traffic Controllers this year.)

Physical Exam. Before you may be appointed, you must pass a rigid physical examination which will be made by a medical examiner designated by and paid for by the government. A detailed list of medical restrictions may be obtained from FAA regional offices.

Still A Student? If you are a student or graduate student, you may be offered a job if you expect to complete your course work within 9 months of filing your application. The work must actually be completed before you start work.

Working For The USA, a pamphlet containing general information about Federal employment, is available at most Federal Job Information Centers, and most large Post Offices. **Ask for Pamphlet BRE 37.**

Qualifications by Grade Level

GS-5	Pass Written Test	Plus	3 yrs. general experience or 4 yrs. of college leading to a Bachelors Degree or an equivalent combination of education and experience
GS-7	Pass Written Test	Plus	3 yrs. general experience or 4 yrs. of college leading to a Bachelors Degree or an equivalent combination of education and experience and 1 yr. of specialized experience or 1 yr. graduate work or superior academic achievement*
	or Pass Written Test With Very High Score	Plus	3 yrs. of general experience or 4 yrs. of college leading to a Bachelors Degree or, an equivalent combination of education and experience
	or Pass Written Test	Plus	ONE OF THE FOLLOWING: civilian or military facility rating in ATC involving active control of air traffic in center or terminal; past or present FAA air carrier dispatcher certificate; past or present instrument flight rating; past or present FAA navigator/Bombardier; past or present co-pilot or pilot rating or equivalent military rating with 350 hours of flight time; past or present rating as an Aerospace Defense Command Intercept Director.

*Superior Academic Achievement means: 1. standing in upper third of class in college or university or major subdivision; 2. average of 2.90 or better on a 4.0 scale (or equivalent) for all courses completed (a) up to the time of application or (b) during last 2 undergraduate years; 3. election to one of the national honorary societies (other than freshman societies) which meet the minimum requirement of the Association of College Honor Societies.

Where to Apply

(Apply to One Area Office Only)

Geographical Area *	U.S. Civil Service Commission with Jurisdiction
Washington, Oregon, Idaho	Seattle Area Office Federal Office Building 1st Avenue & Madison Street Seattle, Washington 98104
California, Arizona, Nevada	Los Angeles Area Office 851 South Broadway Los Angeles, California 90014
Montana, Wyoming, North Dakota, South Dakota, Utah, Colorado	Denver Area Office U.S. Post Office Building 18th and Stout Streets Denver, Colorado 80202
New Mexico, Oklahoma, Arkansas, Louisiana, Texas	Dallas Area Office 1100 Commerce Street 6th Floor Dallas, Texas 75202
Nebraska, Iowa, Kansas, Missouri	Kansas City Area Office 601 East 12th Street, Room 129 Kansas City, Missouri 64106
Minnesota, Wisconsin, Michigan, Illinois, Indiana, Ohio	Chicago Area Office 219 S. Dearborn Street Chicago, Illinois 60604

Geographical Area *	U.S. Civil Service Commission with Jurisdiction
Kentucky, Tennessee, North Carolina, South Carolina, Mississippi, Alabama, Georgia, Florida	Atlanta Area Office Federal Office Building 275 Peachtree Street, N.E. Atlanta, Georgia 30303
New York, New Jersey, Delaware, Pennsylvania, Maryland, West Virginia, Virginia, Washington, D.C.	New York Area Office 26 Federal Plaza New York City, New York 10007
Maine, Vermont, New Hampshire, Massachusetts, Rhode Island, Connecticut	Boston Area Office 3 Center Plaza Boston, Massachusetts 02108
Alaska, Aleutian Islands	Anchorage Area Office 632 Sixth Avenue Anchorage, Alaska 99501
Hawaiian Islands	Honolulu Area Office 1000 Bishop Street Suite 1500 Honolulu, Hawaii 96813
Puerto Rico, Virgin Islands	Puerto Rico Area Office PAN AM Building 255 Ponce de Leon Avenue Hato Rey, Puerto Rico 00917

*See Map

About Announcements

Open and Closed

When applications are being accepted, an announcement is said to be "open," which means that you can apply, take the test and be rated eligible or ineligible for the job. If you are eligible, your name will go on a register, or list of people who are also qualified for the same kind of job.

When there are many names of eligibles on the register in proportion to the number of jobs to be filled, an announcement may be suspended or closed. In this case, no more applications will be accepted until the announcement is open again.

Exceptions:

1. Returning veterans can apply within 120 days after discharge even when an announcement is closed. If the veteran was hospitalized, application must be made within 120 days of discharge from the hospital.
2. Veterans with compensable disabilities may apply at any time.

Because needs for skills vary from time to time and from one area to another, it is possible that an announcement may be open in one location and closed in another.

How to Apply:

Besides this announcement, (#418), you need:

—the latest amendment to this announcement telling you which area offices are accepting applications

—CSC Form AN2300 telling you the locations where the written test is given

—CSC Form 5000AB

Steps to follow:

1. Check the latest amendment given with this announcement to see if the Area Office with jurisdiction over the location where you want to work is accepting applications. If the exam is suspended for that area, you will not be able to apply until the exam is again open in that area.
2. If the examination is open in the area where you want to work, check Form AN2300 and decide where you want to take the written test.

   A resident of any State or territory may be examined in any city named in the list. Select the place where you wish to take the examination from the list. Then enter the city, State, and correct code number on the application card.
3. Send the card (CSC Form 5000 AB) to the Area Office with jurisdiction over the place where you want to work. (Area Offices and their jurisdictions are listed on page 3)
4. The Area Office will schedule you for the test. After you take the test, the Area Office will review your qualifications and send you a "Notice of Rating." If you qualify, the notice of rating will show your numerical score. You will be ranked on a list of eligible candidates and referred in the order of your numerical score.

Where to Get Forms:

Forms and other information can be gotten at Federal Job Information Centers in person, by phone, or by mail. They are located in large cities (see your phone book for address).

Period of Eligibility:

Your eligibility will be established for a period of 1 year from the date of your notice of rating. For continued eligibility, you must submit updated information on your qualifications at intervals of not less than 11 or not more than 12 months.

Location of Eligibility:

You may establish eligibility for locations under the jurisdiction of one area office only. Because of the limited number of positions in Alaska, Hawaii, Guam, and Puerto Rico (including the Virgin Islands), residents of these areas will receive first consideration for employment in these areas. In the absence of well-qualified candidates on any list, candidates on other lists will be considered.

Air Traffic Controller Jobs at GS-9 and Above:

If you are interested in positions at grades GS-9 through GS-12, file a copy of Standard Form 171, card form 50001 ABC and Standard Form 15 (if needed) to the Mid-Level Desk, Number 411, at the U.S. Civil Service Commission Area Office with jurisdiction over the place where you want to work. Only a few of these positions are filled each year.

All qualified applicants will receive consideration for appointment without regard to race, religion, color, national origin, sex, political affiliations or any other non-merit factor.

SAMPLE QUESTIONS

The following sample questions show types of questions that will be used in the written test. They also show how the answers to the questions are to be recorded. Read the directions for each set of questions, and answer them. Record your answers on the Sample Answer Sheets provided on each page of this booklet. Then compare your answers with those given in the Correct Answers to Sample Questions on the same page.

Solve each problem and see which of the suggested answers A, B, C, or D is correct. Darken the space on the Sample Answer Sheet corresponding to the correct answer. If your answer does not exactly agree with any of the first four suggested answers, darken space E.

1. Add:

```
  9 6 3
  2 5 7
  4 1 6
  -----
```

Answers

A) 1,516
B) 1,526
C) 1,636
D) 1,726
E) none of these

2. Subtract:

```
  3 3
    8
  ---
```

A) 25
B) 26
C) 35
D) 36
E) none of these

3. Multiply:

```
  4 5
    5
  ---
```

Answers

A) 200
B) 215
C) 225
D) 235
E) none of these

4. Divide:

40) 1, 2 0 8

A) 3
B) 30
C) 33
D) 40
E) none of these

SAMPLE ANSWER SHEET

	A	B	C	D	E
1	▯	▯	▯	▯	▯
2	▯	▯	▯	▯	▯
3	▯	▯	▯	▯	▯
4	▯	▯	▯	▯	▯
5	▯	▯	▮	▯	▯
6	▯	▯	▯	▯	▯

In questions like No. 5 you are to select the one of the drawings of objects, A, B, C, or D, that would have the TOP, FRONT, and RIGHT views shown in the drawing at the left.

5.

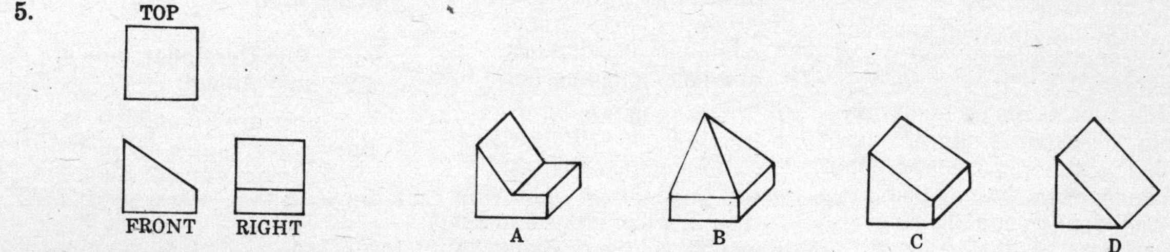

In question No. 5, object C looks like the view marked "TOP" when looked at from directly above, and like the views marked "FRONT" and "RIGHT" when looked at from the front and right side, respectively. Therefore, the space under C has been darkened for question No. 5 on the Sample Answer Sheet.

In questions like No. 6 you are to select the one of the drawings of objects, A, B, C, or D, that could be made from the flat piece drawn at the left, if this flat piece were folded on the dotted lines shown in the drawing.

6.

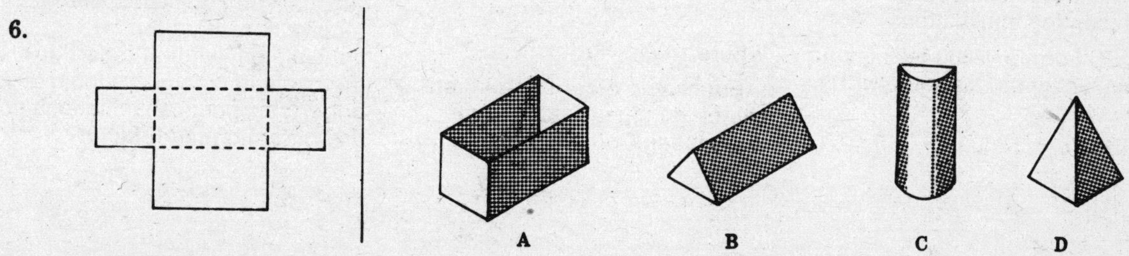

Correct Answers to Sample Questions are: 1, C; 2, A; 3, C; 4, E; 5, C; 6, A.

The problems on these two pages represent highly simplified versions of air-traffic control (ATC) situations. You will be concerned with maintaining adequate time and altitude separations for several aircraft which will

a) be flying at *different altitudes*, and

b) have *different ETA's* (estimated times of arrival) at or over Airport W. However, *all* the aircraft will

c) be flying the *same ground speed* toward Airport W, and

d) be flying on the *same course* toward Airport W.

After studying information presented in Flight Data Displays, determine which of several incoming flights can be permitted to make specified altitude changes while maintaining conformance with a basic traffic rule. For each question, use the flight data given in the display.

Basic traffic rule:

A SEPARATION OF 5 MINUTES IS NECESSARY BETWEEN TWO EN ROUTE AIRCRAFT WHICH ARE EXPECTED TO PASS OVER THE SAME GEOGRAPHICAL POINT AT THE SAME ALTITUDE.

For practice, look at the Sample Flight Data Display shown below.

SAMPLE FLIGHT DATA DISPLAY

Flight Identification	*Cruising Altitude*	*Estimated Time of Arrival (ETA) At or Over Airport W*
E	5000	2:25
F	4000	2:24
G	2000	2:20
H	3000	2:14

Notice that the aircraft are flying at *different altitudes* and that each is expected to arrive at or over, Airport W at a *different time*. However, remember that you are to assume that *ground speed and course* of all flights are the same. Also, consider *rate of climb and rate of descent* as UNKNOWN factors. (In other words, for purposes of these sample questions, make no speculation as to rate of climb or descent; just ignore these two factors completely.)

Answers to questions of this kind will involve a determination of both *time and altitude* separation for the various flights.

Sample Question I is based on information in the Sample Flight Data Display above. Mark your answer on the Sample Answer Sheet. If the correct answer is YES, mark space A, if NO, mark space B. Then compare your answer with the correct answer properly marked in Correct Answers to Sample Questions on page 3.

The question asks whether or not you can safely permit a change in altitude for

I. Flight E to 3000

SAMPLE ANSWER SHEET

	A	B	C	D	E
I	▯	▯	▯	▯	▯

You should have marked space B on the Sample Answer Sheet because Flight E is separated from Flight F by only 1 minute and if Flight E changes from 5000 to 3000 it must pass *through* 4000 which is occupied by Flight F. Flight E *cannot* be permitted to pass through the 4000-foot level without violating the air-traffic-control rule which requires a *minimum of 5 minutes* time separation between *two aircraft flying at the same altitude.*

Now try practice question **II, III, and IV. Mark** your answers on the Sample Answer Sheet and then compare them with the Correct Answers to Sample Questions.

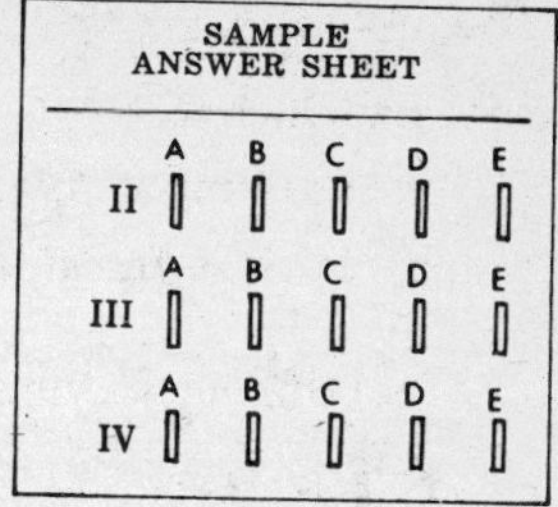

II. Flight G to 4000
III. Flight F to 2000
IV. Flight H to 500

The correct answer to question II is B. Flight G *cannot be permitted to* change from 2000 to 4000 because it is separated by only 4 minutes from Flight F which is flying at 4000.

The correct answer to question III is B. Flight F *cannot* be permitted to change from 4000 to 2000 because (as we have just noticed) it is separated by only 4 minutes from Flight G which is flying at 2000.

The correct answer to question IV is A because Flight H is 6 minutes ahead of the nearest aircraft and *can* be permitted to change to any altitude.

Now try practice questions V, VI, and VII.

SAMPLE ANSWER SHEET

	A	B	C	D	E
V	▯	▯	▯	▯	▯
VI	▯	▯	▯	▯	▯
VII	▯	▯	▯	▯	▯

V. Flight F to 3000
VI. Flight E to 4000
VII. Flight E to 6000

You should have marked A for question V. Flight F *can* safely be permitted to change from 4000 to 3000 because it will not have to move into or through the airspace of the nearest flights, E and G.

You should have marked B for question VI. Flight E *cannot* be permitted to change from 5000 to 4000 because it is separated by only 1 minute from Flight F which is flying at 4000.

The correct answer for question VII is A. Permitting Flight E to change from 5000 to 6000 would assure even greater altitude separation from Flight F which has a time separation of only 1 minute.

Now try the last of the practice questions and compare your answers with the Correct Answers to Sample Questions.

SAMPLE ANSWER SHEET

	A	B	C	D	E
VIII	▯	▯	▯	▯	▯
IX	▯	▯	▯	▯	▯
X	▯	▯	▯	▯	▯

VIII. Flight G to 5000
IX. Flight G to 4000
X. Flight H to 6000

Correct Answers to Sample Questions

	A	B	C	D	E
I	▯	▮	▯	▯	▯
II	▯	▮	▯	▯	▯
III	▯	▮	▯	▯	▯
IV	▮	▯	▯	▯	▯
V	▮	▯	▯	▯	▯
VI	▯	▮	▯	▯	▯
VII	▮	▯	▯	▯	▯
VIII	▯	▮	▯	▯	▯
IX	▯	▮	▯	▯	▯
X	▮	▯	▯	▯	▯

In each of the two following questions, at the left there is a series of seven letters which follow some definite order or pattern, and at the right there are five sets of two letters each. Look at the letters in the series and determine what the order is; then from the suggested answers at the right, select the set that gives the next two letters in the series. Next to the question number on the Sample Answer Sheet darken the space that has the same letter as the set you have chosen.

1. X C X D X E X A) F X B) F G C) X F D) E F E) X G

In question 1 only A could be the answer because the series consists of X's alternating with letters in alphabetical order. Sample question 2 is done in the same way.

2. A R C S E T G A) H I B) H U C) U J D) U I E) I V

Each of the next three questions has two boxes at the left. The symbols in the first box are like each other in some way, and the symbols in the second box are like each other in some way. But whatever it is that makes the symbols alike in one box makes them different from those in the other box. There is a question mark in the second box to indicate that a symbol is missing. You are to choose from the lettered symbols in the third box the one which best fits into the second box.

3.

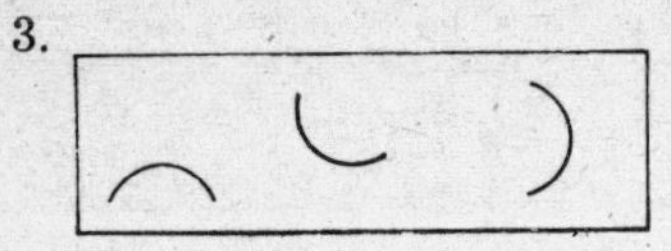

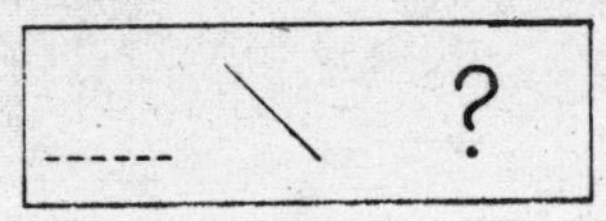

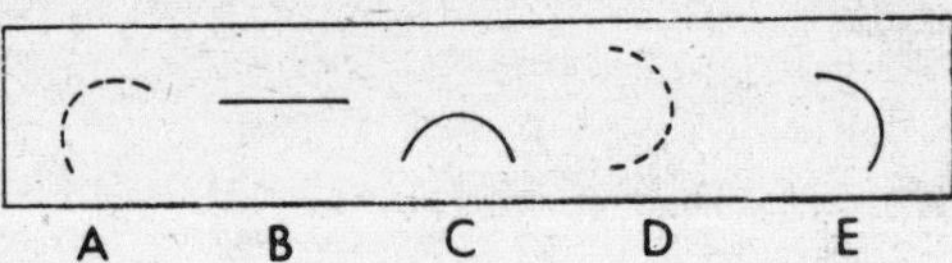

A B C D E

In sample question 3, all the symbols in the first box are curved lines. The second box has two lines, one dotted and one solid. Their *likeness* to each other consists in their straightness; and this straightness makes them *different* from the curves in the other box. The answer must be the *only* one of the five lettered choices that is a straight line, either dotted or solid. Now do questions 4 and 5.

4.

A B C D E

5.

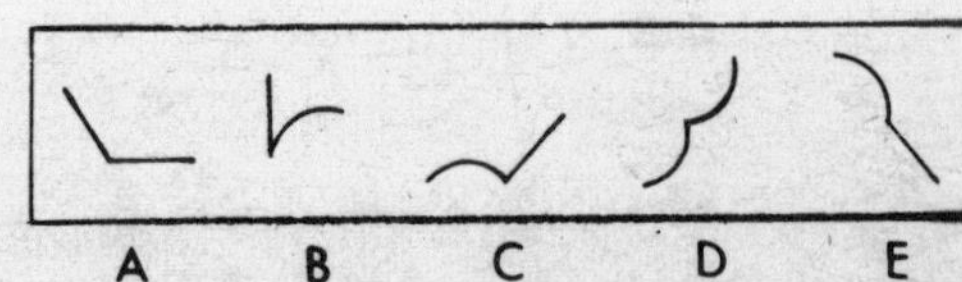

A B C D E

SAMPLE ANSWER SHEET

	A	B	C	D	E
1	▯	▯	▯	▯	▯
2	▯	▯	▯	▯	▯
3	▯	▯	▯	▯	▯
4	▯	▯	▯	▯	▯
5	▯	▯	▯	▯	▯

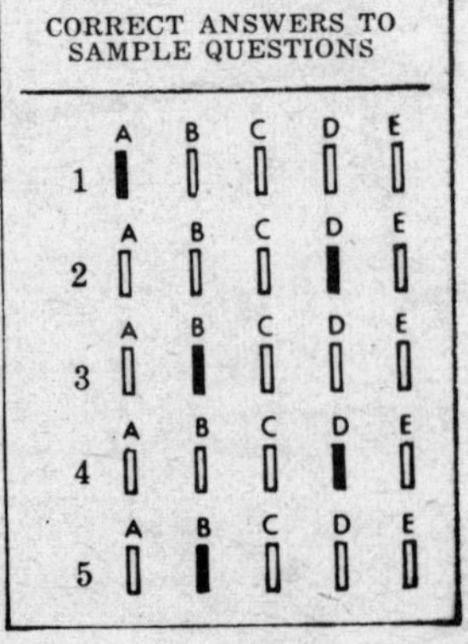

NOTE: There is not supposed to be a *series* or progression in these symbol questions. If you look for a progression in the first box and try to find the missing figure to fill out a similar progression in the second box, you will be wasting time. For example, look at question 3. A competitor who saw that both boxes had a horizontal figure followed by an oblique one might try to find a vertical figure to match the last one in the first box. If he chose D he would be missing the real point of the question. Remember, look for a *likeness* within each box and a *difference* between the two boxes.

As the map shows, there are 11 FAA regions. Be sure to apply where you are willing to work because transfers between regions rarely occur before the controller reaches full performance level.

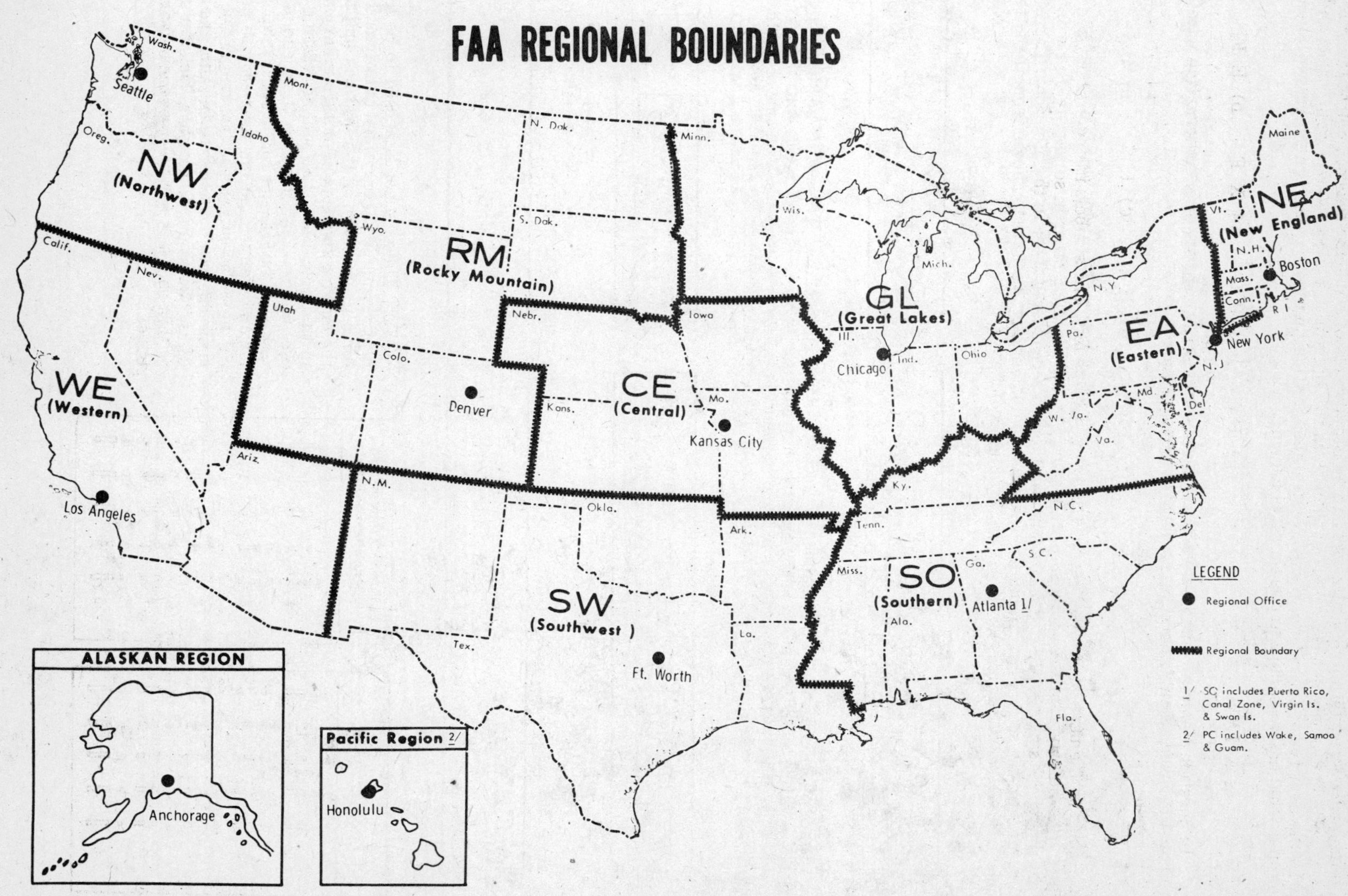

Amendment to Announcement No. 418
AIR TRAFFIC CONTROLLERS
Effective through March 31, 1978

UNITED STATES CIVIL SERVICE COMMISSION
Washington, D.C. 20415

1. Effective January 1, 1978, only those area offices listed below are accepting applications for Air Traffic Controller positions located in their jurisdiction. Applications will not be accepted in any other jurisdiction until further notice.

Anchorage	For positions at GS-5 and GS-7 from residents of Alaska only.
Chicago	All options, GS-7 from January 1 through January 31.
Kansas City	All options, GS-7 from January 1 through January 31.
San Juan	For positions, GS-5 and GS-7 for centers and towers from residents of Puerto Rico and the Virgin Islands only.

2. APPLICANTS ARE LIMITED TO COMPETING IN THE WRITTEN TEST FOR ATC ONCE DURING A QUARTER. IF AN APPLICANT TAKES THE WRITTEN TEST MORE THAN ONCE DURING ANY GIVEN QUARTER, ONLY THE RESULTS FROM THE FIRST WRITTEN TEST WILL BE COUNTED.

3. The Honolulu Area Office will accept Job Interest Cards from individuals interested in GS-5 or GS-7 positions in Hawaii, regardless of residence. These cards may be obtained from the Honolulu Area Office.

4. Because of the limited number of positions in Alaska, Hawaii, Puerto Rico, and the Virgin Islands, residents of these areas may receive first consideration for employment in these areas.

5. The reference on page 4 of Announcement No. 418 to Air Traffic Controller positions at GS-9 and above, applies only to positions with the Department of Defense. (FAA is not hiring at these grade levels.)

6. Please refer to Announcement No. 418 for information on area office addresses and examining jurisdictions.

7. The following area office addresses have changed:

Anchorage:	617 G Street, Alaska 99501
Denver:	1845 Sherman Street, Colorado 80203
Honolulu:	Federal Building, 300 Ala Moana Boulevard, Hawaii 96813
San Juan:	Carlos E. Chardon St., Rm. 124, Hato Rey, Puerto Rico 00918
Seattle:	Federal Bldg., 26th Fl., 915 Second Ave., Washington 98174

8. THIS AMENDMENT SUPERSEDES AND CANCELS ALL PREVIOUS AMENDMENTS TO ANNOUNCEMENT NO. 418. This amendment is effective through March 31, 1978, at which time a revised amendment will be issued.

Issued April 2, 1973 **Amendment to Announcement No. 418**

UNITED STATES CIVIL SERVICE COMMISSION
Washington, D. C. 20415

AIR TRAFFIC CONTROLLER
GS-5 Through GS-9

1. Effective immediately the receipt of applications will be accepted for Air Traffic Controller GS-5/7 positions at *centers* and *towers* only, until further notice.

2. Applications will no longer be accepted for positions at centers, towers, or flight service stations, grade GS-9. The lists of eligibles for this grade will be terminated. Entry to Air Traffic Controller positions will no longer be made to positions in grade GS-9.

3. On the basis of authority provided by the Air Traffic Controller Career Act of 1972, a maximum age limit of 30 at the time of appointment for all candidates has been established for Air Traffic Controller positions at *towers and centers*. Therefore, applications will not be accepted from candidates for these positions who have reached their 31st birthday. Candidates who establish eligibility will be dropped from the list of eligibles for tower and center positions if their ratings do not come within reach for consideration so that they can be entered on duty before they reach age 31. This age limit does not apply to positions at *flight service stations*.

4. Effective with this notice the geographic jurisdictions of Civil Service Commission area offices maintaining registers is revised as follows. This replaces information on page 20 of Announcement No. 418, revised February 1971.

For Positions Located In:	*Send Card Form 5000AB to: U. S. Civil Service Commission*
Washington, Oregon, Idaho	Seattle Area Office Federal Office Building 1st Ave. & Madison St. Seattle, Wash. 98104
California, Arizona, Nevada	Los Angeles Area Office 851 South Broadway Los Angeles, Calif. 90014
Montana, Wyoming, North Dakota, South Dakota, Utah, Colorado	Denver Area Office U. S. Post Office Building 18th & Stout Sts. Denver, Colo. 80202
New Mexico, Oklahoma, Arkansas, Louisiana, Texas	Dallas Area Office 1100 Commerce St. 6th Floor Dallas, Texas, 75202
Nebraska, Iowa, Kansas, Missouri	Kansas Area Office 120 S. Market St. Kansas City, Mo. 64106
Minnesota, Wisconsin, Michigan, Illinois, Indiana, Ohio	Chicago Area Office 219 S. Dearborn St. Chicago, Ill. 60604

For Positions Located In:	*Send Card Form 5000AB to: U. S. Civil Service Commission*
Kentucky, Tennessee, North Carolina, South Carolina, Mississippi, Alabama, Georgia, Florida	Atlanta Area Office Federal Office Building 275 Peachtree St., N.E. Atlanta, Ga. 30303
New York, New Jersey, Delaware, Pennsylvania, Maryland, West Virginia, Virginia, Washington, D. C.	New York Area Office 26 Federal Plaza New York City, N. Y. 10007
Maine, Vermont, New Hampshire, Massachusetts, Rhode Island, Connecticut	Boston Area Office Post Office and Courthouse Bldg. Boston, Mass. 02109
Alaska, Aleutian Islands	Anchorage Area Office 632 Sixth Avenue Anchorage, Alaska 99501
Hawaiian Islands	Honolulu Area Office 1000 Bishop St., Suite 1500 Honolulu, Hawaii 96813
Puerto Rico, Virgin Islands	Puerto Rico Area Office PAN AM Building 255 Ponce de Leon Ave. Hato Rey, P. R. 00917

5. Candidates who meet all requirements will have 12 months eligibility from the date on the notice of rating. Eligibility may be extended an additional 12 months by request one month prior to the expiration of the period of eligibility.

6. Candidates may establish eligibility for locations under the jurisdiction of *one* area office only.
For jobs in Alaska, Hawaii, and Puerto Rico, first preference will be given to local residents.
In the absence of well-qualified candidates on any list, candidates on other lists will be considered.

7. The information in the section "How to Apply" on the inside of the back cover of Announcement No. 418, revised February 1971, is corrected to read "to take the written test, send the form below (or Card Form 5000AB) to the area office of the Civil Service Commission . . .". Also, the reference to "5001AB" in the section "Where to Get Forms" is corrected to read "5000AB." The second paragraph under "How to Apply" is no longer applicable since initial appointments to grade GS-9 will no longer be made.

8. The information on pages 18 and 19 is corrected as follows:
a. Written tests will *not* be held at:

Decatur, Alabama

Oceanside, California
San Luis Obispo, California

Burley, Idaho
Caldwell, Idaho
Preston, Idaho
Weiser, Idaho

Tuscola, Illinois

Jefferson, Indiana

Davenport, Iowa
Denison, Iowa
Keokuk, Iowa

Kansas City, Kansas

Lebanon, Kentucky

Goldwater, Michigan
Holland, Michigan
Ludington, Michigan

Minneapolis, Minnesota
St. Paul, Minnesota

Gulfport, Mississippi

Thompson Falls, Montana

Red Bank, New Jersey

Santa Rosa, New Mexico
White Sands Missile Range, New Mexico

Norwich, New York

Garrison, North Dakota
Valley City, North Dakota

New Philadelphia, Ohio

Ashland, Oregon

Wagner, South Dakota

Fort Stockton, Texas

Beaver, Utah
Delta, Utah
Panguitch, Utah
St. George, Utah

Alexandria, Virginia

Chency, Washington
Port Townsend, Washington

b. Written tests *will* be held at the following additional locations:

Downey, California	60-53	Fort Monmouth, New Jersey	16-14
Fort Snelling, Minnesota	45-12	John Day, Oregon	58-13

9. By previous amendment, notice was given that effective July 19, 1971, the qualifications standards for grade GS-7 were amended, and that applicants may not qualify for grade GS-7 on on the basis of achieving the prescribed scores on the Graduate Record Examination.

10. This amendment supersedes and cancels all previous amendments to Announcement No. 418.

★U.S. Government Printing Office: 1973-783-104/331 Region 8

STEPS TO A JOB IN THE COMPETITIVE FEDERAL SERVICE

STEP 1 FIND OUT ABOUT EXAMINATIONS

Obtain the latest examination announcements for your particular field of interest. Study to find out if you meet the experience and/or educational requirements. Examination announcements may be obtained from college placement offices, or any Civil Service Commission regional office.

STEP 2 APPLY FOR EXAMINATION

After you have determined that you may qualify for a particular kind of position, obtain the application forms specified in the examination announcement. Be sure to mail your application to the address designated in the announcement, and before the deadline.

STEP 3 TAKE THE TEST

If a written test is required, you will have an opportunity to indicate where you want to take the test, and will later be notified when and where to report for the test. Where no written test is required, applicants are rated on experience and education they list on the application forms. It is vital that you exercise care in completing your application forms and include all important facts about your education and experience.

STEP 4 RESULTS OF THE EXAMINATION

To be successful in the examination, an applicant must make a passing score of at least 70 points. After your examination is rated, you will be notified whether you have received an "eligible" or an "ineligible" rating and the numerical score you have earned -- this is called a "Notice of Examination Results" or "Notice of Rating." When you receive an "eligible" notice, you know that your name has been entered on the list of "eligibles" in rank order by score.

STEP 5 HOW JOBS ARE FILLED

When a particular Federal agency has a job to fill, the hiring official of that agency asks the Civil Service Commission for the names of persons who are "eligibles" for that kind of job. The Civil Service Commission then sends to the agency a list of those "eligibles" who rank highest on the list at the time of the request. The hiring official has a choice from among the top 3 "eligibles" for each job to be filled. He may ask the "eligibles" to come in for a personal interview before making his selection. After the hiring official has made his selection, the names of those who were not selected are returned to the list of "eligibles" and again placed in rank order by score for consideration when other vacancies occur.

Federal agencies may obtain from the Civil Service Commission authority to make temporary appointment pending the establishment of a list of eligibles if the Commission has insufficient eligibles available for filling such a position. Accordingly, agencies at times accept applications direct from persons seeking employment in the Federal service.

STEP 6 CHANCES OF EMPLOYMENT

The Federal Government needs approximately 250,000 new employees each year to replace those who retire, die or leave the service for other reasons. Your chances of employment depend on a number of factors:

(1) How well you scored in the examination in comparison with other competitors.
(2) How fast vacancies are occurring and jobs are being filled.
(3) How many "eligibles" there are for that kind of job.
(4) The geographic locations in which you are willing to accept employment. Remember: If you indicate you will accept employment only in certain locations, you are not just indicating a preference -- you will be considered for employment only in the areas where you have indicated you will accept employment. Obviously, your chances of employment are reduced in direct proportion to the extent that you limit your geographical availability.
(5) The minimum salary or grade you indicate you are willing to accept. Remember: If, for example, you indicate the minimum salary or grade you will accept is GS-7, you will not be considered for any position below that level. Conversely, no matter what you indicate as the minimum you will accept, you will be rated for the highest level for which you can qualify.

THE INTERVIEW

The interview is actually an important part of many examinations. This is especially true of job examinations. For many jobs (especially the more important, better-paying jobs) the examination may consist entirely of an oral test, given either to one candidate at a time or to a small group of applicants.

Interview tests are given to obtain information about the technical knowledge and personality of the candidate or candidates. When a written examination has been held --usually before the oral interview--the purpose of the interview is to supplement the information obtained about the candidate from his written examination paper.

Most people walk into an oral examination or interview feeling that the cards are stacked against them, that there is nothing they can do to prepare for the interview.

However, there are certain steps that you can take in advance to prepare yourself for the oral test.

Walking into a room to face a group of strangers places the candidate at a disadvantage, but it is often possible to find out who will conduct the interview. If you are to be interviewed by a private business organization, a little discreet questioning may enable you to learn whom you will face in the interview room.

If you are facing an interview or oral test for a Civil Service position, you will meet an FAA representative and probably a representative of the Civil Service Commission. Another member will represent the department in which the applicant is seeking employment.

Sometimes outside experts are called in, and often a local businessman or someone selected as a representative of the public is invited to sit on the board.

It is always a good idea to learn in advance the identity of the representatives and whatever you can about them. Then when you face them in the interview room, you will have an idea of their individual backgrounds and interests and will know their names.

Five Ways to Prepare for the Oral Test

There is no reason to go into the oral test "cold." The following five steps should help you in getting yourself organized for the test.

1. Review your application. Keep a copy of your application and review it with care before your interview. Often a copy of your application will be the only document about you that the interviewers will have before them, and their questions may be based largely on substantiating the claims made in your application as to your background and experience. Make certain that you have fixed in your mind the experience and education statements in your application, and be especially sure of dates and sequences. You may be asked to review the highlights of your experience and you should be able to do so without fumbling or referring to notes. If you have made any slight exaggerations in your application form about the importance of some job you held or some work you did, be prepared to defend your statements before the board. Any admission that perhaps you "stretched the truth a little" will count heavily against you.

2. Review the purpose of the oral test. A candidate for a higher educational degree goes into the interview room prepared to defend his previously written theses or paper. He knows that the subject matter of the oral test will center on that specific paper, and goes into the room prepared to buttress with oral argument the points made in the paper.

It is more probable that your oral test will involve your suitability for a specific job. Restudy the original announcement of the job test. The qualities, characteristics, or background required for holding the job almost always are stated in the announcement. From that, you can draw important clues to the type of questions you will face.

Let's assume that you are being considered for a supervisory clerical job. The job announcement stated that both a knowledge of modern supervisory practices in business and the personal qualifications of the candidate as a supervisor would be tested. Knowing that, you can readily expect questions on techniques of supervision, especially on how you would deal with a specific situation faced by an office supervisor. Very often these are in the form of hypothetical questions.

On the other hand, if the job you are trying for is of a technical nature, involving little contact with other people, you can expect questions of the "how would you do this?" type, and questions to test your knowledge of techniques and equipment in your field of work.

It's a good rule never to walk into an interview without a full knowledge of the duties and responsibilities of the job you are after.

3. Try to anticipate the questions. Sit down and have a talk with yourself. Try to visualize the questions the board members will ask you. Imagine what questions you would ask if you were a board member, and how you would rate your own answers to them. Measure your own knowledge and background against the job you are seeking and look for areas in which you feel weak. Above all, be realistic and critical.

4. Review for the oral test. The best study preparation for the oral test is general reading in any field in which you think you may be a bit weak. Try especially to use this reading to fill any gaps in your experience background. To get back to our example of the supervisory job, if the job calls for supervision and your personal experience in supervising others is limited, then some general study on supervisory methods and in human relationships could help you. You might also review some supervisory examinations given for other jobs to get an idea of the situation-questions that may be asked of you. The oral representative will be more likely to ask questions of a general nature that will test your understanding and ability, rather than your memory of specific things or methods.

5. Walk in looking healthy. The representatives, consciously or not, will be affected by your general appearance. Get a good night's sleep before the interview. If you feel a cold or other minor ailment coming on (which may be a result of nervous tension brought on by the prospect of the interview), take care of it. If you are inclined to be nervous or shy in strange situations, ask your family doctor to recommend a tranquilizer that you can take shortly before the interview test. Don't prime yourself for the ordeal by taking a drink or tow.

The Day is Here

Give yourself plenty of time. Allow for missing a train or bus, and make certain that you arrive ahead of your schedule time. Very often one or more candidates fail to show up and the representatives may be ready for you even before the exact time listed on your notification card or letter. This is particularly important if your appointment is scheduled for the early morning.

By afternoon, most oral testing representatives are behind their schedule and you may face a long wait. Bring along something to read, or take your copy of your application for a last-minute review. But when you go into the examination room, leave your literature behind. Nothing makes a poorer impression than the candidate who comes in with an armful of papers and magazines and wastes time getting settled.

It shouldn't be necessary to mention the matter of dress, except that many persons ruin their own chances by walking into the examination room needing a shave or haircut, with shoes unshined, and sometimes needing a bath. The moment the door opens and you walk in, the representatives begin getting an impression of you, and your appearance can count for a lot. Avoid flashy dress, and choose conservatice clothes that would fit any business conference. If you don't have the right clothes, borrow them from a friend or relative, or invest in a suit or dress that meets the occasion.

Now Your're In

Finally, your wait is over. Someone calls your name and escorts you to the examination room. From then on, you will be going through the same routine that many persons have lived through before getting their job appointments.

The clerk will introduce you to the representatives. Try to catch every name. Acknowledge the introductions before you sit down. You'll probably find yourself facing a microphone or a tape recorder, or a stenotypist will be there to take down every word. Oral tests are usually recorded in the event that there is an appeal from the representative's rating or other review of the session.

Most often a chairman will start the interview by reviewing the high spots of your education and work experience. This information is taken from your application and is brought up first in order to acquaint the other members with your qualifications and to get that material into the record.

Your job at this stage is to sit there and keep quiet unless you notice an important error or omission. If that happens, speak up.

Next, the chairman will ask you some questions about your present job or your education, mostly to get you talking and to give the board an impression of you as a person. The actual questioning will be started by the chairman or one of the members. Often, each member will cover some one phase of the questioning, and you can expect to have each member of the board question you. Very often, because the time is limited, you will find abrupt switches in the field covered by the questions. Unless a representative discovers some particular strong or weak point, he won't question you at length.

Your Chance to Talk

After each representative has had an opportunity to question you, the chairman will ask if anyone has further questions. If not, he will turn to you and ask whether there is anything you wish to add.

You must be careful at this point. Do not start off on a long speech telling the representative how well qualified you are for the job; and don't try to use psychology on them. Telling them how much you enjoyed meeting them or complimenting them on the fairness of their questions can only hurt your chances.

This opportunity is given you to add anything that may have been overlooked in the questioning, such as some special qualifications, or something you may have accomplished since filing the application that would improve your chances for the job.

If you haven't anything really vital to add, then say "Thanks. I've nothing further to add." Make sure you do not talk yourself out of a good impression.

The Chairman will close the interview by telling you, "That's all, thank you," and that's your clue to leave.

Let's Talk Strategy

You probably feel that the interview or oral test is a battle between you and the examiners or interviewers. To some extent that's true, but you must consider that the examiners have a job to do. Their function is to appraise your qualifications for the job in comparison with those of the other candidates. An uncooperative candidate is working against his own interests. The representatives would like to see you in the best possible light. They are not trying to dig out your secret weaknesses or to embarrass you.

20 Points of Strategy

The following list of 20 points of oral test strategy has been developed from the experience of hundreds of oral tests. Study this list to build up the proper mental attitude and approach for your test.

1. Your physical position. Never lounge or sprawl to show that you are at ease. Sit erect, not too stiffly. Do not smoke unless the chairman gives you permission to do so. Never fuss with your clothing or with ashtrays or papers. You'll probably be a bit nervous, but the board expects that and makes allowances for it.

2. Your outward attitude. Act naturally, not in a cocky manner. Never apologize for weaknesses; concentrate on bringing out your strong points. Board members will think that an outward show of overconfidence may be your means of hiding a weakness.

3. Don't be a comedian. The representatives haven't met to hear your wisecracks or small talk. They consider their hearings a serious matter and expect you to do so too Also, their time is limited and they don't expect to be amused by candidates who come before them.

4. Don't exaggerate. If there is some overmagnification of a statement on your application form, you must defend it. Otherwise, describe your experience and abilities correctly. Sometimes the representatives have the report of an outside investigator before them and may know more about you and your background than you realize. If your experience was as a shipping clerk, you'll find it hard to convince them that you've been a traffic manager.

5. Don't try to take over. Giving the impression that you are trying to dominate the interview will do you no good. Let the representatives give you the clues. Answer their questions with facts, then shut up. Don't try to use up all the interview time by showing how much you know about the answer to the first question.

6. Pay attention. Your whole oral test won't take more than 20 minutes or so. When the chairman or a representative asks you a question, give him your fullest attention. When you reply, answer directly to the one who directed the question to you, but speak clearly enough so that other members can hear you.

7. Be sure you understand the question. Don't anticipate and start answering before the question is finished. If you are not clear about the question, restate it in your own words, or ask the examiner to clarify the question for you. But don't make a habit of quibbling about minor points in the question to show that you can outsmart the examiner.

8. Don't interrupt a member. Sometimes, instead of coming out directly with a question, the examiner will state a situation and then ask his question. Give him enough time to finish before you begin answering.

9. Don't stall on answers. One blank on the rating sheet used by oral examiners says, "Candidate responded readily," another "Candidate hesitated in replies." Answer questions as promptly as you can but take a few seconds first to organize your answer so that you will avoid errors caused by a hasty, ill-considered reply.

10. Don't be overhasty in reply. Answering questions isn't a race between you and the examiners. Don't try to answer every question with a brief, quick-fire reply. Take enough time to give a full, considered answer to every question.

11. Don't try to give the "answer he wants." Many candidates make the mistake of trying to give every examiner the answer he wants, instead of an accurate answer. Most examiners have long experience in giving oral tests; they know when the candidate is trying to play this game with them and mark him down accordingly.

12. Be consistent. Many examiners will take a contrary position merely to see how the candidate reacts. Don't switch sides just to agree with a member. If you think you are right on a given point, stick with it. Don't let the questioning turn into a debate. You can only lose.

13. Admit errors you may make. If some point comes up during the interview or test in which you have made an error of fact or judgment, don't be afraid to admit it. The examiners know that you are on the "hot seat," answering their questions without any chance for prolonged consideration or research. Admit your error, and go on with the test.

14. Don't spend too much time talking about your present job. The examiners know what you are doing now; they are considering you for a better job. Try to word all your answers in terms of the job for which you are being considered.

15. Keep to the point. Don't bring up extraneous remarks or tell any long anecdotes. If you have to tell about some personal experience, keep it short and leave out minor details.

16. Don't overplay your technical knowledge. The examiners either know all the technical language that is involved in your work, or they aren't interested in it. They are interviewing a person, not a walking technical manual.

17. Watch your grammar. Avoid the use of slang and be careful to use your best English during your test or interview. The examiners will be alert for slips of grammar, slang, or poor word usage.

18. Don't bring a pile of exhibits. The oral testroom isn't the place to show your letters of reference, clippings, written papers, etc., unless you have been specifically asked to bring them.

19. Don't try "soft soap." Be pleasant and act naturally, but remember that the interview representatives aren't auditioning you for a TV commercial. You can lose points by overdoing the personality business.

20. If you know one of the examiners, personally or through business, don't play it up or try to hide it. Very often the examiner will tell other representatives that he knows you; sometimes he will agree not to rate you. If he is one of the questioners, treat him exactly like every other board member.

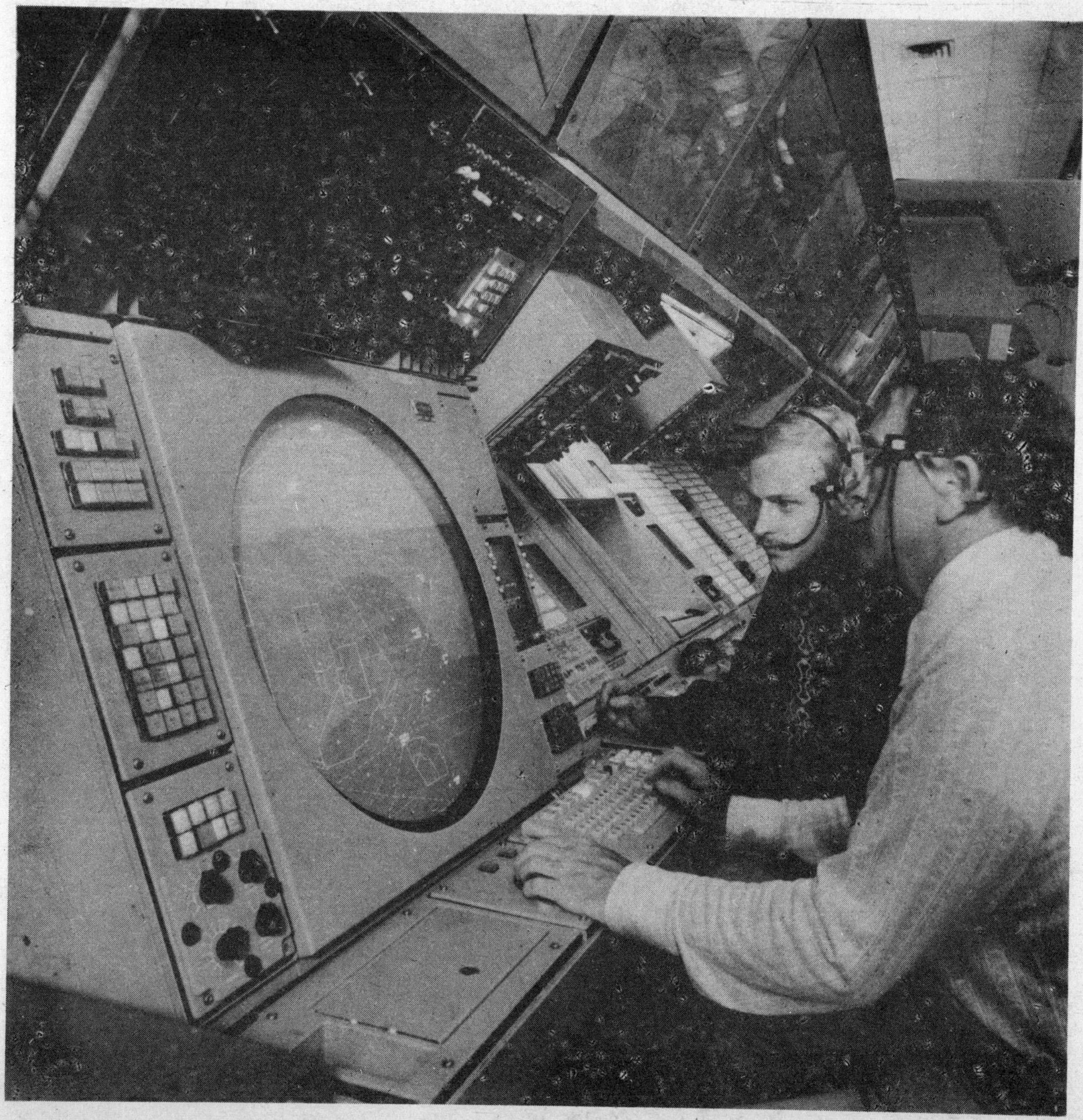

JOB INFORMATION LIST

Air Traffic Control Specialist

NAME OF CANDIDATE

INSTRUCTIONS – This is a reminder of the information which should be covered in each interview. Tell applicant that he will later get much of the material referred to below in written form if he is appointed. Take care that covering this list doesn't use time needed for getting information from applicant.

"√" *each item as you cover it*

	√
1. THE POSITION *(ATC specialties)*	
2. THE BASIC PURPOSE *(Describe briefly)*	
3. THE FAA *(The mission of, and relation to DOT)*	
4. THE ORGANIZATION *(Regions, areas, facilities)*	
5. OTHER FAA FUNCTIONS *(Design equipment, install and maintain it, flight check it; certify pilots, airports, airplanes; plan and establish airways, air navigation facilities; research)*	
6. TYPES OF EQUIPMENT USED BY AIR TRAFFIC CONTROLLERS *(Most advanced communications, radar, digital, etc.)*	
7. LOCATION OF WORK *(Describe working environment and isolated locations of AT Facilities)*	
8. JOB CONDITIONS *(Hours, rotating shifts, overtime, short turnarounds, week-ends and holidays)*	
9. CAREER CONDITIONAL APPOINTMENT *(Three years to "Career," first year probationary)*	
10. STARTING GRADE AND SALARY *(Entrance grade)*	
11. TRAINING *(At Academy in OKC, include per diem travel allowances etc.; on-the-job-training)*	
12. PROMOTION *(Merit promotion systems; stress merit, not automatic)*	
13. MOBILITY *(Working in different environments, i.e., different geographic locations and low to high activity)* RIGHT OF AGENCY TO ADMINISTRATIVELY REASSIGN	
14. FEDERAL EMPLOYEE BENEFITS *(Retirement, annual and sick leave, health insurance, step increases, incentive awards, group life insurance)*	
15. WITHDRAWAL PROCEDURES *(Academy, post-academy)*	

FAA Form 3300-23 (10-70)

GPO 901-639

FAA AC 71-6211

INTERVIEW RECORD AND EVALUATION FOR
Air Traffic Control Specialist

LOCATION

NAME OF CANDIDATE

DATE OF BIRTH

DATE OF INTERVIEW

ADDRESS

TELEPHONE NUMBERS

OFFICE NO.

RESTRICTIONS ON AVAILABILITY *(e.g., location, grade level, date available)*

GRADE LEVEL APPLIED FOR GS–

CANDIDATE'S OPTION PREFERENCE
☐ STATION ☐ CENTER ☐ TOWER

HOME NO.

PART I – INTERVIEW AND EVALUATION

A – APPEARANCE *("X" applicable box(es))*

1. ☐ IMMACULATE 2. ☐ NEAT 3. ☐ DISHEVELED 4. ☐ UNSHAVEN 5. ☐ UNCLEAN 6. ☐ SLOVENLY

7. ☐ OTHER *(If "X," specify)*

B – ORAL EXPRESSION *(Write "Yes" or "No" as applicable in each box)*

DICTION

1. ☐ DEFECTS OR DISTRACTION IN VOICE 2. ☐ CHOOSES WORDS PRECISELY 3. ☐ PRONOUNCES WORDS CORRECTLY

4. ☐ SPEAKS CLEARLY 5. ☐ SLURRS SPEECH 6. ☐ LISPS OR STAMMERS 7. ☐ HARD TO UNDERSTAND

8. ☐ OTHER *(If "Yes," specify)*

FLUENCY

9. ☐ VOCABULARY ADEQUATE 10. ☐ SENTENCE STRUCTURE CLEAR 11. ☐ USES WORDS CORRECTLY 12. ☐ QUESTIONABLE USE OF SLANG OR COLLOQUIALISMS

13. ☐ PRONOUNCES WORDS CORRECTLY 14. ☐ PRONOUNCES WORDS TOO RAPIDLY 15. ☐ OTHER *(If "Yes," specify)*

UNDERSTANDING

16. ☐ MAKES HIMSELF UNDERSTOOD ORALLY 17. ☐ UNDERSTANDS OTHERS READILY 18. ☐ LISTENS TO WHAT OTHERS SAY

19. ☐ COMMENTS *(If "Yes," explain)*

C – ATTITUDE *("X" applicable box(es))*

1. ☐ ENTHUSIASTIC 2. ☐ FRIENDLY 3. ☐ QUIET 4. ☐ TALKATIVE 5. ☐ DISCOURTEOUS 6. ☐ ARGUMENTATIVE

7. ☐ CONFIDENT 8. ☐ CONFUSED 9. ☐ OTHER *(If "X," specify)*

D – STABILITY *(Write "Yes" or "No" as applicable in each box)*

1. ☐ GETS UPSET EASILY 2. ☐ SEEMS HIGHLY NERVOUS 3. ☐ LOOSES SELF-CONTROL READILY 4. ☐ APPEARS SELF POSSESSED

5. ☐ REACTS STRONGLY WHEN DISAGREED WITH 6. ☐ RELAXED 7. ☐ TENSE

E – PERCEPTION AND VITALITY *(Write "Yes" or "No" as applicable in each box)*

1. ☐ SLOW TO UNDERSTAND QUESTIONS 2. ☐ LETS HIS ATTENTION WANDER 3. ☐ IS OBJECTIVE

4. ☐ DISPLAYS SOUND JUDGMENT 5. ☐ SLOW TO RESPOND TO QUESTIONS 6. ☐ APPEARS ALERT AND ENERGETIC

F – MOTIVATION AND INTEREST *(Write "Yes" or "No" as applicable in each box)*

1. ☐ EXPRESSES A POSITIVE INTEREST IN AIR TRAFFIC CONTROL 2. ☐ REASONS FOR DESIRING THIS TYPE OF WORK ARE SOUND

3. ☐ EXPRESSES DESIRE FOR A CAREER THAT IS CONSISTENT WITH THE NEEDS OF AIR TRAFFIC CONTROL 4. ☐ SEEMS INTERESTED IN DOING A JOB WELL 5. ☐ EASILY DISCOURAGED

5. ☐ COMMENTS ON ANY OTHER OBSERVATIONS FELT SIGNIFICANT

FAA Form 3300-22 (10-70) SUPERSEDES FAA FORM 3300-19

PART II – APPRAISAL

INSTRUCTIONS – Read the instructions below before completing evaluation.

1. If you appraise the candidate as "Unacceptable", an objection to this candidate will be sent to the Civil Service Commission.
2. If you appraise the candidate as "Below Average", an objection to this candidate may be sent to the Civil Service Commission.
3. If your appraisal is "Unacceptable" or "Below Average", state your reasons.

APPRAISAL *("X" applicable box)*

1. ☐ UNACCEPTABLE *2.* ☐ BELOW AVERAGE *3.* ☐ AVERAGE *4.* ☐ ABOVE AVERAGE *5.* ☐ EXCELLENT

REASONS FOR "UNACCEPTABLE" OR "BELOW AVERAGE" APPRAISAL

INTERVIEW PANEL RECOMMENDATIONS

	SIGNATURE AND TITLE
PRINCIPAL INTERVIEWER ▶	
INTERVIEWER II ▶	SIGNATURE AND TITLE
INTERVIEWER III ▶	SIGNATURE AND TITLE

FAA AC 71-6212

Part II

First Practice Test

TEAR OUT ALONG THIS LINE AND MARK YOUR ANSWERS AS INSTRUCTED IN THE TEXT.

ANSWER SHEET

1 A B C D E
2 A B C D E
3 A B C D E
4 A B C D E
5 A B C D E
6 A B C D E
7 A B C D E
8 A B C D E
9 A B C D E
10 A B C D F
11 A B C D E
12 A B C D E
13 A B C D E
14 A B C D E
15 A B C D E
16 A B C D E
17 A B C D E
18 A B C D E
19 A B C D E
20 A B C D E
21 A B C D E
22 A B C D E
23 A B C D E
24 A B C D E
25 A B C D E
26 A B C D E
27 A B C D E
28 A B C D E
29 A B C D E
30 A B C D E
31 A B C D E

32 A B C D E
33 A B C D E
34 A B C D E
35 A B C D E
36 A B C D E
37 A B C D E
38 A B C D E
39 A B C D E
40 A B C D E
41 A B C D E
42 A B C D E
43 A B C D E
44 A B C D E
45 A B C D E
46 A B C D E
47 A B C D E
48 A B C D E
49 A B C D E
50 A B C D E
51 A B C D E
52 A B C D E
53 A B C D E
54 A B C D E
55 A B C D E
56 A B C D E
57 A B C D E
58 A B C D E
59 A B C D E
60 A B C D E
61 A B C D E
62 A B C D E

63 A B C D E
64 A B C D E
65 A B C D E
66 A B C D E
67 A B C D E
68 A B C D E
69 A B C D E
70 A B C D E
71 A B C D E
72 A B C D E
73 A B C D E
74 A B C D E
75 A B C D E

1 A B C D E
2 A B C D E
3 A B C D E
4 A B C D E
5 A B C D E
6 A B C D E
7 A B C D E
8 A B C D E
9 A B C D E
10 A B C D F
11 A B C D E
12 A B C D E
13 A B C D E
14 A B C D E
15 A B C D E
16 A B C D E
17 A B C D E

18 A B C D E
19 A B C D E
20 A B C D E
21 A B C D E
22 A B C D E
23 A B C D E
24 A B C D E
25 A B C D E
26 A B C D E
27 A B C D E
28 A B C D E
29 A B C D E
30 A B C D E
31 A B C D E
32 A B C D E
33 A B C D E
34 A B C D E
35 A B C D E
36 A B C D E
37 A B C D E
38 A B C D E
39 A B C D E
40 A B C D E
41 A B C D E
42 A B C D E
43 A B C D E
44 A B C D E
45 A B C D E
46 A B C D E
47 A B C D E
48 A B C D E

49 A B C D E
50 A B C D E
51 A B C D E
52 A B C D E
53 A B C D E
54 A B C D E
55 A B C D E
56 A B C D E
57 A B C D E
58 A B C D E
59 A B C D E
60 A B C D E

1 A B C D E
2 A B C D E
3 A B C D E
4 A B C D E
5 A B C D E
6 A B C D E
7 A B C D E
8 A B C D E
9 A B C D E
10 A B C D F
11 A B C D E
12 A B C D E
13 A B C D E
14 A B C D E
15 A B C D E
16 A B C D E
17 A B C D E
18 A B C D E
19 A B C D E

20 A B C D E
21 A B C D E
22 A B C D E
23 A B C D E
24 A B C D E
25 A B C D E

1 A B C D E
2 A B C D E
3 A B C D E
4 A B C D E
5 A B C D E
6 A B C D E
7 A B C D E
8 A B C D E
9 A B C D E
10 A B C D F
11 A B C D E
12 A B C D E
13 A B C D E
14 A B C D E
15 A B C D E
16 A B C D E
17 A B C D E
18 A B C D E
19 A B C D E
20 A B C D E

1 A B C D E
2 A B C D E
3 A B C D E
4 A B C D E
5 A B C D E

ANSWER SHEET

1 A B C D E
2 A B C D E
3 A B C D E
4 A B C D E
5 A B C D E
6 A B C D E
7 A B C D E
6 A B C D E
7 A B C D E
8 A B C D E
9 A B C D E
10 A B C D E
11 A B C D E
12 A B C D E
13 A B C D E
14 A B C D E
15 A B C D E
16 A B C D E
17 A B C D E
18 A B C D E

19 A B C D E
20 A B C D E

1 A B C D E
2 A B C D E
3 A B C D E
4 A B C D E
5 A B C D E
6 A B C D E
7 A B C D E
8 A B C D E
9 A B C D E
10 A B C D E
11 A B C D E
12 A B C D E
13 A B C D E
14 A B C D E
15 A B C D E
16 A B C D E
17 A B C D E

18 A B C D E
19 A B C D E
20 A B C D E
21 A B C D E
22 A B C D E
23 A B C D E
24 A B C D E
25 A B C D E

1 A B C D E
2 A B C D E
3 A B C D E
4 A B C D E
5 A B C D E
6 A B C D E
7 A B C D E
8 A B C D E
9 A B C D E
10 A B C D E

11 A B C D E
12 A B C D E
13 A B C D E
14 A B C D E
15 A B C D E
16 A B C D E
17 A B C D E
18 A B C D E
19 A B C D E
20 A B C D E
21 A B C D E
22 A B C D E
23 A B C D E
24 A B C D E
25 A B C D E
26 A B C D E
27 A B C D E
28 A B C D E
29 A B C D E

1 A B C D E
2 A B C D E
3 A B C D E
4 A B C D E
5 A B C D E
6 A B C D E
7 A B C D E
8 A B C D E
9 A B C D E
10 A B C D E
11 A B C D E
12 A B C D E
13 A B C D E
14 A B C D E
15 A B C D E
16 A B C D E
17 A B C D E
18 A B C D E
19 A B C D E

20 A B C D E
21 A B C D E
22 A B C D E
23 A B C D E
24 A B C D E
25 A B C D E
26 A B C D E
27 A B C D E
28 A B C D E
29 A B C D E
30 A B C D E
31 A B C D E
32 A B C D E
33 A B C D E
34 A B C D E
35 A B C D E
36 A B C D E
37 A B C D E

THE AIR TRAFFIC CONTROL TEST

The applicant applying for a position as an Air Traffic Controller Specialist must score high on a written test. The test score is used as one of the factors in the determination of eligibility. The following test is duplicated as accurately as possible to the actual test given by the Federal Government. The written test takes approximately two hours; the total time in the examining room is approximately 2 1/2 hours. Candidates for air traffic control work are recruited locally at FAA Regional and Field Offices and the Civil Service Commission and trained at the Aeronautical Center in Oklahoma City.

The Air Traffic Control written test makes it possible for an applicant to be considered for several different occupations through a single examination by measuring a number of abilities common to these occupations. Scores in each area of ability will be weighted according to job requirements. The test includes measures of the ability to understand and use written language; the ability to derive general principles from particular data; the ability to analyze data and derive conclusions; the ability to understand, interpret and solve problems presented in quantitative terms; the ability to derive conclusions from incomplete data supplemented by general knowledge; and the ability to discover the logical sequence of a series of events.

The Air Traffic Control Examination specifically includes several subtests, such as mathematics, abstract reasoning, air traffic control problems and other aptitude assessments. The tests measure how well you can think. These tests contain questions of different types; follow directions as given. It will be to your advantage to answer every question you can since your score will be the number of questions you answer correctly.

APTITUDE TEST

Time: 30 Minutes

Directions: This test contains a number of different types of questions. This is a test to see how well you can think. It is unlikely that you will complete all of the 75 questions but do your best. When taking the actual examination, the official will tell you when to begin. You will be given exactly 30 minutes to work as many of the problems as you can. Be careful not to go too fast and make foolish mistakes since you must try to get as many correct as you can. For each of the following questions, select the choice which best answers the question or completes the statement.

1. A real estate dealer buys a house and lot for $4,400. He pays $125 for painting, $175 for plumbing, and $100 for grading and walks. At what price must he sell the property to make a profit of 12 1/2%?

   A. $6,000
   B. $5,400
   C. $5,600
   D. $5,800

2. Pyrrhic victory is the same as

   A. victory gained at too great a cost
   B. victory as a result of encirclement
   C. total destruction of the enemy
   D. victory as a result of a complete surprise.

3. A democratic practice that characterized the New England colonies was that

   A. there was separation of church and state
   B. a man's qualification for voting was native birth
   C. the business of local government was conducted at town meetings
   D. the choice of governors was left to representative state legislatures.

4. Fetid is the opposite of

   A. in an embryonic state
   B. easily enraged
   C. acclaimed by peers
   D. reduced to skin and bones
   E. having a pleasant odor

5. How many times does six go into 72?

   A. 5 B. 12 C. 15 D. 4

6. An automobile cost $1,200. It depreciated in value 45% the first year, 20% of the reduced value the second year, and 20% of the second reduced value the third year. What was it worth at the end of the third year?

A. $425
B. $432.80
C. $180
D. $422.40

7. Quirt is the same as

A. riding-whip
B. idiosyncrasy
C. witty remark
D. bludgeon

8. Through advertising, manufacturers exercise a high degree of control over consumers' desires. However, the manufacturer assumes enormous risks in attempting to predict what consumers will want and in producing goods in quantity and distributing them in advance of final selection by the consumers.

The paragraph best supports the statement that manufacturers

A. can eliminate risk of overproduction by advertising
B. completely control buyers' needs and desires
C. must depend upon the final consumers for the success of their undertakings
D. distribute goods directly to the consumers
E. can predict with great accuracy the success of any product they put on the market

9 Chimerical is the opposite of

A. nimble
B. realistic
C. powerful
D. underrated
E. remarkable

10. If the income of a certain city is $6,950,000, and 1.81¢ of each dollar is expended for Parks, Libraries and Museums, the total amount spent for Parks, Libraries and Museums will be

A. $25,795
B. $135,795
C. $125,795
D. $12,5799

11. Rara avis is the same as

A. cynosure
B. nonentity
C. gourmet
D. unusual person

12. "Excessive bail shall not be required, nor excessive fines imposed, nor cruel and unusual punishment inflicted" is a quotation from the

A. Constitution of the United States of America
B. Declaration of Independence
C. Articles of Confederation
D. Charter of the United Nations

13. A football team has won 40 games out of 60 played. It has 32 more games to play. How many of these must the team win to make its record 75% for the season?

A. 26
B. 28
C. 29
D. 30
E. 32

14. Turbid is the same as

A. insubordinate
B. distended
C. hooded
D. muddy

15. Apocalyptic is the opposite of

A. concealed
B. pure
C. steep
D. paralyzed
E. authentic

16. Intimidate : Fear ::

A. maintain : satisfaction
B. astonish : wonder
C. sooth : concern
D. feed : hunger
E. awaken : tiredness

17. What is the sum of 8 1/3, 4/5, 5 1/4, and 4 3/8?

A. 18 91/120
B. 17 91/120
C. 18 17/24
D. 17 5/24

18. Truncated is the same as

A. abused
B. lopped off
C. sharpened to a fine point
D. columnar

19. The United States House of Representatives has the power to

A. make treaties
B. appoint judges to the Supreme Court
C. try impeachments
D. originate money bills

20. Stove : Kitchen ::

A. window : bedroom
B. sink : bathroom
C. television : living room
D. trunk : attic
E. pot : pan

21. If 1/3 gallon milk is added to 4/5 gallon, how many quarts of milk will there be?

A. 4 2/15 qts.
B. 4 1/30 qts.
C. 4 8/15 qts.
D. 4 3/5 qts.

22. Sacerdotal is the same as

A. pertaining to the priesthood
B. pertaining to religious sacrifice
C. pertaining to contributions for religious purposes
D. pertaining to the lower back

23. The function of business is to increase the wealth of the country and the value and happiness of life. It does this by supplying the material needs of men and women. When the nation's business is successfully carried on, it renders public service of the highest value.

A. all businesses which render public service are successful
B. human happiness is enhanced only by the increase of material wants
C. the value of life is increased only by the increase of wealth
D. the material needs of men and women are supplied by well-conducted business
E. business is the only field of activity which increases happiness

24. Celebrate : Marriage ::

A. announce : birthday
B. report : injury
C. lament : bereavement
D. face : penalty
E. kiss : groom

25. A man invests $500 at the rate of 6%. How much interest is due him at the end of 3 years and 60 days? (Consider a year as 360 days.)

A. $125
B. $105
C. $85
D. $95

26. Aberrance is the opposite of

A. refusal
B. criticism
C. adherence
D. exhuming
E. easing

27. Margarine : Butter ::

A. cream : milk
B. lace : cotton
C. nylon : silk
D. egg : chicken
E. oak : acorn

28. A mortgage on a house in the amount of $4,000 provides for quarterly payments of $200 plus interest on the unpaid balance at 4 1/2%. The total second payment to be made is

A. $371
B. $285.50
C. $242.75
D. $240.00

29. Saraband is the same as

A. stately dance
B. tiara-like ornament
C. small lute
D. insignia worn on left arm

30. A house can be built by some skilled workmen in 20 days or by a group of boys in 30 days. How many days will it take if all work together?

A. 10
B. 12
C. 12 2/3
D. 13
E. 14

31. A man borrowed $1,200 at 6% on June 1, 1953; on Sept. 25, 1954, he paid the note in full with interest. What was the amount of payment made? (Consider a year as 360 days.)

A. $1,295.40
B. $1,289.55
C. $1,298.35
D. $1,295.00

32. Honest people in one nation find it difficult to understand the viewpoints of honest people in another. Foreign ministries and their ministers exist for the purpose of explaining the viewpoints of one nation in terms understood by the ministries of another. Some of their most important work lies in this direction.

The paragraph best supports the statement that

A. people of different nations may not consider matters in the same light
B. it is unusual for many people to share similar ideas
C. suspicion prevents understanding between nations
D. the chief work of foreign ministries is to guide relations between nations united by a common cause
E. the people of one nation must sympathize with the viewpoints of the people of other nations

33. A certain property is assessed at $55,000, and the tax rate is $4.85 per $1,000. What is the amount of the tax to be paid on this property?

A. $256.75
B. $276.75
C. $286.75
D. $266.75

34. Discrete is the opposite of

A. orderly
B. antisocial
C. crude
D. joking
E. grouped

35. Negligent : Requirement ::

A. careful : position
B. remiss : duty
C. cautious : injury
D. cogent : task
E. easy : hard

36. $120,000 worth of land is assessed at 115% of its value. If the tax rate is $2.80 per $1,000, the amount of tax to be paid is

A. $384.60
B. $386.40
C. $368.80
D. $384.25

37. Saurian is the same as

A. ape-like
B. wicked
C. winged
D. lizard-like

38. Gazelle : Swift ::

A. horse : slow
B. wolf : sly
C. swan : graceful
D. elephant : gray
E. lion : tame

39. Blocks of real estate in a certain area are assessed at $20,000 each. The tax rat is 90¢ per $500. What amount of tax is due on each block?

A. $54.00
B. $48.00
C. $36.00
D. $28.00

40. Ignominy : Disloyalty ::

A. fame : heroism
B. castigation : praise
C. death : victory
D. approbation : consecration
E. derelict : martyr

41. Saturnine : Mercurial ::

A. Saturn : Venus
B. Appenines : Alps
C. redundant : wordy
D. allegro : adagio
E. heavenly : starry

42. The number of cubic feet of soil it takes to fill a flower box 3 ft. long, 8 in. wide, and 1 ft. deep is

A. 2
B. 4 2/3
C. 12
D. 24

43. The first representative form of government to exist in America was established in 1619 in

A. Virginia
B. Rhode Island
C. Georgia
D. Massachusetts

44. Orange : Marmalade ::

A. potato : vegetable
B. jelly : jam
C. tomato : ketchup
D. cake : picnic
E. sandwich : ham

45. If a man can get 1/3 bushel of berries per cubic foot, how many bushels can he get into a box measuring 5 ft. square by 1 ft. deep?

A. 5
B. 9 1/2
C. 9 1/3
D. 8 1/3

46. Sloe-eyed is the same as

A. of gentle look
B. almond-eyed
C. heavy-eyed
D. black-eyed

47. Banish : Apostate ::

A. reward : traitor
B. request : assistance
C. remove : result
D. avoid : truce
E. welcome : ally

48. A carton is 10 ft. long, 4 ft. wide, and 6 in. deep. When packed with machine parts, the carton weighs 60 lbs. How many pounds of machine parts can be packed into a cubic foot of the carton?

A. 10
B. 3
C. 6
D. 8

49. Contumacious is the opposite of

A. swollen
B. scandalous
C. sanguine
D. concise
E. obedient

50. Circle : Sphere ::

A. square : triangle
B. balloon : jet plane
C. heaven : hell
D. wheel : orange
E. pill : drop

51. A certain highway intersection has had A accidents over a ten-year period, resulting in B deaths. What is the yearly average death rate for the intersection?

A. A + B - 10
B. B/10
C. 10 - A/B
D A/10

52. Splayed is the same as

A. hunched
B. spread out
C. splashed
D. knobby

53. If the length and width of a rectangle are each doubled, by what percent is the area increased?

A. 50
B. 75
C. 100
D. 300
E. 400

54. A typist can address approximately R envelopes in a 7-hour day. A list containing S addresses is submitted with a request that all envelopes be typed within T hours. The number of typists needed to complete this task would be

A. $\frac{7RS}{T}$
B. $\frac{S}{7RT}$
C. $\frac{R}{7ST}$
D. $\frac{S}{\frac{R}{7} \times T}$

55. Star Chamber is the same as

A. secret tribunal
B. royal manifesto
C. illegal seizure
D. special jury

56. Clerk X earns $L per year. Clerk Y earns $R less per month. Both earn yearly increments of $T up to S years. At the end of P years, which is less than S years, the excess of Clerk X's earnings over Clerk Y's will be

A. 12PR
B. 12P(L minus R)
C. 12PT(L plus R)
D. P(T plus L minus R)

57. Of the following New England states, the one which does not have an Atlantic seaport is

A. Vermont
B. Rhode Island
C. Connecticut
D. New Hampshire

58. Camaraderie is the opposite of

A. deviation
B. glee
C. aristocracy
D. noise
E. plunder

59. A car traveling a distance of 900 miles averages 50 m.p.h. the first 3 hours of travel, 45 m.p.h. for the 4th and 5th hours, and 40 m.p.h. for the remainder of the trip. How long did it take the car to go 900 miles?

A. 16 1/2 hours
B. 18 1/2 hours
C. 21 1/2 hours
D. 23 hours

60. An airplane on a trans-Atlantic flight took 18 hours to get from New York to its destination, a distance of 3,000 miles. To avoid a storm, however, the pilot went off his course, adding a distance of 200 miles to the flight. How fast did the plane travel?

A. 179.6 m.p.h.
B. 163.4 m.p.h.
C. 166.6 m.p.h.
D. 177.7 m.p.h.

61. Open : Secretive ::

A. mystery : detective
B. tunnel : toll
C. forthright : snide
D. better : best
E. gun : mask

62. Affirm : Hint ::

A. say : deny
B. assert : convince
C. confirm : reject
D. charge : insinuate
E. state : relate

63. Two cars start toward each other along a road between two cities which are 450 miles apart. The speed of the first car is 35 m.p.h. and that of the second 48 m.p.h. How much time will elapse before they meet?

A. 5.42 hours
B. 6.01 hours
C. 4.98 hours
D. 5.25 hours

64. Surrogate is the same as

A. will
B. substitute
C. court clerk
D. criminal court

65. A city pumping station can pump 3,600,000 gallons of water in 24 hours. The pump is operated on an average of 14 hours a day. The population of the city is 15,000. What is the average number of gallons of water pumped every day for each resident of the city?

A. 145 gals.
B. 140 gals.
C. 132 gals.
D. 1,200 gals.

66. Tertian is the same as

A. recurring
B. subordinate
C. intermediate
D. remote in time

67. Dour is the opposite of

A. gay
B. sweet
C. wealthy
D. responsive
E. noiseless

68. Two men working together can build a cabinet in 2 1/2 days. The first man, working alone, can build the cabinet in 6 days. How long would it take the second man to build the cabinet working alone?

A. 5 1/7 days
B. 3 7/8 days
C. 4 2/7 days
D. 4 3/10 days

69. Tessellate is the same as

A. quiver uncontrollably
B. arrange in a checkered pattern
C. adorn with random scraps of metal
D. dry up rapidly

70. Mendacious is the opposite of

A. charitable
B. efficacious
C. truthful
D. destructive
E. brilliant

71. One man can load a truck in 25 minutes; a second can load it in 50 minutes, and a third can load it in 10 minutes. How long would it take the three together to load the truck?

A. 5 3/11 min.
B. 8 1/3 min.
C. 6 1/4 min.
D. 10 min.

72. Trammel is the same as

A. bore holes
B. stamp on
C. impede
D. blend into one mass

73. All of the following have been used to help the American farmer since World War II except

A. a conservation program
B. government subsidies
C. price-support
D. export duties

74. Enervate is the opposite of

A. debilitate
B. fortify
C. introduce
D. conclude
E. escalate

75. If a typist can type 600 letters in 3 days, how many letters can 2 typists complete in one day?

A. 400 letters
B. 90 letters
C. 120 letters
D. 150 letters

APTITUDE TEST ANSWER KEY

1. B
2. A
3. C
4. E
5. B
6. D
7. A
8. C
9. B
10. C
11. D
12. A
13. C
14. D
15. A
16. B
17. A
18. B
19. D
20. B
21. C
22. A
23. D
24. C
25. D
26. C
27. C
28. A
29. A
30. B
31. A
32. A
33. D
34. E
35. B
36. B
37. D
38. C
39. C
40. A
41. D
42. A
43. A
44. C
45. D
46. D
47. E
48. B
49. E
50. D
51. B
52. B
53. D
54. D
55. A
56. A
57. A
58. D
59. C
60. D
61. C
62. D
63. A
64. B
65. B
66. A
67. A
68. C
69. B
70. C
71. C
72. C
73. D
74. B
75. A

MATHEMATICS

Time: 10 Minutes

Directions: The following questions in mathematics test your proficiency in the basic skills. Work as many problems as you can correctly. Select from the lettered choices that choice which best completes the statement or answers the question.

1. Find the sum of 2.04, .003, 42, and 1.6.

   A. .265
   B. 6.525
   C. 8.402
   D. 45.643
   E. none of the above

2. $\begin{array}{r} 7121 \\ +8131 \\ \hline \end{array}$

   A. 14,252
   B. 15,252
   C. 15,352
   D. 15,253
   E. 15,552

3. $\begin{array}{r} 1973 \\ -1562 \\ \hline \end{array}$

   A. 411
   B. 412
   C. 511
   D. 311
   E. none of the above

4. $11\overline{)385}$

   A. 36
   B. 45
   C. 35
   D. 25
   E. 37

5. $\begin{array}{r} 83 \\ \times 12 \\ \hline \end{array}$

   A. 896
   B. 986
   C. 976
   D. 996
   E. 696

6. Subtract the following: (243.24) - (184.2).

A. 59.92
B. 59.02
C. 59.04
D. 59.44
E. none of the above

7.
```
 3009
+4667
```

A. 7676
B. 7666
C. 7667
D. 7776
E. 5676

8.
```
 1101
- 912
```

A. 188
B. 189
C. 289
D. 187
E. 199

9. $25\overline{)8075}$

A. 333
B. 223
C. 233
D. 323
E. none of the above

10.
```
 812
x903
```

A. 723,236
B. 733,336
C. 733,236
D. 633,236
E. 733,237

11. Multiply 23. x 4.003.

A. 920.69
B. 9206.9
C. 9.2069
D. 92.069
E. none of the above

12.
```
 1123
+7272
```

A. 8395
B. 8385
C. 8396
D. 8495
E. 7395

13.
```
 6342
-3219
```

A. 3223
B. 3123
C. 3023
D. 2223
E. none of the above

14. $31\overline{)806}$

A. 25
B. 26
C. 24
D. 36
E. 37

15. 365
x112

A. 41,880
B. 40,770
C. 40,880
D. 40,870
E. none of the above

16. Change the following fraction to its decimal equivalent: $\frac{3}{10}$

A. .003
B. 3.0
C. 30.0
D. .30
E. .03

17. 7935
+1774

A. 9709
B. 9609
C. 9710
D. 9809
E. 9909

18. 10000
- 8754

A. 1346
B. 1246
C. 1146
D. 1245
E. 2246

19. 40,160 ÷ 40 =

A. 1005
B. 1004
C. 1114
D. 1014
E. none of the above

20. $102\overline{)224}$

A. 2.196
B. 2.195
C. 1.195
D. 2.197
E. 3.196

21. Change the decimal .046 to a fraction.

A. 4/10
B. 23/500
C. 46/50
D. 46/100
E. 52/100

22. Which one of these quantities is the smallest?

A. 4/5
B. 7/9
C. .76
D. .54
E. 5/7

23. 9803
-4563

A. 5140
B. 4240
C. 5240
D. 5340
E. 5230

24. 5412
- 981

A. 3331
B. 2431
C. 4431
D. 3431
E. 4432

25. 1200 ÷ 50 =

A. 24
B. 23
C. 34
D. 25
E. none of the above

26. $507\overline{)6112}$

A. 12.055
B. 11.055
C. 12.066
D. 13.055
E. 12.056

27. 10 is what percent of 100?

A. x = 1%
B. x = 10%
C. x = 100%
D. x = 1000%
E. none of the above

28. Change the fraction 1/9 to its decimal equivalent.

A. 1/9 = 11
B. 1/9 = .11 1/9
C. 1/9 = 1 1/9
D. 1/9 = .01 1/9
E. .1234

29. 75,363 - 66,594 =

A. 8869
B. 7769
C. 8768
D. 8769
E. 8669

30. 81,546 - 7,756 =

A. 74,790
B. 63,790
C. 73,790
D. 72,790
E. none of the above

31. 5000 ÷ 8 =

A. 624
B. 625
C. 635
D. 525
E. 626

32. 704 ÷ 4 =

A. 176
B. 175
C. 165
D. 166
E. 276

33. Add 37.03, 11.5627, 3.4005, 3423, and 1.141.

A. 3476.1342
B. 34.761342
C. 53.4765
D. 5347.65
E. none of the above

34. Subtract 4.0037 from 15.3.

A. 11.3037
B. 11.30
C. 11.2963
D. 11.3
E. 12.3037

35. 8,800 - 7,300 =

A. 1400
B. 1501
C. 2500
D. 1500
E. 1510

36. 669 ÷ 3 =

A. 123
B. 223
C. 224
D. 213
E. none of the above

37.
$$\begin{array}{r} 2\ 1/2 \\ 8\ 3/4 \\ +5\ 5/6 \\ \hline \end{array}$$

A. 16 1/2
B. 18 1/2
C. 17 1/2
D. 15 1/2
E. 17 1/4

38. Multiply 23 3/4 by 95.

A. 223
B. 2256 1/4
C. 2255 1/2
D. 226
E. 2257

39. Subtract 4.64324 from 7.

A. 3.35676
B. 2.35676
C. 2.45676
D. 2.36676
E. 2.45776

40. 65,000 - 55,005 =

A. 9995
B. 9895
C. 9095
D. 9955
E. 9785

41.
```
 3 3/4
 1 2/3
+3 1/2
```

A. 9 11/12
B. 8 7/8
C. 8 11/13
D. 8 11/12
E. none of the above

42.
```
 .37
 .09
+.11
```

A. 0.67
B. 1.57
C. 0.57
D. 0.77
E. 2.57

43. Clear $\frac{3/7}{5/14}$

A. 1 1/2
B. 1 1/3
C. 1 1/4
D. 1 1/5
E. 1 1/6

44. Multiply 2.372 by .012.

A. .28464
B. 2.8464
C. .028464
D. 28.464
E. none of the above

45.
```
 5 5/6
 2 2/3
+3 1/3
```

A. 12 5/6
B. 11 5/6
C. 11 5/7
D. 11 2/3
E. 10 5/6

46.
```
 5.88
-3.79
```

A. 2.09
B. 2.19
C. 2.90
D. 2.08
E. 2.10

47.
```
.37
x.2
```

A. 0.075
B. 0.074
C. 1.074
D. 0.174
E. none of the above

48. What is the sum of 12 1/6 - 2 3/8 - 7 2/3 + 19 3/4?

A. 21
B. 21 7/8
C. 21 1/8
D. 22
E. 21 5/6

49. What is the difference between 3/5 and 9/8 expressed decimally?

A. .525
B. .425
C. .520
D. .500
E. .475

50.
```
 10 1/2
  6 1/4
+ 5 2/3
```

A. 23 5/12
B. 21 5/12
C. 22 3/5
D. 22 5/12
E. 22 7/12

51.
```
   9.2
    .25
+31.05
```

A. 41.5
B. 39.5
C. 30.5
D. 40.5
E. 40.6

52.
```
 .932
-.64
```

A. 0.185
B. 0.192
C. 0.292
D. 0.291
E. none of the above

53. Find the product (-8) x (-6).

A. +14
B. -14
C. -48
D. +48
E. none of the above

54. Which of the following fractions is more than 3/4?

A. 35/71
B. 13/20
C. 71/101
D. 19/24
E. 25/50

55.
```
.573
x 32
```

A. 18.336
B. 18.356
C. 18.456
D. 18.355
E. 19.336

56. $\frac{.621}{1.5} =$

A. 0.4
B. 1.4
C. 0.46
D. 0.5
E. none of the above

57. $\frac{62.53}{2.4} =$

A. 25.1
B. 26.1
C. 2.61
D. 26.2
E. 26.4

58. $\frac{18.90}{3} =$

A. 5.3
B. 6.4
C. 6.6
D. 6.3
E. 6.2

59. Change the fraction $\frac{11}{14}$ to its decimal equivalent.

A. $.78\frac{4}{7}$
B. $.8\frac{4}{7}$
C. $7.8\frac{4}{7}$
D. .785
E. none of the above

60. Change the decimal .24 to a fraction.

A. $\frac{3}{25}$
B. $\frac{6}{25}$
C. $\frac{5}{25}$
D. $\frac{4}{25}$
E. $\frac{7}{25}$

MATHEMATICS ANSWER KEY

1. D
2. B
3. A
4. C
5. D
6. C
7. A
8. B
9. D
10. C
11. D
12. A
13. B
14. B
15. C
16. D
17. A
18. B
19. B
20. A
21. B
22. D
23. C
24. C
25. A
26. A
27. B
28. B
29. D
30. C
31. B
32. A
33. A
34. C
35. D
36. B
37. C
38. B
39. B
40. A
41. D
42. C
43. D
44. C
45. B
46. A
47. B
48. B
49. A
50. D
51. D
52. C
53. D
54. D
55. A
56. E
57. B
58. D
59. A
60. B

VERBAL ABILITIES TEST

Time: 15 Minutes

Directions: This test is designed to measure your ability to read and understand the meaning of words and the ideas associated with them, to understand the meanings of whole sentences and paragraphs, and to present the information or ideas clearly. Each item includes a paragraph which must be read accurately so that you can promptly analyze its contents and meaning or follow its instructions exactly. In this type of questioning, you should select from the multi-choice answers the correct one that best summarizes the paragraph.

Radio has just about reached in 20 years the goal toward which print has been working for 500; to extend its audience to include the entire population. In 1966, in the United States, nine out of ten families had radios--45 million sets going an average of five hours a day.

1. According to the above paragraph:

    A. the entire nation has radio sets
    B. nine out of ten individuals listen an average of five hours a day to the radio
    C. the radio-listening public grew much more rapidly than did the reading public
    D. there are more radios in the United States than in other countries
    E. the total possible radio audience is larger than the reading public

What gave this country the isolation it enjoyed in the 19th century was the statesmanship of Jefferson, Adams, Madison, and Monroe on this side of the Atlantic and of men like Canning on the other side. American independence from the European system did not exist in the two centuries before the Monroe Doctrine of 1823, and it has not existed in the century which began in 1914.

2. According to the above paragraph:

    A. America enjoyed greater isolation from European affairs from 1823 to 1914 than before or after
    B. the isolation of this country from European affairs was, prior to 1914, the result of our geographic location
    C. Canning was a statesman living in the 20th century
    D. America is less isolated today than it has ever been
    E. the statesmanship of Washington helped to keep America free from foreign entanglements.

One effect of specialization in industry is the loss of versatility which it has brought to the individual worker. Often, each laborer is trained to do a particular task and no other. The result is that he is almost entirely dependent for employment upon the demand for labor of his particular type. If anything happens to interrupt that demand he is deprived of employment.

3. This paragraph indicates that

A. the unemployment problem is a direct result of specialization in industry
B. the demand for labor of a particular type is constantly changing
C. the average laborer is not capable of learning more than one particular task at a time
D. some cases of unemployment may be due to the lack of versatility of the worker
E. too much specialization is as dangerous as too little.

Never was management needed more than now. The most essential characteristic of management is organization, and the organization must be such that management can distribute enough responsibility and authority upon it to maintain the balance and perspective necessary to make such weighty decisions as are thrust upon it today.

4. The above paragraph is a plea for

A. better business
B. adequately controlled responsibility
C. well regulated authority
D. better management through organization
E. less perspective and more balance.

During the last century and a half the economic life of the western world has been transformed by a series of remarkable inventions and the general application of science to the productive process. A revolution, more profound in its effect than any armed revolt that ever shook the foundations of a political state, has been achieved in the three realms of manufacture, agriculture, and communication.

5. The paragraph notes that science

A. has revolutionized the productive process
B. has shaken the foundations of manufacturing, agriculture and communication
C. is the tool of the inventor
D. has been an important factor in the founding of the agricultural process
E. is becoming more and more the determining factor in modern civilization.

The judgments of science are distinguished from the judgments of opinion by being more impartial, more objective, more precise, more subject to verification by any competent observer, and by being made by those who by their nature and training should be better judges.

6. Which of the following does the paragraph note is a distinguishing feature of the judgments of science?

A. they can be verified by all observers
B. they can be tested by advanced laboratory methods
C. no opinion is accepted until validated
D. no truth is accepted a priori
E. they are usually propounded by experts in their fields

It may be said that the problem in adult education seems to be not the piling up of facts but practice in thinking.

7. According to the above paragraph

   A. adult education should stress ability to think
   B. educational methods for adults and young people should differ
   C. adults do not seem to retain new facts
   D. a well-educated adult is one who thinks but does not have a store of information
   E. adults seem to think more than young people

Approximately 19,000 fatal accidents in 1965 were sustained in industry. There were approximately 130 non-fatal injuries to each fatal injury.

8. According to the above paragraph, the number of non-fatal accidents during 1965 was approximately:

   A. 146,000
   B. 190,000
   C. 1,150,000
   D. 2,500,000
   E. 3,200,000

One of the results of the increasing size of business organizations has been to make less and less practical any great amount of personal contact between superior and subordinate. Consequently, one finds in business today a greater dependence upon records and reports as a means whereby the executive may secure information and exercise control over the operations of the various departments.

9. According to this paragraph, the increasing size of business organizations

   A. has caused a complete cleavage between employer and employee
   B. makes for impracticality in relationships between the employer and employee
   C. has tended toward class distinctions in large organizations
   D. has resulted in a more indirect means of controlling the operations of various departments
   E. has made evaluation of the work of the employee more objective.

For mediocre executives who do not have a flair for positive administration, the implantation in subordinates of anxiety about job retention is a safe, if somewhat unimaginative, method of insuring a modicum of efficiency in the working organization.

10. Of the following, the most accurate statement according to this paragraph is that

   A. implanting anxiety about job retention is a method usually employed by the mediocre executive to improve the efficiency of his organization
   B. an organization will operate with at least some efficiency if employees realize that unsatisfactory work performance may subject them to dismissal
   C. successful executives with a flair for positive administration relieve their subordinates of any concern for their job security
   D. the implantation of anxiety about job security in subordinates should not be used as a method of improving efficiency

E. anxiety in executives tends to make them think that it is present in employees also.

A scientific law is related to the perceptions and conceptions formed by the perceptive and reasoning facilities in man; it is meaningless except in its associations with these; it is the resume or brief expression of the relationships and sequences of certain groups of these perceptions and conceptions, and exists only when formulated by man.

11. An assumption that is most in accord with this paragraph is that a scientific law

A. may have meaning apart from the human mind if it is a summation of related scientific facts
B. is essentially a product of the human mind
C. may be related to man's reasoning faculties and yet not be based on experience
D. is as variable as the human mind
E. may exist without the human mind, but has no meaning until perceived.

We find many instances in early science of the use of the "a priori" method of scientific investigation. Scientists thought it proper to carry over the generalizations from one field to another. It was assumed that the planets revolved in circles on account of the geometrical simplicity of the circle. Even Newton assumed that there must be seven primary colors corresponding to the seven tones of the musical scale.

12. According to the paragraph one might best conclude that

A. Newton sometimes used the "a priori" method of investigation
B. scientists no longer consider it proper to carry over generalizations from one field to another
C. the planets revolve about the earth in ellipses rather than in circles
D. even great men like Newton sometimes make mistakes
E. the number of notes in the musical scale has no connection with the number of primary colors.

In a lightning-like military advance, similar to that used by the Germans, the use of persistent chemicals is unnecessary and might be of considerable detriment to a force advancing over a broad front.

13. According to the above paragraph:

A. chemicals should not be used by a defending army
B. the Germans advanced in a narrow area
C. an advancing army may harm itself through the use of chemicals
D. chemicals are unnecessary if warfare is well-organized
E. chemical warfare is only effective if used by an advancing army.

The X-ray has gone into business. Developed primarily to aid in diagnosing human ills, the machine now works in packing plants, in foundries, in service stations, and in a dozen ways contributes to precision and accuracy in industry.

14. According to the above paragraph, the X-ray:

    A. was first developed to aid business
    B. is more of a help to business than to medicine
    C. is being used to improve the functioning of business
    D. is more accurate for packing plants than for foundries
    E. increases the output of such industries as service stations.

In large organizations some standardized yet simple and inexpensive method of giving employees information regarding company policies and rules, as well as specific instructions regarding their actual duties, is practically essential. This is the purpose of all office manuals of whatever type.

15. The above paragraph notes that office manuals

    A. are all about the same
    B. should be simple enough for the average employee to understand
    C. are necessary to large organizations
    D. act as constant reminders to the employee of his duties
    E. are the only means by which the executive of a large organization can reach his subordinates.

Items 16-18 are to be answered solely on the basis of the information contained in the following passage:

It is common knowledge that ability to do a particular job and performance on the job do not always go hand in hand. Persons with great potential abilities sometimes fall down on the job because of laziness or lack of interest in the job, while persons with mediocre talents have often achieved excellent results through their industry and their loyalty to the interests of their employers. It is clear, therefore, that the final test of any employee is his performance on the job.

16. The most accurate of the following statements, on the basis of the above paragraph, is that

    A. employees who lack ability are usually not industrious
    B. an employee's attitudes are more important than his abilities
    C. mediocre employees who are interested in their work are preferable to employees who possess great ability
    D. superior capacity for performance should be supplemented with proper attitudes.

17. On the basis of the above paragraph, the employee of most value to his employer is not necessarily the one who

    A. best understands the significance of his duties
    B. achieves excellent results
    C. possesses the greatest talents
    D. produces the greatest amount of work.

18. According to the above paragraph, an employee's efficiency is best determined by an

    A. appraisal of his interest in his work
    B. evaluation of the work performed by him
    C. appraisal of his loyalty to his employer
    D. evaluation of his potential ability to perform his work.

For the United States, Canada has become the most important country in the world yet there are few countries about which Americans know less. Canada is the third largest country in the world; only Russia and China are larger. The area of Canada is more than a quarter of the whole British Empire.

19. According to the above paragraph:

    A. the British Empire is smaller than Russia or China
    B. the territory of China is greater than that of Canada
    C. Americans know more about Canada than about China or Russia
    D. the United States is the most important nation in the world as far as Canada is concerned
    E. the Canadian population is more than one quarter the population of the British Empire.

Although the rural crime reporting area is much less developed than that for cities and towns, current data are collected in sufficient volume to justify the generalization that rural crime rates are lower than those of urban communities.

20. According to the above paragraph:

    A. better reporting of crime occurs in rural areas than in cities
    B. there appears to be a lower proportion of crime in rural areas than in cities
    C. cities have more crime than towns
    D. crime depends on the amount of reporting
    E. no conclusions can be drawn regarding crime in rural areas because of inadequate reporting.

Knowledge of the composition of food materials has been greatly enlarged as the result of the determination of fuel value per unit weight, the discovery of vitamins and an approach to their quantitative estimation and detailed analytical studies of individual constituents.

21. The one of the following statements which best characterizes the above paragraph is

    A. the composition of food materials has been greatly enlarged
    B. food value per unit weight has added greatly to our knowledge of vitamins
    C. quantitative estimation of fuel value in individual foods has added to our knowledge of their individual constituents
    D. investigation into the composition of food materials has been aided by detailed analytical studies of their individual constituents
    E. the determination of the unit weight in individual foods has increased our knowledge of the nature of their fuel contents.

Formerly it was thought that whole wheat and graham breads were far superior to white bread made from highly refined wheat flour. However, it is now believed that the general use of milk solids in white bread has significantly narrowed the nutritional gap between the two types of bread. About the only dietary advantages that can now be claimed for whole wheat bread are its higher content of iron and vitamin B, both of which are also easily obtainable from many other common foods.

22. The paragraph notes that

 A. white bread is fattening because of its milk content
 B. whole wheat bread is not much more nutritious than white bread
 C. whole wheat bread contains roughage
 D. white bread has the dietary disadvantage that it contains neither iron nor vitamin B
 E. contrary to popular misconception, white bread is not inferior in quality to bread made from graham or whole wheat flour.

The view is widely held that butter is more digestible and better absorbed than other fats because of its low melting point. There is little scientific authority for such a view. As margarine is made today, its melting point is close to that of butter, and tests show only the slightest degree of difference in digestibility of fats of equally low melting points.

23. According to the paragraph one could most reasonably conclude that

 A. butter is more easily digested than magarine
 B. the concept that butter has a lower melting point than other fats is a common misconception, disproved by scientists
 C. there is not much difference in the digestibility of butter and margarine
 D. most people prefer butter to margarine
 E. it sometimes becomes necessary to use a substitute for butter

When from a sufficient although partial classification of facts a simple principle has been discovered which describes the relationship and sequences of any group, then this principle or law itself generally leads to the discovery of a still wider range of hitherto unregarded phenomena in the same or associated fields.

24. Which of the following phrases most adequately describes the preceding paragraph?

 A. relationship between group classifications
 B. establishment of principles derived from group relationships and sequences
 C. association of phenomena in a wide range of varied fields
 D. establishment of general laws in hitherto undiscovered fields
 E. discovery of hitherto unregarded phenomena in their relationships and sequences to varied groups.

A hundred years ago, the steamboat was the center of life in the thriving Mississippi towns. Came the railroads; river traffic dwindled and the white-painted vessels rotted at the wharves. During the World War, the government decided to relieve rail congestion by reviving the long-forgotten waterways.

25. According to the above paragraph:

    A. the railroads were once the center of thriving river towns on the Mississippi River
    B. the volume of river transportation was greater than the volume of rail transportation during the World War
    C. growth of river transportation greatly increased the congestion on the railroads
    D. business found river transportation more profitable than railroad transportation during the World War
    E. in the past century the volume of transportation on the Mississippi has varied.

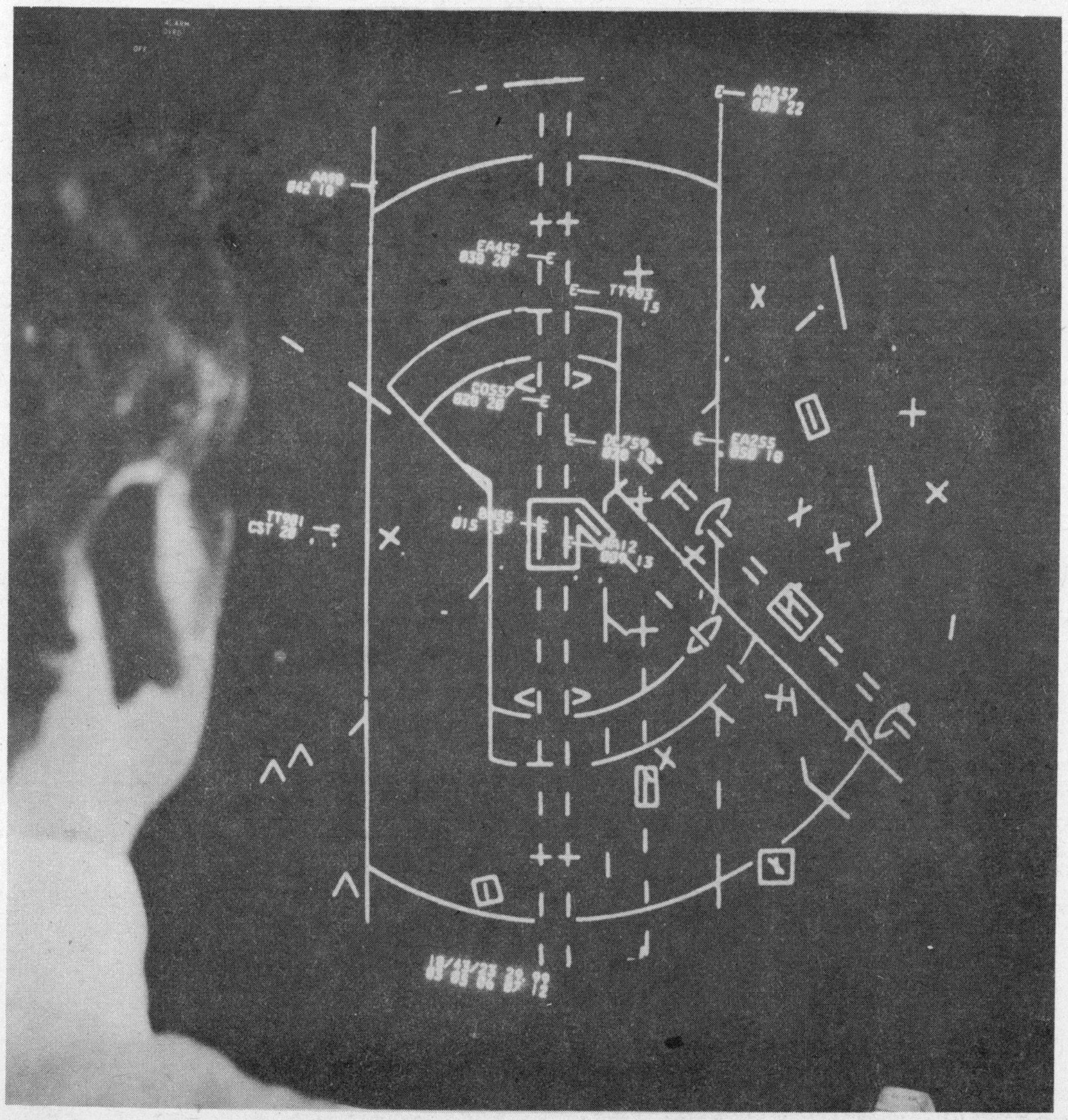

VERBAL ABILITIES TEST ANSWER KEY

1. (C)
2. (A)
3. (D)
4. (D)
5. (A)
6. (E)
7. (A)
8. (D)
9. (D)
10. (B)
11. (B)
12. (A)
13. (C)
14. (C)
15. (C)
16. (D)
17. (C)
18. (B)
19. (B)
20. (B)
21. (D)
22. (B)
23. (C)
24. (B)
25. (E)

LETTER SERIES

Time: 25 Minutes

Directions: Select from the choices offered in each of the following, the one which is correct or most nearly correct.

Two Test Questions Analyzed

In each of these questions there is a series of letters which follow some definite order, followed by five sets of two letters each. Look at the letters in the series and determine what the order is; then from the suggested answers that follow, select the set that gives the next two letters in the series in their correct order.

1. X C X D X E X

   A. F X
   B. F G
   C. X F
   D. E F
   E. X G

The series consists of X's alternating with letters in alphabetical order. The next two letters would be F and X; therefore (A) is the correct answer.

2. A B D C E F H

   A. G H
   B. I G
   C. G I
   D. K L
   E. I H

If you compare this series with the alphabet, you will find that it goes along in pairs, the first pair in their usual order and the next pair in reverse order. The last letter given in the series is the second letter of the pair G - H, which is in reverse order. The first missing letter must, therefore, be G. The next pair of letters would be I - J, in that order; the second of the missing letters is I. The alternative you look for, then, is G I, which is lettered (C).

Suggestion: In solving alphabetic series and progressions it is a good idea (you may have found it out yourself) to write out the alphabet and keep it in front of you. The key to each series can be picked out much more easily that way.

A	B	C	D	E	F	G	H	I	J	K	L	M	N	O	P	Q	R	S	T	U	V	W	X	Y	Z
1	2	3	4	5	6	7	8	9	10	11	12	13	14	15	16	17	18	19	20	21	22	23	24	25	26

1. B D F H J L

A. N
B. P
C. R
D. T
E. none of these

2. G H F G E F

A. B
B. C
C. D
D. E
E. none of these

3. A A B A C A D A

A. A E
B. D A
C. E A
D. E E
E. F A

4. B H C G E F H E

A. J F
B. K C
C. K D
D. L D
E. L F

5. C M D O E Q F S G

A. T
B. W
C. U
D. Y

6. G O L H P M I

A. Q N
B. Q J
C. N J
D. N Q
E. J N

7. J M K N L O M

A. P
B. K
C. O
D. Q

8. J O L Q N S

A. P
B. X
C. U
D. O

9. D J H N L R

A. P
B. T
C. X
D. V

10. C D C E C F C G C

A. H C
B. I C
C. I D
D. D H

11. X C X D X E X

A. F X
B. F G
C. X F
D. E F

12. B D F H L N R T

A. X Z
B. Z X
C. V Z
D. U Y

13. J K L K L M L M N M N O N

A. O P
B. M N
C. N O
D. P O

14. A B C B D F C F I D H L E

A. I O
B. I N
C. J O
D. J N

15. A B C D D D G F E J H F

A. J M
B. M J
C. L J
D. L I

16. M L H K J H I

A. H G
B. F H
C. H F
D. H H
E. G H

17. M R M Q M P M

A. O M
B. M N
C. M O
D. N O
E. O N

18. M M J L L J K

A. J J
B. J I
C. K I
D. I K
E. K J

19. F E D F E D F

A. D F
B. F D
C. E D
D. E F
E. D E

20. J J I H H G F

A. E E
B. E D
C. F E
D. F D
E. E C

LETTER SERIES ANSWER KEY

1. (A)
2. (C)
3. (C)
4. (D)
5. (C)
6. (A)
7. (A)
8. (A)
9. (A)
10. (A)
11. (A)
12. (A)
13. (A)
14. (C)
15. (B)
16. (D)
17. (A)
18. (E)
19. (C)
20. (C)

PROBLEM SOLVING TEST

Directions: This test is to see how well you listen to directions and follow instructions. You should have someone read the questions to you. This test contains different types of questions and you must follow the instructions carefully. Write the letter closest to your drawing. *

READ THE FOLLOWING:

1. Draw a square and then draw a diagonal from the upper left-hand corner; then draw a line from the mid-point of the diagonal to the top of the square.

2. Draw two isosceles triangles sharing the same base with one on top of the other. Draw a rectangle within the upper triangle.

3. Draw a right triangle. On the hypotenuse of the triangle draw two triangles which have one point in common.

4. Draw a rectangle with length greater than width and then draw lines from the two bottom corners to the mid-point of the top side. Now draw a figure symmetrical to the one you have just drawn, outside of the rectangle.

5. Draw a right triangle. Draw perpendiculars from the middle of the hypotenuse of the right triangle and from the point where the base and the hypotenuse intersect. Draw these perpendiculars until the point where they intersect, then draw a line from this point to the point where the side of the triangle and the hypotenuse intersect.

* On the actual test, these questions will be read to you, and you will draw your figures along side four possible answers, as on the following pages. In order to make this test as challenging as possible, we recommend if at all practicable that someone read these questions to you and that you draw your figures on a blank sheet of paper.

ANSWER KEY

1. (A)
2. (B)
3. (D)
4. (B)
5. (A)

ACTION WORK SHEET
FOR PROBLEM SOLVING TEST

(Once more, we recommend you cover these figures when drawing your own.)

DRAW HERE: LISTEN CAREFULLY

1. ____

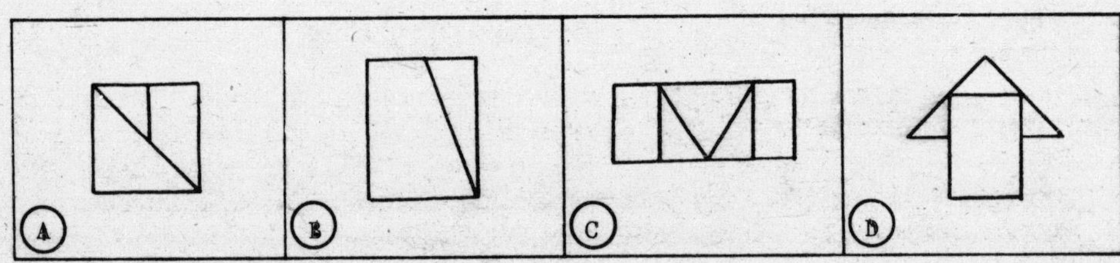

2. ____

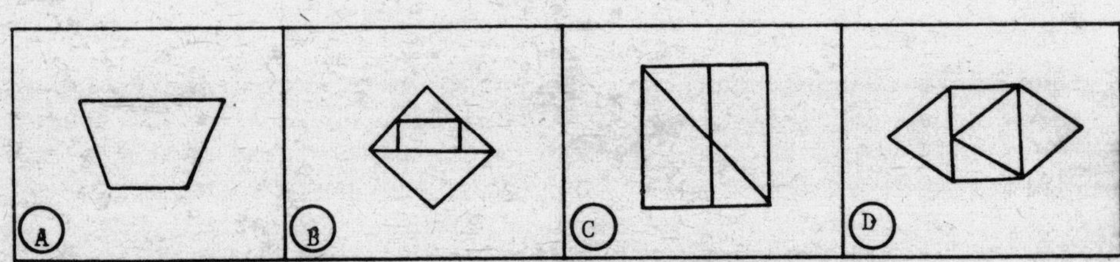

3. ____

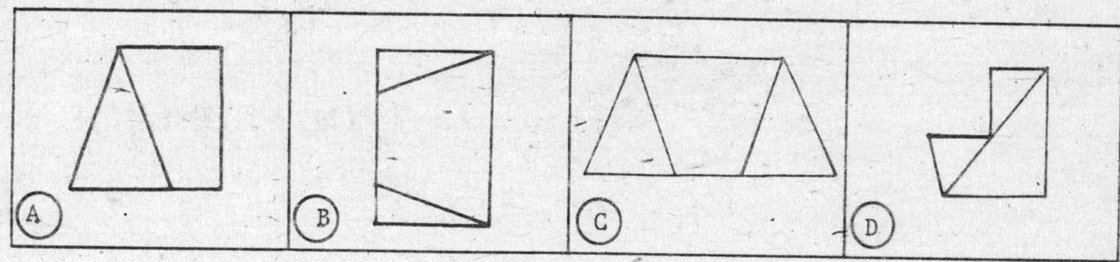

4. ____

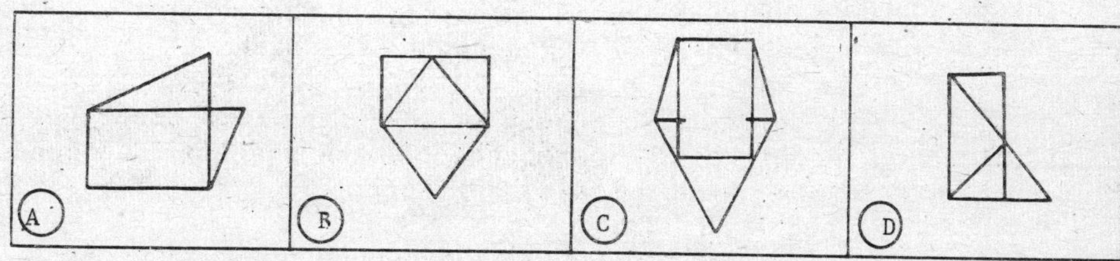

5. ____

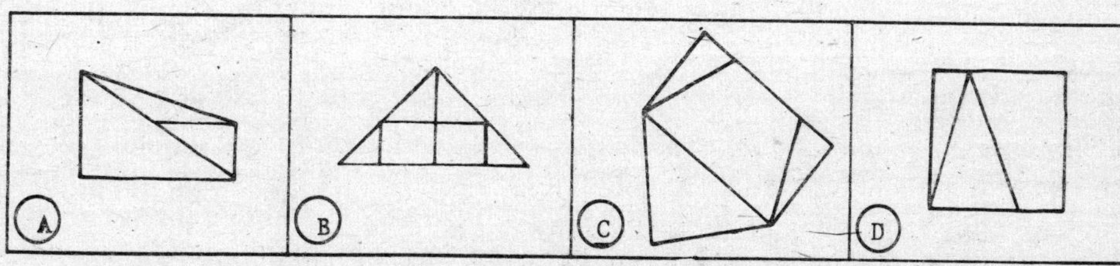

AIR TRAFFIC CONTROL PROBLEMS

The problems that follow represent highly simplified procedures of air traffic control situations. You will be concerned with maintaining adequate time and altitude separations for several aircraft which will:

(1) be flying at different altitudes
(2) have different ETA's (estimated times of arrival) at or over the airport
(3) by flying the same ground speed toward the airport
(4) by flying on the same course toward the airport

After studying information presented in Flight Data Displays, determine which of several incoming flights can be permitted to make specified altitude changes while maintaining conformance with a basic traffic rule. For each question, use the flight data given in the display.

The aircraft are flying at different altitudes and each is expected to arrive at, or over, the airport at a different time. However, remember that you are to assume that ground speed and course of all flights are the same. The rate of climb and rate of descent are not involved in the problems. Answers to questions of this kind will involve a determination of both time and altitude separation for the various flights.

It is essential to keep in mind the basic traffic rule that follows.

Basic Traffic Rule

A SEPARATION OF 5 MINUTES IS NECESSARY BETWEEN TWO EN ROUTE AIRCRAFT WHICH ARE EXPECTED TO PASS OVER THE SAME GEOGRAPHICAL POINT AT THE SAME ALTITUDE.

Now look at the Flight Data Display table.

FLIGHT DATA DISPLAY

Flight Identification	Cruising Altitude	Estimated Time of Arrival (ETA) At or Over Airport
102	30,000	19:00
104	28,000	18:58
106	32,000	18:55
108	29,000	18:51

CAN YOU, AS AN AIR TRAFFIC CONTROLLER, SAFELY PERMIT A CHANGE IN CRUISING ALTITUDE?

DIRECTIONS: Questions are based on information in the Flight Data Display on the preceding page. If the answer is YES, circle the letter A, if NO, the letter B. Correct answers appear at the end of the test.

1. Flight 102 to 28,000 A. Yes B. No
2. Flight 108 to 27,000 A. Yes B. No
3. Flight 104 to 29,000 A. Yes B. No
4. Flight 106 to 30,000 A. Yes B. No
5. Flight 108 to 33,000 A. Yes B. No
6. Flight 106 to 29,000 A. Yes B. No
7. Flight 102 to 33,000 A. Yes B. No
8. Flight 104 to 31,000 A. Yes B. No
9. Flight 102 to 26,000 A. Yes B. No
10. Flight 106 to 28,000 A. Yes B. No

FLIGHT DATA DISPLAY

Flight Identification	Cruising Altitude	Estimated Time of Arrival (ETA) At or Over Airport
113	14,000	4:02
115	13,000	4:00
117	16,000	3:57
119	15,000	3:58

11. Flight 117 to 17,000 A. Yes B. No
12. Flight 113 to 13,500 A. Yes B. No
13. Flight 115 to 11,000 A. Yes B. No
14. Flight 117 to 14,000 A. Yes B. No
15. Flight 119 to 13,500 A. Yes B. No
16. Flight 113 to 16,000 A. Yes B. No
17. Flight 119 to 17,000 A. Yes B. No
18. Flight 115 to 16,000 A. Yes B. No
19. Flight 113 to 15,000 A. Yes B. No
20. Flight 119 to 13,000 A. Yes B. No

EXPLANATORY ANSWERS

1. (B) Flight 102 cannot be permitted to change to 28,000 because Flight 104 is there and is only two minutes ahead of 102.

2. (A) Flight 108 can change to 27,000 because it is more than five minutes ahead of Flight 104 which is at the 28,000 altitude which it must pass through.

3. (A) Flight 104 can go to 29,000 because it is seven minutes behind Flight 108.

4. (A) Flight 106 can go to 30,000 because it is five minutes ahead of Flight 102 which is at that altitude.

5. (B) Flight 108 cannot go to 33,000 because it is only four minutes ahead of Flight 106 which is travelling at 32,000 which Flight 108 would have to fly through.

6. (B) Flight 106 cannot go to 29,000 because although it is five minutes ahead of Flight 102 which is at 30,000, it is four minutes behind Flight 108 which is at 29,000.

7. (A) Flight 102 can go to 33,000 because it is five minutes behind Flight 106 which is at 32,000.

8. (B) Flight 104 cannot go to 31,000 because it is only two minutes ahead of Flight 102 which is at the altitude of 30,000 which it must pass through.

9. (B) Flight 102 cannot go to 26,000 because it is only two minutes behind Flight 104 which is at the altitude of 28,000 which it must pass through.

10. (B) Flight 106 cannot go to 28,000 because it is only four minutes behind Flight 108 which is at 29,000 and only three minutes ahead of Flight 104 which is at 28,000.

11. (A) Flight 117 can go to 17,000 because there is no other Flight at that altitude.

12. (A) Flight 113 can go to 13,500 because there is no other Flight at that altitude.

13. (A) Flight 115 can go to 11,000 because there is no other Flight at that altitude.

14. (B) Flight 117 cannot go to 14,000 because it is only one minute ahead of Flight 119 which is at the altitude of 15,000 which it must pass through.

15. (B) Flight 119 cannot go to 13,500 because it is only four minutes ahead of Flight 113 which is at the altitude of 14,000 which it must pass through.

16. (B) Flight 113 cannot go to 16,000 because it is only four minutes behind Flight 119 which is at the altitude of 15,000 which it must pass through.

17. (B) Flight 119 cannot go to 17,000 because it is only one minute behind Flight 117 which is at the altitude of 16,000 which it must pass through.

18. (B) Flight 115 cannot possibly go to 16,000 as it is only two minutes ahead of Flight 113 at 14,000, only two minutes behind Flight 119 at 15,000 and only three minutes behind Flight 117 at 16,000.

19. (B) Flight 113 cannot go to 15,000 because it is only four minutes behind Flight 119 which is at that altitude.

20. (B) Flight 119 cannot go to 13,000 because it is only four minutes ahead of Flight 113 which is at the altitude of 14,000 which must pass through and only two minutes ahead of Flight 115 which is at 13,000.

1.	B	11.	A
2.	A	12.	A
3.	A	13.	A
4.	A	14.	B
5.	B	15.	B
6.	B	16.	B
7.	A	17.	B
8.	B	18.	B
9.	B	19.	B
10.	B	20.	B

SYMBOL CLASSIFICATION

IN tests of this type each question contains three boxes in which there are a number of symbols. Each symbol in the first box is like the others in that box in some way. And each symbol in the second box is like the other in some way. But there is always some difference between the symbols in the first box and the symbols in the second box. Some characteristic feature is different. The first box has three symbols and the second box has two symbols, with one missing symbol represented by a question mark. You are to decide what the difference between the symbols in the first box and the symbols in the second box is, and then choose the lettered symbol (A), (B), (C), (D), or (E), in the third box, which can best take the place of the missing symbol in the second box.

TWO TEST QUESTIONS ANALYZED

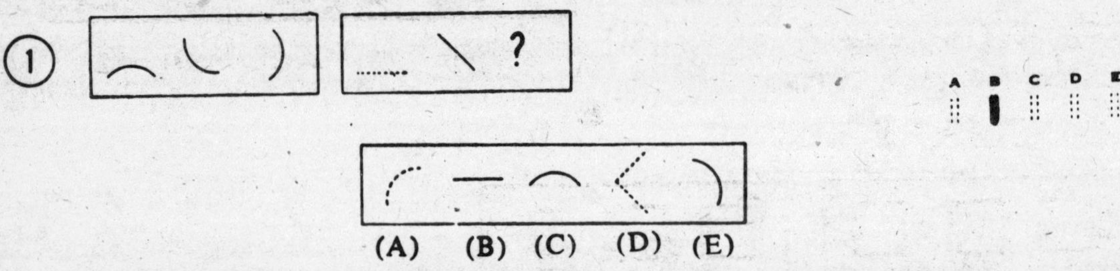

A B C D E

In question 1 all the symbols in the first box are curved, while the symbols in the second box are straight. Of the lettered symbols in the third box, only (B) is straight, so (B) is the correct answer. (Note that although one symbol in the second box is made of dashes, the other is not. The type of line, therefore, is not the feature that distinguishes this box from the first.)

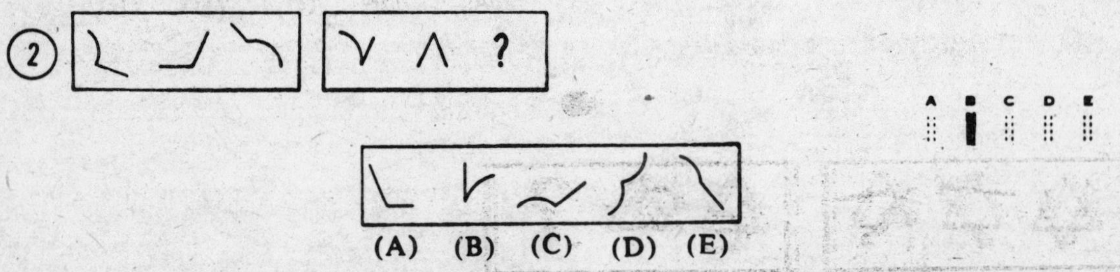

A B C D E

In question 2 the given symbols consist of two lines making an angle. There are curved lines and straight lines in each box; therefore the difference that must be found cannot be the difference between curved and straight. The angles formed in the first box are *obtuse;* those in the second box are *acute*. Now a check of the alternatives shows that only one of them consists of lines making an acute angle; the correct answer is therefore (B).

TEST QUESTIONS FOR PRACTICE

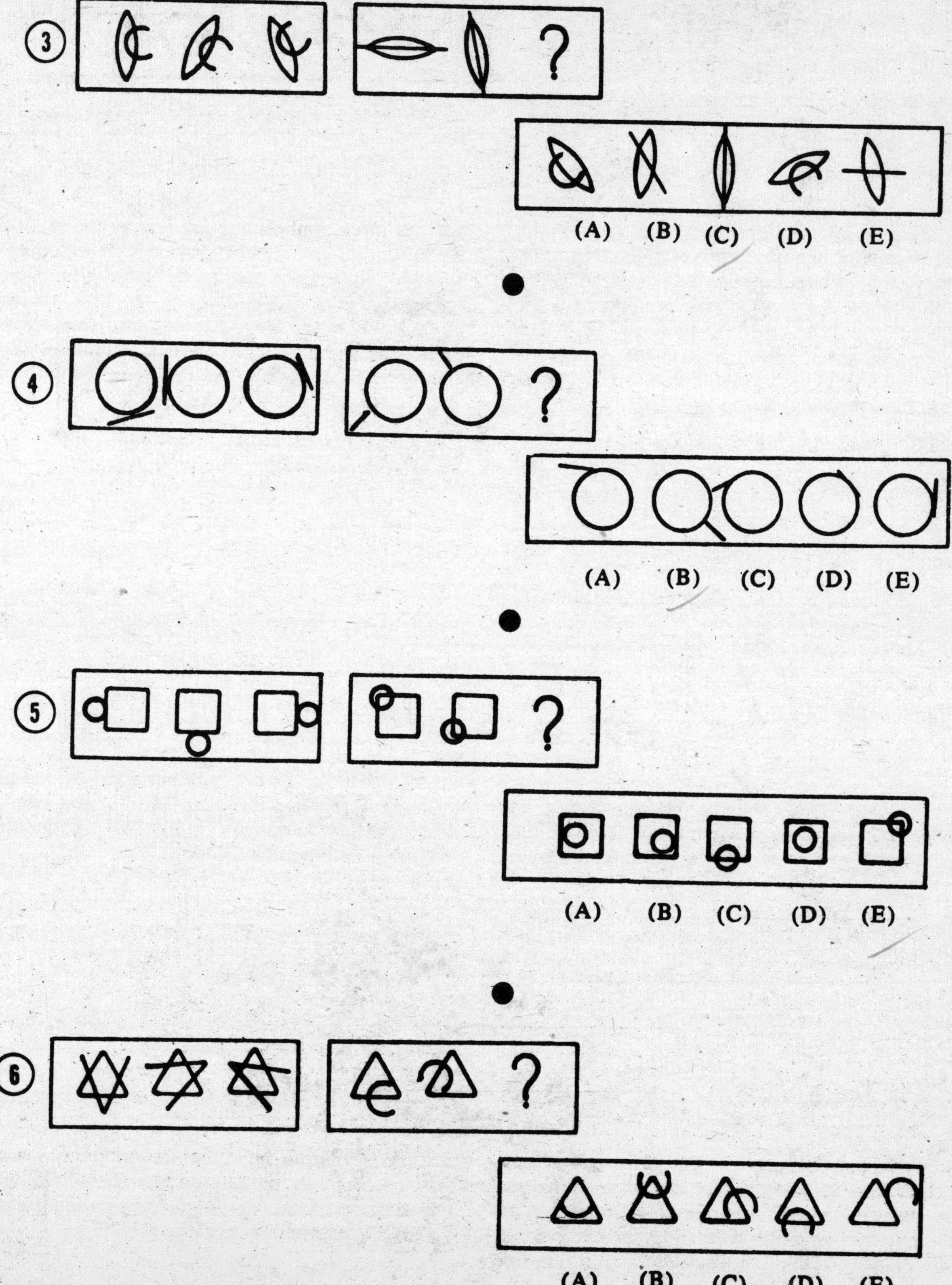

7
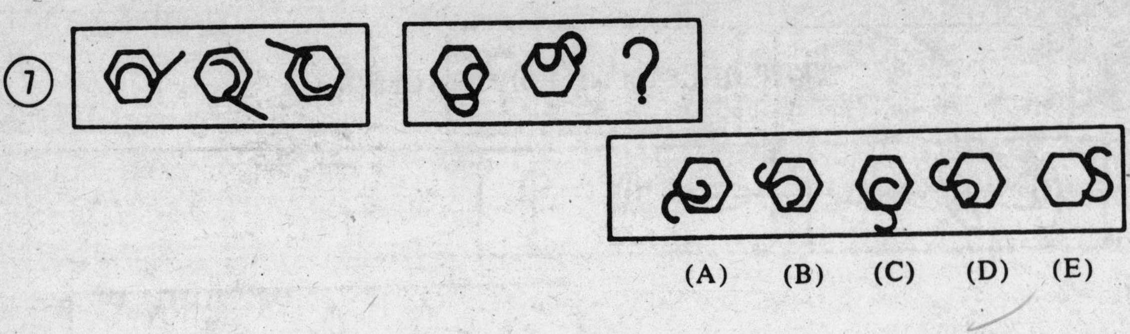

8
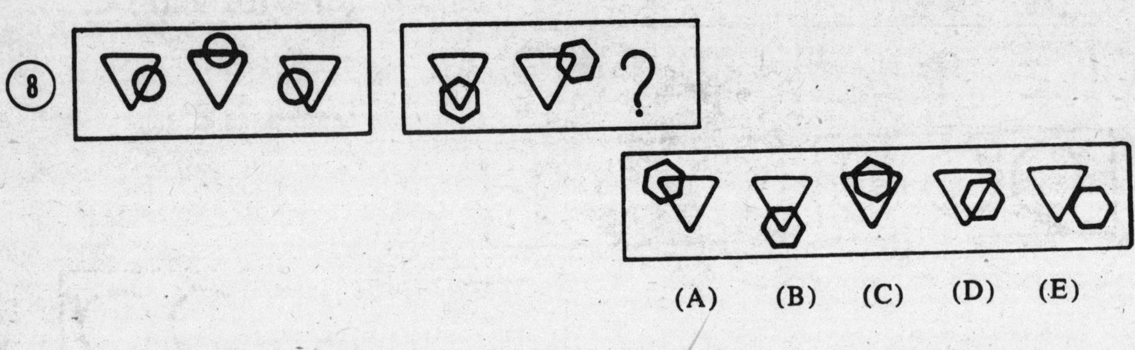

9
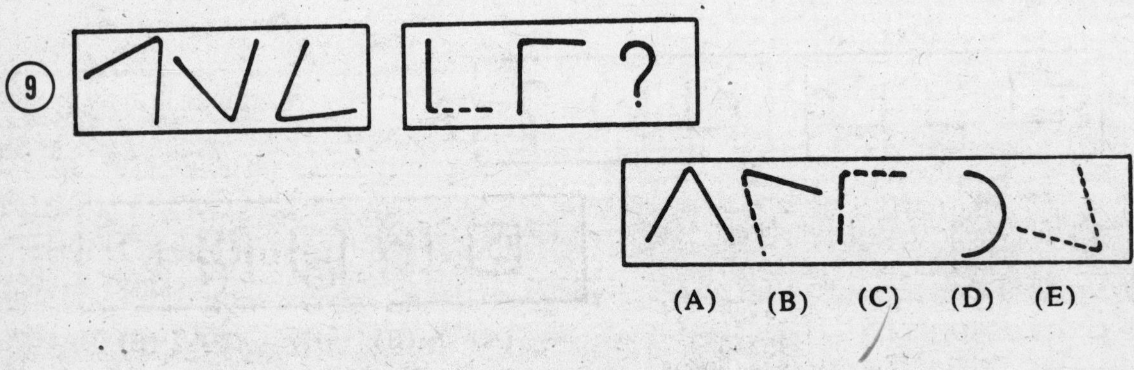

10
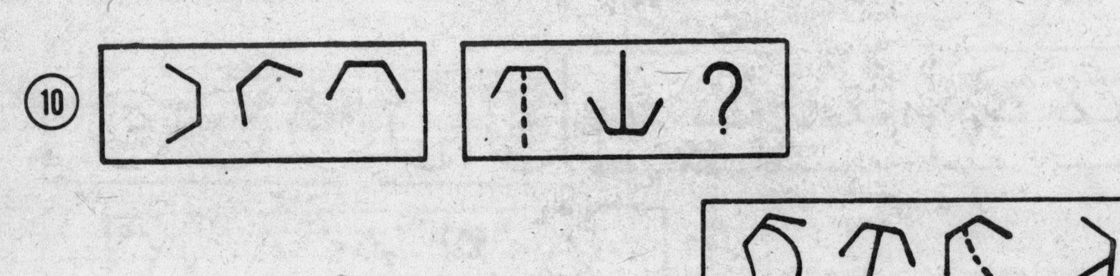

(A) (B) (C) (D) (E)

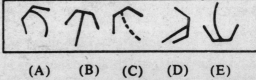

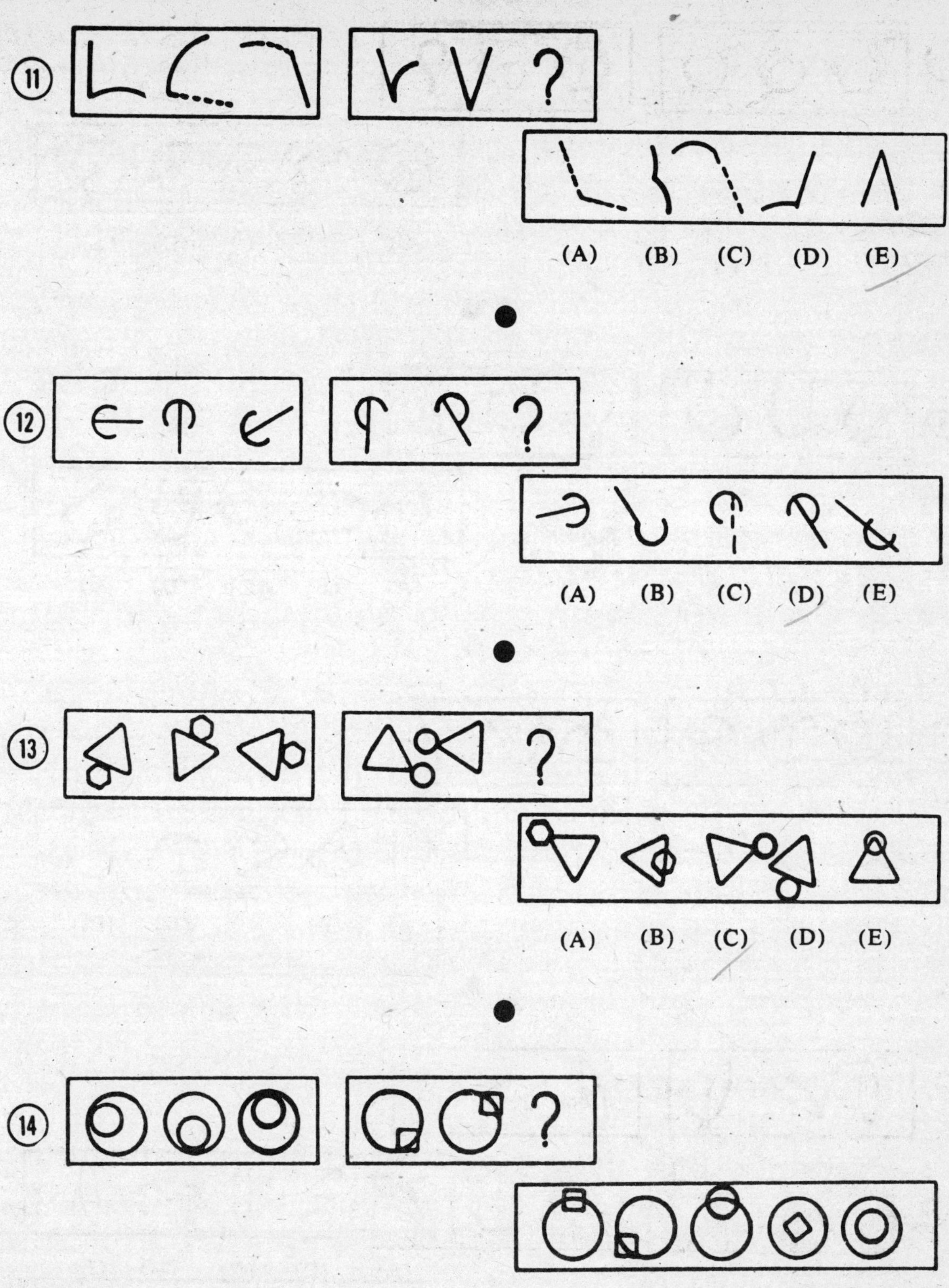
11
?
(A) (B) (C) (D) (E)
12
?
(A) (B) (C) (D) (E)
13
?
(A) (B) (C) (D) (E)
14
?
(A) (B) (C) (D) (E)

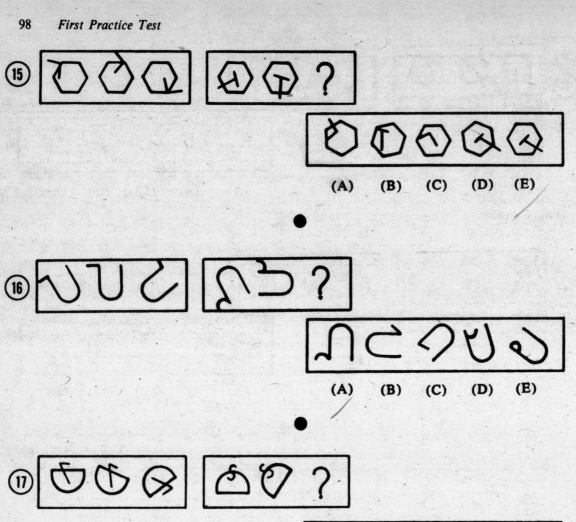

15

?

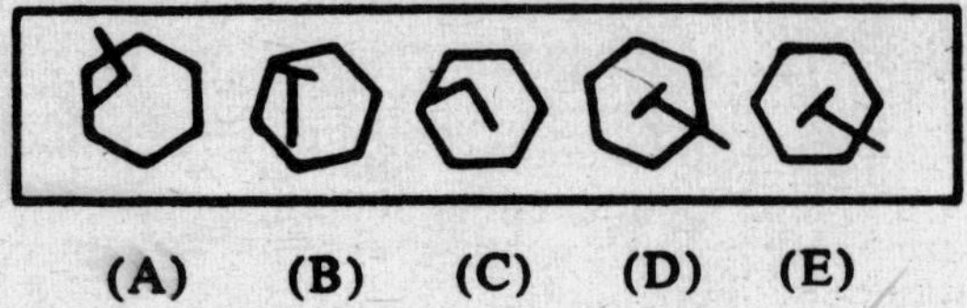

(A) (B) (C) (D) (E)

•

16

?

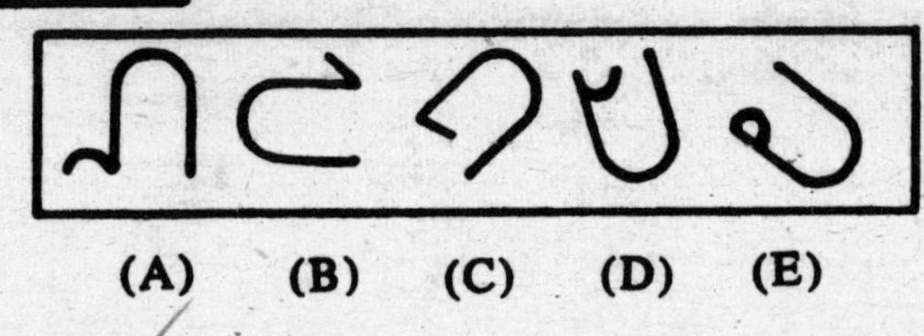

(A) (B) (C) (D) (E)

•

17

?

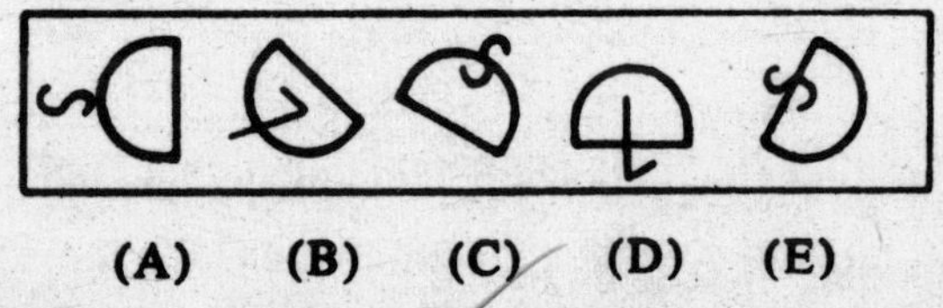

(A) (B) (C) (D) (E)

•

18

?

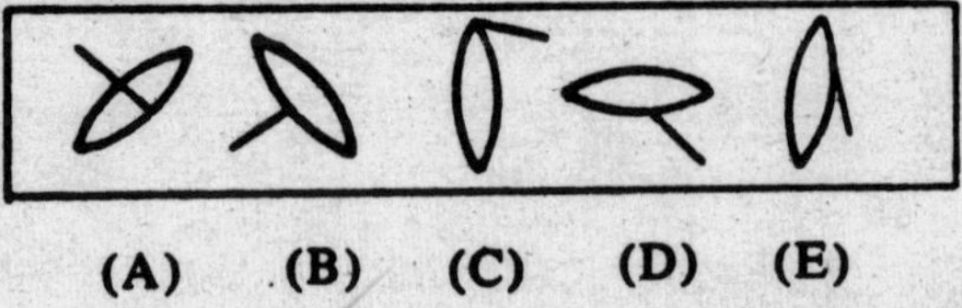

(A) (B) (C) (D) (E)

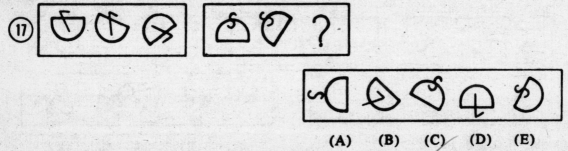

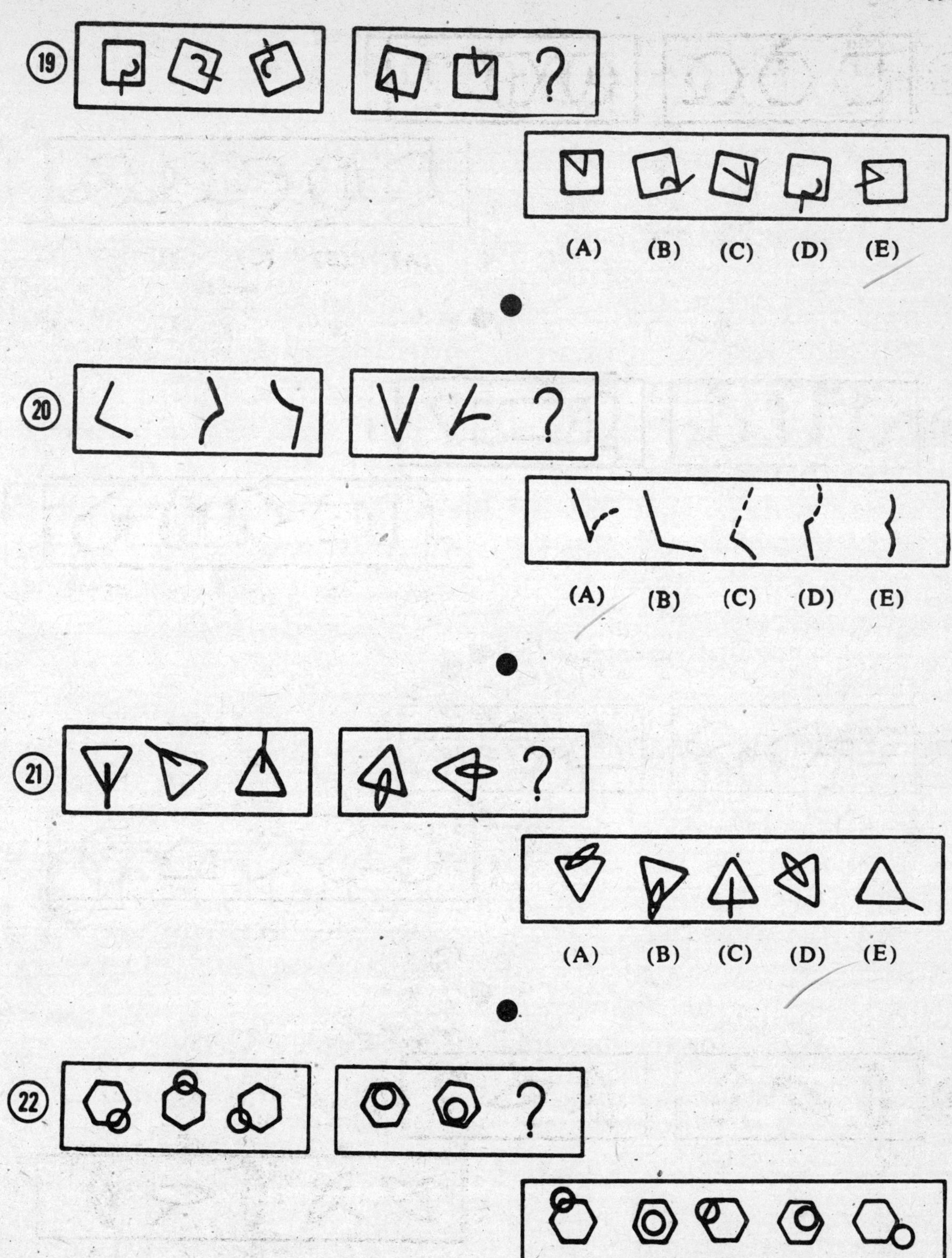
19
?
(A) (B) (C) (D) (E)
20
?
(A) (B) (C) (D) (E)
21
?
(A) (B) (C) (D) (E)
22
?
(A) (B) (C) (D) (E)

23

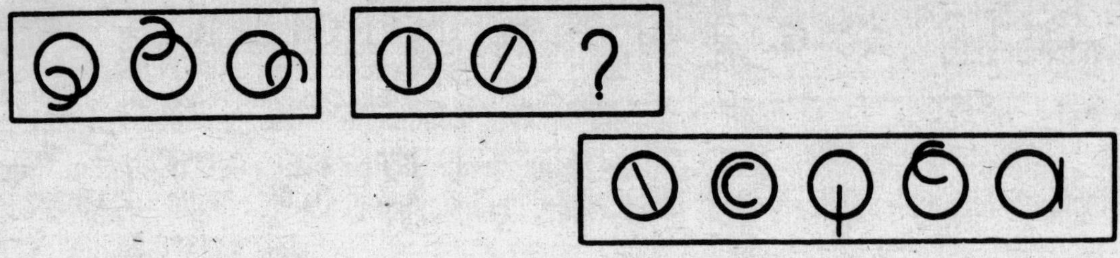

(A) (B) (C) (D) (E)

24

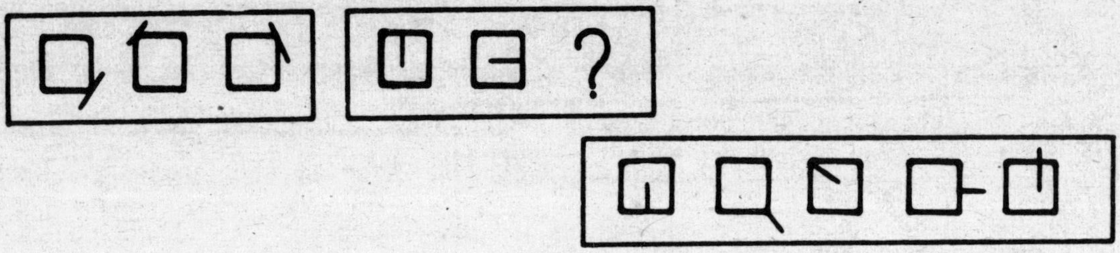

(A) (B) (C) (D) (E)

25

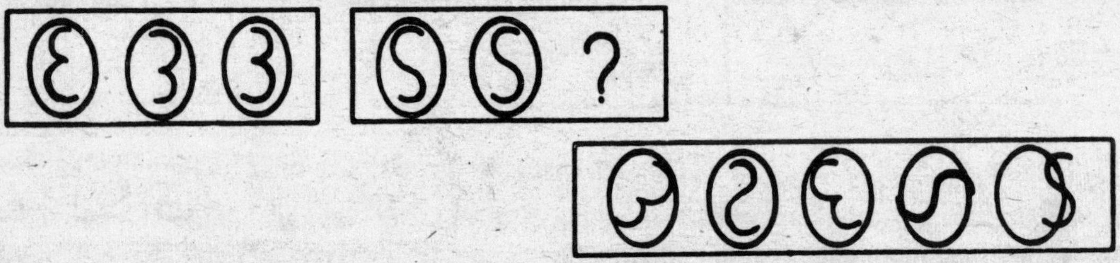

(A) (B) (C) (D) (E)

Correct Answers For The Foregoing Questions

(Please make every effort to answer the questions on your own before looking at these answers. You'll make faster progress by following this rule.)

1. B	6. C	11. E	16. A	21. D
2. B	7. D	12. D	17. C	22. D
3. C	8. A	13. C	18. B	23. A
4. B	9. C	14. B	19. E	24. A
5. E	10. B	15. E	20. A	25. B

SCORE .... %

NO. CORRECT ÷ NO. OF QUESTIONS

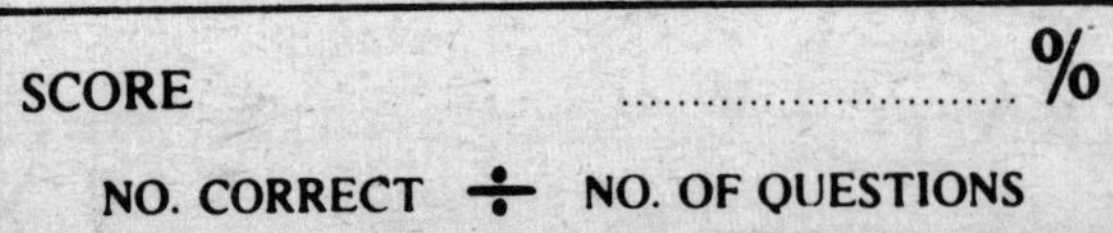

SYMBOL SERIES

The questions in this section are simple enough, but to acquire speed and accuracy in answering them requires practice. Try to do all the questions, and then compare your answers with the correct answers at the end of the chapter. If you have less than 70% correct, plan to do the chapter again in two weeks and compare your new score with your first attempt.

DIRECTIONS AND SUGGESTIONS

QUESTIONS 1 and 2 consist of a series of five symbols at the left and five other symbols labeled (A), (B), (C), (D), and (E) at the right. In each question, first study the series of symbols at the left; then from the symbols at the right, labeled (A), (B), (C), (D), and (E) select the one which continues the series most completely.

Each symbol in series question 1 has two coils. The symbols differ from one another in the number of loops that each coil has. In the first symbol, each coil has five loops; in the second, the left-hand one has four and the right-hand one has five; in the third, each coil has four. In this series, first the left-hand coil loses a loop and then the right-hand coil loses one.

Since the fifth symbol has three loops in each coil, the net symbol in this series must have two loops in the left-hand coil and three in the right-hand coil. Since symbol (A) is the only one which has two loops in the left-hand coil and three in the right-hand coil, (A) is the answer.

Question 2 is harder. The first five symbols show an alternation from small to large to small; and a quarter-turn in a......... clockwise direction each time. The answer should be a large circle, therefore (which eliminates (B) from the alternatives), with the larger rectangle at the bottom of the circle (which eliminates (D) and (E)). A second look at (A) shows that the rectangles within it are larger than any of the rectangles in the other circles; this change has no basis in the series. Thus (C) is left as the correct answer.

1 : (A) (B) (C) (D) (E)

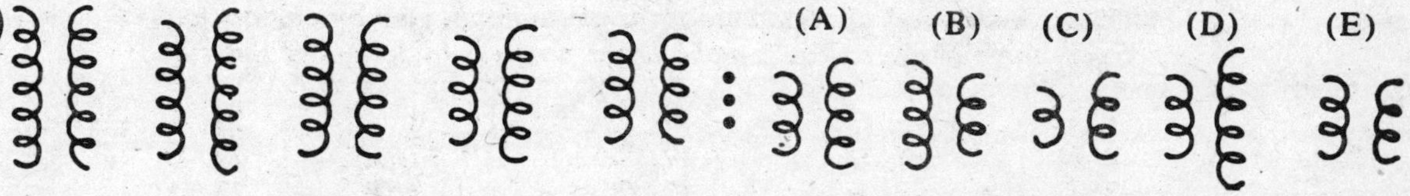

2 : (A) (B) (C) (D) (E)

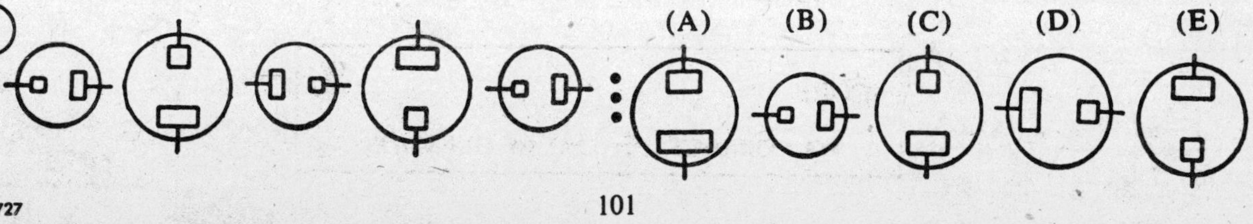

TEST QUESTIONS FOR PRACTICE

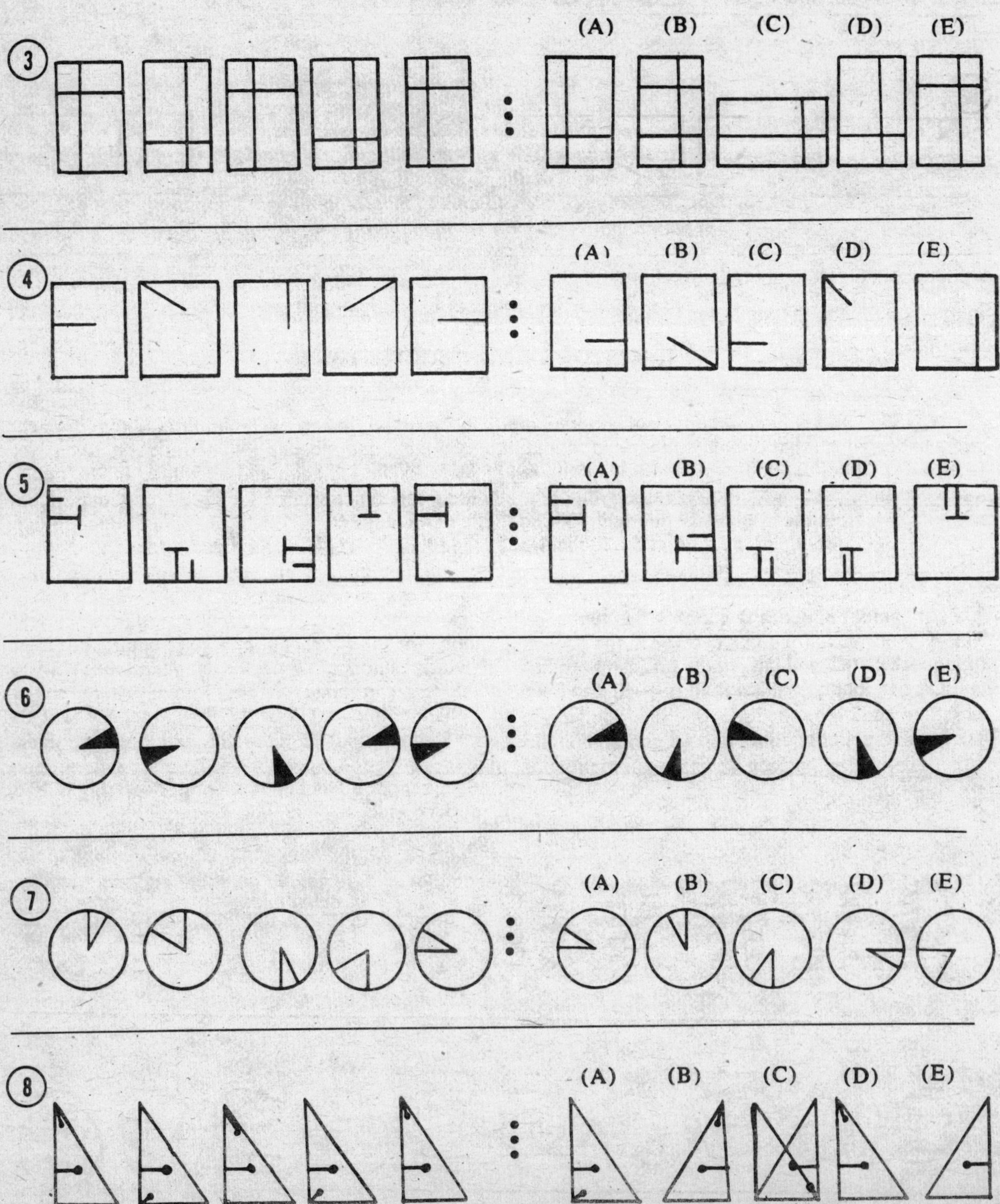

9
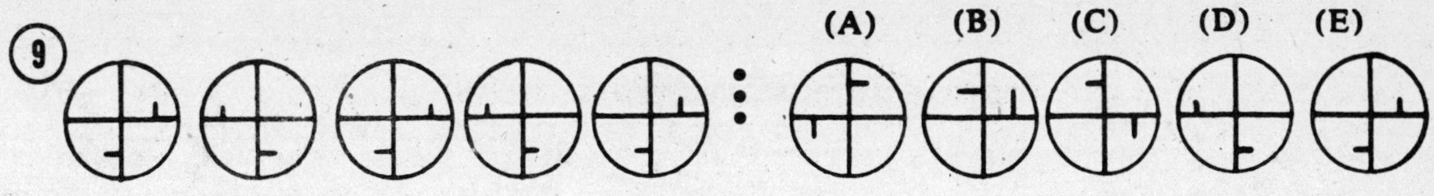

10
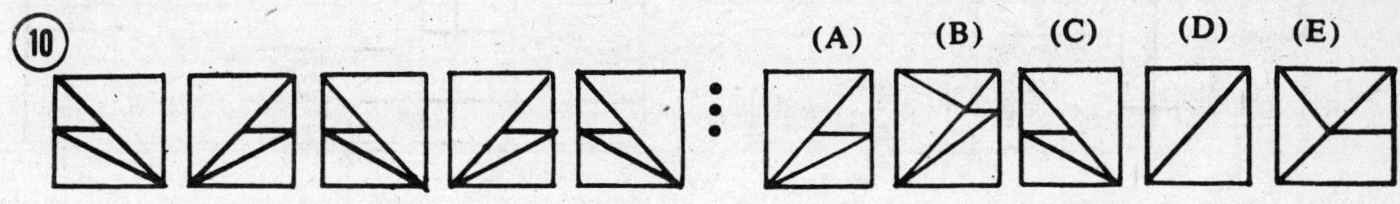

11
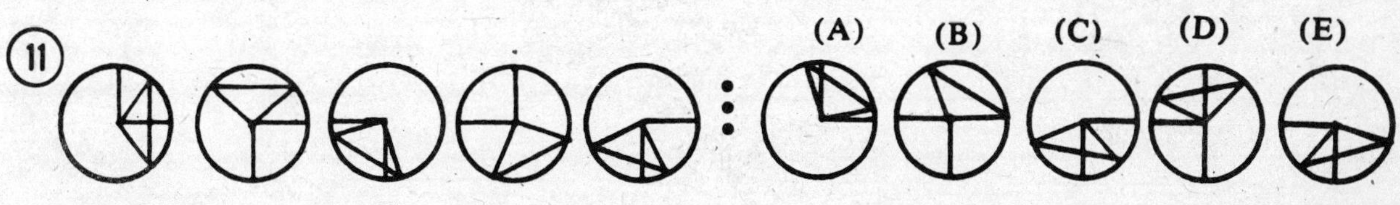

12
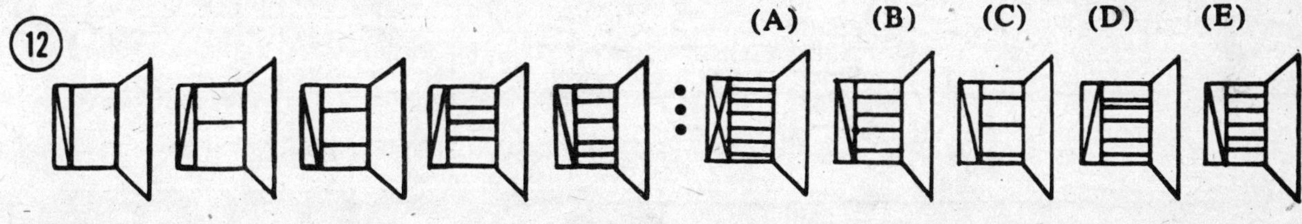

13
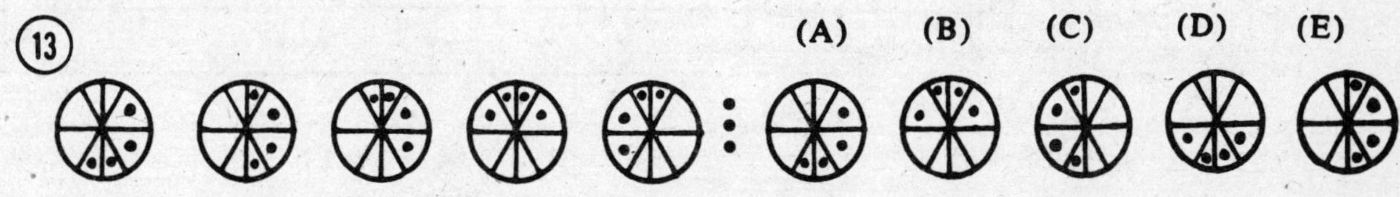

14

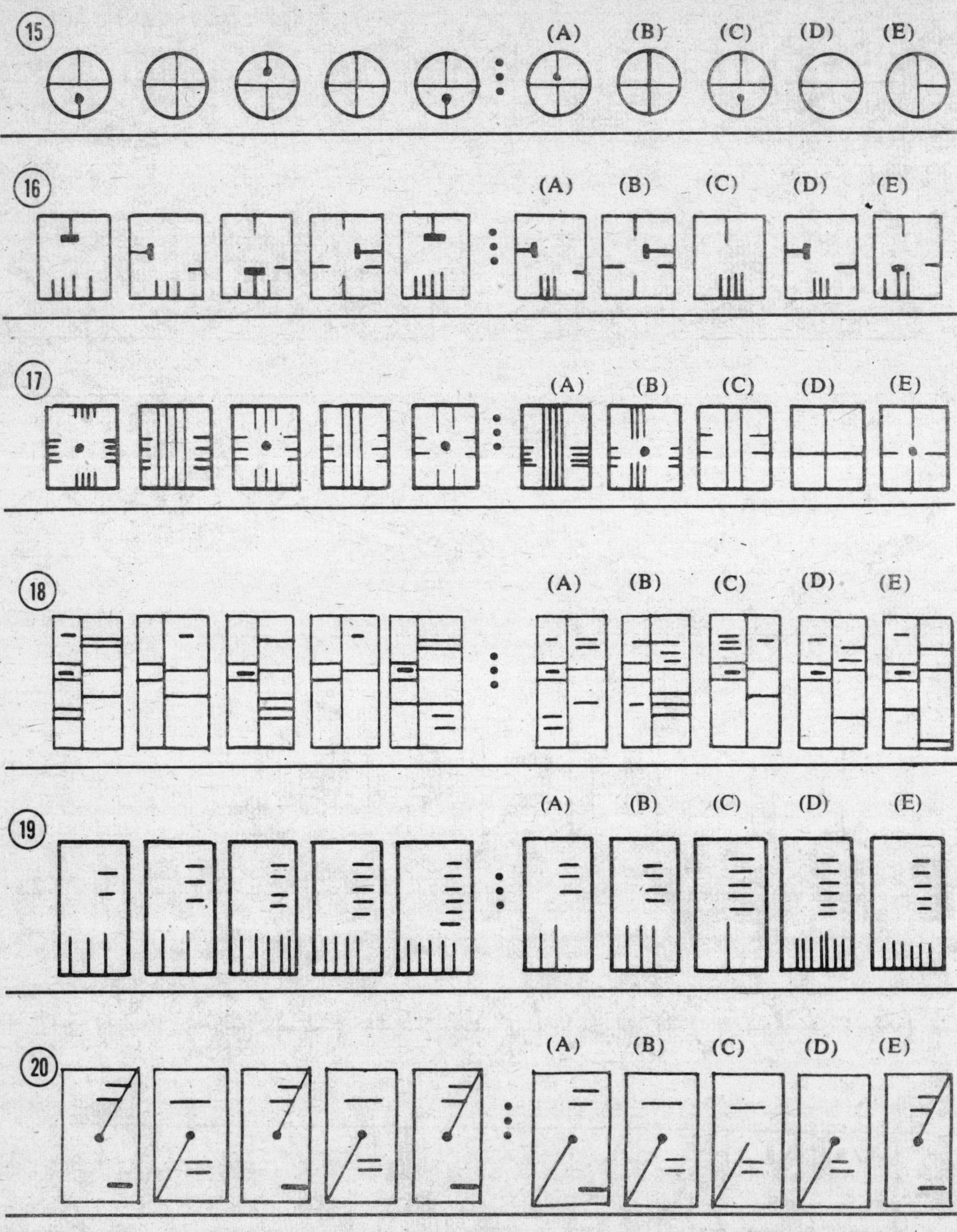

15
(A)
(B)
(C)
(D)
(E)
16
(A)
(B)
(C)
(D)
(E)
17
(A)
(B)
(C)
(D)
(E)
18
(A)
(B)
(C)
(D)
(E)
19
(A)
(B)
(C)
(D)
(E)
20
(A)
(B)
(C)
(D)
(E)

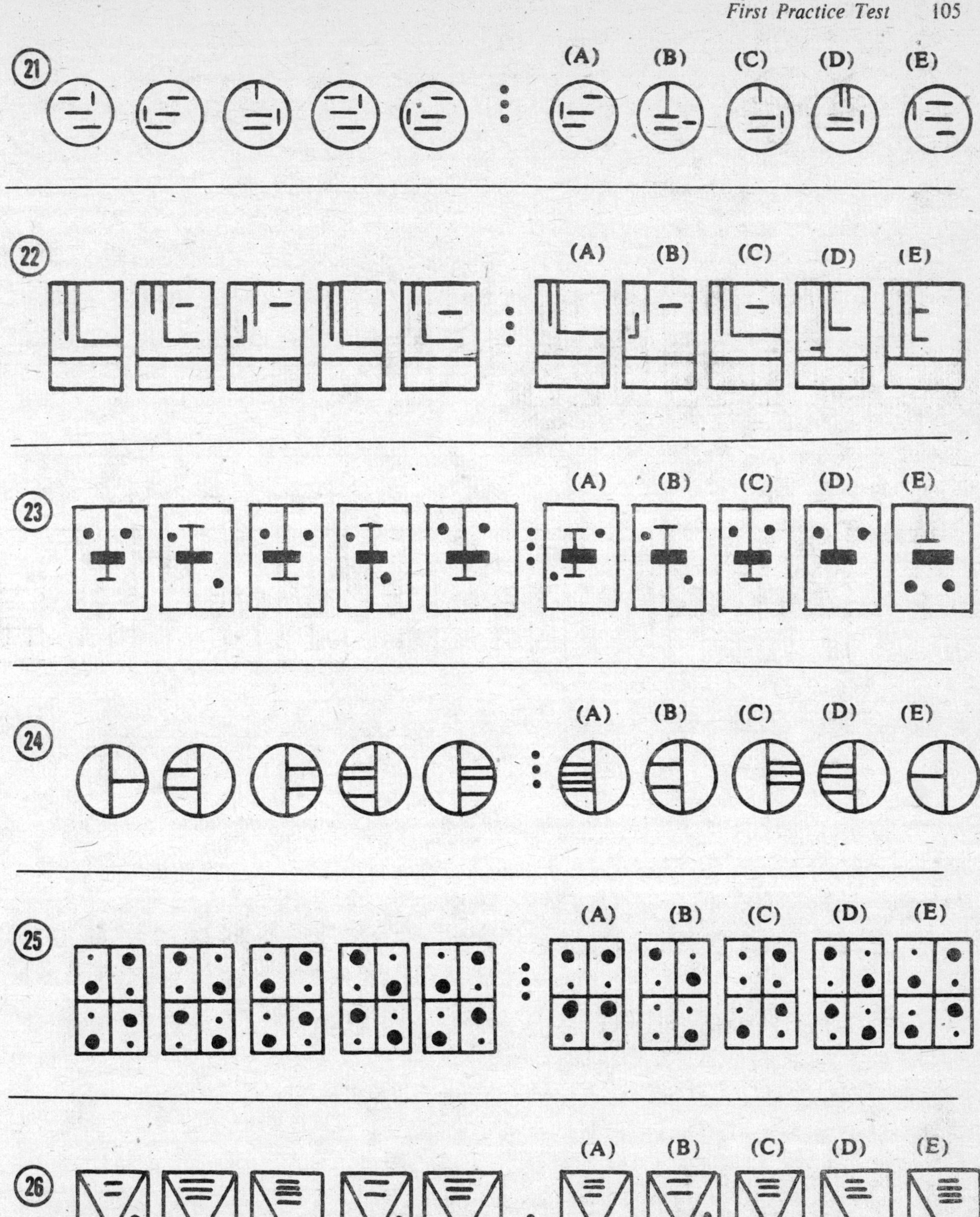
21
(A)
(B)
(C)
(D)
(E)
22
(A)
(B)
(C)
(D)
(E)
23
(A)
(B)
(C)
(D)
(E)
24
(A)
(B)
(C)
(D)
(E)
25
(A)
(B)
(C)
(D)
(E)
26
(A)
(B)
(C)
(D)
(E)

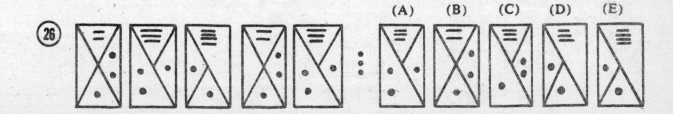

27 (A) (B) (C) (D) (E)

28 (A) (B) (C) (D) (E)

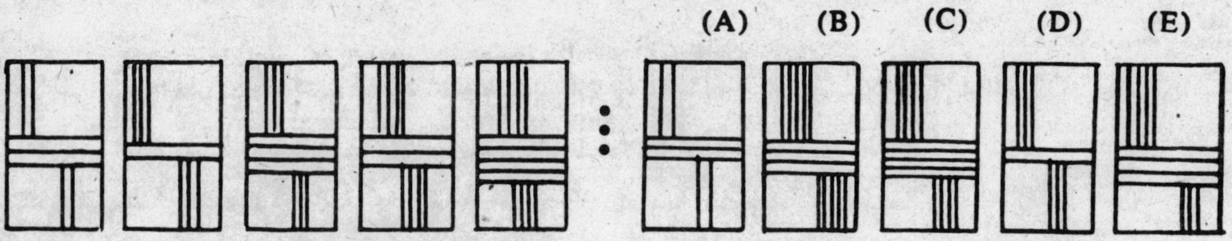

29 (A) (B) (C) (D) (E)

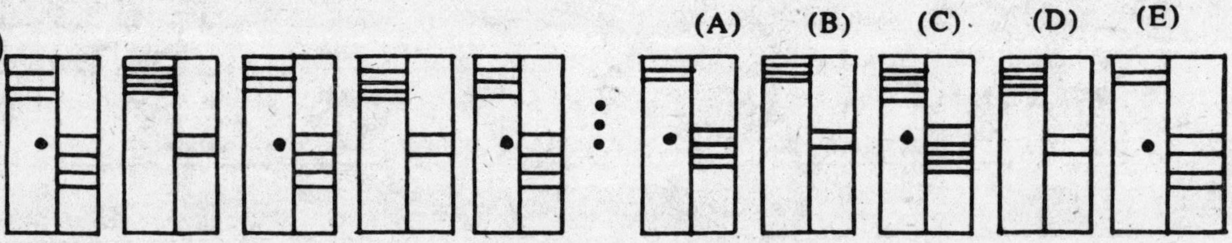

Correct Answers For The Foregoing Questions

(Please make every effort to answer the questions on your own before looking at these answers. You'll make faster progress by following this rule.)

1. A	7. E	13. C	19. E	25. D
2. C	8. A	14. E	20. B	26. E
3. D	9. D	15. B	21. C	27. A
4. B	10. A	16. A	22. B	28. B
5. C	11. B	17. C	23. B	29. D
6. D	12. D	18. B	24. A	

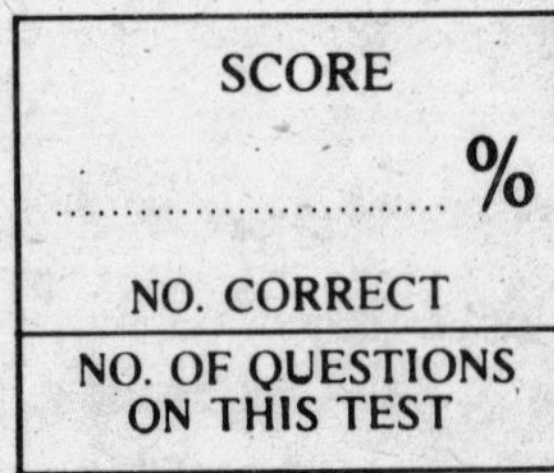
SCORE

.... %

NO. CORRECT

NO. OF QUESTIONS ON THIS TEST

FIGURE ANALOGIES

Your ability to see the differences between, and the relationship between various abstract symbols is one indication of your ability to learn. It is a measure of your ability to meet new situations and evaluate them. The following practice questions will help to familiarize you with this type of question. As in other analogy problems—verbal analogies and numerical series—the best approach is to translate into words the exact relationship between the key figures. Be sure to avoid the traps of similar figures which do not have the same relationship.

IN the following problems, the symbols in columns 1 and 2 have a relationship to each other. Select from the symbols in columns A, B, C, D and E the symbol which has the same relationship to the symbol in column 3, as the symbol in column 2 has to the symbol in column 1:

1 : 2 : : 3 : ? (A) (B) (C) (D) (E)

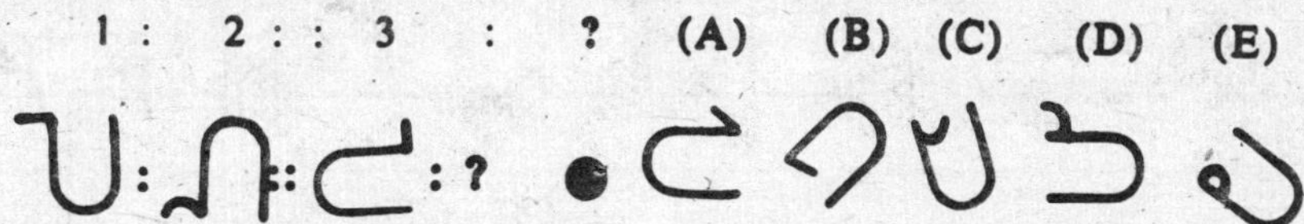

The correct answer is (D)

TEST QUESTIONS FOR PRACTICE

1 : 2 : : 3 : ? (A) (B) (C) (D)

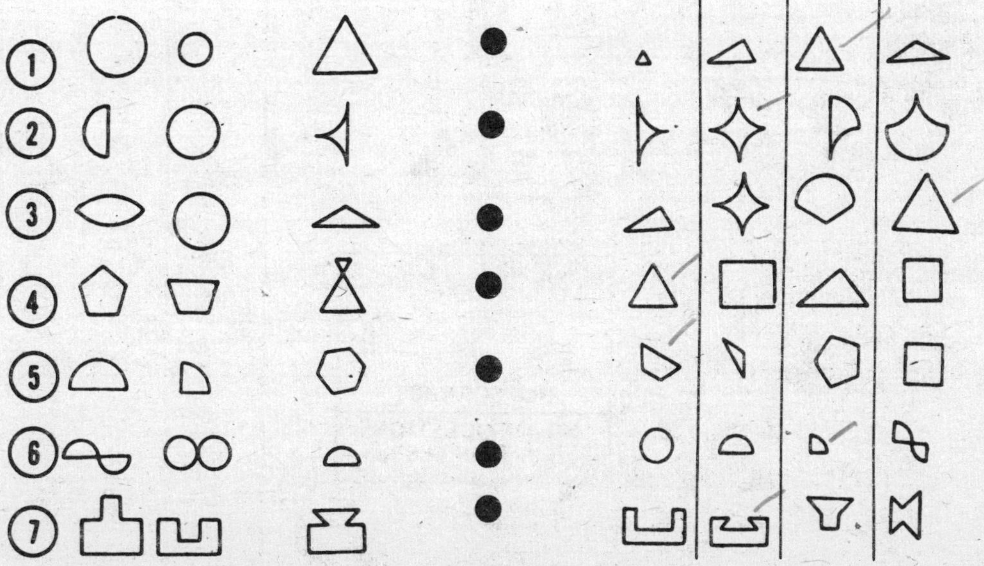

1

2

3

4

5

6

7

S727

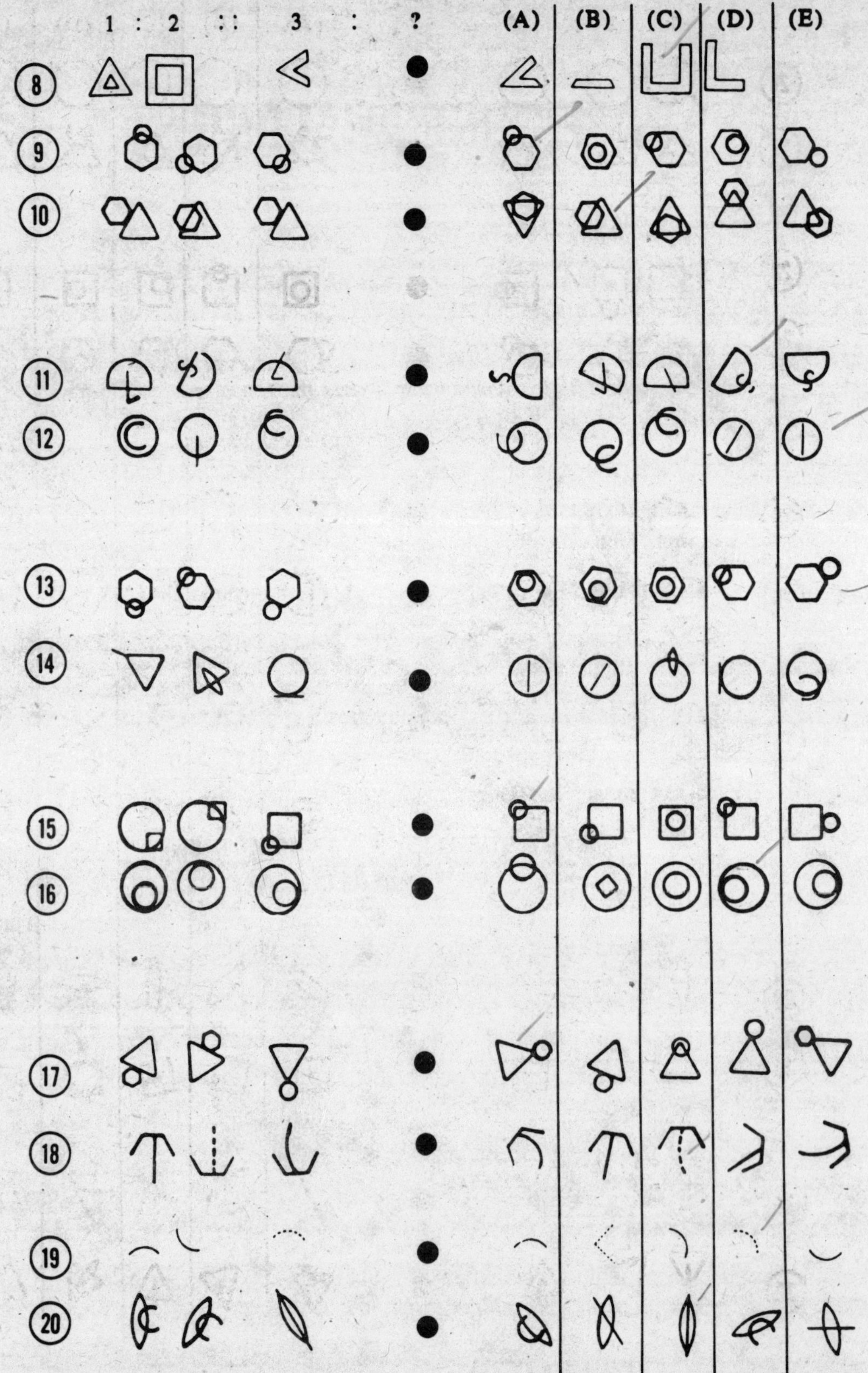
1 : 2 :: 3 : ?
(A)
(B)
(C)
(D)
(E)
8
9
10
11
12
13
14
15
16
17
18
19
20

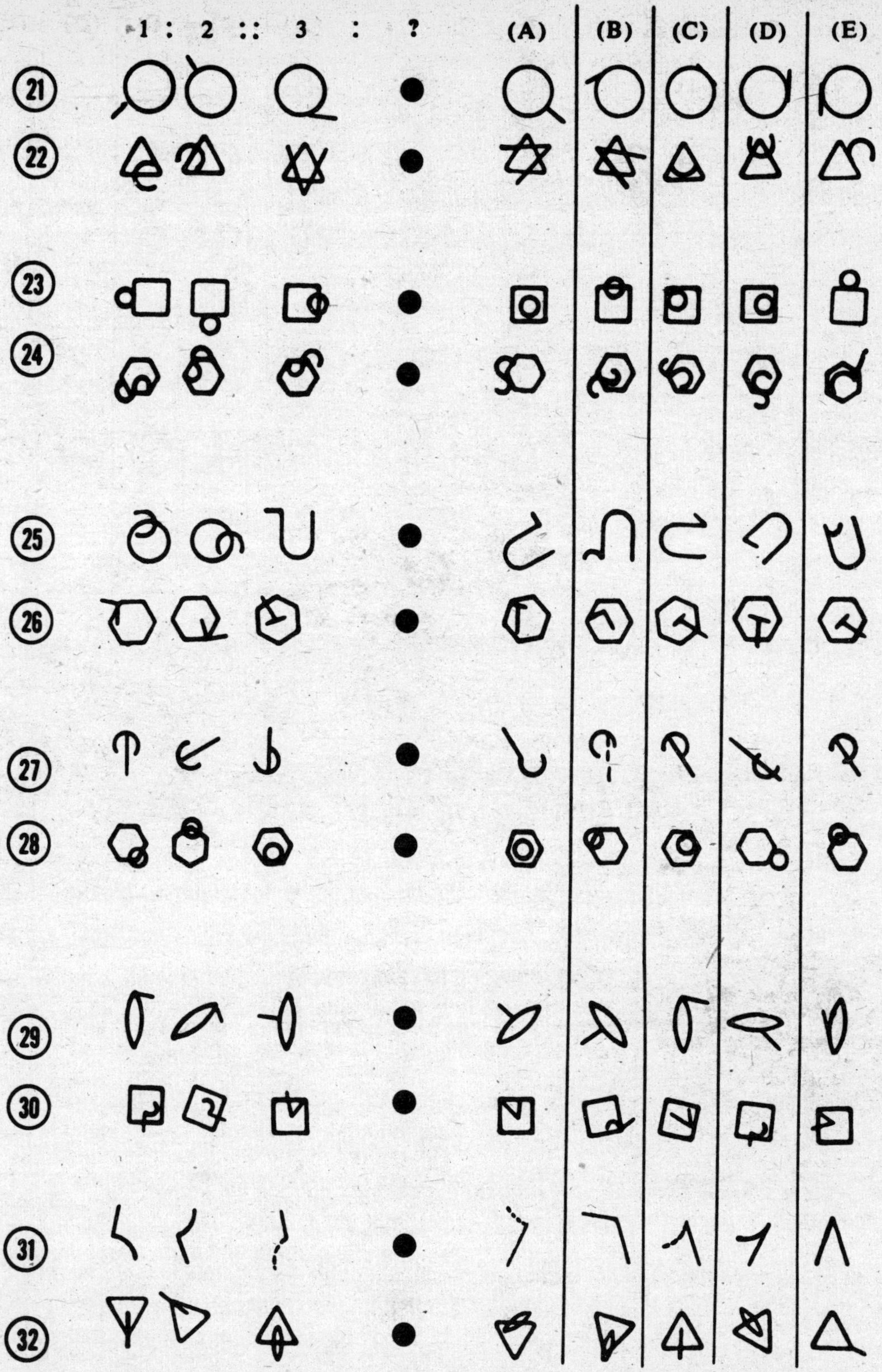

1 : 2 :: 3 : ? (A) (B) (C) (D) (E)

21

22

23

24

25

26

27

28

29

30

31

32

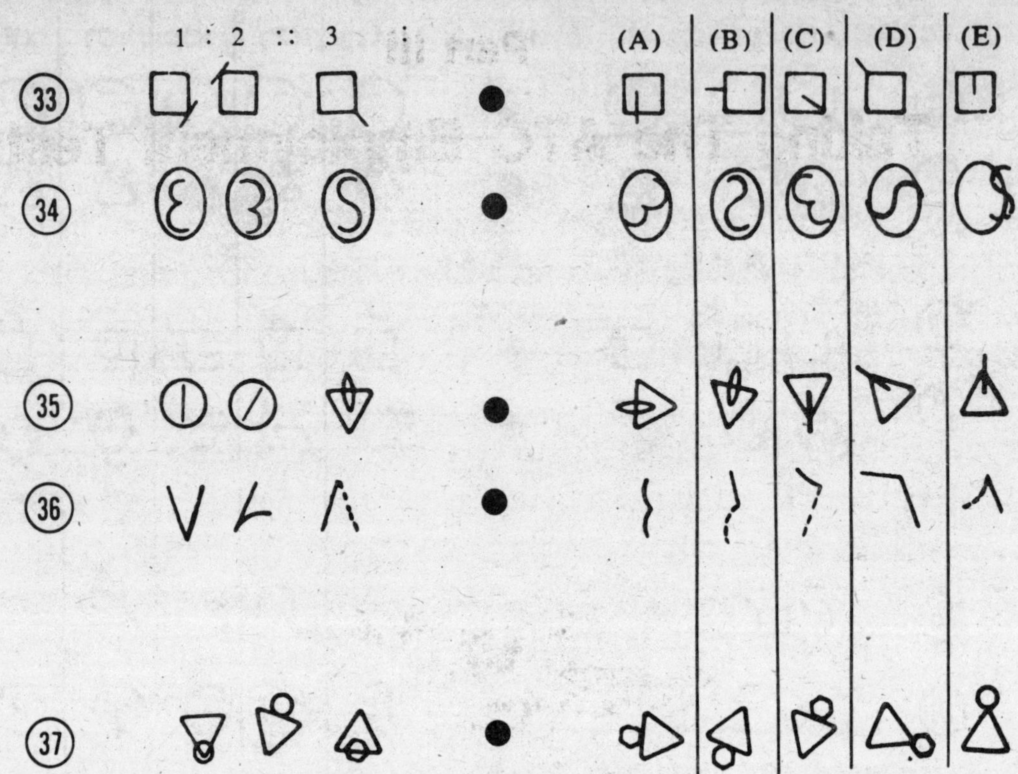

Correct Answers For The Foregoing Questions

(Please make every effort to answer the questions on your own before looking at these answers. You'll make faster progress by following this rule.)

1. C
2. B
3. D
4. A
5. A
6. A
7. B
8. C
9. A
10. B
11. D
12. E
13. E
14. D
15. A
16. D
17. D
18. C
19. D
20. C
21. D
22. B
23. B
24. C
25. A
26. E
27. C
28. C
29. A
30. E
31. A
32. A
33. D
34. B
35. B
36. E
37. D

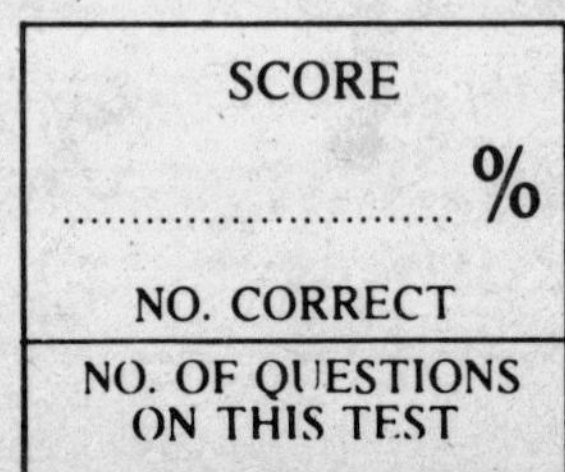

Part III

Taking The ATC Employment Test

TAKING THE ATC EMPLOYMENT TEST

Competitors should give themselves every fair advantage in preparing for and taking the written test by following the practices and techniques suggested below:

1. Since the test is not a knowledge test such as the ones given in school, studying for the examination the night before will not be helpful. A good night's rest is a better idea.

2. The sample questions included in this book should be studied carefully. Also, the instructions included in each section of the actual test should be read as carefully as time will allow. A reasonable amount of time is allotted for this purpose in the examination room.

3. Each competitor should bring two medium No. 2 pencils already sharpened. Also, although the examiner will periodically indicate the time, it may be advisable to bring a watch as an aid in keeping track of the time during the examination.

4. Competitors should take into consideration possible difficulties in finding a parking place or in locating the examination room. Extra time should be allowed to avoid running the risk of arriving too late to be admitted to the examination.

5. Competitors must have all required forms completely filled out or they will not be admitted to the examination.

Following the above recommendations should help competitors to be relaxed and ready to concentrate fully on the test material.

TIME LIMITS

A definite time limit has been set for each part of the test. These time limits are ample but will not be enough if competitors waste their time on questions for which they do not know the answer. Before each part the examiner will announce the number of questions in that part and the length of time allowed. When the time is announced competitors should check their watches or the room clock, if there is one, so that they know when the time will be up. While competitors are taking the test they should occasionally check the time. The examiner will mention the time 10 minutes before it is up. After this reminder competitors should finish the questions in that section and try to allow a few minutes for making final decisions and checking their answers before the time is up.

HOW TO MARK THE ANSWER SHEET

Competitors will be instructed to select the best choice of the suggested alternative answers for each question and to record this choice on a separate answer sheet. The question numbers on the answer sheet run across the page. Each answer must be shown by completely darkening the space corresponding to the letter that is the same as the letter of the correct answer. To avoid inaccurate scoring, the mark MUST be kept within the space and marks that have to be erased should be completely erased. Only one answer should be marked for each question since the scoring machine scores double answers as errors. All answers must be marked on the answer sheet; answers in the test booklet do not count. On the other hand, any figuring that needs to be done in answering a question should be done in the test booklet, NOT on the answer sheet.

HOW TO ANSWER THE QUESTIONS

If competitors first answer the questions that they know, they will not risk having time called before they have answered those questions for which they know the answers. When the answer is known after the first careful reading of a question, that answer should be marked on the answer sheet and the competitor should proceed to the next question without pausing. When a question appears especially difficult and is left until later, care should be taken that the corresponding number on the answer sheet is left unmarked.

GUESSING

In this test the examiner will tell the competitors, "It will be to your advantage to answer every question you can since your score will be the number of questions you answer correctly." This statement means that guessing is not penalized and that the score is the actual number of right answers. It is advisable therefore to make an intelligent guess about the answer to a difficult question.

ADDITIONAL SUGGESTIONS

Oral directions by the examiner and written directions in the test booklet are given to help the competitor and should be followed closely. When the examiner is giving directions before the test, competitors should feel free to call for an explanation if they need one. They should not risk making mistakes because the directions are not clear to them. Those competitors who have taken certain courses in education and psychology may have been warned by their instructors to avoid using words such as "none," "always," "every" and "all" in making test questions for prospective students. It is often difficult to write an answer in such terms and a consensus exists that the correct answer usually contains words like "mostly," "may be," "often" and other indefinite expressions. The wrong choices are popularly supposed to be tipped off by "always," "every," etc. This is not the case in Civil Service examinations like the Air Traffic Controller Test. If a choice seems good it should not be ruled out simply because it contains a word that is not "supposed" to be in a correct answer.

The written test consists of several sections which measure the abilities that are considered essential in carrying out the duties of the air traffic control. Since certain sections of the test apply more to some occupations than to others, part scores on the written test will be weighted and combined under different weighting patterns to obtain six basic ratings, each representing the combination of abilities appropriate for certain occupations.

THE AIR TRAFFIC CONTROL PROBLEMS

As an introduction to the air traffic system, a sample situation is presented. Future references in this report will relate back to that situation. The air traffic controller is repeatedly faced with similar situations in a multitude of ways when completing his day-to-day duty assignments.

> "Trans World Airlines Flight 1 (TW1) desires to depart the Kansas City Airport (MCI) and proceed to the Indianapolis Airport (IND) at an altitude of 29,000 feet. A solid cloud layer exists from 1,000 feet above the ground to an altitude of 30,000 feet between the MCI and IND Airports."

Obviously in the above situation some type of an electronic navigational system is required in order to insure that TW1 can fly to the destination airport, and some type of control must be provided to insure the flight maintains separation from other flights also flying in the clouds. The Federal Aviation Administration provides the navigational and control system. The control services are provided by air traffic controllers and the system is called air traffic control (ATC).

The purpose of ATC is to provide safe, orderly and expeditious flight conditions for an aircraft from departure to destination airport. Air traffic control is primarily concerned with Instrument Flight Rules (IFR) flights. Aircraft operating under these rules are considered by the controller as always "being in the clouds" and the pilot relies on the controller to provide separation from other IFR flights. This is accomplished by the controller issuing the pilot control instructions such as headings, routes and altitudes.

Another system pilots may operate under is called Visual Flight Rules (VFR). Under this system, the pilot provides his own separation from all other aircraft by visual means. Minimum conditions which must exist to operate under VFR are 3-5 miles forward visibility and 1,000 feet above, 500 feet below and 2,000 feet horizontally from a cloud layer. Controllers are not normally concerned with VFR flights. However, an IFR flight could fly in VFR conditions and operate on an IFR flight plan to take advantage of the ATC system. As a matter of record, almost all commercial and military flights now file and fly IFR regardless of the meteorological conditions.

There are some principles which must be established in order for the ATC system to operate. They are as follows:

1. A navigational system must exist. This is accomplished by ground stations transmitting electronic signals which can be received in the aircraft. This results in the establishment of definable airways and air routes.

2. A pilot/controller communication system must exist. It is imperative that the controller maintain direct radio communications with the pilot in order to provide timely instructions. This is accomplished by discrete radio frequencies provided at individual controller positions.

3. Separation standards are established. There are a myriad number of rules which establish minimum separation standards that the controller must adhere to. Some of the more basic ones are listed as examples:

   A. Nonradar Separation. This refers to time and distance separation.

      (1) Longitudinal--aircraft behind one another or on crossing courses. Basic separation rule—10 minutes.

(2) Lateral--aircraft beside one another on different routes. Basic separation rule--8 miles.

(3) Vertical--aircraft above one another. Basic separation rule--1,000/2,000 feet.

(4) Distance Measuring Equipment (DME)--special airborne and ground equipment will further reduce the longitudinal separation minimum listed in (1) above. Basic separation rule--20 miles.

B. Radar Separation. This refers to distance separation and is determined by the controller interpreting a radar display. Minimum radar separation between aircraft is 3 or 5 miles.

4. The same controller provides control instructions to all aircraft in a given airspace (sector). This is required in order to insure no conflict exists regarding airspace usage. Therefore, the same controller provides control instructions to all aircraft (military, commercial, civilian) operating within a given sector.

5. A coordination system must exist. Due to the complexity of the ATC system and the continual changing of the air traffic picture (aircraft entering/exiting a sector), an immediate coordination system must exist for the controllers. This is provided by a number of telephone lines available at the control sector for coordination purposes.

6. ATC facilities must be established. After establishment these facilities must be adequately staffed with qualified specialists to provide control services to the pilot. Additionally, definite areas of responsibilities must be established for each facility including Letters of Agreement, designated airspaces, area boundaries and other special operating procedures.

Continuing with the illustration, all required Kansas City Center flight progress strips for our TW1 flight in a "simulated" environment.

Segment of Training = 300 Hours

Reference Material - P-1 Manual, Kansas City Center Maps (2)
Kansas City Center Handbook 7210.3C

SAMPLE FLIGHT PROGRESS STRIPS FOR TW1

The symbology depicted on the flight progress strips below is as follows:

TW1:	Aircraft Call Sign
B707/A:	Aircraft Type
T475:	Aircraft Air Speed
391:	Computer Number
01:	First Progress Strip Prepared by the Computer
MCI:	Flight Progress Strip Designator
P1845:	Aircraft Proposed Departure Time
R290:	Pilot's Required Altitude in Hundreds of Feet
MCI J24 IND:	Proposed Route of Flight

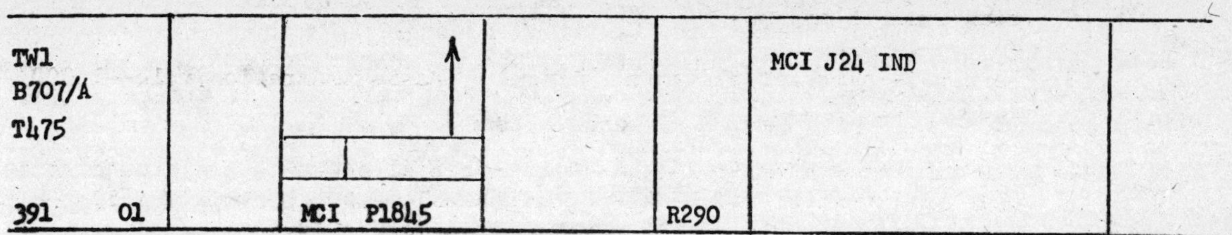

TW1 B707/A T475 391 01		MCI P1845		R290	MCI J24 IND	

Depicts the format for a proposal flight plan (aircraft on the ground and departure clearance not in effect).

TW1 B707/A T475 G337 391 02	MKC 1857	19 16 HLV	290		MCI J24 IND	

Here the aircraft has departed and will pass Hallsville, Missouri, VORTAC on its assigned route on or about 1916 (Greenwich Mean Time) at an assigned altitude of 29,000' (altitudes written in 100's of feet...last two zeros deleted) enroute to Indianapolis.

TW1 B707/A T475 G570 391 03	HLV 1916	19 30 STL	290		MCI J24 IND	*ZID

This strip is posted for the St. Louis sector and is basically the same as #2 above. The extra notation at the far right indicates that the flight plan has been forwarded by computer to Indianapolis Center.

Further attention is now given to the ATC facilities. These facilities are control towers, control centers and flight service stations. They are further described as follows:

1. Control tower (Twr). This facility is generally located on the larger airports. The staffing will average between 10 and 50 controllers. The tower airspace normally extends outward to a 20-mile radius of the airport and from the ground to an altitude of about 9,000 feet.

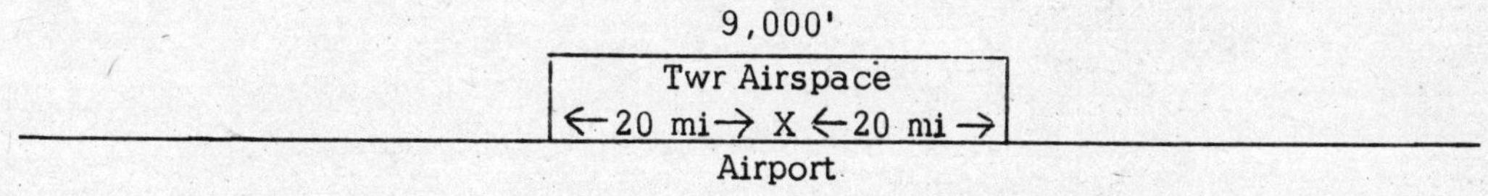

The tower controller provides both radar (if available) and nonradar control and has direct pilot/controller radio communications. Some of the larger towers now have computers.

2. Control Center. The center is generally located a considerable distance from the airports (example: Kansas City Center at Olathe). The staffing will average between 350-450 controllers. The center airspace extends outward from the tower 20-mile radius and upward from the tower 9,000 foot ceiling. At smaller airports with no control tower the center airspace extends all the way to the ground.

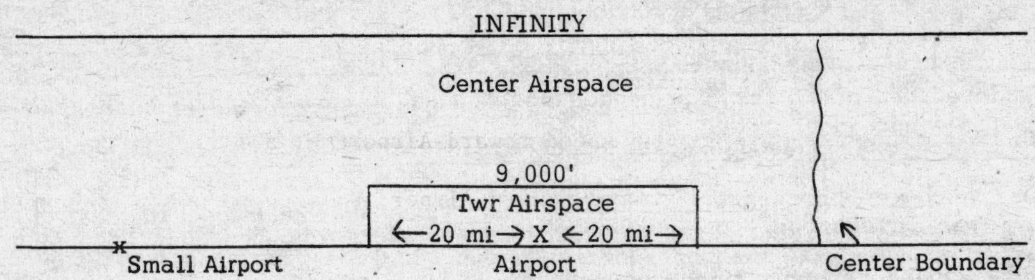

The center controller provides both radar and nonradar control, and has direct pilot/controller radio communications. Computer and teletype services are available.

3. Flight Service Station (FSS). The flight service station is not a control facility. This facility provides services such as flight following, weather briefings and information pertaining to airport conditions to both VFR and IFR pilots. The FSS will also relay IFR flight plans from pilots to center/tower controllers and control instructions from the controllers to pilots. The facility has direct pilot/specialist radio communications and a teletype system. An FSS may be located at large or small airports.

In our original situation involving Trans World Airlines Flight 1, the following sequences of events would take place regarding ATC.

1. TW1 pilot files flight plan with the Kansas City FSS

2. The Kansas City FSS relays the flight plan to MCI Twr and Kansas City Center

3. TW1 pilot requests clearance (routing and altitude) from MCI Twr.

4. MCI Twr advises Kansas City Center who issues clearance

5. MCI Twr advises Kansas City Center of departure time and flight is coordinated with all involved controllers.

TW1 flight must be provided separation from all conflicting flights from ground to cleared altitude when climbing from the MCI airport, other enroute aircraft at assigned altitude and all flights from assigned altitude to ground when descending to the IND airport. Facilities involved in this flight would be Kansas City FSS, MCI Twr, Kansas City Center, Indianapolis Center and Indianapolis Twr.

All of the above information identifies a most complex ATC system and since a controller may be providing control instructions to as many as 15 or 20 aircraft at a time, the workload adds to the system complexity. For these reasons a most comprehensive training program, including a demanding evaluation system, must be administered to the center student controller.

SELECTED AIR TRAFFIC CONTROL PROBLEMS

The problems on these pages represent highly simplified versions of air-traffic control (ATC) situations. You will be concerned with maintaining adequate time and altitude separations for several aircraft which will

A. be flying at different altitudes, and

B. have different ETA's (estimated times of arrival) at or over Airport W. However, all the aircraft will

C. be flying the same ground speed toward Airport W, and

D. be flying on the same course toward Airport W.

After studying information presented in Flight Data Displays, determine which of several incoming flights can be permitted to make specified altitude changes while maintaining conformance with a basic traffic rule. For each question, use the flight data given in the display.

Basic traffic rule:

A SEPARATION OF 5 MINUTES IS NECESSARY BETWEEN TWO EN ROUTE AIRCRAFT WHICH ARE EXPECTED TO PASS OVER THE SAME GEOGRAPHICAL POINT AT THE SAME ALTITUDE.

For practice, look at the Sample Flight Data Display shown below:

SAMPLE FLIGHT DATA DISPLAY

Flight Identification	Cruising Altitude	Estimated Time of Arrival (ETA) At or Over Airport W
E	5000	2:25
F	4000	2:24
G	2000	2:20
H	3000	2:14

Notice that the aircraft are flying at different altitudes and that each is expected to arrive at, or over, Airport W at a different time. However, remember that you are to assume that ground speed and course of all flights are the same. Also, consider rate of climb and rate of descent as UNKNOWN factors. (In other words, for purposes of these sample questions, make no speculation as to rate of climb or descent; just ignore these two factors completely.)

Answers to questions of this kind will involve a determination of both time and altitude separation for the various flights.

Sample Question 1 is based on information in the Sample Flight Data Display above. Indicate your answer next to the question. On the test, if the correct answer is YES, circle A, if NO, circle B.

The question asks whether or not you can safely permit a change in altitude for

1. Flight E to 3000 A. Yes B. No

You should have circled B because Flight E is separated from Flight F by only 1 minute and if Flight E changes from 5000 to 3000 it must pass through 4000 which is occupied by Flight F. Flight E cannot be permitted to pass through the 4000-foot level without violating the air-traffic-control rule which requires a minimum of 5 minutes time separation between two aircraft flying at the same altitude.

Now try practice questions 2, 3, and 4. Mark your answers and then compare them with the correct answers.

2. Flight G to 4000 A. Yes B. No

3. Flight F to 2000 A. Yes B. No

4. Flight H to 5000 A. Yes B. No

The correct answer to question 2 is B. Flight G cannot be permitted to change from 2000 to 4000 because it is separated by only 4 minutes from Flight F which is flying at 4000.

The correct answer to question 3 is B. Flight F cannot be permitted to change from 4000 to 2000 because (as we have just noticed) it is separated by only 4 minutes from Flight G which is flying at 2000.

The correct answer to question 4 is A because Flight H is 6 minutes ahead of the nearest aircraft and can be permitted to change to any altitude.

Now try practice questions 5, 6, and 7.

5. Flight F to 3000 A. Yes B. No

6. Flight E to 4000 A. Yes B. No

7. Flight E to 6000 A. Yes B. No

You should have marked A for question 5. Flight F can safely be permitted to change from 4000 to 3000 because it will not have to move into or through the airspace of the nearest flights, E and G.

You should have marked B for question 6. Flight E cannot be permitted to change from 5000 to 4000 because it is separated by only 1 minute from Flight F which is flying at 4000.

The correct answer for question 7 is A. Permitting Flight E to change from 5000 to 6000 would assure even greater altitude separation from Flight F which has a time separation of only 1 minute.

PROBLEM SOLVING QUESTIONS

As stated previously, the problem-solving question is the type least frequently met with on employment and Civil Service tests; it is, of course, quite common on school and college examinations. Usually, though not always, this type of question deals with mathematics and geometry problems; however, problems in physics, chemistry engineering, logic, and other subjects are found, depending upon the scope of the examination and the subject area of the test.

There is one essential ingredient for answering all problem-solving questions: knowledge of the subject matter. Indeed, this axiom applies to all types of questions in all categories, but it is never more vital than when solving a problem. Equally important is a thorough knowledge of the basic principles and processes connected with the subject area.

Assuming that you possess this basic knowledge, there are ten steps that you can take toward a successful solution of all types of problems:

1. Fast reading of problem for subject and purpose.

2. A second, careful reading to determine extent and limits of the question.

3. Rereading to determine what facts are stated in the question.

4. Eliminating "red herrings."

5. Restating problem, with only the relevant data.

6. Determining how to solve the problem and what formulas or principles to apply.

7. Determining how best to apply these principles and formulas.

8. Precise application of relevant principles and formulas.

9. Careful, step-by-step solution of problem.

10. Review and checking of all processes outlined in steps 2 to 9, above.

Let us see how these ten success steps can be applied to a real problem. The example we have chosen consists of a relatively simple problem, one that will not be found on a more specialized exam, such as physics, engineering, mathematics, etc., but one that can be understood by anyone, not only by those who are taking a test in one of the science subjects. No <u>specialized</u> knowledge is needed to solve the following problem.

<u>Analysis of a Problem-Solving Question</u>

There are three pipes leading into a pool. One 8-inch in diameter pipe, of iron, can fill the pool in 20 minutes; a second, 5-inch in diameter pipe, of concrete, can fill the pool in 30 minutes; and a third pipe, 10-inch in diameter, of steel, can fill the pool in 10 minutes. How long would it take the three pipes together to fill the pool which measures 10 X 22 X 45 ft.

<u>Applying Step 1</u>, above, we read the problem quickly to determine the subject matter and the purpose of the question. We can see that the <u>subject</u> is a so-called "time and work" problem (i.e., a given object does a given work in a given amount of time).

The purpose of the question is to find out the amount of time it would take the given objects (pipes) to do the given job (filling the pool).

According to Step 2, we read the problem again, carefully this time, to find out exactly what we are asked to do. In the question we are asked to figure out how long it would take all three pipes together to fill the pool.

It is extremely important that all problems be read with great care to determine the extent and limit of the question. In other words, what exactly are you asked to find out? Many exam-takers have found to their sorrow that they have answered a problem quite correctly but answered the wrong part of the problem. This is especially true of problems involving several elements such as height, weight, distance, temperature, etc. On such a problem--if the question is not read carefully--you may find out the correct height and weight, but the question actually asked you to find the distance. So, study the question carefully and determine exactly what you are asked to do.

Step 3 tells us to reread the problem carefully and see what facts are stated. In our example the facts we have to work with are these:

Three pipes leading into a pool that measures 10 X 22 X 45 ft.
No. 1 is iron, 8-inch dia. and fills pool in 20 minutes
No. 2, concrete, 5-inch dia., fills pool in 30 minutes
No. 3, steel, 10-inch dia., fills pool in 10 minutes

Our facts are: a pool of a certain capacity; three pipes of varying capacity; each fills the same pool at different rates of speed.

The first thing we have to watch out for is the tricky arrangement of even this simple question. Notice that the pipes are not listed in either increasing or decreasing capacity; but rather, they are listed so that the pipe with the medium capacity is given first; the one with the slowest capacity is listed second; and the pipe with the fastest capacity is given last. In other words, there is no order to the listing. This is an important point to watch out for, especially in questions of greater complexity. One's mind tends to be orderly and assumes automatically that a listing of any type follows some sort of order or rule. However, as we have seen, this is not the case with problems that have to be solved as part of an examination.

In our relatively simple example, the time values are identical; that is, they are all given in minutes. However, the question could have been worded in varying values so that the time for one of the pipes could have been listed in hours or seconds or days, etc. Or, in our problem, one of the pipes may only fill the pool halfway or 3/5 or some other varying figure. This is also true of problems where some facts may be stated in feet, others in inches, or in ounces and pounds, etc. Always make sure that the given facts are stated in identical values; if they are not, one or more facts must be converted so that you are working with a common value factor. These are extremely important points to watch out for in problem-solving questions.

Note also that our problem contains "red herring" information which must be identified and eliminated before the problem can be solved with speed and economy. Upon closer study of the problem, we can see that the size of the pool is immaterial as far as the question is concerned. We are told that the pipes fill the pool; therefore, it is immaterial how big the pool is. It could be twice as large or half the size--it does not matter. The important fact is that it is filled to capacity--by each pipe at a given rate. So we may safely eliminate the size of the pool as irrelevant data.

But wait. How does the material of the pipes affect our answer? It may affect the rate of flow of the water, and it probably does, but we are not directly concerned with that. We already know the rate of flow for each pipe.

And, finally, upon closer examination, we find that the diameter of the pipes will not affect our answer in any manner. It would not matter, so far as this problem is concerned, if one of the pipes were 12 feet in diameter, or if they all had the same diameter. We are told how long it takes each pipe to fill the pool. That is all that concerns us.

So we have found, upon careful examination of the problem, that some of the data is irrelevant and should be eliminated to avoid confusion. We can now restate the problem (Step 5) in our minds, if not on paper, so that all "red herrings" are eliminated. This will enable us to concentrate on the problem itself which, simplified (but still identical to the original) will read:

> One pipe fills a pool in 20 minutes; a second can fill it in 30 minutes; a third can fill it in 10 minutes. How long does it take all three pipes together to fill the pool?

Now that we have reduced the problem to its basic elements and eliminated the irrelevancies, our next task (Step 6) is to determine how best to solve it by applying the correct basic formulas or principles.

By examining the problem, we should come to the conclusion that the principle that applies here is that of fractions. That is, the first pipe, which fills the pool in 20 minutes, fills 1/20 of the pool in 1 minute. Accordingly, the second pipe fills 1/30 of the pool in 1 minute; and the third pipe fills 1/10 of the pool in 1 minute.

Therefore, (Step 7) by adding the 1-minute flow of all three pipes together we will be able to see how much of the pool is filled in 1 minute. Thus (Step 8, applying the principle and Step 9, step-by-step solution):

$$1/20+1/30+1/10 = \frac{3+2+6}{60} = \frac{11}{60} \text{ in 1 minute}$$

Therefore:

After having found the common denominator 60, we find that in 1 minute all three pipes working together will fill 11/60 of the pool.

However, we cannot stop here. We do not want to know how long it takes to fill 11/60 of the pool. We need to know how long it takes to fill the whole pool.

If we know our principles and formulas, we know that if 11/60 of the pool is filled in 1 minute, the reciprocal of the fraction will tell us how many minutes will be required to fill the whole pool. The reciprocal of 11/60 is 60/11.

Therefore:

$$\frac{60}{11} = 5\frac{5}{11} \text{ minutes (our answer).}$$

As we have just seen, we must identify the principle that applies to the solution of the problem. In our case it is fractions. It may also be, in other problems, πr^2 - or Rate X Time = Distance or Ohm's law or any other mathematical, geometric, or scientific principle or law--depending upon the given problem.

In our simple example, of course, knowledge of the total principle was not as vital as it would be in other, more complex problems. Had we not known about the reciprocal of fractions, we might have been able to solve the problem by some application of logic--but it would have taken us much longer, and there would have been a greater chance of error. We could, for example, have taken the 11/60 (one minute) and seen how many times 11/60 it would take to make 60/60 (the whole pool). We would have found that it takes 5 times plus 5/11. However, without the knowledge of the basic principle--fractions--we would have had a difficult, if not impossible task. And it certainly would have consumed a lot of valuable time.

We have solved the problem (Steps 1 through 9) and all that remains is the last, but very important, 10th Step: checking our work carefully. This is of utmost importance if you want to get a good score on your test. Very often you will find, upon rechecking and reviewing, that you omitted an important point in your solution or made a fatal mistake in your haste to solve the problem. Check your facts and figures carefully; go over your computations; make sure that all facts are accounted for; and be certain that you have answered the questions completely.

Even though we may seem to be repetitious, we must point out again the most vital factor in solving problems--one that is not listed in our ten success steps: a thorough understanding of the subject matter of the question category and knowledge of the underlying principles connected with the subject matter. Only study and more study, practice and more practice, will give you this understanding and knowledge. Thorough preparation is all-important for every kind of test, but it is vital for the problem-solving type.

Some sample questions on problem-solving follow:

1. "Some specialists are willing to give their services to the Government entirely free of charge; some feel that a nominal salary, such as will cover traveling expenses, is sufficient for a position that is recognized as being somewhat honorary in nature; many other specialists value their time so highly that they will not devote any of it to public service that does not repay them at a rate commensurate with the fees that they can obtain from a good private clientele."

This quotation best supports the statement that the use of specialists by the Government

A. is rare because of the high cost of securing such persons
B. may be influenced by the willingness of specialists to serve
C. enables them to secure higher salaries in private fields
D. has become increasingly common during the past few years
E. always conflicts with private demands for their services

2. "What constitutes skill in any line of work is not always easy to determine; economy of time must be carefully distinguished from economy of energy, as the quickest method may require the greatest expenditure of muscular effort, and may not be essential or at all desirable."

This quotation best supports the statement that

A. the most efficiently executed task is not always the one done in the shortest time
B. energy and time cannot both be preserved in performing a single task
C. a task is well done when it is performed in the shortest time
D. skill in performing a task should not be acquired at the expense of time

3. Draw a horizontal line across your paper in the space allotted for question number three, draw vertical lines about half an inch long, through the horizontal line, breaking the horizontal line into eight approximately equal sections numbering the sections one through eight. Draw the horizontal line representing section seven vertically under section two, draw the horizontal line representing section four horizontally under section six, take the line in section eight and place it horizontally under section two connecting the end of seven and eight together, move the line in section one to section six placing it horizontally under line four, draw the line in section six horizontally under section two connecting one end of six to one end of seven, take the line in section two and draw it vertically under section six connecting lines four and one at the end, draw the line in section five vertically under section two connecting the ends of lines six and eight, draw the line in section three vertically under section six so that one end touches line four at the end and the other end touches line one at the end, now number each line in the squares consistent with the section it came from.

4. Read the following sentence:

If you understand this sentence completely, you will have no problem answering this question.

-     - - -   - - - - - - -

Take the last letter in the last word in the longest line above and place it above the sixth dash from the left, take the fourth letter from the right in the fourteenth word of the sentence and put it above the last dash on the right, take the first letter of the third word and place it above the first dash on the left, take the sixth letter in the last word before the comma and put it above the third dash from the right, take the next to last letter in the word problem and place it above the fourth dash from the left, take the first letter in the sixth word and place it above the fifth dash from the left and the second dash from the right, take the sixth letter from the right of the third word from the left of the longest line of the sentence and place it above the fourth and fifth dashes from the right and the third dash from the left, now guess what letter goes above the vacant dash.

5. "Individual differences in mental traits assume importance in fitting people to jobs because such personal characteristics are persistent and are relatively little influenced by training and experience."

The quotation best supports the statement that training and experience

A. are limited in their effectiveness in fitting people to jobs
B. do not increase a person's fitness for a job
C. have no effect upon a persons mental traits
D. have relatively little effect upon the individual's chances for success
E. should be based on the mental traits of an individual

6. "In the relations of man to nature, the procuring of food and shelter is fundamental. With the migration of man to various climates, ever new adjustments to the food supply and to the climate became necessary."

The quotation best supports the statement that the means by which man supplies his material needs are

A. accidental
B. varied
C. limited
D. inadequate

ANSWER KEY TO PROBLEM SOLVING QUESTIONS

1. B

2. A

3.

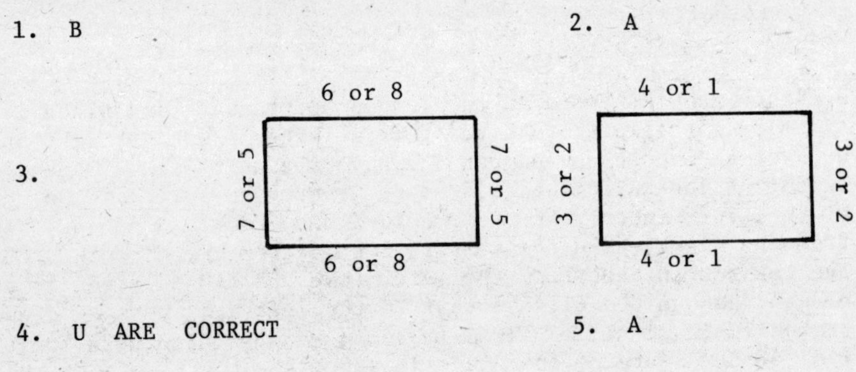

4. U ARE CORRECT

5. A

6. B

JUDGMENT AND REASONING QUESTIONS

This is perhaps the broadest category of all. Questions may range from general knowledge questions about current events, history, sociology, politics, etc., to specific areas dealing with the candidate's chosen field of work or with matters related to that field.

Questions of this type are usually of the multiple-choice form, although other forms of objective-type questions may appear on a particular test.

The only way the exam-taker can adequately prepare himself for general questions of this type is by having a genuine curiosity about everything, by reading good books, newspapers, and magazines, by following current political and social trends. In other words, be alert to what's going on in the world, think about it, examine it, and question it. For the more specific questions in this category, obviously the preparation must consist of a good background and knowledge of the field in which you take the examination.

The difficulty level of the questions will usually depend on the type of position for which you are applying and on the educational and professional requirement called for in the examination announcement.

Below, we will give examples of some typical questions in this category. However, they are only "typical" in the sense of being in the same category; it is impossible here to predict the questions <u>you</u> may be asked on <u>your</u> test. "General Information" is a virtually limitless category, and it is impossible to guess even vaguely at the general areas that may be covered by your test. The specific questions --relating to job knowledge--are simpler to guess at, but even there it is impossible to know what part of the job knowledge the questions may cover.

Here are some types of general questions:

1. Mass production results in lower prices chiefly because

A. the cost of making each unit is lowered
B. a larger amount of material is used
C. competition becomes keener
D. demand for the product increases
E. the articles produced are of an inferior quality

2. The fact that the sun seems to rise in the east and set in the west is proof that

A. only the sun is in motion
B. only the earth is in motion
C. either the sun or the earth is in motion
D. the east and the west are merely abstract concepts
E. there are 12 hours in the average day

3. Which of the following groups gives the correct order of succession to the Presidency of the United States?

A. Vice-President--Secretary of State--Secretary of Treasury
B. Vice-President--Speaker of the House--President <u>pro tempore</u> of the Senate
C. Vice-President--Secretary of State--Secretary of Defense
D. Vice-President--President <u>pro tempore</u> of the Senate--Speaker of the House

4. Although accuracy and speed are both important for an employee in the performance of his work, accuracy should be considered more important mainly because

A. most supervisors insist on accurate work
B. much time is lost in correcting errors
C. a rapid rate of work cannot be maintained for any length of time
D. speedy workers are usually inaccurate

5. In starting a load, a horse has to pull harder than he does to keep it moving, because

A. the load weighs less when it is moving
B. there is no friction after the load is moving
C. the horse has to overcome the tendency of the wagon to remain at rest
D. the wheels stick to the axles
E. the horse becomes accustomed to pulling the load

6. Rare manuscripts are reproduced on photographic film

A. to reduce the possibility of loss by fire
B. so that the text may be available without any disturbance to the original manuscript
C. so that they may be stored in smaller space
D. to facilitate ready reference
E. to aid scholars in research

7. Which of the following is the best source of current business information

A. almanac
B. dictionary
C. city directory
D. telephone directory
E. newspaper

The seven questions above fall in the "General Information" category because no specific professional or technical knowledge is required to solve them. We will now go through the steps of solving this type of question by analyzing the last problem of the preceding group, question No. 7.

First, it is important to analyze the question. Notice, the "key" adjectives: best, current, and business. Of the five possible choices, the correct one must have the three qualities. It must be "the best source of current business information."

Ask yourself the following questions regarding the choices: (1) Is it a source of information? (2) Is it a source of business information? (3) Is it a source of current information? (4) Is it the best source of current business information?

Let us analyze the five choices:

(A) almanac: (a) The almanac is a source of information. (b) The almanac could be called a source of current information since an almanac is generally issued annually, and for a time has current information. (c) However, an almanac is generally not a source of business information. An almanac is defined as "a book containing a calendar of days, weeks, and months, with the times of the rising and setting of the sun, moon, etc." Therefore, "almanac" is not the proper choice.

(B) dictionary: (a) The dictionary is a source of information. (b) The dictionary is a source of business information because it gives us the meaning of words, including business terms. (c) Some dictionaries may be a source of current information, right after they come off the press, but any dictionary is not always a source of current information. Therefore, the dictionary is not the proper answer.

(C) city directory: (a) The city directory is a source of information. (b) The city directory is a source of business information, because it gives us the names, addresses and business occupations of city inhabitants. (c) The city directory is a source of current information because it gives the present or current addresses and occupations of people living in the city. So far in our analysis, we see that the city directory is a source of current business information. (d) Now the question is: Is it the best source of current business information? Let us examine the other choices before we decide.

(D) telephone directory: (a) The telephone directory is a source of information. (b) The telephone directory is a source of business information because it gives the names, addresses, business and phone numbers of city inhabitants. (c) The telephone directory is a source of current information because like the city directory, it indicates the present or current addresses, etc. of city inhabitants, since copies are issued twice a year. (d) Again the question remains: Is it the best source of current business information? Let us examine the last choice.

(E) newspaper: (a) The newspaper is a source of information. (b) The newspaper is a source of business information, since almost all newspapers have a business section. (c) The newspaper is a source of current information, since it is issued daily, in most cases.

At this point, it is clear that of the five choices, three of them, the city directory, telephone directory, and the newspaper, are all sources of current business information.

We must now decide which is the best. Compared to the city directory and the telephone directory, it becomes very apparent that the newspaper is the best source of current business information. Therefore, the correct answer is (E).

We could, of course, go on and on, giving examples of specific questions asked of applicants for a specific position. However, even that would serve little purpose, because chances are that we would not be able to list the specific question you may be asked on your test. All we can suggest is that you study your particular subject and that you apply what you know about it when you answer your questions. Once you are familiar with your subject, use that knowledge as you would any other knowledge: examine the question carefully; make sure that you understand it fully; look for the key words in the question; and answer it by using the same methods of reasoning you would use with any other type of question.

CORRECT ANSWERS TO JUDGMENT AND REASONING QUESTIONS

1. A
2. C
3. B
4. B
5. C
6. B
7. E

PROJECTED
ALTITUDE
PREDICTED
ALTITUDE
CURRENT
ALTITUDE

Part IV

Second Practice Test

TEAR OUT ALONG THIS LINE AND MARK YOUR ANSWERS AS INSTRUCTED IN THE TEXT.

ANSWER SHEET

1 A B C D E
2 A B C D E
3 A B C D E
4 A B C D E
5 A B C D E
6 A B C D E
7 A B C D E
8 A B C D E
9 A B C D E
10 A B C D E
11 A B C D E
12 A B C D E
13 A B C D E
14 A B C D E
15 A B C D E
16 A B C D E
17 A B C D E
18 A B C D E
19 A B C D E
20 A B C D E
21 A B C D E
22 A B C D E
23 A B C D E
24 A B C D E
25 A B C D E
26 A B C D E
27 A B C D E
28 A B C D E
29 A B C D E
30 A B C D E
31 A B C D E
32 A B C D E
33 A B C D E
34 A B C D E
35 A B C D E
36 A B C D E
37 A B C D E
38 A B C D E
39 A B C D E
40 A B C D E
41 A B C D E
42 A B C D E
43 A B C D E
44 A B C D E
45 A B C D E
46 A B C D E
47 A B C D E
48 A B C D E
49 A B C D E
50 A B C D E
51 A B C D E
52 A B C D E
53 A B C D E
54 A B C D E
55 A B C D E
56 A B C D E
57 A B C D E
58 A B C D E
59 A B C D E
60 A B C D E
61 A B C D E
62 A B C D E
63 A B C D E
64 A B C D E
65 A B C D E
66 A B C D E
67 A B C D E
68 A B C D E
69 A B C D E
70 A B C D E
71 A B C D E
72 A B C D E
73 A B C D E
74 A B C D E
75 A B C D E

1 A B C D E
2 A B C D E
3 A B C D E
4 A B C D E
5 A B C D E
6 A B C D E
7 A B C D E
8 A B C D E
9 A B C D E
10 A B C D E
11 A B C D E
12 A B C D E
13 A B C D E
14 A B C D E
15 A B C D E
16 A B C D E
17 A B C D E
18 A B C D E
19 A B C D E
20 A B C D E
21 A B C D E
22 A B C D E
23 A B C D E
24 A B C D E
25 A B C D E
26 A B C D E
27 A B C D E
28 A B C D E
29 A B C D E
30 A B C D E
31 A B C D E
32 A B C D E
33 A B C D E
34 A B C D E
35 A B C D E
36 A B C D E
37 A B C D E
38 A B C D E
39 A B C D E
40 A B C D E
41 A B C D E
42 A B C D E
43 A B C D E
44 A B C D E
45 A B C D E
46 A B C D E
47 A B C D E
48 A B C D E
49 A B C D E
50 A B C D E
51 A B C D E
52 A B C D E
53 A B C D E
54 A B C D E
55 A B C D E
56 A B C D E
57 A B C D E
58 A B C D E
59 A B C D E
60 A B C D E

1 A B C D E
2 A B C D E
3 A B C D E
4 A B C D E
5 A B C D E
6 A B C D E
7 A B C D E
8 A B C D E
9 A B C D E
10 A B C D E
11 A B C D E
12 A B C D E
13 A B C D E
14 A B C D E
15 A B C D E
16 A B C D E
17 A B C D E
18 A B C D E
19 A B C D E
20 A B C D E
21 A B C D E
22 A B C D E
23 A B C D E
24 A B C D E
25 A B C D E

1 A B C D E
2 A B C D E
3 A B C D E
4 A B C D E
5 A B C D E
6 A B C D E
7 A B C D E
8 A B C D E
9 A B C D E
10 A B C D E
11 A B C D E
12 A B C D E
13 A B C D E
14 A B C D E
15 A B C D E
16 A B C D E
17 A B C D E
18 A B C D E
19 A B C D E
20 A B C D E

ANSWER SHEET

	A	B	C	D	E
1					
2					
3					
4					
5					
6					
7					
8					
9					
10					
11					
12					
13					
14					
15					
16					
17					
18					
19					
20					

	A	B	C	D	E
1					
2					
3					
4					
5					

	A	B	C	D	E
1					
2					
3					
4					
5					
6					
7					
8					
9					
10					
11					
12					
13					
14					
15					
16					
17					
18					
19					
20					
21					
22					
23					
24					
25					
26					
27					
28					
29					
30					
31					
32					
33					
34					
35					
36					
37					
38					
39					
40					
41					
42					
43					
44					
45					
46					
47					
48					
49					
50					
51					
52					
53					
54					
55					
56					
57					
58					
59					
60					
61					
62					
63					
64					
65					
66					

	A	B	C	D	E
1					
2					
3					
4					
5					
6					
7					
8					
9					
10					
11					
12					
13					
14					
15					
16					
17					
18					
19					
20					
21					
22					
23					
24					
25					

THE AIR TRAFFIC CONTROL TEST

The applicant applying for a position as an Air Traffic Controller Specialist must score high on a written test. The test score is used as one of the factors in the determination of eligibility. The following test is duplicated as accurately as possible to the actual test given by the Federal Government. The written test takes approximately two hours; the total time in the examining room is approximately 2 1/2 hours. Candidates for air traffic control work are recruited locally at FAA Regional and Field Offices and the Civil Service Commission and trained at the Aeronautical Center in Oklahoma City.

The Air Traffic Control written test makes it possible for an applicant to be considered for several different occupations through a single examination by measuring a number of abilities common to these occupations. Scores in each area of ability will be weighted according to job requirements. The test includes measures of the ability to understand and use written language; the ability to derive general principles from particular data; the ability to analyze data and derive conclusions; the ability to understand, interpret and solve problems presented in quantitative terms; the ability to derive conclusions from incomplete data supplemented by general knowledge; and the ability to discover the logical sequence of a series of events.

The Air Traffic Control Examination specifically includes several subtests, such as mathematics, abstract reasoning, air traffic control problems and other aptitude assessments. The tests measure how well you can think. These tests contain questions of different types; follow directions as given. It will be to your advantage to answer every question you can since your score will be the number of questions you answer correctly.

APTITUDE TEST

Time: 30 Minutes

Directions: This test contains a number of different types of questions. This is a test to see how well you can think. It is unlikely that you will complete all of the 75 questions but do your best. When taking the actual examination, the official will tell you when to begin. You will be given exactly 30 minutes to work as many of the problems as you can. Be careful not to go too fast and make foolish mistakes since you must try to get as many correct as you can. For each of the following questions, select the choice which best answers the question or completes the statement.

1. If 12 factory workers produce 120 units in 20 days, how many units can 18 workers produce in 50 days?

   A. 375
   B. 350
   C. 325
   D. 450

2. Vitiate is the same as

   A. enliven
   B. create
   C. impair
   D. defame

3. Theodore Roosevelt applied the term "Muckrakers" at the turn of the century to the

   A. traction magnates Whitney, Yerkers, and Widener
   B. writers Tarbell, Sinclair and Steffens
   C. meat tycoons Armour, Swift and Morris
   D. steel and oil monopolists Carnegie, Morgan and Vanderbilt.

4. If 15 construction workers earn $2,800 in 18 days, how much will 8 workers earn in 25 days?

   A. $2,900
   B. $2,074
   C. $1,843
   D. $2,650

5. Poltroon is the opposite of

   A. plutocrat
   B. hero
   C. amateur
   D. partisan
   E. sage

6. A vase is packed in a carton with a 10" diameter and is surrounded by packing 2" thick at the mouth. If the diameter of the base is 1/2 the diameter of the mouth, what is the diameter of the base?

   A. 3"
   B. 4"
   C. 6"
   D. 8"
   E. none of these

7. Population figures for a certain area show there are 1 1/2 times as many single men as single women in the area. Total population is 18,000. There are 1,122 married couples, with 756 children. How many single men are there in the area?

   A. 5,893
   B. 9,874
   C. 3,498
   D. 9,000

8. Watershed is the same as

   A. artificial passage for water
   B. sudden copious rainfall
   C. drainage area
   D. line marking ebb or flow of tide

9. The distance s in feet that a body falls in t seconds is given by the formula $s = 16t^2$. If a body has been falling for 4 seconds, how far will it fall during the 5th second?

   A. 64 feet
   B. 80 feet
   C. 144 feet
   D. 176 feet
   E. 256 feet

10. A dairyman has 4 gallons of milk worth 25¢ a quart. How much water must he add to make it worth 18¢ a quart?

    A. 1.2 gallons
    B. 3.7 quarts
    C. 6.2 quarts
    D. 3 gallons

11. The colony of Rhode Island was founded for the purpose of securing

    A. an asylum for debtors and criminals
    B. freedom of worship
    C. mineral wealth
    D. protection from the Indians

12. Throw : Ball ::

    A. kill : bullet
    B. shoot : gun
    C. question : answer
    D. hit : run
    E. stab : knife

13. A car dealer sold 3 different makes of cars. The price of the first make was $1,800, of the second $2,200, and the third $2,600. The income from these sales was $26,400. If the number of each make sold was the same, how many cars were sold?

A. 12
B. 10
C. 8
D. 6

14. A 5-quart solution of nitric acid and water is 60% acid. If a gallon of water is added, what percent of the resulting solution is acid?

A. 25
B. 33 1/3
C. 40
D. 48
E. 50

15. Speedy : Greyhound ::

A. innocent : lamb
B. animate : animal
C. voracious : tiger
D. clever : fox
E. sluggish : sloth

16. If it takes 3 men 56 minutes to fill a trench 4' x 6' x 5', and two of the men work twice as rapidly as the third, the number of minutes that it will take the two faster men alone to fill this trench is

A. 70 minutes
B. 60 minutes
C. 50 minutes
D. impossible to determine from the above data

17. Welkin is the same as

A. sky
B. countryside
C. fire gong
D. church bells

18. Punctilious is the opposite of

A. late
B. scrupulous
C. disorganized
D. apathetic
E. repulsive

19. Your office wishes to purchase an adding machine. Company X offers you a standard model, less discounts of 10% and 5%. Company Y offers you the same model at the same list price, less discounts of 5% and 10%. Of the two plans, the total discount given by Company X, compared to that given by Company Y, is

A. much larger
B. slightly larger
C. equal
D. slightly less

20. Bowdlerize is the same as

A. ratiocinate
B. interpolate
C. asservate
D. expurgate

21. How much vinegar selling at $2.60 per gallon must be mixed with a certain amount of vinegar selling at $2.20 a gallon to make 15 quarts selling at $36.60?

A. 10
B. 9
C. 8
D. 7
E. 6

22. The dimensions of an office are 25 feet by 15 feet. It is to be fitted with desks 4 feet by 3 feet. The distance between the front of one desk and the rear of another should be 3 feet while the distance between the sides of 2 desks should be 4 feet. Assuming that no desk is placed closer than 1 ft. from any wall, the optimum number that can be placed in the office is

A. 6
B. 8
C. 10
D. 12

23. The Japan Current affects the climate of Alaska in a way similar to the way in which the Gulf Stream affects the climate of

A. Norway
B. Labrador
C. Scotland
D. France

24. Vilify is the opposite of

A. sing the praises of
B. show satisfaction with
C. regard with distrust
D. welcome with glee
E. accept halfheartedly

25. Two pieces of meat which together weighed 40 lbs. were sold for the same sum. What did the 12¢ piece weigh if they were worth 18¢ and 12¢ a pound?

A. 24
B. 20
C. 30
D. 40

26. Welter is the same as

A. ridge
B. turmoil
C. vault of heaven
D. conglomeration

27. Impeach : Dismiss ::

A. arraign : convict
B. exonerate : charge
C. imprison : jail
D. plant : reap
E. president : Johnson

28. How many houses worth $12,000 each can a real estate agent buy for 1,000 bungalows worth $900 each?

A. 75
B. 74
C. 73
D. 72

29. Triangle : Pyramid ::

A. cone : circle
B. corner : angle
C. tube : cylinder
D. pentagon : quadrilateral
E. square : box

30. Suppose that the amount of money that the Fire Department has saved the citizens of the City of New York in 1940 is estimated at P dollars. If this sum is to be increased at least 100 percent in 1941, then the saving in 1941 must be at least

A. equivalent to the ratio between P and 100
B. commensurate with a sum derived by arithmetic manipulation involving P, 100, and a third value not given in the problem
C. 100 times P dollars
D. twice P dollars
E. a sum of money not accurately described in any of the foregoing options

31. Suppose that the loss of water pressure in a hose due to friction is uniformly L pounds per square inch for every foot of hose. Of the following, the best estimate of the total loss in terms of pressure per square inch in a hose H feet long is

A. H plus L pounds
B. H times L pounds
C. H divided by L pounds
D. L divided by H pounds
E. none of the foregoing

32. Wherefore is the same as

A. whilom
B. why
C. whence
D. whither

33. Irascible is the opposite of

A. placid
B. fortuitous
C. shameless
D. entrancing
E. yielding

34. Emulate : Mimic ::

A. slander : defame
B. praise : flatter
C. aggravate : promote
D. complain : condemn
E. express : imply

35. Carafe is the same as

A. glass water bottle
B. means of transportation
C. wineskin
D. bony case covering back of animal

36. Hand : Nail ::

A. paw : claw
B. foot : toe
C. head : hair
D. ear : nose
E. jaw : tooth

37. The velocity of a fire engine which is traveling to a fire is computed by

A. multiplying distance by time
B. dividing distance by time
C. squaring the force with which the earth attracts the engine
D. means of the moment of inertia
E. use of the Pythagorean Theorem

38. Acanthus is the same as

A. leaf-like architectural ornamentation
B. gummy substance used in stiffening fabrics
C. ethereal spirit
D. ornamental vessel

39. Square : Diamond ::

A. cube : sugar
B. circle : ellipse
C. innocence : jewelry
D. rectangle : square
E. prizefight : baseball

40. Suppose that R persons were rescued from burning buildings by firemen in 1940. Suppose also that P persons perished in burning buildings in 1940. If R is less than S but greater than T and P is less than both M and N, it may safely be concluded that

A. the sum of R and T is greater than S
B. the sum of M and N is greater than P
C. R is between M and N times as great as P
D. R exceeds P to an indeterminate degree lying somewhere between S and N
E. none of the foregoing options is correct

41. Gelid is the opposite of

A. chilly
B. solid
C. mature
D. pallid
E. boiling

42. Seventy 58" x 34" desks must be stored in a warehouse. If as many desks as possible are stored on the floor of a 15' x 25' room, how many desks will still require storage?

A. 46
B. 25
C. 45
D. 43
E. none of these

43. In an experiment, a sprinkler system discharging W gallons of water per hour extinguished a fire covering a floor of A square yards in T minutes. The amount of water actually used to put out the fire was

A. W times T divided by 60
B. 60 times W divided by T
C. 60 times W times T
D. T divided by the fraction whose numerator is W and denominator 60
E. none of the foregoing

44. Alfresco is the same as

A. fresh food
B. spring flood
C. water color
D. in the open air

45. Woodsman : Axe ::

A. mechanic : wrench
B. soldier : gun
C. draftsman : ruler
D. doctor : prescription
E. carpenter : saw

46. Suppose that a ladder consists of four sections, each R feet in length. When the ladder is extended, adjacent sections overlap for a distance of S feet to strengthen the interlocking. The total overall length of the ladder, when fully opened, is

A. 4 R feet
B. 4 R minus 3 S feet
C. 4 R minus 4 S feet
D. 4 R minus 6 S feet
E. none of the foregoing

47. Two nations that fought on the side of the Allies in World War I but on the side of the Axis in World War II were

A. Italy and Bulgaria
B. Rumania and Hungary
C. Turkey and Bulgaria
D. Japan and Italy

48. Condign is the opposite of

A. unavoidable
B. unsatisfactory
C. unguarded
D. unsuitable
E. severe

49. Bigotry : Hatred ::

A. sweetness : bitterness
B. segregation : integration
C. equality : government
D. sugar : grain
E. fanaticism : intolerance

50. In the New York City Fire Department there are A firemen, D lieutenants, E captains, and G chiefs of various ranks. Suppose that, for comparative purposes, promotional opportunities are evaluated as the ratio of the number of promotional positions to the number of positions at the entrance level. In accordance with this method, promotional opportunities in the uniformed force of the Fire Department in New York City are evaluated as

A. G divided by the sum of A plus D plus E
B. the sum of D plus E plus G divided by the number of firemen
C. A divided by the sum of D plus E plus G
D. the sum of A plus D divided by the sum of E plus G
E. a fraction about which it is known only that the numerator is greater than the denominator

51. Animadversion is the same as

A. vitality
B. ire
C. taboo
D. stricture

52. Assist : Save ::

A. agree : oppose
B. rely : descry
C. hurt : aid
D. declare : deny
E. request : command

53. Suppose that the number of fires occurring in a particular type of dwelling decreased C percent in 1939, as compared with 1938, but then increased C percent in 1940, as compared with 1939. Then the number of fires occurring in that type of dwelling during 1940, as compared with 1938, is

A. decreased by the percent equal to C squared divided by 100
B. unchanged
C. increased by the percent equal to the fraction whose numerator is 100 minus C and denominator is 100
D. decreased by the percent equal to the square of the fraction C over 100
E. dependent on the temporal distance between 1938 and 1939 as contrasted with that between 1939 and 1940.

54. 2 : 5 ::

A. 5 : 7
B. 6 : 17
C. 6 : 15
D. 5 : 14
E. 21 : 51

55. Doubleheader : Trident ::

A. twin : troika
B. ballgame : three bagger
C. chewing gum : toothpaste
D. freak : zoo
E. two : square

56. In the year 1940, fires occurred in K "Type Z" multiple dwellings. It is known that L percent of the M multiple dwellings in New York City are of "Type Z". The fraction of "Type Z" multiple dwellings in which fires occurred during 1940 is

A. K divided by L times M
B. L times M divided by 100 K
C. K divided by the quantity 100 times L times M
D. 100 K divided by the quantity L times M
E. none of the foregoing

57. Aplomb is the same as

A. self-assurance
B. stodginess
C. foppishness
D. sturdiness

58. Unctuous is the opposite of

A. benign
B. coarse
C. supple
D. sullen
E. dilated

59. Bouquet : Flower ::

A. key : door
B. air : balloon
C. skin : body
D. chain : link
E. eye : pigment

60. Suppose that the amount of money spent for supplies in 1946 for a division in a City department was $15,650. This represented an increase of 12% over the amount spent for supplies for this division in 1945. The amount of money spent for supplies for this division in 1945 was most nearly

A. $13,973
B. $13,772
C. $14,346
D. $13,872

61. Letter : Word ::

A. club : people
B. homework : school
C. page : book
D. product : factory
E. picture : crayon

62. 36 : 4 ::

A. 3 : 27
B. 9 : 1
C. 4 : 12
D. 12 : 4
E. 5 : 2

63. Suppose that a group of five clerks have been assigned to insert 24,000 letters into envelopes. The clerks perform this work at the following rates of speed: Clerk A, 1100 letters an hour; Clerk B, 1450 letters an hour; Clerk C, 1200 letters an hour; Clerk D, 1300 letters an hour; Clerk E, 1250 letters an hour. At the end of two hours of work, Clerks C and D are assigned to another task. From the time that Clerks C and D were taken off the assignment, the number of hours required for the remaining clerks to complete this assignment is

A. less than 3 hours
B. 3 hours
C. more than 3 hours, but less than 4 hours
D. more than 4 hours

64. Apocryphal is the same as

A. awesome
B. disease-bearing
C. of doubtful authority
D. threatening

65. Feckless is the opposite of

A. spotted
B. fatuous
C. fawning
D. strong
E. reckless

66. Six gross of special drawing pencils were purchased for use in a City department. If the pencils were used at the rate of 24 a week, the maximum number of weeks that the six gross of pencils would last is

A. 6 weeks
B. 12 weeks
C. 24 weeks
D. 36 weeks

67. Artifact is the same as

A. product of human workmanship
B. stratagem
C. duplication
D. artful or skillful contrivance

68. A mechanic repairs 16 cars per 8-hour day. Another mechanic in the same shop repairs 1 1/2 times this number in 3/4 the time. Theoretically, how long will it take to repair 16 cars in the shop?

A. 2 2/3 hours
B. 2 9/10 hours
C. 3 hours
D. 2 1/2 hours
E. none of these

69. A stock clerk had 600 pads on hand. He then issued 3/8 of his supply of pads to Division X, 1/4 to Division Y, and 1/6 to Division Z. The number of pads remaining in stock is

A. 48
B. 125
C. 240
D. 475

70. Atavistic is the same as

A. overeager
B. narrow-minded
C. reverting to a primitive type
D. pertaining to an uncle

71. Polemic is the opposite of

A. apologetic
B. corresponding
C. abrupt
D. restless
E. challenging

72. If a certain job can be performed by 18 clerks in 26 days, the number of clerks needed to perform the job in 12 days is

A. 24 clerks
B. 30 clerks
C. 39 clerks
D. 52 clerks

73. Baize is the same as

A. cereal plant
B. medicinal plant
C. tree marking
D. soft fabric

74. Hoi Polloi is the opposite of

A. natives
B. foreigners
C. nobility
D. military
E. city dwellers

75. A department vehicle has completed the first 5 miles of a 10 mile trip in 10 minutes. To complete the entire trip at an average rate of 45 miles per hour, the vehicle must travel the remaining 5 miles in

A. 3 minutes
B. 5 minutes
C. 10 minutes
D. 15 minutes
E. 20 minutes

APTITUDE TEST ANSWER KEY

1. D
2. C
3. B
4. B
5. B
6. A
7. D
8. C
9. C
10. C
11. B
12. B
13. A
14. B
15. E
16. A
17. A
18. C
19. C
20. D
21. B
22. B
23. C
24. A
25. A
26. B
27. A
28. A
29. E
30. D
31. B
32. B
33. A
34. B
35. A
36. A
37. B
38. A
39. B
40. B
41. E
42. C
43. A
44. D
45. E
46. B
47. D
48. D
49. E
50. B
51. D
52. E
53. A
54. C
55. A
56. D
57. A
58. B
59. D
60. A
61. C
62. B
63. B
64. C
65. D
66. D
67. A
68. A
69. B
70. C
71. B
72. C
73. D
74. C
75. B

MATHEMATICS

Time: 10 Minutes

Directions: The following questions in mathematics test your proficiency in the basic skills. Work as many problems as you can correctly. Select from the lettered choices that choice which best completes the statement or answers the question.

1. Add 2.31, .037, 4, and 5.0017.

   A. 7.7487
   B. 11.7487
   C. 7.7887
   D. 11.3487
   E. 11.3488

2. Multiply 2/3 X 2 4/7 X 5/9.

   A. 10/11
   B. 20/21
   C. 5/6
   D. 5/7
   E. 5/8

3. Add $73.69, $4.31, $19.58, $35.72.

   A. $134.30
   B. $123.30
   C. $133.30
   D. $132.30
   E. $233.30

4.
$$\begin{array}{r} 6402 \\ 3394 \\ 6786 \\ 735 \\ \underline{8092} \end{array}$$

   A. 24,409
   B. 25,309
   C. 25,409
   D. 25,408
   E. none of the above

5. Divide 7 by 50.

A. 7 1/7
B. .14
C. .07
D. 1.40
E. .04

6. Change 5/11 to a decimal of 2 places.

A. .456
B. .45 1/2
C. .45
D. .45 5/11
E. none of the above

7. $2.98 from $5 =

A. $1.02
B. $2.03
C. $2.04
D. $2.02
E. $3.02

8. 546.741 from 837.602 =

A. 291.861
B. 290.861
C. 390.861
D. 290.862
E. 280.861

9. Divide 2/3 by 2 1/4.

A. 8/27
B. 2/7
C. 4/13
D. 1/4
E. none of the above

10. $\frac{2}{5} \div .6 =$

A. $\frac{2}{30}$
B. $\frac{2}{3}$
C. $\frac{4}{5}$
D. $\frac{12}{5}$
E. none of the above

11. .035 x 100 =

A. 2.5
B. 3.6
C. 3.5
D. 1.5
E. 3.7

12. 4.21 x 4.6 =

A. 18.366
B. 19.336
C. 19.368
D. 19.366
E. 19.338

13. From 18.432 subtract 6.84.

A. 17.748
B. 11.632
C. 11.592
D. 11.752
E. 11.743

14. What is the product of $4\frac{2}{3}$ times $3\frac{1}{2}$?

A. $\frac{49}{3}$
B. $\frac{14}{3}$
C. $\frac{24}{3}$
D. $\frac{27}{3}$
E. $\frac{29}{3}$

15. 5.123 x 39 =

A. 198.797
B. 199.797
C. 199.788
D. 199.777
E. none of the above

16. 3265 divided by 5 =

A. 654
B. 653
C. 655
D. 553
E. 635

17. 1386 ÷ 22 =

A. 64
B. 53
C. 61
D. 63
E. 62

18. Multiply 48 x 3.1.

A. 144.1
B. 148.8
C. 148.4
D. 142.4
E. none of the above

19. Change the following decimal to a fraction: .625

A. $.625 = \frac{5}{8}$
B. $.625 = \frac{7}{8}$
C. $.625 = \frac{2}{3}$
D. $.625 = \frac{5}{6}$
E. $.625 = \frac{1}{8}$

20. 575.82 ÷ 6.3 =

A. 92.4
B. 91.5
C. 91.4
D. 91.3
E. 90.4

21. Add 4 5/12, 2 1/3, 5 1/4.

A. 11
B. 10
C. 13
D. 12
E. 14

22. 3/8 + 3/4 + 1/3 =

A. 1 11/24
B. 1 11/25
C. 1 1/2
D. 2 11/24
E. none of the above

23. Which is the larger fraction: 3/4 or 2/3?

A. 2/3
B. 3/4

24. How much is 9 times 7; divided by 3; plus 136; minus 150?

A. 6
B. 5
C. 7
D. 8
E. 9

25. Add 2/3, 12 1/8, 9 1/4.

A. 22 1/2
B. 22 1/24
C. 22 1/3
D. 22 3/4
E. none of the above

26. Subtract 1/8 from 1/4.

A. 1/4
B. 1/8
C. 1/6
D. 1/12
E. 2/3

27. 4 1/2 from 8 2/3 =

A. 4 1/6
B. 4 1/12
C. 4 5/8
D. 4 1/8
E. 4 2/3

28. Find the average of: 72; 86; 92; 80; 95.

A. 85
B. 86
C. 81
D. 84
E. 90

29. What is 7/8 of 56?

A. 48
B. 46
C. 49
D. 50
E. none of the above

30. 13 1/2 - 8 3/4 =

A. 4 1/2
B. 4 2/3
C. 4 3/4
D. 4 1/3
E. 4 1/6

31. 5/12 x 3/5 =

A. 1/2
B. 1/3
C. 5/8
D. 1/4
E. 2/3

32. 9 1/2 multiplied by 2 1/2 =

A. 18 1/2
B. 22 3/4
C. 19 1/3
D. 23 3/4
E. 23 1/4

33. Which is the largest: 3/10; 3%; .33; .003?

A. 3/10
B. .33
C. 3%
D. .003

34. Express 1/20 as a decimal.

A. .05
B. .005
C. .0005
D. .10
E. none of the above

35. 21/7 x 42 =

A. 122
B. 124
C. 126
D. 212
E. 200

36. Divide 3/4 by 3/8.

A. 1
B. 4
C. 2
D. 3
E. 6

37. 27 divided by 3/4 =

A. 34
B. 30
C. 27
D. 36
E. none of the above

38. Write .5% as a decimal.

A. .05
B. .005
C. .0005
D. .5
E. 5.0

39. 1 2/3 divided by 3 3/4 =

A. 4/9
B. 7/9
C. 1/2
D. 5/9
E. 3/4

40. Add $36.47, $18.92, $28.64, $94.55.

A. $179.58
B. $175.78
C. $177.58
D. $178.58
E. $168.58

41.
```
 7403
 2384
 5786
  357
 1725
 ----
```

A. 16,655
B. 17,555
C. 17,656
D. 17,655
E. none of the above

42. How much is 10 times 7; divided by 7; plus 90; minus 90?

A. 20
B. 12
C. 10
D. 15
E. 25

43.
```
  $5.00
 - 1.97
 ------
```

A. $3.03
B. $2.03
C. $1.03
D. $3.02
E. $3.05

44. 623.647 from 715.432 =

A. 92.785
B. 91.785
C. 91.685
D. 91.786
E. none of the above

45. Find the average of: 76; 85; 93; 91; 80.

A. 84
B. 75
C. 83
D. 85
E. 90

46. .075 x 100 =

A. .75
B. .0075
C. 7.5
D. .075
E. none of the above

47. 8.15 multiplied by 8.5 =

A. 68.275
B. 69.375
C. 69.275
D. 69.285
E. 69.277

48. What is 4/9 of 72?

A. 30
B. 32
C. 36
D. 28
E. 33

49. 3.754 x 69 =

A. 258.026
B. 259.026
C. 259.022
D. 259.126
E. none of the above

50. $6\overline{)4356}$ =

A. 726
B. 770
C. 722
D. 725
E. 626

51. 51 is how many times 8 1/2?

A. 5
B. 4
C. 8
D. 6
E. 7

52. 5475 divided by 15 =

A. 366
B. 365
C. 265
D. 367
E. none of the above

53. 1.127 ÷ 4.9 =

A. .23
B. .24
C. .22
D. .25
E. .21

54. Which is the largest: 2.50; 2 3/4; 225%; 2 1/2?

A. 2.50
B. 2 1/2
C. 2 3/4
D. 225%
E. none of the above

55. Add 7 5/6, 6 1/2, 7 2/3.

A. 21
B. 20
C. 23
D. 22
E. 24

56. 3/5 + 5/8 + 7/10 =

A. 1 37/40
B. 1 39/40
C. 1 1/2
D. 2 37/40
E. 1 3/4

57. Express 1/25 as a decimal.

A. .02
B. .03
C. .04
D. .05
E. .06

58. 7/16 + 4 1/2 + 3/8 =

A. 4 5/16
B. 5 7/8
C. 5 5/16
D. 5 5/12
E. none of the above

59. 50 is what percent of 25?

A. 100%
B. 200%
C. 150%
D. 50%
E. 25%

60. 1/6 from 1/3 =

A. 1/3
B. 2/3
C. 1/4
D. 1/6
E. 1/2

MATHEMATICS ANSWER KEY

1.	D	21.	D	41.	D
2.	B	22.	A	42.	C
3.	C	23.	B	43.	A
4.	C	24.	C	44.	B
5.	B	25.	B	45.	D
6.	C	26.	B	46.	C
7.	D	27.	A	47.	C
8.	B	28.	A	48.	B
9.	A	29.	C	49.	B
10.	B	30.	C	50.	A
11.	C	31.	D	51.	D
12.	D	32.	D	52.	B
13.	C	33.	B	53.	A
14.	A	34.	A	54.	C
15.	B	35.	C	55.	D
16.	B	36.	C	56.	A
17.	D	37.	D	57.	C
18.	B	38.	B	58.	C
19.	A	39.	A	59.	B
20.	C	40.	D	60.	D

VERBAL ABILITIES TEST

Time: 15 Minutes

Directions: This test is designed to measure your ability to read and understand the meaning of words and the ideas associated with them, to understand the meanings of whole sentences and paragraphs; and to present the information or ideas clearly. Each item includes a paragraph which must be read accurately so that you can promptly analyze its contents and meaning or follow its instructions exactly. In this type of questioning, you should select from the multi-choice answers the correct one that best summarizes the paragraph.

I consider that a man's brain originally is like a little empty attic, and you have to stock it with such furniture as you choose. A fool takes in all the lumber of every sort that he comes across, so that the knowledge which might be useful to him gets crowded out, or at best is jumbled up with a lot of other things, so that he has a difficulty in laying his hands upon it. It is a mistake to think of the brain as a little room with elastic walls which can be distended to any extent. Remember there comes a time with every addition of knowledge, you can forget something that you knew before.

1. According to the preceding paragraph, knowledge

   A. should be sought for its own sake
   B. is always valuable
   C. should be avoided
   D. should be acquired only if it is necessary
   E. may be acquired without limitation.

Interest is essentially an attitude of continuing attentiveness, found where activity is satisfactorily self-expressive. Whenever work is so circumscribed that the chance for self-expression or development is denied, monotony is present.

2. On the basis of this paragraph, it is most accurate to state that

   A. tasks which are repetitive in nature do not permit self-expression and therefore create monotony
   B. interest in one's work is increased by financial and non-financial incentives
   C. jobs which are monotonous can be made self-expressive by substituting satisfactory working conditions

D. workers whose tasks afford them no opportunity for self-expression find such tasks to be monotonous
E. work is monotonous unless there is activity which satisfies the worker.

During the past few years business has made rapid strides in applying to the field of office management the same fundamental principles of procedure and method that have been in successful use for years in production work. Indeed, present-day competition, resulting as it has in smaller margins of profit, has made it essential to give the most careful attention to the efficient organization and management of internal administrative affairs in order that individual productivity may be increased and unit costs reduced.

3. According to the above paragraph

A. office management always lags behind production work
B. present day competition has increased individual productivity
C. efficient office management seeks to reduce gross costs
D. the margin of profit widens as individual productivity is increased
E. similar principles have met with equal success in the fields of office management and production work.

More produce is artificially ripened by treatment with ethylene gas, which makes possible shipment in "the firm green condition," and the sale of fruit and vegetables before they would naturally be in season. This method of ripening is prohibited only when it is applied to oranges so unripe as to contain less than 8 parts of sugar to 1 of acid.

4. It can be reasonably concluded from the preceding paragraph that

A. artificial ripening is not harmful unless applied to oranges containing less than 8 parts of sugar to 1 of acid
B. fruits and vegetables are usually shipped in the firm green condition
C. oranges are ripe when they contain more than 8 parts of sugar to 1 of acid
D. the law does not prohibit the use of ethylene ripening in most cases
E. it is dangerous to eat fruit and vegetables out of season, since they are often artificially ripened.

In a recent questionnaire circulated among the students of a certain college, there was a general agreement among the students questioned that the greatest single influence of the movies has been to give them a better understanding of the people and customs of other parts of the world. The degree of approval given this statement was a third greater than that accorded to the second most important influence, that of a desire for greater freedom in social relations.

5. Judging from the data derived from the above-mentioned questionnaire, the chief single influence of the movies

A. is an emphasis upon crime and crime prevention
B. reveals the astounding information that the larger majority of college students attend the movies regularly
C. is a tendency to create a desire for greater freedom of social relations among college students
D. is the dissemination of the broad cultural aspects of lands other than our own
E. is the graphic presentation of foreign folklore.

Specialization is made possible by the process of exchange. The farmer specializes in the raising of certain food products and raw materials. He produces in the course of a year's time many more bushels of corn than he and his family can possibly consume. On the other hand, being a specialist, he has no time to make for himself a wide variety of other products such as food, clothing, shelter, newspapers, machinery and many other goods which he needs. What he does is to exchange his corn for those products. So it is with all other producers.

6. Which of the following does the above paragraph indicate is one of the principal results of specialization?

   A. the process of exchange has been greatly accelerated
   B. the farmer produces more corn than he and his family can possibly consume
   C. the farmer can no longer make his own clothes
   D. the farmer's produce must be sent to the open market for distribution
   E. food products become the specialized field of the farmer.

Salt has always been important in our diet as a flavoring for food, but it is only recently that doctors have come to recognize it as an absolute necessity. Most living things contain salt and it is almost impossible to eat a normal diet without getting some. However, that "some" may not be enough, and now doctors recommend that those who normally use little salt step up their salt consumption in hot weather, when more than the usual salt is required by the body.

7. According to the preceding paragraph one could assume most correctly that

   A. salt is necessary if life is to be maintained
   B. people living on a normal diet have an intake of salt which is sufficient to maintain good health
   C. salt is more essential to the body in summer than in winter
   D. all organic life contains salt in one form or another
   E. up to very recently, the most important function of salt has been its use in the flavoring of foods.

The capacity of the banks to grant loans depends, in the long run, on the amount of money deposited with them by the public. In the short run, however, it is a well known fact that the banks not only can but do lend more than is deposited with them. If such lending is carried to excess, it leads to inflation.

8. On the basis of the preceding paragraph it is most reasonable to conclude that

   A. banks often indulge in the vicious practice of lending more than is deposited with them
   B. in the long run, a sound banking policy operates for the mutual advantage of the bankers and the public
   C. inflation is usually the result of excess lending by the banks
   D. the public must guard against inflation
   E. bank lending is always in direct ratio with bank deposits.

Even when sheep raising is a principal business and not a farm by-product it is extremely difficult to approach uniformity in the quality of the wool. On one sheep there are at least four qualities. Often, throughout a flock, no two sheep in one season yield exactly the same grade of wool. In addition, since the quality is influenced by the food the sheep eat, the soil over which they graze, and the weather, no two flocks in one year produce the same quality of wool, and the same flock will change from year to year.

9. On the basis of the preceding paragraph one could most reasonably conclude that

   A. soil is a factor in the quality of sheep-wool
   B. sheep raising is usually a by-product of the meat-producing business
   C. no two sheep in one season yield exactly the same grade of wool
   D. there is a consistent change in the seasonal quality of wool
   E. flocks of sheep will change from year to year.

Neither the revolution in manufacture nor that in agriculture could have proceeded without the series of brilliant inventions in transportation and communication which have bound country to city, nation to nation, and continent to continent.

10. Judging from the contents of the preceding paragraph it can most precisely be indicated that

   A. nations have been brought together more closely by transportation than by manufacture and agriculture
   B. progress in communication and transportation has been essential to progress in manufacturing and agriculture
   C. changes in manufacture and agriculture are characterized by a revolutionary process
   D. industrial changes must be preceded by brilliant inventions in communication
   E. both industry and transportation serve to bind country to city, nation to nation and continent to continent.

Rivers and water courses afford a very convenient and accessible source of supply; and one of the principal reasons for towns in olden times having been established by the banks of rivers is supposed to have been the facility with which, in such a situation, an ample supply of water was secured.

11. According to the preceding paragraph, rivers and water courses are

   A. valuable
   B. useful
   C. convenient sources of water supply for towns
   D. the main support of ancient towns
   E. valuable only for ancient towns.

The direct lighting arrangement is exemplified by the individual desk light or the ceiling light with the ordinary reflector which diffuses all of the rays downward. Such lighting arrangements are considered the least satisfactory of any, due principally to the fact that there is almost sure to be a glare of some sort on the working surface.

12. The above paragraph indicates that direct lighting is least satisfactory as a method of lighting chiefly because

A. the light is diffused causing eye strain
B. the shade on the individual desk lamp is not constructed along scientific lines
C. the working surface is usually obscured by the glare
D. the ordinary reflector causes the rays to fall perpendicularly
E. direct lighting is injurious to the eyes.

The principal advantage of wood over steel office equipment is the fact that, in the case of files in a burning building, for example, while the wooden exterior of the cabinet may burn somewhat, the papers will not be charred so quickly as when they are in a steel cabinet. This is due to the fact that wood burns slowly and does not transmit heat, while steel, although it does not burn, is a conductor of heat, with the result that, under similar circumstances, papers would be charred more quickly in a steel cabinet.

13. Judging from this information alone, the principal advantage of wood over steel office equipment is

A. in case of fire, papers will not be destroyed in a wooden cabinet
B. wooden equipment is cheaper to replace
C. steel does not resist fire as well as wood
D. steel equipment is heavy and cannot be moved about very easily
E. wood is a poor conductor of heat.

In a general way, the size and form of the brain is determined by the size and form of the cranial cavity. Some skulls are relatively long and narrow, others short and broad, and these variations correspond to general variations in the shape of the brain. But conformation of the skull, as seen from the outside is not an accurate indication of the conformation of the brain within.

14. The paragraph notes that

A. intelligence in humans is, in a general way, correlated with the volume of the cranial cavity
B. the size and form of the external skull is not an accurate indication of the conformation of the cranial cavity
C. as we go up the rungs of the ladder of evolution, we note a gradual increase in the size of the brain
D. there is no connection between the size of the skull and the size of the brain
E. the size and form of the brain is an inherited trait, just as is the conformation of the cranial cavity.

Whether or not the nerve impulses in various nerve fibers differ in kind is a question of great interest in physiology. The usually accepted view is that they are identical in character in all fibers and vary only in intensity.

15. Judging from the information contained in the foregoing paragraph it could be most correctly assumed that

A. nerve fibers are the product of neural impulses
B. nerve fibers are usually accepted as differing in kind
C. the nature of neural impulses is still a moot question
D. the student of physiology accepts the view that nerve impulses sometimes differ in intensity
E. the character of nerve fibers is accepted as being constant.

In 1895, of the 300 cars owned only four were manufactured in this country. Of the 22 million registered on January 1, 1927, all but an infinitesimal number were manufactured in American plants.

16. The paragraph notes that registered automobiles in this country in 1927

    A. were far in excess of those manufactured abroad in 1895
    B. were manufactured in the United States
    C. increased considerably over the preceding decade
    D. improved greatly in construction over the 1895 model
    E. were almost exclusively of domestic construction.

The labor required to produce a bushel of wheat was reduced from three hours in 1830 to ten minutes in 1896; and it has been estimated that fifty men, employing modern farm machinery and the new methods of agriculture, can do the work of five hundred peasants toiling under the conditions of the eighteenth century.

17. On the basis of the facts presented above one could best conclude that

    A. the increase of efficiency in agriculture is almost as great as that in manufacturing
    B. peasants in the eighteenth century worked much harder than do our farmers today
    C. modern farm machinery has resulted in serious unemployment among farmers
    D. 18 times as much wheat was produced in 1896 as in 1830
    E. modern farm machinery is labor-saving.

Questions 18 and 19 are to be answered solely on the basis of the information contained in the following paragraph:

Forms are printed sheets of paper on which information is to be entered. While what is printed on the form is most important, the kind of paper used in making the form is also important. The kind of paper should be selected with regard to the use to which the form will be subjected. Printing a form on an unnecessarily expensive grade of paper is wasteful. On the other hand, using too cheap or flimsy a form can materially interfere with satisfactory performance of the work the form is being planned to do. Thus a form printed on both sides normally requires a heavier paper than a form printed only on one side. Forms to be used as permanent records, or which are expected to have a very long life in files, require a quality of paper which will not disintegrate or discolor with age. A form which will go through a great deal of handling requires a strong tough paper, while thinness is a necessary qualification where the making of several carbon copies of a form will be required.

18. According to this paragraph, the type of paper used for making forms

    A. should be chosen in accordance with the use to which the form will be put
    B. should be chosen before the type of printing to be used has been decided upon
    C. is as important as the information which is printed on it
    D. should be strong enough to be used for any purpose.

19. According to this paragraph, forms that are

    A. printed on both sides are usually economical and desirable
    B. to be filed permanently should not deteriorate as time goes on
    C. expected to last for a long time should be handled carefully
    D. to be filed should not be printed on inexpensive paper

The railroads, building trades, mineral industries, and automotive works normally take two-thirds of our annual production of steel. The remaining third has been around 16 million tons. For this last third of our output the farmers have been the best customers with farm machinery tools and wire constituting their chief demands.

20. Judging from the above facts it would be most reasonable to assume that

    A. there is an increasing demand for the newer and more efficient farm machinery and tools
    B. the growth of the steel industry has made possible the growth of all of our basic industries that depend upon steel
    C. the farmers are our best steel customers
    D. our normal annual steel output is about 48 million tons
    E. only one-third of our steel output is exported with the remaining two-thirds consumed by our own industries.

The term "agent of a foreign principal" means any person who acts or engages or agrees to act as a public-relations counsel, publicity agent, or as agent, servant, representative, or attorney for a foreign principal or for any domestic organization subsidized directly or indirectly in whole or in part by a foreign principal. Such term shall not include a duly accredited diplomatic or consular officer of a foreign government who is so recognized by the Department of State of the United States.

21. According to this paragraph

    A. no foreign official can be termed an "agent of a foreign principal" unless he is so recognized by the Department of State
    B. a person who acts as a public-relations counsel for a foreign principal, must be subsidized by that principal before he can be termed its "agent"
    C. if a foreign publicity agent is subsidized directly by a domestic organization, he may be termed an "agent of a domestic principal"
    D. outside of accredited and recognized diplomatic officials, persons acting as agents for foreign countries are termed "agents of a foreign principal"
    E. consular officers and accredited diplomats are exempted from the term "agent of a foreign principal"

For the most part, in humid climates, a thick growth of vegetation protects the moist soil from the wind with a cover of leaves and stems and a mattress of interlacing roots. But in arid regions either vegetation is wholly lacking, or scant growths are found huddled in detached clumps, leaving inter-space of unprotected ground. Little or no moisture is present to cause the particles to cohere, and they are therefore readily lifted and drifted by the wind.

22. According to the paragraph

    A. vegetation is always present in humid climates
    B. lack of moisture decreases cohesion of earth particles in arid regions
    C. moisture is an important element in soil and rock erosion

D. the wind is the chief agent in the dispersal of the top-soil layer
E. tree roots are closely associated with the thick growth of vegetation in moist climates.

A hurricane acts as a syphon on a grand scale, drawing water and air to its center. It raises water in the same way that liquid rises in a straw used in sipping a drink. It is not just the central core of the hurricane that produces this effect, but the whole hurricane area, more than 100 miles in diameter. The hurricane is a low-pressure area and the pressure gets lower as the center is approached. The lower the pressure gets the higher it raises the level of the ocean.

23. The above paragraph intimates that

A. hurricanes can be controlled
B. all low-pressure areas result in hurricanes for that area
C. the pressure is inversely proportional to the height the water level of the ocean rises
D. hurricanes are comparatively few in this section of the country
E. the physical principles governing a hurricane are not adequately known.

It has been at times suggested that it is incongruous for the government to employ one lawyer to prosecute and another to defend the same prisoner. This is a superficial point of view, for it overlooks the principle that the Government should be as anxious to shield the innocent as it is to punish the guilty.

24. According to this paragraph

A. it is not properly within the scope of the government to provide criminals with both prosecuting and defending lawyers
B. a person held for a crime, if he be poor need never fear that he will not be adequately defended, because the government makes provision for competent lawyers to aid him in his defense
C. although sometimes criticised, it is governmental policy to provide legal defense for indigent persons accused of crime
D. a great government should feel obligated to shield the innocent as well as punish the guilty
E. it is an incongruous point of view that the government should concurrently shield the innocent and punish the guilty.

There exists today an unparalleled opportunity for those nations and groups which look forward with clear vision to bring about an early return to sane perspectives and relationships based upon full comprehension that the members of the family of nations must live together amicably and work together in peace--or be broken in an utterly destructive misuse of the power and the instruments which, properly used, bear beneficial witness to the amazing constructive capacity of mankind.

25. The above paragraph signifies that

A. peace is based upon the rightful use of forces which, if abused, destroy mankind
B. world peace is based upon vision
C. nations must have vision
D. nations, like individuals, look for direction to leaders
E. peace is a will-o-the-wisp; the solution is only visionary.

VERBAL ABILITIES TEST ANSWER KEY

1. (D)
2. (D)
3. (D)
4. (D)
5. (D)
6. (B)
7. (C)
8. (C)
9. (A)
10. (B)
11. (C)
12. (D)
13. (E)
14. (B)
15. (C)
16. (E)
17. (E)
18. (A)
19. (B)
20. (D)
21. (D)
22. (B)
23. (C)
24. (C)
25. (A)

LETTER SERIES

Time: 25 Minutes

Directions: Select from the choices offered in each of the following, the one which is correct or most nearly correct.

Two Test Questions Analyzed

In each of these questions there is a series of letters which follow some definite order, followed by five sets of two letters each. Look at the letters in the series and determine what the order is; then from the suggested answers that follow, select the set that gives the next two letters in the series in their correct order.

1. X C X D X E X

   A. F X
   B. F G
   C. X F
   D. E F
   E. X G

The series consists of X's alternating with letters in alphabetical order. The next two letters would be F and X; therefore (A) is the correct answer.

2. A B D C E F H

   A. G H
   B. I G
   C. G I
   D. K L
   E. I H

If you compare this series with the alphabet, you will find that it goes along in pairs, the first pair in their usual order and the next pair in reverse order. The last letter given in the series is the second letter of the pair G - H, which is in reverse order. The first missing letter must, therefore, be G. The next pair of letters would be I - J, in that order; the second of the missing letters is I. The alternative you look for, then, is G I, which is lettered (C).

Suggestion: In solving alphabetic series and progressions it is a good idea (you may have found it out yourself) to write out the alphabet and keep it in front of you. The key to each series can be picked out much more easily that way.

A	B	C	D	E	F	G	H	I	J	K	L	M	N	O	P	Q	R	S	T	U	V	W	X	Y	Z
1	2	3	4	5	6	7	8	9	10	11	12	13	14	15	16	17	18	19	20	21	22	23	24	25	26

1. B A C A D A E A F A G A

A. H A
B. A H
C. K A
D. L A

2. A B D C B D D B D E B D F B D G B

A. H D
B. D G
C. D B
D. D H

3. J I H G F E D C

A. B C
B. C B
C. B A
D. A B

4. Z Y X W V U T S R

A. P Q
B. Q P
C. O P
D. N P

5. X X W X V X U X T X S X R

A. X O
B. Q X
C. X P
D. X Q

6. K L N M O P R Q S T

A. V U
B. U V
C. W V
D. V W

7. A B C F E D G H I L K J M

A. O N
B. N O
C. O M
D. M O

8. Z Y W X V U S T R Q O P N M

A. K J
B. J K
C. K L
D. L K

9. Y Z X W U V T S Q R P O M N

A. K J
B. L K
C. K L
D. J K

10. Z Y X U V W T S R O P Q N M L

A. I K
B. K I
C. I J
D. K J

11. A C E G I K M O Q

A. S U
B. S T
C. R S
D. R T

12. Z X V T R P N L

A. K L
B. K J
C. H J
D. J H

13. Z W T Q N K H

A. E B
B. E C
C. F B
D. F C

14. A D G J M P S

A. V W
B. U W
C. U V
D. V Y

15. A D F I K N P S

A. W U
B. U W
C. U X
D. U V

16. Z C E D G I H K M L

A. O P
B. O Q
C. Q P
D. P Q

17. Z X V W T Q R O K L

A. J K
B. K J
C. L K
D. I E

18. B A D C F E H G J I L

A. K N
B. K M
C. N K
D. L K

19. Y Z W X U V S T Q R O P M

A. L K
B. K L
C. N L
D. N K

20. A B D C E F H G I J L K M N

A. R P
B. P O
C. O P
D. P Q

LETTER SERIES ANSWER KEY

1. (A)
2. (D)
3. (C)
4. (B)
5. (D)
6. (A)
7. (B)
8. (C)
9. (B)
10. (C)
11. (A)
12. (D)
13. (A)
14. (D)
15. (C)
16. (B)
17. (D)
18. (A)
19. (D)
20. (B)

AIR TRAFFIC CONTROL PROBLEMS

The problems that follow represent highly simplified procedures of air traffic control situations. You will be concerned with maintaining adequate time and altitude separations for several aircraft which will:

(1) be flying at different altitudes
(2) have different ETA's (estimated times of arrival) at or over the airport
(3) by flying the same ground speed toward the airport
(4) by flying on the same course toward the airport

After studying information presented in Flight Data Displays, determine which of several incoming flights can be permitted to make specified altitude changes while maintaining conformance with a basic traffic rule. For each question, use the flight data given in the display.

The aircraft are flying at different altitudes and each is expected to arrive at, or over, the airport at a different time. However, remember that you are to assume that ground speed and course of all flights are the same. The rate of climb and rate of descent are not involved in the problems. Answers to questions of this kind will involve a determination of both time and altitude separation for the various flights.

It is essential to keep in mind the basic traffic rule that follows.

<u>Basic Traffic Rule</u>

A SEPARATION OF 5 MINUTES IS NECESSARY BETWEEN TWO EN ROUTE AIRCRAFT WHICH ARE EXPECTED TO PASS OVER THE SAME GEOGRAPHICAL POINT AT THE SAME ALTITUDE.

Now look at the Flight Data Display table.

FLIGHT DATA DISPLAY

Flight Identification	Cruising Altitude	Estimated Time of Arrival (ETA) At or Over Airport
460	24,000	7:15
510	23,000	7:12
703	21,500	7:17
848	25,500	7:08

CAN YOU, AS AN AIR TRAFFIC CONTROLLER, SAFELY PERMIT A CHANGE IN CRUISING ALTITUDE?

DIRECTIONS: Questions are based on information in the Flight Data Display on the preceding page. If the answer is YES, circle the letter A, if NO, the letter B. Correct answers appear at the end of the test.

1. Flight 460 to 22,000 A. Yes B. No
2. Flight 510 to 20,000 A. Yes B. No
3. Flight 703 to 25,000 A. Yes B. No
4. Flight 848 to 23,500 A. Yes B. No
5. Flight 510 to 25,000 A. Yes B. No
6. Flight 703 to 25,500 A. Yes B. No
7. Flight 460 to 26,000 A. Yes B. No
8. Flight 510 to 21,000 A. Yes B. No
9. Flight 848 to 21,000 A. Yes B. No
10. Flight 703 to 23,500 A. Yes B. No

FLIGHT DATA DISPLAY

Flight Identification	Cruising Altitude	Estimated Time of Arrival (ETA) At or Over Airport
56	9,500	2:58
105	10,500	2:51
256	11,000	2:47
305	13,000	2:56

CAN YOU, AS AN AIR TRAFFIC CONTROLLER, SAFELY PERMIT A CHANGE IN CRUISING ALTITUDE?

11. Flight 56 to 11,000 A. Yes B. No
12. Flight 256 to 9,500 A. Yes B. No
13. Flight 56 to 12,500 A. Yes B. No
14. Flight 105 to 9,000 A. Yes B. No
15. Flight 305 to 10,000 A. Yes B. No
16. Flight 256 to 13,500 A. Yes B. No
17. Flight 105 to 12,000 A. Yes B. No
18. Flight 305 to 12,000 A. Yes B. No
19. Flight 105 to 13,500 A. Yes B. No
20. Flight 256 to 9,000 A. Yes B. No

EXPLANATORY ANSWERS

1. (B) Flight 460 cannot go to 22,000 because it is only three minutes behind Flight 510 which is at the altitude of 23,000 which it must pass through.

2. (A) Flight 510 can go to 20,000 because it is five minutes ahead of Flight 703 which is at the altitude of 21,500 which it must pass through.

3. (B) Flight 703 cannot go to 25,000 because it is only two minutes behind Flight 460 which is at the altitude of 24,000 which it must pass through.

4. (A) Flight 848 can go to 23,500 because it is seven minutes ahead of Flight 460 which is at the altitude of 24,000 which it must pass through.

5. (B) Flight 510 cannot go to 25,000 because it is only three minutes ahead of Flight 460 which is at the altitude of 24,000 which it must pass through.

6. (B) Flight 703 cannot go to 25,500 because it is only two minutes behind Flight 460 which is at the altitude of 24,000 which it must pass through.

7. (A) Flight 460 can go to 26,000 because it is seven minutes behind Flight 848 which is at the altitude of 25,500 which it must pass through.

8. (B) Flight 510 cannot go to 27,000 because it is only three minutes ahead of Flight 460 at 24,000 and only four minutes behind Flight 848 at 25,500 and it must pass through both of those altitudes.

9. (B) Flight 848 cannot go to 21,000 because it is only four minutes ahead of Flight 510 which is at the altitude of 23,000 which it must pass through.

10. (A) Flight 703 can go to 23,500 because it is five minutes behind Flight 510 which is at the altitude of 23,000 which it must pass through.

11. (A) Flight 56 can go to 11,000 because it is seven minutes behind Flight 105 at an altitude of 10,500 which it must pass through and eleven minutes behind Flight 256 at 11,000.

12. (B) Flight 256 cannot go to 9,500 because it is only four minutes ahead of Flight 105 which is at an altitude of 10,500 which it must pass through.

13. (A) Flight 56 can go to 12,500 because it is seven minutes behind Flight 105 which is at an altitude of 10,500 and eleven minutes behind Flight 256 which is at an altitude of 11,000 and it must pass through both these altitudes.

14. (A) Flight 105 can go to 9,000 because it is seven minutes ahead of Flight 56 which is at an altitude of 9,500 which it must pass through.

15. (A) Flight 305 can go to 10,000 because it is nine minutes behind Flight 256 which is at an altitude of 11,000 and five minutes behind Flight 105 which is at an altitude of 10,500 and it must pass through both these altitudes.

16. (A) Flight 256 can go to 13,500 because it is nine minutes ahead of Flight 305 which is at an altitude of 13,000.

17. (B) Flight 105 cannot go to 12,000 because it is only four minutes behind Flight 256 which is at an altitude of 11,000 which it must pass through.

18. (A) Flight 305 can go to 12,000 because it will not cross the altitude of any other flight.

19. (B) Flight 105 cannot go to 13,500 because it is only four minutes behind Flight 256 which is at an altitude of 11,000 which it must pass through.

20. (B) Flight 256 cannot go to 9,000 because it is only four minutes ahead of Flight 105 which is at an altitude of 10,500 which it must pass through.

1. B
2. A
3. B
4. A
5. B
6. B
7. A
8. B
9. B
10. A
11. A
12. B
13. A
14. A
15. A
16. A
17. B
18. A
19. B
20. B

PROBLEM SOLVING TEST

Directions: This test is to see how well you listen to directions and follow instructions. You should have someone read the questions to you. This test contains different types of questions and you must follow the instructions carefully. Write the letter closest to your drawing. *

READ THE FOLLOWING:

1. Draw an isosceles triangle with the height pointing to the left and then connect the two sides with a straight line a short distance from the height.

2. Draw a rectangle with length greater than width, then draw a diagonal from the lower left hand corner. Draw a perpendicular from the diagonal to the right side of the rectangle at the mid-point and then from the same point on the diagonal draw a line to the lower right hand corner of the rectangle.

3. Draw a rectangle with width greater than length and draw a similar rectangle within the first one having one side in common. Draw a diagonal from the upper left hand corner of the second rectangle.

4. Draw a square, and then within this square draw another square with each corner of the second square touching a midpoint of a side of the first square. Draw a line which will be a diagonal for the second square and a perpendicular for the first square.

5. Draw a square and then a triangle on top of the square using one side of the square as one of the triangle's sides. Draw two diagonals in the square and then a perpendicular from the bottom of the square to the height of the triangle.

* On the actual test, these questions will be read to you, and you will draw your figures along side those of four others as on the following pages. As an aid to you, in order to make this test as challenging as possible, we recommend if at all practicable someone reads these questions to you and draw your figures on a blank sheet of paper.

ANSWER KEY

1. (B)
2. (A)
3. (A)
4. (C)
5. (A)

ACTION WORK SHEET
FOR PROBLEM SOLVING TEST

(Once more, we recommend you cover these figures when drawing your own.)

DRAW HERE: LISTEN CAREFULLY

1. ____

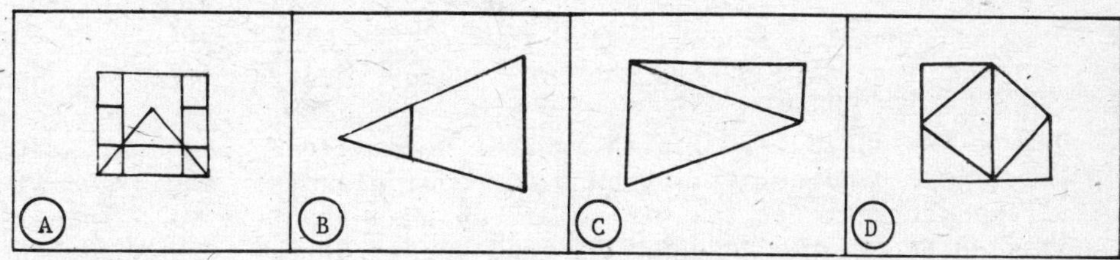

2. ____

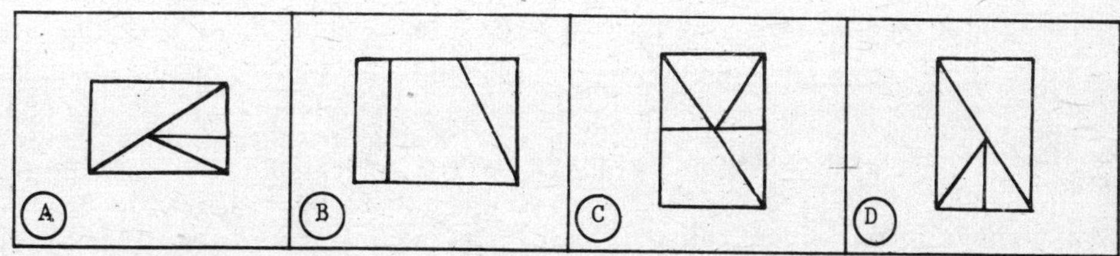

3. ____

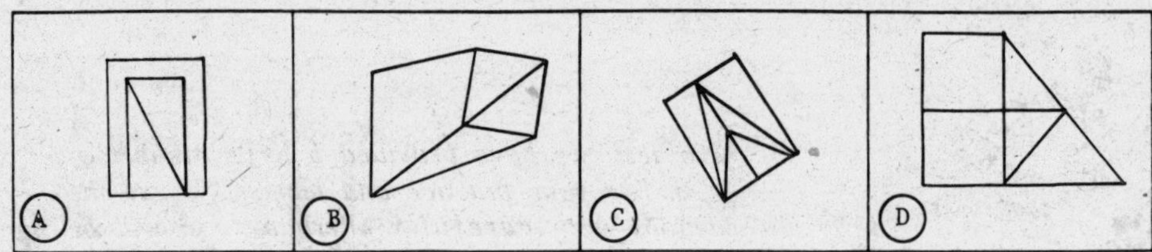

4. ____

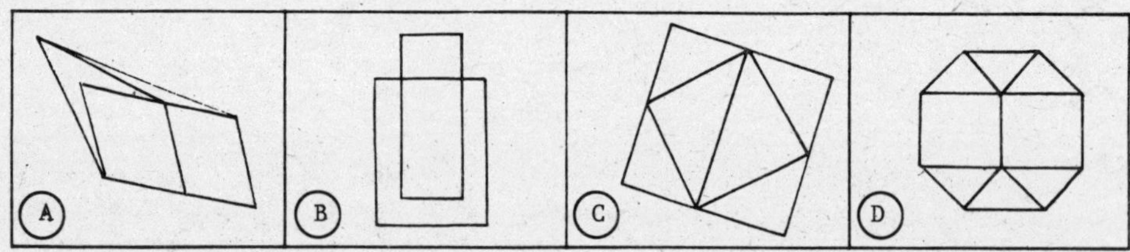

5. ____

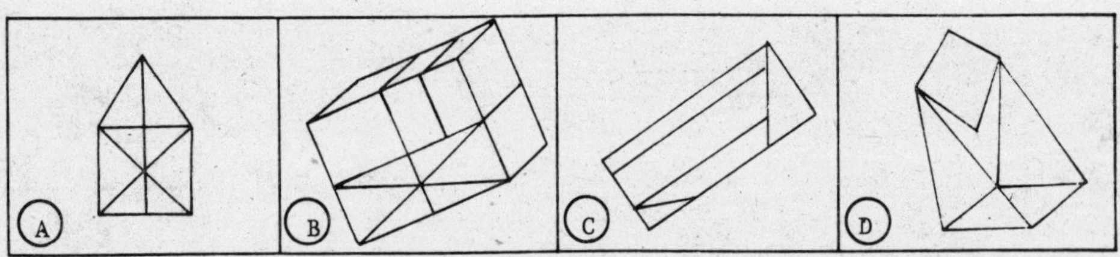

ABSTRACT REASONING

Since this type of question may be stressed on your test, we have provided a large number of questions for your practice and learning. Read the instructions very carefully. Perhaps you will be helped if we tell you that all ten symbols are of one general class, and that each of the three in the first two boxes represent variants of that class.

In each of these questions, look at the symbols in the first two boxes. Something about the three symbols in the first box makes them alike; something about the two symbols in the other box with the question mark makes them alike. Look for some characteristic that is common to all symbols in the same box, yet makes them different from the symbols in the other box. Among the five answer choices, find the symbol that can best be substituted for the question mark, because it is *like* the symbols in the second box, and, *for the same reason*, different from those in the first box.

0

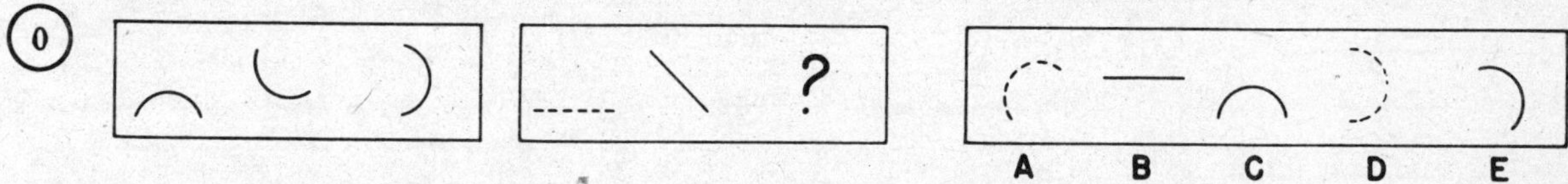

In same question 0, all the symbols in the first box are curved lines. The second box has two lines, one dotted and one solid. Their *likeness* to each other consists in their straightness; and this straightness makes them *different* from the curves in the other box. The answer must be the *only* one of the five lettered choices that is a straight line, either dotted or solid. Now do questions 11 and 12.

1

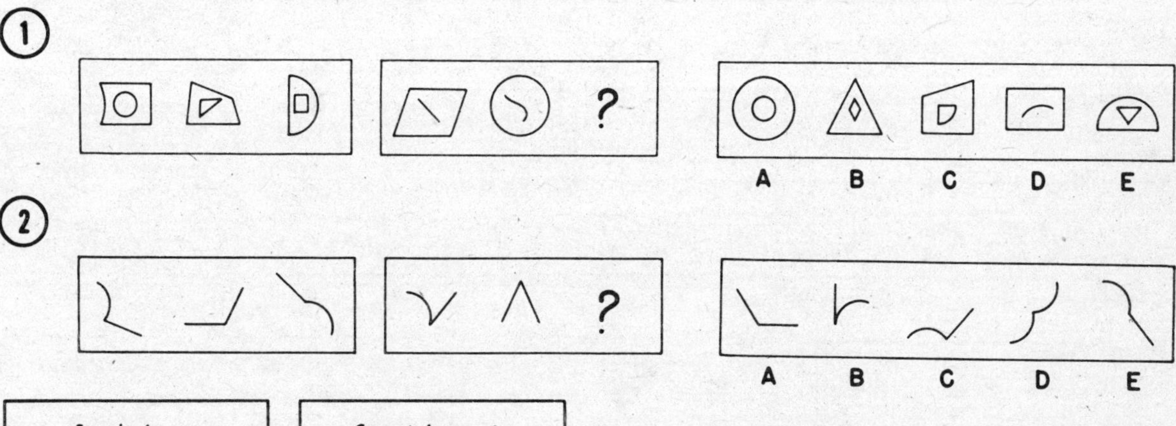

Sample Answer Sheet

	A	B	C	D	E
0					
1					
2					

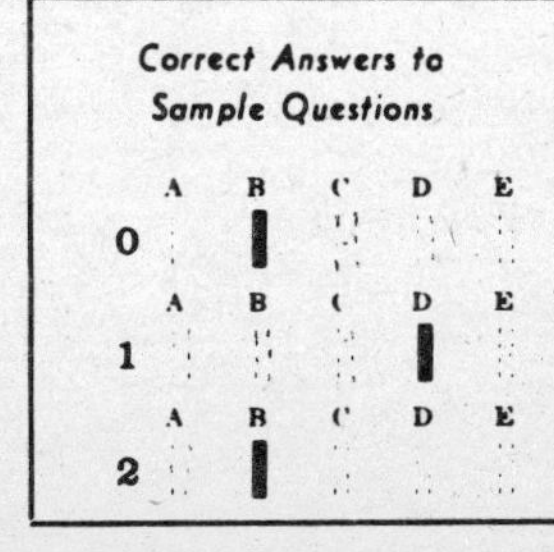

NOTE.—There is not supposed to be a *series* or progression in these symbol questions. If you look for a progression in the first box and try to find the missing figure to fill out a similar progression in the second box, you will be wasting time. For example, look at question 0. A competitor who saw that both boxes had a horizontal figure followed by an oblique one might try to find a vertical figure to match the last one in the first box. If he chose D he would be missing the real point of the question. Remember, look for a *likeness* within each box and a *difference* between the two boxes.

PRACTICE QUESTIONS IN ABSTRACT REASONING

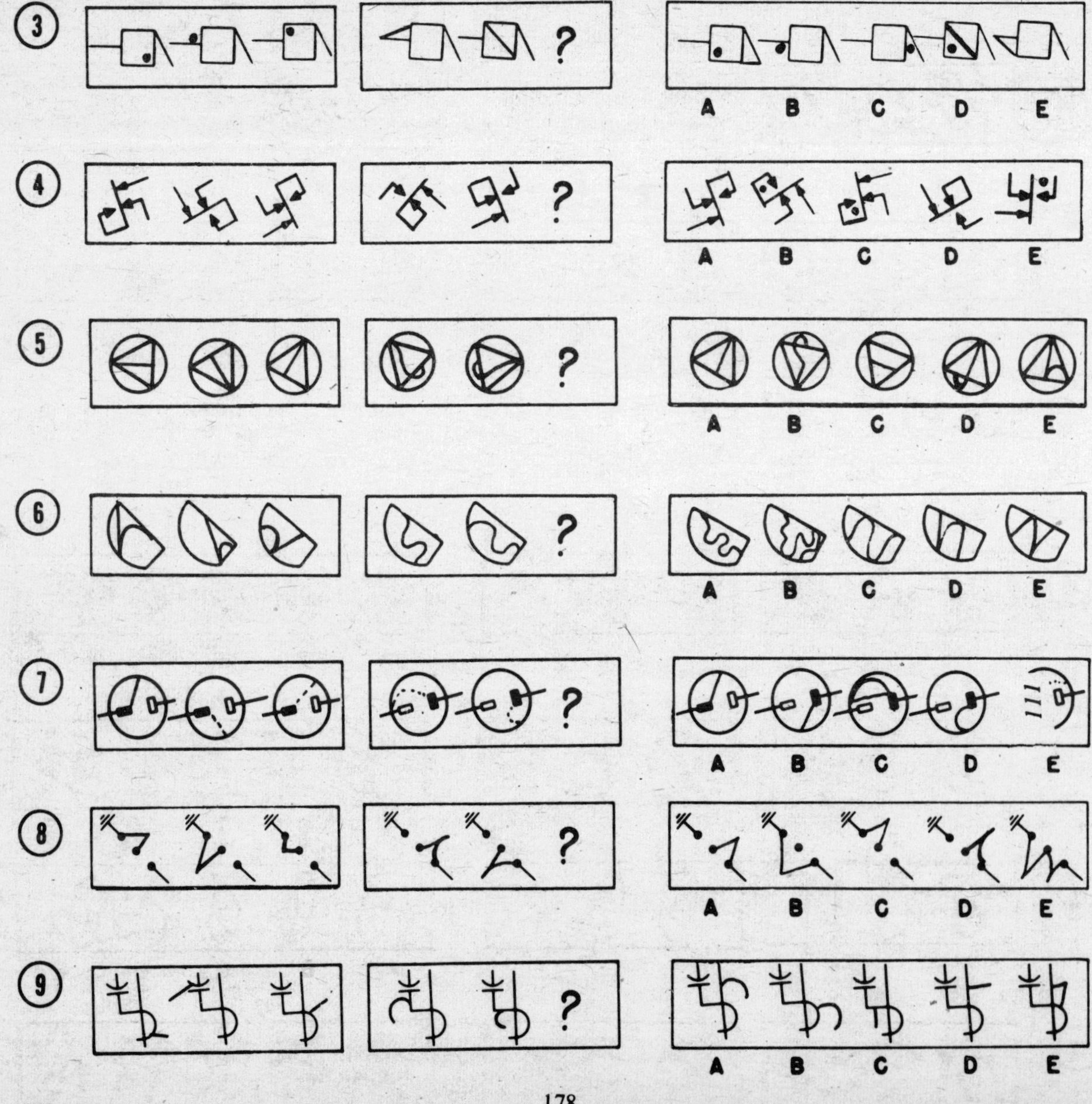

10
?
A B C D E
11
?
A B C D E
12
?
A B C D E
13
?
A B C D E
14
?
A B C D E
15
?
A B C D E
16
?
A B C D E
17
?
A B C D E
18
?
A B C D E
19
?
A B C D E

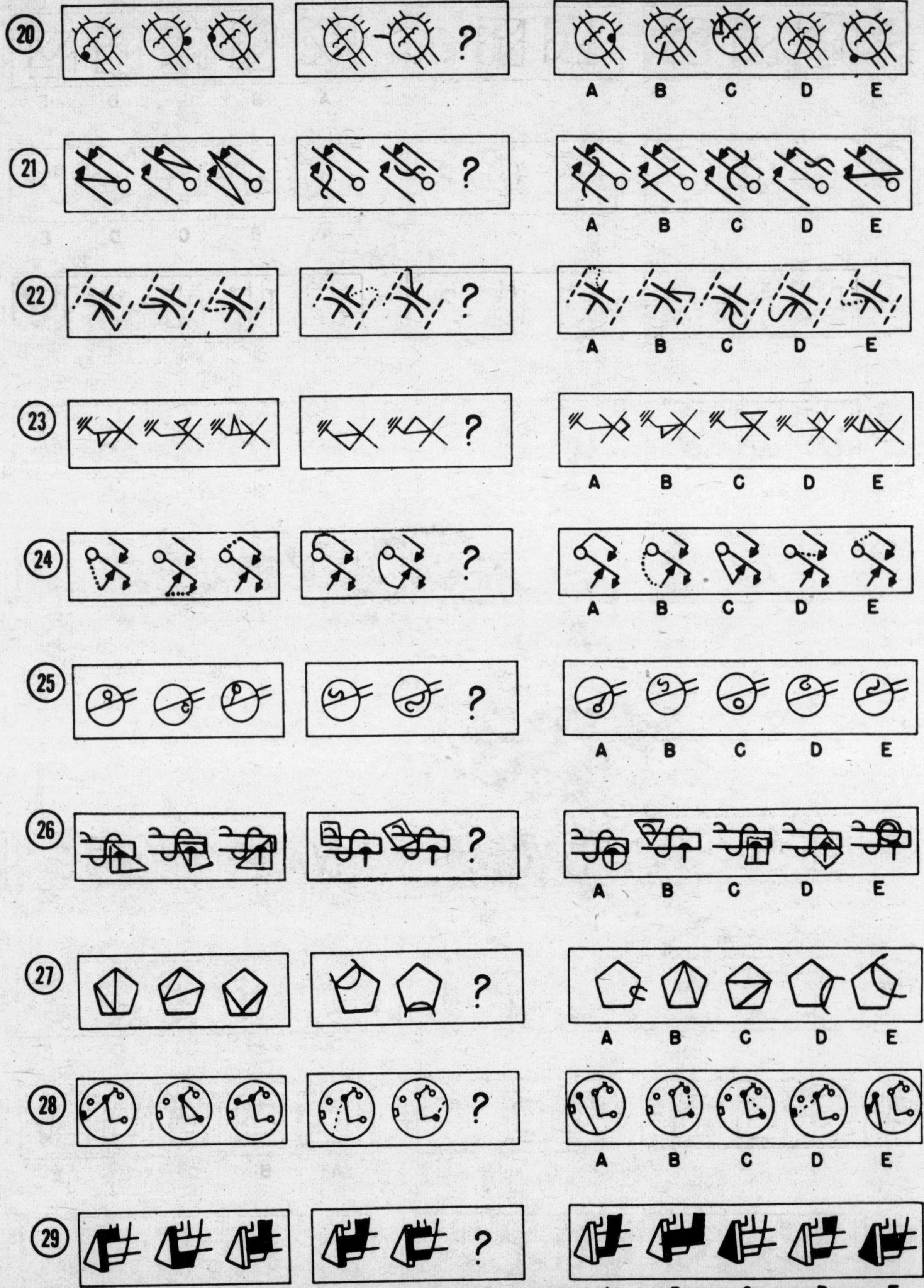
20
?
A B C D E
21
?
A B C D E
22
?
A B C D E
23
?
A B C D E
24
?
A B C D E
25
?
A B C D E
26
?
A B C D E
27
?
A B C D E
28
?
A B C D E
29
?
A B C D E

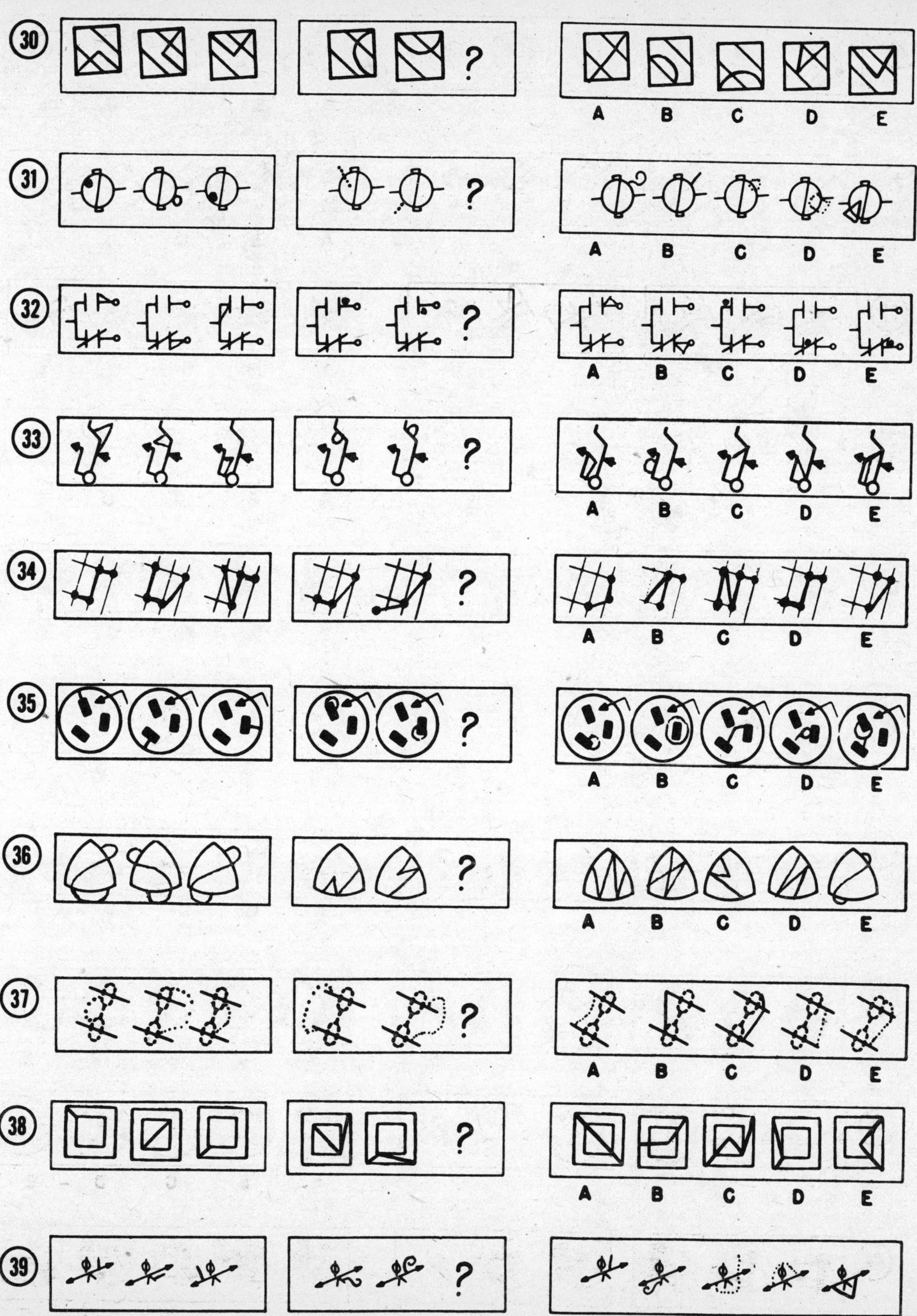
30
?
A
B
C
D
E
31
?
A
B
C
D
E
32
?
A
B
C
D
E
33
?
A
B
C
D
E
34
?
A
B
C
D
E
35
?
A
B
C
D
E
36
?
A
B
C
D
E
37
?
A
B
C
D
E
38
?
A
B
C
D
E
39
?
A
B
C
D
E

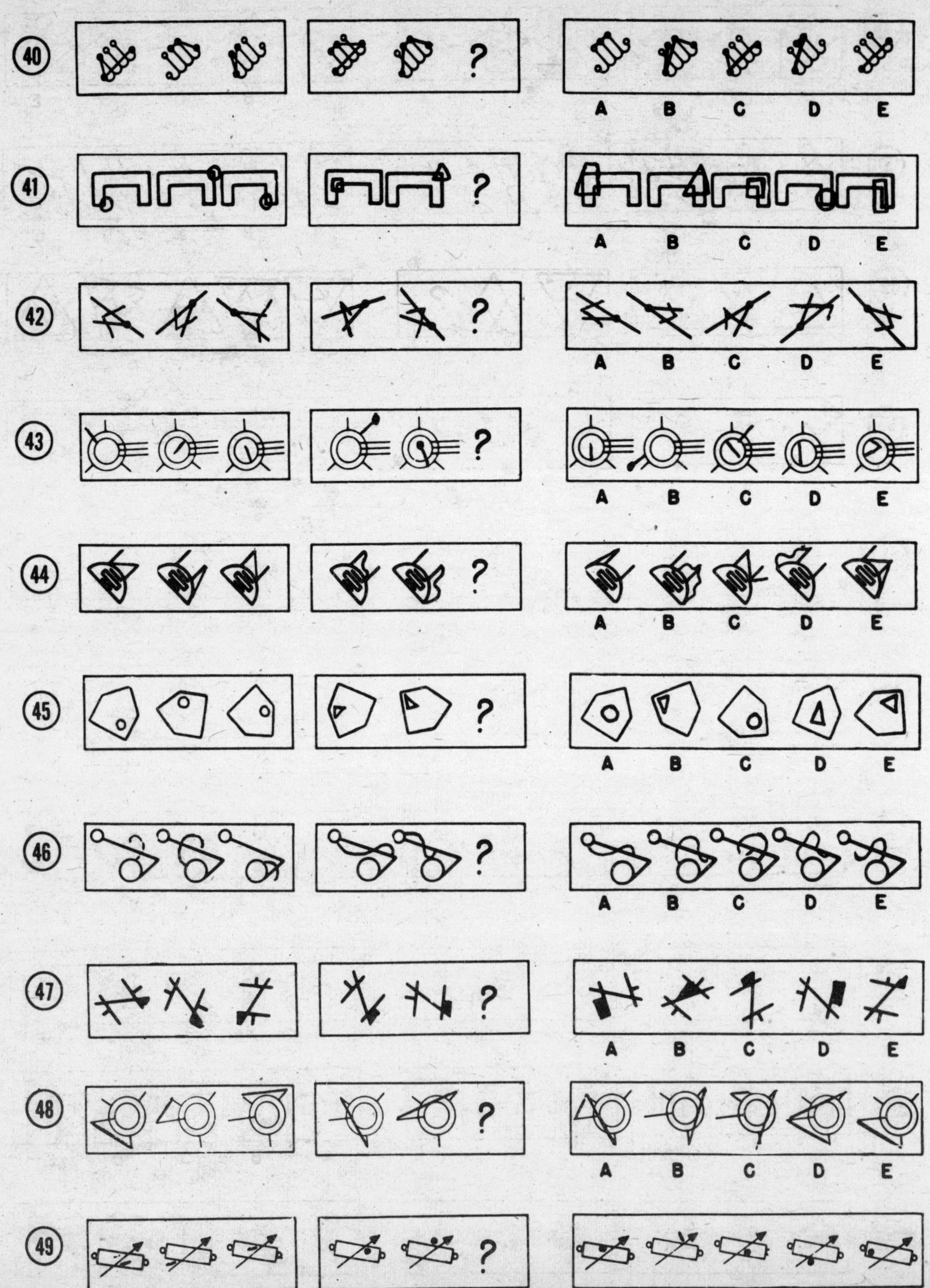
40
?
A B C D E
41
?
A B C D E
42
?
A B C D E
43
?
A B C D E
44
?
A B C D E
45
?
A B C D E
46
?
A B C D E
47
?
A B C D E
48
?
A B C D E
49
?
A B C D E

50
?
A B C D E
51
?
A B C D E
52
?
A B C D E
53
?
A B C D E
54
?
A B C D E
55
?
A B C D E
56
?
A B C D E
57
?
A B C D E
58
?
A B C D E
59
?
A B C D E

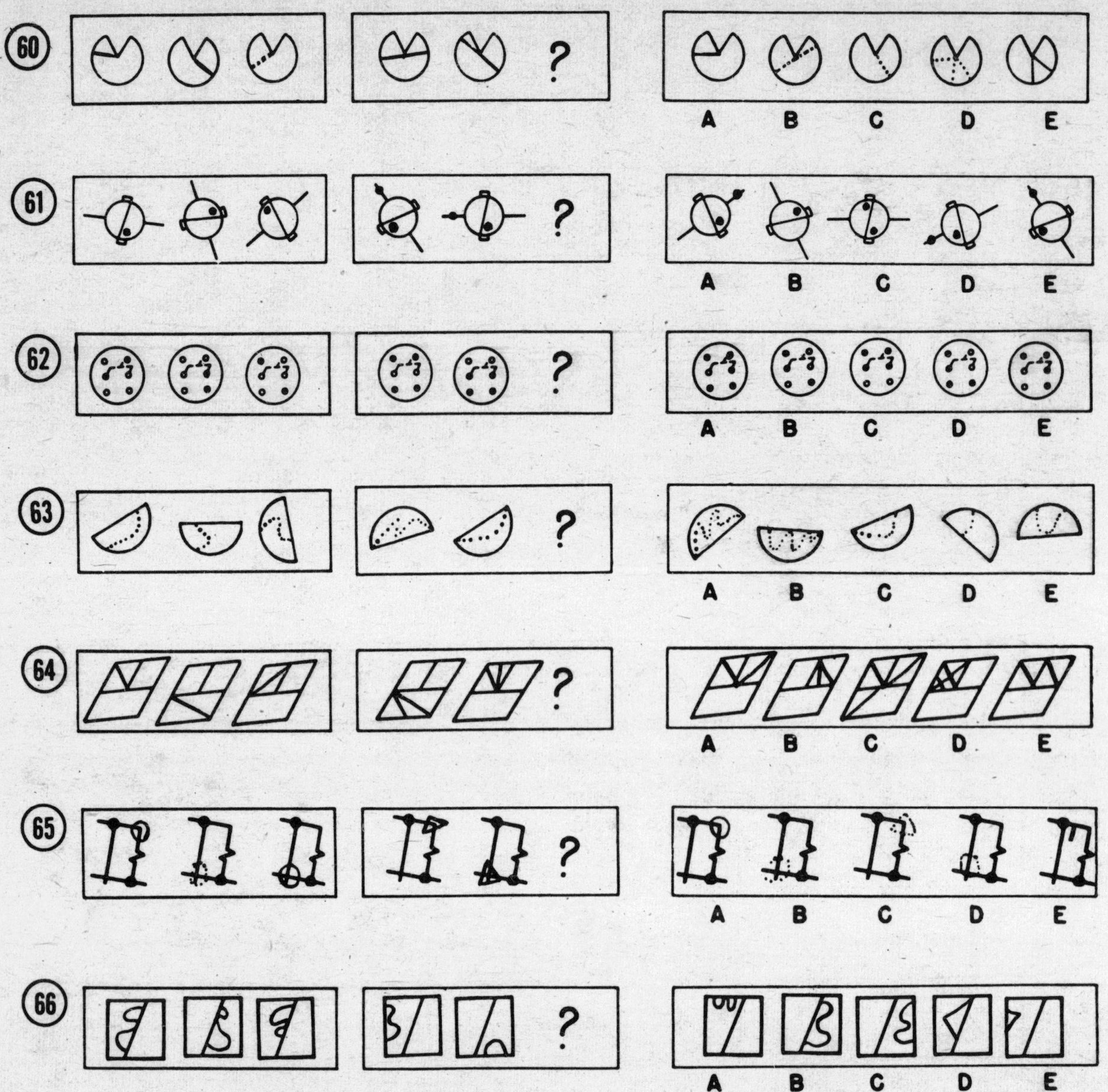

Correct Answers For The Foregoing Questions

(Please try to answer the questions on your own before looking at our answers. You'll do much better on your test if you follow this rule.)

0. B	9. A	18. B	27. D	36. C	45. B	54. E	63. A
1. D	10. C	19. D	28. A	37. A	46. A	55. D	64. B
2. B	11. A	20. B	29. B	38. D	47. C	56. D	65. C
3. E	12. D	21. D	30. C	39. B	48. B	57. C	66. C
4. D	13. A	22. A	31. B	40. B	49. D	58. E	
5. B	14. E	23. C	32. C	41. C	50. A	59. D	
6. A	15. C	24. B	33. B	42. C	51. A	60. B	
7. D	16. E	25. E	34. A	43. B	52. A	61. E	
8. D	17. B	26. B	35. A	44. D	53. D	62. C	

FIGURE CLASSIFICATION

The spatial relations problems in this chapter are designed by the test-makers to measure your reasoning ability without depending on educational background. The answers do not depend on your vocabulary, your reading ability, or your other verbal skills. They do depend on how well you understand the task and the directions. That's why, to afford plenty of practice, we've constructed a large number of these items, and have arranged them as a series of tests. Each test is just about as long and as difficult as the sub-test you will encounter. Observe the time limits; space and schedule your test-taking; record your progress.

FIGURE CLASSIFICATION QUESTIONS EXPLAINED

DIRECTIONS: In this type of test, each problem consists of two groups of figures labeled 1 and 2. These two groups are followed by five answer figures, lettered A, B, C, D, and E. For each problem you must decide what characteristic each of the figures in Group 1 has that none of the figures in Group 2 has. Then select the lettered answer figure that has this characteristic.

Now look at the sample problems and the explanations we have provided. That should make the DIRECTIONS quite clear.

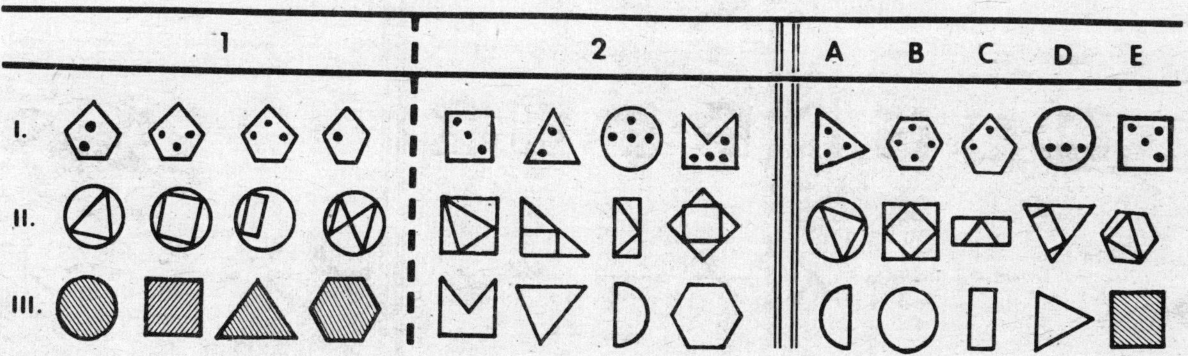

EXPLANATION: In Sample problem I all the figures in Group 1 are pentagons, but none of the figures in Group 2 is a pentagon, so C is the answer.

In Sample problem II, all the figures in Group 1 include a circle, but none of the figures in Group 2 include a circle: so A is the answer.

In Sample problem III, all the figures in Group I are shaded figures, but none in Group 2 is a shaded figure. So the correct lettered answer figure is E.

Correct Answers To Each Test Are Given. After Each Test

FIGURE CLASSIFICATION TEST

20 Minutes

DIRECTIONS: In this type of test, each problem consists of two groups of figures labeled 1 and 2. These two groups are followed by five answer figures, lettered A, B, C, D, and E. For each problem you must decide what characteristic each of the figures in Group 1 has that none of the figures in Group 2 has. Then select the lettered answer figure that has this characteristic.

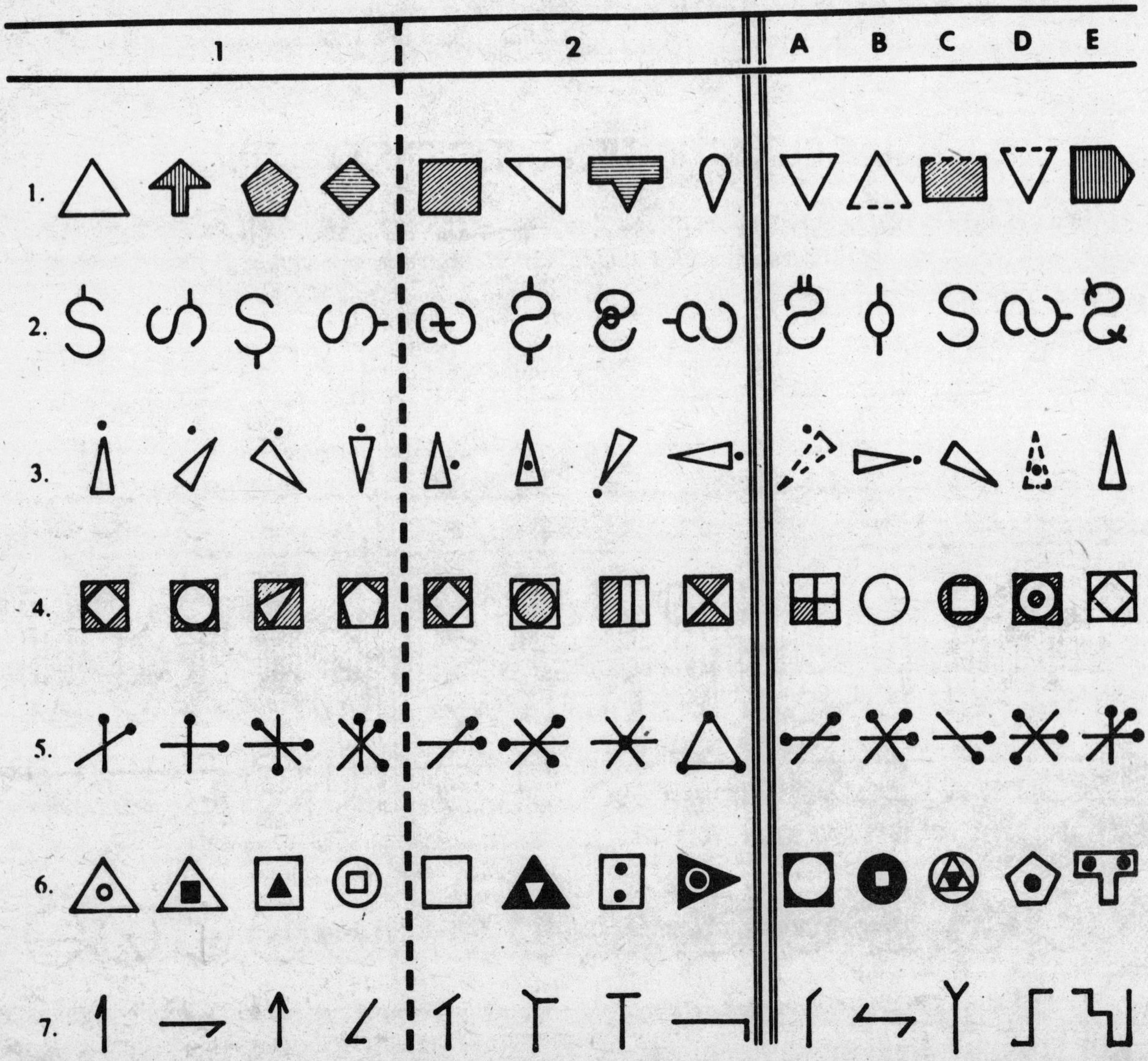

	1	2	A	B	C	D	E
1.							
2.							
3.							
4.							
5.							
6.							
7.							

S1207

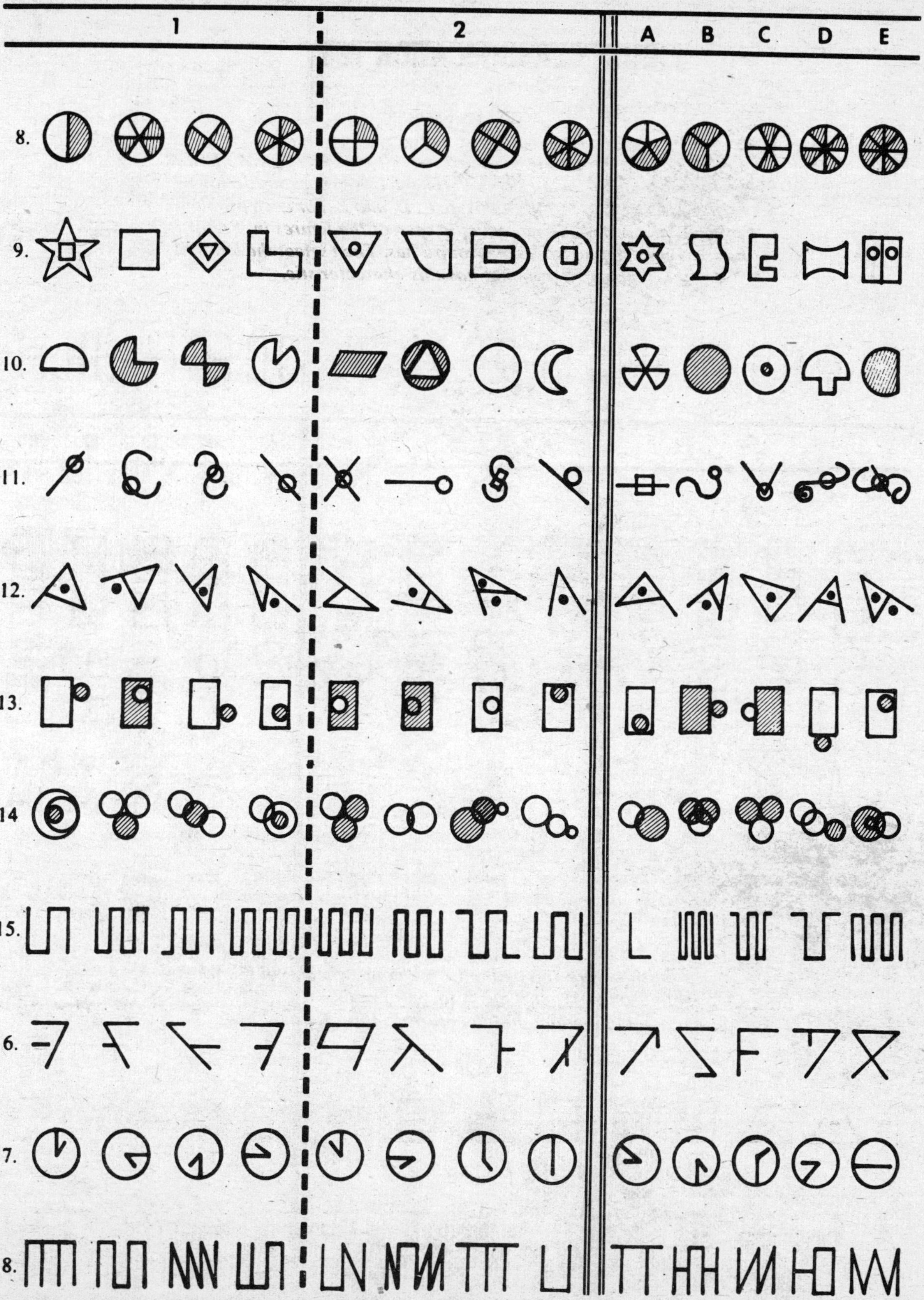

1	2	A	B	C	D	E
8.						
9.						
10.						
11.						
12.						
13.						
14						
15.						
16.						
17.						
18.						

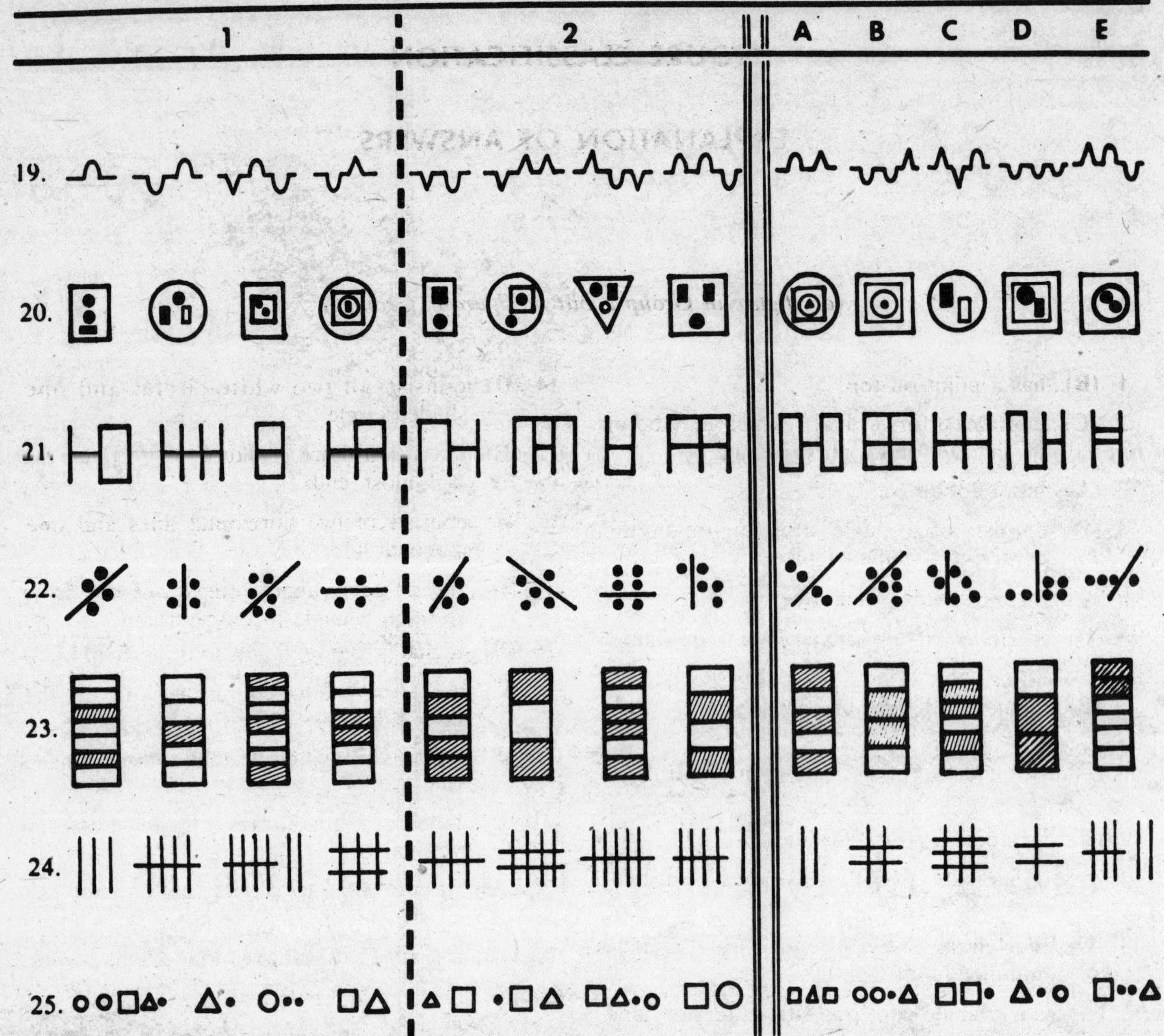

END OF SECTION

If you finish before the allotted time is up, check your work on this section only. When time is up, proceed directly to the next section and do not return to this section.

FIGURE CLASSIFICATION

EXPLANATION OF ANSWERS

Every figure in Group I, but no figure in Group II...

1. **(B)**...has a point on top.
2. **(C)**...contains a forward "S" (which may be on its side, but not a mirror image).
3. **(A)**...has a dot above.
4. **(C)**...consists of a single white figure in the center of a shaded figure.
5. **(E)**...includes one vertical line.
6. **(D)**...is a *single* figure (of any color or shape) on a white background.
7. **(B)**...includes no right or obtuse angles (only acute angles).
8. **(D)**...is divided equally between white and black area.
9. **(C)**...includes only straight lines.
10. **(A)**...is a circle with "pie-shaped" sector(s) removed.
11. **(D)**...is a circle with a line or curve running completely through it.
12. **(A)**...is a triangle with one side extended, and one dot anywhere.
13. **(E)**...is a rectangle with a different-colored circle attached to its rightmost side.
14. **(D)**...consists of two white circles and one shaded circle.
15. **(E)**...ends on a down stroke: ——┐ (at the rightmost end).
16. **(B)**...consists of two horizontal lines and one diagonal line.
17. **(D)**...has an acute angle going *clockwise* from the long "hand" to the short one.
18. **(B)**...includes four (and only four) vertical lines.
19. **(C)**...has no two adjacent protrusions on the same side of the line.
20. **(B)**...consists of two circles and two rectangles (only).
21. **(D)**...has three horizontal lengths (between verticals).
22. **(A)**...has the same number of dots on each side of the line.
23. **(E)**...has more white boxes than shaded ones.
24. **(D)**...has an odd number of lines.
25. **(C)**...has the parts arranged so that all circles come to the left of everything else, all squares come to the left of triangles and dots, and all triangles precede dots.

SCORE 1
.... %
NO. CORRECT
NO. OF QUESTIONS ON THIS TEST

SCORE 2
.... %
NO. CORRECT
NO. OF QUESTIONS ON THIS TEST

SCORE 3
.... %
NO. CORRECT
NO. OF QUESTIONS ON THIS TEST

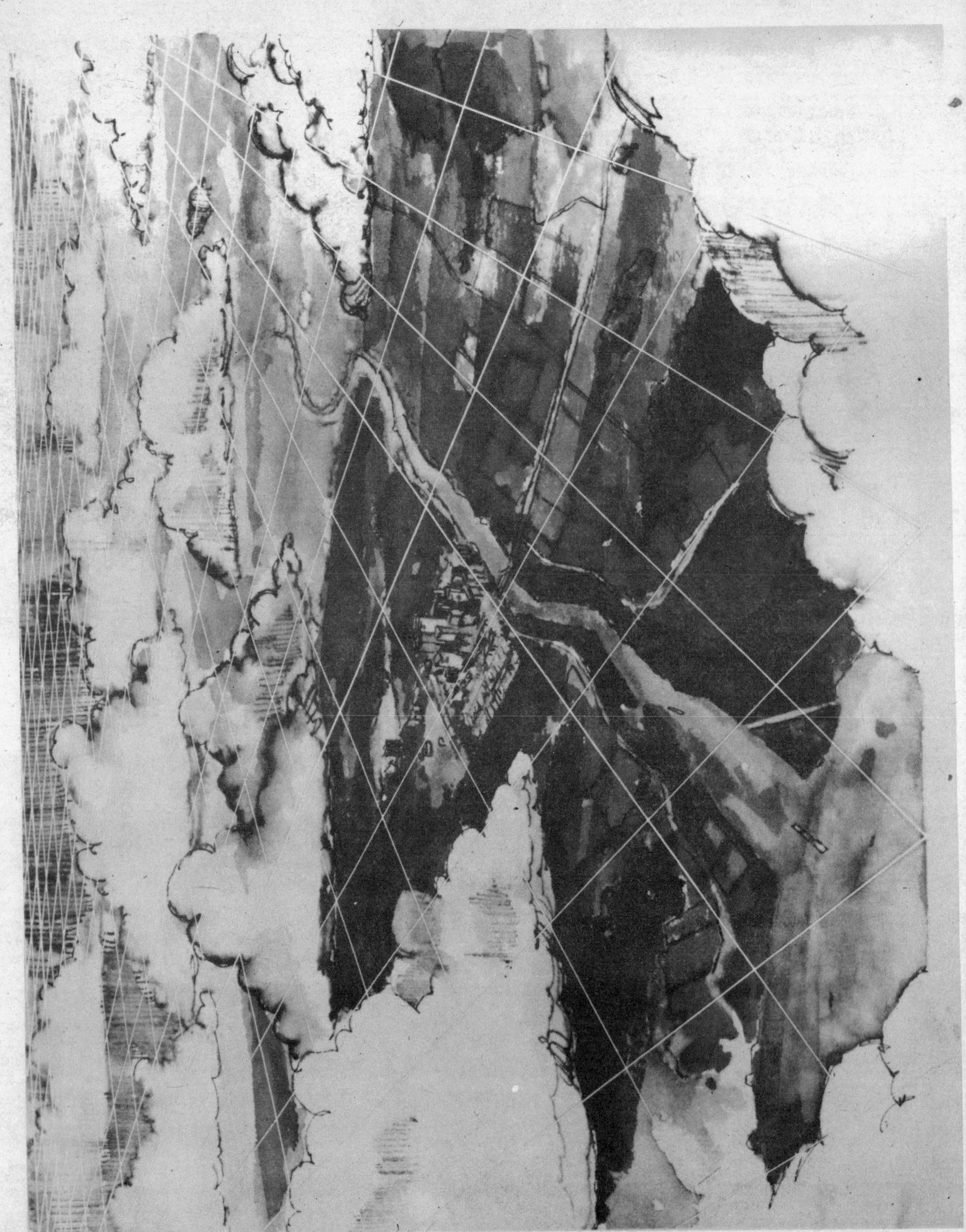

Part V

Third Practice Test

ANSWER SHEET

1 A B C D E
2 A B C D E
3 A B C D E
4 A B C D E
5 A B C D E
6 A B C D E
7 A B C D E
8 A B C D E
9 A B C D E
10 A B C D E
11 A B C D E
12 A B C D E
13 A B C D E
14 A B C D E
15 A B C D E
16 A B C D E
17 A B C D E
18 A B C D E
19 A B C D E
20 A B C D E
21 A B C D E
22 A B C D E
23 A B C D E
24 A B C D E
25 A B C D E
26 A B C D E
27 A B C D E
28 A B C D E
29 A B C D E
30 A B C D E
31 A B C D E
32 A B C D E
33 A B C D E
34 A B C D E
35 A B C D E
36 A B C D E
37 A B C D E
38 A B C D E
39 A B C D E
40 A B C D E
41 A B C D E
42 A B C D E
43 A B C D E
44 A B C D E
45 A B C D E
46 A B C D E
47 A B C D E
48 A B C D E
49 A B C D E
50 A B C D E
51 A B C D E
52 A B C D E
53 A B C D E
54 A B C D E
55 A B C D E
56 A B C D E
57 A B C D E
58 A B C D E
59 A B C D E
60 A B C D E
61 A B C D E
62 A B C D E
63 A B C D E
64 A B C D E
65 A B C D E
66 A B C D E
67 A B C D E
68 A B C D E
69 A B C D E
70 A B C D E
71 A B C D E
72 A B C D E
73 A B C D E
74 A B C D E
75 A B C D E

1 A B C D E
2 A B C D E
3 A B C D E
4 A B C D E
5 A B C D E
6 A B C D E
7 A B C D E
8 A B C D E
9 A B C D E
10 A B C D E
11 A B C D E
12 A B C D E
13 A B C D E
14 A B C D E
15 A B C D E
16 A B C D E
17 A B C D E
18 A B C D E
19 A B C D E
20 A B C D E
21 A B C D E
22 A B C D E
23 A B C D E
24 A B C D E
25 A B C D E
26 A B C D E
27 A B C D E
28 A B C D E
29 A B C D E
30 A B C D E
31 A B C D E
32 A B C D E
33 A B C D E
34 A B C D E
35 A B C D E
36 A B C D E
37 A B C D E
38 A B C D E
39 A B C D E
40 A B C D E
41 A B C D E
42 A B C D E
43 A B C D E
44 A B C D E
45 A B C D E
46 A B C D E
47 A B C D E
48 A B C D E
49 A B C D E
50 A B C D E
51 A B C D E
52 A B C D E
53 A B C D E
54 A B C D E
55 A B C D E
56 A B C D E
57 A B C D E
58 A B C D E
59 A B C D E
60 A B C D E

1 A B C D E
2 A B C D E
3 A B C D E
4 A B C D E
5 A B C D E
6 A B C D E
7 A B C D E
8 A B C D E
9 A B C D E
10 A B C D E
11 A B C D E
12 A B C D E
13 A B C D E
14 A B C D E
15 A B C D E
16 A B C D E
17 A B C D E
18 A B C D E
19 A B C D E
20 A B C D E
21 A B C D E
22 A B C D E
23 A B C D E
24 A B C D E
25 A B C D E

TEAR OUT ALONG THIS LINE AND MARK YOUR ANSWERS AS INSTRUCTED IN THE TEXT.

TEAR OUT ALONG THIS LINE AND MARK YOUR ANSWERS AS INSTRUCTED IN THE TEXT.

ANSWER SHEET

1 A B C D E
2 A B C D E
3 A B C D E
4 A B C D E
5 A B C D E
6 A B C D E
7 A B C D E
8 A B C D E
9 A B C D E
10 A B C D F
11 A B C D E
12 A B C D E
13 A B C D E
14 A B C D E
15 A B C D E
16 A B C D E
17 A B C D E
18 A B C D E
19 A B C D E
20 A B C D E

1 A B C D E
2 A B C D E
3 A B C D E
4 A B C D E
5 A B C D E
6 A B C D E
7 A B C D E
8 A B C D E
9 A B C D E
10 A B C D E
11 A B C D E
12 A B C D E
13 A B C D E
14 A B C D E
15 A B C D E
16 A B C D E
17 A B C D E
18 A B C D E
19 A B C D E
20 A B C D E

1 A B C D E
2 A B C D E
3 A B C D E
4 A B C D E
5 A B C D E

1 A B C D E
2 A B C D E
3 A B C D E
4 A B C D E
5 A B C D E
6 A B C D E
7 A B C D E
8 A B C D E
9 A B C D E
10 A B C D F
11 A B C D E
12 A B C D E
13 A B C D E
14 A B C D E
15 A B C D E
16 A B C D E
17 A B C D E
18 A B C D E
19 A B C D E
20 A B C D E
21 A B C D E

1 A B C D E
2 A B C D E
3 A B C D E
4 A B C D E
5 A B C D E
6 A B C D E
7 A B C D E
8 A B C D E
9 A B C D E
10 A B C D E
11 A B C D E
12 A B C D E
13 A B C D E
14 A B C D E
15 A B C D E
16 A B C D E
17 A B C D E
18 A B C D E
19 A B C D E
20 A B C D E
21 A B C D E
22 A B C D E
23 A B C D E
24 A B C D E
25 A B C D E

THE AIR TRAFFIC CONTROL TEST

The applicant applying for a position as an Air Traffic Controller Specialist must score high on a written test. The test score is used as one of the factors in the determination of eligibility. The following test is duplicated as accurately as possible to the actual test given by the Federal Government. The written test takes approximately two hours; the total time in the examining room is approximately 2 1/2 hours. Candidates for air traffic control work are recruited locally at FAA Regional and Field Offices and the Civil Service Commission and trained at the Aeronautical Center in Oklahoma City.

The Air Traffic Control written test makes it possible for an applicant to be considered for several different occupations through a single examination by measuring a number of abilities common to these occupations. Scores in each area of ability will be weighted according to job requirements. The test includes measures of the ability to understand and use written language; the ability to derive general principles from particular data; the ability to analyze data and derive conclusions; the ability to understand, interpret and solve problems presented in quantitative terms; the ability to derive conclusions from incomplete data supplemented by general knowledge; and the ability to discover the logical sequence of a series of events.

The Air Traffic Control Examination specifically includes several subtests, such as mathematics, abstract reasoning, air traffic control problems and other aptitude assessments. The tests measure how well you can think. These tests contain questions of different types; follow directions as given. It will be to your advantage to answer every question you can since your score will be the number of questions you answer correctly.

APTITUDE TEST

Time: 30 Minutes

Directions: This test contains a number of different types of questions. This is a test to see how well you can think. It is unlikely that you will complete all of the 75 questions but do your best. When taking the actual examination, the official will tell you when to begin. You will be given exactly 30 minutes to work as many of the problems as you can. Be careful not to go too fast and make foolish mistakes since you must try to get as many correct as you can. For each of the following questions, select the choice which best answers the question or completes the statement.

1. Assume that the average time required for a department vehicle to reach the scene of an emergency is M minutes. Solely on the basis of this fact, the one of the following which is the most reasonable inference is that in

   A. no case did a vehicle reach the scene of an emergency in less than M minutes
   B. no case did a vehicle reach the scene of an emergency in more than M minutes
   C. every case a vehicle reached the scene of an emergency in exactly M minues
   D. some cases vehicles reached the scene of an emergency after M minutes had elapsed
   E. a majority of cases vehicles reached the scene of an emergency in a period of time equal to M divided by two.

2. Unassuaged is the same as

   A. unseen
   B. unrelieved
   C. unconvinced
   D. unwashed

3. Immediate and unconditional freeing of the slaves before the Civil War was demanded by

   A. Stephen A. Douglas
   B. William Lloyd Garrison
   C. Andrew Jackson
   D. Abraham Lincoln

4. "A proper record shall be kept of the dimension and capacity of each bin or space in quarters that is used for the storage of coal." Suppose that it is necessary to determine the capacity of a bin measuring 12 feet by 10 feet by 6 feet. The additional information required is

A. the weight of a cubic foot of coal
B. the volume of the bin
C. the area of the base of the bin
D. which dimension is the height
E. the corresponding volume of coal required to fill the bin

5. Two cars going in the same direction, one at 30 miles per hour, and the other at 40 miles per hour, are 15 miles apart. How many hours will it take the faster car to catch up with the slower car?

A. 1/2
B. 1
C. 1 1/4
D. 1 1/2
E. 2

6. Palliate is the opposite of

A. apologize
B. hesitate
C. wait impatiently
D. decide finally
E. cure completely

7. Suppose that the average number of violations per day during a period of P days is M. The total number of violations during the period of P days is expressed as

A. M
B. P
C. the product of P and M
D. the sum of M and P
E. the quotient M divided by P

8. Coadjutor is the same as

A. assistant
B. partner
C. arbitrator
D. extra judge

9. Control : Order ::

A. joke : clown
B. teacher : pupil
C. disorder : climax
D. anarchy : chaos
E. government : legislator

10. The fraction corresponding to the decimal .40 is

A. 1/25
B. 1/4
C. 1/8
D. 2/5
E. 1/40

11. The Northwest Ordinance is significant in part because it provided a framework for the

A. organization of city government
B. Constitution of the United States
C. admission of new states to the union
D. Articles of Confederation

12. Consonant is the opposite of

A. insuperable
B. dissonant
C. nonexistent
D. clear
E. abundant

13. When 5.1 is divided by 0.017 the quotient is

A. 30
B. 300
C. 3,000
D. 30,000
E. 300,000

14. The development of a country's water power is advocated as a means of conserving natural resources CHIEFLY because such a hydroelectric policy would tend to

A. stimulate the growth of industries in hitherto isolated regions
B. encourage the substitution of machinery for hand labor
C. provide a larger market for coal
D. make cheap electricity available in rural areas
E. lessen the use of irreplaceable fuel materials

15. Doughty is the same as

A. flabby and pale
B. strong and valiant
C. weak and craven
D. crude and boorish

16. One percent of $23,000 is

A. $.023
B. $2.30
C. $23
D. $230
E. $2,300

17. Concise is the opposite of

A. wordy
B. mundane
C. ignorant
D. sturdy
E. wrong

18. Wood : Carve ::

A. trees : sway
B. Paper : burn
C. clay : mold
D. pipe : blow
E. statue : model

19. The sum of $82.79; $103.06 and $697.88 is, most nearly,

A. $1628
B. $791
C. $873
D. $1395
E. $885

20. President Monroe's primary reason for stating the Monroe Doctrine was to

A. make the United States of America a world power
B. stop European interference in the already independent countries of America
C. give the United States of America control over the Latin American countries
D. help in the economic development of Latin America

21. State : Border ::

A. nation : state
B. flag : loyalty
C. Idaho : Montana
D. planet : satellite
E. property : fence

22. A clerk is requested to file 800 cards. If he can file cards at the rate of 80 cards an hour, the number of cards remaining to be filed after 7 hours of work is

A. 40
B. 140
C. 240
D. 260
E. 560

23. Soldier : Regiment ::

A. navy : army
B. lake : river
C. star : constellation
D. amphibian : frog
E. flock : geese

24. Apogee : Perigee ::

A. dog : pedigree
B. opposite : composite
C. paradoxical : incredible
D. effigy : statue
E. inappropriate : apposite

25. An officer's weekly salary is increased from $80.00 to $90.00. The per cent of increase is, most nearly,

A. 10 per cent
B. 11 1/9 per cent
C. 12 1/2 per cent
D. 14 1/7 per cent
E. 20 per cent

26. Entomology is the same as

A. study of plant fossils
B. study of relics of man
C. study of insects
D. study of derivatives

27. Fecund is the opposite of

A. sinister
B. pure
C. young
D. barren
E. beneficial

28. If an engine pumps G gallons of water per minute, then the number of gallons pumped in half an hour may be found by

A. taking one-half of G
B. dividing 60 by G
C. multiplying G by 60 then dividing the product by two
D. dividing 30 by G

29. Asylum : Refugee ::

A. flight : escape
B. peace : war
C. lunatic : insanity
D. accident : injury
E. destination : traveler

30. Compendious is the opposite of

A. profound
B. inflated
C. simple
D. ambiguous
E. vague

31. Suppose there were 69 men on the payroll of your department on June 1, 1969. This is a decrease of 8% from the number of men on the payroll June 1, 1968. The number of men on the payroll on June 1, 1968 was

A. 75
B. 74
C. 76
D. 77

32. Euphemistic is the same as

A. having good digestion
B. less offensive in phrasing
C. exhibiting great enjoyment
D. excessively elegant in style

33. Fortuitous is the opposite of

A. unfortunate
B. designed
C. stupid
D. fearful
E. pious

34. If change is made of three dollars in nickels and dimes, giving twice as many nickels as dimes, it will consist of

A. $1.50 in nickels and $1.50 in dimes
B. $1.00 in nickels and $2.00 in dimes
C. $2.00 in nickels and $1.00 in dimes
D. $1.80 in nickels and $1.20 in dimes

35. A Railroad Clerk having $2.00 in nickels, $1.00 in dimes and $2.00 in quarters, has

A. twice as many nickels as dimes
B. twice as many quarters as dimes
C. five times as many nickels as quarters
D. the same number of nickels as quarters

36. Euphoria is the same as

A. sense of well-being
B. assumption of friendliness
C. ability to speak well
D. eagerness to agree

37. Worried : Hysterical ::

A. hot : cold
B. happy : ecstatic
C. lonely : crowded
D. happy : serious
E. skilled : careful

38. To say that the number of arrests made by members of the uniformed force has been increased by 50 per cent means that the number of arrests has been

A. increased by 1/2
B. doubled
C. multiplied by 5
D. multiplied by 50

39. Complaints by the owners of large cars that they cannot see an already-parked small car in a parking lot until they have begun to pull into a space, are BEST justified if

    A. there are few empty parking spaces in the lot
    B. the small car has been parked for a long time
    C. the owners of large cars have poor vision
    D. there is a designated parking area for small cars
    E. there are few other small cars in the lot

40. Saturnine is the opposite of

    A. earthy
    B. cheerful
    C. complicated
    D. maudlin
    E. honest

41. It is estimated that 10 officers can do a certain job in 10 hours. If only 5 officers are available, the job will probably take

    A. 5 hours
    B. 10 hours
    C. 15 hours
    D. 20 hours

42. Exceptionable is the same as

    A. not better than average
    B. objectionable
    C. out of the ordinary
    D. captious

43. The first major industry to come under Federal governmental regulation in the United States was

    A. mining
    B. ship building
    C. railroad transportation
    D. textile manufacturing

44. If the number of men in a uniformed force is to be increased by 150, and this increase represents an increase of 5 per cent over the present force, then the number of men in the force at present is most nearly

    A. 1500
    B. 3000
    C. 5000
    D. 7500

45. Word : Charade ::

    A. phrase : act
    B. idea : philosophy
    C. fun : party
    D. message : code
    E. graph : chart

46. Player : Team ::

    A. fawn : doe
    B. book : story
    C. ball : bat
    D. fish : school
    E. tennis : racket

47. If a vehicle is to complete a 20 mile trip at an average rate of 30 miles per hour, it must complete the trip in

    A. 20 minutes
    B. 30 minutes
    C. 40 minutes
    D. 50 minutes

48. Excoriate is the same as

A. rack
B. expel
C. disembarrass
D. flay

49. Banana : Bunch ::

A. city : state
B. world : earth
C. president : nation
D. people : continent
E. universe : planet

50. Suppose that a uniformed force, during a certain period of time, has made 150 arrests and has issued 400 summonses. If the number of arrests were doubled and the number of summonses reduced by one-half, the ratio of arrests to summonses would be

A. 1 to 3
B. 4 to 1
C. 1 1/2 to 1
D. 2 1/2 to 4

51. After 15 gallons of gasoline are removed from a tank, the gauge drops from 1/5 to 3/20. What is the capacity, in gallons, of the tank?

A. 300
B. 310
C. 320
D. 350
E. 380

52. Frangible is the opposite of

A. argumentative
B. docile
C. insincere
D. indestructible
E. inedible

53. A stolen vehicle traveling at 60 miles per hour passes by a police car, which is standing still with the engine running. The police car immediately starts out in pursuit, and one minute later, having covered a distance of half a mile, it reaches a speed of 90 miles per hour, and continues at this speed. In how many minutes after the stolen vehicle passes the police car, will the police car overtake it?

A. 1 minute
B. 1 1/2 minutes
C. 2 minutes
D. 3 minutes

54. A country that is newly settled usually produces very little art, music or literature. The MOST REASONABLE explanation of this fact is that

A. its people have had few experiences to draw on
B. there is little use for such work
C. suitable materials for such work must be imported
D. the physical development of the country absorbs most of the interest and energy of the people
E. there is as yet no governmental encouragement of the arts

55. Farrier is the same as

A. ship's carpenter
B. litter of pigs
C. blacksmith
D. trainman

56. Moth : Clothing ::

A. egg : larva
B. suit : dress
C. hole : repair
D. stigma : reputation
E. mouse : closet

57. Lethargy is the opposite of

A. acidity
B. prodigy
C. rigidity
D. alertness
E. corpulence

58. Fecund is the same as

A. fruitful
B. decaying
C. offensive
D. feverish

59. In 1969 the Department of Sanitation towed away 8,430 cars which were abandoned or illegally parked on New York City streets. If the value of the abandoned cars was $1,038,200 and that of the illegally parked cars was $6,234,800, then the average value of one of the towed cars was most nearly

A. $400
B. $720
C. $860
D. $1,100

60. Endemic is the opposite of

A. decorative
B. frustrating
C. terrorizing
D. dry
E. universal

61. Lincoln : Nebraska ::

A. Washington : D.C.
B. Trenton : New Jersey
C. New York : U.S.
D. Chicago : New York
E. city : state

62. Two per cent of all school children are problem children. Some 80% of these problem children become delinquents, and about 80% of the delinquent children become criminals. If the school population is 1,000,000 children, the number of this group who will eventually become criminals, according to this analysis, is

A. 12,800
B. 1,280
C. 640
D. 128

63. Fettle is the same as

A. gala occasion
B. shackle
C. thriving condition
D. part of a horse's leg

64. Of the following pairs, the one in which the items are incorrectly paired is

A. dynamite - Nobel
B. elevator - Otis
C. safety lamp - Drake
D. linotype - Mergenthaler

65. A patrol car began a trip with 12 gallons of gasoline in the tank and ended with 7 1/2 gallons. The car traveled 17.3 miles for each gallon of gasoline. During the trip gasoline was bought for $2.32 at a cost of 29¢ per gallon. The total number of miles traveled during this trip was most nearly

A. 79
B. 196
C. 216
D. 229

66. Compendious is the opposite of

A. profound
B. inflated
C. simple
D. ambiguous
E. vague

67. Buzz : Hum ::

A. noise : explosion
B. reverberation : peal
C. tinkle : clang
D. echo : sound
E. crack : whip

68. Fey is the same as

A. appearing to be under a spell
B. happy-go-lucky
C. not clairvoyant
D. lacking vision

69. A radio motor patrol car finds it necessary to travel 90 miles per hour for a period of 1 minute and 40 seconds. The number of miles which the car travels during this period is

A. 1 5/6
B. 2
C. 2 1/2
D. 3 3/4

70. The CHIEF reason why every society has certain words and concepts that are never precisely translated into the language of another society is that

A. the art of good translation is as yet not sufficiently developed
B. there is too great a disparity between the intellectual levels attained by different societies
C. every society possesses cultural elements which are unique to itself
D. words and concepts never express the true nature of a society
E. every society has some ideas which it does not wish to share with other societies

71. Fiduciary is the same as

A. faithful
B. speculative
C. yielding interest
D. holding in trust

72. Boxer : Gloves ::

A. swimmer : water
B. librarian : glasses
C. businessman : bills
D. fruit : pedlar
E. bacteriologist : microscope

73. A radio motor patrol car has to travel a distance of 15 miles in an emergency. If it does the first two thirds of the distance at 40 m.p.h. and the last third at 60 m.p.h. the total number of minutes required for the entire run is most nearly

A. 15
B. 20
C. 22 1/2
D. 25

74. If prices are reduced 25% and sales increase 20%, what is the net effect upon gross receipts?

A. they increase by 5%
B. they decrease by 5%
C. they remain the same
D. they increase by 10%
E. they decrease by 10%

75. Atelier is the same as

A. hat shop
B. tea shop
C. jeweler
D. workshop

APTITUDE TEST ANSWER KEY

1. (D)
2. (B)
3. (B)
4. (A)
5. (D)
6. (E)
7. (C)
8. (A)
9. (D)
10. (D)
11. (C)
12. (B)
13. (B)
14. (E)
15. (B)
16. (D)
17. (A)
18. (C)
19. (E)
20. (B)
21. (E)
22. (C)
23. (C)
24. (E)
25. (C)
26. (B)
27. (D)
28. (C)
29. (E)
30. (C)
31. (A)
32. (B)
33. (B)
34. (A)
35. (C)
36. (A)
37. (B)
38. (A)
39. (D)
40. (B)
41. (D)
42. (B)
43. (C)
44. (B)
45. (D)
46. (D)
47. (C)
48. (D)
49. (A)
50. (C)
51. (A)
52. (D)
53. (C)
54. (D)
55. (C)
56. (D)
57. (D)
58. (A)
59. (C)
60. (E)
61. (B)
62. (A)
63. (C)
64. (C)
65. (C)
66. (B)
67. (C)
68. (A)
69. (C)
70. (C)
71. (D)
72. (E)
73. (B)
74. (E)
75. (D)

MATHEMATICS

Time: 10 Minutes

Directions: The following questions in mathematics test your proficiency in the basic skills. Work as many problems as you can correctly. Select from the lettered choices that choice which best completes the statement or answers the question.

1. $\begin{array}{r} 896 \\ \underline{\times 708} \end{array}$

   A. 643,386
   B. 634,386
   C. 634,368
   D. 643,368
   E. none of the above

2. $9\overline{)4266}$

   A. 447
   B. 477
   C. 474
   D. 475
   E. none of the above

3. Add the following: 40¢, $2.75, $186.21, $24,865, $.74, $8.42, $2,475.28, $11,998.24.

   A. $38,537.04
   B. $39,537.04
   C. $38,533.40
   D. $39,573.40
   E. none of the above

4. $\begin{array}{r} \$125.25 \\ .50 \\ 70.86 \\ \underline{6.07} \end{array}$

   A. $201.68
   B. $202.69
   C. $200.68
   D. $202.68
   E. none of the above

5. $1,250.37
   \- 48.98

A. $1,201.39
B. $1,201.49
C. $1,200.39
D. $1,201.38
E. none of the above

6. Perform the indicated operations and express your answer in its simplest form: 5/8 divided by 20/3 times 7/19 divided by 63/38 times 16/21 divided by 1/14.

A. 2/9
B. 1/2
C. 1/3
D. 5/9
E. none of the above

7. 29/476.92

A. 16.4445
B. 17.4445
C. 16.4555
D. 17.4455
E. none of the above

8. 7962.27
   x .06

A. 4777.362
B. 477.6732
C. 4787.632
D. 477.7362
E. none of the above

9. Perform the indicated operations: .020301 times 2.15 divided by .00000063.

A. 69218.19
B. 69821.19
C. 69281.91
D. 69281.19
E. none of the above

10. 28
    19
    17
    24

A. 87
B. 88
C. 90
D. 89
E. none of the above

11. 3.7/2339.86

A. 632.4
B. 62.34
C. 642.3
D. 63.24
E. none of the above

12. 4 1/2
    5 3/4
    3 2/3

A. 13 10/13
B. 12 3/4
C. 13 2/3
D. 12 1/2
E. none of the above

13. Add the following fractions: 1 1/2, 2 1/16, 9 1/3, 2 1/4, 6 1/5.

A. 21 8/20
B. 21 1/2
C. 20
D. 20 9/20
E. none of the above

14. 45,286
x 4 1/5

A. 190,021 1/5
B. 190,234
C. 190,201 1/5
D. 190,202 2/5
E. none of the above

15. 8 1/6
-5 2/3

A. 3 2/3
B. 2 1/3
C. 3 1/6
D. 2 1/2
E. none of the above

16. 1/9 x 2/3 x 7/8 =

A. 6/108
B. 7/108
C. 14/27
D. 14/108
E. none of the above

17. 4 1/3/1/4 =

A. 3/52
B. 5/52
C. 17 1/3
D. 12/52
E. none of the above

18. Perform the indicated operations and express your answer in inches: 12 feet minus 7 inches, plus 2 feet 1 inch, minus 7 feet, minus 1 yard, plus 2 yards 1 foot 3 inches.

A. 130 inches
B. 128 inches
C. 129 inches
D. 131 inches
E. none of the above

19. Find 6 2/3% of $13.50.

A. $.89
B. $.91
C. $.88
D. $.95
E. none of the above

20. Reduce 11/16 to a decimal.

A. .8675
B. .6875
C. .6785
D. .6576
E. none of the above

21. Add: 7 years, 3 months + 5 years, 6 months + 8 years, 11 months.

A. 20 yrs.
B. 20 yrs. 8 mos.
C. 21 yrs. 9 mos.
D. 21 yrs. 8 mos.
E. none of the above

22. 7 ft. 4 in.
x 6 in.

A. 582 sq. in.
B. 825 sq. in.
C. 528 sq. in.
D. 568 sq. in.
E. none of the above

23. 1/5 of 295 =

A. 55
B. 49
C. 57
D. 59
E. none of the above

24. Find the cost of 2 dozen boxes of pencils at $3.60 per 1/4 dozen boxes.

A. $28.80
B. $29.50
C. $20.88
D. $28.08
E. none of the above

25. 26.456
- 2.6465

A. 24.8095
B. 23.0895
C. 24.8059
D. 23.8095
E. none of the above

26. 6/7 x 48.14 =

A. 40.27
B. 41.26
C. 40.26
D. 41.28
E. none of the above

27. When 5.1 is divided by 0.017 the quotient is

A. 30
B. 300
C. 3,000
D. 30,000
E. none of the above

28. .84 + 7.2 + .008 =

A. 8.048
B. 7.148
C. 7.048
D. 8.148
E. none of the above

29. One percent of $23,000 is

A. $.023
B. $2.30
C. $23
D. $2300
E. none of the above

30.
```
 3 1/4
 4 1/8
 4 1/2
```

A. 11 5/8
B. 11 3/4
C. 11 7/8
D. 12
E. none of the above

31. $\frac{12.02 \times .0001}{.02} =$

A. 6.01
B. .601
C. .61
D. 6.1
E. none of the above

32. The sum of $82.79; $103.06 and $697.88 is, most nearly,

A. $1628
B. $791
C. $873
D. $1395
E. none of the above

33.
```
 58,769
- 4,028
```

A. 54,641
B. 44,741
C. 54,741
D. 53,741
E. none of the above

34.
```
  5 ft.  4 in.
 19 ft.  9 in.
  9 ft.  3 in.
        10 in.
```

A. 44 ft. 4 in.
B. 35 ft. 2 in.
C. 33 ft. 2 in.
D. 30 ft. 26 in.
E. none of the above

35. The sum of 2345 and 4483 is

A. 6288
B. 6828
C. 6882
D. 8628
E. none of the above

36.
```
48,207
x  926
```

A. 44,639,682
B. 45,739,682
C. 45,638,682
D. 46,739,682
E. none of the above

37. The difference between 2876 and 1453 is

A. 1342
B. 1324
C. 1234
D. 1423
E. none of the above

38.
```
 427
 936
 502
 884
```

A. 2,836
B. 2,751
C. 3,027
D. 2,749
E. none of the above

39. If each of 5 sections has 15 cans, the total for all five sections is

A. 70
B. 65
C. 60
D. 80
E. none of the above

40.
```
 8276.91
-5382.17
```

A. 2895.76
B. 2884.74
C. 2894.76
D. 1874.74
E. none of the above

41. Five tons of snow will weigh how many pounds?

A. 1,000 lbs.
B. 10,000 lbs.
C. 100 lbs.
D. 5,000 lbs.
E. none of the above

42. $.7\overline{)913.5}$

A. 130.5
B. 1305.
C. 13.05
D. 1.305
E. none of the above

43. A man who works 8 hours a day for 6 days will work a total of how many hours?

A. 40 hours
B. 45 hours
C. 50 hours
D. 47 hours
E. none of the above

44. 31.18 x 186.7 =

A. 58213.060
B. 5836.3060
C. 5821.3060
D. 582130.60
E. none of the above

45. If a load of snow contains 3 tons, it will weigh how many lbs.?

A. 3,000 lbs.
B. 1,500 lbs.
C. 12,000 lbs.
D. 6,000 lbs.
E. none of the above

46. 8.6 - 2.19 =

A. 6.41
B. 5.87
C. 2.67
D. 58.7
E. none of the above

47. The sum of 284.5, 3016.24, 8.9736, and 94.15 is, most nearly,

A. 3402.9
B. 3403.0
C. 3403.9
D. 4036.1
E. none of the above

48.
```
 7,258
 8,456
 2,313
 6,548
```

A. 24,576
B. 25,575
C. 24,577
D. 24,674
E. none of the above

49. If 8394.6 is divided by 29.17, the result is most nearly

A. 288
B. 347
C. 2880
D. 3470
E. none of the above

50.
```
 10 2/3
- 9 1/2
```

A. 1 1/3
B. 1 1/2
C. 1 1/6
D. 13/32
E. none of the above

51. If two numbers are multiplied together, the result is 3752. If one of the two numbers is 56, the other number is

A. 41
B. 15
C. 109
D. 76
E. none of the above

52.
```
12,689
x   37
```

A. 569,493
B. 468,493
C. 469,493
D. 568,493
E. none of the above

53. The sum of the fractions 1/4, 2/3, 3/8, 5/6, and 3/4 is

A. 20/33
B. 1 19/24
C. 2 1/4
D. 2 7/8
E. none of the above

54. 3/4/$\overline{9/16}$

A. 27/64
B. 3/4
C. 5/8
D. 7/16
E. none of the above

55.
78,523
21,457
3,256
1,478

A. 104,715
B. 105,714
C. 104,814
D. 105,814
E. none of the above

56. 5/8 x 2/3 =

A. 15/16
B. 1/2
C. 5/12
D. 7/22
E. none of the above

57. Convert 7/8 to %.

A. 112%
B. 875%
C. 90%
D. 87 1/2%
E. none of the above

58.
7/8
5/8
3/4
1/2

A. 2 3/4
B. 2 7/16
C. 2 1/2
D. 2 9/16
E. none of the above

59. 126/$\overline{189}$

A. 1.59
B. 1.64
C. 1.5
D. 1.43
E. none of the above

60. 3/8 x 40 =

A. 20
B. 65
C. 15
D. 55
E. none of the above

MATHEMATICS ANSWER KEY

1. C
2. C
3. B
4. D
5. A
6. A
7. E
8. D
9. D
10. B
11. A
12. E
13. E
14. C
15. D
16. B
17. A
18. C
19. E
20. B
21. D
22. C
23. D
24. A
25. D
26. E
27. B
28. A
29. E
30. C
31. E
32. C
33. C
34. B
35. B
36. A
37. D
38. D
39. E
40. E
41. B
42. B
43. E
44. C
45. D
46. A
47. C
48. E
49. A
50. C
51. E
52. C
53. D
54. B
55. E
56. C
57. D
58. A
59. C
60. C

VERBAL ABILITIES TEST

Time: 15 Minutes

Directions: This test is designed to measure your ability to read and understand the meaning of words and the ideas associated with them, to understand the meanings of whole sentences and paragraphs, and to present the information or ideas clearly. Each item includes a paragraph which must be read accurately so that you can promptly analyze its contents and meaning or follow its instructions exactly. In this type of questioning, you should select from the multi-choice answers the correct one that best summarizes the paragraph.

Since the government can spend only what it obtains from the people and this amount is ultimately limited by their capacity and willingness to pay taxes, it is very important that they should be given full information about the work of the government.

1. According to this paragraph

   A. governmental employees should be trained not only in their own work, but also in how to perform the duties of other employees in their agency
   B. taxation by the government rests upon the consent of the people
   C. the release of full information on the work of the government will increase the efficiency of governmental operations
   D. the work of the government, in recent years, has been restricted because of reduced tax collections

Just as municipal corporations acting in government capacity are free from liability, so also are charitable corporations or associations exempt from liability when carrying on welfare or charitable enterprises, not for profit.

2. According to the above paragraph it follows that

   A. municipal and charitable corporations are exempt from liability
   B. a private hospital or clinic which treats indigent patients without making a charge would not be liable for injuries caused
   C. some charitable organizations operate for profit
   D. municipal corporations do not operate for profit
   E. an individual hurt in an automobile accident by a city chauffeur cannot sue a city if the latter is incorporated.

A hundred years ago the ownership of real estate was a fairly reliable index of "ability to pay" and was therefore an equitable basis for the levying of taxes. But, with the rise of the present complex economic order with its far-reaching associations and subtle relationships, property has assumed many novel and intangible forms which fall quite outside the incidence of the tax on real estate.

3. According to the import of the foregoing paragraph one can conclude most accurately that

   A. the best basis for the levying of taxes is "ability to pay"
   B. since property is not always easily recognizable as such, the government is faced with the problem of tax evasion
   C. in our present complex economic order, ownership of property can no longer be considered a reliable index of "ability to pay"
   D. a tax based on "ability to pay" would result in greater equality in the distribution of wealth
   E. real estate today is only one kind of property.

Questions 4-6 are to be answered solely on the information contained in the following paragraph:

The equipment in a mail room may include a mail metering machine. This machine simultaneously stamps, postmarks, seals, and counts letters as fast as the operator can feed them. It can also print the proper postage directly on a gummed strip to be affixed to bulky items. It is equipped with a meter which is removed from the machine and sent to the post office to be set for a given number of stampings of any denomination. The setting of the meter must be paid for in advance. One of the advantages of metered mail is that it by-passes the cancellation operation and thereby facilitates handling by the post office. Mail metering also makes the pilfering of stamps impossible, but does not prevent the passage of personal mail in company envelopes through the meters unless there is established a rigid control or censorship over outgoing mail.

4. According to this paragraph, the post office

   A. is responsible for training new clerks in the use of mail metering machines
   B. usually recommends that both large and small firms adopt the use of mail metering machines
   C. is responsible for setting the meter to print a fixed number of stampings
   D. examines the mail metering machines to see that they are properly installed in the mail room.

5. According to this paragraph, the use of mail metering machines

   A. requires the employment of more clerks in a mail room than does the use of postage stamps
   B. interferes with the handling of large quantities of outgoing mail
   C. does not prevent employees from sending their personal letters at company expense
   D. usually involves smaller expenditures for mail room equipment than does the use of postage stamps.

6. On the basis of this paragraph, it is most accurate to state that

   A. mail metering machines are often used for opening envelopes
   B. postage stamps are generally used when bulky packages are to be mailed
   C. the use of metered mail tends to interfere with rapid mail handlings by the post office
   D. mail metering machines can seal and count letters at the same time.

Statutes to prevent and penalize adulteration of foods and to provide for sanitation of them are in force in every state. Such legislation has been upheld as proper under the police power of the state, as it is obviously designed to promote the health and general welfare of the people.

7. It is reasonable to conclude from the above paragraph that

   A. the state provides for drastic measures to deal with offenders of the pure food laws
   B. to make laws for the purpose of promoting the general health and general welfare of the people, is a proper function of the state
   C. adulterated food is an outstanding menace to public health
   D. every state has adequately provided for the prevention of adulteration of foods, by enforcement of suitable legislation
   E. the right of the state to penalize adulteration of foods has never been questioned.

Many industrial processes are dangerous to the health of the worker and may give rise to occupational disease. The state, as the guardian of public health and welfare, has a legitimate interest in conserving the vitality of industrial workers and may, to this end, make appropriate laws, and give to boards or departments authority to make regulations to carry out the law. Such laws and rules may prohibit dangerous conditions, regulate the plant or the person, or compensate for injuries received.

8. It can best be inferred from the preceding paragraph that

   A. workmen's compensation laws are in force in practically all the states
   B. the state makes laws that prohibit industrial processes that it considers dangerous to the health of the worker
   C. Government regulation of industry is highly desirable
   D. the state is interested in lessening the occurrence of occupational disease
   E. the state compensates the worker for injuries received while carrying out the duties of his occupation.

Certain occult chemical changes, such as fermentation, have been somewhat lately found to be due to the action of innumerable living micro-organisms, known under the general name of bacteria; and the decomposition of sewage has been recently discovered to result from a similar cause.

9. According to the preceding paragraph certain occult chemical changes are due to

   A. oxidation
   B. fermentation
   C. decomposition
   D. bacteria
   E. sewage

The dangers of the ancient triple menace of the operating room--shock, hemorrhage and infection--have been virtually eliminated. Transfusion of blood is employed to combat shock and hemorrhage. It also is used to build up a patient so weakened by disease that operation otherwise would be impossible.

10. The principle idea expressed in the preceding paragraph is

    A. asepsis has removed the danger from infection
    B. operations are no longer as dangerous as formerly
    C. a blood transfusion usually precedes a serious operation
    D. operating technique has greatly improved due to the rise in standards of medical schools
    E. hemorrhages are very rare.

Answer questions 11-17 on the basis of the information appearing in the paragraph below:

The first consideration in shooting a revolver is how to stand in a steady position. You may almost face the target in assuming a comfortable shooting stance, or you may face away from the target as much as ninety degrees, and still find it possible to stand easily and quietly. The principal point to observe is to spread the feet apart at least eight inches. This varies with the individual according to the length of his legs. Stand firmly on both feet. Do not bend either leg at the knee and be careful to develop a stance which does not allow the body to lean backward or forward. Ease and naturalness in posture with body muscles relaxed is the secret of good shooting form. The shooting arm should be straight, with the weight of the pistol supported not so much by the arm as by the muscles of the shoulder. Do not tense any muscle of the arm or hand while holding the revolver; especially avoid locking the elbow. The grip of the gun should be seated in the hand so that an imaginary line drawn along the forearm would pass through the bore of the gun. The heel of the hand should reach around the stock far enough to go past the center line of the gun. The thumb can be either alongside the hammer, on top of the frame, or it can be pointed downward toward the tip of the trigger finger. The high position is preferable, because when you are shooting rapid fire the thumb will have a shorter distance to move to reach the hammer spur.

11. One of the following subjects discussed in the above paragraph is the proper method of

    A. leading a moving target
    B. squeezing the trigger
    C. gripping the revolver
    D. using revolver sights.

12. According to the above paragraph, the secret of good shooting form is

    A. proper sighting of the target
    B. a relaxed and natural position
    C. firing slowly and carefully
    D. keeping the thumb alongside the hammer.

13. For proper shooting stance, it is recommended that the weight of the pistol be supported by

    A. the muscles of the shoulder
    B. locking the elbow
    C. the muscles of the forearm
    D. tensing the wrist muscles.

14. The chief advantage of employing a high thumb position in firing a revolver is to

    A. maintain a more uniform grip
    B. achieve greater accuracy
    C. achieve better recoil control
    D. facilitate more rapid shooting.

15. When firing a revolver at a target, the angle at which you should face the target

    A. is 45 degrees
    B. is 90 degrees
    C. is greater for taller persons
    D. varies naturally from person to person.

16. According to the above paragraph, the revolver should be held in such a manner that the

    A. bore of the revolver is slightly below the heel of the hand
    B. revolver, horizontally, is level with the shoulder
    C. center line of the revolver is a continuation of the forearm
    D. revolver is at a 45 degree angle with the target.

17. Of the following, the most accurate statement concerning proper shooting position is that the

    A. left knee should be bent slightly
    B. feet should be spread at least eight inches apart
    C. you should lean slightly forward as you fire each shot
    D. weight of the body should be on the right foot.

The rates of vibration that can be perceived by the ear as musical tones lies between fairly well-defined limits, although in this organ, as in the case of the eye, there are individual variations, which are more marked in the case of the ear, since its range of appreciation is larger.

18. The paragraph points out that the ear

    A. is limited in its sense for vibration by the nature of its variations;
    B. is the most sensitive of the auditory organs
    C. differs from the visual sense in its broader range of appreciation
    D. is sensitive to a great range of musical tones
    E. depends for its sense on the rate of vibration of a limited range of sound waves.

It is probably safe to assume that the majority of individuals reach the limits set by nature to mental growth, somewhere between the ages of fourteen and a half and sixteen years. From this time on they cease to show increased capacity to meet those novel situations which, for their solution, make demands on native ability rather than mere experience. Growth in intellectual effectiveness after 16 is ascribed to wider experience and more information, rather than an increase in general mental capacity.

19. According to the import of the preceding paragraph, one can assume with greater accuracy that the majority of individuals between the ages of fourteen and a half and sixteen years

    A. make demands on mere experience rather than on native ability
    B. are still in the adolescent state
    C. show an increase rather than a decrease in general mental capacity
    D. reach the capacity of their mental growth as set by nature
    E. cease to show increased capacity to meet novel situations.

Old age insurance, under which benefits are paid as a right and not on the basis of need to upwards of thirty millions of workers, is the one feature of the Social Security Act that is wholly administered by the Federal Government.

20. This paragraph indicates most nearly that

    A. under the Social Security Act, the Federal Government administers old age insurance to any who deserve it
    B. the States have no part in administering Social Security old age insurance
    C. thirty million workers are eligible for old age insurance
    D. the Social Security Act is administered by the Federal Government
    E. every year thirty million workers receive old age insurance.

The indiscriminate or continual use of any drug, without the supervision of a capable physician, is very dangerous. Even those drugs not usually considered harmful, if taken for a period of years, may result in a form of chronic poisoning. One should not have a prescription refilled unless the physician prescribes a given amount because he wishes use of a drug to be discontinued after a certain time. One should never use the prescription which a physician has prescribed for another patient because although the symptoms may seem to be the same, there may be differences apparent to the expert, but which the layman does not see, and which imply an entirely different ailment and different medication.

21. The paragraph notes that

    A. the use of drugs is very dangerous
    B. if a physician prescribes a drug, it is safe to refill the prescription
    C. the people with similar symptoms are usually suffering from the same ailment
    D. a drug which is not harmful when taken for a limited time, may be dangerous when taken over a longer period of time
    E. a good physician will never prescribe a dangerous drug.

The editor, publisher, business manager, or owner must file, in duplicate, not later than October 1 of each year on Form 3526 a sworn statement showing the ownership and management of their publication. The statement must be published in the second issue of the publication printed next after the statement has been filed. Copies of Form 3526 are furnished by the local postmaster. The two copies of Form 3526 and one copy of the issue in which the statement is published must be filed with the postmaster at the office where the publication has original second-class mail privileges.

22. To comply with the above regulation, a publisher must

 A. file a copy of form 3526, and an issue of his publication containing statement of ownership, this issue being the second one printed after original filing date
 B. notify the postmaster not later than October 1 of each year that he intends to file, and then submit the second subsequent issue bearing statement of ownership
 C. swear to ownership and management of the publication, and print statement of same in publication
 D. contact post office where publication has original second-class privileges, and file what is necessary at their direction
 E. file two copies of Form 3526 to post office where privilege was originally obtained before October 1 of each year, and print statement of ownership in second issue subsequent to filing date, and file with same post office.

What constitutes skill in any line of work is not always easy to determine; economy of time must be carefully distinguished from economy of energy, as the quickest method may require the greatest expenditure of muscular effort, and may not be essential or at all desirable.

23. The paragraph best supports the statement that

 A. the most efficiently executed task is not always the one done in the shortest time
 B. energy and time cannot both be conserved in performing a single task
 C. if a task requires muscular energy it is not being performed economically
 D. skill in performing a task should not be acquired at the expense of time
 E. a task is well done when it is performed in the shortest time.

The function of business is to increase the wealth of the country and the value and happiness of life. It does this by supplying the material needs of men and women. When the nation's business is successfully carried on, it renders public service of the highest value.

24. The paragraph best supports the statement that

 A. all businesses which render public service are successful
 B. human happiness is enhanced only by the increase of material wants
 C. the value of life is increased only by the increase of wealth
 D. the material needs of men and women are supplied by well-conducted business
 E. business is the only field of activity which increases happiness.

Education should not stop when the individual has been prepared to make a livelihood and to live in modern society. Living would be mere existence were there no appreciation and enjoyment of the riches of art, literature, and science.

25. The paragraph best supports the statement that true education

A. is focused on the routine problems of life
B. prepares one for full enjoyment of life
C. deals chiefly with art, literature and science
D. is not possible for one who does not enjoy scientific literature
E. disregards practical ends

VERBAL ABILITIES TEST ANSWER KEY

1. (B)
2. (B)
3. (E)
4. (C)
5. (C)
6. (D)
7. (B)
8. (D)
9. (D)
10. (B)
11. (C)
12. (B)
13. (A)
14. (D)
15. (D)
16. (C)
17. (B)
18. (C)
19. (D)
20. (B)
21. (D)
22. (E)
23. (A)
24. (D)
25. (B)

LETTER SERIES

Time: 25 Minutes

Directions: Select from the choices offered in each of the following, the one which is correct or most nearly correct.

Two Test Questions Analyzed

In each of these questions there is a series of letters which follow some definite order, followed by five sets of two letters each. Look at the letters in the series and determine what the order is; then from the suggested answers that follow, select the set that gives the next letters in the series in their correct order.

1. X C X D X E X

A. F X
B. F G
C. X F
D. E F
E. X G

The series consists of X's alternating with letters in alphabetical order. The next two letters would be F and X; therefore (A) is the correct answer.

2. A B D C E F H

A. G H
B. I G
C. G I
D. K L
E. I H

If you compare this series with the alphabet, you will find that it goes along in pairs, the first pair in their usual order and the next pair in reverse order. The last letter given in the series is the second letter of the pair G - H, which is in reverse order. The first missing letter must, therefore, be G. The next pair of letters would be I - J in that order; the second of the missing letters is I. The alternative you look for, then, is G I, which is lettered (C).

Suggestion: In solving alphabetic series and progressions it is a good idea (you may have found it out yourself) to write out the alphabet and keep it in front of you. The key to each series can be picked out much more easily that way.

A	B	C	D	E	F	G	H	I	J	K	L	M	N	O	P	Q	R	S	T	U	V	W	X	Y	Z
1	2	3	4	5	6	7	8	9	10	11	12	13	14	15	16	17	18	19	20	21	22	23	24	25	26

1. A B C D F E G H I J L K M

A. O N
B. N O
C. P O
D. O P

2. Z Y X U V W T S R

A. O P
B. P O
C. O N
D. N O

3. A B C B C D C D E D E F E

A. G H
B. G F
C. E F
D. F G

4. C M D O E Q F S G

A. T
B. W
C. U
D. Y

5. D J H N L R

A. P
B. T
C. X
D. V

6. J O L Q N S

A. P
B. X
C. U
D. O

7. J M K N L O M

A. P
B. K
C. O
D. Q

8. A A B A C A D A

A. A E
B. D A
C. E A
D. E E

9. B H C G E F H E

A. J F
B. K C
C. K D
D. L D

10. S R L Q P M O

A. P L
B. N N
C. L N
D. N L

11. R O F P N F N

A. L F
B. N M
C. F L
D. M L
E. M F

12. F F E H H G J J

A. H L
B. I L
C. L L
D. L I
E. I I

13. O E G P I K Q

A. R M
B. O Q
C. L S
D. M O
E. L M

14. S Q P P M O J

A. N G
B. L I
C. N I
D. G L
E. J N

15. K A P J F U I

A. L Z
B. Z H
C. K Z
D. K H
E. H K

16. U U S Q Q O M

A. K K
B. M K
C. K I
D. I G
E. M M

17. W V T S P O K

A. F E
B. J I
C. F A
D. J F
E. J E

18. Q J P I N H K

A. G K
B. G G
C. J D
D. D J
E. G D

19. G E I G K I M

A. K N
B. J O
C. K O
D. L N
E. J N

20. I J K G H I E

A. F G
B. G H
C. E F
D. F D
E. G E

LETTER SERIES ANSWER KEY

1. (B)
2. (A)
3. (D)
4. (C)
5. (A)
6. (A)
7. (A)
8. (C)
9. (D)
10. (B)
11. (E)
12. (B)
13. (D)
14. (A)
15. (C)
16. (B)
17. (E)
18. (B)
19. (C)
20. (A)

AIR TRAFFIC CONTROL PROBLEMS

The problems that follow represent highly simplified procedures of air traffic control situations. You will be concerned with maintaining adequate time and altitude separations for several aircraft which will:

(1) be flying at different altitudes
(2) have different ETA's (estimated times of arrival) at or over the airport
(3) be flying the same ground speed toward the airport
(4) be flying on the same course toward the airport

After studying information presented in Flight Data Displays, determine which of several incoming flights can be permitted to make specified altitude changes while maintaining conformance with a basic traffic rule. For each question, use the flight data given in the display.

The aircraft are flying at different altitudes and each is expected to arrive at, or over, the airport at a different time. However, remember that you are to assume that ground speed and course of all flights are the same. The rate of climb and rate of descent are not involved in the problems. Answers to questions of this kind will involve a determination of both time and altitude separation for the various flights.

It is essential to keep in mind the basic traffic rule that follows.

Basic Traffic rule

A SEPARATION OF 5 MINUTES IS NECESSARY BETWEEN TWO EN ROUTE AIRCRAFT WHICH ARE EXPECTED TO PASS OVER THE SAME GEOGRAPHICAL POINT AT THE SAME ALTITUDE.

Now look at the Flight Data Display table.

FLIGHT DATA DISPLAY

Flight Identification	Cruising Altitude	Estimated Time of Arrival (ETA) At or Over Airport
475	7,000	1:20
542	5,500	1:26
638	4,600	1:27
657	6,400	1:23

CAN YOU, AS AN AIR TRAFFIC CONTROLLER, SAFELY PERMIT A CHANGE IN CRUISING ALTITUDE?

DIRECTIONS: Questions are based on the information in the Flight Data Display on the preceding page. If the answer is YES, circle the letter A, if NO, the letter B. Correct answers appear at the end of the test.

1. Flight 475 to 5,500 A. Yes B. No

2. Flight 542 to 7,500 A. Yes B. No

3. Flight 657 to 5,000 A. Yes B. No

4. Flight 638 to 4,000 A. Yes B. No

5. Flight 657 to 7,000 A. Yes B. No

6. Flight 542 to 7,000 A. Yes B. No

7. Flight 657 to 5,800 A. Yes B. No

8. Flight 638 to 6,500 A. Yes B. No

9. Flight 475 to 4,500 A. Yes B. No

10. Flight 638 to 5,400 A. Yes B. No

FLIGHT DATA DISPLAY

Flight Identification	Cruising Altitude	Estimated Time of Arrival (ETA) At or Over Airport)
238	18,000	12:44
332	15,000	12:39
341	16,000	12:48
455	19,000	12:41

11. Flight 341 to 17,000 A. Yes B. No

12. Flight 238 to 15,000 A. Yes B. No

13. Flight 455 to 17,000 A. Yes B. No

14. Flight 238 to 20,000 A. Yes B. No

15. Flight 332 to 17,000 A. Yes B. No

16. Flight 455 to 18,000 A. Yes B. No

17. Flight 341 to 14,000 A. Yes B. No

18. Flight 332 to 18,000 A. Yes B. No

19. Flight 455 to 14,000 A. Yes B. No

20. Flight 332 to 20,000 A. Yes B. No

EXPLANATORY ANSWERS

1. (B) Flight 475 cannot go to 5,500 because it is only three minutes ahead of Flight 657 which is at the altitude of 6,400 which it must pass through.

2. (B) Flight 542 cannot go to 7,500 because it is only three minutes behind Flight 657 which is at the altitude of 6,400 which it must pass through.

3. (B) Flight 657 cannot go to 5,000 because it is only three minutes ahead of Flight 542 which is at the altitude of 5,500 which it must pass through.

4. (A) Flight 638 can go to 4,000 because there is no other Flight at that altitude and it will not cross the path of any other Flights.

5. (B) Flight 657 cannot go to 7,000 because it is only three minutes behind Flight 475 which is at that altitude.

6. (B) Flight 542 cannot go to 7,000 because it is only three minutes behind Flight 657 which is at the altitude of 6,400 which it must pass through.

7. (A) Flight 657 can go to 5,800 because no other Flight is at that altitude and it will not cross the path of any other Flight.

8. (B) Flight 638 cannot go to 6,500 because it is only one minute behind Flight 542 at 5,500 and four minutes behind Flight 657 at 6,400 and it would have to pass through both these altitudes.

9. (B) Flight 475 cannot go to 4,500 because it is only three minutes ahead of Flight 657 which is at the altitude of 6,400 which it must pass through.

10. (A) Flight 638 can go to 5,400 because there is no other Flight at that altitude and it will not cross the path of any other Flight.

11. (A) Flight 341 can go to 17,000 because there are no other flights at that altitude and it does not cross the path of any other Flight.

12. (B) Flight 238 cannot go to 15,000 because it is only four minutes ahead of Flight 341 which is at the altitude of 16,000 which it must pass through.

13. (B) Flight 455 cannot go to 17,000 because it is only three minutes ahead of Flight 238 which is at the altitude of 18,000 which it must pass through.

14. (B) Flight 238 cannot go to 20,000 because it is only three minutes behind Flight 455 which is at the altitude of 19,000 which it must pass through.

15. (A) Flight 332 can go to 17,000 because it is nine minutes ahead of Flight 341 which is at the altitude of 16,000 which it must pass through.

16. (B) Flight 455 cannot go to 18,000 because it is only three minutes ahead of Flight 238 which is at that altitude.

17. (A) Flight 341 can go to 14,000 because it is nine minutes behind Flight 332 which is at the altitude of 15,000 which it must pass through.

18. (A) Flight 332 can go to 18,000 because it is nine minutes ahead of Flight 341 at 16,000 and five minutes ahead of Flight 238 at 18,000.

19. (B) Flight 455 cannot go to 14,000 because it is only three minutes ahead of Flight 238 at 18,000 and only two minutes behind Flight 332 at 15,000 and it must pass through both altitudes.

20. (B) Flight 332 cannot go to 20,000 because it is only two minutes ahead of Flight 455 which is at the altitude of 19,000 which it must pass through.

1.	B	11.	A
2.	B	12.	B
3.	B	13.	B
4.	A	14.	B
5.	B	15.	A
6.	B	16.	B
7.	A	17.	A
8.	B	18.	A
9.	B	19.	B
10.	A	20.	B

PROBLEM SOLVING TEST

Directions: This test is to see how well you listen to directions and follow instructions. You should have someone read the questions to you. This test contains different types of questions and you must follow the instructions carefully. Write the letter closest to your drawing. *

READ THE FOLLOWING:

1. Draw an isosceles triangle and then draw a parallelogram within the triangle so that the parallelogram is constructed from the mid-points of all three sides.

2. Draw a rectangle with width greater than length and then draw an isosceles triangle within the rectangle with all corners of the triangle touching a side of the rectangle.

3. Draw a right scalene triangle and then from the mid-point of the base draw a line to the hypotenuse. Now from this point draw a line to the vertex.

4. Draw a rectangle with length greater than width and then connect the mid-points of all the sides making a parallelogram.

5. Draw an isosceles triangle and then draw a line tangent to the top of the triangle Connect both end points of the base with the tangent line and then draw a perpendicular from the mid-point of the base.

*** On the actual test, these questions will be read to you, and you will draw your figures along side four possible answers, as on the following pages. In order to make this test as challenging as possible, we recommend if at all practicable that someone read these questions to you and that you draw your figures on a blank sheet of paper.**

ANSWER KEY

1. (B)
2. (A)
3. (D)
4. (C)
5. (D)

ACTION WORK SHEET
FOR PROBLEM SOLVING TEST

(Once more, we recommend you cover these figures when drawing your own.)

DRAW HERE: LISTEN CAREFULLY

1. ____

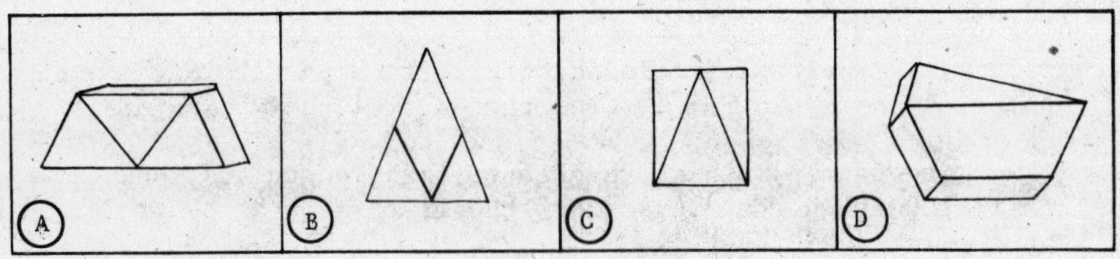

2. ____

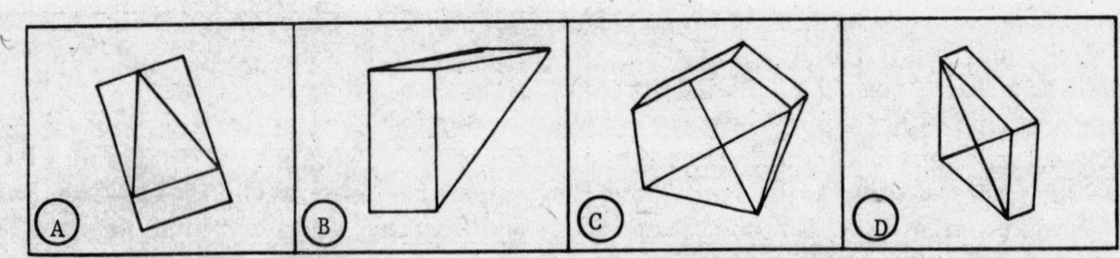

3. ____

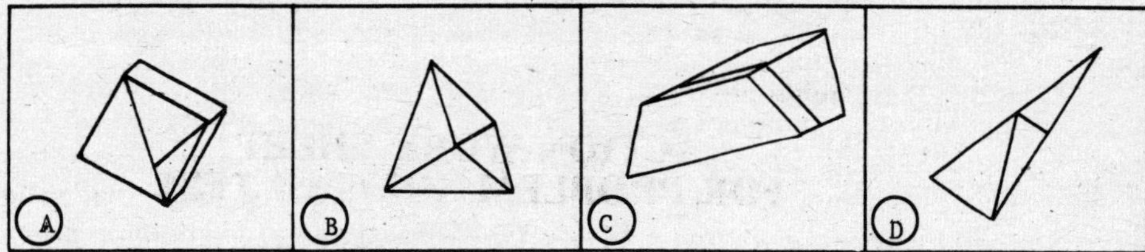

4. ____

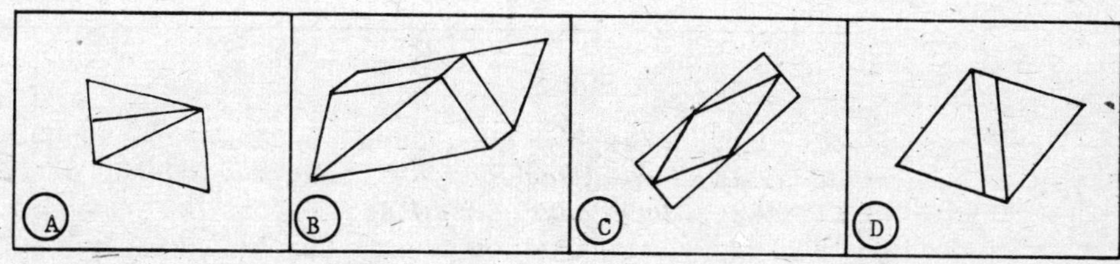

5. ____

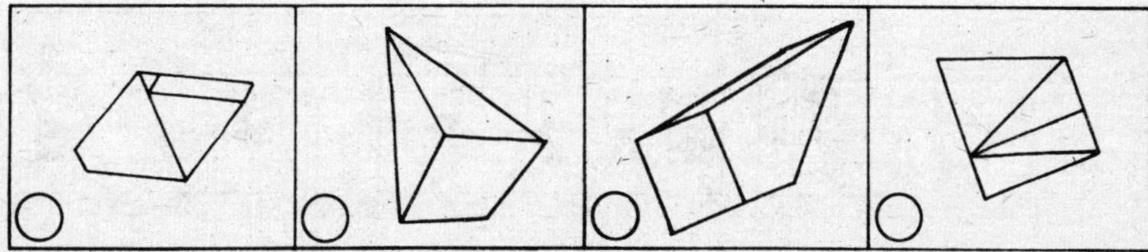

ABSTRACT REASONING

Your ability to see the differences between, and the relationship between various abstract symbols is one indication of your ability to learn. It is a measure of your ability to meet new situations and evaluate them. The following practice questions will help to familiarize you with this type of question. As in other analogy problems—verbal analogies and numerical series—the best approach is to translate into words the exact relationship between the key figures. Be sure to avoid the traps of similar figures which do not have the same relationship.

TEST I. ABSTRACT REASONING

Time: 20 Minutes

DIRECTIONS: In each of these questions, look at the symbols in the first two boxes. Something about the three symbols in the first box makes them alike; something about the two symbols in the other box with the question mark makes them alike. Look for some characteristic that is common to all symbols in the same box, yet makes them different from the symbols in the other box. Among the five answer choices, find the symbol that can best be substituted for the question mark, because it is like the symbols in the second box, and, for the same reason, different from those in the first box.

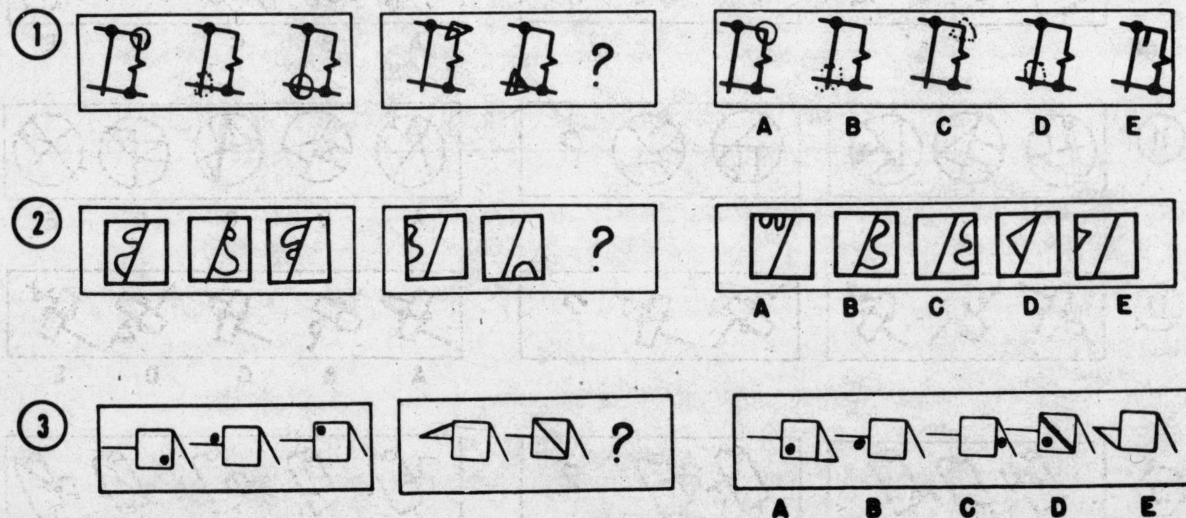

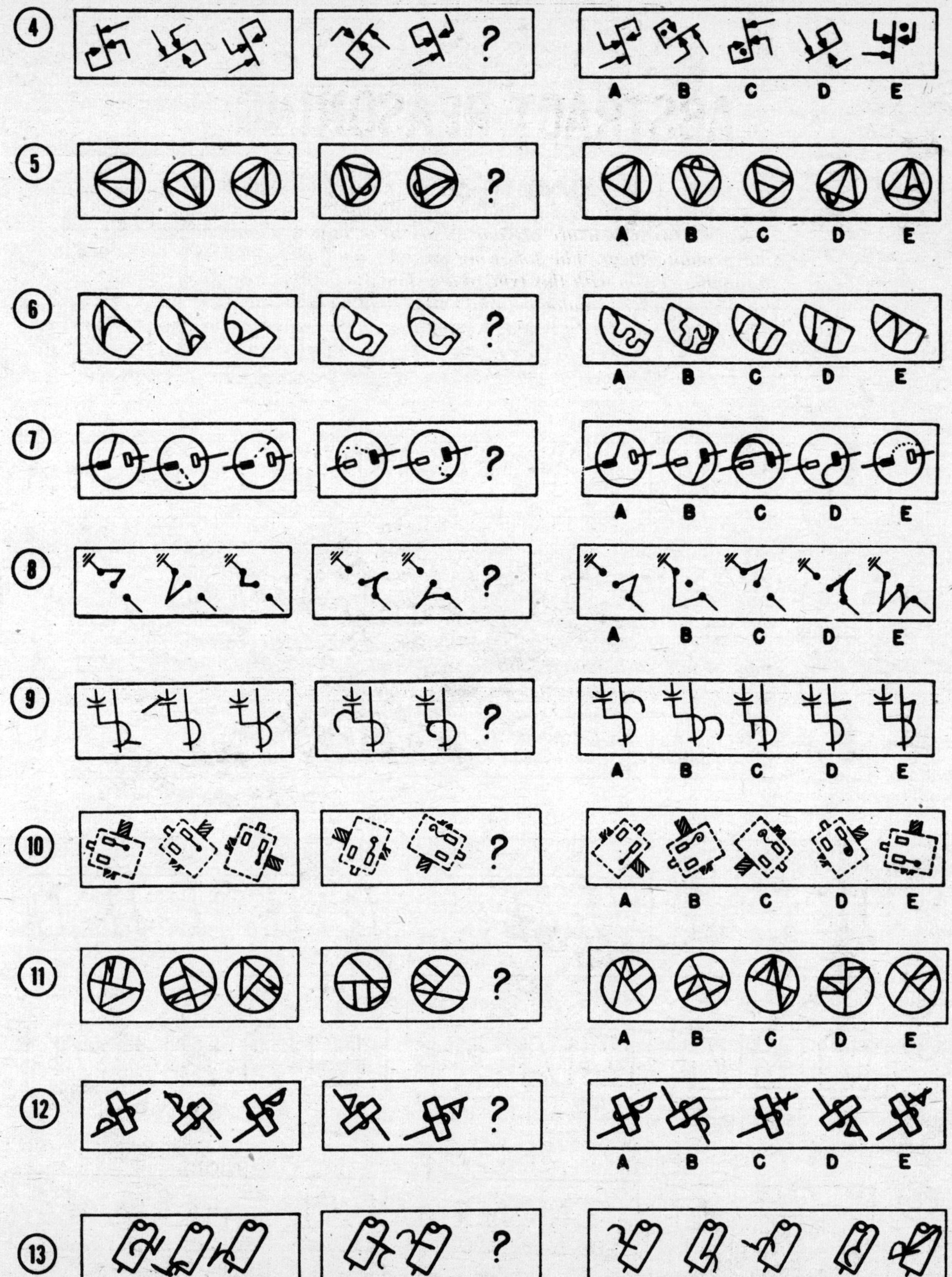
4
?
A B C D E
5
?
A B C D E
6
?
A B C D E
7
?
A B C D E
8
?
A B C D E
9
?
A B C D E
10
?
A B C D E
11
?
A B C D E
12
?
A B C D E
13
?
A B C D E

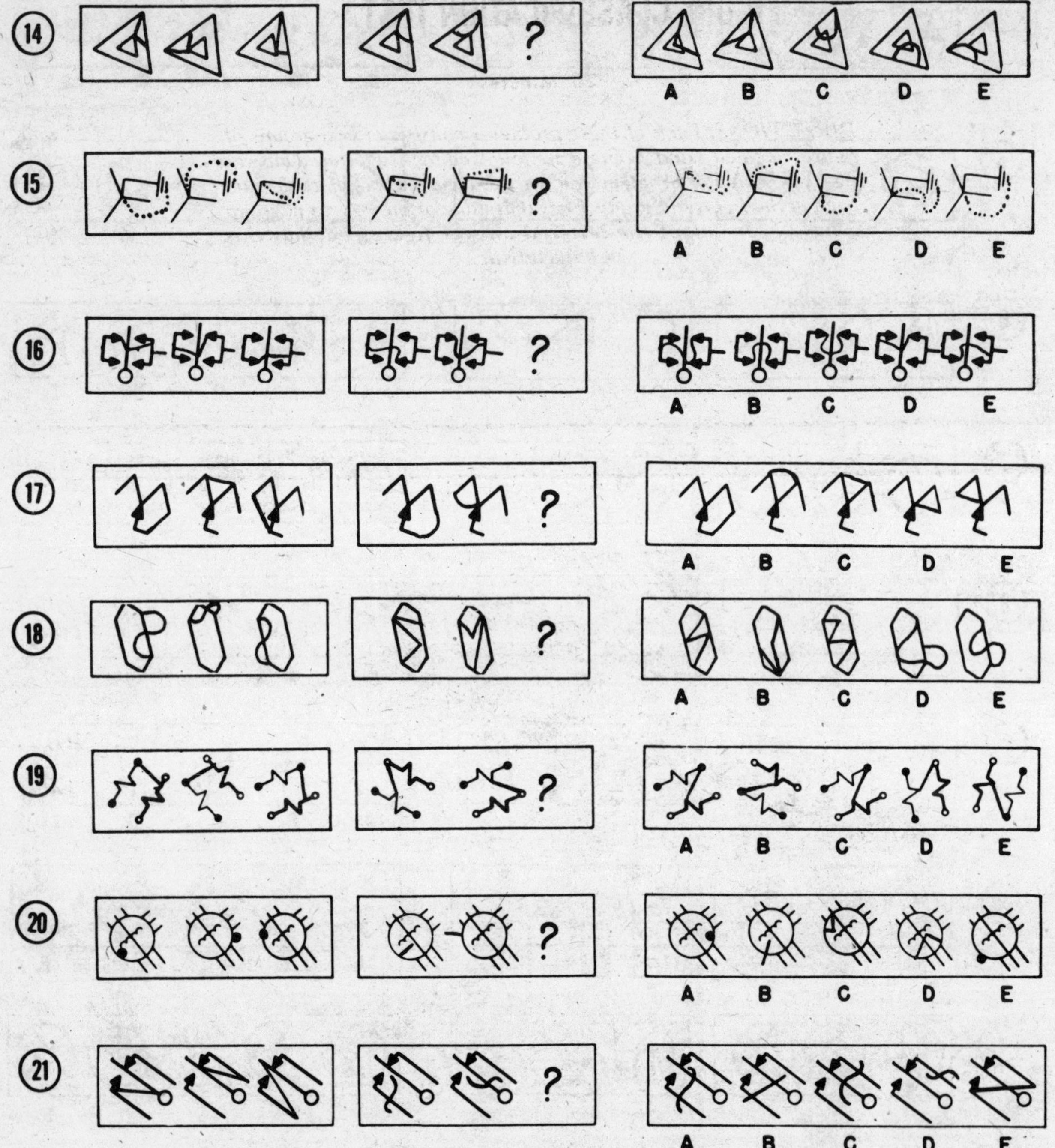

Correct Answers For The Foregoing Questions

1.C	4.D	7.D	10.C	13.A	16.E	19.D
2.C	5.B	8.D	11.A	14.E	17.B	20.B
3.E	6.A	9.A	12.D	15.C	18.B	21.D

FIGURE CLASSIFICATION TEST

20 Minutes

DIRECTIONS: Each of these problems consists of two groups of figures, labeled 1 and 2. These are followed by five lettered answer figures. For each problem you are to decide what characteristic each of the figures in group 1 has that none of the figures in group 2 has. Then select the lettered answer figure that has this characteristic.

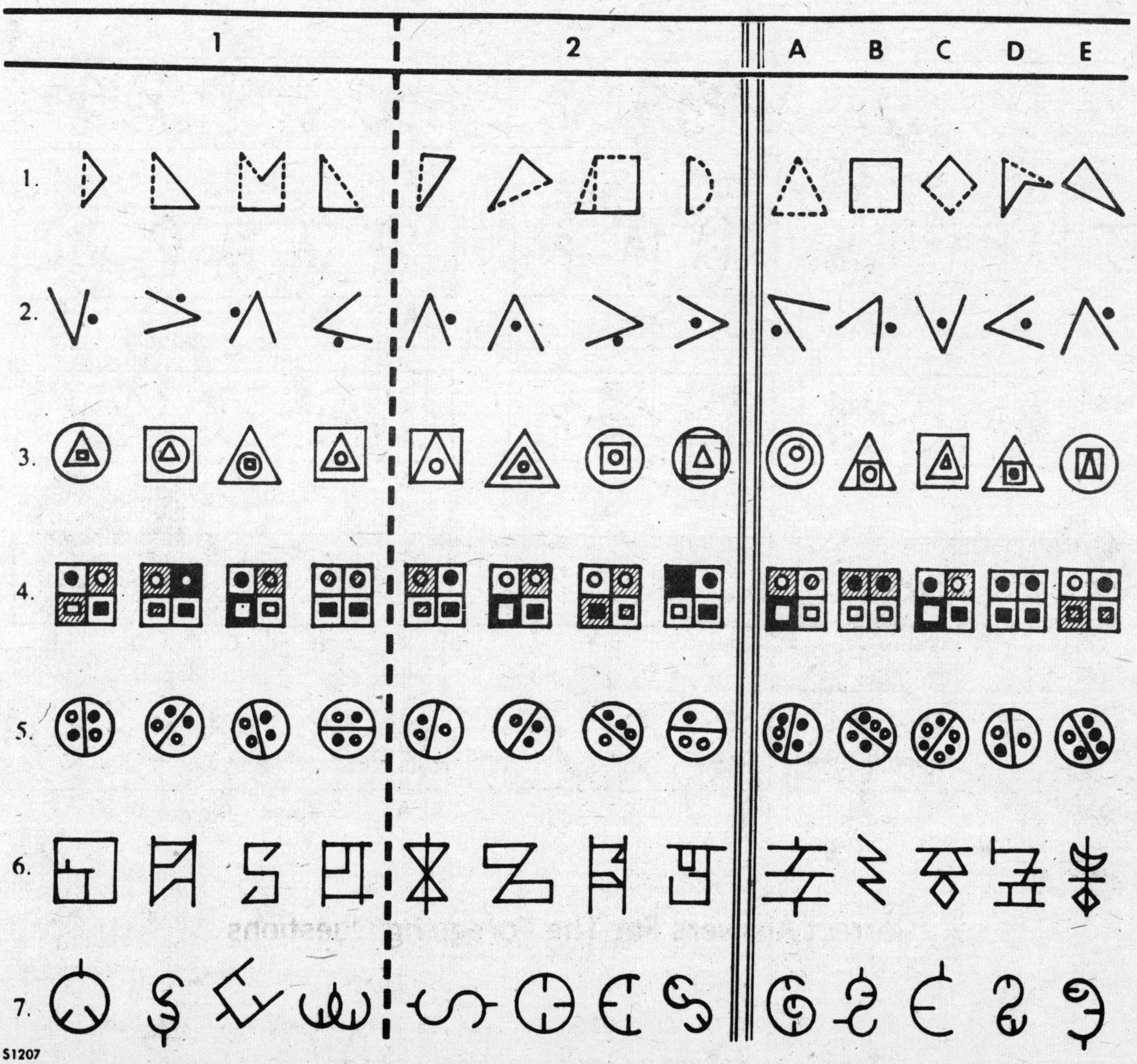

1	2	A	B	C	D	E
1.						
2.						
3.						
4.						
5.						
6.						
7.						

S1207

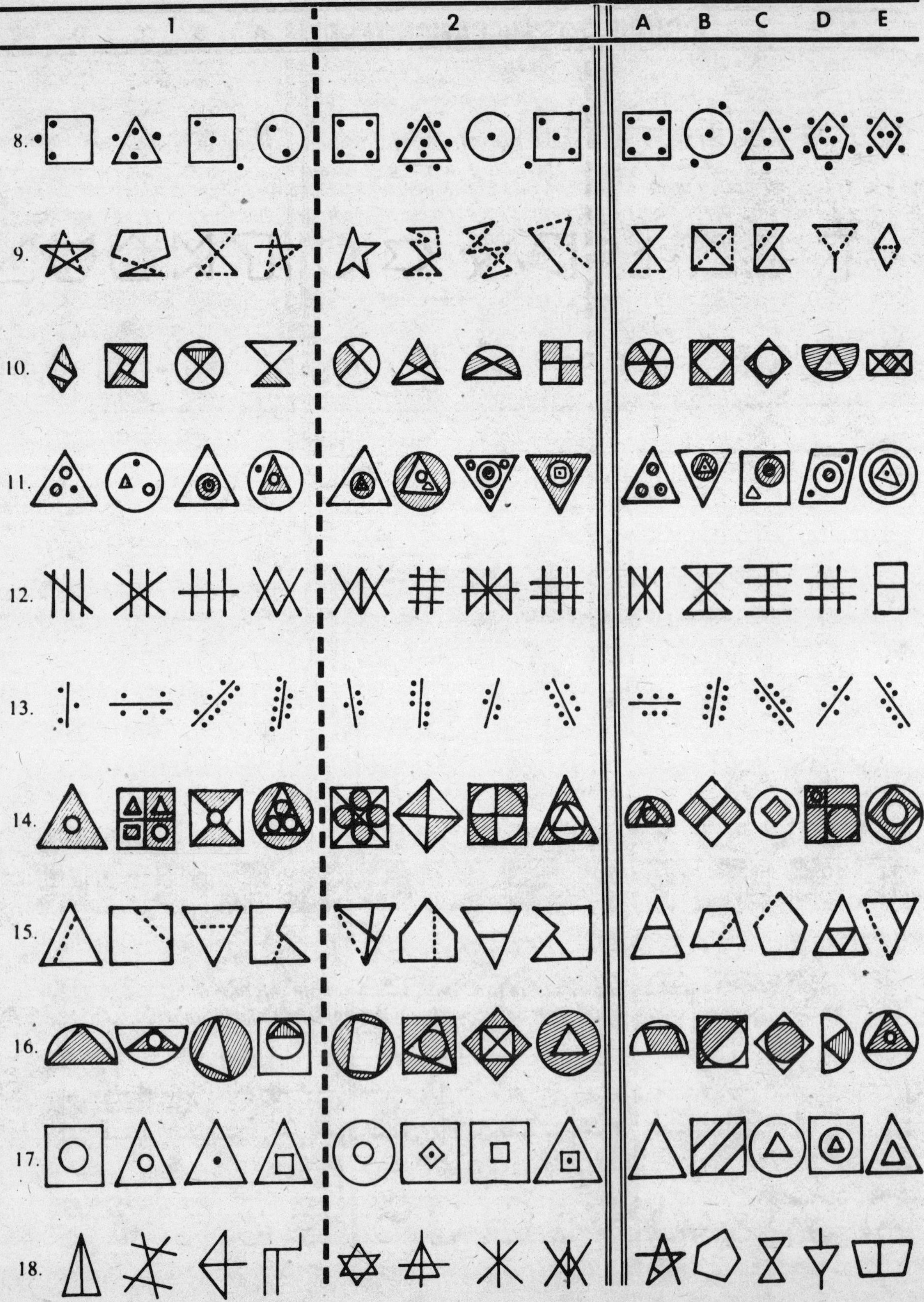
1
2
A B C D E
8.
9.
10.
11.
12.
13.
14.
15.
16.
17.
18.

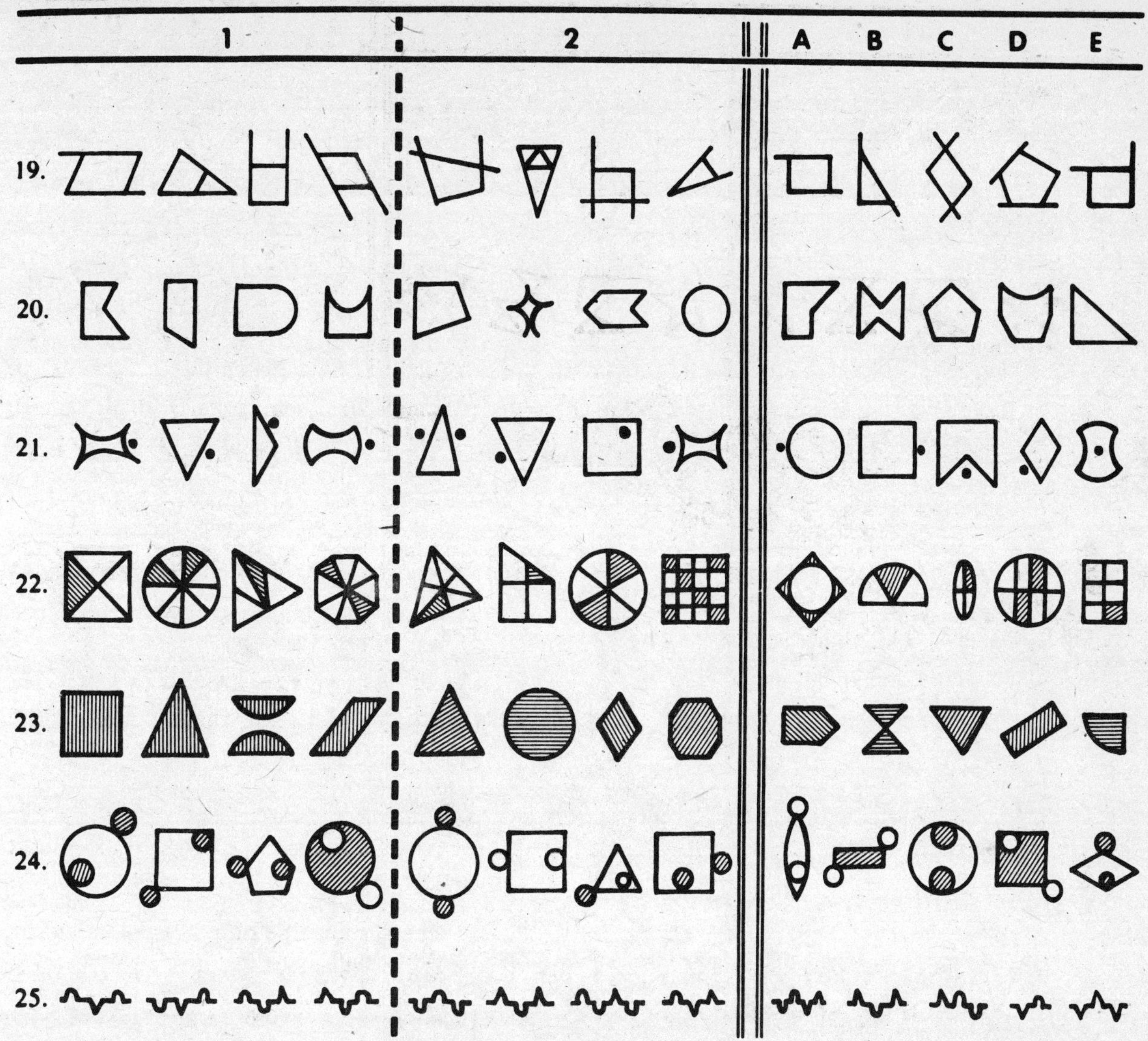

END OF SECTION

If you finish before the allotted time is up, work on this part only. When time is up, proceed directly to the next part and do not return to this part.

FIGURE CLASSIFICATION

EXPLANATION OF ANSWERS

Every figure in Group I, but no figure in Group II...

1. **(D)**...includes an upward angle made by a solid line and adotted line.
2. **(A)**...has the dot on the right side when the V is rotated clockwise.
3. **(D)**...has three different figures, one inside the other without touching.
4. **(B)**...has four white regions, two shaded ones, two black ones.
5. **(C)**...has an equal number of white and/or black dots on either side of the line.
6. **(A)**...has three horizontal lines.
7. **(E)**...has two lines attached inside and one line outside.
8. **(E)**...has two two dots inside the figure.
9. **(B)**...has a dotted line crossing over a solid line.
10. **(B)**...includes at least one shaded triangle.
11. **(E)**...consists of a triangle, two circles, and a dot.
12. **(D)**...has four lines.
13. **(C)**...has an odd number of dots.
14. **(E)**...contains at least one empty white circle.
15. **(B)**...is a solid figure with one triangular piece cut off by a dotted line.
16. **(B)**...includes a semicircle (with its diameter) and a triangle.
17. **(C)**...has a figure, inside of which is one different type of figure (consider a dot a figure).
18. **(C)**...can be drawn with only four straight lines.
19. **(A)**...is a quadrilateral with only two opposite sides extended.
20. **(A)**...includes three sides of a rectangle.
21. **(B)**...has only one dot which is to the right of the main figure.
22. **(C)**...is one-quarter shaded in area.
23. **(D)**...has vertical shading.
24. **(D)**...has one circle inside, and one outside attached at opposite ends of the main figure; circles must be of a color different from the main figure.
25. **(C)**...has two curved humps and one pointed one.

SCORE 1	SCORE 2	SCORE 3
.... %	.... %	.... %
NO. CORRECT	NO. CORRECT	NO. CORRECT
NO. OF QUESTIONS ON THIS TEST	NO. OF QUESTIONS ON THIS TEST	NO. OF QUESTIONS ON THIS TEST

Part VI

How To Become An Air Traffic Control Specialist

COMPETITIVE EXAMINING SYSTEM

The U. S. Civil Service Commission operates Area Offices and over 100 Federal Job Information and Testing Centers throughout the country. These offices provide complete one-stop information service on filing procedures and employment opportunities in the Federal service. Toll-free WATTS telephone service is provided within each state.

Area Offices also announce and conduct examinations, direct and coordinate recruiting activities, and evaluate and refer eligible to employing agencies in their geographic areas. Basically, they serve as the liason between the public and Federal employers.

How to Apply for a Federal Job

The Federal Government is the nation's largest employer with almost three million civilian employees working in hundreds of different jobs. The first step in applying for a Federal job is to decide what kind of position you are interested in and qualified for. The people at the FEDERAL JOB INFORMATION CENTERS can give you information on what jobs are available and what qualifications are required.

The Civil Service Commission (CSC) examines applicants to determine the person best qualified for each position. An examination consists of a review of the applicant's work experience, education, training and sometimes, but not always, a written test. For example, scientists, engineers, and trades workers are rated by exams which do not require written tests. The Professional and Administrative Career Exam (PACE) which covers over 200 different jobs, requires a written test. Stenos and typists take a written test of clerical ability and then either demonstrate typing and shorthand skills or present proof of proficiency.

After you have completed the examination process, you will be advised of the status of your application by an acknowledgment letter or by a Notice of Rating which may contain a numerical rating. If you are rated eligible, it means that you have met the minimum general qualifications, and your name has been added to the list of candidates maintained by the Civil Service Commission. When an agency decides to hire a new employee, CSC sends the agency the names of candidates selected from those on the list at the time who meet the specific requirements of the job to be filled. The agency may select one of the top three candidates for each job. The names of people not selected are returned to the Commission for reconsideration when other vacancies occur. Your chances for employment depend on:

1. How well you rated in comparison to others.

2. How many vacancies there are.

3. How many applicants there are.

4. Where you are willing to work.

5. The salary you will accept. (Highest paying jobs are often filled by promotion).

Steps to a Government Career

You should begin the application process two or three months before graduation since your qualification brief must be reviewed, the test (if one is required) must be taken and scored, and in some cases, your references, teachers, and former supervisors contacted before your eligibility is established.

Step 1 - Find Out About Career Opportunities

Obtain a copy of the most current ANNOUNCEMENT which covers the position in which you are interested from your college placement office or the nearest FJITC. Carefully review the announcement to determine if you meet the experience and/or education requirements.

Step 2 - Submit Your Application

If you qualify for a position, obtain and complete the application forms specified in the announcement and mail to the designated address, prior to any deadlines listed.

Step 3 - Take the Test

If a written test is required, you may select any of the testing points listed in the announcement. You will be given instructions on when and where to report for the test. When a written test is not required, your application will be rated on your experience, education, and other pertinent information.

Step 4 - Notification of Results

When your application is evaluated, you will be notified whether you have been rated as eligible or ineligible for the positions covered by the announcement or whether your application will be held and rated at a later time for a specific vacancy. If you receive an eligible notice, your name is entered on the list of eligibles in rank order by score.

MEASURING YOURSELF AGAINST THE JOB

Written Test

Unless you have had experience in Air Traffic Control or directly related work, you will have to take a written test. Sample questions of the type found on the test, which takes about 2 1/2 hours, are included in this book. If you have had previous experience, you do not have to take the written test. You may apply for grade GS-9.

Rating

Your qualifications for the job will be rated on the basis of 100, with a minimum score of 70 necessary for you to be rated eligible.

For GS-5, ratings will be based on the written test score.
For GS-7, ratings will be based on the written test and your experience, education and training in relation to the requirements of the job.
For GS-9, ratings will be based on an evaluation of the kind, amount, and pertinence of qualifying Air Traffic Control experience, education and training.

General experience is progressively responsible work which demonstrates your potential for learning and performing Air Traffic Control work. The work could be administrative, technical or other types of employment. You may substitute education for experience, up to four years of college for three years of experience.

Specialized experience is experience in military or civilian Air Traffic Control or comparable experience (for example, military activities involving direct control of aircraft and missiles) which shows that you have the knowledge, skills and abilities required to perform Air Traffic Control work at the grade level you're applying for.

Interview. As in the case with any employment, you will be asked to report for an interview. This is critically important in the hiring process.

Physical exam. Before you may be appointed, you must pass a rigid physical examination which will be made by a medical examiner designated by and paid for by the government. A detailed list of medical restrictions may be obtained from FAA regional offices.

Still a student? If you are a student or graduate student, you may be offered a job if you expect to complete your course work within 9 months of filing your application. The work must actually be completed before you start work.

Working for the USA, a pamphlet containing general information about Federal employment, is available at most Federal Job Information Centers, and most large Post Offices. Ask for Pamphlet 4.

QUALIFICATIONS BY GRADE LEVEL

GS 5	Pass Written Test	Plus	3 yrs. general experience or 4 yrs. of college or combination of both

GS 7	Pass Written Test	Plus	3 yrs. general experience or 4 yrs. of college or combination of both and 1 yr. of specialized experience or 1 yr. graduate work or superior academic achievement*
	OR		
	Pass Written Test With Very High Score	Plus	3 yrs. general experience or 4 yrs. of college or combination of both
	OR		
	Pass Written Test	Plus	ONE OF THE FOLLOWING: civilian or military rating in ATC involving active control of air traffic in center or terminal; past or present FAA air carrier dispatcher certificate; past or present instrument flight rating; past or present FAA navigator/Bombardier; past or present co-pilot or pilot rating or equivalent military rating with 350 hours of flight time; past or present rating as an Aerospace Defense Command Intercept Director.
GS 9	(No Written Test)		3 yrs. general experience or 4 years of college and 2 yrs. specialized experience or 1 yr. specialized experience combined with 1 yr. graduate work

*Superior Academic Achievement means:

1) standing in upper third of class in college or university or major subdivision;
2) average of 2.90 or better on a 4.0 scale (or equivalent) for all courses completed (a) up to the time of application or (b) during last 2 undergraduate years;
3) election to one of the national honorary societies (other than freshman societies) which meet the minimum requirement of the Association of College Honor Societies;
4) 600 on an Advanced Test of the Graduate Record Examination or 600 or better on an area test administered prior to October 1, 1969.

PREPARING FORM SF 171

Standard Form 171 is designed to place before appointing officials sufficient information concerning a candidate's background and experience to permit an intelligent evaluation of his abilities. It has, like any other general form, its limitations. The intelligent applicant can remedy these deficiencies, however, and make a modest but highly useful personal representative of his 171.

There are several general rules which should be observed when filling out the application form. Of these, four are most important:

A. Be honest.

B. Be specific.

C. Be neat.

D. Use good judgment.

Be Honest

Not only is honesty a high moral precept, but it is also the test of all engineering practices. The surest way to discredit yourself in the eyes of a possible employer is to enlarge upon or embroider the truth, and don't think that "forgetfulness" is any excuse. Inaccuracy is as useless a habit as dishonesty and there is no place in this government for people who do not know or cannot remember. Practiced application examiners are sensitive to all embroideries of fact and the lives of many people have been changed because they saw fit to claim, either directly or by inference, more than their records warranted. There is no better guide to a person's integrity than his accuracy in the statement of his background and experience. The fact that he may be technically correct means very little if he has permitted an unwarranted implication to be drawn. Don't be guilty of mis-, mal-, or over-statement. False statement anywhere on the 171 is, of course, punishable by law.

Be Specific

Be adequate but also be specific. This is not a contradiction in terms. Most people object, with good reason, to wading through long-winded statements of experience when shorter ones would have done as well. The boxes under Item 20 are adequate for a general statement of the duties of most jobs. They give the applicant an opportunity to summarize his work. He is not expected to include his job sheet in the blank which is provided. Nor is he expected to write a monograph on his profession, but by all means attach supplemental statements if necessary to fully describe your duties or education.

Remember that other people have to read what you write. Make their task as easy and as pleasant for them as you can; since after all, you are the person who has the most to gain.

Be Neat

There are few better indications of a person's work habits than the neatness of his application. It is not necessary that the application be typewritten, although this unquestionably helps. Most people do not object to carbon copies if they are legible. The large number of uses of the 171 today makes it fairly mandatory that some sort of duplication be used. Legible carbon copies are better received than photostats. Mimeographed applications are not recommended since there is a tendency on the part of many people to feel that you are making a wholesale circularization in the hope that one "feeler" may click. If you are applying for a job involving clerical work or typing, be sure that you have typed your application neatly with no strikeovers or misspelled words.

Be sure that your application contains no major ink blots, cigarette burns, stains or dirt from pocket wear and tear. There is no excuse for slovenliness. You wouldn't hire a cook who used dirty dishes. Most people will not hire an applicant with a dirty 171.

Use Good Judgment

Think of the man who will read your application. Do not become so involved in yourself that you forget him. He will probably not be interested in you if you are a confirmed egotist who has written "I did this" and "I did that" in endless detail.

Don't be flippant. A sober, thoughtful application is a dozen times better than a "wise" one. For every candidate who has the deftness of touch of clever phraseology, there are forty who think they have--and fall flat on their faces because of it. And he certainly will not want you if you are so verbose that you have submitted an encyclopedia, nicely tabbed and footnoted, when a couple of pages would have said everything worth saying. Sheer bulk will get you nowhere these days.

Your application is your best foot forward. It speaks for you when you can't be there. Try to realize that it must say exactly what you intend it to say and that appointing officers cannot fill the gaps you have left, or overlook the claims you have made. No substitute has yet been found for good judgment and the chances are you won't find one either.

ITEM BY ITEM

What Form Should you Use?

Standard Form 171 has been revised on several different occasions. The latest revision is dated September 1971, U. S. Civil Service Commission. In submitting your qualifications, you should attempt to obtain the latest possible revision. Application forms are available at Post Offices and Government Personnel Offices.

Suggestions for Filling out Standard Form 171

Items 1A through D: Standard Form 171 has many purposes, one of which is, of course, application for Civil Service Examinations. Question #1 is primarily for this type of applicant. You are expected to provide the name of the examination you want to take and, if you know it, the announcement number, as Engineer Technician, GS-5 through GS-12 Announcement Circular 424, the type of option, such as Electronic Engineer; and the place of employment for which you are applying. In some instances, the latter will be specified on the examination; in others, only general areas will be indicated.

Since you are applying directly to a government agency, rather than to the Civil Service Commission, it is not as important that Question #1 be answered in detail. If you have a specific position or type of position in mind, you should so indicate. The applicant who knows what he wants is always more highly regarded than the scatter-gun enthusiast.

Items 2 through 9: The only question here which may give you trouble is legal or voting residence. Persons with veteran's preference are not required to prove their residence, but they are asked to indicate it for statistical purposes. If you do not have veteran's preference, it is important that you answer this question, as your certification to a position in the District of Columbia depends in part upon the quota for the state in which you reside. Roughly speaking, legal residence is the place where you are actually domiciled, or a fixed permanent residence to which you intend to return. Voting residence is established if you have been accepted as a voter for one year prior to the closing date of the Civil Service examination for which you are applying, and the Commission holds that as far as Civil Service is concerned when voting residence is established, legal residence is thereby also established.

Item 11: Do not omit either of the elements of this question. It is important to appointing officers to know how long you have been in your present grade since most promotions cannot be made unless a person has worked a stated period of time at the next lower level.

Item 15: Whether, or how, you answer Item 15 is optional. Remember: no one will presume anything which you have not specifically stated, and your failure to indicate that you would accept employment of less than six months in duration is the best reason in the world for passing over you if a five-month job becomes vacant. Similarly, you will not be considered for a lower salary figure than you indicate under 13.

The latter is one of the most disputed points of the 171. Many candidates hesitate to name the lowest figure they would accept since they feel that many other considerations than salary enter such a determination.

These involve place of employment, type of work, hours, etc. Others feel that by naming a figure lower than they are now receiving they are revealing "bargaining" information which is important to them in such matters as within-grade salary increases. Many list the lowest grade they would accept, leaving the several hundred dollars variance between grades for later discussion. Others simply write in the word "open" in the blank. What you may wish to do will depend on your personal situation. The Civil Service Commission will not rate you for examinations for grades below the figure indicated but will consider you for all you are qualified for above. Most government personnel technicians can spot a candidate who is "window shopping" or one who is more interested in the promotion than in the work, and "too tough" an attitude here on the part of the applicant undoubtedly contributes to this impression. So, USE YOUR BEST JUDGMENT IN ANSWERING Item 15.

Aiming Your Application

Some people aim their applications at the specific job or type of work for which they are applying. This has definite merit in that it gives the applicant an opportunity to "point up" certain types of experience rather than other types which are less useful. Many even go so far as to prepare a different Form 171 for each type of work they can do.

Like all systems, this one has its disadvantages. Naturally, a "pointed" application in the employee's official file is likely to limit his consideration for other types of positions which may be available.

Here are some general guidelines to follow:

Read the General Instructions carefully. You won't be wasting your time.

You are asked to provide the name and title of your immediate supervisor in order that your work under him may be checked, if desired, by the appointing officials. If your old supervisor is no longer with the organization, and you know his present address, include it.

If, while with the same organization you change jobs, use a separate box for each job. The time you think you save in lumping several jobs together will be spent, if you are lucky, in revising the form later to show the required information; or in sitting out the old job waiting for the offer which never comes.

Don't overlook your "reason for desiring to change employment" and make sure it's the right one. Doubletalk answers such as "changed jobs" or "more money" particularly when you move to a job making less, are just that--doubletalk. You or someone else will be asked for more specific reasons; so include the right ones at the start.

Your description of your work would not, if you are now with the Federal Government, be a rewrite of your job sheet. Classification words and phrases are technical ones and designed for a purpose--which is not job applications. Attempt to describe your work in the space provided. If you feel that it is desirable or necessary, you can add supplementary material providing you note in the appropriate box that it exists and where it may be found. Be orderly about it. The attached material, done preferably on white bond, should be securely fastened to the center of the application. Each page should be headed with your name and address, and should be numbered at the bottom since it is difficult to find page numbers when they are hidden in the binding. A separate page should be used for the supplement to each box on the Form 171.

Employment Experience

The following outline and information should be followed in describing any previous technician experience:

1. Name of Employer and Dates of Employment or Job Number on Form 171.

2. Organization Chart (may be brief penciled sketch) showing your position in organization, including number and kind of subordinate positions and positions above yours.

3. Give dates of promotions or changes in assignment, if any.

4. Furnish breakdowns for each position (consider duties performed after promotion or change in assignments as a new position if duties performed were more responsible or different as follows:

   a. Number of hours a week or percentage of time devoted to each kind of engineering (see optional branches listed at head of announcement) if more than one optional branch of engineering technology was involved.

   b. List the engineering technology function or functions performed by you as design, specification writing, surveying, estimating, etc., giving best estimate or number of hours a week devoted to each function or percentage of time.

   c. List engineering technology techniques used by you in solving problems including highest level of mathematics required for the solution of your engineering technology problems.

   d. Give brief description of your work giving some idea of size of project in terms of cost, size of building, kind of machines, equipment you worked with, difficulty of work, unusual problems encountered and methods of solving them. For example:

   "I designed a new rhombic antenna for the _____ transmitter site in connection with antenna modifications that were necessary for conversion of radio telegraph circuits to radio teletype. The Regional Office requested that station maintenance personnel design and install this new rhombic as we originally recommended in our plans for antenna modifications.

"My first step in designing the rhombic antenna was to determine what antenna gain would be required to produce a satisfactory radio field intensity at the receiving point for this circuit with the transmitter power and frequencies available. This was done by estimating the minimum radio field intensity needed to allow an intelligible signal for radio teletype service in the presence of radio noise at the receiving point 24 hours a day and 365 days per year. I made this by referring to "world radio noise distribution charts" and "minimum radio field intensity charts" contained in the Bureau of Standards Circular 462 "Ionospheric Radio Propagation." These charts are of a general nature showing hourly and seasonal variations for different radio frequencies making it necessary to analyze each chart carefully in applying it to this design problem. Having estimated the minimum radio field intensity required at the receiving point, I calculated the required gain factor for the transmitting antenna by applying the minimum field intensity figure, absorption factor, noise factor, transmission frequencies and transmitter power to field intensity charts contained in Circular 462. These charts are also of a general nature and require analyzing for hourly and seasonal variations to insure the best possible circuit at all times. The factor required for this antenna was _____ db.

"Having determined the antenna gain required, next I calculated the optimum vertical path angle for this circuit based on the frequency channels available. This was done by a graphical solution using the procedure contained in Circular 462. In working out this solution I selected median values for the various ionospheric layer minimum heights from CRPL (Central Radio Propagation Laboratory) charts and then graphically determined the various departure angles by applying these median layer heights to transmission curves. From these path angles I calculated the optimum angle for this particular circuit by analyzing the hourly and seasonal variations in properties of the ionosphere such as layer heights, layer density, layer thickness, layer absorption, and other ionospheric disturbances for this transmission path. Having now calculated the optimum path angle and the antenna gain required, I computed the necessary physical dimensions of the rhombic antenna such as the height, leg lengths and tilt angle by using a rhombic antenna design chart contained in the handbook "Reference Data for Radio Engineers." This design chart is used by applying certain known parameters such as vertical path angle, transmitting frequency and antenna gain and then reading directly from the chart physical dimensions of the rhombic antenna. However, in designing a rhombic antenna system for simultaneous multifrequency operation (necessary to provide a continuous circuit uninterrupted by hourly and seasonal variations in the ionosphere), it was necessary that I engineer an optimum design that would provide satisfactory gain and vertical path angle for all transmitting frequencies. I accomplished this by engineering several designs and evaluating each design for quality of circuit operation, taking into account the many variations in propagation conditions attendent to simultaneous multi-frequency operation. The optimum path angle was _____ degrees for this antenna. The physical dimensions for this antenna were height _____ feet, leg length _____ feet and tilt angle _____ degrees.

"I designed a terminating impedance unit for the rhombic antenna using the procedure contained in the text "Rhombic Antenna Design" by Harper. This was done by reviewing the theory of terminating impedance for rhombic antennas and then selecting a value that would give the most uniform terminal impedance at the operating frequencies available. I made this selection by considering the theory involved and by using empirical tables contained in Harper's text. The terminating impedance required was _____ ohms.

"I designed the transmission line for connecting the antenna to the transmitter output by reviewing the theory of transmission lines for rhombic antennas given in Harper's text. I selected a suitable characteristic impedance for the transmitter and applying the basic theory involved. The physical dimensions, such as wire size, type and spacing, were determined by using design formulas and charts contained in "Radio Data for Radio Engineers."

<u>Salary and earnings</u> are useful clues in an evaluation of your work. Do not omit them. Your earnings should be "net". Do not try to show "gross" in instances where you operate your own business just to impress people. This is covered under Rule 1 on Page 1 and may be an example of the type of inference that does you more harm than good. The amount you declare for income tax purposes is the amount you should show on Form 171.

If there are insufficient boxes under Item 20 for the jobs you have held, you may use the prepared Continuation Sheet for this purpose (Form 171A). If it is not available, white bond is adequate providing you supply the same information required in the original 171.

Item 21: Any special knowledge or qualifications pertinent to the position which cannot be described adequately in the space provided can be continued on the next page or on a supplemental sheet. You should indicate your professional engineering technician registration here, i.e., "Engineer-in-Training, State of Colorado, #1234, October 1974" or, "Registered Engineer, State of Colorado, #1234, October 1974." Do not clutter your application with a lot of needless material. Keep your application pertinent to the general type position for which you are applying.

Item 22: Education--Highest Grade Completed, refers to years of grade school and high school combined. If you finished eight grades of primary school and four years of high school, you should write figure "12" in the space provided.

Under college education, do not fail to indicate your major subject or "specialty", e.g., engineering. Indicate also the number of semester hours for which you received credit. This does not mean the number of hours spent in classroom. If your college used some other system of establishing credits than semester hours, so indicate and explain.

Do not overlook your chief undergraduate and graduate college subjects if you did college work. A space is provided for each.

If you claim correspondence school credit, indicate it as such. Also indicate how many courses you took and completed.

Item 25: This is probably the question that applicants most frequently muff. Item 25 asks for three references, other than supervisors shown under Item 20, "who have definite knowledge of your qualifications and fitness for the position for which you are applying". Despite this admonition, many applicants continue to give character references who have no particular knowledge of their special abilities. There is no objection to naming your family doctor, for example, providing he is well informed concerning, and in a position to judge accurately, your professional ability. It does not add materially to your chances because he can report you are healthy or sociable.

Give accurate addresses. It matters not that John Doe will put in a substantial word in your behalf if all you know about him is that he lives in Southern, Indiana. Remember also that "United States Army" or "Navy Department" are not adequate addresses.

Give the names of persons who are, as far as possible, easily accessible by telephone to the appointing officials. A telephone call or a personal visit is always more satisfactory to the appointing officers than a letter, but people in San Francisco or Seattle cannot be called from Washington, D. C., without running up heavy long distance charges. So, if these are the best references you can provide, your appointment will have to wait until the mail gets through.

Don't give the names of persons as high in public life or so inaccessible that it is difficult to reach them. The backing of a President of the United States is a tribute to anyone, but few personnel officers can get the Chief Executive on the telephone these busy days. Besides, the inclusion of his name is likely to smack of ostentation on your part.

Items 26 through 36: Most of these questions relate to your legal qualifications (i.e., loyalty, moral turpitude) as distinct from your professional or technical qualifications for Federal employment. They should be read and answered with great care, as an X in the wrong box might bar you from any consideration.

Some Don'ts

Don't include your picture. It's been years since a photograph was required.

Don't indicate your religion either directly or indirectly. This is a practice--and a bad one--of some applicants who prepare printed personal history statements. People are more interested in what you can do than how you worship.

Don't include material you don't want to lose. If your paper gets the circulation you hope it will, a lot of people will be handling it, and the chances of it being misplaced increase thereby. Have all important documents photostated and, if necessary, attach the photostat.

Don't expect to get your application back. You may, but dont' count on it. So, KEEP A COPY. Dates and rates of pay of earlier employment you will find will be harder and harder to recall with each succeeding year. Keep a record of all your applications. Not only will it help you in making out the new ones, but it will keep you from any misstatements which faulty memory might otherwise cause.

Finally: Compare your application, item by item, with the suggestions in this paper. Have you overlooked anything? Have you said what you intended to say? Have you been to the best of your ability, accurate?

Don't make the mistake of thinking that you can do a slipshod job because no one will read the blank-blank thing anyway. That's where you'll be wrong--and you'll probably never know the difference. Applications are read and, what is more, studied. You'll save yourself grief by doing a good job the first time out.

STANDARD FORM 171

PERSONAL QUALIFICATIONS STATEMENT

IMPORTANT

READ THE FOLLOWING INSTRUCTIONS CAREFULLY BEFORE FILLING OUT YOUR STATEMENT

All requested information must be furnished. The information you give will be used to determine your qualifications for employment.

It is IMPORTANT that you answer all questions on your Statement *fully* and *accurately;* failure to do so may delay its consideration and could mean loss of employment opportunities.

If an item does not apply to you, or if there is no information to be given, please write in the letters "N.A." for Not Applicable.

GENERAL INSTRUCTIONS

- Use typewriter if available. Otherwise, write legibly or print clearly in dark ink.
- If you are applying for a specific civil service examination, follow exactly the directions in the examination announcement as well as the instructions for filling out this form.
- For a written examination, the admission card tells you what to do with this Statement.
- If the examination involves no written test, mail this Statement to the office named in the examination announcement. Be sure to mail to the same office any other forms required in the announcement.
- Notify the office with which you file this Statement of any change in your name or address.

INSTRUCTION RELATING TO SPECIFIC ITEMS

ITEM 13. LOWEST GRADE OR SALARY

- Enter the lowest grade OR the lowest salary you will accept. You will not be considered for any lower grade or salary; you *will* be considered for higher grades or salary. If you enter grade, do not enter salary.

ITEM 19. ACTIVE MILITARY SERVICE AND VETERAN PREFERENCE

- Five-point preference is granted to veterans if they are honorably separated from the armed forces; (a) after active duty during the periods April 6, 1917, to July 2, 1921, or December 7, 1941, to July 1, 1955; (b) after more than 180 consecutive days of active duty after January 31, 1955 (not counting service under an initial period of active duty for training under the "6-month" Reserve or National Guard programs); or (c) after service in a campaign for which a campaign badge has been authorized.
- If you claim five-point preference, you are not required to furnish records to support your claim until the time of appointment.
- Ten-point preference is granted in some cases to disabled veterans, including veterans awarded the Purple Heart, to widows of veterans, to wives of disabled veterans, and to mothers of deceased or disabled veterans. See Standard Form 15, Claim for 10-Point Veteran Preference.
- If you claim ten-point preference, complete Standard Form 15 and attach it, together with the proof called for in that form, to this Statement.

ITEM 20. EXPERIENCE

- Take time to fill in these experience blocks carefully and completely. Your qualifications rating depends in a large part on your experience and employment history. *Failure to give complete details may delay consideration of your Statement.* Answers given in this item may be verified with former employers.
- When the block contains experience in more than one type of work (examples: carpentry and painting, or personnel and budget) estimate and indicate the approximate percentage of time spent in each type of work. Place these percentages in parentheses at the end of the description of the duties.

PLEASE READ ADDITIONAL INSTRUCTIONS ON BACK OF THIS SHEET

ITEM 20. EXPERIENCE—(Continued)

- *Block 1*—Describe your present position in this block. Indicate in this block if you are now unemployed or if you have never been employed.
- *Blocks 2 and 3*—Describe in Block 2 the position you held just before your present position, and continue to work backwards using Block 3.
- *Need for additional blocks*—If you need more experience blocks, use Standard Form 171-A, Continuation Sheet, or a plain piece of paper. If you use plain paper, each experience block must contain all of the information requested in Item 20 of the printed Statement. If there is not enough space in any of the experience blocks to describe the positions held, continue the description on a plain piece of paper. Identify each plain sheet at the top by showing your name, birth date, examination or position title, and the block under Item 20 from which the description is continued. Attach these supplemental sheets to the top of page 3 at place marked, "Attach Supplemental Sheets or Forms Here."
- *Description of duties, responsibilities, and accomplishments*—Describe each job briefly, including required skills and abilities. Include description of any specialties and special assignments; your authority and responsibility; your relationships to others; accomplishments; and any other factors which help describe the job.
- *General Information*—If supervision over other employees was one of your duties, be sure to indicate the number and kind (and grades, if Federal Government) of employees supervised by you, and explain your duties as a supervisor under description of duties.
- Indicate in each block of Item 20 the name under which you were employed if it was different from the name in Item 4 of this Statement. Show former name in parentheses after "Description of duties and accomplishments in your work."
- Use separate blocks if your duties, responsibilities, or salary level changed materially while working for the same employer. Treat each such change as a separate position.
- Include your military or merchant marine service in separate blocks in its proper order and describe major duty assignments.
- Experience acquired more than 15 years ago may be summarized in one block if it is not applicable to the type of position applied for.
- Account for periods of unemployment in separate blocks in order.
- Indicate estimated number of hours worked per week in the space provided if you were on part-time work.
- Section 3311 of title 5, United States Code, provides that in examinations in which experience is a factor, credit will be granted for any pertinent religious, civic, welfare, service, and organizational activity which you have performed either with or without compensation. You *may*, if you wish, report such experience at the end of your employment history if you feel that it represents qualifying experience for the position(s) for which you are applying. Show actual time spent in such activity.

ITEMS 27 AND 28. MEMBERSHIP IN ORGANIZATIONS

- Answer these questions carefully. Admitted past membership and participation in an organization of the type to which this question refers does not by itself disqualify you for Government employment. Consideration will be given to the nature of the organization, the extent of your participation, and any other relevant facts and circumstances.

ITEMS 34 AND 35. RELATIVES EMPLOYED BY THE UNITED STATES GOVERNMENT

- A Federal official (civilian or military) may not appoint any of his relatives or recommend them for appointment in his agency, and a relative who is appointed in violation of this restriction can not be paid. Thus it is necessary to have information about your relatives who are working for the Government. In listing relative(s) in answer to question 34 include: father, mother, son, daughter, brother, sister, uncle, aunt, first cousin, nephew, niece, husband, wife, father-in-law, mother-in-law, son-in-law, daughter-in-law, brother-in-law, sister-in-law, stepfather, stepmother, stepson, stepdaughter, stepbrother, stepsister, half brother, and half sister.
- Question 35 is needed because of restrictions in making a career or career-conditional appointment in the competitive service when a person is not entitled to veteran preference and two or more members of his family are already serving in the competitive service under a career or career-conditional appointment.

CERTIFICATION

- Be careful that you have answered all questions on your Statement correctly and considered all statements fully so that your eligibility can be decided on all the facts. Read the certification carefully before you sign and date your Statement.
- Sign your name in ink.
- Use one given name, initial or initials, and surname.

PLEASE DETACH THIS INSTRUCTION SHEET BEFORE SUBMITTING YOUR STATEMENT

STANDARD FORM 171

PERSONAL QUALIFICATIONS STATEMENT

Office of Management and Budget
Approved 50-RO387

1A. Kind of position *(job)* you are filing for *(or title of announcement)*

B. Announcement No.

C. Options for which you wish to be considered *(if listed in announcement)*

D. Primary place(s) you wish to be employed

2. Home phone *(including Area Code)*

3. Office phone *(including Area Code)*

4. Name *(Last) (First) (Middle) (Maiden, if any)* ☐ Mr. ☐ Miss ☐ Mrs.
and Address *(Number, Street, City, State and ZIP Code)*

5. Legal or voting residence *(State)*

6. Height without shoes
_____ Feet _____ Inches

7. Weight

8. Birthplace *(City and State, or foreign country)*

9. Birth date *(Month, day, year)*

10. Social Security Account Number

11. If you have ever been employed by the Federal Government as a civilian, give your last classification series, grade, and job title.

Dates of service in that grade
From To

12. If you are currently on a list of eligibles for appointment to a Federal position, give the name of the announcement, the name of the office maintaining the list, the date on your notice of rating, and your rating.

13. Lowest pay or grade you will accept

PAY		GRADE
$ per	OR	

14. When will you be available?

DO NOT WRITE IN THIS BLOCK
FOR USE OF EXAMINING OFFICE ONLY

	Material	Entered Register:
☐ Appor.	☐ Submitted	
☐ Nonappor.	☐ Returned	

Notations:

Form Reviewed:

Form Approved:

Option	Grade	Earned Rating	Preference	Aug. Rating
			☐ 5 points *(Tent.)*	
			☐ 10 Points Comp.Dis.	
			☐ Other 10 Points	
			☐ Disal.	
			☐ Being Investi-gated	
Initials and Date				

ANNOUNCEMENT NO.

STATEMENT NO.

THIS SPACE FOR USE OF APPOINTING OFFICER ONLY
Preference has been verified through proof that the separation was under honorable conditions, and other proof as required.

☐ 5-Pt. ☐ 10-Pt. Comp. Disab. ☐ 10-Pt. Other

Signature and Title

Agency | Date

☐ Refer for medical action

15. Will you accept temporary employment for:
(Acceptance or refusal of temporary employment will not affect your consideration for other appointments.)

	YES	NO
1 month or less?		
1 to 4 months?		
4 to 12 months?		

16. Where will you accept a job?

	YES	NO
Washington, D.C.		
Any place in the United States.		
Outside of the United States.		
Only in *(specify)*:		

17. Will you accept less than full time work?
(Less than 40 hours per week) ☐ Yes ☐ No

18. Are you willing to travel? *(Check one)*

NO	SOME	OFTEN

19. VETERAN PREFERENCE. Answer all parts. If a part does not apply to you, answer "No." (Yes / No)

A. Have you ever served on active duty in the United States military service? *(Exclude tours of active duty for training as a reservist or Guardsman.)*

B. Have you ever been discharged from the armed services under other than honorable conditions? (You may omit any such discharge changed to honorable by a Discharge Review Board or similar authority.) . . . .
If "Yes," give details in Item 37.

C. Do you claim 5-point preference based on active duty in the armed forces? . . . .
If "Yes," you will be required to furnish records to support your claim at the time you are appointed.

D. Do you claim 10-point preference? . . . .
If "Yes," check type of preference claimed and complete and attach Standard Form 15. "Claim for 10-point Veteran Preference," together with the proof called for in that form
TYPE: ☐ Compensable disability ☐ Disability ☐ Wife ☐ Widow ☐ Mother

E. List Dates, Branch, and Serial or Service Number of All Active Service *(Enter "N/A" if not applicable)*

From	To	Branch of Service	Serial or Service Number

THE FEDERAL GOVERNMENT IS AN EQUAL OPPORTUNITY EMPLOYER

Standard Form 171
September 1971 U.S. Civil Service Commission
171-104

Page 1

PLEASE BE SURE TO READ ATTACHED INSTRUCTIONS BEFORE COMPLETING ITEM 20

20. EXPERIENCE *(Start with your PRESENT position and work back. Account for periods of unemployment in separate blocks in order.)*

May inquiry be made of your present employer regarding your character, qualifications, and record of employment?.................... ☐ Yes ☐ No
(A "No" will not affect your consideration for employment opportunities except for HEARING EXAMINER positions.)

1	Dates of employment *(month, year)* From To PRESENT TIME		Exact title of position		If Federal service, civilian or military grade
Salary or earnings Starting $ per Present $ per		Avg. hrs. per week	Place of employment City: State:	Number and kind of employees supervised	Kind of business or organization *(manufacturing, accounting, insurance, etc.)*
Name of immediate supervisor			Name of employer *(firm, organization, etc.)* and address *(including ZIP Code, if known)*		
Area Code and phone No. if known					
Reason for wanting to leave					
Description of duties, responsibilities, and accomplishments					
					For agency use *(skill codes, etc.)*

2	Dates of employment *(month, year)* From To		Exact title of position		If Federal service, civilian or military grade
Salary or earnings Starting $ per Final $ per		Avg. hrs. per week	Place of employment City: State:	Number and kind of employees supervised	Kind of business or organization *(manufacturing, accounting, insurance, etc.)*
Name of immediate supervisor			Name of employer *(firm, organization, etc.)* and address *(including ZIP Code, if known)*		
Area Code and phone No. if known					
Reason for leaving					
Description of duties, responsibilities, and accomplishments					
					For agency use *(skill codes, etc.)*

3	Dates of employment *(month, year)* From To		Exact title of position		If Federal service, civilian or military grade
Salary or earnings Starting $ per Final $ per		Avg. hrs. per week	Place of employment City: State:	Number and kind of employees supervised	Kind of business or organization *(manufacturing, accounting, insurance, etc.)*
Name of immediate supervisor			Name of employer *(firm, organization, etc.)* and address *(including ZIP Code, if known)*		
Area Code and phone No. if known					
Reason for leaving					
Description of duties, responsibilities, and accomplishments					
					For agency use *(skill codes, etc.)*

IF YOU NEED ADDITIONAL EXPERIENCE BLOCKS USE STANDARD FORM 171-A OR BLANK SHEETS SEE INSTRUCTION SHEET

ATTACH SUPPLEMENTAL SHEETS OR FORMS HERE

• ANSWER ALL QUESTIONS CORRECTLY AND FULLY

21 A. Special qualifications and skills *(skills with machines; patents or inventions; your most important publications (do not submit copies unless requested); your public speaking and publications experience; membership in professional or scientific societies; etc.)*

B. Kind of License or Certificate *(For example, pilot, registered nurse, lawyer, radio operator, C.P.A.; etc.)*	C. State or other licensing authority	D. Year of first license or certificate	E. Year of latest license or certificate	F. Approximate number of words per minute: Typing	Shorthand

22. A. Did you graduate from high school, or will you graduate within the next nine months?				B. Name and location *(city and State)* of last high school attended
YES	MONTH/YEAR	NO	HIGHEST GRADE COMPLETED	

C. Name and location *(city, State, and ZIP Code if known)* of college or university. *(If you expect to graduate within 9 months, give MONTH and year you expect degree.)*	Dates attended		Years Completed		No. of credits compl.		Type of degree *(B.A., etc.)*	Year of degree
	From	To	Day	Night	Semester hours	Quarter hours		

D. Chief undergraduate college subjects	No. of credits compl.		E. Chief graduate college subjects	No. of credits compl.	
	Semester hours	Quarter hours		Semester hours	Quarter hours

F. Major field of study at highest level of college work

G. Other schools or training *(for example, trade, vocational, armed forces, or business)*. Give for each the name and location *(city, State, and ZIP Code if known)* of school, dates attended, subjects studied, number of classroom hours of instruction per week, certificates, and any other pertinent data.

23. HONORS, AWARDS, AND FELLOWSHIPS RECEIVED

24. LANGUAGES OTHER THAN ENGLISH

List the languages and indicate your knowledge of each by placing "X" in proper columns	Reading			Speaking			Understanding			Writing		
	Excl	Good	Fair	Excl	Good	Fair	Excl	Good	Fair	Excl	Good	Fair

25. REFERENCES. List three persons who are NOT related to you and who have definite knowledge of your qualifications and fitness for the position for which you are applying. Do not repeat names of supervisors listed under Item 20, EXPERIENCE.

FULL NAME	PRESENT BUSINESS OR HOME ADDRESS *(Number, Street, City, State and ZIP Code)*	BUSINESS OR OCCUPATION

ANSWER ITEMS 26 THROUGH 36 BY PLACING AN "X" IN THE PROPER COLUMN	Yes	No
26. Are you a citizen of the United States? If "No," give country of which you are a citizen:		
Before answering these questions read Items 27 and 28 in the attached instructions. Are you now, or within the last ten years have you been, a member of:		
27. The Communist Party, U.S.A., or any subdivision of the Communist Party, U.S.A.?		
28. An organization that to your present knowledge seeks the overthrow of the constitutional form of government of the United States by force or violence or other unlawful means? *If your answer to Item 27 or 28 is "Yes," write your answers to the following questions in Item 37 or on a separate piece of paper: (A) The name of the organization? (B) The dates of your membership? (C) Your understanding of the aims and purposes of the organization at the time of your membership?*		
29. To insure that you are not placed in a position which might impair your health, or which might be a hazard to you or to others, we need information about the following: Do you have, or have you had, heart disease, a nervous breakdown, epilepsy, tuberculosis, or diabetes? *If your answer is "Yes," concerning any one of these, identify which one(s) and give details in Item 37.*		
30. Within the last five years have you been fired from any job for any reason?		
31. Within the last five years have you quit a job after being notified that you would be fired? *If your answer to 30 or 31 above is "Yes," give details in Item 37. Show the name and address (including ZIP Code) of employer, approximate date, and reasons in each case. This information should agree with your answers in Item 20, EXPERIENCE.*		
32. Have you ever been convicted of an offense against the law or forfeited collateral, or are you now under charges for any offense against the law? (You may omit: (1) traffic violations for which you paid a fine of $30.00 or less; and (2) any offense committed before your 21st birthday which was finally adjudicated in a juvenile court or under a Youth Offender law.)		
33. While in the military service were you ever convicted by general court-martial? *If your answer to 32 or 33 is "Yes," give details in Item 37. Show for each offense: (1) date; (2) charge; (3) place; (4) court; and (5) action taken.*		
34. Does the United States Government employ in a civilian capacity or as a member of the Armed Forces any relative of yours (by blood or marriage)? (See Items 34 and 35 in the attached instruction sheet.)		
35. Do you live with, or within the past 12 months have you lived with, any of these relatives who are employed in a civilian capacity? *If your answer to 34 is "Yes," give in Item 37 for such relatives: (1) full name; (2) present address (including ZIP Code); (3) relationship; (4) department, agency, or branch of the Armed Forces. If your answer to 35 is "Yes," also give the kind of appointment held by the relative(s) you live with or have lived with within the past 12 months.*		
36. Do you receive or do you have a pending application for retirement or retainer pay, pension, or other compensation based upon military, Federal civilian, or District of Columbia Government service? *If your answer is "Yes," give details in Item 37.*		

Your Statement cannot be processed until you have answered all questions, including Items 26 through 36 above. Be sure you have placed an "X" to the left of EVERY marker (◀) above, either in the "Yes" or the "No" column.

37. Space for detailed answers. Indicate Item number to which answers apply.

Item No.	

If more space is required, use full sheets of paper approximately the same size as this page. Write on EACH sheet your name, birth date. and *announcement or position* title. Attach all sheets to this Statement at the top of Page 3.

ATTENTION — THIS STATEMENT MUST BE SIGNED

Read the following paragraph carefully before signing this Statement

A false answer to any question in this Statement may be grounds for not employing you, or for dismissing you after you begin work, and may be punishable by fine or imprisonment (U.S. Code, Title 18, Sec. 1001). All statements are subject to investigation, including a check of your fingerprints, police records, and former employers. All the information you give will be considered in reviewing your Statement and is subject to investigation. A false answer to items 27 or 28 could deprive you of your right to an annuity when you reach retirement age in addition to the penalties described above.

CERTIFICATION I CERTIFY that all of the statements made in this Statement are true, complete, and correct to the best of my knowledge and belief, and are made in good faith.	SIGNATURE *(Sign in ink)*	DATE SIGNED

GPO c48—16—81484-2 474-401

SUPPLEMENTAL FEDERAL APPLICATION STATEMENT

(This supplemental form is to be used with Standard Form 171, Personal Qualifications Statement, Standard Form 173, Job Qualifications Statement, and any other Federal application form which contains questions concerning your membership in organizations, convictions, and medical history.)

CONVICTIONS—(Item 32 on SF-171, May 1975 edition, and Item 19 on SF-173, July 1968 edition.)
The following question replaces the conviction question on the qualifications statement and must be answered by all applicants.
Have you ever been convicted of an offense against the law or forfeited collateral, or are you now under charges for any offense against the law? [You may omit: (a) traffic violations for which you paid a fine of $30.00 or less; (b) any offense committed before your 18th birthday which was finally adjudicated in a juvenile court or under a youth offender law; (c) any conviction the record of which has been expunged under Federal or State law; and (d) any conviction set aside under the Federal Youth Corrections Act or similar State authority.]............

YES	NO

LOYALTY—(Items 27, 28, and 29 on SF-171, May 1975 edition, and Item 15 on SF-173, July 1968 edition.)
Recent court decisions have prohibited routine inquiry into an individual's membership in certain organizations. As a result, questions on the Federal application form concerning membership in (a) the Communist Party, U.S.A., or (b) organizations advocating the overthrow of the Government of the United States or any of its subdivisions, should not be answered. However, if you are under consideration for appointment to sensitive positions for which such associations would be of relevant concern, you may be asked to provide such information. DO NOT ANSWER THE QUESTIONS—CROSS THEM OUT ON THE QUALIFICATIONS STATEMENT.

MEDICAL—(Item 16 on SF-173, July 1968 edition, and not on the SF-171, May 1975 edition.)
The Civil Service Commission has determined that medical questions which ask applicants for their history of heart disease, nervous breakdowns, epilepsy, tuberculosis, or diabetes be asked only on the appropriate medical forms—not on the application itself. DO NOT ANSWER THE QUESTION—CROSS IT OUT ON THE QUALIFICATIONS STATEMENT.

PRIVACY ACT NOTICE

AUTHORITY TO COLLECT PERSONAL INFORMATION—This information is provided pursuant to Public Law 93-579 (Privacy Act of 1974), December 31, 1974, for individuals completing Federal employment application forms. Sections 1302, 3301, and 3304 of Title 5 of the United States Code give the U. S. Civil Service Commission the authority to recruit, examine, and evaluate applicants' qualifications for employment in the Federal service. Use of the employment application forms is necessary for performing these functions.

PURPOSES AND USES—The principal purpose of employment application forms is to collect information needed to determine qualifications, suitability, and availability of applicants for Federal employment and of current Federal employees for reassignment, reinstatement, transfer, or promotion. Your completed application may be used to examine, rate, and/or assess your qualifications; to determine if you are entitled under certain laws and regulations such as Veterans Preference, and restrictions based on citizenship, members of family already employed, and residence requirements; and to contact you concerning availability and/or for an interview. All or part of your completed Federal employment application form may be disclosed outside the U. S. Civil Service Commission to:

1. Federal agencies upon request for a list of eligibles to consider for appointment, reassignment, reinstatement, transfer, or promotion.
2. State and local government agencies, congressional offices, public international organizations, and other public offices, if you have indicated availability for such employment consideration.
3. Federal agency investigators to determine your suitability for Federal employment.
4. Federal, State, or local agencies to create other personnel records after you have been appointed.
5. Appropriate Federal, State, or local law enforcement agencies charged with the responsibility of investigating a violation or potential violation of the law.
6. Appropriate Federal, State, or local agencies maintaining records on you to obtain information relevant to an agency decision about you.
7. A requesting Federal, State, or local agency to the extent the information is relevant to the requesting agency's decision.
8. Federal agency selecting officials involved with internal personnel management functions.
9. Your college or university placement offices if you are appointed to a career position in some occupations at certain grade levels.
10. Anyone requesting statistical information (without your personal identification) under the Freedom of Information Act.
11. A congressional office in response to an inquiry from the congressional office made at your request.

EFFECTS OF NONDISCLOSURE—Omission of an item means you might not receive full consideration for a position in which this information is needed.

INFORMATION REGARDING DISCLOSURE OF YOUR SOCIAL SECURITY NUMBER UNDER PUBLIC LAW 93-579, SECTION 7(b)—Disclosure by you of your Social Security Number (SSN) is mandatory to obtain the services, benefits, or processes that you are seeking. Solicitation of the SSN by the United States Civil Service Commission is authorized under provisions of Executive Order 9397, dated November 22, 1943. The SSN is used as an identifier throughout your Federal career from the time of application through retirement. It will be used by the Civil Service Commission and other Federal agencies in connection with lawful requests for information about you from your former employers, educational institutions, and financial or other organizations. The information gathered through the use of the number will be used only as necessary in personnel administration processes carried out in accordance with established regulations and published notices of systems and records. The SSN also will be used for the selection of persons to be included in statistical studies of personnel management matters. The use of the SSN is made necessary because of the large number of present and former Federal employees and applicants who have identical names and birth dates, and whose identities can only be distinguished by the SSN.

ATTENTION — THIS STATEMENT MUST BE SIGNED

Read the following paragraph carefully before signing this Statement

A false answer to the question in this Supplement may be grounds for not employing you, or for dismissing you after you begin work, and may be punishable by fine or imprisonment (U.S. Code, Title 18, Sec. 1001). The statement is subject to investigation, including a check of your fingerprints, police records, and former employers. All the information you give will be considered in reviewing your Statement and is subject to investigation.

CERTIFICATION	SIGNATURE *(Sign in ink)*	DATE SIGNED
I CERTIFY that the statement made in this supplement is true, complete, and correct to the best of my knowledge and belief, and is made in good faith.		

U.S. Civil Service Commission ☆ U.S. GOVERNMENT PRINTING OFFICE: 1977—723-281/253 3-1 CSC Form 1276 (Sept. 1976)

Part VII

Appendices

APPENDIX A—NAVAIDS
INTRODUCTION *

The National Airspace System (NAS) is a common system of airways and control procedures which have been developed to accommodate both civil and military aircraft. It is a working arrangement of people, equipment and procedures designed to obtain maximum safety in the use of United States airspace; the NAS is also a plan to improve the system by continuously incorporating additional equipment and capabilities. The objective is an ULTIMATE SYSTEM where all aircraft can operate as quickly and safely in poor weather as well as in good.

Not only must each specialist be proficient in his or her own option, but know much about the pilot's environment in the daily contacts that bring pilots and controllers together. The developmental specialist does not need the knowledge and ability of an experienced pilot or navigator, but an understanding of some of the basic principles and methods of navigation used in instrument or visual flight is desirable. In order to do this, the developmental specialist must be able to use the charts and publications pertinent to air navigation and acquire a basic knowledge of the functions and uses of the radio navigation aids used in the NAS.

*This FAA training material is not required information for the Air Traffic Control Employment Examination but is considered useful and important to air traffic control work.

GLOSSARY

The following terms are used frequently in this manual. Your progress in this course depends upon a thorough understanding of them.

1. ***Aeronautical Chart***: A map designed especially for use in air navigation that shows in detail the earth's surface, featuring terrain in topographical detail, navigational aids, airways and other pertinent cultural features.

2. ***Azimuth/Bearing***: These share a common definition in the dictionary, but in aviation usage, their meanings and uses differ slightly.

   a. Azimuth is direction, stated in number of angular degrees, *from* a reference line, usually north. In ATC, it is frequently and most usually used in reference to radar displays. It is also used in conjunction with Very High Frequency (VHF) or Ultra High Frequency (UHF) navigational aids.

   b. Bearing can be used interchangeably with azimuth, but is usually used to refer to the position of an object or point *from* the position of another object or point. The term bearing is normally used in conjunction with Low or Medium Frequency navigational (L/MF) aids and Direction Finding (DF) equipment. Remember, a bearing is always *from*.

3. ***Celestial Navigation***: Navigation by determination of position by exactly timed sextant observations of celestial bodies.

4. ***Coordinates***: Description of a point or position in degrees, minutes and seconds of latitude and longitude on or over the surface of the earth.

5. ***Course***: The intended direction of flight on a horizontal plane; an aircraft's proposed track over the ground not corrected for wind.

6. ***Dead Reckoning***: A slang term derived from Deductive Reckoning, applied to navigation and position determination based on heading flown, elapsed time and estimated ground speed.

7. ***Deviation***: A form of magnetic compass error caused by magnetic influences in aircraft structure and equipment.

8. ***Equator***: An imaginary line on the earth's surface, equidistant between the North and South Poles, dividing the Earth into the Northern and Southern Hemispheres. This is the zero degree reference line from which north and south parallels of latitude are measured.

9. ***Fix, Radio***: A definite position of an aircraft determined by reference to navigational aids and aircraft instruments. For instance, a radio fix determined from airborne instruments using the Oklahoma City Very High Frequency Omnidirectional Range/Tacan (VORTAC) indicates "OKC-210150". This tells a pilot that he is bearing 210° from the OKC VORTAC at a distance of 150 nautical miles.

10. ***Great Circle***: As applied in navigation to a route or direction, it is the shortest distance between two points, crossing all meridians at a different angle.

11. ***Heading***: The direction an aircraft is pointing, which has included a correction for offcourse wind to make good a proposed track. It may be magnetic, true or compass. Normally, when a pilot flies a

heading as directed by ATC, he is flying an uncorrected compass reading. The controller has given him a heading to fly which includes the necessary wind corrections to make good a track over the ground.

12. ***Homing***: Flight toward a radio navigational aid. Homing is usually used in conjunction with non-directional aids. It is also navigation by using an airborne Automatic Direction Finder (or equivalent) as a primary means of maintaining a course without correcting for wind.

13. ***Isogonic Line***: A line of equal magnetic variation. (See Variation)

14. ***Knots***: A speed of one nautical mile per hour. All airspeeds and wind velocities (aloft or surface—actual or forecast) are reported in knots. (See Mile.)

15. ***Latitude***: Distance north or south of the Equator, measured in degrees, minutes and seconds of arc. Parallels of latitude are shown on aeronautical charts as circles on the Earth's surface, parallel to and north or south of the Equator.

16. ***Longitude***: Distance east or west of the Prime Meridian measured in degrees, minutes and seconds of arc. Meridians of longitude are shown on aeronautical charts as north—south lines which, if extended, pass through the Earth's poles.

17. ***Mile***: Unit for measuring distance in feet.

    a. *Nautical Mile*: A measure of distance equal to one minute of latitude. It is always used in IFR flight planning—mileages and airspeeds, and all distances on IFR flight planning charts are in nautical miles.

    b. *Statute Mile*: A unit of 5,280 feet. It is generally used in VFR flight planning and operations and in reporting visibilities, surface and aloft.

18. ***National Airspace System***: NAS. The common system of air navigation and traffic service encompassing communication and control facilities, airways, controlled airspace, special use airspace, and flight procedures authorized by Federal Aviation Regulations for aviation.

19. ***Pilotage***: Navigation by reference to visible landmarks.

20. ***Prime Meridian***: The meridian that passes through Greenwich, England, that is used as the zero degree reference line from which east and west longitude is measured. This meridian is also referred to as the Greenwich Meridian and is the reference line from which we measure time zones.

21. ***Radial***: Used exclusively to describe a *magnetic bearing from* omnidirectional Very or Ultra High Frequency navigational aids. All these navaids' zero degree radials are aligned to magnetic north.

22. ***Range***: Distance. Range is primarily used to denote distance in the radar environment. The word distance is used in conjunction with navigation of any kind.

23. ***Reciprocal***: A corresponding but opposite value. It is usually used to describe a radial or heading—the 010° radial is the reciprocal of the 190° radial, or the reciprocal heading of 060° is 240°. (A 180° difference in each instance.)

24. ***Relative Bearing***: The bearing of a point, object or navigational aid relative to the nose (heading) of an aircraft.

25. ***Rhumb Line***: A curved line on the earth's surface, crossing all meridians at a constant angle.

26. ***Track***: The actual flight path of an aircraft over the ground.

27. ***Tracking***: Flight away from a radio navigational aid. Usually used in conjunction with non-directional aids. Tracking does not include a correction for wind.

28. ***Variation***: The angular difference between true north and magnetic north at any given place.

29. ***Wind Correction Angle***: The number of degrees right or left of course that a pilot must steer to compensate for off-course wind in order to stay on course.

CHAPTER 1
BASIC NAVIGATION

1-1. CHART PROJECTIONS FOR AIR NAVIGATION

While it is impossible to exactly represent a sphere upon a plane, there are some surfaces that can be spread out on a plane without stretching or tearing. Such surfaces are called developable surfaces. The cone and cylinder are two well-known developable surfaces. Those like the sphere are called nondevelopable.

Since the sphere cannot be directly developed into a plane surface, it is customary to first project the reference lines of a sphere upon some developable surface such as a cone or cylinder. This is done by mathematical analysis, but the process may be visualized by supposing a tiny light at the corner of a transparent sphere, projecting a shadow network of meridians and parallels upon a tangent cone or cylinder. When this developable surface has been unrolled into a plane, we have a more or less satisfactory representation of the reference line of the sphere upon a plane surface. If projected upon a cone, the system of lines representing the meridians and parallels of the sphere is known as a conic chart projection.

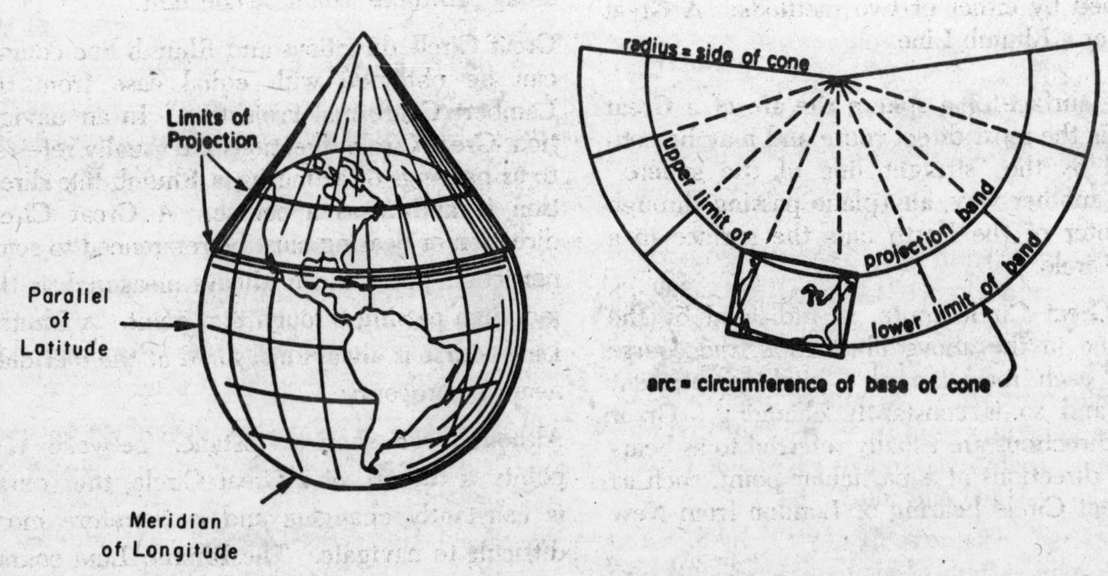

FIGURE 1-1. Development of the Lambert Conformal Conic Projection.

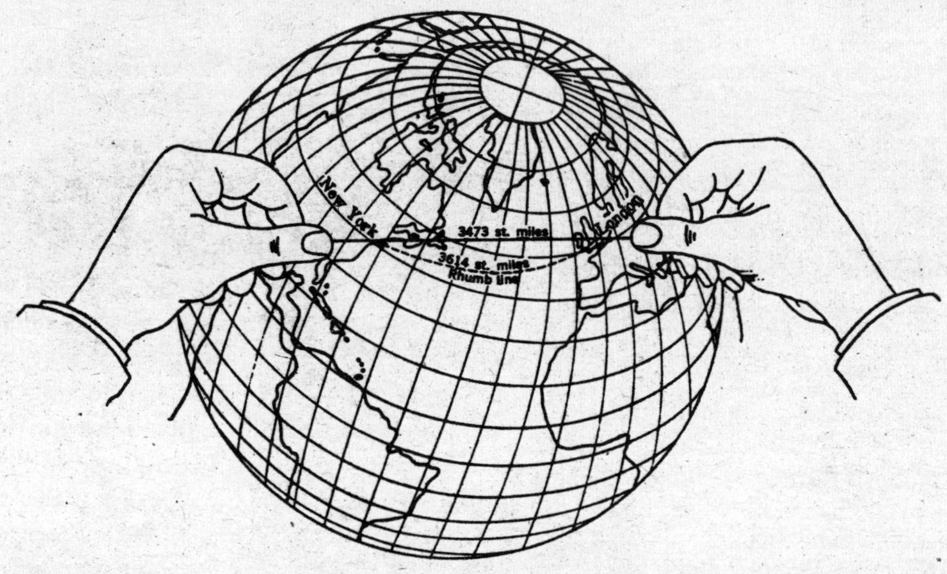

FIGURE 1-2. Great Circle versus Rhumb Line.

1-2. DISTANCE AND DIRECTION ON A SPHERE

Any two points on the surface of the Earth may be joined by either of two methods: A Great Circle or a Rhumb Line.

On the surface of a sphere the arc of a Great Circle is the most direct route and may be considered as the "straight line of the sphere." Stated another way, any plane passing through the center of the Earth cuts the surface in a Great Circle.

On a Great Circle route, as indicated by the solid line in the above illustration, the course crosses each meridian at a slightly different angle, and so is constantly changing. Great Circle directions are usually referred to as bearings or directions at a particular point, such as the Great Circle bearing of London from New York.

Besides the Great Circle illustrated above, there is the Rhumb Line. If you were to draw a line intersecting all meridians between New York and London at the same angle, as indicated by the dashed line in the Figure 1-2, your course along this route would be constant.

Great Circle directions and Rhumb line courses can be obtained with equal ease from the Lambert Conformal Projection. In air navigation, Great Circle directions are usually referred to as bearings or azimuths; a Rhumb line direction is known as a course. A Great Circle direction or bearing must be referenced to some particular point and is always measured as the meridian passing through that point. A Rhumb Line course is always measured at the meridian nearest mid-course.

Although the shortest distance between two points is the arc of a Great Circle, the course is constantly changing and is therefore more difficult to navigate. The Rhumb Line course provides a constant course but is somewhat circuitous and always longer.

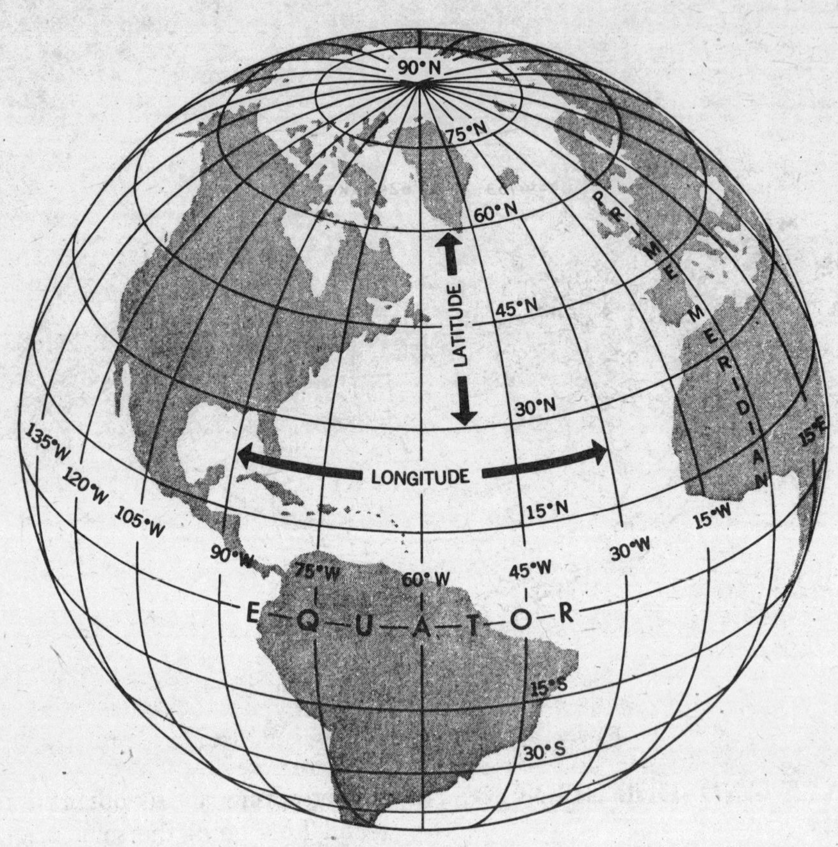

FIGURE 1-3. Parallels of latitude indicate North and South latitude. Meridians indicate East and West longitude.

1-3. LOCATING POSITIONS

When imaginary lines of latitude and longitude are drawn around the Earth, measurements of position, direction and distance become relatively simple. The parallels of latitude running east and west enable us to measure distance in degrees of latitude north or south of the Equator. The meridians of longitude running north and south enable us to measure distance in degrees of longitude east or west of the Prime Meridian.

A degree is divided into 60 minutes (60'). A minute is subdivided into 60 seconds (60"). One minute of latitude equals one nautical mile. These subdivisions are for angular measurement, and are in no way related to the measurement of time.

The United States lies between approximately 67° and 125° West Longitude and between 25° and 49° North Latitude. Any specific point can be located by reference to its latitude and longitude. When the terms latitude and longitude are omitted in giving a position, normal procedure is to state the latitude first, then the longitude.

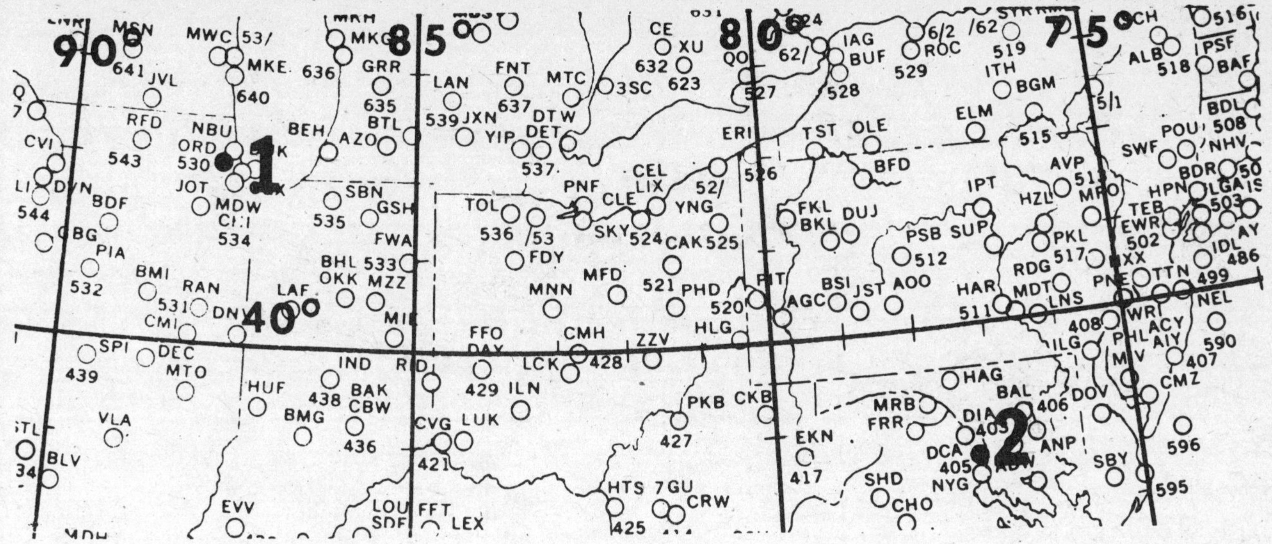

FIGURE 1-4

Chicago is approximately 42 degrees North Latitude, 88 degrees West Longitude, or approximately 42° 00' 00" 88 00' 00" (Number 1 in Figure 1-4.); Washington, D.C., approximately 39 degrees North Latitude, 77 degrees West Longitude, or 39° 00' 00" 77 00' 00" (Number 2 in Figure 1-4). Position can be more specific, such as radio broadcast station WKY, Oklahoma City, 35 33' 24", 97 30' 25". (Not shown.)

1-4. TRUE COURSE

In navigation, True Course is the basis for planning the desired flight. True Course is the desired track over the ground, measured from True North. To find True Course, a straight line is first drawn between two points as in Figure 1-5, A and B.

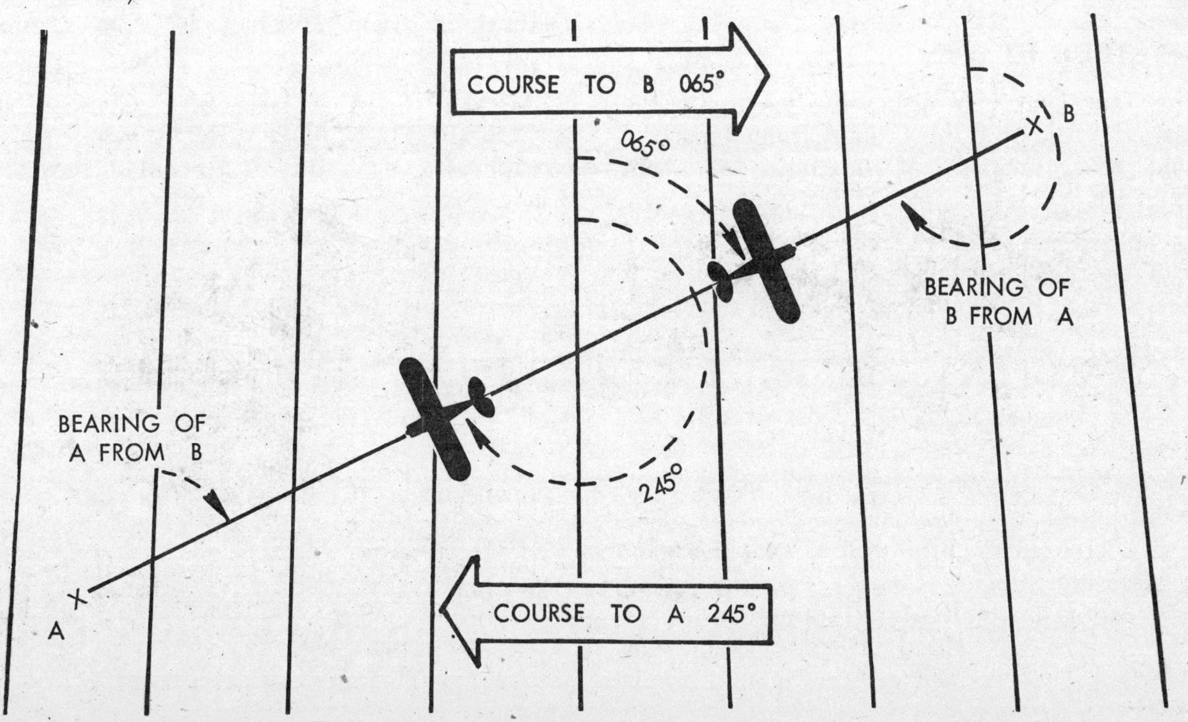

FIGURE 1-5. Courses and Bearings.

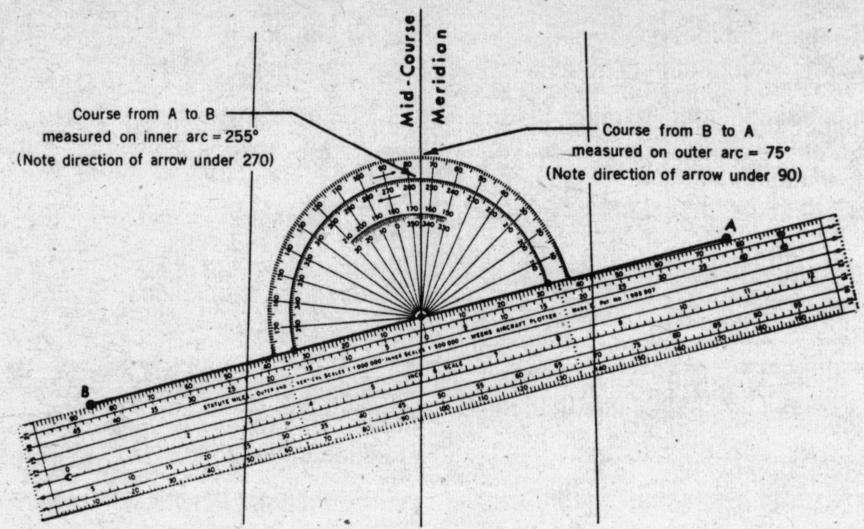

FIGURE 1-6. Measuring the true courses with a common type of protractor.

Align the base of the protractor portion of the plotter with this line. Place the small hole at the base of the protractor on the meridian nearest the half-way point. The True Course may be read at the point where this meridian intersects the inner scale of the protractor. In our example, the inner scale is used because the flight is proceeding from right to left. The outer scale would be used if the flight were from left to right. (Fig. 1-6.).

1-5. TRUE HEADING

The True Course furnishes the pilot with the desired track over the ground from departure point to destination. If the flight were conducted in a calm wind condition, or if the wind direction paralleled the True Course, True Course and True Heading would be the same. But since flight is seldom conducted under these conditions, a pilot must check on forecast wind direction and speed to figure a Wind Correction Angle.

Figure 1-7 shows the effect of wind on True Course.

Definition: True Heading is True Course corrected for wind.

REMEMBER! ANY HEADING CONTAINS A CORRECTION FOR WIND. When radar controllers give an aircraft a heading, they are

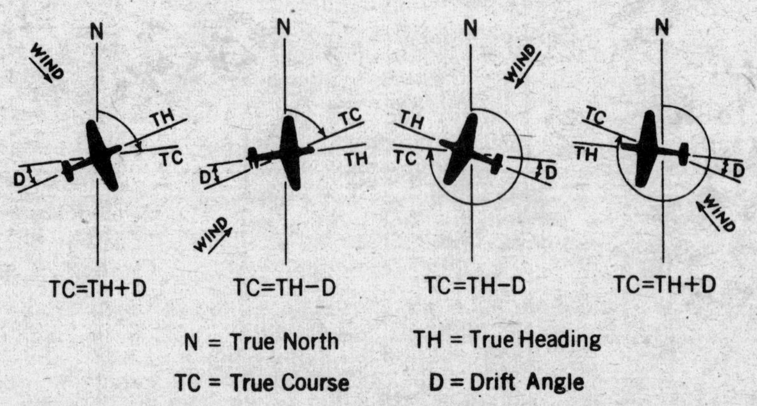

FIGURE 1-7. Combining true heading and wind correction to find true course.

automatically including a correction for wind so that aircraft can make good a desired track over the ground.

The allowance or correction for wind must be added or subtracted, depending on wind direction in relation to the True Course. Figure 1-8 demonstrates application of this rule:

FOR WIND FROM THE RIGHT,
ADD THE CORRECTION.

FOR WIND FROM THE LEFT,
SUBTRACT THE CORRECTION, or

ADD WIND RIGHT –
SUBTRACT WIND LEFT.

Look at Figure 1-8. Suppose that an aircraft desires to fly a True Course of 270°. A northerly wind requires an allowance of +5° (wind from the right) to compensate for drift. True Heading would be True Course of 270° + 5° wind correction, or 275°.

For the return trip, True Course is 090°, with the wind remaining the same. The wind correction must be subtracted: 090° – 5° = 085°. Winds aloft (or surface) are reported in knots in relation to True North. If you are going to figure speeds or courses, be sure you have all values in knots or in miles, and all courses and winds in true or magnetic values.

The conversion factor for knots and miles is 1.15. To convert nautical miles to statute miles, multiply nautical by 1.15. To convert Statute miles to nautical miles, divide statute by 1.15.

1-6. VARIATION

In order for the pilot to maintain a heading or course, he must refer to his magnetic compass, an instrument essential to any navigation problem. And because the compass is a magnetic instrument, it is subject to the varying influence of the Earth's magnetic field.

The north magnetic pole is located close to 71°N, 96°W—about 1,300 miles from the geographical location of the true north pole.

The earth itself is not uniformly magnetized. In the United States, for example, the compass needle usually points in the general direction of the magnetic north pole, *but* may vary greatly in certain localities. Consequently, the exact amount of variation at thousands of selected locations in the U.S. has been determined by the U.S. Coast and Geodetic Survey. The amount and direction of Variation is shown on aeronautical charts in dashed lines (called Isogonic lines) connecting points of equal variation. Figure 1-9 shows the Variation across the U.S.

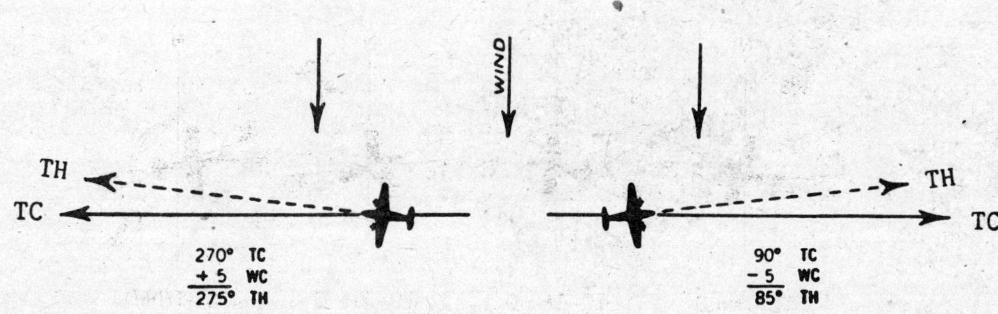

FIGURE 1-8. Wind correction angle reversed for opposite courses.

1-7. CORRECTION FOR VARIATION

As you can see in Fig. 1-9, on the west coast of the United States, the compass needle will point to the east of true north, and on the east coast, it will point to west of true north. Magnetic and True north coincide along an Agonic line (or line of equal or no variation) running through the western Great Lakes and the southern Appalachians to off the east coast of Florida. Since courses are measured by geographic meridians which point toward true north and flown by reference to the magnetic compass which points along the magnetic meridian (in the general direction of magnetic north), the True Course must be converted into magnetic direction, or Magnetic Course. (If a wind correction has been figured and you have a True Heading to work with, application of a correction for Variation will result in a Magnetic Heading.)

Conversion from True to Magnetic, whether working with course or heading, is done by adding or subtracting the variation indicated by the nearest Isogonic line on the chart.

Memory Aid:

EAST IS LEAST—WEST IS BEST
(SUBTRACT EAST) – (ADD WEST)

When True Course has been corrected for wind drift, True Heading is the result. Correcting True Heading for the effects of Variation results in Magnetic Heading. One more correction remains before we can arrive at a value useable in air navigation – Deviation.

1-8. DEVIATION

The compass is a thoroughly reliable instrument upon which the pilot may depend if he is aware of its idiosyncrasies. When the aircraft is in steady straight and level flight and the pilot disagrees with the compass reading, you may be fairly sure that any error lies in his judgment and not in the compass.

Deviation of the Magnetic Compass results from magnetic influences in the aircraft structure, differs for each aircraft, for different headings of the same aircraft and varies according to electrical equipment in use.

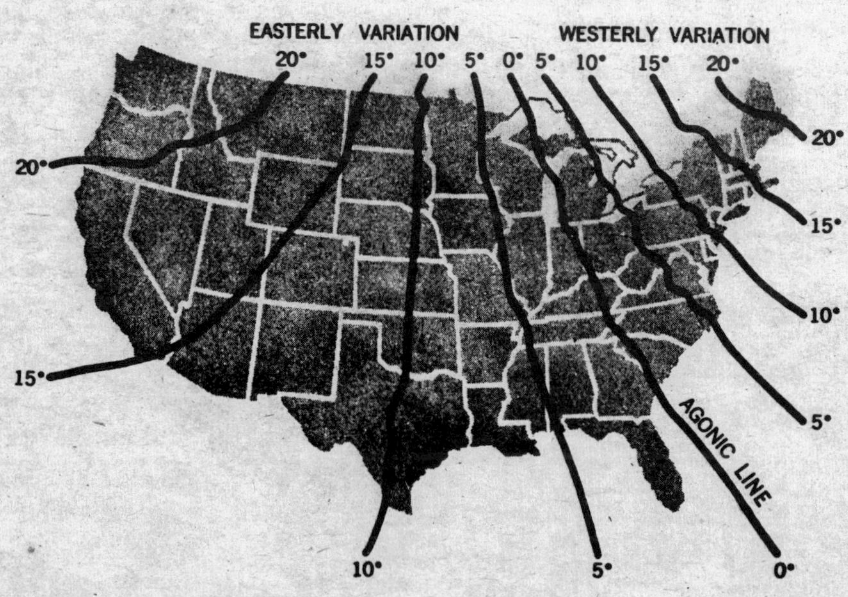

FIGURE 1-9. Isogonic Chart. The lines are "isogonic lines" which connect geographical points with identical magnetic variation.

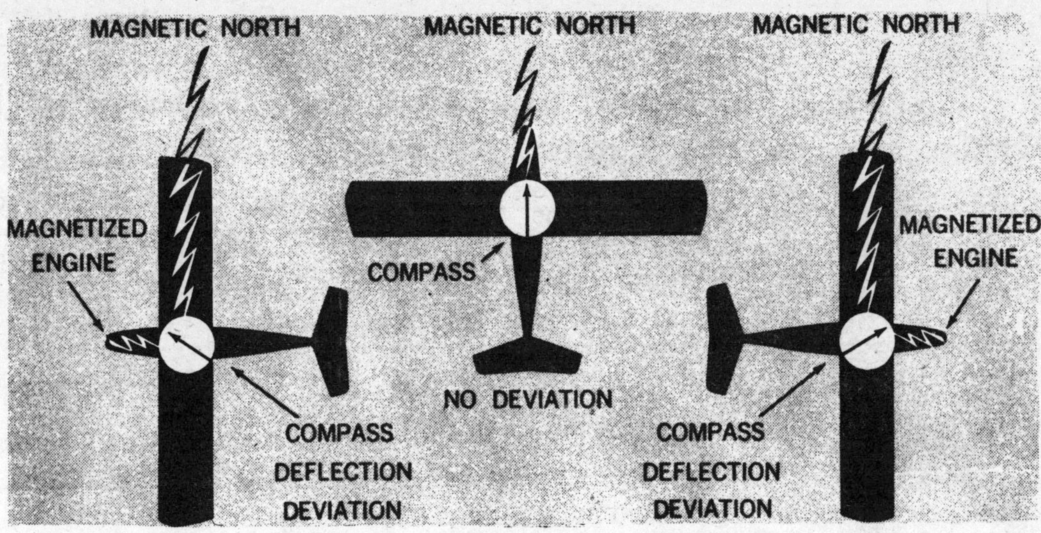

FIGURE 1-10. Magnetized portions of the plane cause the compass to deviate from its normal indication.

To determine Deviation, an aircraft's nose is aligned first with Magnetic North, and readings of compass indications with various electrical components in operation recorded. The aircraft's heading is then moved around the compass in 30° increments and readings taken again for each increment. Resulting readings are recorded on a "deviation card" in the aircraft's cockpit near the magnetic compass. There may be one or more readings posted on the "deviation card", depending upon the amount of and sophistication of the equipment on board the aircraft. Figure 1-11 below is an example of a simple "deviation card" which might be found on a light aircraft.

For Example:

To correctly fly a magnetic heading of north or 360°, correction for deviation would require flying a Compass Heading of 003°.

When you have corrected Magnetic Heading for Deviation, you will have Compass Heading, the value you will fly or keep in the window of your magnetic compass.

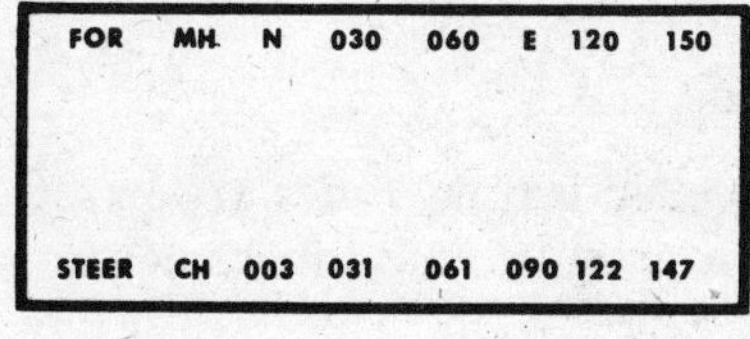

FOR MH	N	030	060	E	120	150
STEER CH	003	031	061	090	122	147

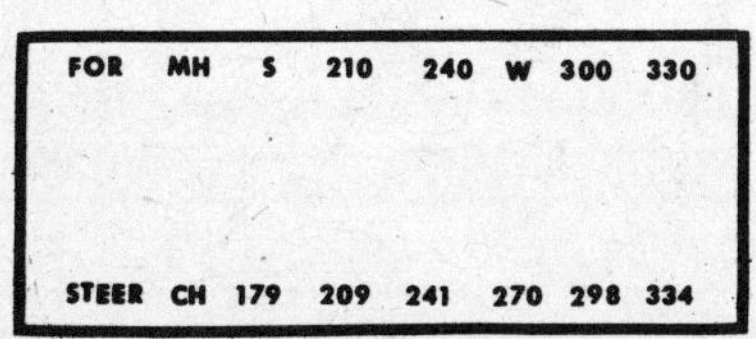

FOR MH	S	210	240	W	300	330
STEER CH	179	209	241	270	298	334

FIGURE 1-11. Deviation Card.

1-9. CONVERSION OF COMPASS HEADING BACK TO TRUE COURSE OR ANY INTERMEDIATE VALUE

Figure 1-12 illustrates not only the steps involved in converting True Course to Compass Heading but how to retrace our steps and convert Compass Heading back to a True Course. If we have arrived at a Compass Heading of 069°, as in our example above, we can recompute True Heading by adding the 15° wind correction back on, subtracting the 4° deviation correction and adding the 10° variation correction.

	TRUE	VARIATION (CORRECTION)	MAGNETIC	DEVIATION (CORRECTION)	COMPASS
COURSE	TC 090°	+ or − -10°	MC 080°	+ or − +4°	CC 084°
WIND (CORRECTION)	+ or − -15°		+ or − -15°		+ or − -15°
HEADING	TH 075°	+ or − -10°	MH 065°	+ or − +4°	CH 069°

FIGURE 1-12. A graphic depiction of procedures normally taken to convert a plotted *true course* (TC), to a desired *compass heading* (CH).

1-10. TIME ZONES

Meridians are used in designating time zones. A day is defined as the time required for the earth to make one complete revolution of 360°. Since the day is divided into 24 hours, we can say that the earth revolves at the rate of 15° per hour.

Noon is the time when the sun lies directly above a meridian; with the exception of certain local changes for convenience, a time zone is established which extends 7½° either side of that meridian. Figure 1-13 shows the meridians in the U.S. upon which our time zones are established (solid lines), the actual time zones in use today (alternating gray and white areas), and the hypothetical time zones which are based on the meridians (dashed lines).

The standard practice is to establish a time zone for each 15° of longitude which makes a difference of exactly one hour between each zone. We have four such zones in the United States: Eastern, based on the 75° meridian; Central, on the 90° meridian; Mountain, on the 105° meridian; and Pacific, on the 120° meridian. Measurement of these meridians begins at the 0° or Prime Meridian which runs through Greenwich, England.

Refer to Figure 1-13. When the sun is directly above the 90° meridian, it is noon Central Standard Time. At the same time, it is 1:00 P.M. Eastern Standard Time, 11:00 A.M Mountain Standard Time and 10:00 Pacific Standard Time.

1-11. GREENWICH TIME

In aviation, a standard time to use as we fly across one or more time zones is necessary to eliminate confusion which may arise over time zones or A.M. and P.M. The time at the Prime or Greenwich Meridian is used as the standard and is called Greenwich Time or Greenwich Mean Time.

As we have said, time zones are based on meridians measured in 15° increments from the Prime or Greenwich Meridian. These meridians are considered in degrees east or west of the Prime Meridian, and count as one hour of time. If you know the time at one meridian, you can determine the time at another meridian by counting (in 15° increments) the intervening meridians.

Time *increases* one hour per 15° increment when we measure from west to east, and *decreases* by one hour per 15° increment when

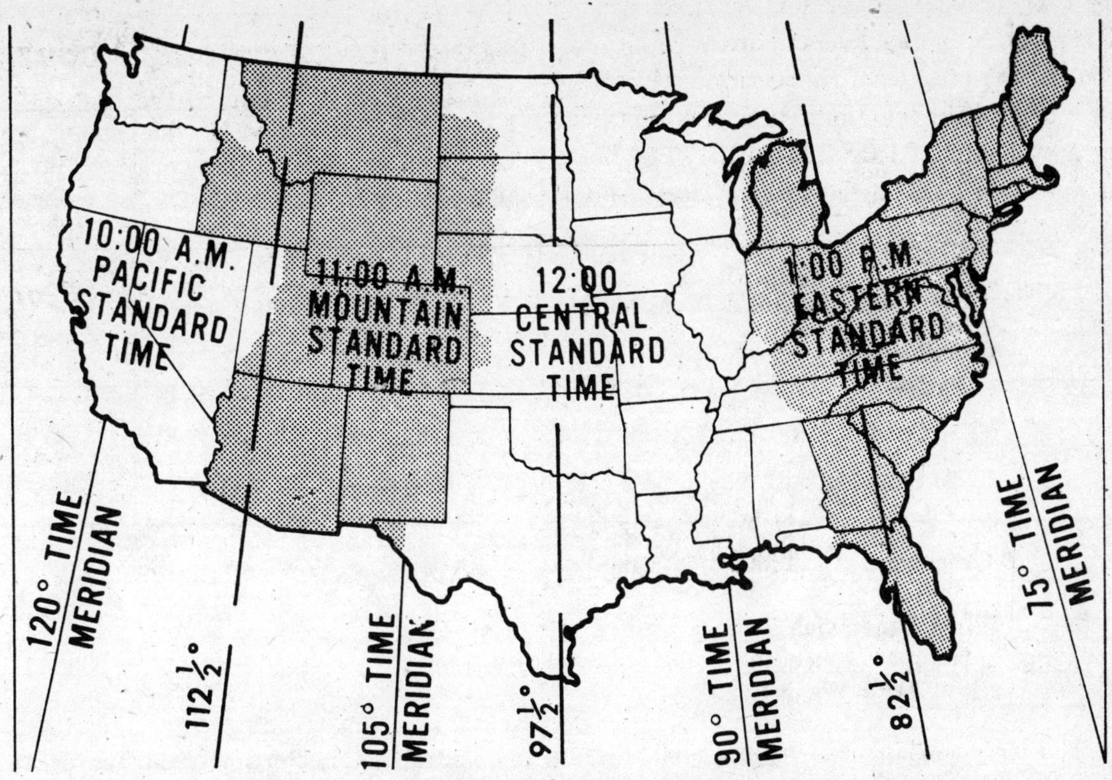

FIGURE 1-13. When the sun is directly above a meridian, the time at points on that meridian is *"noon"*. This is the basis on which time zones are established.

we measure from east to west. If Greenwich Time is considered the 0° or base time, the first time zone west of Greenwich is based on the 15°W meridian. Time there is one hour earlier and this zone is referred to as the −1 zone *because* time there is one hour less. However, since we want to convert that time back to Greenwich Time, we must add the hour back on.

Following through with this idea, the time zones in the United States may be designated as:

Zone	Meridian Based on	Zone Name	Factor to Add to Convert Time to Greenwich
−5	75°	Eastern	+5
−6	90°	Central	+6
−7	105°	Mountain	+7
−8	120°	Pacific	+8

Remember, these time zones are west of Greenwich, so time is earlier, and we must add the appropriate value to their local times to obtain Greenwich Time.

The first step in converting local time to Greenwich Time is to find local time on the 24-hour clock. This simply means that we take the number of the hour and add two zeros.

8:00 A.M. is 0800; 10:30 A.M. is 1030. (The two zeros added to the hours figure reserve those units for minutes when necessary.) For the hours after noon, continue to name them as they are counted. 1:00 P.M. is the 13th hour and would be 1300 on the 24-hour clock. 6:00 P.M. is the 18th hour or 1800. (Simply add 12 to the hours after noon for a short cut.)

The last step is to add to the time on the 24-hour clock the value of the time zone (i.e., Central Time Zone = +6). Here's an illustration:

Zone	Pacific	Mountain	Central	Eastern	Greenwich
Conversion Factor	Add 8	Add 7	Add 6	Add 5	0 or Base
Local	11:00 P.M.	12:00 P.M.	1:00 P.M.	2:00 P.M.	7:00 P.M.
24-Hour Clock	1100	1200	1300	1400	1900
Greenwich	1900	1900	1900	1900	1900

When Greenwich Time is figured and it results in a figure exceeding 2400, subtract 2400 and add a day. For instance:

Zone	Pacific	Mountain	Central	Eastern	Greenwich
Conversion Factor	Add 8	Add 7	Add 6	Add 5	0 or Base
Local Time	7:35 P.M. Saturday	8:35 P.M. Saturday	9:35 P.M. Saturday	10:35 P.M Saturday	03:35 A.M. Sunday
24-hour Clock (Local)	1935	2035	2135	2235	
Greenwich Time	2735 –2400 0335 GMT	2735 –2400 0335	2735 –2400 0335	2735 –2400 0335	0335

Greenwich Mean Time is used for all operational times in aviation, and in the weather system to designate observation and forecast validation times.

1-12. DATE CHANGE

When crossing the International Date Line, the 180° meridian, West to East, subtract one day; going from East to West, add one day.

WORK SHEET

BASIC NAVIGATION

Complete the following questions without reference to the preceding material. Upon completion, compare your answers with the correct answers at the end of this manual. For those questions you have answered incorrectly, we suggest you review the appropriate paragraphs in the study material.

QUESTIONS

1. The deflection of the compass needle caused by magnetic influences within the aircraft is called:

   (1) Variation

   (2) Deviation

2. When it is 10:00 P.M. CST in Oklahoma City (90th Meridian Time), Greenwich Mean Time is:

   (1) 0400, the following day.

   (2) 0400, the previous day.

   (3) 1600, the same day.

   (4) 1600, the previous day.

3. Any two points on the surface of the Earth may be joined by either a Great Circle or a Rhumb Line. Which of the two is the most direct route? ....

4. A time zone is established for how many degrees of longitude?

   (1) 7½ degrees (3) 15 degrees

   (2) 30 degrees (4) 5 degrees

5. The angle between true north and magnetic north is called:

   (1) Deviation

   (2) True Heading

   (3) Isogonic Line

   (4) Variation

6. Which of the following is the factor to be applied in changing a course to a heading?

   (1) Deviation

   (2) Wind Correction Angle

   (3) Variation

   (4) Relative Bearing

7. The purpose of projecting the reference lines of a sphere upon a cone is:

   (1) to develop a cylinder

   (2) so that they can be mathematically analyzed.

   (3) to produce a developable surface.

   (4) spread it out on a plane.

8. Parallels of Longitude and Meridians of Latitude enable us to measure distance and locate positions on the Earth.

   (1) True (2) False

9. Conversion of True Course to Compass Heading requires corrections for:

   (1) Variation, Deviation.

   (2) Deviation, Wind.

   (3) Wind, Variation, Deviation.

   (4) Wind Variation.

10. Time zones are measured from the:

    (1) International Date Line.

    (2) Equator.

    (3) Prime Meridian.

    (4) 90 degree meridian.

CHAPTER 2
AERONAUTICAL CHARTS

2-1. VFR CHARTS — GENERAL

Aeronautical charts depict information essential to safety of flight and good traffic control. You must become familiar with each type so that you can select the proper chart when seeking information. FAA personnel shall always refer to *officially-published* charts and documents for aeronautical information. Other agencies and/or pilots may use privately published or military Flight Information Publications. (FLIP).

2-2. SECTIONAL CHARTS

Sectional charts are used for plotting courses and locating geographical points for VFR flying. They are scaled 1:500,000 or 8 statute miles (about 7 nautical miles) to the inch and show the greatest detail. See Figures 2-1, 2, 3.

2-3. WORLD AERONAUTICAL CHARTS (WAC)

WAC's are also basically used in VFR flight but show less detail than the Sectionals. WAC's are scaled 1:1,000,000 or 16 statute miles (about 14 nautical miles) to the inch. See Figures 2-4, 5, 6.

2-4. IFR CHARTS — GENERAL

The remaining charts we will study here are specifically designed for use in IFR flight, and mileage scales vary from chart to chart within a series.

2-5. ENROUTE LOW ALTITUDE — U.S.

These are used in preflight and inflight in the NAS. They show airway structure, airspace designation, navigational aids, mileages, frequencies, enroute altitude information (MEA, MRA, MOCA), airport locations, and special use airspace such as Restricted and Warning Areas and ISJTA's. See Figures 2-7 and 8.

2-6. AREA CHARTS

Area Charts depict airways, navigational aids, non-standard holding patterns, MEA's, and radio frequencies for selected terminal areas, using the same symbology as the Enroute Low Altitude Charts and on a larger scale. (No example shown.)

2-7. AREA NAVIGATION (RNAV), CHARTS

RNAV charts are for preflight and inflight use on established area navigation routes. RNAV routes are superimposed on Enroute Charts and show RNAV information in a contrasting color. Area navigation is based on the present VOR/VORTAC system and this chart facilitates transition to and from the current system. See Figures 2-9 and 2-10.

2-8. ENROUTE HIGH ALTITUDE — U.S.

These are similar to the Low Altitude series discussed earlier, but show information necessary for preflight and inflight use in the NAS at and above 18,000'MSL. See Figures 2-11 and 2-12.

2-9. STANDARD INSTRUMENT APPROACH PROCEDURES (SIAP)

These specify details of instrument approaches. Some of the information shown includes a detailed sketch of airport layout and approach including minimum altitudes, bearings, weather minima and obstructions. See Figures 2-13-18.

2-10. HIGH ALTITUDE INSTRUMENT APPROACH CHARTS

These show basically the same information as the SIAP but apply to jet approaches to the airport and aid in transitioning from the high altitude structure to the low altitude for approach. See Figure 2-18.

2-11. STANDARD INSTRUMENT DEPARTURES (SID's)

SID's depict the officially approved special routes out of major terminals, and are published in booklet form. See Figures 2-19 and 20.

2-12. STANDARD TERMINAL ARRIVAL ROUTES (STAR's)

STAR's depict officially approved special routes out of major terminal routes, and are published in booklet form. See Figures 2-21 and 22.

Both SID's and STAR's are assigned special computer codes to facilitate their entry into the NAS computer network. These codes appear on the page describing the SID or STAR.

2-13. PROHIBITED, RESTRICTED AND WARNING AREAS

These areas are established and charted to show pilots hazards or potential hazards presented by activities within the designated areas. Each area is assigned to an air traffic facility for purposes of coordination during periods of activity. Information about each area regarding periods of activity and controlling agency appear on the chart the area appears on.

2-14. PROHIBITED AREA

A Prohibited Area is an area in which flight is not permitted. This area is designated by Executive Order of the President of the United States.

2-15. RESTRICTED AREA

A Restricted Area is designated when activities (usually invisible) hazardous to flight, such as aerial gunnery, bombing or guided missile or artillery firing, are conducted. These areas are effective at various times and between various altitudes. No person is permitted to operate an aircraft within an active Restricted Area unless prior permission for such operation has been issued by the appropriate authority. The FAA Administrator designates Restricted Areas, and instructions governing flight in Restricted Areas are found in Federal Aviation Regulation 73.

2-16. WARNING AREA

Activities conducted within Warning Areas are generally the same as those conducted within Restricted Areas. However Warning Areas are located outside the continental limits of the United States and thus no restrictions or prohibitions to flight may be imposed. All pilots should be discouraged from penetrating Warning Areas during periods of activity because of the hazard to flight. The FAA Administrator also designates Warning Areas.

2-17. MILITARY OPERATIONS AREA (MOA)

An airspace area established for the purpose of segregating certain military training activities from airspace containing IFR aircraft. Nonparticipating IFR traffic may be cleared through an active MOA if IFR separation can be provided by ATC. VFR pilots should exercise caution while flying within an active MOA. These areas are depicted on sectional, VFR terminal and low altitude enroute charts.

2-18. AIRMAN'S INFORMATION MANUAL (AIM)

The AIM is written in layman's language and contains much aeronautical information useful to pilots. It is divided into four parts: Part 1, Basic Flight Manual and ATC Procedures; Part 2, Airport Directory; Part 3, Operational Data and Notices to Airmen; and Part 4, Graphic Notices and Supplemental Data.

The AIM is an excellent reference manual for all Air Traffic Control Specialists. At least one copy is available at all Air Traffic facilities, and Specialists are familiar with its contents.

DALLAS - FT WORTH

SECTIONAL AERONAUTICAL CHART
SCALE 1:500,000

Lambert Conformal Conic Projection Standard Parallels 33°20′ and 38°40

Topographic data corrected to April 1976

16TH EDITION *July 15, 1976*

Includes airspace amendments effective *July 15, 1976*
and all other aeronautical data received by May 27, 1976

Consult appropriate NOTAMs and Flight Information
Publications for supplemental data and current information

This chart will become *OBSOLETE FOR USE IN NAVIGATION* upon publication of the next edition scheduled for *JANUARY 27, 1977*

PUBLISHED IN ACCORDANCE WITH INTER-AGENCY AIR CARTOGRAPHIC COMMITTEE SPECIFICATIONS AND AGREEMENTS APPROVED BY

DEPARTMENT OF DEFENSE ★ FEDERAL AVIATION ADMINISTRATION ★ DEPARTMENT OF COMMERCE

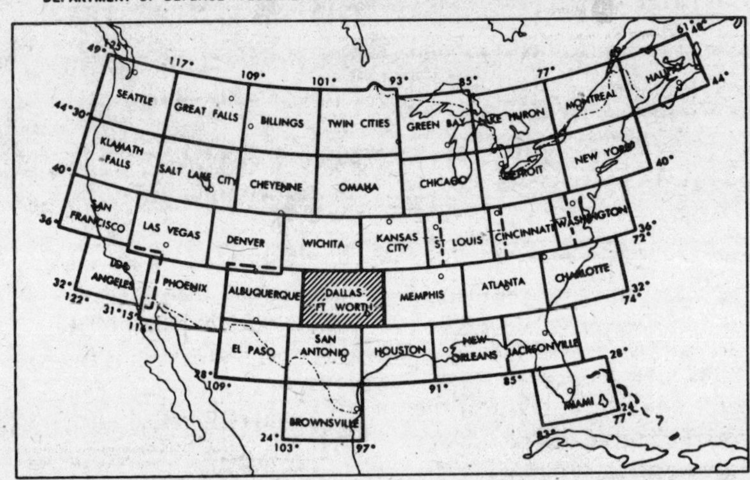

CONTOUR INTERVAL
500 feet

—— 500 ——
Basic

HIGHEST TERRAIN elevation is
3815 **feet**
located at 34°52′N – 101°59′W

3815
3000
2000
1000
Sea Level

Critical elevation . . . . ∙4254

Approximate elevation . . . . ×3200

Doubtful locations are indicated by omission of the point locator (dot or "x")

POWER TRANSMISSION LINE

MAXIMUM TERRAIN ELEVATIONS

Maximum Terrain elevation figures, centered in the area bounded by ticked lines of latitude and longitude, are elevations in THOUSANDS and HUNDREDS of feet required to safely clear the terrain, BUT DO NOT INCLUDE ELEVATIONS OF VERTICAL OBSTRUCTIONS.

The value is computed by adding the safety factor (100 feet or ½ contour interval when interval exceeds 200 feet on source data) to the highest terrain, and raising the sum to the next 100 foot level.

3100 feet 31

CONVERSION OF ELEVATIONS

FEET (Thousands) 0 2 4 6 8 10 12 14 16 18 20 22 24 26 28 30

METERS (Thousands) 0 1 2 3 4 5 6 7 8 9

Published at Washington, D.C.

U.S. Department of Commerce
National Oceanic and Atmospheric Administration
National Ocean Survey

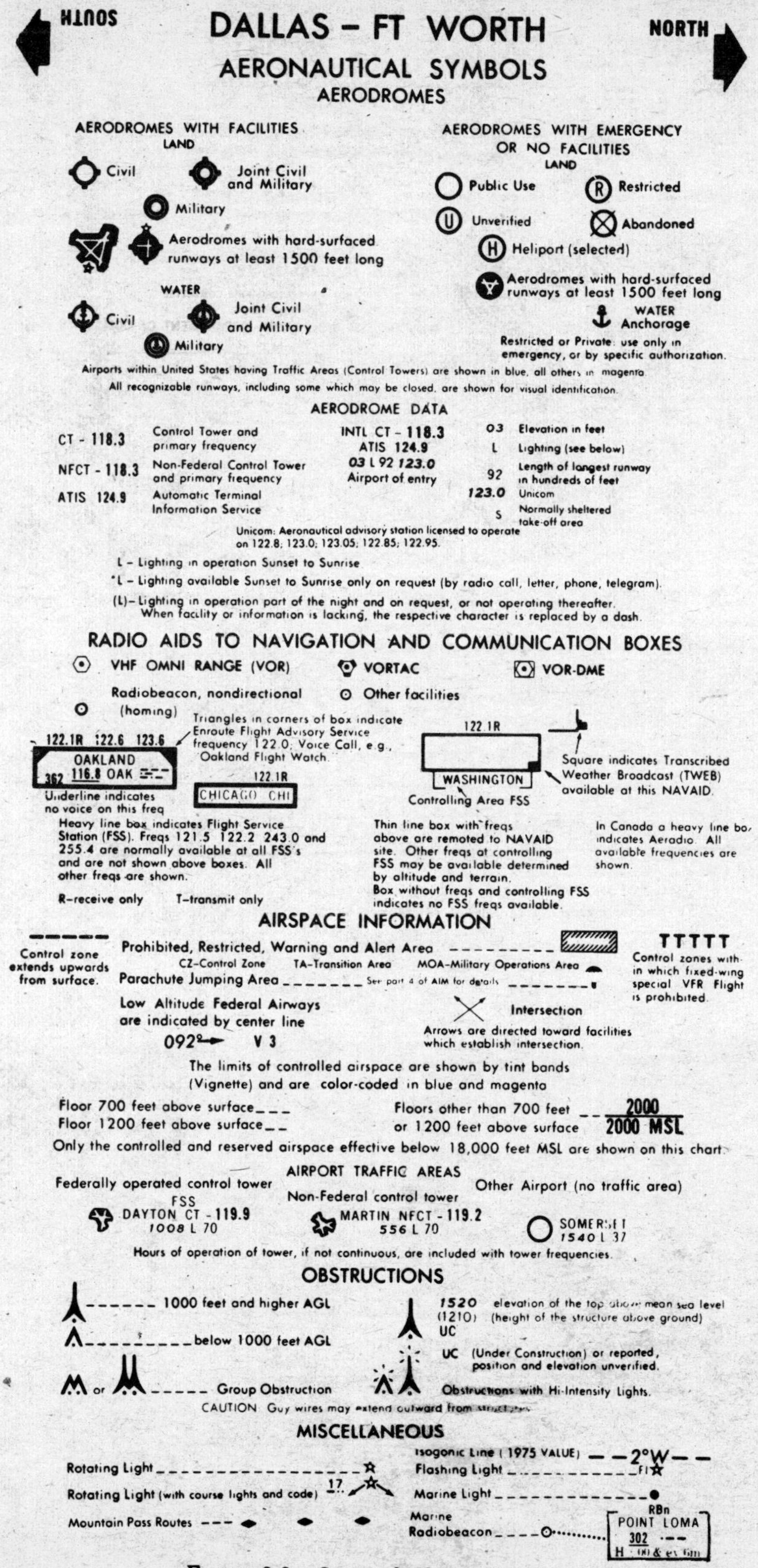

DALLAS – FT WORTH

NORTH

AERONAUTICAL SYMBOLS

AERODROMES

AERODROMES WITH FACILITIES

LAND

Civil — Joint Civil and Military

Military

Aerodromes with hard-surfaced runways at least 1500 feet long

WATER

Civil — Joint Civil and Military

Military

AERODROMES WITH EMERGENCY OR NO FACILITIES

LAND

Public Use — Restricted

Unverified — Abandoned

Heliport (selected)

Aerodromes with hard-surfaced runways at least 1500 feet long

WATER Anchorage

Restricted or Private: use only in emergency, or by specific authorization.

Airports within United States having Traffic Areas (Control Towers) are shown in blue, all others in magenta.

All recognizable runways, including some which may be closed, are shown for visual identification.

AERODROME DATA

CT - 118.3 — Control Tower and primary frequency

NFCT - 118.3 — Non-Federal Control Tower and primary frequency

ATIS 124.9 — Automatic Terminal Information Service

INTL CT - 118.3
ATIS 124.9
03 L 92 123.0
Airport of entry

03 — Elevation in feet

L — Lighting (see below)

92 — Length of longest runway in hundreds of feet

123.0 — Unicom

S — Normally sheltered take-off area

Unicom: Aeronautical advisory station licensed to operate on 122.8, 123.0, 123.05, 122.85, 122.95.

L – Lighting in operation Sunset to Sunrise

*L – Lighting available Sunset to Sunrise only on request (by radio call, letter, phone, telegram).

(L) – Lighting in operation part of the night and on request, or not operating thereafter.
When facility or information is lacking, the respective character is replaced by a dash.

RADIO AIDS TO NAVIGATION AND COMMUNICATION BOXES

VHF OMNI RANGE (VOR) — VORTAC — VOR-DME

Radiobeacon, nondirectional (homing) — Other facilities

122.1R 122.6 123.6
OAKLAND
362 116.8 OAK

Triangles in corners of box indicate Enroute Flight Advisory Service frequency 122.0. Voice Call, e.g., Oakland Flight Watch.

Underline indicates no voice on this freq

122.1R
CHICAGO CHI

122.1R
WASHINGTON

Controlling Area FSS

Square indicates Transcribed Weather Broadcast (TWEB) available at this NAVAID.

Heavy line box indicates Flight Service Station (FSS). Freqs 121.5 122.2 243.0 and 255.4 are normally available at all FSS's and are not shown above boxes. All other freqs are shown.

R–receive only T–transmit only

Thin line box with freqs above are remoted to NAVAID site. Other freqs at controlling FSS may be available determined by altitude and terrain.
Box without freqs and controlling FSS indicates no FSS freqs available.

In Canada a heavy line box indicates Aeradio. All available frequencies are shown.

AIRSPACE INFORMATION

Control zone extends upwards from surface.

Prohibited, Restricted, Warning and Alert Area

CZ–Control Zone TA–Transition Area MOA–Military Operations Area

Parachute Jumping Area — See part 4 of AIM for details

TTTTT
Control zones within which fixed-wing special VFR Flight is prohibited.

Low Altitude Federal Airways are indicated by center line

092° V 3

Intersection

Arrows are directed toward facilities which establish intersection.

The limits of controlled airspace are shown by tint bands (Vignette) and are color-coded in blue and magenta

Floor 700 feet above surface

Floor 1200 feet above surface

Floors other than 700 feet or 1200 feet above surface — 2000 / 2000 MSL

Only the controlled and reserved airspace effective below 18,000 feet MSL are shown on this chart.

AIRPORT TRAFFIC AREAS

Federally operated control tower
FSS
DAYTON CT - 119.9
1008 L 70

Non-Federal control tower
MARTIN NFCT - 119.2
556 L 70

Other Airport (no traffic area)
SOMERSET
1540 L 37

Hours of operation of tower, if not continuous, are included with tower frequencies.

OBSTRUCTIONS

1000 feet and higher AGL

below 1000 feet AGL

Group Obstruction

1520 elevation of the top above mean sea level
(1210) (height of the structure above ground)
UC

UC (Under Construction) or reported, position and elevation unverified.

Obstructions with Hi-Intensity Lights.

CAUTION Guy wires may extend outward from structures

MISCELLANEOUS

Rotating Light

Rotating Light (with course lights and code) 17

Mountain Pass Routes

Isogonic Line (1975 VALUE) — 2°W —

Flashing Light — Fl

Marine Light

Marine Radiobeacon
RBn
POINT LOMA
302
H

FIGURE 2-2. Sectional Chart Legend.

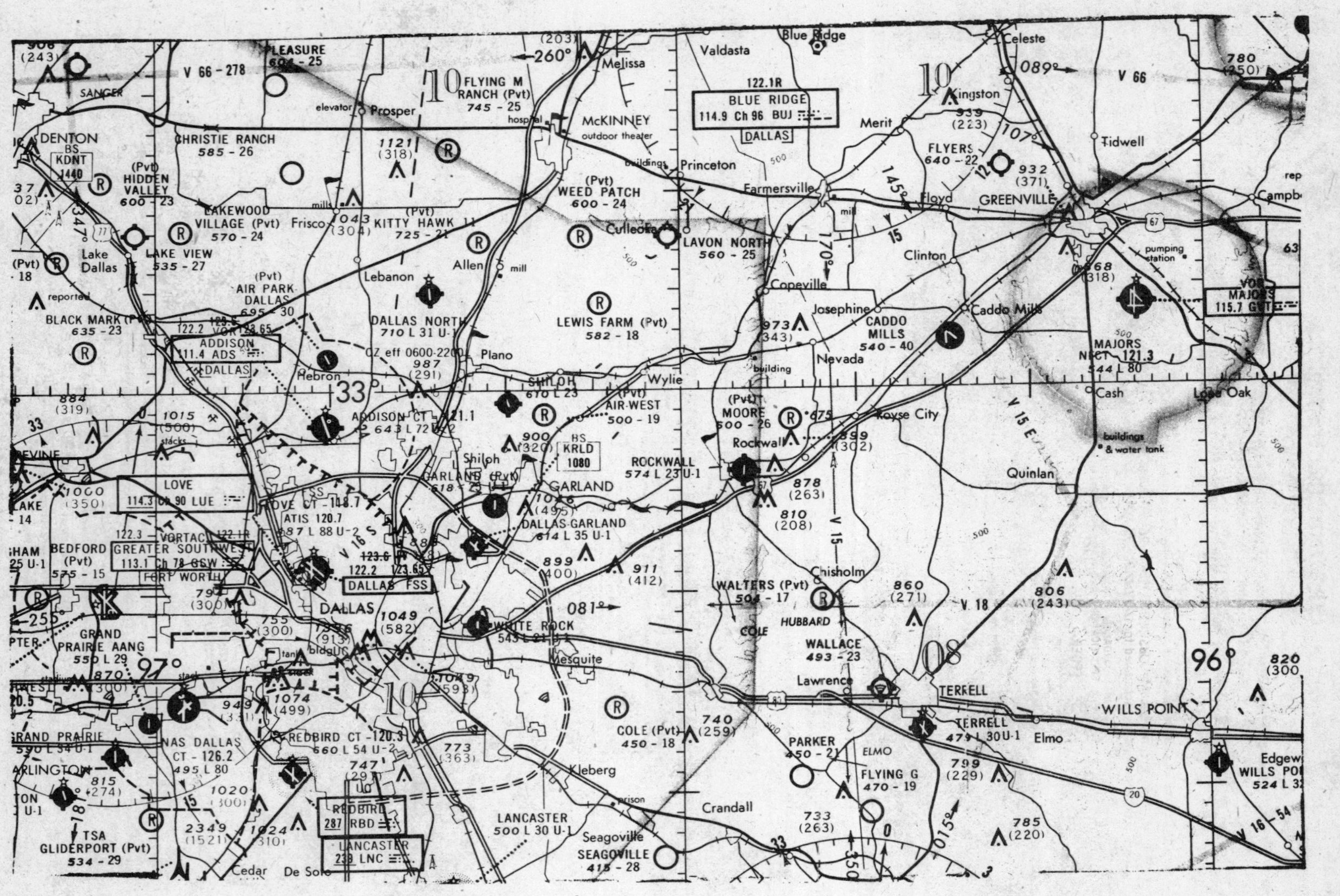

FIGURE 2-3. Sectional Chart.

SOUTH

CH-25

NORTH

WORLD AERONAUTICAL CHART
SCALE 1:1,000,000

Lambert Conformal Conic Projection Standard Parallels 25°20′ and 30°40′
Topographic data corrected to June 1972

3RD *EDITION* corrected to include airspace amendments effective *February 1, 1973*
and all other aeronautical data received by December 15, 1972
Consult appropriate NOTAMS and Flight Information
Publications for supplemental data and current information.

This chart will become *OBSOLETE FOR USE IN NAVIGATION* upon publication of the next edition scheduled for *JANUARY 31, 1974*

PUBLISHED IN ACCORDANCE WITH INTER-AGENCY AIR CARTOGRAPHIC COMMITTEE SPECIFICATIONS AND AGREEMENTS, APPROVED BY:

DEPARTMENT OF DEFENSE FEDERAL AVIATION ADMINISTRATION DEPARTMENT OF COMMERCE

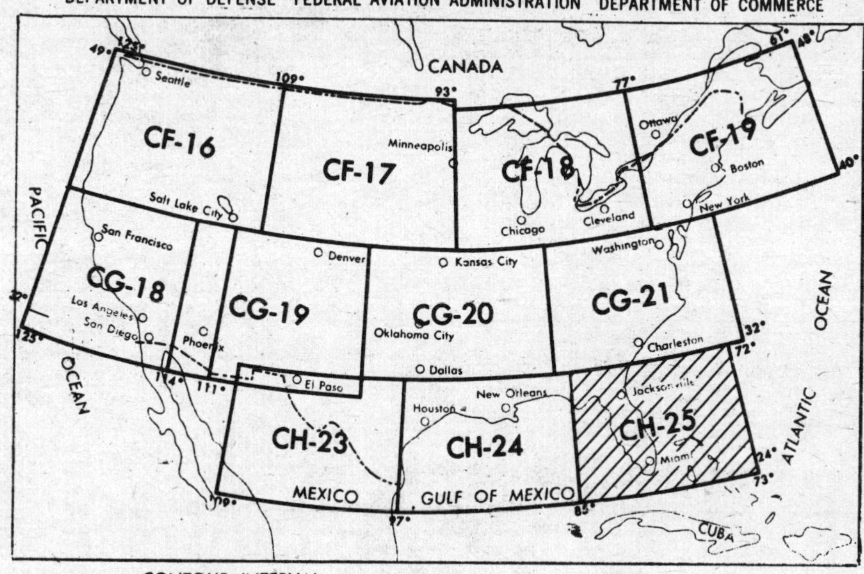

CONTOUR INTERVAL
1000 feet

HIGHEST TERRAIN elevation is
725 feet
located at 32°11′N-84°42′W

Critical elevation *4254*
Approximate elevation *3200*
Doubtful locations are indicated by omission of the point locator (dot or "x")

725
Sea Level

POWER TRANSMISSION LINE •----•----•--

MAXIMUM TERRAIN ELEVATIONS

Maximum Terrain elevation figures, centered in the area completely bounded by ticked lines of latitude and longitude, are represented in THOUSANDS and HUNDREDS of feet BUT DO NOT INCLUDE ELEVATIONS OF VERTICAL OBSTRUCTIONS.

3100 feet _ _ _ _ _ _ _ 31

CONVERSION OF ELEVATIONS

FEET (Thousands) 0 2 4 6 8 10 12 14 16 18 20 22 24 26 28 30
METERS (Thousands) 0 1 2 3 4 5 6 7 8 9

Published at Washington, D.C.
U.S. Department of Commerce
National Oceanic and Atmospheric Administration
National Ocean Survey

FIGURE 2-4. WAC Chart Cover.

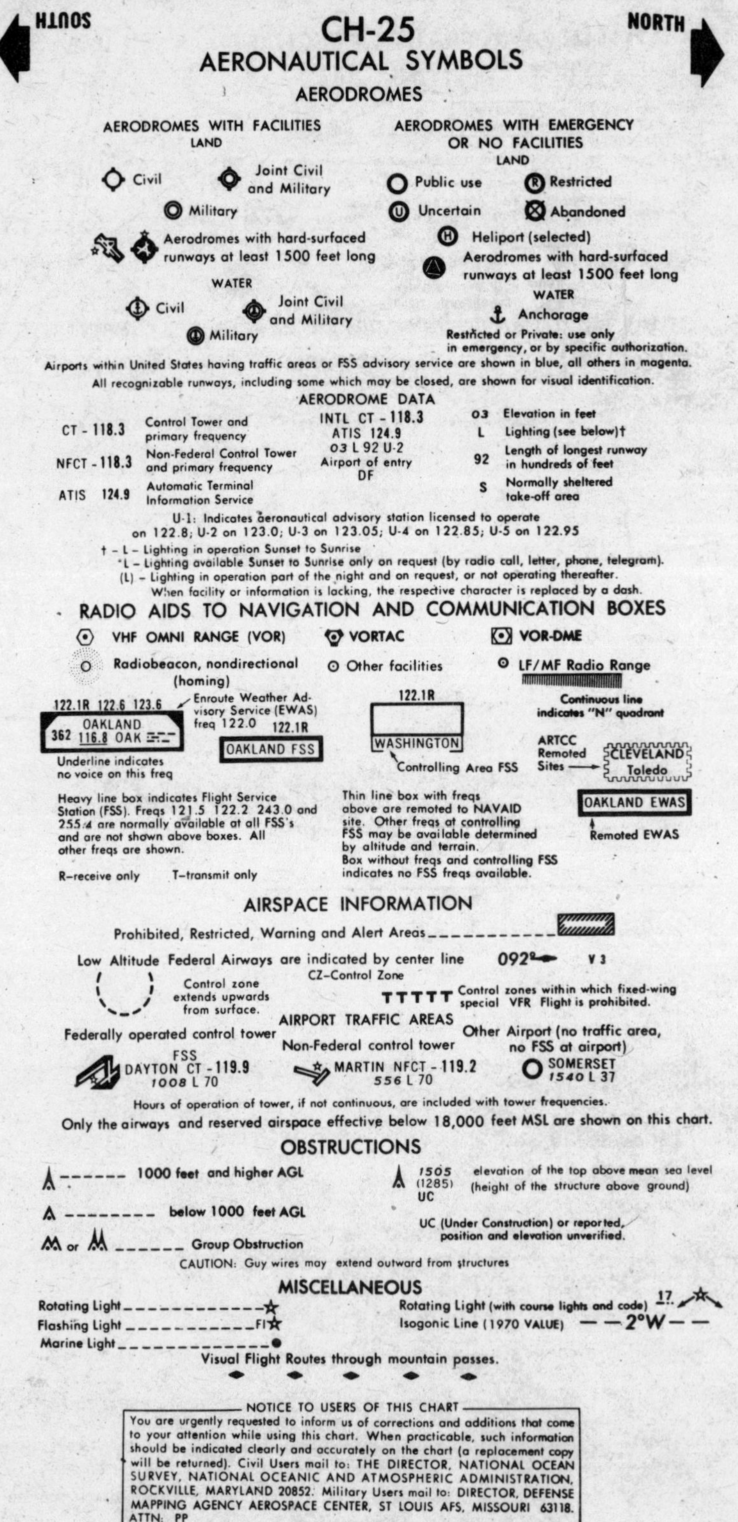
SOUTH
CH-25
NORTH
AERONAUTICAL SYMBOLS
AERODROMES
AERODROMES WITH FACILITIES
LAND
Civil
Joint Civil and Military
Military
Aerodromes with hard-surfaced runways at least 1500 feet long
WATER
Civil
Joint Civil and Military
Military
AERODROMES WITH EMERGENCY OR NO FACILITIES
LAND
Public use
Restricted
Uncertain
Abandoned
Heliport (selected)
Aerodromes with hard-surfaced runways at least 1500 feet long
WATER
Anchorage
Restricted or Private: use only in emergency, or by specific authorization.
Airports within United States having traffic areas or FSS advisory service are shown in blue, all others in magenta.
All recognizable runways, including some which may be closed, are shown for visual identification.
AERODROME DATA
CT - 118.3 Control Tower and primary frequency
NFCT - 118.3 Non-Federal Control Tower and primary frequency
ATIS 124.9 Automatic Terminal Information Service
INTL CT - 118.3
ATIS 124.9
03 L 92 U-2
Airport of entry
DF
03 Elevation in feet
L Lighting (see below)†
92 Length of longest runway in hundreds of feet
S Normally sheltered take-off area
U-1: Indicates aeronautical advisory station licensed to operate on 122.8; U-2 on 123.0; U-3 on 123.05; U-4 on 122.85; U-5 on 122.95
† - L - Lighting in operation Sunset to Sunrise
*L - Lighting available Sunset to Sunrise only on request (by radio call, letter, phone, telegram).
(L) - Lighting in operation part of the night and on request, or not operating thereafter.
When facility or information is lacking, the respective character is replaced by a dash.
RADIO AIDS TO NAVIGATION AND COMMUNICATION BOXES
VHF OMNI RANGE (VOR)
VORTAC
VOR-DME
Radiobeacon, nondirectional (homing)
Other facilities
LF/MF Radio Range
Continuous line indicates "N" quadrant
122.1R 122.6 123.6
OAKLAND
362 116.8 OAK
Enroute Weather Advisory Service (EWAS) freq 122.0
122.1R
OAKLAND FSS
Underline indicates no voice on this freq
122.1R
WASHINGTON
Controlling Area FSS
ARTCC Remoted Sites
CLEVELAND
Toledo
OAKLAND EWAS
Remoted EWAS
Heavy line box indicates Flight Service Station (FSS). Freqs 121.5 122.2 243.0 and 255.4 are normally available at all FSS's and are not shown above boxes. All other freqs are shown.
R–receive only T–transmit only
Thin line box with freqs above are remoted to NAVAID site. Other freqs at controlling FSS may be available determined by altitude and terrain.
Box without freqs and controlling FSS indicates no FSS freqs available.
AIRSPACE INFORMATION
Prohibited, Restricted, Warning and Alert Areas
Low Altitude Federal Airways are indicated by center line
092°
V 3
CZ–Control Zone
Control zone extends upwards from surface.
TTTTT Control zones within which fixed-wing special VFR Flight is prohibited.
AIRPORT TRAFFIC AREAS
Federally operated control tower
Non-Federal control tower
Other Airport (no traffic area, no FSS at airport)
FSS
DAYTON CT - 119.9
1008 L 70
MARTIN NFCT - 119.2
556 L 70
SOMERSET
1540 L 37
Hours of operation of tower, if not continuous, are included with tower frequencies.
Only the airways and reserved airspace effective below 18,000 feet MSL are shown on this chart.
OBSTRUCTIONS
1000 feet and higher AGL
below 1000 feet AGL
or Group Obstruction
1505 (1285) UC
elevation of the top above mean sea level (height of the structure above ground)
UC (Under Construction) or reported, position and elevation unverified.
CAUTION: Guy wires may extend outward from structures
MISCELLANEOUS
Rotating Light
Flashing Light Fl
Marine Light
Rotating Light (with course lights and code) 17
Isogonic Line (1970 VALUE) 2°W
Visual Flight Routes through mountain passes.
NOTICE TO USERS OF THIS CHART
You are urgently requested to inform us of corrections and additions that come to your attention while using this chart. When practicable, such information should be indicated clearly and accurately on the chart (a replacement copy will be returned). Civil Users mail to: THE DIRECTOR, NATIONAL OCEAN SURVEY, NATIONAL OCEANIC AND ATMOSPHERIC ADMINISTRATION, ROCKVILLE, MARYLAND 20852. Military Users mail to: DIRECTOR, DEFENSE MAPPING AGENCY AEROSPACE CENTER, ST LOUIS AFS, MISSOURI 63118. ATTN: PP

FIGURE 2-5. WAC Chart Legend.

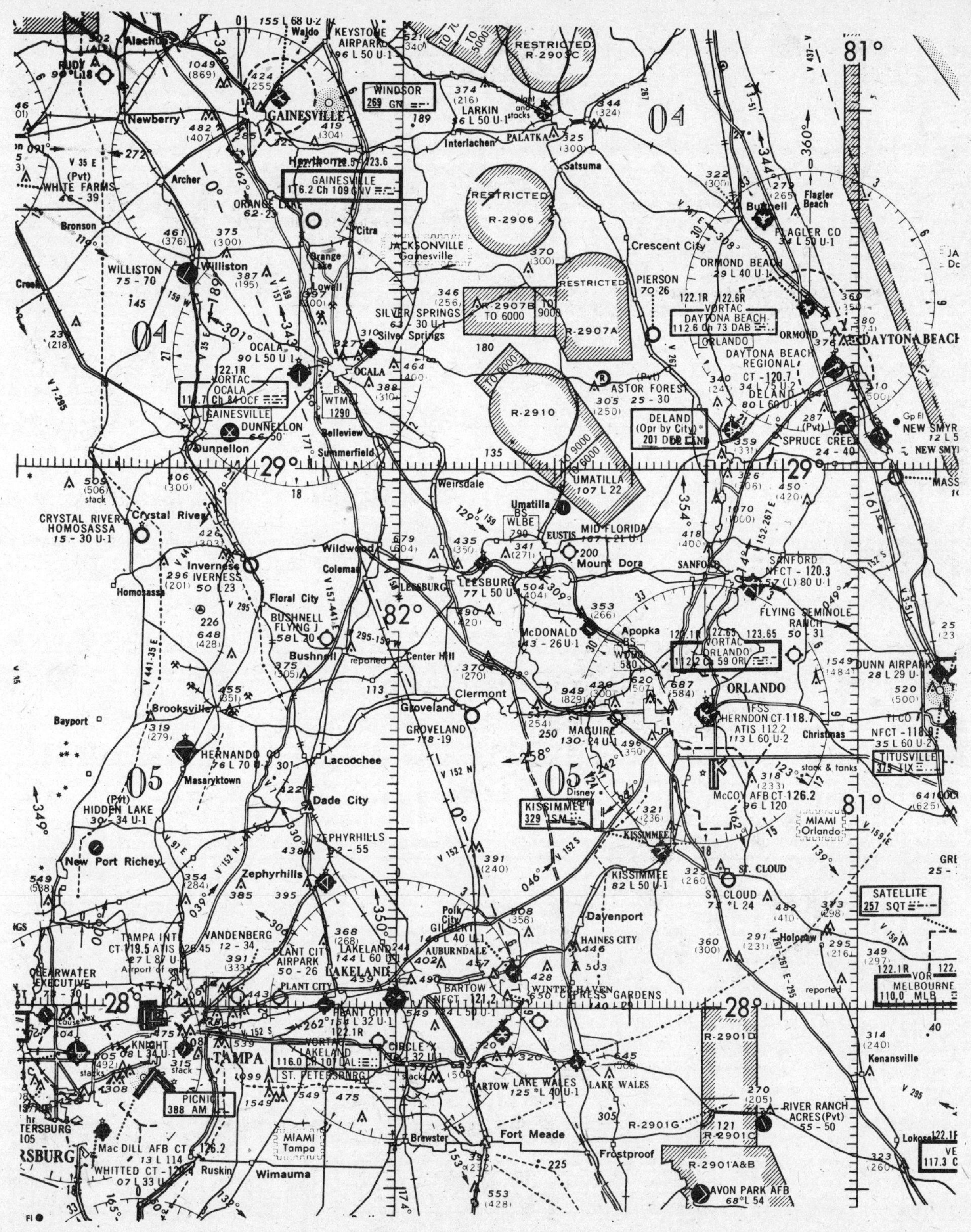

FIGURE 2-6. WAC Chart.

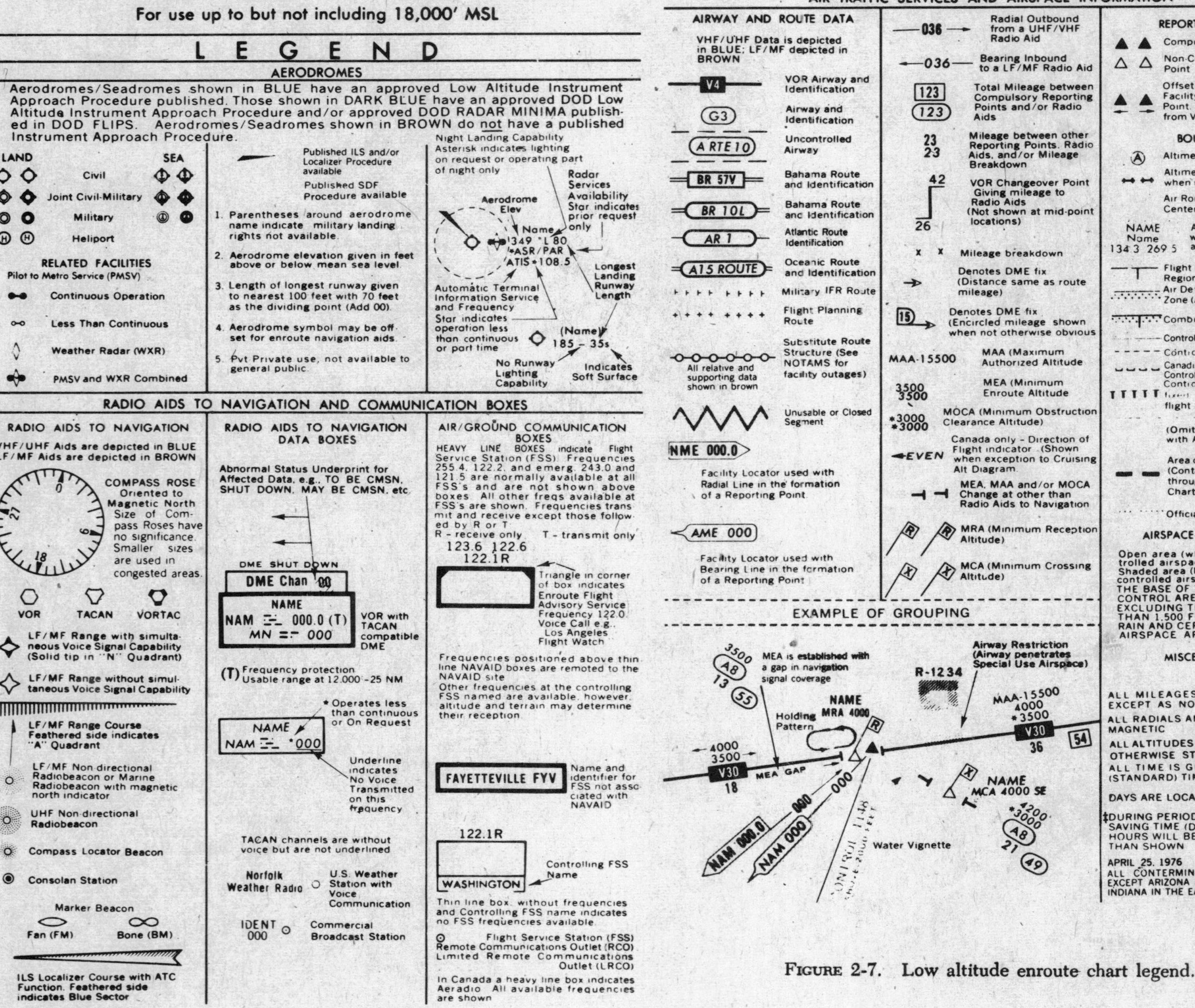

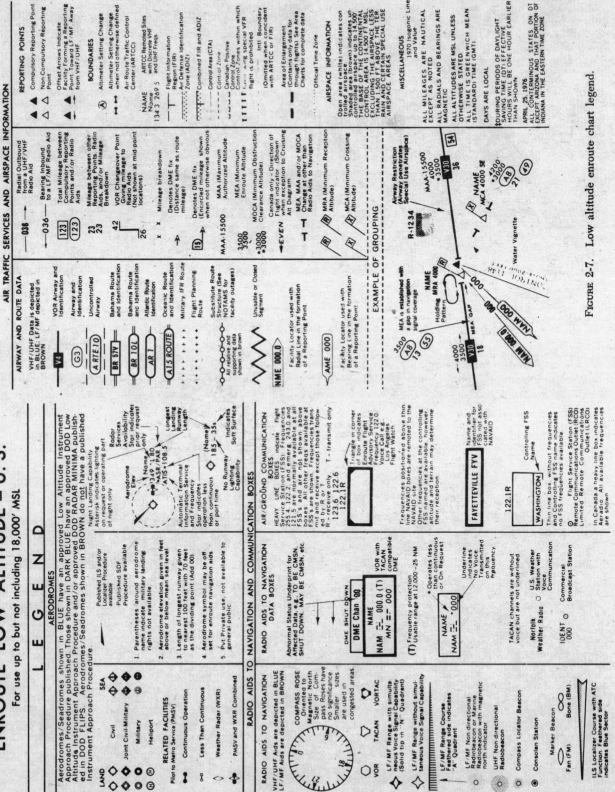

FIGURE 2-7. Low altitude enroute chart legend.

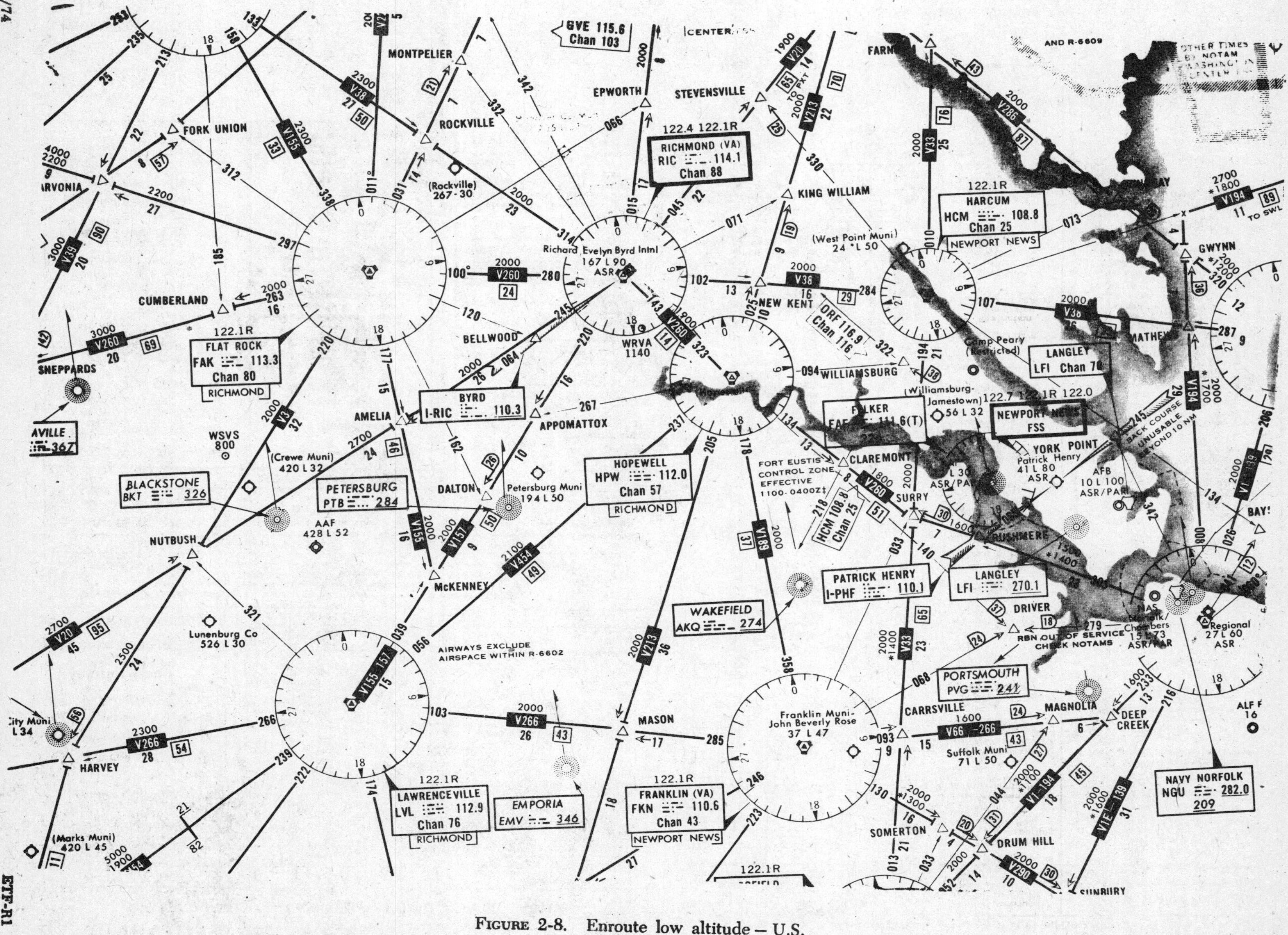

FIGURE 2-8. Enroute low altitude – U.S.

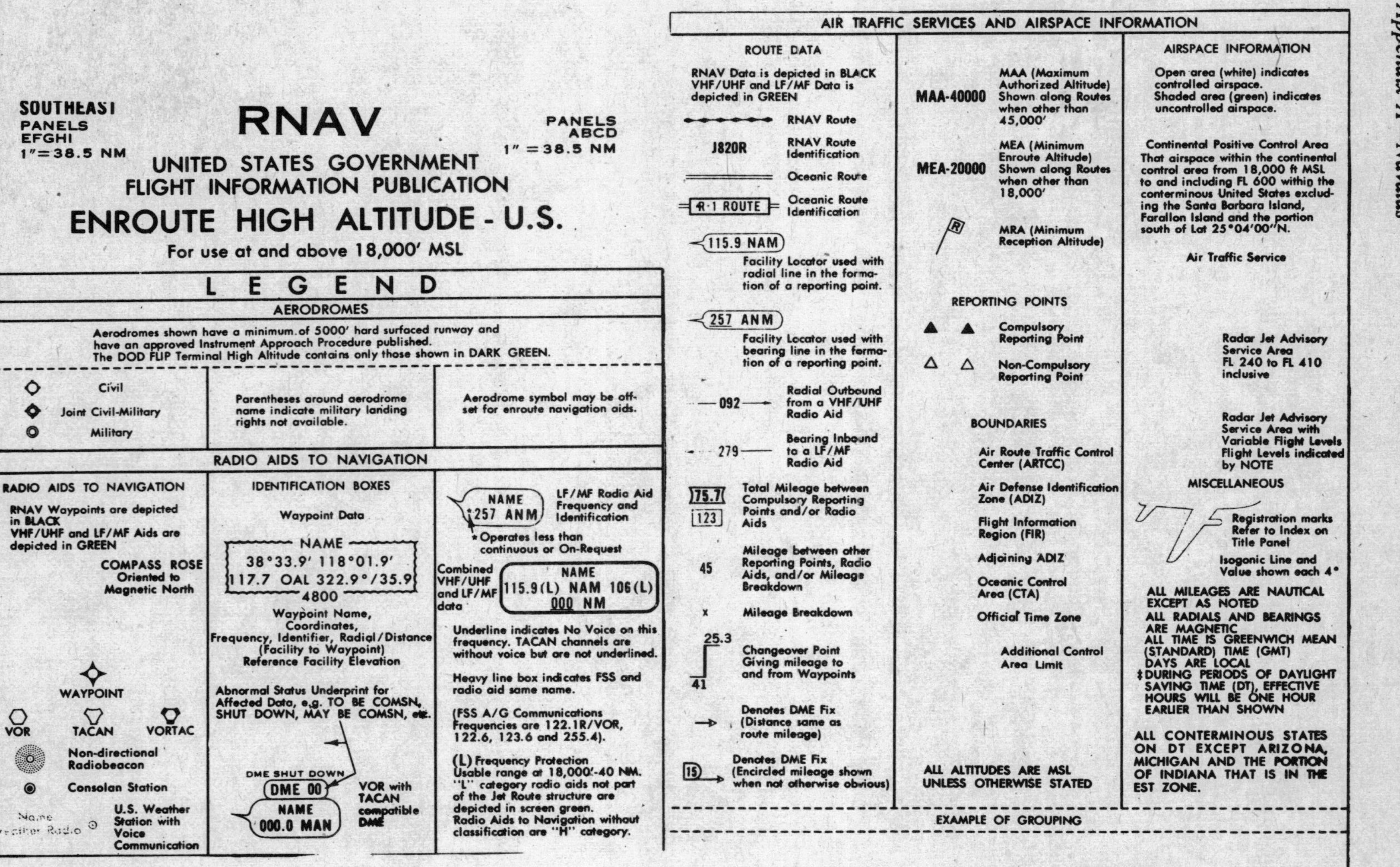
SOUTHEAST
PANELS
EFGHI
1"=38.5 NM
RNAV
PANELS
ABCD
1" =38.5 NM
UNITED STATES GOVERNMENT
FLIGHT INFORMATION PUBLICATION
ENROUTE HIGH ALTITUDE - U.S.
For use at and above 18,000' MSL
L E G E N D
AERODROMES
Aerodromes shown have a minimum of 5000' hard surfaced runway and have an approved Instrument Approach Procedure published.
The DOD FLIP Terminal High Altitude contains only those shown in DARK GREEN.
Civil
Joint Civil-Military
Military
Parentheses around aerodrome name indicate military landing rights not available.
Aerodrome symbol may be offset for enroute navigation aids.
RADIO AIDS TO NAVIGATION
RADIO AIDS TO NAVIGATION
RNAV Waypoints are depicted in BLACK
VHF/UHF and LF/MF Aids are depicted in GREEN
COMPASS ROSE
Oriented to
Magnetic North
WAYPOINT
VOR
TACAN
VORTAC
Non-directional Radiobeacon
Consolan Station
Name Weather Radio
U.S. Weather Station with Voice Communication
IDENTIFICATION BOXES
Waypoint Data
NAME
38°33.9' 118°01.9'
117.7 OAL 322.9°/35.9
4800
Waypoint Name,
Coordinates,
Frequency, Identifier, Radial/Distance
(Facility to Waypoint)
Reference Facility Elevation
Abnormal Status Underprint for Affected Data, e.g. TO BE COMSN, SHUT DOWN, MAY BE COMSN, etc.
DME SHUT DOWN
DME 00
NAME
000.0 MAN
VOR with TACAN compatible DME
NAME
257 ANM
LF/MF Radio Aid Frequency and Identification
* Operates less than continuous or On-Request
Combined VHF/UHF and LF/MF data
NAME
115.9(L) NAM 106(L)
000 NM
Underline indicates No Voice on this frequency. TACAN channels are without voice but are not underlined.
Heavy line box indicates FSS and radio aid same name.
(FSS A/G Communications Frequencies are 122.1R/VOR, 122.6, 123.6 and 255.4).
(L) Frequency Protection
Usable range at 18,000'-40 NM.
"L" category radio aids not part of the Jet Route structure are depicted in screen green.
Radio Aids to Navigation without classification are "H" category.
AIR TRAFFIC SERVICES AND AIRSPACE INFORMATION
ROUTE DATA
RNAV Data is depicted in BLACK
VHF/UHF and LF/MF Data is depicted in GREEN
RNAV Route
J820R
RNAV Route Identification
Oceanic Route
R-1 ROUTE
Oceanic Route Identification
115.9 NAM
Facility Locator used with radial line in the formation of a reporting point.
257 ANM
Facility Locator used with bearing line in the formation of a reporting point.
092
Radial Outbound from a VHF/UHF Radio Aid
279
Bearing Inbound to a LF/MF Radio Aid
75.7
123
Total Mileage between Compulsory Reporting Points and/or Radio Aids
45
Mileage between other Reporting Points, Radio Aids, and/or Mileage Breakdown
x
Mileage Breakdown
25.3
41
Changeover Point Giving mileage to and from Waypoints
Denotes DME Fix (Distance same as route mileage)
15
Denotes DME Fix (Encircled mileage shown when not otherwise obvious)
MAA-40000
MAA (Maximum Authorized Altitude) Shown along Routes when other than 45,000'
MEA-20000
MEA (Minimum Enroute Altitude) Shown along Routes when other than 18,000'
R
MRA (Minimum Reception Altitude)
REPORTING POINTS
Compulsory Reporting Point
Non-Compulsory Reporting Point
BOUNDARIES
Air Route Traffic Control Center (ARTCC)
Air Defense Identification Zone (ADIZ)
Flight Information Region (FIR)
Adjoining ADIZ
Oceanic Control Area (CTA)
Official Time Zone
Additional Control Area Limit
ALL ALTITUDES ARE MSL UNLESS OTHERWISE STATED
AIRSPACE INFORMATION
Open area (white) indicates controlled airspace.
Shaded area (green) indicates uncontrolled airspace.
Continental Positive Control Area
That airspace within the continental control area from 18,000 ft MSL to and including FL 600 within the conterminous United States excluding the Santa Barbara Island, Farallon Island and the portion south of Lat 25°04'00"N.
Air Traffic Service
Radar Jet Advisory Service Area FL 240 to FL 410 inclusive
Radar Jet Advisory Service Area with Variable Flight Levels Flight Levels indicated by NOTE
MISCELLANEOUS
Registration marks Refer to Index on Title Panel
Isogonic Line and Value shown each 4°
ALL MILEAGES ARE NAUTICAL EXCEPT AS NOTED
ALL RADIALS AND BEARINGS ARE MAGNETIC
ALL TIME IS GREENWICH MEAN (STANDARD) TIME (GMT)
DAYS ARE LOCAL
‡DURING PERIODS OF DAYLIGHT SAVING TIME (DT), EFFECTIVE HOURS WILL BE ONE HOUR EARLIER THAN SHOWN
ALL CONTERMINOUS STATES ON DT EXCEPT ARIZONA, MICHIGAN AND THE PORTION OF INDIANA THAT IS IN THE EST ZONE.
EXAMPLE OF GROUPING
Track Angle
056°
236°
95
62.9
059°
MAA-40000
MEA-20000
J802-858R
157.9
239°
3/74
ETF-R1

FIGURE 2-9. RNAV Chart Legend.

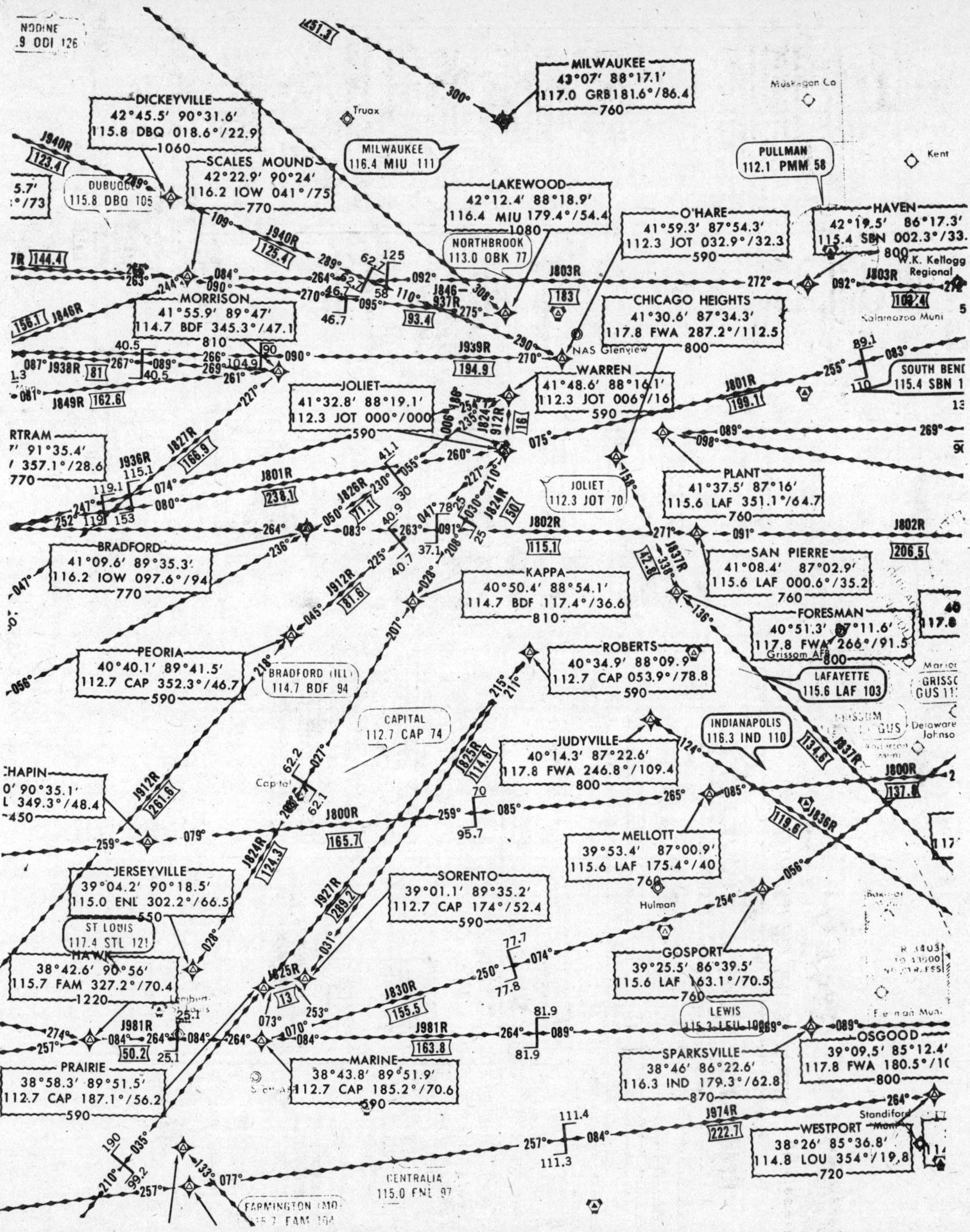

FIGURE 2-10. RNAV Chart.

ENROUTE HIGH ALTITUDE - U.S.

For use at and above 18,000′ MSL

L E G E N D

AERODROMES

Aerodromes shown have a minimum of 5000′ hard surfaced runway.
Aerodromes in BLUE have an approved Instrument Approach Procedure published.
The DOD FLIP Terminal High Altitude contains only those shown in DARK BLUE.

Civil
Joint Civil-Military
Military

Parentheses around aerodrome name indicates military landing rights not available.

Aerodrome symbol may be displaced for enroute navigational aids.

RADIO AIDS TO NAVIGATION

RADIO AIDS TO NAVIGATION

VHF/UHF Aids are depicted in BLUE
LF/MF Aids are depicted in BROWN

COMPASS ROSE Oriented to Magnetic North

VOR TACAN VORTAC

LF/MF Range with simultaneous Voice Signal Capability (Solid tip in "N" Quadrant)

LF/MF Range without simultaneous Voice Signal Capability

090°

LF/MF Range Course
Feathered side indicates "A" Quadrant

LF/MF Non-directional Radiobeacon or Marine Radiobeacon

UHF Non-directional Radiobeacon

Consolan Station

Name Weather Radio — U.S. Weather Station with Voice Communication

IDENTIFICATION BOXES

Abnormal Status Underprint for Affected Data, e.g. TO BE CMSN, SHUT DOWN, MAY BE CMSN, etc.

DME SHUTDOWN
DME 00
NAME 000.0 MAN — VOR with TACAN compatible DME

NAME •257 ANM — LF/MF Radio Aid Identification and Frequency

Operates less than continuous or On-Request

Combined VHF/UHF and LF/MF data.

LWAS- Enroute Weather Advisory Service. Frequency 122.0 MHz. Voice Call e.g. "Los Angeles EWAS"

NAME
115.9 (L) NAM 106 (L)
000 NM

Underline indicates No Voice on this frequency. TACAN Channels are without Voice but are not underlined.

Heavy line box indicates FSS and radio aid same name.

(FSS freqs available are 255.4, 122.2, selected discrete freqs, and emerg. 243.0 and 121.5)

(L) Frequency Protection
Usable range at 18,000′–40 NM
"L" category radio aids located off Jet routes are depicted in screen blue.
Radio Aids to Navigation Without Classification are "H" Category

AIR TRAFFIC SERVICES AND AIRSPACE INFORMATION

ROUTE DATA

VHF/UHF Data is depicted in BLUE;
LF/MF Data is depicted in BROWN

Jet Route
Oceanic Route
Substitute Route Structure

(Via or by-passing temporarily shutdown navigational aids).
See NOTAMS or appropriate publications for specific information.

Unusable Route Segment
Military IFR Route
Flight Planning Route
J1 — Jet Route Identification
J6 — Preferred Single Direction Jet Route.
HL500 — Canadian High Level Airway Identification.
A15 ROUTE — Oceanic Route Identification

115.9 NAM — Facility Locator used with Radial Line in the formation of a Reporting point

257 ANM — Facility Locator used with Bearing Line in the formation of a Reporting Point

— 092 → Radial Outbound from a VHF/UHF Navigational Aid

← 279 — Bearing Inbound to a LF/MF Navigational Aid

123, 146 — Total Mileage between Compulsory Reporting Points and/or Radio Aids

23, 45 — Mileage between other Reporting Points, Radio Aids, and/or Mileage Breakdown

42 / 26 — VOR Changeover Point Giving mileage to Radio Aids (Not shown when less than 5 NM from the midpoint in either direction

Mileage Breakdown

Denotes DME fix, (Distance same as route mileage)

15 — Denotes DME fix (Encircled mileage shown when not otherwise obvious)

MAA-40000 — MAA (Maximum Authorized Altitude) Shown along Routes when other than 45,000′

MEA-20000 — MEA (Minimum Enroute Altitude) Shown along Routes when other than 18,000′

MEA and/or MAA Change at other than Radio Aids to Navigation

MRA (Minimum Reception Altitude)

REPORTING POINTS

Compulsory Reporting Point

Non-Compulsory Reporting Point

Offset Arrows Indicate Facility Forming a Reporting Point. Toward LF/MF Away From VHF/UHF Radio Aid

Radar Jet Advisory Service Area FL 240 to FL 410 inclusive.

Radar Jet Advisory Service Area with Variable Flight Levels. Flight Levels Indicated by NOTE.

ALL ALTITUDES ARE MSL UNLESS OTHERWISE STATED.

BOUNDARIES

Air Route Traffic Control Center (ARTCC)
Air Defense Identification Zone (ADIZ)
Flight Information Region (FIR)
Upper Information Region (UIR)
Adjoining ADIZ
Combined FIR and UIR
Oceanic Control Area (CTA)
International Boundary (Not shown when coincident with ARTC or FIR)
Official Time Zone

AIRSPACE INFORMATION

Open area (white) indicates controlled airspace.
Shaded area (brown) indicates uncontrolled airspace.

Continental Positive Control Area

That airspace within the continental control area from 18,000 ft MSL to and including FL 600 within the conterminous United States excluding the Santa Barbara Island, Farallon Island and the portion south of Lat 25°04′00″N

Air Traffic Service

CTA/FIR
NAME OCEANIC

Additional Control Area Limit

MISCELLANEOUS

Registration marks Refer to Index on Title Panel

12°E — 1970 Isogonic Line and Value shown each 4°

ALL MILEAGES ARE NAUTICAL EXCEPT AS NOTED
ALL RADIALS AND BEARINGS ARE MAGNETIC
ALL TIME IS GREENWICH MEAN (STANDARD) TIME (GMT)
DAYS ARE LOCAL
‡DURING PERIODS OF DAYLIGHT SAVING TIME (DT), EFFECTIVE HOURS WILL BE ONE HOUR EARLIER THAN SHOWN

EXAMPLE OF GROUPING

Effective Times of Single Direction Routes

1200–0400Z

090° J6 70 216 049 J78 76 MAA-40000 MEA-26000 60 270 45 146 065 115.9 NAM 106

Jet Route centerlines are shown through facilities which are not part of that specific route.

Holding Pattern

FIGURE 2-11. High altitude enroute chart legend.

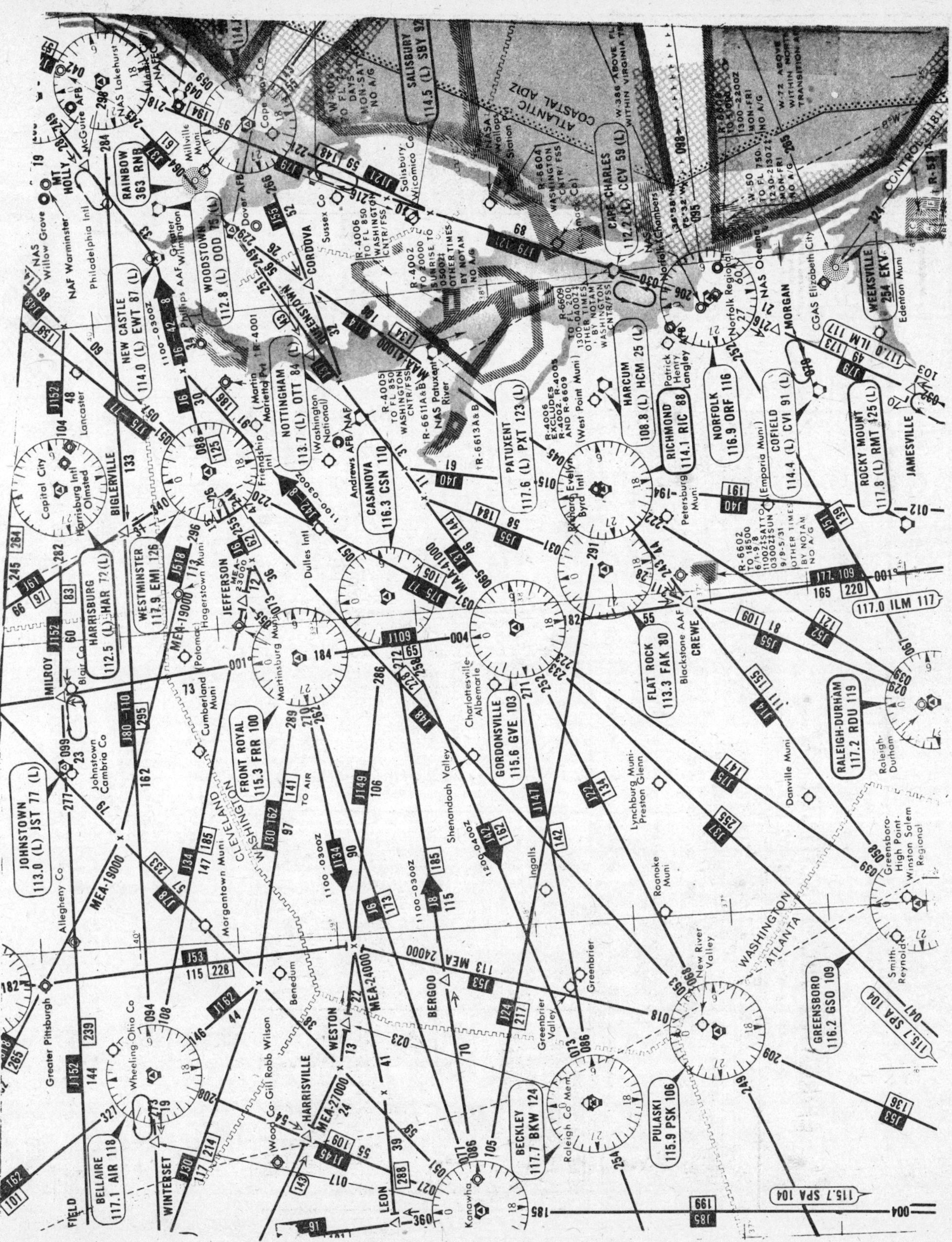

FIGURE 2-12. High altitude enroute chart.

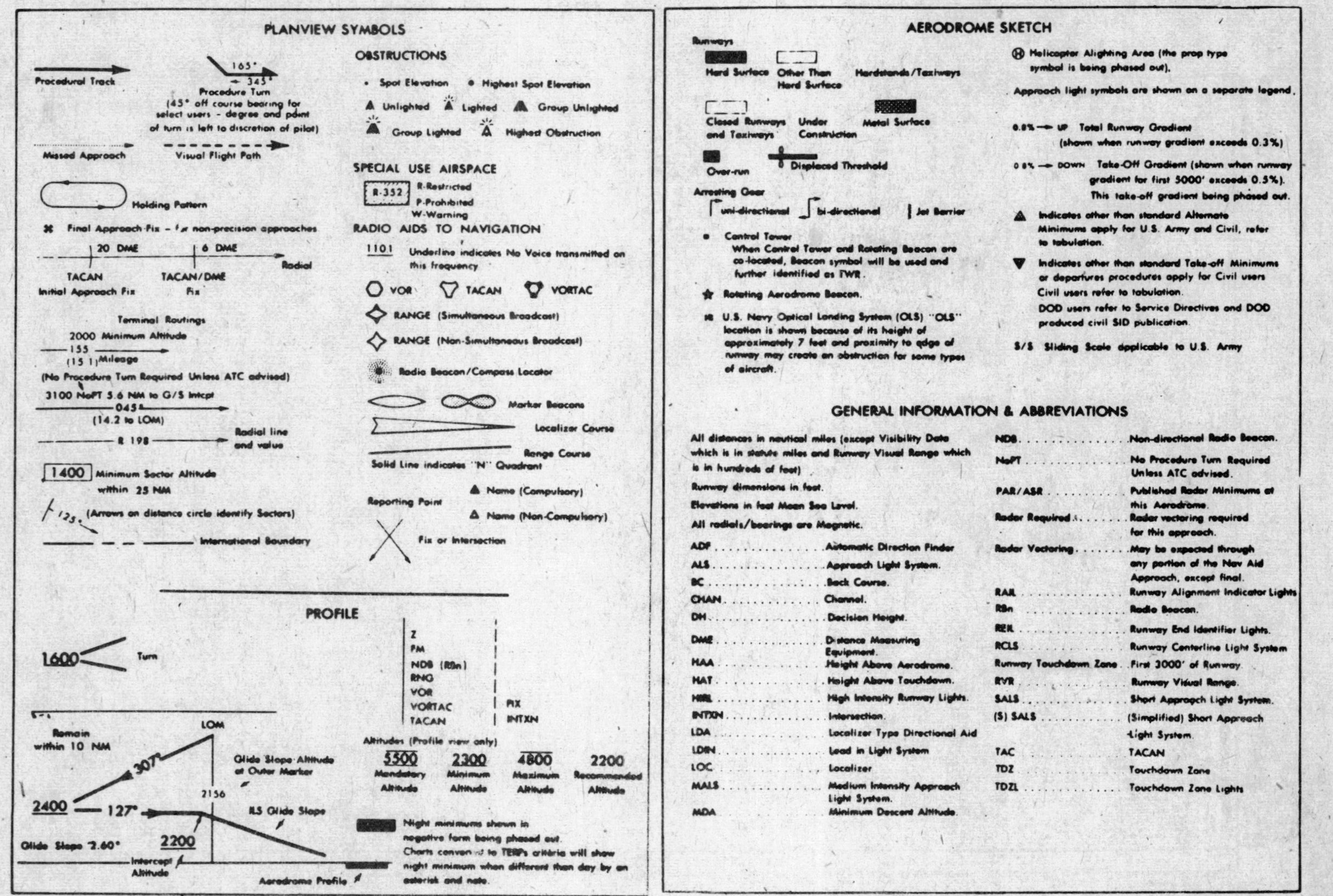

FIGURE 2-13. SIAP Chart Legend.

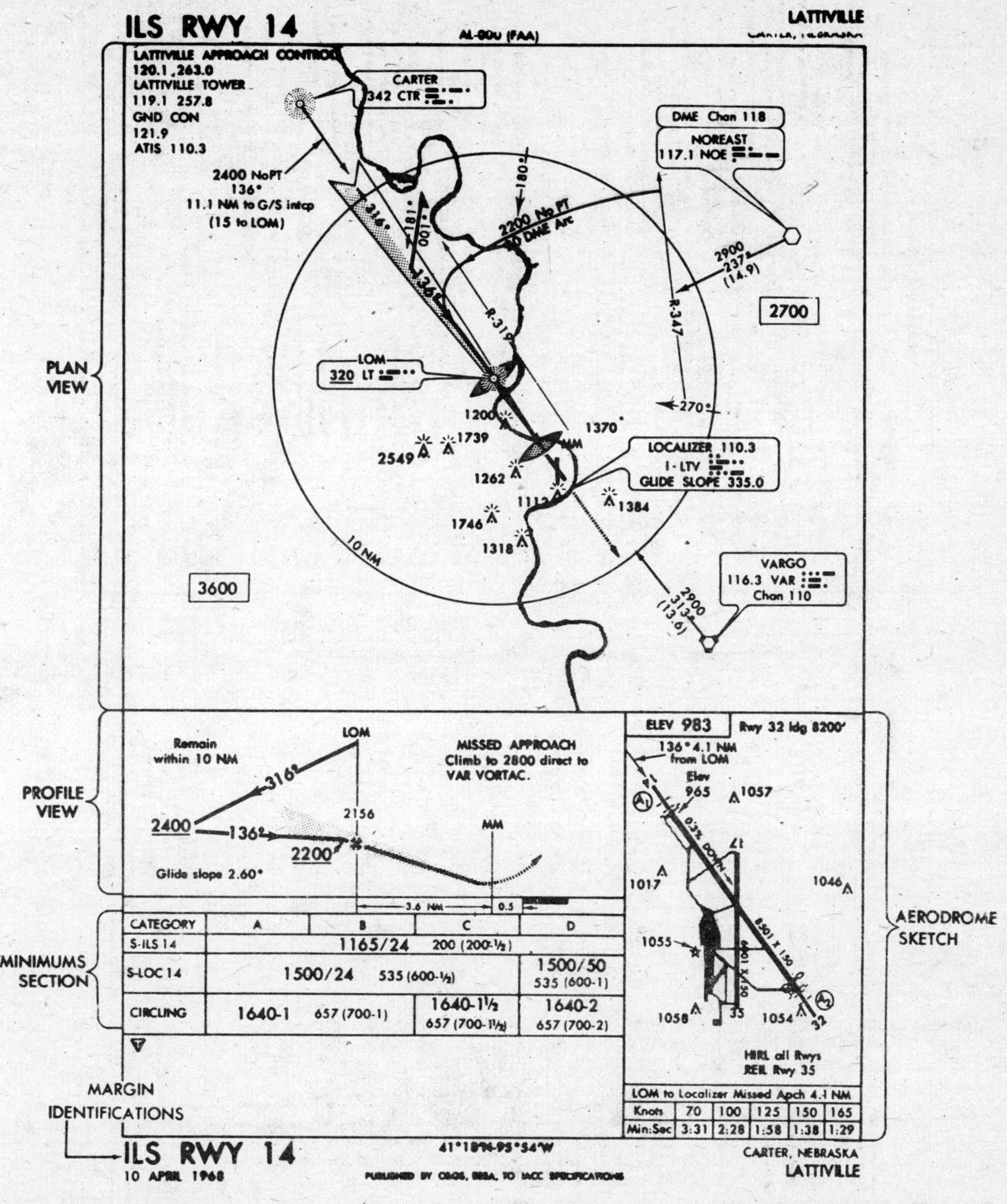

FIGURE 2-14. Breakdown of an SIAP Chart.

PLAN VIEW
Lattiville Airport
Carter, Nebraska

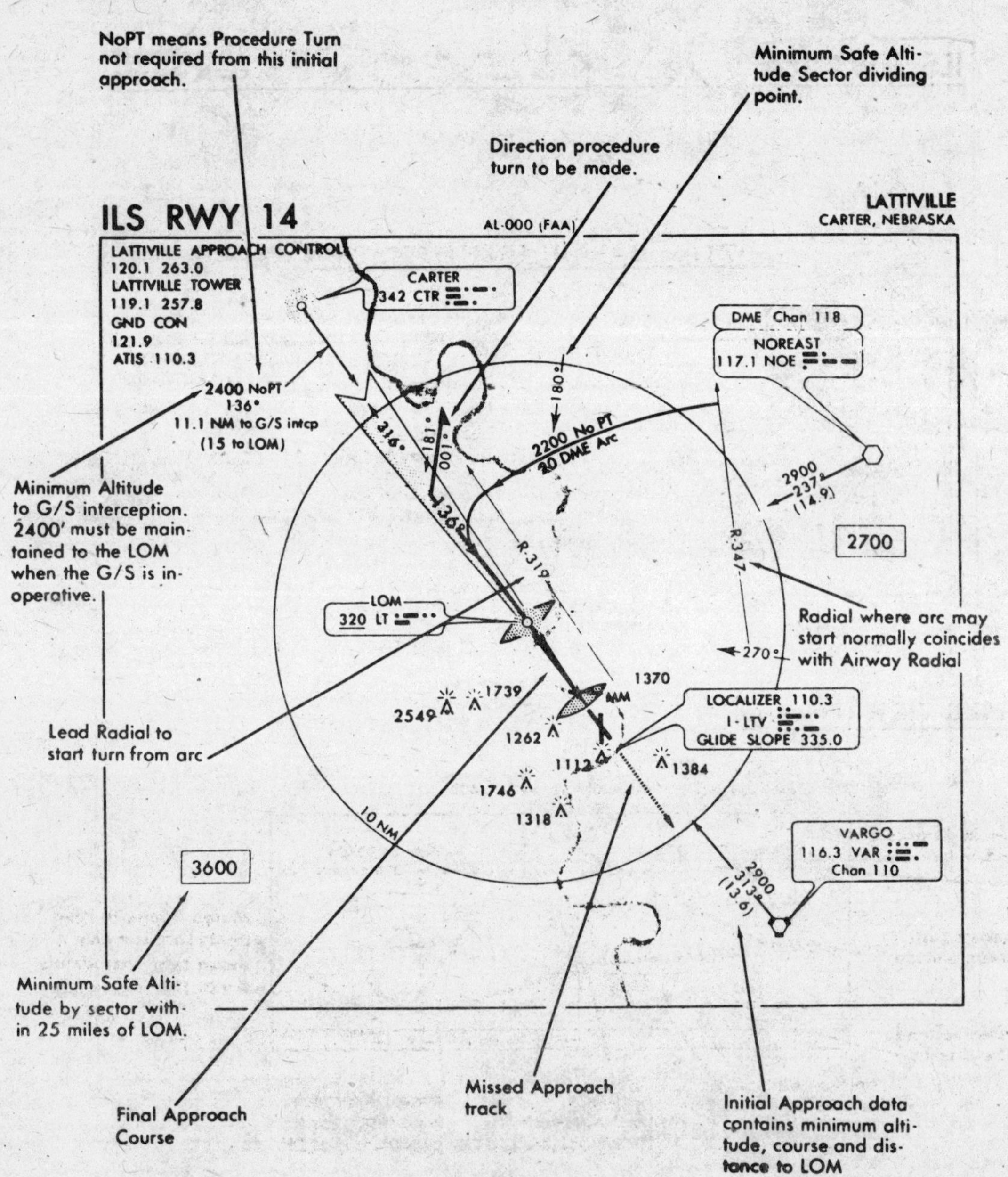
NoPT means Procedure Turn not required from this initial approach.
Minimum Safe Altitude Sector dividing point.
Direction procedure turn to be made.
ILS RWY 14
AL-000 (FAA)
LATTIVILLE
CARTER, NEBRASKA
LATTIVILLE APPROACH CONTROL
120.1 263.0
LATTIVILLE TOWER
119.1 257.8
GND CON
121.9
ATIS 110.3
CARTER
342 CTR
DME Chan 118
NOREAST
117.1 NOE
2400 NoPT
136°
11.1 NM to G/S intcp
(15 to LOM)
316°
181°
001°
180°
2200 No PT
20 DME Arc
136°
R-319
R-347
2900
237°
(14.9)
2700
Minimum Altitude to G/S interception. 2400′ must be maintained to the LOM when the G/S is inoperative.
LOM
320 LT
Radial where arc may start normally coincides with Airway Radial
270°
1370
1739
2549
MM
LOCALIZER 110.3
I-LTV
GLIDE SLOPE 335.0
1262
Lead Radial to start turn from arc
1112
1384
1746
1318
10 NM
VARGO
116.3 VAR
Chan 110
3600
2900
313°
(13.6)
Minimum Safe Altitude by sector within 25 miles of LOM.
Missed Approach track
Final Approach Course
Initial Approach data contains minimum altitude, course and distance to LOM

FIGURE 2-15.

TOP MARGIN IDENTIFICATION

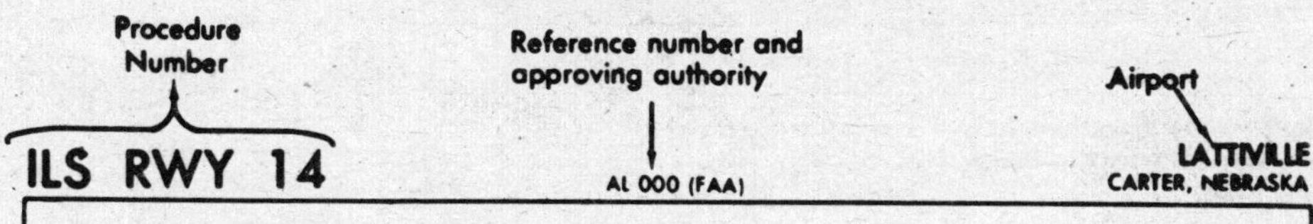

BOTTOM MARGIN IDENTIFICATION

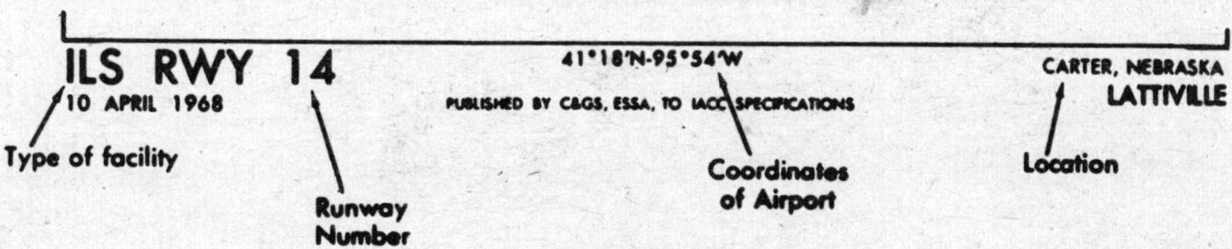

FIGURE 24.

PROFILE VIEW (Precision)

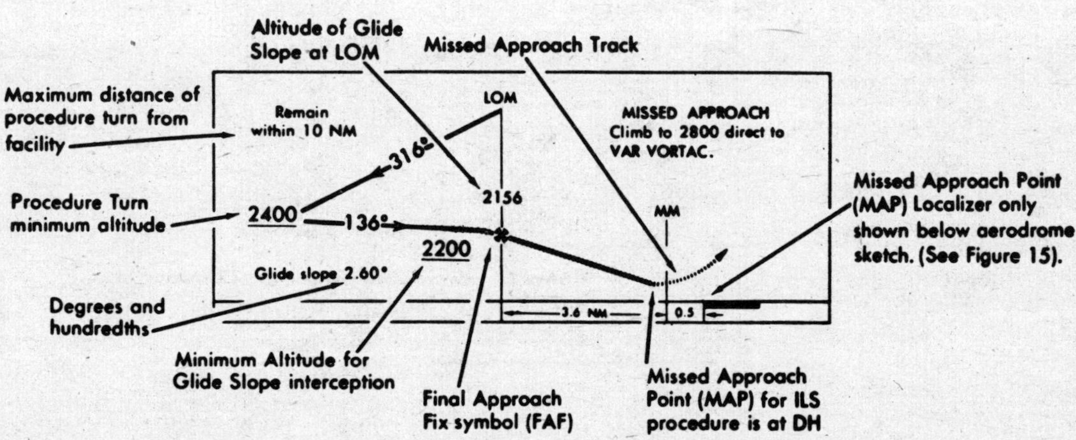

FIGURE 2-16.

MINIMUMS SECTION (and notes).

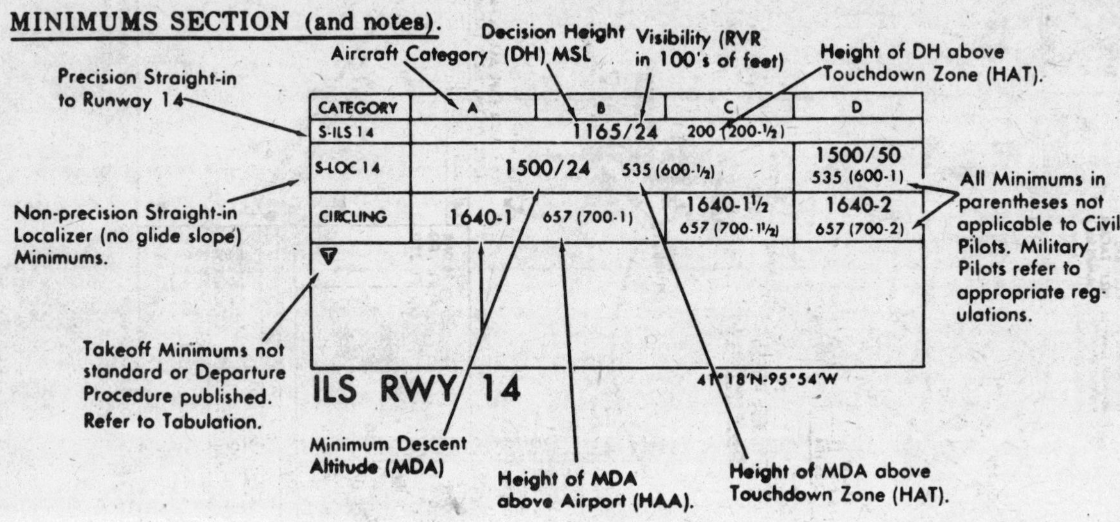

Aerodrome Data.

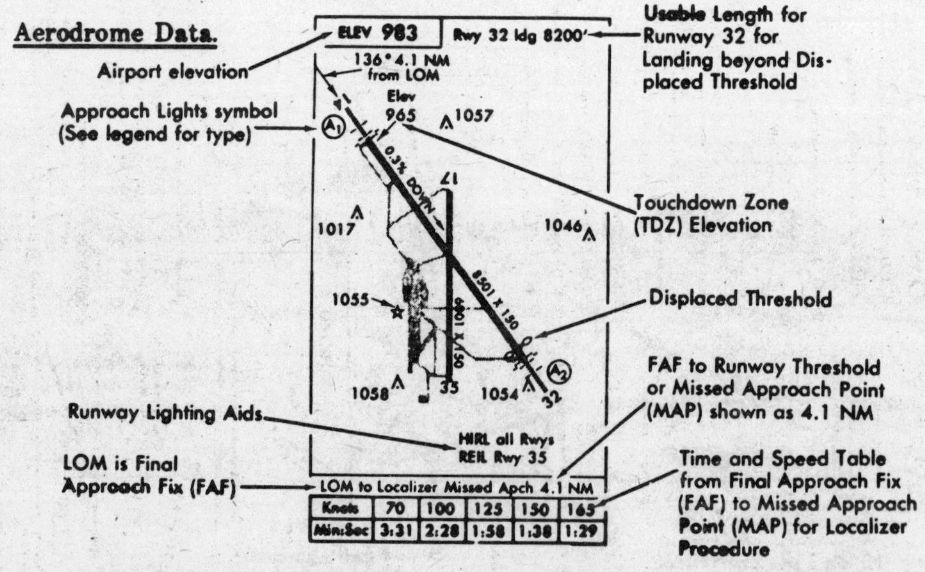

FIGURE 2-17.

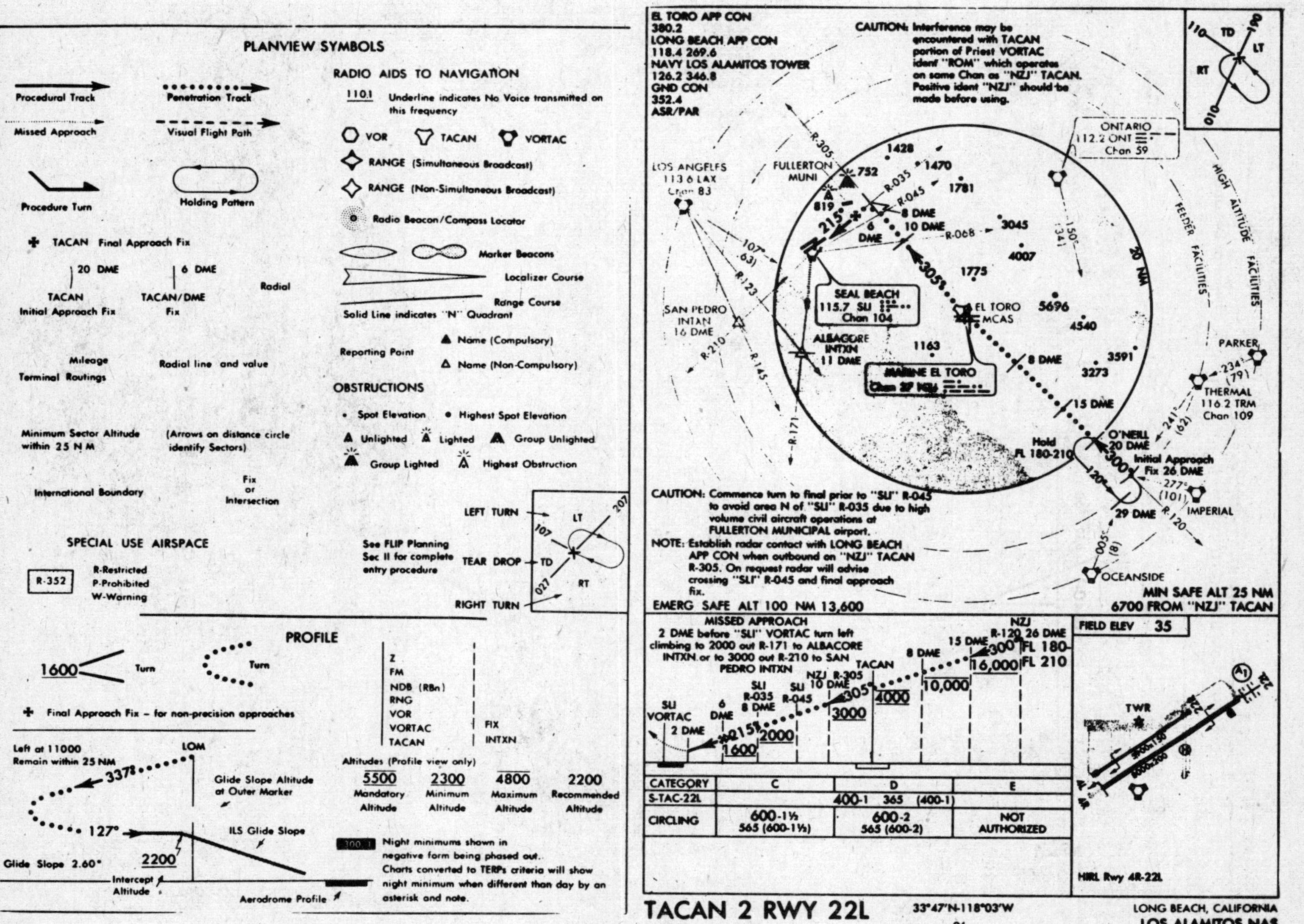

FIGURE 2-18. High Altitude Approach Chart and Legend.

WEST

UNITED STATES GOVERNMENT

STANDARD INSTRUMENT DEPARTURES

SIDs

FOR CIVIL AERODROMES

WESTERN UNITED STATES

(WEST OF MISSISSIPPI RIVER)

EFFECTIVE 0901Z 23 MAY 1974

TO 0901Z 18 JUL 1974

NOTE

DOD OBSTRUCTION CRITERIA HAVE NOT BEEN APPLIED TO THE SIDS HEREIN. SIDS WHICH PROVIDE DOD OBSTRUCTION CLEARANCE INFORMATION FOR MILITARY AND JOINT CIVIL/MILITARY AERODROMES, IF PUBLISHED, ARE AVAILABLE IN THE BASE OPERATIONS OF THESE AERODROMES. USAF/USN PILOTS WILL USE DOD PRODUCED SIDS WHERE AVAILABLE. U. S. ARMY PILOTS REFER TO AR 95-1.

PUBLISHED BY NATIONAL OCEAN SURVEY
NATIONAL OCEANIC AND ATMOSPHERIC ADMINISTRATION
PUBLISHED IN ACCORDANCE WITH INTER-AGENCY AIR CARTOGRAPHIC COMMITTEE
SPECIFICATIONS AND AGREEMENTS APPROVED BY:

DEPARTMENT OF DEFENSE ★ FEDERAL AVIATION ADMINISTRATION ★ DEPARTMENT OF COMMERCE

LEGEND

STANDARD INSTRUMENT DEPARTURE (SID) CHARTS

RADIO AIDS TO NAVIGATION

VOR
TACAN
VORTAC
WAYPOINT (RNAV)
NDB (Non-directional Radio Beacon)
RANGE (Simultaneous Voice)
RANGE (Non-Simultaneous Voice)
LOM (Compass Locator)
MARKER BEACONS
LOCALIZER COURSE

AERODROMES

Helicopter

RUNWAYS

Hardsurface
Metal Surface
Closed
Under Construction
Other Than Hard Surface
Over-run / Hardstands / Taxiways

ROUTES

Departure Route
Transition Route

SPECIAL USE AIRSPACE

R-5
R-Restricted
P-Prohibited
W-Warning
A-Alert

MISCELLANEOUS SYMBOLS

Intersections
Compulsory Reporting Point
DME Fix
Radial line and value
Distance Not To Scale
Arresting Gear
Jet Barrier
Displaced Threshold
Control Tower
Take Off Gradient
Changeover Point
Airway Identification

Outer Marker (OM)-continuous dashes
Middle Marker (MM)-alternate dots and dashes.
117.6-frequency underlined indicates no voice capability.
All radials/bearings are magnetic.
All mileages are nautical.
Runway dimensions in feet.
Elevation in feet-MSL.

FIGURE 2-19. SID cover page and legend.

INSTRUMENT APPROACH PROCEDURES (CHARTS)
WESTERN UNITED STATES

▽ IFR TAKE-OFF MINIMUMS AND DEPARTURE PROCEDURES

FAR 91.116(c) prescribes take-off rules and establishes standard take-off minimums as follows:

(1) Aircraft having two engines or less – one statute mile.

(2) Aircraft having more than two engines – one-half statute mile.

Aerodromes within this geographical area with IFR take-off minimums other than standard are listed below alphabetically by aerodrome name. Departure procedures and/or ceiling visibility minimums are established to assist pilots conducting IFR flight in avoiding obstructions during climb to the minimum enroute altitude.

Take-off minimums and departure procedures apply to all runways unless otherwise specified.

AERODROME NAME — TAKE-OFF MINIMUMS

ARCATA .... Rwy 1, 500-1
Arcata-Eureka, California — Rwy 13, 300-1
Rwy 31, RVR/24
Rwy 1, left turn within 1 NM. Rwy 13, right turn within 1 NM. All aircraft climb on ACV R-178 CW through R-291 to V27.

AURORA STATE
Aurora, Oregon
Climb runway heading to 500 then direct to UBG VORTAC before proceeding on course. V23 climb on course.

BAKER MUNI 600-1
Baker Oregon
Climb visually over the airport to 3900, climb on BKE R-297 within 10 NM to cross BKE VORTAC at or above: SE bound V4, V4S, 7000; W bound V182, 10,000; NW bound V4, 7000; NW bound V357, 6000. All maneuvering N side of BKE R-297.

BARSTOW-DAGGETT .... Rwys 21, 25, 800-1
Daggett, California
Rwys 21, 25, turn right and cross airport NE bound. Climb direct to DAG VORTAC thence on assigned route.

BELLINGHAM INTL
Bellingham, Washington
Climb direct to BLI VORTAC before proceeding on course; V23 SE bound, climb visually to 400 over the airport before proceeding on course.

BEND MUNI
Bend, Oregon
Turn left, climb direct to RDM VORTAC, continue climb on R-141 within 10 NM to cross RDM VORTAC at or above 5000: NW bound V165, 8000; W bound V121/V536, 5300.

BERMUDA DUNES
Bermuda Dunes, California
Rwy 29 turn right and cross airport SE bound. Climb direct to TRM VORTAC continue climb on R-107 within 10 NM to MCA for direction of flight.

BISBEE-DOUGLAS INTL
Douglas, Arizona
Climb to 5700 in holding pattern thence assigned route.

BISHOP .... 2 miles
Bishop, California
Climb visually within 2 NM of Bishop Airport to Cross BIH VOR at or above 8000, Climb SE bound on R-140 to 10,000, turn left, proceed to BIH VOR continuing climb in a one minute holding pattern on R-140 (320° inbound), right turns to the following MCAs: NW bound direct to Nichols Int, 13,000; N bound direct to Coaldale VORTAC, 15,500; SW bound direct to Friant VORTAC, 15,000.

BLYTHE
Blythe, California
Rwy 26 requires a climb rate of 280 ft. per NM to 1500 feet.
Departures 180° CW through 040° and 070° CW through 095°, climb direct to BLH VORTAC, climb W bound on V64-460 to 2000, W bound continue climb on course. E bound, N bound and S bound turn left, continue climb direct BLH VORTAC.

BOEING FIELD INTL KING COUNTY
Seattle, Washington
Climb visually over the airport to 300 then direct to SEA VORTAC, continue climb on R-227 within 10 NM to cross SEA VORTAC at or above: E bound V2N, 4300; E bound V2, 2000; E bound V2S/V4, 4000; SE bound V4S, 4000, or comply withpublished BFI SIDs.

(Continued on page 2)

BARSTOW ONE DEPARTURE (8YB1.8YB)

WILL ROGERS WORLD
OKLAHOMA CITY, OKLAHOMA

ROGERS GND CON
121.9 348.6
ROGERS TOWER
118.3 257.8
OKE CITY DEP CON
124.6 385.5
ATIS 125.6

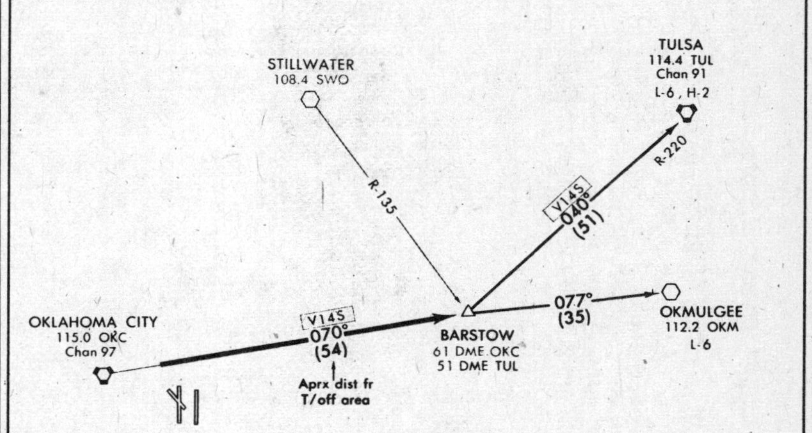

STILLWATER
108.4 SWO
R-135

TULSA
114.4 TUL
Chan 91
L-6, H-2
R-220
V14S
040°
(51)

OKLAHOMA CITY
115.0 OKC
Chan 97
V14S
070°
(54)
Aprx dist fr T/off area

BARSTOW
61 DME OKC
51 DME TUL

077°
(35)

OKMULGEE
112.2 OKM
L-6

DEPARTURE ROUTE DESCRIPTION

(Specified heading or routing). To intercept and proceed via the OKC R-070 to the BARSTOW INT. Then via (transition) or (assigned route). Maintain (altitude assigned by ATC).

OKMULGEE TRANSITION (8YB1.OKM): Via the BARSTOW INT direct to OKM VOR.

TULSA TRANSITION (8YB1.TUL): Via BARSTOW INT and TUL R-220 to TUL VORTAC.

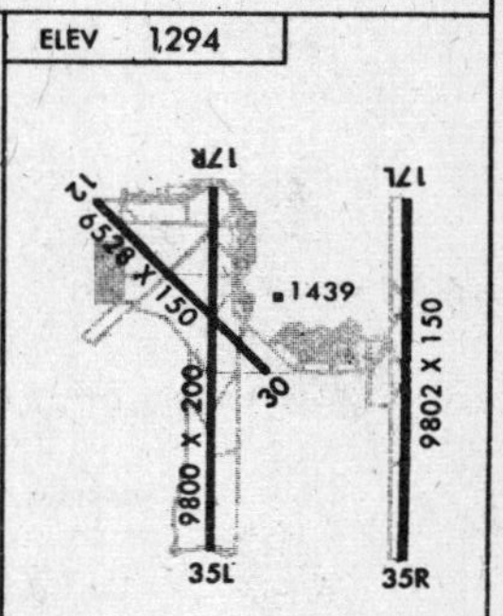

ELEV 1294
17R 12 6528 X 150 .1439 30 9800 X 200 35L
17L 9802 X 150 35R

BARSTOW ONE DEPARTURE (8YB1.8YB)
177

OKLAHOMA CITY, OKLAHOMA
WILL ROGERS WORLD

FIGURE 2-20. IFR Take Off Minimums and SID

3/74

UNITED STATES GOVERNMENT

STANDARD TERMINAL ARRIVAL ROUTES

STARs

UNITED STATES

INCLUDING PUERTO RICO AND THE VIRGIN ISLANDS

EFFECTIVE 0901Z **25 APR 1974**
TO 0901Z **20 JUN 1974**

PUBLISHED BY NATIONAL OCEAN SURVEY
NATIONAL OCEANIC AND ATMOSPHERIC ADMINISTRATION
PUBLISHED IN ACCORDANCE WITH INTER-AGENCY AIR CARTOGRAPHIC COMMITTEE
SPECIFICATIONS AND AGREEMENTS APPROVED BY:
DEPARTMENT OF DEFENSE ★ FEDERAL AVIATION ADMINISTRATION ★ DEPARTMENT OF COMMERCE

LEGEND

STANDARD TERMINAL ARRIVAL ROUTE (STAR) CHARTS

RADIO AIDS TO NAVIGATION

VOR
TACAN
VORTAC
WAYPOINT (RNAV)
RANGE (Simultaneous Broadcast)
NDB (Non-directional Radio Beacon)
LOM (Compass Locator)
Marker Beacons
Localizer Course
SDF Course

NAME
000.0 NAM 00
DME or TACAN Channel
Underline indicates no voice transmitted on this frequency

R-275 Radial line and value

Reporting Point △ Non-Compulsory ▲ Compulsory

DME Fix
5 DME Mileage (when not obvious)

VOR Changeover Point

ROUTES

4500 MEA
*3500 MCCA
270°
(65) Mileage
Arrival Route

Transition Route

MCA (Minimum Crossing Altitude)

x Mileage Breakdown

Altitude change at other than Radio Aids

(65) Mileage between Radio Aids, Reporting Points and Route Breaks

V12 J80 Airway/Route Identification

Holding Pattern

SPECIAL USE AIRSPACE

R-352
R-Restricted
P-Prohibited
W-Warning
A-Alert

AERODROMES

Civil
Joint Civil-Military
Military
Heliport

Entry facility/fix identified by name and symbol only.
All radials/bearings are magnetic
All mileages are nautical
All altitudes in feet–MSL
MEA – Minimum Enroute Altitude
MOCA – Minimum Obstruction Clearance Altitude

ETF-R1

FIGURE 2-21. Star Cover Page and Legend.

CITRUS TWO ARRIVAL (4CW.4CW2)

29

LOS ANGELES INTERNATIONAL
LOS ANGELES, CALIFORNIA

IOS ANGELES APP CON
124.9 269.0
ATIS 135.65

NOTE: Rwy 24L/R ILS and Jumbo DME fix shown for information only.

NOTE: B-747 aircraft restricted to Rwys 6 and 24. Rwy 7R-25L closed to DC-10 and L-1011 over 325,000 pounds. DC-10 and L-1011 not authorized Rwy 7L-25R.

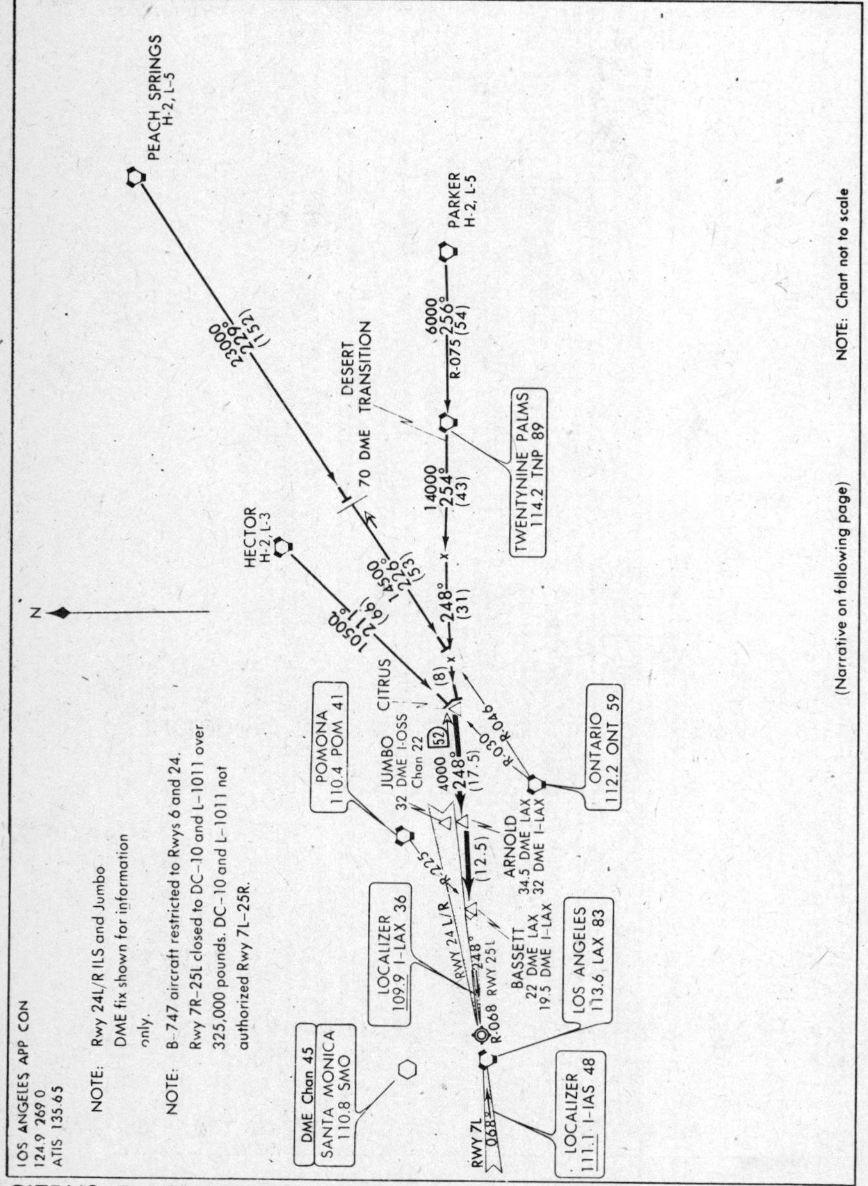

PEACH SPRINGS H-2, L-5
23000 229° (152)
HECTOR H-2, L-3
10500 211° (66)
70 DME DESERT TRANSITION
14500 226° (53)
PARKER H-2, L-5
6000 256° R-075 (54)
TWENTYNINE PALMS 114.2 TNP 89
14000 254° (43)
248° (31)
(8)
CITRUS
JUMBO 32 DME I-OSS Chan 22
4000 52 248° (17.5)
R-030
R-046
ONTARIO 112.2 ONT 59
POMONA 110.4 POM 41
R-225
ARNOLD 34.5 DME LAX 32 DME I-LAX
(12.5)
BASSETT 22 DME LAX 19.5 DME I-LAX
RWY 24 L/R
248° RWY 25L
R-068
LOCALIZER 109.9 I-LAX 36
LOS ANGELES 113.6 LAX 83
DME Chan 45
SANTA MONICA 110.8 SMO
RWY 7L 068°
LOCALIZER 111.1 I-IAS 48
N

NOTE: Chart not to scale

(Narrative on following page)

CITRUS TWO ARRIVAL (4CW.4CW2)
29
LOS ANGELES, CALIFORNIA
LOS ANGELES INTERNATIONAL

CITRUS TWO ARRIVAL (4CW.4CW2)

30

LOS ANGELES INTERNATIONAL
LOS ANGELES, CALIFORNIA

ARRIVAL ROUTE DESCRIPTION

DESERT TRANSITION (TNP.4CW2): From over TWENTYNINE PALMS VORTAC via TWENTYNINE PALMS R-254 and LOS ANGELES R-068 to CITRUS INT. Thence....

HECTOR TRANSITION (HEC.4CW2): From over HECTOR VORTAC via HECTOR R-211 and ONTARIO R-030 to CITRUS INT. Thence....

PARKER TRANSITION (PKE.4CW2): From over PARKER VORTAC via PARKER R-256 and TWENTYNINE PALMS R-075 to TWENTYNINE PALMS VORTAC. Via TWENTYNINE PALMS R-254 and LOS ANGELES R-068 to CITRUS INT. Thence....

PEACH SPRINGS TRANSITION (PGS.4CW2): From over PEACH SPRINGS VORTAC via PEACH SPRINGS R-229 and ONTARIO R-046 and LOS ANGELES R-068 to CITRUS INT. Thence....

....From CITRUS INT via LOS ANGELES ILS Rnwy 25L Localizer east course/ LAX R-068 via ARNOLD DME Fix to BASSETT INT.

Runways 24 and 25: From BASSETT INT expect ILS approach procedure to LOS ANGELES airport.

Runways 6 and 7: From BASSETT INT expect routing via direct SANTA MONICA VOR, thence via vector to Rnwy 7/6 final approach course to LOS ANGELES airport.

CITRUS TWO ARRIVAL (4CW.4CW2)
30
LOS ANGELES, CALIFORNIA
LOS ANGELES INTERNATIONAL

FIGURE 2-22. Star.

WORKSHEET — CHARTS

Refer to the preceding chapter when answering these questions.

Compare your answers with the correct answers at the end of this manual. For those questions you have answered incorrectly, it is suggested you review the appropriate paragraphs in the study material.

The following questions are based on the Sectional Chart in Fig. 2-3 and the legends in Figures 2-1 and 2.

1. The length of the longest runway at Redbird Airport is:

   a. 6600 feet

   b. 12,300 feet

   c. 5000 feet

   d. 5400 feet

2. What is the primary tower frequency at the Addison Airport? ....

3. How high above sea level is the obstruction 2 miles south of the city of Greenville?

   a. 868 feet

   b. 318 feet

   c. 932 feet

   d. 371 feet

4. What is the field elevation of Majors Airport?

   a. 500 feet

   b. 800 feet

   c. 544 feet

   d. 200 feet

5. Lighting is available at Caddo Mills Airport.

   True

   False

The following questions are based on the En Route Low altitude Chart Figure 2-8 and the legends in Fig. 2-7.

6. What is the frequency and Channel of the Flat Rock VORTAC? ....

7. What is the MEA between Nutbush and Amelia intersections on V20?

   a. 2000

   b. 2700

   c. 2500

   d. 1500

8. What is the distance between King William and the New Kent intersection on V213?

   a. 13

   b. 19

   c. 9

   d. 10

9. Which radial from the Hopewell VORTAC forms V189 southeast-bound?

   a. 358

   b. 134

   c. 205

   d. 178

10. Give the VORTACs and radials that form Stevensville Intersection on V20.

    a. RIC 045 and FAK 075

    b. HPW 015 and RIC 045

    c. RIC 045 and HCM 330

    d. RIC 045 and HCM 320

11. What does this symbol mean?

    21

    82

a. Unusable or closed segment of an airway.

b. Frequency protection in miles.

c. Substitute route

d. VOR changeover point giving mileage to radio aids.

12. What radio aids to navigation and what types of radar service are available at Richard Evelyn Byrd Airport.

a. ILS with no radar available and VORTAC

b. LF/MF Non-directional Radio Beacon and ILS

c. ASR, PAR and VORTAC

d. ILS, ASR and VORTAC

Refer to the SIAP illustrations (Figures 2-13 through 2-17) to answer the following questions.

13. What is the distance from the LOM to the approach end of runway 14 at the Lattiville Airport?

a. 4.1 miles

b. 3.6 miles

c. 2.6 miles

d. 0.5 miles

14. What is the inbound ILS heading to the Lattiville Airport?

a. 316

b. 320

c. 136

d. 319

15. When may an aircraft descend below 2200 feet on the ILS APCH to Lattiville Airport?

a. After completing procedure turn.

b. After passing the LOM inbound.

c. After passing the MM inbound.

d. Any time after intercepting the localizer course.

16. What is the minimum safe altitude 15 miles west of the LOM?

a. 3600 feet

b. 2400 feet

c. 2700 feet

d. 3200 feet

17. What is the frequency of the Lattiville localizer?

a. 320 kHz

b. 116.3 MHz

c. 110.3 MHz

d. 335.0 MHz

18. What are the circling minimums for a Category "C" civil aircraft executing an ILS runway 14 approach to Lattiville Airport?

a. 1165/24

b. 1640-1

c. 700 – 1½

d. 1640 – 1 1/2

The following questions are based on the Jet Approach and Landing chart and legend in Figure 2-18.

19. What is the field elevation at Los Alamitos NAS?

a. 215 feet

b. 35 feet

c. 1600 feet

d. 22 feet.

20. At what altitude must an aircraft cross the NZJ TACAN on approach to Los Alamitos NAS?

a. below 4000 feet

b. 4000 feet or below

c. at 4000 feet

d. at 3000 feet

21. What is the emergency safe altitude within 100 miles of the NZJ TACAN?

    a. 6700 feet

    b. FL210

    c. not specified

    d. 13,600 feet

22. What TACAN and radial will be used on final approach to Los Alamitos NAS in the approach illustrated in Figure 2-18?

    a. SLI 215R

    b. NZJ 305R

    c. NZJ 300R

    d. SLI 035R

23. At what altitudes may aircraft hold at the O'Neil intersection?

    a. FL180-210

    b. FL300

    c. FL180-FL 300

    d. 12,000

24. What is the highest spot elevation within 20 miles of the NZJ TACAN?

    a. 752 feet

    b. 5696 feet

    c. 6700 feet

    d. 12,600 feet

Refer to Figures 2-9 and 2-10, RNAV Charts and legends.

25. Match the following by placing the letter from Column B in the blank before the appropriate item in Column A.

Column A	Column B
............(1) Reference Facility Elevation for Sorento waypoint.	a. Kansas City Center
............(2) Facility's area in which Judyville waypoint is located.	b. 354 degrees at 19.8 nm
............(3) Coordinates of Dickeyville waypoint.	c. J800R
............(4) RNAV Route number between Mellott and Chapin waypoints.	d. JOT, 112.3
............(5) MAA between Sparkville and Marine waypoints on J981R.	e. 124.3 nm
............(6) Total mileage between Kappa and Jerseyville waypoints.	f. 45,000'
............(7) Reference facility and its frequency for Joliet waypoint.	g. 031 degrees
............(8) Track angle from Sorento waypoint on J825R.	h. 42° 45.5', 90° 31.6'
............(9) Radial and distance from LOU to Westport waypoint.	i. 18,000'
..........(10) MEA on J802R between Bradford and San Pierre waypoints.	j. 590'

Refer to Figures 2-19 and 2-20, Standard Instrument Department Chart and Legend.

26. Aerodromes with IFR take-off minimums other than standard are listed in the SID booklet; take-off minimums are established to assist pilots in .... Departure procedures and /or ceiling-visibility minimums are established for flight up to the ....

27. Tulsa appears on which IFR High and Low Altitude charts?

    (1) Low .... (2) High ....

28. What is the elevation of Oklahoma City Will Rogers Airport? ....

29. Takeoff minimums and departures apply to all runways at Oklahoma City, Will Rogers.

    (1) True (2) False

30. What radials make up the Barstow Instersection?

    (1) OKC070 and OKM077
    (2) OKM077 and SWO135
    (3) TUL040 and OKC070
    (4) OKC070 and SWO135

Refer to Figures 2-21 and 2-22, Standard Terminal Arrival Routes and Legend.

31. What is the ILS course heading for Runway 25L? ....

32. What is the mileage between Citrus and Arnold Intersections? ....

33. What is the frequency of the Los Angeles ATIS? ....

34. What is the MEA between Twentynine Palms VORTAC and Citrus Intersection?
....

35. What radials compose Citrus Intersection? (3) ....
....

CHAPTER 3
INSTRUMENTS

3-1. MAGNETIC COMPASS

A magnetic compass is the basic air navigation instrument. It indicates the direction in which an aircraft is flying with respect to the magnetic north pole. The magnetic compass is filled with liquid in which a card element carrying a system of magnetized needles is suspended, on a pivot, and free to align itself with the earth's magnetic field. The card is normally marked in 5 degree increments, with cardinal headings of north, south, east, and west usually shown in large letters. The remaining indications are usually labeled in 30 degree increments numerically, with smaller increments of 5 degrees marked by small vertical lines. (See Figure 3-1.)

While the compass is thoroughly dependable, it has a few errors the pilot must be aware of if he is to use it accurately. Variation and deviation have been discussed in Chapter 1; there remain the *northerly turning error* and the *acceleration error*. For accurate reading from the compass, the aircraft must remain in straight and level flight for at least a short time to allow the fluid in the bowl to return to the horizontal plane. Especially when aiding disoriented pilots, advise them to maintain straight and level flight before giving you any necessary magnetic compass readings.

FIGURE 3-1. Magnetic Compass.

3-2. AIRCRAFT CLOCK

The safe, orderly and expeditious flow of air traffic hinges on both pilots and controllers having the correct time; accuracy of IFR and VFR navigation is dependent on timing for estimating enroute or arrival times. When requested, pilots will be given a time check on departure and prior to being cleared for a timed approach. ATCS's are expected to know how to set a standard clock and a tumbler (direct-reading) clock to within 3 seconds of Naval Observatory time and to know when and how to give a time check. Time is given to the nearest quarter minute in a time check.

3-3. ALTIMETER

The altimeter is an aneroid barometer which measures the weight of the column of air above it and indicates that weight in terms of altitude instead of inches of mercury. It consists of a small, airtight chamber from which most of the air has been removed. The pressure, or weight, of the column of air tends to collapse the chamber, but this tendency is resisted by a small spring. As the pressure increases, the chamber is compressed; as it decreases, the chamber is expanded again by the spring. The slight motion produced is magnified mechanically and indicated in terms of altitude that would produce a corresponding change in pressure under *standard* pressure and temperature conditions.

Three hands indicate the altitude on this altimeter. The shortest hand indicates tens of thousands, the middle hand indicates thousands, and the long hand indicates hundreds of feet. The altitude depicted in Figure 3-2 is 10,160'. On the side of the dial there is a barometric scale in which is set the current altimeter setting. In Figure 3-2, this scale is set to 29.92" of mercury.

Current altimeter settings may be obtained from an air traffic facility prior to takeoff, and the altimeter should be reset periodically during flight to conform to the setting for the nearest weather observation station along his route. Altimeter settings are always given in inches of mercury and must not be confused with barometric pressure which is reported in millibars, contains certain corrections and should *never* be given to aircraft for use in setting altimeters. When the current altimeter setting for a particular airport has been entered in the altimeter, the instrument will indicate very closely the field elevation above sea level when the aircraft is on the ground.

3-4. RADIO ALTIMETER

The radio altimeter, also referred to as terrain clearance or absolute altimeter, differs from the aneroid type in that it measures the actual altitude of an aircraft above the terrain. A radio wave is sent to the ground and the interval required for it to reach the ground and be reflected back to the aircraft is timed. The signal returned is calibrated and altitude information is displayed to the pilot in the cockpit on a direct-reading instrument face. Extremely exact readings of altitude are possible and of great assistance to the pilot making instrument approaches in low weather conditions.

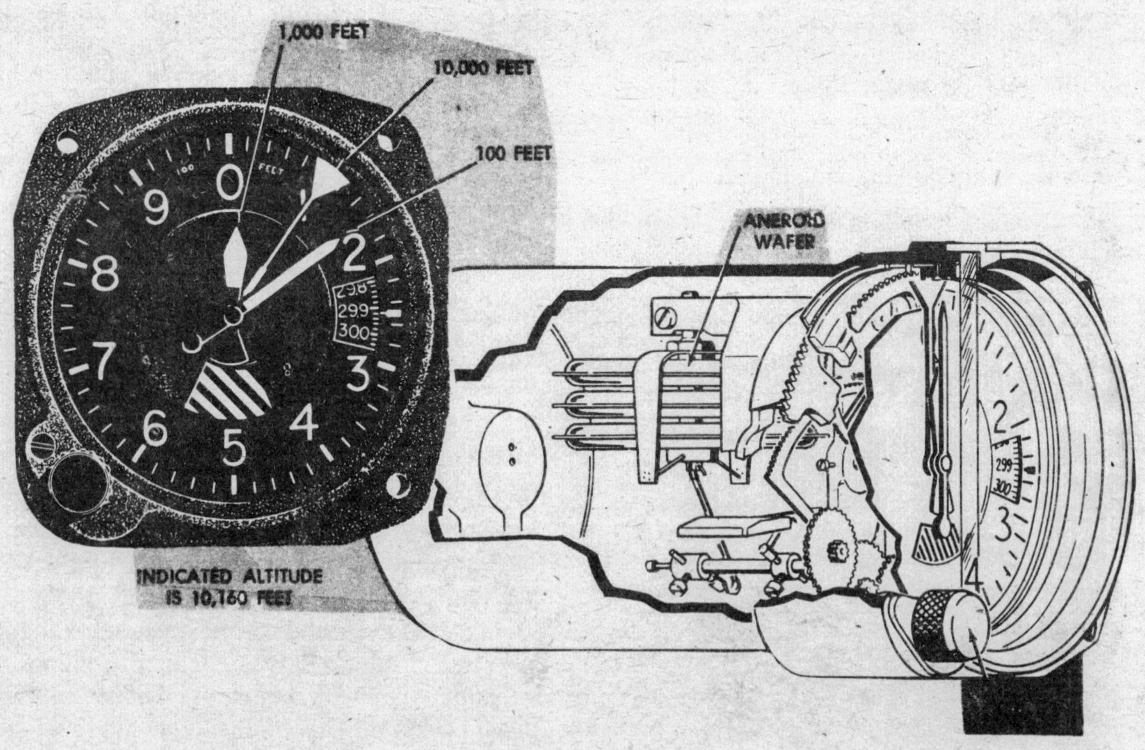

FIGURE 3-2. Aircraft Altimeter

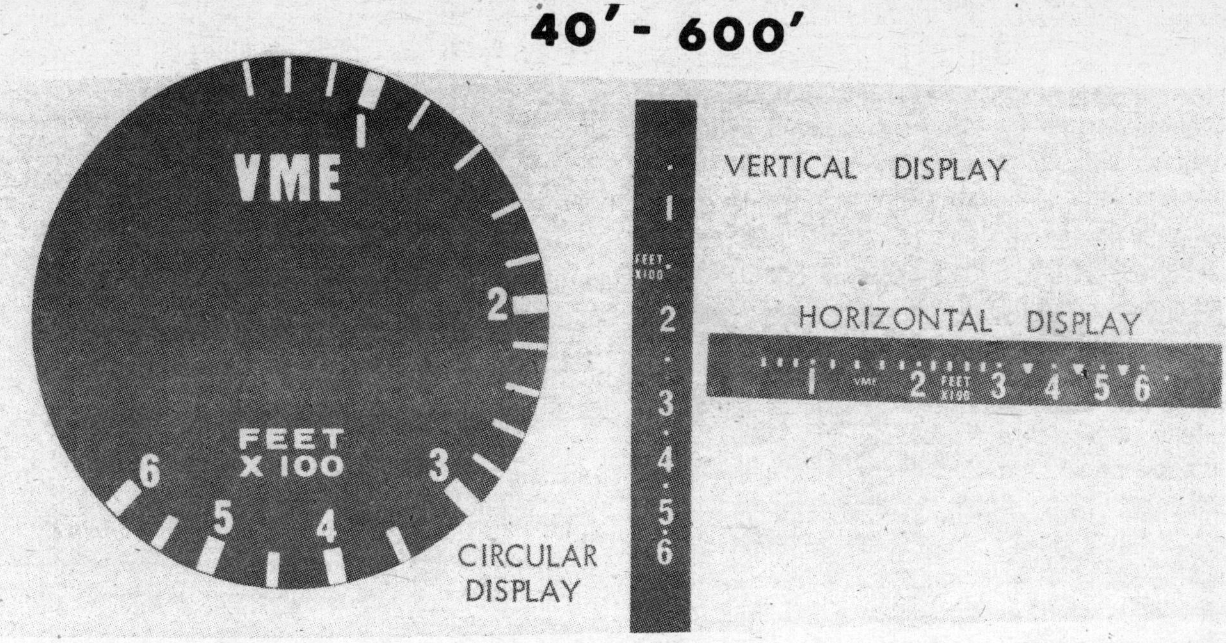

FIGURE 3-3. Radio Altimeter Displays.

3-5. ALTIMETER SETTING INDICATOR

The instrument most usually used in Air Traffic facilities for altimeter settings is the Altimeter Setting Indicator, shown in Figure 3-3, which gives a direct reading. Temporary errors are compensated for by adding or subtracting a correction obtained by comparing the instrument reading with that of a mercurial barometer.

Occasionally, an aircraft altimeter is installed as a backup unit for use when the Altimeter Setting Indicator is out of service. Altimeter setting information is obtained from the altimeter by using a prescribed method.

An error in setting an altimeter will result in incorrect display of altitude, about 100 feet per .1" (one-tenth inch) setting error.

FIGURE 3-4. Altimeter Setting Indicator.

3-6. ALTITUDE

Various kinds of altitude information are available from the altimeter, and it is important that you understand how they are derived and their uses.

Indicated Altitude is the altitude shown on the face of the altimeter when set to the current altimeter setting, and indicates a height above sea level (MSL). Indicated altitude is used by all pilots flying below 18,000 feet MSL. It provides all aircraft in a given area that are using the same altimeter setting a standard reference plane upon which vertical separation may be predicated.

Pressure Altitude is the altitude shown on the face of the altimeter when it has been set to standard sea level pressure, 29.92" hq. Pressure altitude is used for flight at Flight Levels at or above 18,000' MSL as required by FAR's and in determining certain aircraft performance figures.

Density Altitude is Pressure Altitude corrected for nonstandard temperature. Aircraft performance data is based on performance at standard pressure and temperature and since these conditions rarely exist, aircraft performance can be seriously affected, especially if the temperature is higher than standard (15 degrees C. or 59 degrees F.) Density altitude is used in computing aircraft takeoff, inflight and landing performance and can be of crucial importance to flight safety. High airport elevation, high temperature and high relative humidity can add up to a serious impairment of aircraft performance characteristics.

Absolute Altitude is height above the surface. This height may be indicated directly on a radio altimeter. Absolute altitude is essential information for flights over mountainous terrain and may be approximately computed from indicated altitude and chart elevation data.

True altitude is true height above sea level. This is a mathematical value determined by computer and therefore based upon standard atmospheric conditions assumed in the computer solution.

If existing temperature is ***higher*** than standard (15°C. or 59°F.), the true altitude is higher than the indicated; if the temperature is lower than standard, the true altitude is lower. At higher temperatures the air has expanded and is lighter (thinner) than standard per unit volume. The change of pressure per thousand feet will therefore be less. When the air is colder than standard, it is heavier and the opposite is true. When temperatures are very low, the True Altitude may be as much as 20 percent lower than Indicated Altitude. Normal departures from standard temperature can result in altimeter errors of several hundred feet. If the temperature between the surface and the aircraft does not decrease at the standard rate of 2 degrees per 1,000 feet, or if the pressure at flight level is nonstandard, reliance on a computer solution to determine obstruction clearance can be very hazardous. Pilot reports of temperatures aloft can be of great value to a pilot in flight planning over mountainous terrain for this reason.

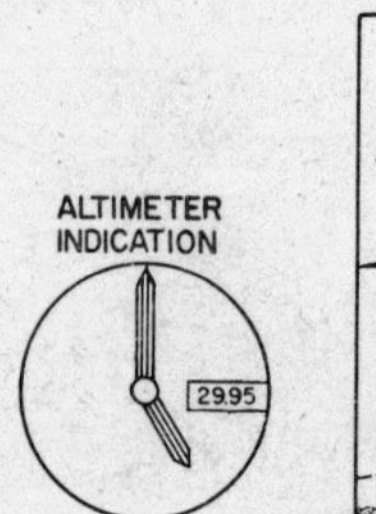

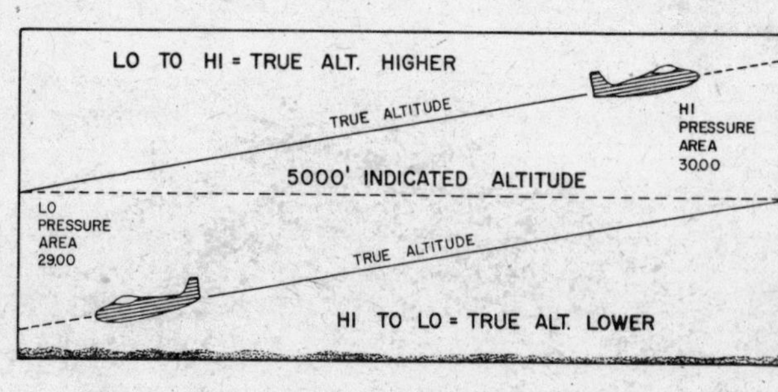

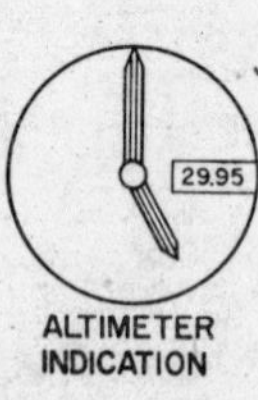

FIGURE 3-5. The Effect of Pressure on Altitude.

WORKSHEET

Complete the following questions without reference to the preceding study material. Upon completion, compare your answers with the correct answers at the end of this manual. For those questions you have answered incorrectly, we suggest that you review the appropriate paragraphs in the study material.

1. The compass is the primary navigation instrument and indicates the direction the aircraft is heading with respect to:

   (1) True North

   (2) Deviation

   (3) Magnetic North

   (4) Variation

2. If a pilot were operating at an indicated altitude of 3,000′ in an area where the current local altimeter setting is 29.50″ and his altimeter was set to 30.00″, the altitude of the aircraft would be (disregarding corrections for temperature):

   (1) 1,500′ MSL

   (2) 2,500′ MSL

   (3) 3,000′ MSL

   (4) 3,500′ MSL

3. Federal Aviation Regulations Require that aircraft operating at or above 18,000 MSL use an altimeter setting of:

   (1) 30.00″ hg.

   (2) True Altitude

   (3) 30.02″ hg.

   (4) 29.92″ hg.

4. The Radio Altimeter displays the actual altitude of the aircraft above:

   (1) Mean Sea Level.

   (2) A reference data level.

   (3) The terrain.

   (4) 18,000′.

5. Match the correct definition to the term by placing the letter from Col. B in the blanks preceding Column A.

Column A	Column B
.... Pressure Altitude	a. Shown on the face of the altimeter when set to current altimeter setting.
.... Density Altitude	b. Pressure Altitude correct for nonstandard temperature.
.... Absolute Altitude	c. Shown on the face of the altimeter when set to Standard Sea Level Pressure 29.92″ hg.
.... Indicated Altitude	d. Height above the surface or terrain.
.... True Altitude	e. Height above sea level.

CHAPTER 4
INSTRUMENT LANDING SYSTEM (ILS)

4-1. INTRODUCTION

The ILS is the most precise navigation system in use today. The accuracy of the aid and the critical portion of flight for which it is used requires the specialist to have a working knowledge of its components and use. Flying the ILS is the pilot's responsibility. However, the specialist with a good knowledge of the components and the presentation the pilot uses will be better able to use the system to expedite arriving and departing aircraft safely.

4-2. GENERAL

The Instrument Landing System is designed to provide an approach path for exact alignment and descent of an aircraft on final approach to a runway.

The ground equipment consists of two highly directional transmitting systems and, along the approach, three (or fewer) marker beacons. The directional transmitters are known as the localizer and glide slope transmitters.

4-3. FUNCTIONS

a. The system may be divided functionally into three parts:

Guidance information—localizer, glide slope

Range information—marker beacons

Visual information—approach lights, touchdown and centerline lights, runway lights

b. Compass locators located at the outer marker or middle marker may be substituted for these marker beacons. DME when located at the glide slope antenna may be substituted for the outer marker.

c. At some locations a complete ILS system has been installed on each end of a runway (on the approach end of runway 4 and the approach end of runway 22 for example.) When such is the case, the ILS systems are not operated simultaneously during IFR weather conditions. In other words, if instrument approaches are being conducted to runway 4, the ILS system on the opposite end of runway 4 (runway 22) will be shut down.

4-4. LOCALIZER

a. The localizer transmitter, operating on one of the twenty ILS channels within the frequency range of 108.1 MHz to 111.9 MHz, emits signals which provide the pilot with course guidance to the runway centerline. Some localizers have voice capability.

b. The approach course of the localizer, which is used with other functional parts, e.g., glide slope, marker beacons, etc., is called the front course. The localizer signal emitted from the transmitter at the far end of the runway is adjusted to produce an angular width between 3° and 6°, as necessary, to provide a linear width of approximately 700' at the runway approach threshold.

c. The course line along the extended centerline of a runway, in the opposite direction to "b", above, is called the back course. **CAUTION**—unless an aircraft's ILS equipment includes reverse sensing capability, when flying inbound on the back course it is necessary to steer the aircraft in the direction opposite to the direction of the needle deflection on the airborne instrument when making corrections from off-course to on-course. This "flying away from the needle" is also required when flying *outbound* on the front course of the localizer.

d. Identification is in International Morse Code and consists of a three-letter identifier preceded by the letter I (••) transmitted on the localizer frequency.

Example: I-DIA

e. The localizer provides course guidance throughout the descent path to the runway threshold from a distance of 18 NM from the antenna between an altitude of 1000' above the highest terrain along the course line and 4500' above the elevation of the antenna site. Proper off-course indications are provided throughout the following angular areas of the operational service volume:

1. To 10° either side of the course along a radius of 18 NM from the antenna, and
2. From 10°—35° either side of the course along a radius of 10 NM.

f. Generally, proper off-course indications are provided to 90° either side of the localizer course; however, some facilities cannot provide angular coverage to that extent because of siting characteristics or antenna configurations or both. Therefore, instrument indications of possible courses in the area from 35°—90° should be disregarded. All unrestricted localizer facilities provide acceptable course guidance information within the areas described in e above.

g. Momentary localizer flag activity and course aberrations may be observed when other aircraft cross over the localizer antenna or are in a position to affect the radiated signal.

4-5. GLIDE SLOPE

a. The UHF glide slope transmitter, operating on one of the twenty ILS channels within the frequency range 329.3 MHz to 335.0 MHz radiates its signals primarily in the direction of the localizer front course. Normally, a glide slope transmitter is not installed with the intent of radiating signals toward the localizer back course; however, there are a few runways at which an additional glide slope transmitter is installed to radiate signals primarily directed toward the localizer back course to provide vertical guidance. The two glide slope transmitters will operate on the same channel but are interlocked to avoid simultaneous radiation to support either the front course or the back course, but not both at the same time. Approach and landing charts for the runways which have glide slopes on the localizer back course will be depicted accordingly.

Caution: Spurious glide slope signals may exist in the area of the localizer back course approach which can cause the glide slope flag alarm to disappear and present unreliable glide slope information. A pilot will disregard all glide slope signal indications when making a localizer back course approach unless glide slope is specified on the approach and landing chart.

b. The glide slope transmitter is located between 750' and 1250' from the approach end of the runway (down the runway) and offset 400-600' from the runway centerline. It transmits a glide path beam 1.4° wide. The term "glide path" means that portion of the glide slope that intersects the localizer.

e. The glide path projection angle is normally adjusted to 3 degrees above horizontal so that it intersects the middle marker at about 200 feet and the outer marker at about 1400 feet above the runway elevation.

d. In addition to the desired glide path, false course and reversal in sensing will occur at vertical angles considerably greater than the usable path. The proper use of the glide ness as the glide path interception is approached and interpret correctly the "fly-up" and "fly-down" instrument indications to avoid the possibility of attempting to follow one of the higher angle courses. Provided that procedures are correctly followed and pilots are properly indoctrinated in glide path instrumentation, the fact that these high angle courses exist should cause no difficulty in the glide path navigation.

e. Every effort should be made to remain on the indicated glide path (reference: FAR 97.87(d)(3). Extreme caution should be exercised to avoid deviations below the glide path so that the predetermined obstacle/terrain clearance provided by an ILS instrument approach procedure is maintained.

f. A glide slope facility provides a path which flares from 18-27 feet above the runway. Therefore, the glide path should **not be** expected to provide guidance completely to a touchdown point on the runway.

4-6. MARKER BEACON

a. ILS marker beacons have a rated power output of 3 watts or less and an antenna array designed to produce an elliptical pattern with dimensions, at 1000 feet above the antenna, of approximately 2400 feet in width and 4200 feet in length. Airborne marker beacon receivers with a selective sensitivity feature should always be operated in the "low" sensitivity position for proper reception of ILS marker beacons.

b. Ordinarily, there are two marker beacons associated with an instrument landing system; the outer marker and middle marker. However, some locations may employ a third marker beacon to indicate the point at which the decision height should occur when used with a Category II ILS.

c. The outer marker (OM) normally indicates a position at which an aircraft at the appropriate altitude on the localizer course will intercept the ILS glide path. The OM is modulated at 400 Hz and identified with continuous dashes at the rate of two dashes per second.

d. The middle marker (MM) indicates a position at which an aircraft is approximately 3500 feet from the landing threshold. This will also be the position at which an aircraft on the glide path will be at an altitude of approximately 200 feet above the elevation of the touchdown zone. The MM is modulated at 1300 Hz and identified with alternate dots and dashes keyed at the rate of 95 dot/dash combinations per minute.

e. The inner marker (IM), where installed, will indicate a point at which an aircraft is at a designated decision height (DH) on the glide path between the middle marker and landing threshold. The IM is modulated at 3000 Hz and identified with continuous dots keyed at the rate of six dots per second.

f. A back course marker, where installed, normally indicates the ILS back course final approach fix where approach descent is commenced. The back course marker is modulated at 3000 Hz and identified with two dots at a rate of 72 to 95 two-dot combinations per minute.

4-7. COMPASS LOCATOR

a. Compass locator transmitters are often situated at the middle and outer marker sites. The transmitters have a power of less than 25 watts, a range of at least 15 miles and operate between 200 and 415 kHz. At some locations, higher-powered radio beacons, up to 400 watts are used as outer marker compass locators. Compass locators aid in transitioning from the airway system to the ILS, can be used for ADF approaches and generally carry Transcribed Weather Broadcast information.

b. Compass locators transmit two-letter identification groups. The outer locator transmits the first two letters of the localizer identification group, and the middle locator transmits the last two letters of the localizer identification group.

4-8. ILS MINIMUMS

ILS Minimums with all components operative normally establish a DH (Decision Height MSL) with a HAT (Height Above Touchdown) of 200 feet, and a visibility of one-half statute mile.

ILS

[FAA INSTRUMENT LANDING SYSTEM]

STANDARD CHARACTERISTICS AND TERMINOLOGY

ILS approach charts should be consulted to obtain variations of individual systems.

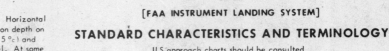

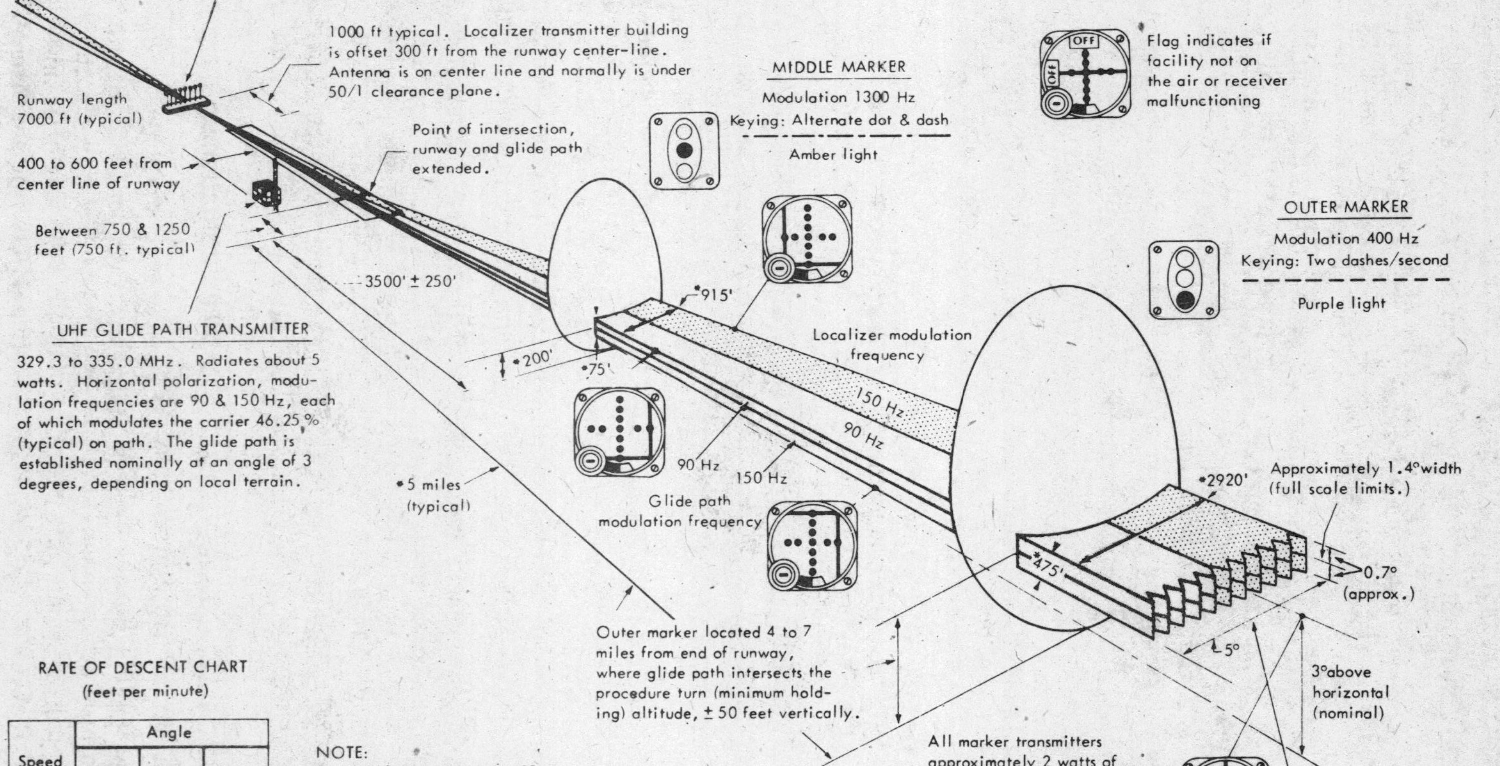

VHF LOCALIZER
108.1 to 111.9 MHz odd tenths only. Radiates about 100 watts. Horizontal polarization. Modulation frequencies 90 and 150 Hz. Modulation depth on course 20% for each frequency. Code identification (1020 Hz, 5%) and voice communication (modulated 50%) provided on same channel. At some localizers, where terrain (siting) difficulties are encountered, an additional antenna (slotted waveguide type) provides the necessary course straightness.
1000 ft typical. Localizer transmitter building is offset 300 ft from the runway center-line. Antenna is on center line and normally is under 50/1 clearance plane.
Runway length 7000 ft (typical)
400 to 600 feet from center line of runway
Point of intersection, runway and glide path extended.
Between 750 & 1250 feet (750 ft. typical)
3500' ± 250'
UHF GLIDE PATH TRANSMITTER
329.3 to 335.0 MHz. Radiates about 5 watts. Horizontal polarization, modulation frequencies are 90 & 150 Hz, each of which modulates the carrier 46.25% (typical) on path. The glide path is established nominally at an angle of 3 degrees, depending on local terrain.
•200'
•75'
•915'
•5 miles (typical)
MIDDLE MARKER
Modulation 1300 Hz
Keying: Alternate dot & dash
Amber light
Flag indicates if facility not on the air or receiver malfunctioning
OFF
OUTER MARKER
Modulation 400 Hz
Keying: Two dashes/second
Purple light
Localizer modulation frequency
150 Hz
90 Hz
90 Hz
150 Hz
Glide path modulation frequency
•2920'
•475'
Approximately 1.4° width (full scale limits.)
0.7° (approx.)
5°
3° above horizontal (nominal)
Outer marker located 4 to 7 miles from end of runway, where glide path intersects the procedure turn (minimum holding) altitude, ± 50 feet vertically.
All marker transmitters approximately 2 watts of 75 MHz modulated about 95%
Course width varies; 5° at most locations (full scale limits)
• Figures marked with asterisk are typical. Actual figures vary with deviations in distances to markers, glide angles and localizer widths.

RATE OF DESCENT CHART
(feet per minute)

Speed (Knots)	Angle 2 1/2°	2 3/4°	3°
90	400	440	475
110	485	535	585
130	575	630	690
150	665	730	795
160	707	778	849

NOTE:
Compass locators, rated at 25 watts output. 200 to 415 kHz, are installed at most outer and middle markers. A 1020 Hz tone, modulating the carrier about 95 %, is keyed with the first two letters of the ILS identification on the outer locator and the last two letters on the middle locator. At some locators, simultaneous voice transmissions from the control tower are provided, with appropriate reduction in identification percentage.

FIGURE 4-1. FAA Instrument Landing System.

4-9. ILS FREQUENCIES

The ILS Localizer operates in the VHF band between 108.10 and 111.95 mHz. The ILS Glide Slope operates in the UHF band on a paired frequency. Frequency pairing is listed in Part 1 of the AIM; selecting the VHF Localizer frequency automatically tunes in the paired UHF Glide Slope frequency.

4-10. STANDARD APPROACH LIGHTING SYSTEM TYPE ALSF-1

The standard U.S. ALS consists of a number of light bars installed symmetrically about the extended runway centerline starting at the landing threshold and extending a distance of 3000 feet outward into the approach zone. The longitudinal spacing of these light bars is 100 feet. The system provides roll guidance, a distinctive marker at 1000 feet, and a distinctive threshold (See Figure 4-2). Their purpose is to aid the pilot in establishing visual contact with the ground.

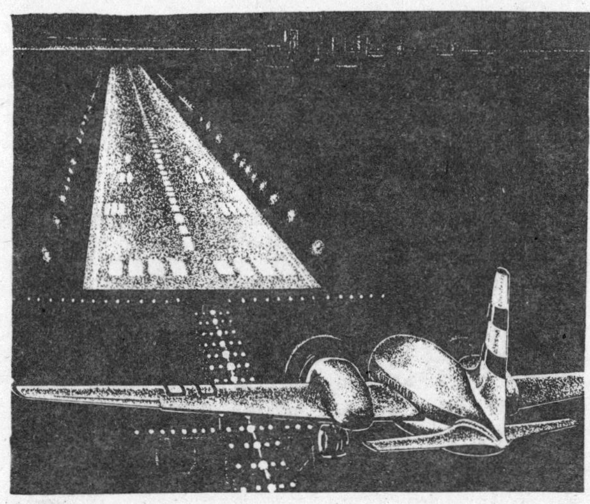

FIGURE 4-2. Standard U.S. ALS.

4-11. AIRBORNE EQUIPMENT

A. *Antenna Equipment*

The antenna array for ILS airborne installations consists of a dipole antenna mounted well forward on the fuselage of the aircraft to serve as the localizer antenna. The glide slope antenna is a straight dipole antenna mounted either in the same location as the localizer antenna or in the nose of the aircraft.

B. *Localizer and Glide Slope Receivers*

The localizer receiver is remotely controlled from a small control panel on the instrument panel of the cockpit and incorporates an ON-OFF switch, volume control and channel selector.

C. *Localizer—Glide Slope Indicator*

Also located in the instrument panel of the aircraft in full view of the pilot, output from the localizer and glide slope transmitters is displayed on this indicator. (Figure 4-3). The vertical needle, labeled the Course Deviation needle, shows the position of the localizer course with respect to the aircraft's position, which is represented by a circle or a small aircraft in the center of the instrument face. The horizontal needle indicates the relative position of the instrument face. The horizontal needle indicates the relative position of the glide slope. (If insufficient signal for accurate readings is received or either transmitter fails, red flags appear near the affected needles.)

Sensitivity of this equipment is such that when the aircraft is approximately two and one half degrees to the right or left of the centerline of the runway, the vertical needle will indicate a full-scale deflection. This sensitivity permits the use of the indicator for highly accurate course guidance. If the needle is no further off center than one-quarter scale, the aircraft will likely be able to complete the approach to landing with no problems. The glide slope needle has equally high sensitivity, and if the aircraft is as much as one-half degree above

FIGURE 4-3. Localizer – Glide Slope Indicator.

or below the glide slope, the horizontal needle will register a full-scale deflection.

D. *ILS Marker Beacon Receivers*

A three-light indicator is also mounted on the instrument panel. Activation of these lights is controlled by the modulated frequency of the particular signal being received; the OM is modulated at 400 cps and activates the purple light; the MM is modulated at 1,300 cps and activates the amber light; and the white light is activated by an IM (Inner Marker) if the facility is so equipped. These lights along with aural signals transmitted by the markers give pilots a double-check on distance as they pass over the markers.

4-12. ILS MONITOR SYSTEM

The high performance level and dependability demand of the ILS transmitting equipment require a reliable monitor system to notify specialists of any malfunction. A monitor panel is installed in the tower cab or flight service station at locations where a tower is not in operation to alert specialists to any malfunction of the localizer, glide slope, markers or DME, if so equipped, by an aural alarm and light to show which component has failed. Localizer and glide slope are equipped with standby transmitters which automatically switch into operation when the regular transmitters fail. A typical ILS monitor panel is shown in Figure 4-4.

4-13. FLYING THE ILS

A. Executing instrument approaches using the ILS is a relatively simple procedure if the pilot understands the functions of the various components of the system. The Localizer-Glide Slope Indicator (Fig. 4-3) furnishes the pilot with the necessary information to align his aircraft with the centerline of the runway and to maintain the proper glide angle on approach The pilot knows that when flying TOWARD the airport on the FRONT course of the localizer, if his aircraft is to the right of the center line, the vertical needle will be deflected to the left of center. To return to course, he must FLY TOWARD THE NEEDLE to return to the centerline of the runway. Conversely, if his aircraft is left of centerline, the vertical needle will be deflected to the right and again the pilot will FLY TOWARD THE

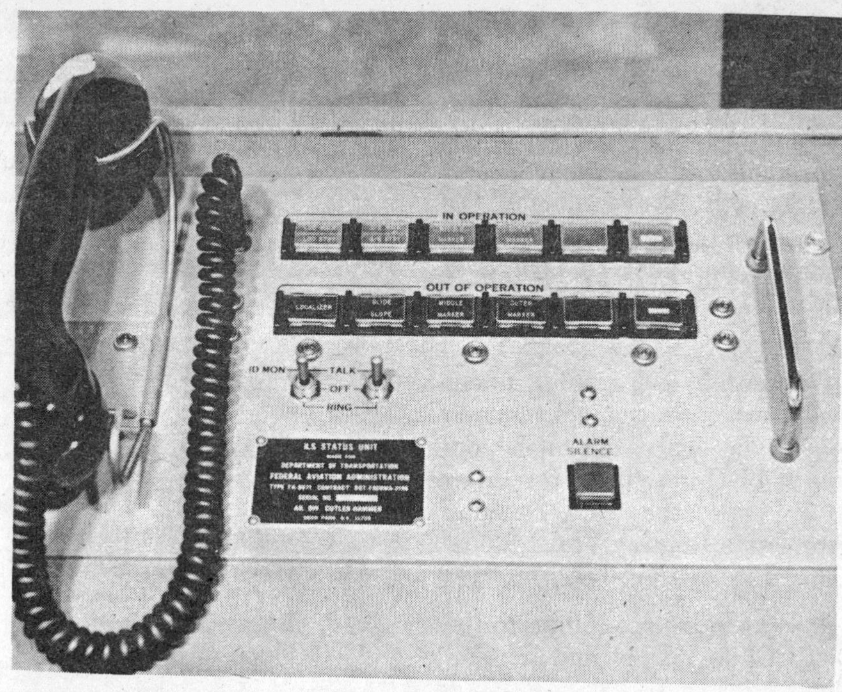

FIGURE 4-4. Solid State ILS Monitor Panel.

NEEDLE to bring it back to the center. To fly AWAY from the airport on the BACK course of the ILS, he will still fly towards the needle. REMEMBER:

WHEN FLYING INBOUND ON THE FRONT COURSE OR OUTBOUND ON THE BACK COURSE, FLY TOWARD THE NEEDLE.

B. This procedure is reversed when flying the reciprocal direction (making what is called *a back-course* approach.) The aircraft has reversed its position and direction of flight, but the equipment will continue to furnish the same information, and thus indicate in reverse. When inbound on the back course or outbound on the front course, the pilot must fly AWAY from the needle to return to the centerline. This is known as *reverse sensing* and will not cause any problem if the pilot remembers that if the aircraft's position and heading are reversed, the indications on his instrument will be reversed.

C. Reaction of the glide slope needle is similar to that of the localizer needle except that indications received from the glide slope can only be relied upon when the aircraft is inbound on the front course of the localizer. If the aircraft is below the proper glide slope, the horizontal needle will be deflected upward, indicating that the glide slope is above the aircraft's position; again, the pilot will have to fly toward the needle.

Corrections made to center either needle must be minor.

4-14. CATEGORY II ILS

Linkage of the ILS and automatic pilot system, computer-assisted, and improved ground equipment, have resulted in a highly sophisticated approach and landing aid called Category II ILS, or CAT II. An electronic computer interprets the signals received and sends out impulses to the various servomotors of the autopilot system. The servomotors operate ailerons, rudder, elevators, and throttles to guide the aircraft even more precisely than possible under manual control. The system must control the aircraft in a uniform manner, regardless of the strength of the radio signals being received, control airspeed positively without surges of engine power, maintain and coordinate operation of the elevators with the operation of the throttles, and it must be capable of instant disconnection to permit the pilot to take over control of the aircraft in case of a malfunction, emergency, or other necessity.

CAT II permits approach and landing under extremely low weather conditions and research is continuing to someday make *all*-weather operations a reality. CAT II approach procedures already provide for approaches to a Decision Height of 100 feet with a Runway Visual Range reading of 1200.

CAT II components include, in addition to the normal Localizer, Glide Slope and marker beacons:

A. Airborne:
   1. Autopilot/Coupler
   2. Flight Director System (incorporating a computer)
   3. Automatic Throttle System

B. Ground:
   1. Electronic Guidance System
      a. VHF 75 mHz Inner Marker
   2. Visual Guidance System
      a. Approach Lighting System
      b. Touchdown Zone Lighting System
      c. Centerline Lighting System
      d. High Intensity Runway Edge Lighting System
      e. Taxiway Turnoff Lighting System
      f. All-Weather Runway Markings

C. Other Requirements
   1. Runway Visual Range (RVR—measures visibility) or Transmissometer (also measures visibility)
   2. Radar (Radio) Altimeter Setting Height (AGL value)
   3. Remote Monitoring Capability for Glide Slope, Localizer, Marker Beacons and Approach Lighting System.
   4. Inspection Procedures for the Visual Guidance System
   5. Critical Areas designated, marked and lighted. (A Critical Area is a place near the localizer transmitter where vehicular traffic may interfere with transmitted signals.)

Additional information on Category II ILS requirements may be found in FAA Advisory Circular 120-29.

WORK SHEET — INSTRUMENT LANDING SYSTEM

Complete the following questions without reference to the preceding study material. Compare your answers with the correct answers at the end of this manual. For those questions you have answered incorrectly, it is suggested you review the appropriate paragraphs in the study material.

Questions

1. List the 3 functions of the ILS System and what each consists of.

   ....

   ....

   ....

2. A pilot making an approach using the ILS observes an alternate dot and dash keying of his marker indicator light. He knows that the distance to the end of the runway is about

   (1) 750 - 1,250 feet.

   (2) 2,000 feet.

   (3) 3,500 feet.

   (4) 4 - 7 miles.

3. The distance in miles from the outer marker of an ILS to the end of the runway is about

   (1) 1 to 4.

   (2) 2 to 5.

   (3) 3 to 6.

   (4) 4 to 7.

4. A pilot of an aircraft inbound on the front course of an ILS notes that the vertical needle of the cross-pointer indicator is right of center. The horizontal needle is below center. The position of the aircraft with respect to being "on-course" is:

   (1) right and high.

   (2) left and low.

   (3) left and high.

   (4) right and low.

5. A pilot making a front course ILS approach notes that the vertical needle of the cross-pointer indicator is left of center. The horizontal needle is below center. To return to "on-course", the pilot should:

   (1) turn right and climb.

   (2) turn left and descend.

   (3) turn right and descend.

   (4) turn left and climb.

6. A pilot is making a front course ILS approach to Will Rogers Airport. Checking the vertical needle of the GP-LOC Indicator, the pilot saw it indicating a full deflection to the right.

   (a) Which direction (right or left) was the aircraft off course? ....

   ....

   ....

   (b) How many degrees does full deflection of the vertical needle represent?

   ....

   ....

   ....

7. When Distance Measuring Equipment is used in conjunction with the ILS, there would be no apparent need for using the:

   (1) compass locators.

   (2) glide path.

   (3) localizer.

   (4) marker beacons.

8. Oklahoma City Approach Control wishes to contact the pilot of an aircraft making an ILS approach to Will Rogers Field. He may be able to contact the pilot via voice communications on:

   (1) the localizer frequency.

   (2) the glide path frequency.

   (3) the marker frequency.

   (4) the compass locater frequency.

9. A pilot has tuned to a VHF radio frequency and hears the identification "I—OKC" in Morse code. He knows that he has tuned to:

   (1) A VOR.

   (2) A TACAN.

   (3) the localizer of the ILS.

   (4) the compass locator of an ILS.

10. The glide slope is:

   (1) Always the same.

   (2) Tuned in separately in the 329 - 335 MHz band.

   (3) Automatically tuned to the correct frequency when the localizer frequency is selected and tuned in by the pilot.

   (4) In the 108 - 112 MHz band.

11. A pilot is making an ILS approach and has both the vertical and horizontal needles of the LOC/GP Indicator centered. A flag suddenly appears at the base of the horizontal needle. What does the appearance of the flag signify? ....

....

12. If the middle marker were inoperative, would it be possible to make an ILS approach? Explain ....

....

....

13. Name three functions of ILS compass locators. ....

....

14. The glide path is adjusted to project an angle of approximately ....° above horizontal so that it intersects the MM at about .... feet and the OM at about .... feet above the runway elevation.

15. Why are high intensity approach lights important to pilots making instrument approaches? ....

....

....

CHAPTER 5
LOW/MEDIUM FEQUENCY RADIO NAVIGATIONAL AIDS, HOMING, UHF/VHF DIRECTION FINDING EQUIPMENT

5-1. LOW/MEDIUM FREQUENCY NAVIGATIONAL AIDS

The term *radio beacon* is a general designation for a low or medium frequency aid intended for use in airborne radio direction finding (homing), instrument approaches and as an aid to a more precise holding pattern where holding is required. Radio beacons operate in the 200-415 kHz frequency band and radiate a circular or non-directional signal pattern like a commercial broadcast station, permitting reception form any point within the facility's service range.

5-2. CLASSIFICATION

Beacons are classified as follows:

Type, MH – **Power**, less than 50 watts – **Normal Range**, approximately 25 miles

Type, H – **Power**, 50 to 1,999 watts – **Normal Range**, approximately 50 miles

Type, HH – **Power**, 2,000 watts or greater – **Normal Range**, approximately 75 miles

Type, L – **Power**,under 25 watts – **Normal Range**, approximately 15 miles

The H facilities listed transmit a continuous three-letter identification code except during voice transmissions. The L facility is more commonly referred to as an LOM, or Locator, Outer Marker, and is always associated with the ILS. L facilities transmit a continuous two-letter identification. Unless the letter W (without voice) is included in the class designator (HW, for instance) voice transmissions may be made on them.

5-3. HOMING

Nearly everyone is familiar with the fact that by rotating a portable radio volume can be varied. If the radio is rotated through a full circle, there will be two volume peaks (when the antenna loop is pointed toward the station) and two distinct low spots or nulls (when the loop is at right angles to the station.) This principle is used in radio direction finding or homing.

In its simplest form, a loop antenna is attached to an aircraft in a fixed position and the aircraft is turned to locate the nulls, which are sharper than the peaks and therefore more useful. With a manually rotated loop, the null can be found without turning the aircraft, and the bearing is indicated by a pointer on an azimuth dial.

Unlike flying a straight course, homing normally results in a curved course due to the effect of wind. (Figure 5-1. The actual path of the aircraft would actually curve more nearer the station.) Careful navigation procedures using an ADF and gyrocompass can largely eliminate this error.

5-4. AUTOMATIC DIRECTION FINDER

The most efficient type of airborne direction finding equipment is the Automatic Direction Finder (ADF). (Figure 5-2.) The loop is automatically rotated and maintained in a null position by an electric motor. In this equipment, the 180 degree ambiguity found in other types is eliminated. A single-ended pointer gives the pilot continuous information on the bearing of the station in relation to aircraft heading. This equipment can be used for

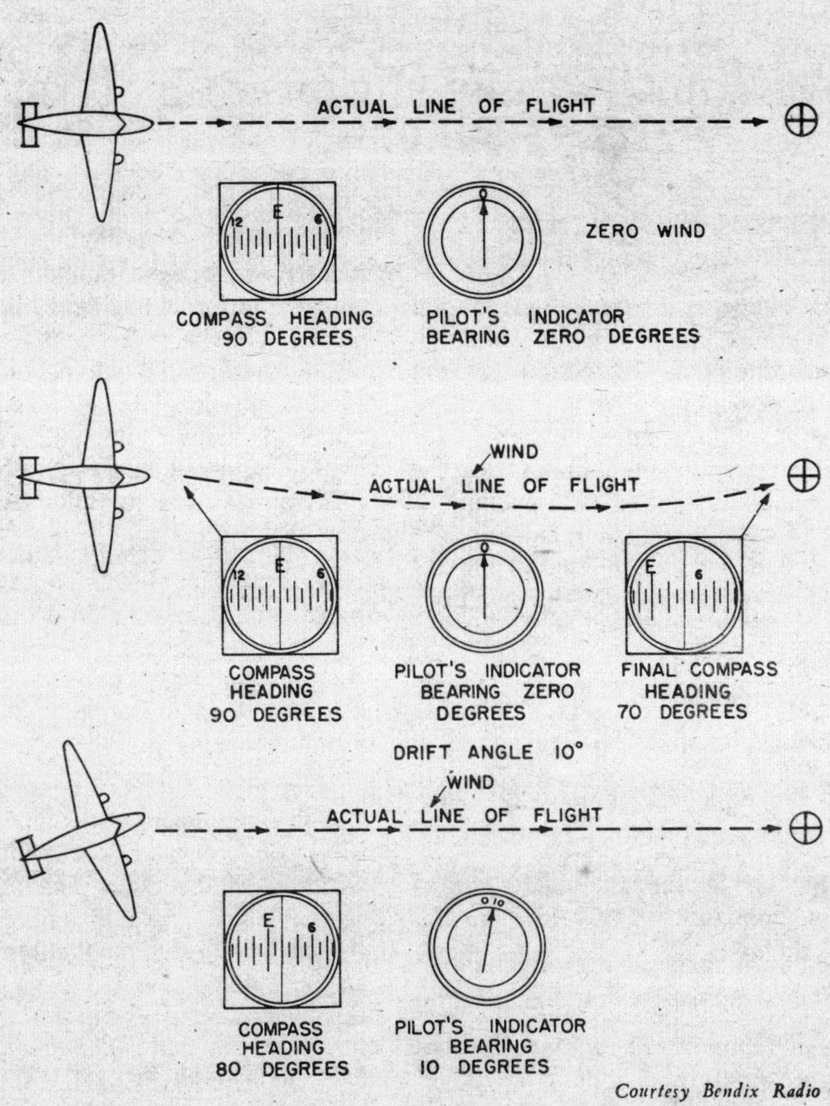

Courtesy Bendix Radio

Figure 5-1.

FIGURE 5-2. ADF receiver.

homing on a particular station, whether in the L/MF or commercial broadcast band. In Figure 5-2 above, the radio beacon selected is bearing 257 degrees from the nose of the aircraft.

5-5. VHF/UHF DIRECTION FINDING EQUIPMENT

The acronym ADF is commonly used to refer to airborne direction-finding equipment, whether automatic or not. The term DF refers to ground-based equipment which indicates an aircraft's bearing from the equipment site. When the aircraft transmits on a specified UHF or VHF frequency which has been selected (tuned in) on the DF, an indication of its bearing from the receiver is given by a strobe line either on a specially equipped radarscope or on a specialized cathode ray tube display called a Direction Finder. Both the radarscope and DF scope have compass roses (oriented to magnetic north) around them and the strobe line then indicates the magnetic bearing of the aircraft from the station. Many air traffic facilities are equipped with DF, and it is, with the possible exception of radar, the specialist's best tool to aid lost aircraft. (Figure 5-3). For more information regarding DF, see Direction Finder Services, Manual S-12.

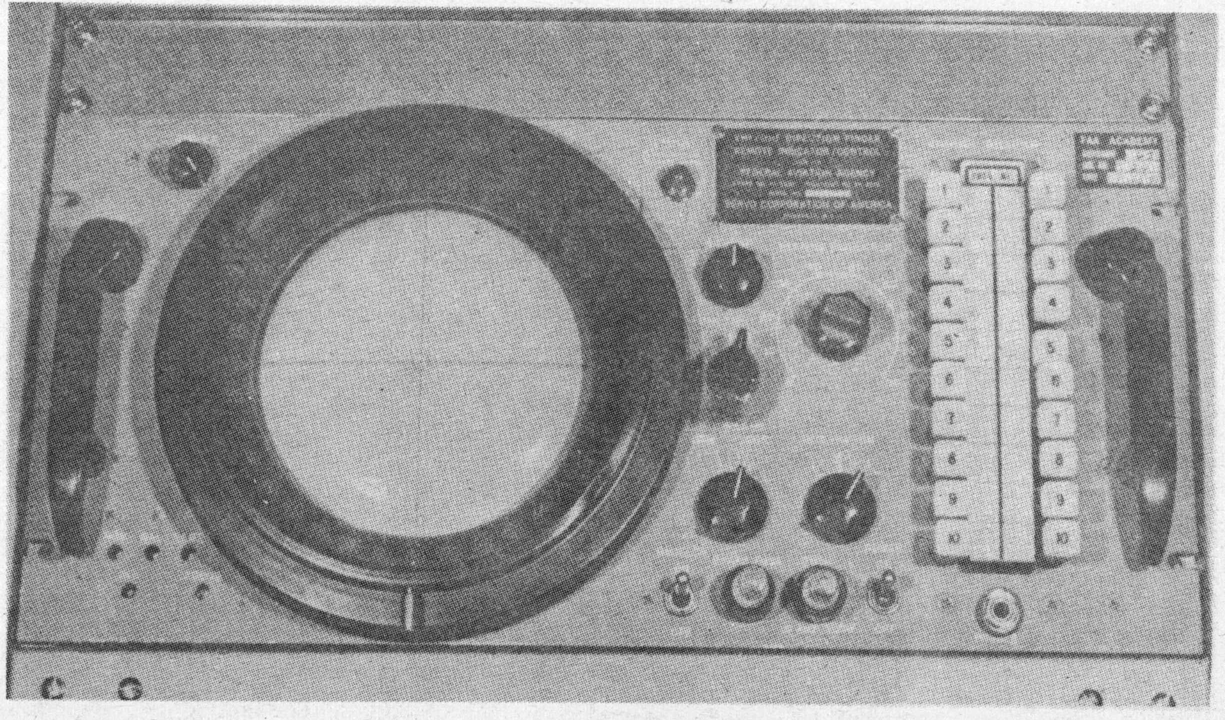

FIGURE 5-3

CHAPTER 5 — WORKSHEET

1. Radio beacons radiate:
   (1) a directional signal pattern.
   (2) a continuous two-letter identification.
   (3) schedule weather broadcasts.
   (4) a non-directional signal pattern.

2. Homing normally results in a .... course, due to the effect of ....

3. ADF is considered the most efficient direction finding equipment. List three reasons why.
   1. ....
   2. ....
   3. ....

4. Airborne direction finding equipment indicates the .... of the facility from the .... Ground-based DF equipment indicates the .... of the aircraft ....

5. DF equipment is oriented to .... North, receives signals in the ..../......... bands, and indicates a .... of the transmitting aircraft.

CHAPTER 6
RADAR

6-1. RADAR

Radar, a contraction of the words *Radio Detection And Ranging,* is the primary air traffic control aid. Radar furnishes the control specialist with the actual position of aircraft by means of transmitting an electronic pulse and timing the reflected echo's return. This information is presented to the specialist on the cathode ray tube or radar scope of the radar console.

Radar information is presented to the controller in a number of different ways, but the PPI (Plan Position Indicator) is the basis of all air traffic control displays.

6-2. AIRPORT SURVEILLANCE RADAR (ASR)

There are several types of surveillance radar available to the terminal radar specialist. Terminal equipment built to FAA specifications is the ASR series (ASR-6, ASR-7).

ASR is medium range radar for the control of traffic in the vicinity of an airport with a normal range of about 60 miles. Moving targets, fixed targets and precipitation areas are displayed.

The presentation of this information is called a PPI (Plan Position Indicator) display, and is a circular-type projection with the antenna site normally in the center of the display. Since the antenna scans a full 360 degrees, the azimuth and *range* of aircraft are displayed. (No altitude information is available.) By observing the relative movement of the target, the controller may determine the approximate heading and speed of the aircraft.

An inherent disadvantage is the return from *terrain* features close to the antenna site. This is called *ground clutter,* and can cover targets in some areas. This can be largely eliminated by the use of MTI, Moving Target Indicator, which filters out signals returned from stationary objects. A map of the area is electronically superimposed on the scope face with the targets. This is referred to as VIDEO MAPPING. This map shows navaids and airways as well as landmarks. With the aid of this map, a cursor or strobe and the compass rose around the edge of the scope, the specialist is able to determine the exact position of a target. With this information he is able to give headings to a pilot that will enable the pilot to make an approach to a runway without the use of any other navigational aids. This feature is one of the major advantages of radar.

6-3. AIR ROUTE SURVEILLANCE RADAR (ARSR)

The ARSR-1, first installed in the latter part of 1958, was the first long-range radar to be designed primarily for use in air traffic control. Maximum range of the equipment is 200 miles. On the ARSR-2, the controller may select a presentation of 25, 50, 100, or the full 200 miles. Aircraft may be detected to well above 40,000 feet. The ARSR-2 operates in the 1280-1350 mHz band and is a dual channel system. While one channel is being used, the other is on standby, providing a backup in the event the channel in use does not operate properly.

The presentation of the ARSR is similar to that of the ASR in that the antenna scans 360 degrees giving aircraft azimuth and range.

Again, observing the relative movement of the target, the controller may determine the approximate heading and speed of the aircraft. (No altitude information is available.)

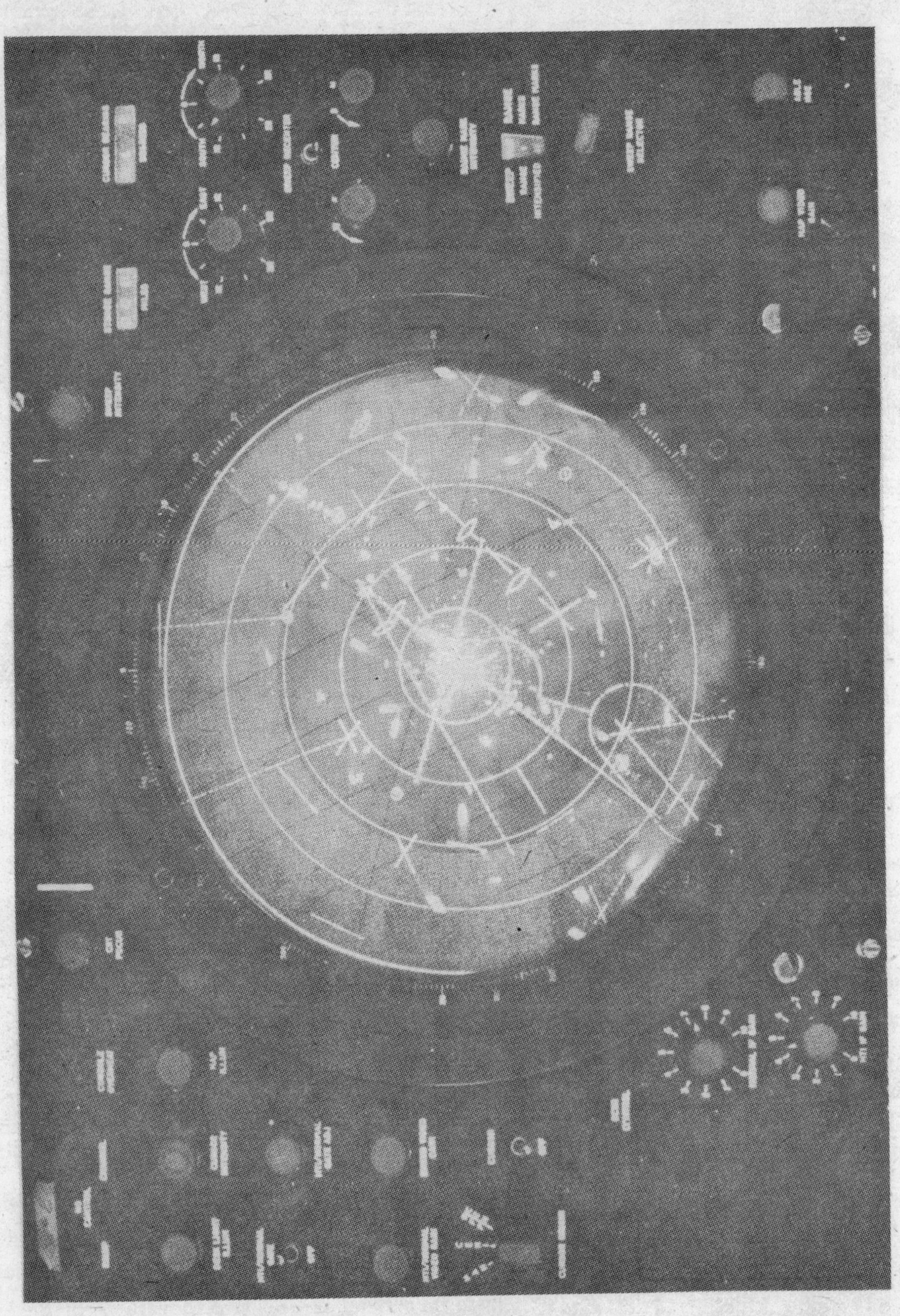

FIGURE 6-1. An ASR-5 presentation showing video mapping.

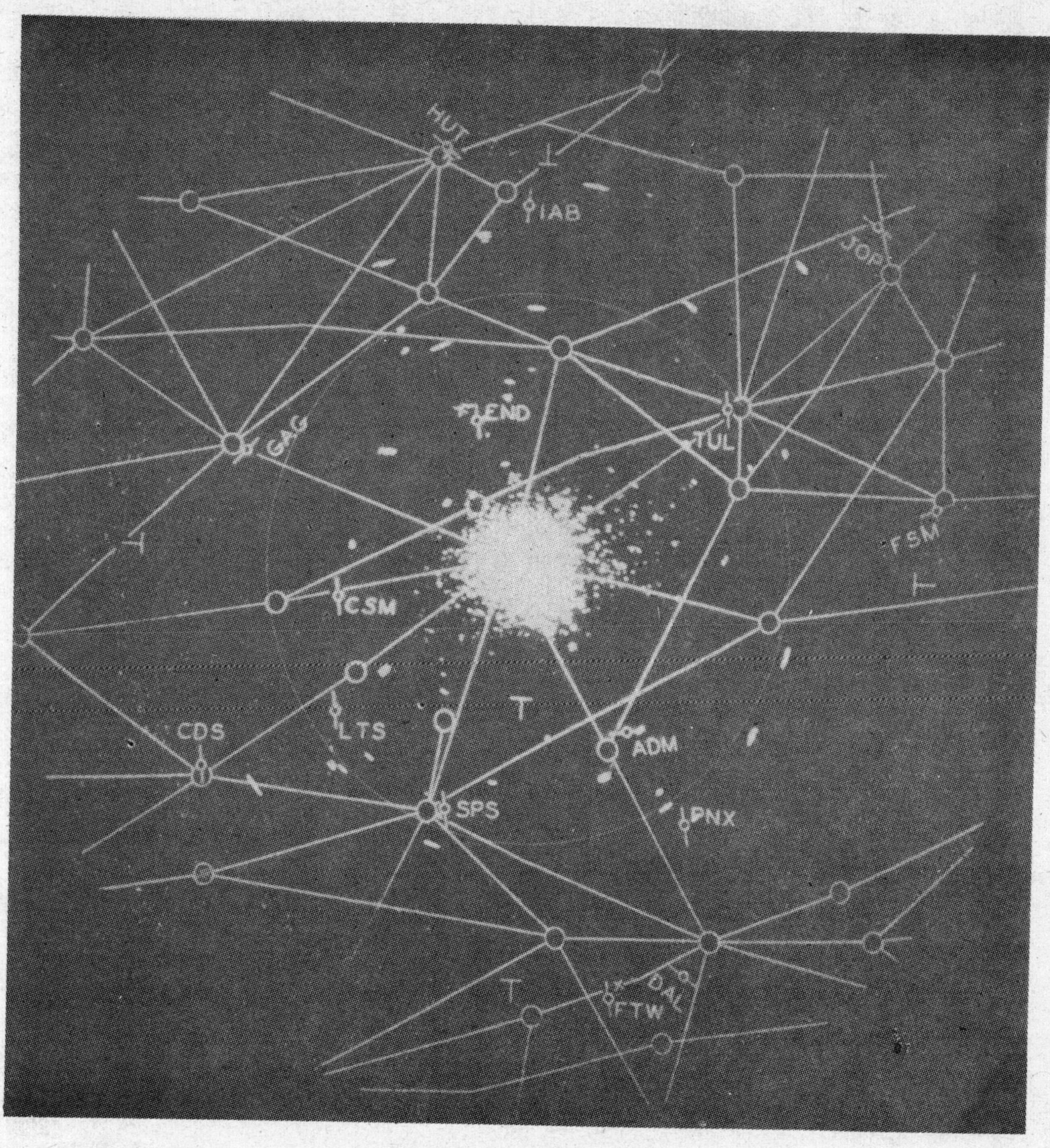

FIGURE 6-2. An ARSR presentation. The light area in the center of the scope is ground clutter. Ground clutter may be reduced and practically eliminated by using the MTI (Moving Target Indicator) feature.

The display of precipitation areas provides a means for the controller to assist aircraft in avoiding these areas while en route. A *video map* is provided on the scope with airway layout, navigational aids and airports depicted to assist in aircraft orientation over the entire 200 miles of range.

Two minor disadvantages of ARSR are ground clutter and decreasing accuracy with increasing range.

6-4. PRECISION APPROACH RADAR (PAR)

Precision approach radar is designed to be used as a *landing aid* rather than an aid to sequencing and spacing. PAR equipment may be used as a primary landing aid, or it may be used to monitor other types of approaches. PAR searches the final approach to a runway. It is designed to display **azimuth, range** and *elevation* over a small area and is effective as a landing aid in *extremely* poor weather It is accurate enough to detect variations of *300 feet in range,* and at one mile, variation of *10 feet in elevation* and *20 feet in azimuth* can be observed. Approaches usually begin within ten miles of the airport, so the limited range of the PAR does not hinder its intended use.

The principle underlying precision approach equipment is the same as any other radar. The major difference is the method of presentation. The scope is divided into two parts. The *upper half* presents elevation and range information, and the *lower half* presents azimuth and range. Targets move from right to left.

Two antennas are used in the PAR array, one scanning a vertical plane, and the other scanning horizontally. Since *range* is limited to *10 miles, azimuth to 20 degrees,* and *elevation to 7 degrees,* only the area of final approach is covered.

One of the disadvantages of PAR is that it normally can be used on only one runway at a time, and is usually installed so that instrument approaches to the main instrument runway can be monitored.

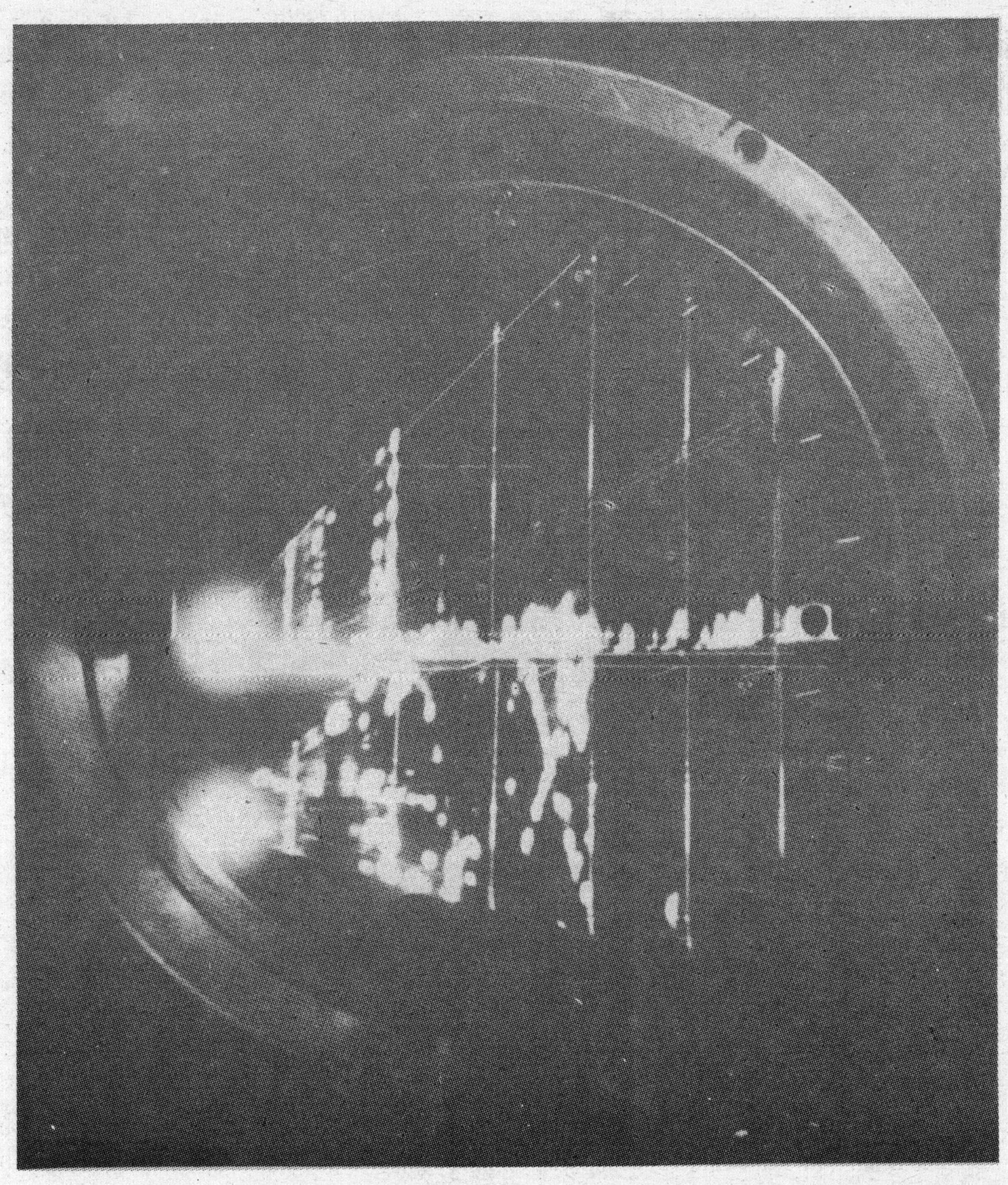

FIGURE 6-3. A PAR presentation. Notice the mapping showing the glide slope on the upper portion of the scope and the runway centerline extension on the lower portion.

6-5. AIRPORT SURFACE DETECTION EQUIPMENT (ASDE)

ASDE is designed to *scan the ground* rather than the sky and provide specialists with an unobstructed view of the airport. A sixteen-inch scope is used in the ASDE to display a *one* to *four* mile radius. The result presented to the specialist is a sharply defined relief map of the entire surface of the airport showing movement of aircraft and vehicular traffic. Taxiing operations can be conducted as close as 50 feet between aircraft in trail, and with as little as 15 foot wing tip separation. Thus the specialist has a way to observe the entire surface of the airport even though it is hidden by darkness, fog or other restriction to visibility.

FIGURE 6-4. ASDE. Look at the map and the radar picture side by side; note the faithful reproduction by radar of details needed for control of ground traffic.

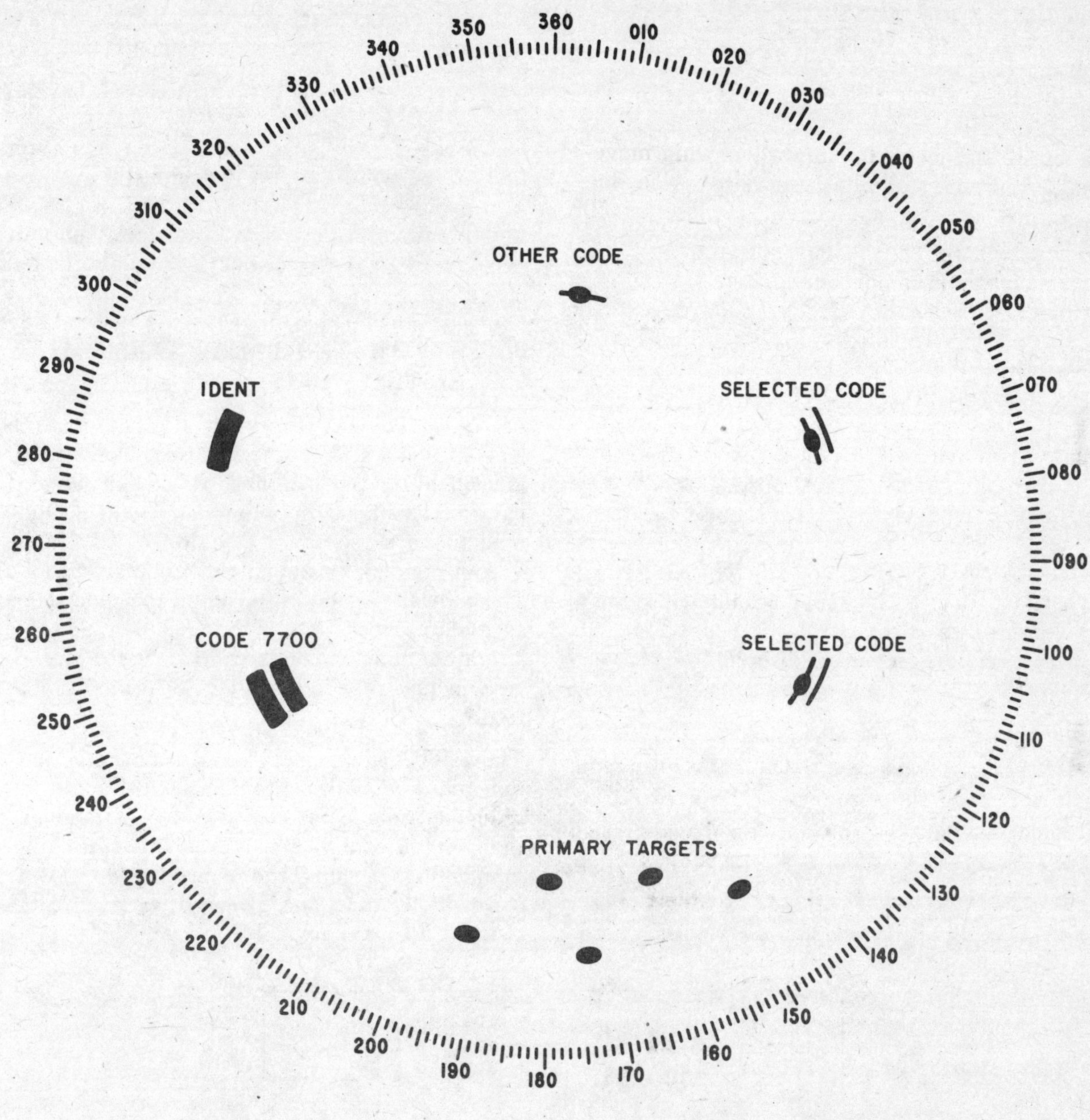

FIGURE 6-5. Secondary Surveillance Radar. This presentation differs from the normal radar target presentation in that one or more 'slashes' may be displayed from the same aircraft return. This presentation may vary with the aircraft's reply or the selection of the desired return by the controller.

6-6. SECONDARY SURVEILLANCE RADAR (AIR TRAFFIC CONTROL RADAR BEACON SYSTEM—ATCRBS)

Secondary Surveillance Radar is the international term for the Air Traffic Control Radar Beacon System. Secondary Surveillance Radar is a *separate* system, capable of independent operation. However, in normal air traffic control use, it is slaved with ASR and ARSR and displayed combined on a PPI. (Primary radar returns may be turned down or off momentarily when weather, for instance, is impairing the display, to leave an unimpaired beacon-only display.) Secondary radar (radar beacon or beacon) displays differ from primary radar displays in that they are returns from an airborne transponder rather than a reflected signal; targets differ, too, in that primary targets appear as elongated spots or "blips" on the radarscope while beacon targets appear as *segments of an arc or slashes.* Depending on the transponder code being transmitted, the beacon targets consist of from one to eight slashes. A control panel on the radar equipment permits the controller to select specific codes he wants to display, and he may differentiate between by having them transmit or *squawk* different codes.

Secondary Surveillance Radar helps overcome the following shortcomings of Primary Radar. Primary radar return and displayed target strength depend on aircraft reflectivity (size, configuration and heading), weather conditions (especially precipitation), radio interference, ground clutter, and blind spots in antenna coverage. All can affect the return of the reflected radar signal.

Since Secondary Surveillance Radar targets are not *reflected* but *transmitted* signals, they are not as vulnerable to degrading effects as severely as primary radar returns.

Secondary Surveillance Radar is an important tool of the controller, as it enables him to use his airspace more effectively, aiding in aircraft identification, assists him in helping aircraft avoid weather and assisting lost or disoriented aircraft.

6-7. AUTOMATED RADAR TERMINAL SYSTEM (ARTS)

ARTS is designed to provide terminal controllers with an alphanumeric display of aircraft identification and ground speed on aircraft equipped with transponders, and with altitude readout on those aircraft equipped with Mode C transponders (automatic altitude reporting). The information is displayed on the radarscope as a data block and automatically tracks the aircraft target. (This system is like the ATCRBS in that it is independent of primary radar return.)

The ARTS equipment has lessened coordination required within terminal facilities and has reduced pilot/controller verbal communications significantly. This reduction in communicating permits the controller to devote more of his time and attention to control decisions and planning.

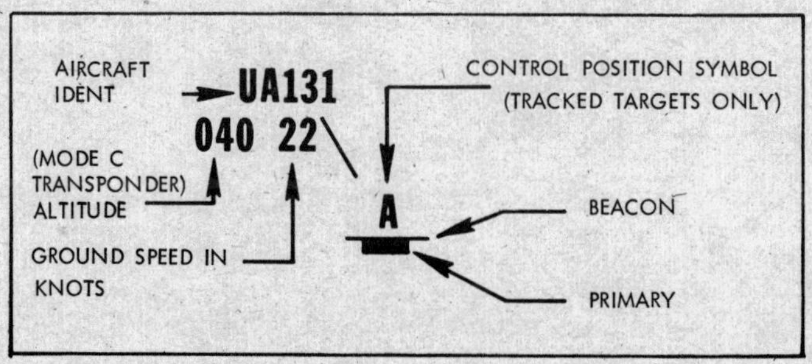

FIGURE 6-6. ARTS. Full Data Block.

WORK SHEET — RADAR

Complete the following questions without reference to the preceding study material.

Compare your answers with the correct answers at the end of this manual. For those questions you have answered incorrectly, it is suggested you review the appropriate paragraphs in the study material.

Questions:

1. What type of equipment is the basis of all air traffic control radar display? ....

....

2. The pilot of an aircraft under ASR observation knows that the radar controller can give him information as to his actual:
   (1) azimuth and range from the airport.
   (2) azimuth, altitude and range from the VOR.
   (3) elevation, azimuth, and distance from the airport.
   (4) elevation, azimuth and distance from the airport.

3. What is the normal range of ASR?

....

4. One disadvantage of the ASR is ground clutter. What causes this and where is it most prevalent? ....

....

5. What information does Video Mapping usually provide? ....

....

6. What type radar was the first long range radar primarily designated for air traffic control? ....

....

7. What is the maximum range of the ARSR-2? .... This radar will detect aircraft up to what altitude? ....

8. Why is it important for the radar controller to be able to observe storm and precipitation areas? ....

....

9. List two minor disadvantages of the ARSR display. ....

....

10. During PAR approaches, specialists normally provide pilots with the following information:
    (1) azimuth and distance.
    (2) bearing and range.
    (3) azimuth, distance and deviation.
    (4) azimuth, range and elevation.

11. Which radar is designed primarily as a landing aid? ....

12. PAR is accurate enough to detect variations in range of:
    (1) 1 mile.
    (2) 500 feet.
    (3) 1/4 mile.
    (4) 300 feet.

13. The radius of an ASDE display is?
    (1) 7 degrees.
    (2) 10 miles.
    (3) 1 to 4 miles.
    (4) 50 miles.

14. ASDE provides specialists with a display of:

    (1) 50 miles of the antenna.

    (2) 20 degrees horizontally and 7 degrees vertically.

    (3) airport surface.

    (4) 10 miles of the antenna.

15. What is the primary difference between secondary radar and primary radar?............

    ....

CHAPTER 7
VHF/UHF OMNI-DIRECTIONAL FACILITIES

7-1. OMNI-DIRECTIONAL FACILITIES

The VHF omni-directional range (VOR) is the primary radio aid to air navigation today.

Omni is from the Latin word *omnis,* meaning *all,* and the omni facilities produce directional guidance in *all* directions. Theoretically speaking, an infinite number of courses are produced by these facilities, but in actual practice, only 360 are usable under optimum conditions. Deficiencies in siting or in equipment will make some of the 360 courses unusable. Unusable or *scalloping* courses will be advertised in the AIM or as a NOTAM and should not be used for navigational or air traffic control purposes.

Courses produced by omni facilities radiate from the station like spokes from the hub of a wheel and are called *radials.* It is important to remember that the radials are *always from the station.*

7-2. PRINCIPLE OF OPERATION

The principle of the omnidirectional range is based on the comparison of the phase differences between two radiated audio frequency signals, the difference in phase varying with change in azimuth. One of the two signals is non-directional; it has a constant phase throughout 360° of azimuth and is called the ***REFERENCE*** phase. The other signal rotates at a speed of 1,800 RPM, varies in phase with azimuth and is called the ***VARIABLE*** phase.

The rotating signal is initially set so that at *magnetic north* both the reference and the variable signals are exactly in phase: In all other directions, the positive maximum of the variable signal will occur at some time later than the maximum of the reference signal. The fraction of the cycle which elapses between the occurrence of the two maxima at any point in azimuth, will identify the azimuth angle of that point, Fig. 7-1.

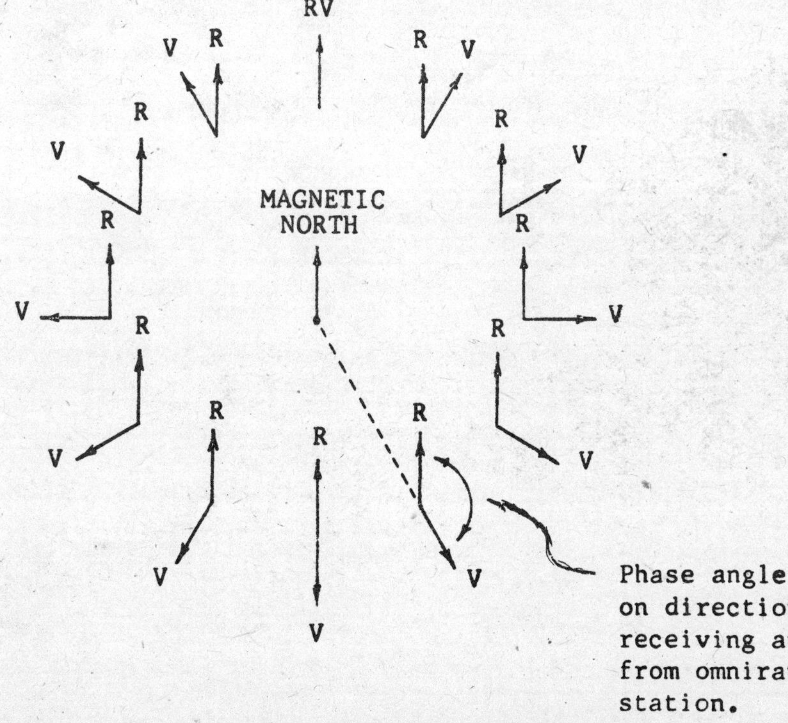

FIGURE 7-1. Phase Angle Relationship.

To help visualize the method of determining bearing from the transmitter, let's use as an example the rotating airport beacon. Suppose the identification flasher cam is so adjusted that the green airport identification light flashes each time the light beam sweeps past magnetic north and the beacon rotates clockwise at 6 RPM (one revolution each 10 seconds or 36° per second).

To determine our direction from the beacon, we could use a stop watch, starting the watch at the instant we see the start of the green flash and stopping it when the rotating beam sweeps past our position. Then, by multiplying the number of seconds shown on the stop watch by 36, we can obtain our magnetic bearing from the beacon.

Suppose that exactly five seconds elapse from the start of the green flash until the rotating beam flashes; 5 × 36 = 180 and our bearing from the beacon is 180 degrees.

If we move to the right (*counter-clockwise*), the elapsed time would be less, and our bearing would be less than 180°. The converse would be true if we moved our position to the left (*clockwise*). In effect, the reference and variable voltages of the omni facility provide the same information electronically that the flasher and beacon supply visually in this example.

7-3. TYPES AND FREQUENCIES

Three types or combinations of omnidirectional facilities are in operation today; therefore, careful use of terminology when referring to these facilities is necessary. These facilities and their operating frequencies are:

a. *VOR* – VHF omni-directional radio range which provides *bearing* (azimuth) information. VOR facilities operate on frequencies between 108.0 and 117.95 MHz. Frequency assignment between 108.0 and 112.0 is in the even tenth decimal to preclude any confliction with ILS localizer frequency assignment.

b. *TACAN* – UHF omni-directional radio range which provides bearing (azimuth) and range information. TACAN facilities operate between 960 and 1215 MHz. VOR receivers are unable to receive navigational signals from TACAN facilities.

FIGURE 7-2. A VOR installation (Left) – A VORTAC installation (Right).

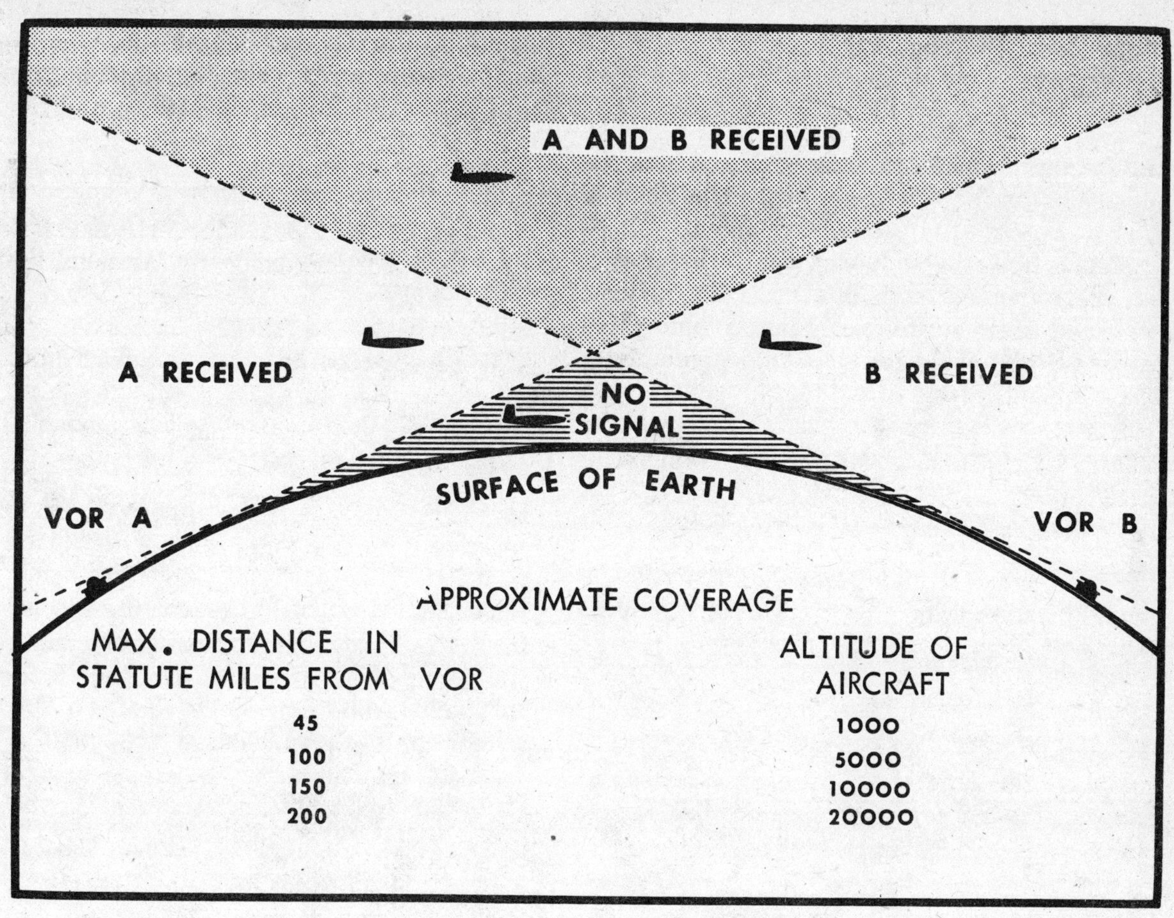

FIGURE 7-3. Diagram of the *line of sight* transmission characteristics.

c. *VORTAC*—A combination of VOR and TACAN. This facility provides bearing (azimuth) information *on VHF* (108-117.95 MHz), as well as bearing (azimuth) and range information on UHF (960-1215 MHz). TACAN-equipped aircraft can receive both bearing and range information from the TACAN portion. Aircraft equipped with VOR/DME use the bearing information from the VOR and obtain range information from the TACAN portion.

7-4. RECEPTION DISTANCE

All VHF/UHF omnifacility signals follow an approximate *line-of-sight* course. (Figure 7-3). *Reception* distance *increases* with *altitude* to a reliable operating range of about 40 miles at Minimum Enroute Altitude (1,000 ft. above terrain). Omni facilities are spaced approximately 90 miles apart to assure navigation coverage over the airway. They are relatively free of atmospheric and precipitation static. Below are the UHF/VHF band ranges assuming no intervening obstructions between transmitter and receiver.

Feet Above Ground Station	Nautical Miles Reception Distance
1000	39
3000	69
5000	87
10000	122
15000	152
20000	174

7-5. FACILITY CLASSIFICATION

Omni facilities are divided into three classes which specify the intended interference-free service volume of the facilities. Service volume consists of the altitude and distance limits of the facility wherein no interference will be received from adjoining aids with the same or closely spaced frequency assignment. It is apparent from the following table that this is not the maximum range of the facility. Use of these facilities outside the service volume is not intended, and could result in undependable or incorrect indications in the aircraft.

NOTE: H = High, L = Low T = Terminal

VOR/VORTAC/TACAN NAVAIDS

Normal Usable Altitudes and Radius Distances

Class	Altitudes	Distance (miles)
T	12,000' and below	25
L	Below 18,000'	40
H	Below 18,000'	40
H	14,500' – 17,999'	100*
H	18,000' – FL450	130
H	Above FL450	100

*Applicable only within the conterminous U.S.

7-6. FACILITY IDENTIFICATION

The only positive method of identifying a VOR is by its three-letter Morse Code identification. Reliance on determining the identification of an omnirange should never be placed on listening to voice transmissions by the Flight Service Station (FSS) or control facility involved. Many FSS's remotely operate several omnis which have different names, and in some cases none have the name of the *parent* FSS. (During periods of maintenance, the coded identification is removed.)

Voice identification has been added to numerous VHF omniranges. The transmission consists of a voice announcement, "*Okmulgee V-O-R*", alternating with the usual coded identification. If no air/ground communications facility is associated with the omnirange, "*Airville Unattended V-O-R*" will be heard. At some locations, the coded identification is supplemented with VOR voice identification transmitting continuously in the background.

7-7. AIRBORNE VOR INSTRUMENTS

The basic indicators used in VOR navigation today, the Course Selector, the Ambiguity Meter, and the Course Deviation Indicator, are usually combined into a single instrument package which often incorporates a two-way radio communication feature as well. Figures 7-4A through 7-4D illustrate typical models in use today in light aircraft.

In the illustrated models, the VOR frequency selector is on the right side of the instrument face. In Figure 7-4A, the right-hand knob selects the decimal figure and the second knob from the right the units and tens digit, with the figure *1* stationary in the hundreds digit. In Figure 7-4D, the outer knob on the right selects the units and tens digits, and the inner knob the tenths.

After the pilot has selected the VOR frequency, to positively identify the station selected, he activates the Ident feature. The small lever in the lower right corner of the set (Figure 7-4A) is moved upwards and the ON-OFF/Volume knob adjusted so he can aurally monitor the VOR identification. In Figure 7-4D, the Ident knob, top center, is turned to *ON* and the ON-OFF/Volume knob (smaller knob inside the Ident knob) adjusted until the identification is heard. Once the VOR has been positively identified, the Ident feature is usually turned off. In the models shown, VOR voice transmissions can be received as long as the ON-OFF/Volume control switches are on and adjusted properly.

A. The pilot's next step is to select a radial. In Figure 7-4B, the radial is selected by turning the knob (Course Selector or Omni Bearing Selector) in the lower left corner of the instrument face until the desired radial appears under the small triangle at the bottom of the circular dial, OR by

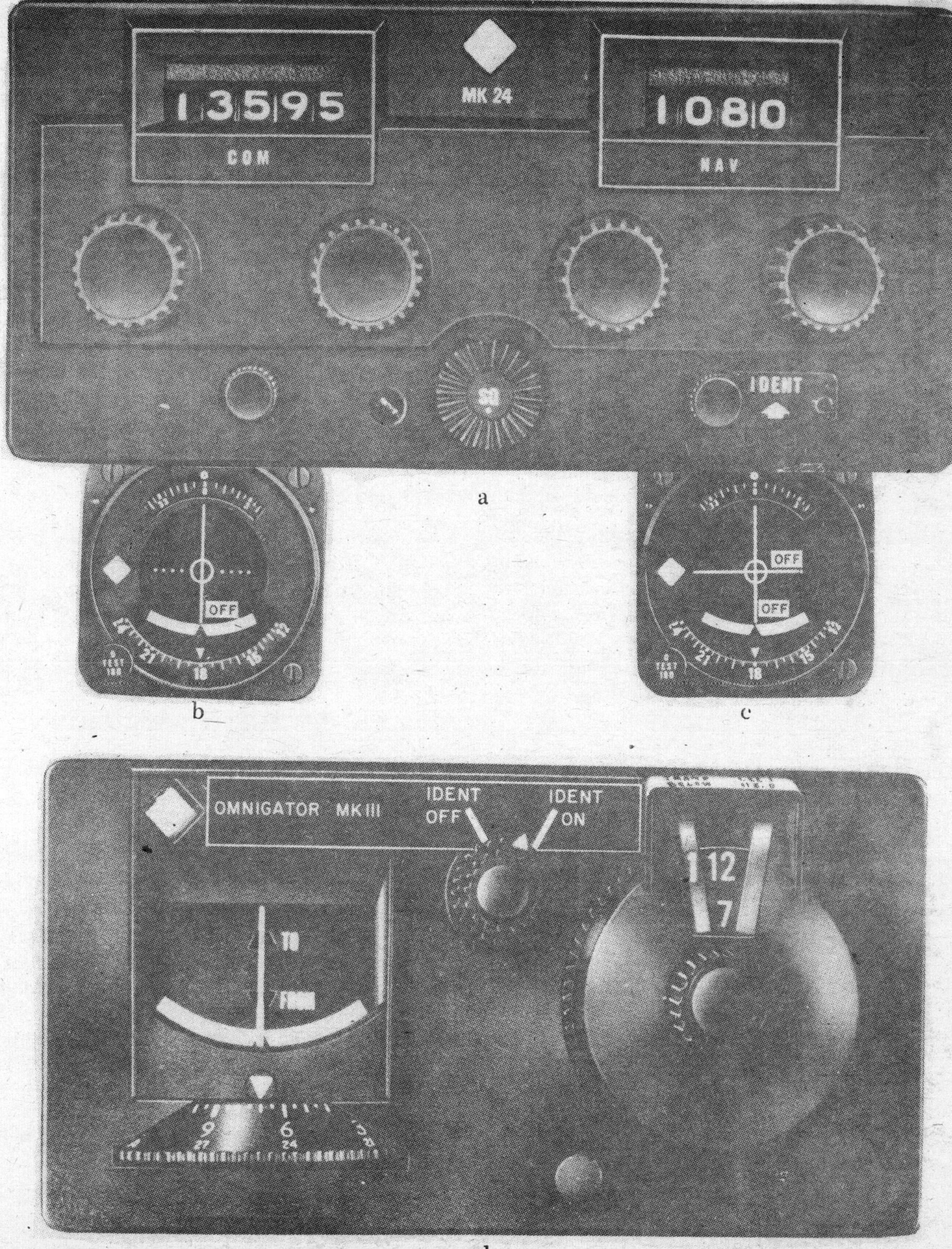
1 3 5 9 5
COM
MK 24
1 0 8 0
NAV
IDENT
a
OFF
b
OFF
OFF
c
OMNIGATOR MK III
IDENT OFF
IDENT ON
112
7
TO
FROM
d

FIGURE 7-4.

turning the knob until the vertical needle centers. The method used depends on whether the pilot wants to intercept a radial he is not presently on or wants to know what radial he is on at the time of selection.

The Course Selector knobs in the illustrations are labeled *0 TEST 180,* and incorporate a feature that permits the pilot to check receiver accuracy. Designated VOR test facilities (VOT) and airborne checkpoints are listed in the Airman's Information Manual.

In Figure 7-4D, the radial is selected by turning the horizontally-mounted dial on the lower left section of the equipment until the selected radial is under the white triangle. This may be tested by tuning to a VOT and rotating the Course Selector to either) degrees or 180 degrees. Accurate equipment will show a centered needle. If the needle is off-center to either side, the amount of inaccuracy is noted, and applied as a correction factor in navigation. The MK III, like the MK 24, can also be checked for accuracy by using airborne check points.

B. Once a radial has been selected, the pilot checks the Ambiguity Meter (also called the *TO-FROM* Indicator) which shows whether the radial selected, *IF FLOWN*, would take him *TO* or *FROM* the *VOR*. It *does not* indicate whether the aircraft is headed to or from the station.

The Ambiguity Meter may be either a small needle that points to TO or FROM, a small window in which the words TO or FROM may appear (Figure 7-4B and C) or a white flag that appears in a TO or FROM window (Figure 7-4D). If the signal is too weak for accurate navigation or fails, or if the aircraft is approximately 90 degrees either side of the selected radial and no true indication of TO or FROM is possible, the indicator will show blank, OFF or, if a pointer, neutral.

C. The Course Deviation Indicator (or Left-Right Needle) shows the pilot whether his aircraft is to the right or left of or on the selected radial. When the Indicator is centered the aircraft is crossing or on the selected radial or its reciprocal. As long as the heading of the aircraft is generally within 90 degrees of the radial selected, the indicator or needle will move in the direction the aircraft must fly to return to the selected radial.

The Course Deviation Indicator is a vertical needle or bar which, on most instruments, is pivoted from the top so that it can swing right or left of center, and is usually in the same instrument as the Course or Omni Bearing Selector. (Some instruments, as shown in Figure 7-4C, also incorporate a horizontal needle for use with ILS.)

Since there is no provision in the airborne VOR equipment to tell what direction the aircraft is heading, it is normally necessary to compare VOR instrument readings with the aircraft heading on the Magnetic Compass to navigate by VOR.

7-8. FLYING THE VOR

When flying TO a facility, the pilot first tunes in and aurally identifies the station. Next, he manually rotates the Course Selector until the Course Deviation Indicator centers and the Ambiguity Meter reads TO. (The deviation indicator will center twice, if rotated 360°; once to indicate the radial the aircraft is on (FM on Ambiguity meter), and again to indicate to the pilot a heading which, if flown (no-wind conditions), would take him to the VOR (TO on ambiguity meter).) Flying towards the needle of the Course Deviation Indicator will keep the aircraft on the desired radial, automatically compensating for wind drift (as long as the aircraft's heading is generally within 90 degrees of the course selected.)

When the aircraft passes over the VOR, the Course Deviation Indicator (needle) will fluctuate for a few seconds and then settle down near center. Simultaneously, the TO-FROM

Indicator changes to FROM, indicating that the radial on the Course Selector will take the aircraft *from* the station.

When flying FROM a facility, the desired course is selected on the Course Selector. The Ambiguity Meter should display a FROM indication and the pilot can maintain his desired track by flying toward the needle of the Course Deviation Indicator when necessary to keep it centered.

7-9. REVERSE SENSING

If the radial selected on the Course Selector and the Aircraft's heading differ by more than 90 degrees, the indications of the Deviation Indicator are reversed, and the pilot must fly away from the needle to return to course. For true or correct sensing, the aircraft's heading or Course Selector should generally agree; that is, the compass reading and radial flown must be within 90 degrees of each other. The compass shows the aircraft's heading, but the Course Selector tells the pilot whether the course (radial) selected will, if flown, take him to or from the facility. The direction the aircraft is heading is not recognized by the VOR receiver equipment; the equipment will always show what radial the aircraft is on (*or* its reciprocal) when the needle is centered, and whether flying a heading which is in general agreement with the radial selected will take you to or from the station. (Figure 7-5).

7-10. RESTRICTIONS AND LIMITATIONS

The sensitivity of the VOR receiver and Course Deviation Indicator is such that course width (full left to full right) is 20 degrees. (Figure 7-5).

While Course alignment accuracy of omni facilities is generally within ±2°, some facilities may have courses with larger errors. Where the error is more 2.5° from the theoretical position of the radial, the course will be reported unusable by NOTAM, either in the Notam Summary or in the AIM. Minor irregularities, course roughness, infrequent brief flag alarms, course deflections, or limited distance (range) also may be noted.

During periods of routine or emergency maintenance, the coded identification will be removed from a VOR. The removal of identification serves as a warning to pilots that the facility has been officially taken over by maintenance personnel and may be unreliable even though on the air intermittently or constantly.

7-11. VOR AIRWAY SYSTEM

VOR airways are numbered similarly to U. S. highways. Airways which run generally north and south have odd numbers and those which run generally east and west have even numbers. As in the highway numbering system, a segment of an airway which is common to two or more routes carries the numbers of all the airways which coincide for that segment. For example, between Chicago and South Bend, (*V* (*Victor*) *6* (Chicago-Cleveland) and *V* (*Victor*) *10* (Chicago-South Bend) are common and aeronautical charts show both airway numbers. When an airway has one or more numbers along a particular segment, a pilot filing a flight plan along that route need indicate only the number of the route that he is using. If his flight will be from Chicago to Cleveland, for instance, he will specify Victor 6. If his flight is from Chicago to South Bend, he will specify Victor 10.

Alternate airways are identified by their relative position from the main airway; *Victor 9 West* indicates an alternate airway associated with and lying to the west of Victor 9.

High altitude routes are called Jet Routes, referred to as *"J 78" or "J 46"*, and are numbered by the same method as the airways in the lower altitude strata. Jet routes begin above 18,000 feet and extend to FL 450.

Area Navigation routes are numbered like the other airways, and are spoken like the jet routes, except that the word *"Romeo"* is added -*"J 478 Romeo."*

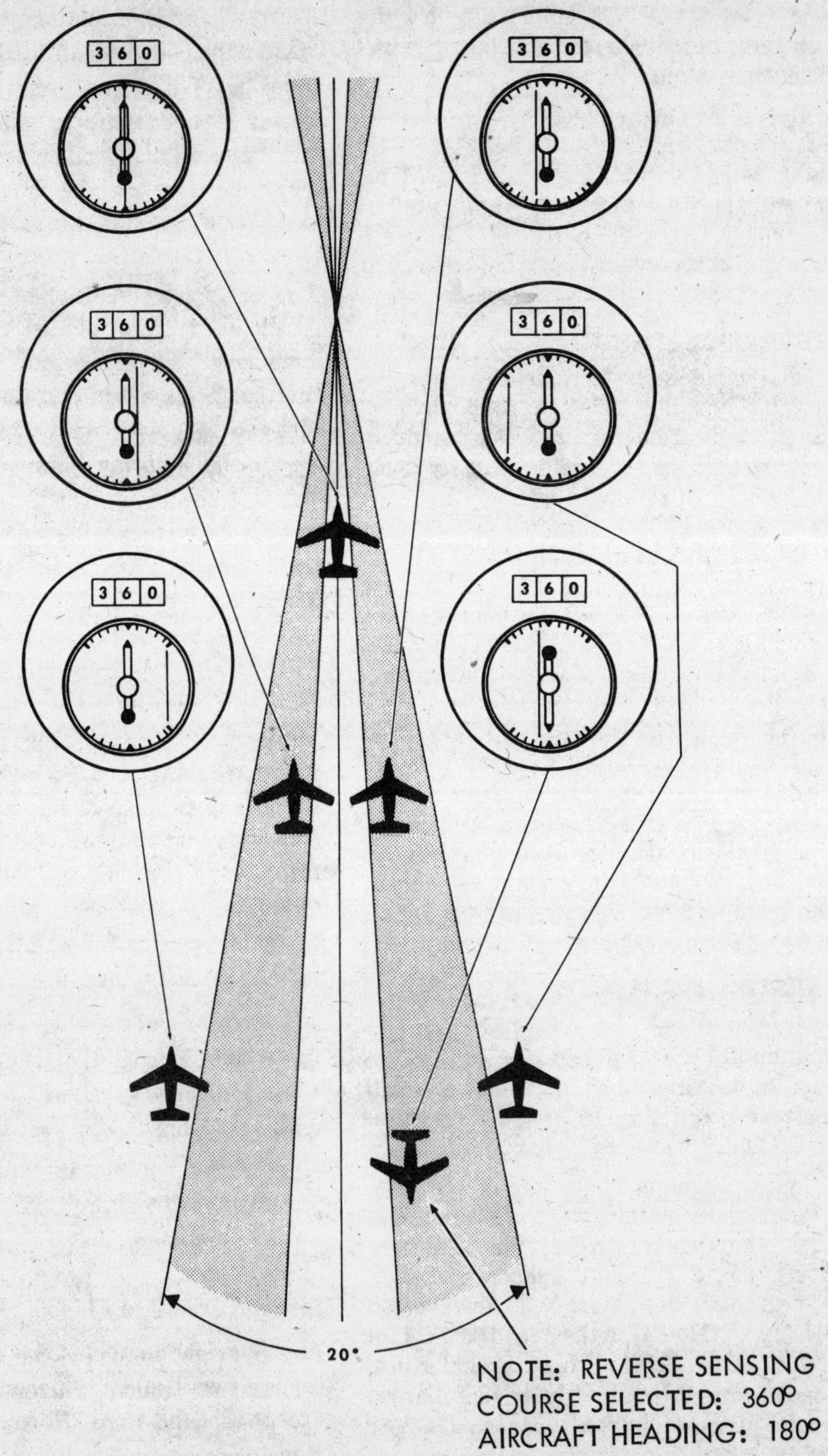

FIGURE 7-5. Relation of Course Width to Deviation Indicator.

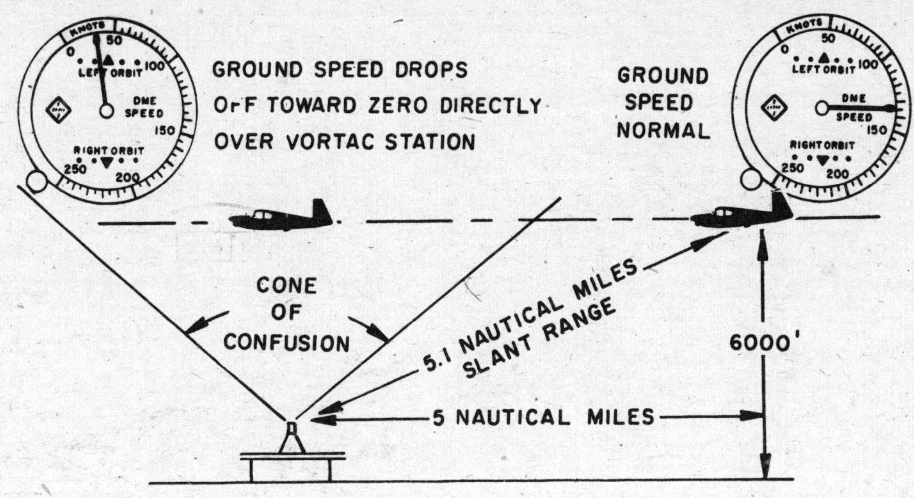

FIGURE 7-6.

7-12. DISTANCE MEASURING EQUIPMENT (DME)

A. *Introduction*

Distance and direction from a known ground point are two items of information necessary for a pilot to establish position and navigate and for a controller to maintain separation between aircraft. Until the advent of Distance Measuring Equipment, a pilot could find his bearing from a selected VOR or L/MF facility, but in order to determine his actual position (bearing *and* range), it was necessary to tune to another facility and determine position by cross-reference, a time-consuming procedure. With DME, the pilot has range from a DME-equipped station displayed instantly, accurately and constantly, and his bearing from VOR, TACAN or ILS.

B. *Principle of Operation*

DME capability requires special equipment both in the aircraft and on the ground. The airborne equipment consists of:

1. The control unit – an ON-OFF switch and channel selector

2. Indicators – located on the instrument panel, provides a continuous display of distance to the pilot, in nautical miles, of the slant-range distance from the airplane to the ground station. (Figure 7-6).

3. Interrogator – interrogates the ground station; that is, transmits radio signals to the ground station which trigger reply signals from it. (Figure 7-7). These reply signals, picked up by the aircraft's transmit/receive antenna, are fed to the interrogator for amplification, verification and distance measurement. By computing the elapsed time between transmission of the interrogation signals and the receipt of reply signals, the interrogator determines the distance between the airplane and the ground station. In some models of DME, these same signals can be displayed as Ground Speed.

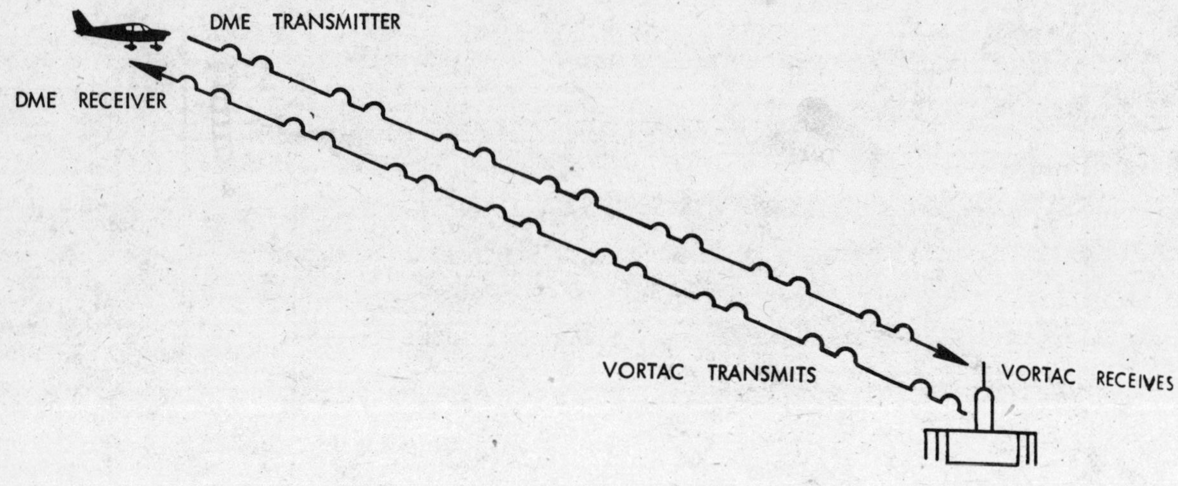

FIGURE 7-7.

4. Antenna – located on the bottom of the aircraft to minimize adverse effects possible if the body of the aircraft should inadvertently get between the antenna and ground station.

The ground station equipment is called a Transponder, and answers specific radio signals from the airborne interrogator.

DME operates in the UHF band between 960 and 1215 mHz, with normal line of sight limitations. Reliable signals may be received at distances up to 196 miles at an altitude of 17,000 feet or more, with an accuracy of no more than 2% error. Except in the immediate vicinity of the ground station or at a relatively high altitude, the error introduced by the slant measurement is minor and usually may be ignored.

C. Types of Facilities

DME information is available from VORTAC and TACAN facilities. Some VORs and ILS's have collocated DME facilities and are designated as VOR/DME's or ILS/DME's.

D. Advantages

DME offers many advantages to the pilot and to the controller. By giving instant, accurate and constant range information to the pilot, DME assists him in checking ETA's and ground speeds, can be used to fly directly to off-airway airports (out a specific navaid radial a specific number of miles), precisely indicate intersections, find best winds aloft (wherever his groundspeed is highest), maintaining precise holding patterns without timing, and facilitates in ATC radar identification by giving the pilot a pinpointed position to give the radar controller.

DME aids the controller by making a greater portion of his airspace usable. DME-equipped aircraft can hold at any point within reception range of a DME-equipped facility, and are not limited to intersections or radio fixes based on two facilities. They can fly arcs about navaids, restricted use airspace, or congested traffic areas, aiding in reducing general airway and terminal area congestion.

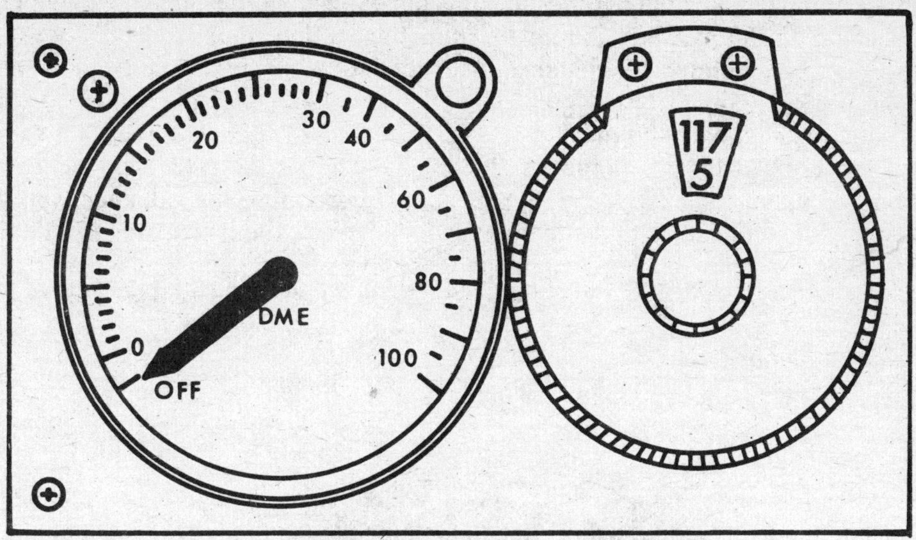

FIGURE 7-8a.

Figure 7-8a—Typical DME Indicator—Dial on the left indicates nautical miles on a variable-scale face. The DME Channel Selector indicates the frequency of the navaid collocated with the DME in use, and automatically selects the proper DME frequency.

Figure 7-8b—Typical DME/GSI Indicator—On this model, the pilot can select either a distance display or a ground speed display. With the Ground speed displayed, the pilot, to find best winds aloft, need only find the altitude that gives the best groundspeed. Also note that this unit can display distance on two scales: 0 to 35 nautical miles, used primarily during instrument approaches, and 30 to 100 nautical miles for enroute navigation.

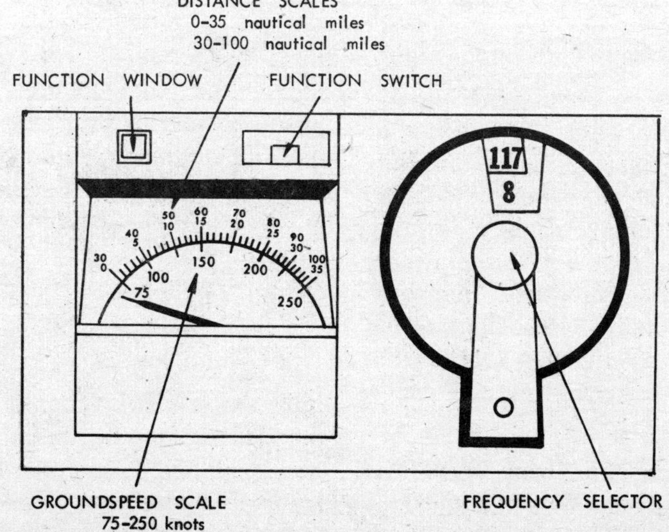

FIGURE 7-8b.

To read out the amount of flying time in minutes to or from the VORTAC station, rotate knob (1) until value in window (2) matches DME distance indication (3). At this point, groundspeed needle automatically pointing out ground-speed on inner dial (4) also points out minutes-to-station on outer dial (5). In the example of Figure 7-9, it can be seen that traveling at a speed of 400 knots, 125 nautical miles from the station, it will take 19 minutes to fly to the station.

NOTE: Other distances may also be set in, making it possible, for example, to determine in advance the time between the next two VORTAC stations.

FIGURE 7-9. Distance/Ground-Speed Indicator Display.

Figure 7-10a—Another Typical DME/GSI Indicator Face—This model has the same basic features as the instrument in Figure 7-8b, and Figure 7-10b is a closeup of the indications with the function selector switch in its various position.

7-13. AREA NAVIGATION (RNAV)

A. *Introduction*

The concept of Area Navigation is not new. Pilots who have used VOR and DME to establish checkpoints along a course line plotted directly from departure point to destination are practicing area navigation. The more sophisticated Area Navigation allows a pilot not only to fly a course to a predetermined point without overflying intermediate navigation aids, but allows him to set up his own navigation aids, airways, checkpoints, intersections and approach aids to navigate by.

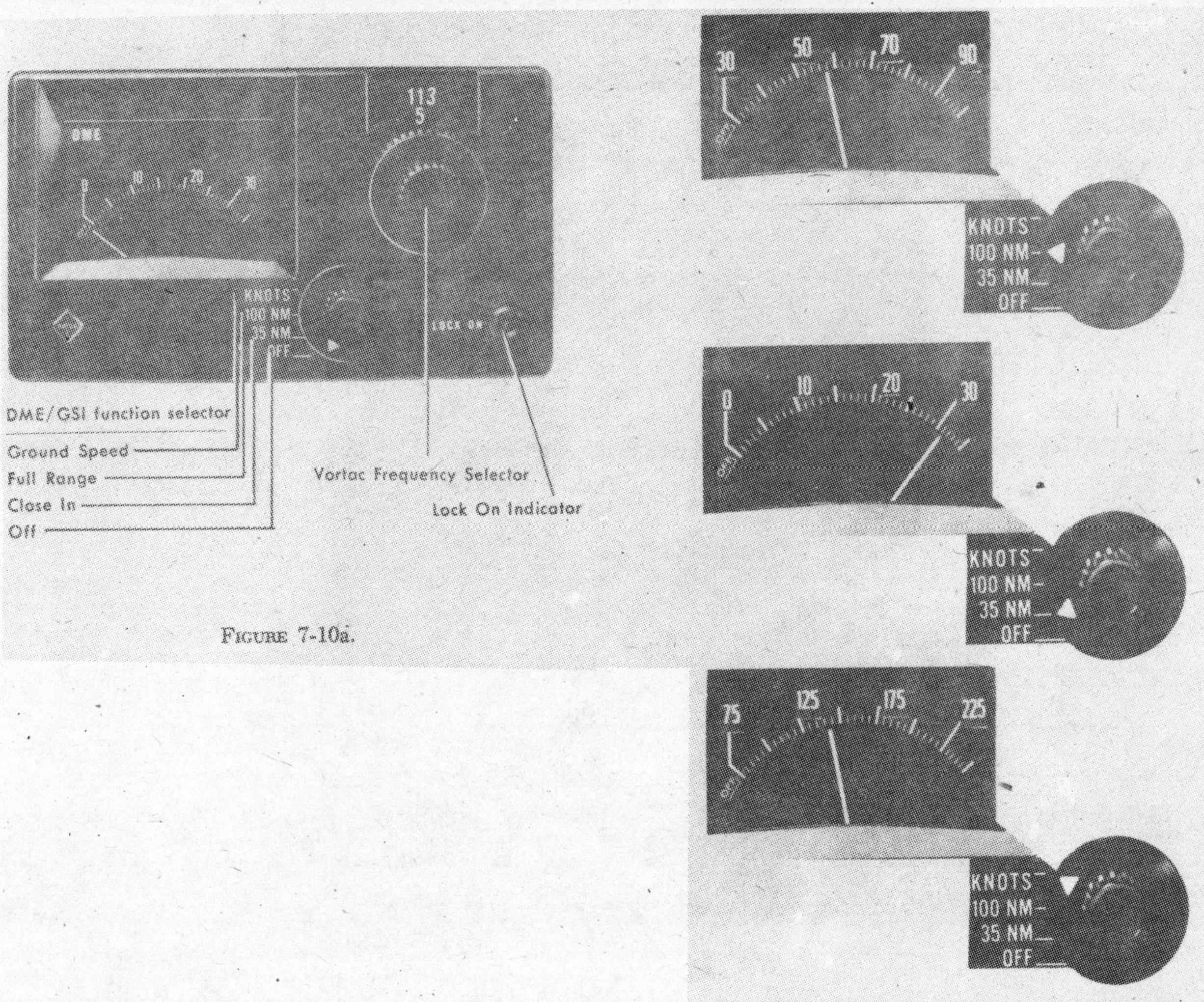

FIGURE 7-10a.

FIGURE 7-10b.

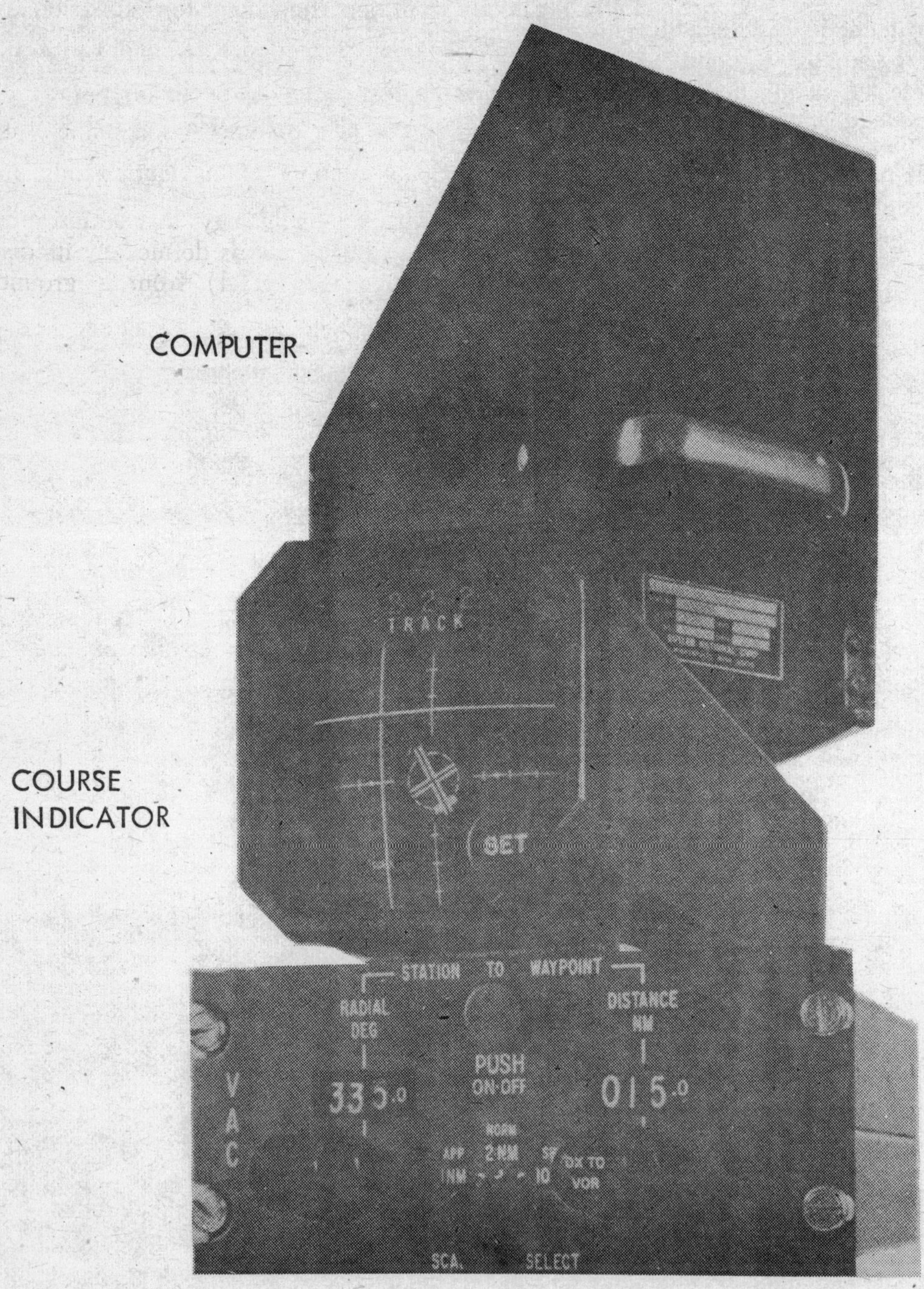

FIGURE 7-11. Typical RNAV Installation.

B. Aircraft Equipment

To use Area Navigation the aircraft must be properly equipped. A typical installation includes:

A. Vector Analog Computer

B. Way Point Selector

C. Pictorial Course Indicator. (See Figures 7-11 and 7-12).

C. How It Works

Horizontal navigational information is based upon input from VOR/DME, VORTAC or TACAN. Simply expressed, the Analog Computer electronically moves the navaid to any desired location within receiving range. Sometimes called a *phantom station*, in generally accepted RNAV terminology this location is known as a *waypoint* and is defined by its distance and bearing (radial) from a ground station.

Course Indicator

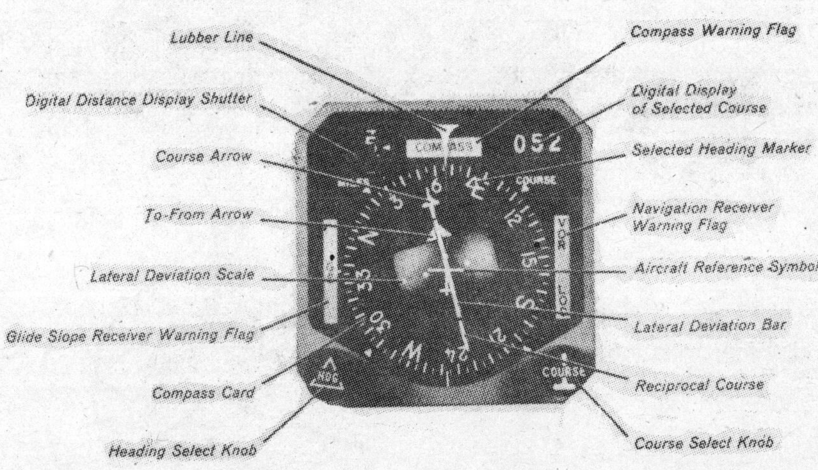

FIGURE 7-12. Typical RNAV pictorial course indicator.

In Figure 7-13, the value of side (A) is the measured DME distance to the VORTAC. Side (B), the distance from the VORTAC to the waypoint, and angle (1), the bearing from the VORTAC to the waypoint, are set in the cockpit computer. The bearing from the VORTAC to the aircraft, angle (2), is measured by the VOR receiver. The airborne computer compares angles (1) and (2) and determines angle (3). With this information, the computer continually solves for side (C), which is the distance in nautical miles and the magnetic course from the aircraft to the waypoint. This information will be continuously displayed for the pilot. Area Navigation (RNAV) route descriptions appear in AIM, Part 3. They are numbered in a manner similar to Victor and jet airways with the suffic "R" identifying them as Area Navigation routes (J803R, V707R).

D. *Advantages of Area Navigation*

1. Pilots can fly accurate straight-line courses between geographical points without having to dogleg over or between VORTAC's. On a flight of even moderate length, a significant reduction of enroute time results.
2. Useable airspace is greatly expanded by providing routes which are not limited by facility location.
3. Holding and orbiting are simplified.
4. Course deviation for weather avoidance may be accomplished more effectively. With Area Navigation, the pilot (with ATC approval) can alter his course without radar vectors and remain constantly aware of his position.
5. Changes in routing such as the assignment of a parallel route can be accomplished without radar vectors.
6. Multiple and one-way routes may be established to reduce congestion on heavily traveled airways. Traffic may be segregated by aircraft speed and characteristics.
7. A capacity is provided for instrument letdown and approach to airports not equipped with approach facilities or for which RNAV approach procedures are presently published.
8. There will be a reduction in the number of communications between controller and pilot.

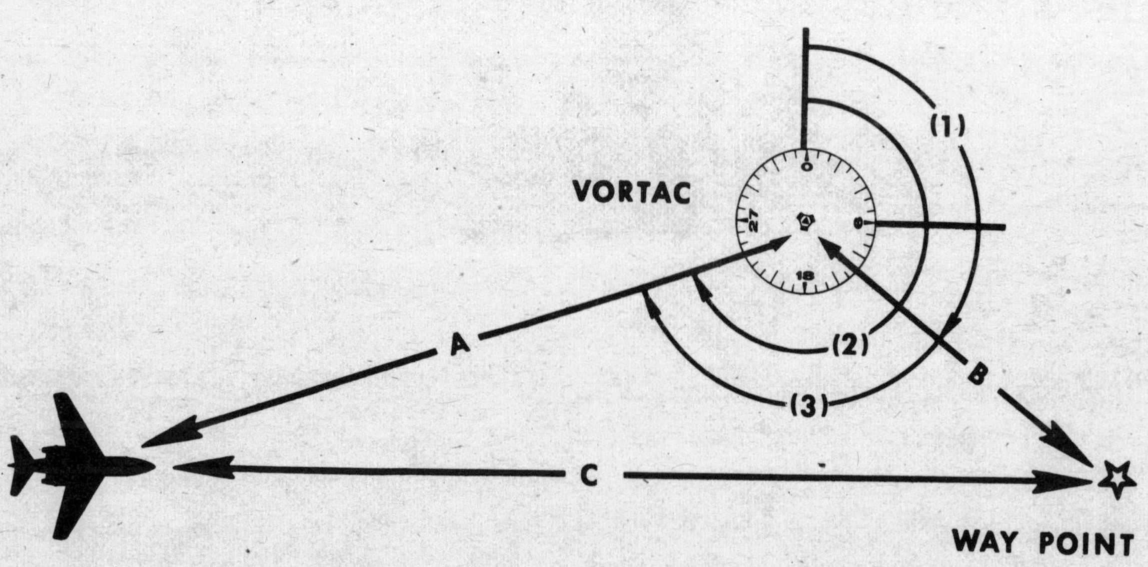

FIGURE 7-13. Analog or course line computer geometry.

WORKSHEET — OMNI-DIRECTIONAL FACILITIES, DME, RNAV

Complete the following questions without referring to the preceding study material.

Compare your answers with the correct answers at the end of the manual. For those questions you have answered incorrectly, it is suggested you review the appropriate paragraphs in the study material.

1. VORs operate in the VHF frequency band from:

   (1) 104-108 mHz.

   (2) 108-112 mHz.

   (3) 112-118 mHz.

   (4) 108-117.95 mHz

2. The number of magnetic courses provided by a VORTAC is:

   (1) 357.

   (2) 180.

   (3) 359.

   (4) theoretically infinite.

3. A pilot is flying at one thousand feet above the terrain on a VOR radial. At this altitude, he can expect to receive the course signals for approximately:

   (1) 40 miles.

   (2) 90 miles.

   (3) 100 miles.

   (4) 150 miles.

4. List the three basic instruments used for VOR navigation.

   (1) ....

   (2) ....

   (3) ....

5. The aircraft instrument which shows a pilot whether flying the selected course will take him "TO" or "FROM" the station is the:

   (1) ambiguity meter.

   (2) course selector.

   (3) deviation indicator.

   (4) magnetic compass.

6. A pilot has tuned to a VOR. The course selector reads 90 degrees when the deviation indicator is centered and the ambiguity meter reads "TO". The magnetic heading of the aircraft is 80 degrees.

   The pilot knows that his magnetic course to the station is:

   (1) 260 degrees.

   (2) 80 degrees.

   (3) 90 degrees.

   (4) 270 degrees.

7. When an aircraft drifts left or right of a selected radial, the information is shown on the:

   (1) course deviation indicator.

   (2) course selector.

   (3) ambiguity meter.

   (4) magnetic compass.

8. A pilot wishes to fly 270-degree radial to a specific station. After tuning to the proper frequency, the 270-degree radial is selected on:

   (1) ambiguity meter.

   (2) course selector.

   (3) Course deviation indicator.

   (4) magnetic compass.

9. The course deviation indicator shows that the aircraft is left or right of the selected course to a maximum of:

   (1) 5 degrees.

   (2) 10 degrees.

   (3) 15 degrees.

   (4) 20 degrees.

10. The radials of a VOR are:

    (1) magnetic toward the station.

    (2) true toward the station.

    (3) magnetic from the station.

    (4) true from the station.

11. Flying 195 degrees "TO" a VOR, you notice that the ambiguity meter and course deviation indicator are fluctuating rapidly. After a short time both indicators become steady. The deviation indicator returns to center but the ambiguity meter is now pointing to "FROM". You know that:

    (1) the VOR is unreliable.

    (2) your aircraft has passed over the station.

    (3) insufficient signal was being received.

    (4) the VOR signals were momentarily interrupted.

12. Station passage of a TACAN facility is presumed to have occurred:

    (1) When changing course after reaching the station.

    (2) When the DME indicates a distance approximately the same as the absolute altitude of the aircraft and is starting to indicate an increase in distance or range.

    (3) When the approximate range is 2.75 miles.

    (4) When the TO-FROM and the Deviation Indicators start to fluctuate.

13. A pilot flying an aircraft equipped with a functioning TACAN receiver can obtain azimuth and distance information by tuning in a VORTAC.

    True or False.

14. TACAN operates in the ....

    frequency band between ....MHz

    and ....MHz.

15. Place the letter(s) of the NAVAID in the blank preceding the appropriate term.

A. VOR, B. DME, C. RNAV, D. TACAN.

.... 1. Provides(s) constant Azimuth and range information in properly equipped aircraft.

.... 2. Operate(s) in VHF frequency band.

.... 3. Heading and course must agree generally within 90 degrees.

.... 4. Some airborne equipment also displays ground speed information.

.... 5. Permit(s) flying arcs about or orbiting of NAVAIDS.

.... 6. Usable range of nearly 200 miles at a line-of-sight altitude.

.... 7. Emits aural three-letter coded identification.

.... 8. Usually has voice capability.

.... 9. Operate(s) in the UHF frequency band.

............10. Utilizes a computer to analyze received radio information.

WORKSHEET ANSWERS

Chapter 1. Basic Navigation

1. (2) Deviation
2. (1) 0400 the following day
3. Great Circle
4. (3) 15 degrees
5. (4) Variation
6. (2) Wind Correction Angle
7. (3) to produce a developable surface.
8. (2) Parallels of Latitude, Meridians of Longitude
9. (3) Wind, Variation, Deviation
10. (3) Prime Meridian

Answers, Chapter 2, Charts and Publications

1. d
2. 121.1
3. a
4. c
5. False
6. 113.3, Ch. 80
7. b
8. c
9. d
10. c
11. d
12. d
13. a
14. c
15. b
16. a
17. c
18. d
19. b
20. c
21. d
22. d
23. a
24. b
25. (1) 590
    (2) Kansas City Center
    (3) 44° 45.5', 90° 31.6'.
    (4) J800R
    (5) 45,000' (See Legend)
    (6) 124.3 nm
    (7) JOT 112.3
    (8) 031 degrees
    (9) 354 degree, 19.8 NM
    (10) 18,000' (See Legend)
26. obstruction clearance,, Minimum Enroute Altitude
27. L-6, H-2
28. 1,294'
29. (1) True
30. OKC070R/SW0135R
31. 248 degrees
32. 17.5
33. 135.65
34. 14,000'
35. HEC211R, ONT030R, LAX068R

Answers Chapter 3 Worksheet

1. 3
2. 2
3. 4
4. 3
5. c, b, d, a,e

Chapter 4, ILS Worksheet Answers

1. A. Guidance information–Localizer, Glide Slope

   B. Range – Marker Beacon

   C. Visual Information – Lights
2. 3
3. 4
4. 3
5. 2
6. a. Left

   b. 2.5°
7. 4
8. 1
9. 3
10. 3
11. inadequate signal strength or failure of GS transmitter
12. Yes – merely a checkpoint for distance
13. TWEB, ADF Approaches, Transition from airways to ILS
14. 3°, 200, 1400
15. Aid in transitioning to visual contact with the ground.

Chapter 5 Worksheet

1. D
2. Curved, wind
3. 1. 180° ambiguity is eliminated

   2. loop (antenna) is automatically rotated

   3. gives the pilot continuous bearing information
4. bearing, nose of the aircraft
   bearing, from the equipment
5. magnetic, VHF/UHF, bearing from the station

Chapter 6 Radar Worksheet

1. PPI (Plan Position Indicator)
2. (1) azimuth and range
3. about 60 miles
4. return from terrain features close to the antenna, in the center of the scope
5. navaids, airways, landmarks, map of the area
6. ARSR-1
7. 200 miles, to above 40,000'
8. to assist pilots in weather avoidance
9. ground clutter, decreasing accuracy with increasing range
10. azimuth, range and elevation
11. Precision Approach Radar (PAR)
12. (4) 300 feet
13. one to four mile radius
14. (3) airport surface
15. Primary radar is a reflected signal; secondary radar is a signal transmitted from an airborne transponder.

Chapter 7 – Worksheet Answers

1. (4) 108 – 117.95 mHz
2. (4) theoretically infinite
3. (1) 40 NM
4. Course selector, ambiguity meter, course deviation indicator
5. (1) ambiguity meter
6. (3) 90 degrees

7. (1) course deviation indicator
8. (2) course selector
9. (2) 10 degrees
10. (3) magnetic from the station
11. (2) Your aircraft has passed over the station
12. (2)
13. True
14. UHF, 960-1215 mHz
15. 1 – C, D
    2 – A, C (VHF + UHF)
    3 – A, D
    4 – B
    5 – B, C
    6 – B
    7 – A, D
    8 – A
    9 – B, D
    10 – B, C

☆ U.S. GOVERNMENT PRINTING OFFICE 1977—771 -089/737

APPENDIX B—WEATHER FOR CONTROLLERS
PREFACE *

This publication has been prepared by the Air Traffic Branch and designed to support the training requirements of the National Air Traffic Training Program.

This reference material provides supplementary information on the weather services as administered in the National Air Traffic Training Program. It is to be used by the air traffic control specialist as an adjunct to his formal training. It has been prepared in coordination with the Weather Service Coordinator and Training Consultant at the FAA Academy.

*This FAA training material is not required information for the Air Traffic Control Employment Examination but is considered useful and important to air traffic control work.

INTRODUCTION

What do you as a controller need to know about weather? Despite the development of weather satellites, radar, aircraft design, radio aids, and navigation techniques, safety in flight is still subject to conditions of limited visibility, turbulence and icing. You must have a fundamental knowledge of the atmosphere and weather behavior to aid pilots in avoiding hazardous flight conditions.

This manual is not intended for meteorologists or flight service specialists, but is designed for controllers. It presents selected items of weather information necessary to perform your job as a controller.

This manual contains the following subjects:

1. Aids used by the National Weather Service and FAA to provide controllers with weather information.

2. Special knowledge the controller needs to understand commonly used weather terms.

3. Weather causes.

4. Aviation weather hazards.

5. Interpretation of sequence reports, area forecasts, terminal forecasts, and other pertinent data.

Throughout the United States a network of airport weather stations report current weather. At most of these stations, trained personnel are always on duty making observations and sending hourly reports to central points. Since weather near the earth's surface often results from conditions at high altitudes, selected stations periodically release and track balloons to determine wind direction and speed at the upper levels. A complete record of temperature, pressure, and humidity at upper levels is obtained by National Weather Service (NWS) radiosonde stations which release balloons.

This information with other data collected by radio, telephone, and other means is assembled and plotted on weather maps. These maps provide specific information concerning the weather all over the country and give meteorologists data for making weather predictions.

The NWS also issues daily forecasts especially designed to indicate flying conditions anticipated for the following 12 or 24 hours.

CHAPTER 1
WEATHER CAUSES

SECTION 1
ATMOSPHERE

1. GENERAL

Our study of Weather Causes is not a complete course in meteorology. It is a review of basic meteorology and furnishes you with sufficient background to effectively use weather information. It covers atmospheric properties, the structure of the atmosphere, atmospheric processes, and weather producing systems.

2. LAYERS

The atmosphere is divided into five layers with each layer having certain features. For our purpose we will emphasize the troposphere and the stratosphere, since most aircraft flights occur in these layers.

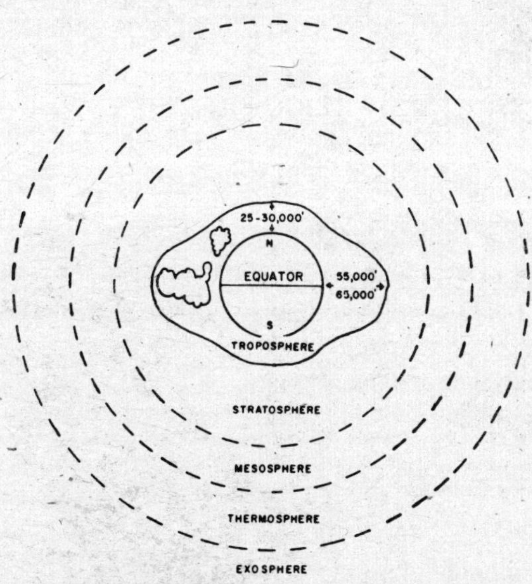

Vertical structure of the atmosphere showing one division into layers or spheres based on temperature.

FIGURE 1-1

3. TROPOSPHERE

Trosphere is that layer of air beginning at the ground and ending at an average altitude of 7 miles. Thickness varies from equator to poles and from season to season. It is thicker over the equator than over the poles and also has a greater thickness in summer. The troposphere contains about three-quarters of the atmosphere by weight, and almost all of the weather. The boundary between the troposphere and the stratosphere is the tropopause. Its significance is that high speed winds (called "jet stream") producing clear air turbulence are often found near the tropopause.

4. STRATOSPHERE

Stratosphere is that layer just above the tropopause. The average altitude of the stratosphere is 7 miles at the base and 22 miles at the top. Characteristics of the layer are a slight increase in temperature with height and near absence of water vapor. Occasionally, however, a strong thunderstorm will break through the tropopause into the lower stratosphere.

5.-6. RESERVED

SECTION 2
ATMOSPHERIC PRESSURE

7. PRESSURE

Atmospheric pressure is a measure of weight that a column of air exerts on an object. This pressure is measured with a barometer.

8. MERCURIAL BAROMETER

Mercurial barometer balances a column of mercury in an evacuated glass tube against the weight of the column of air above it. The length of the column of mercury is a measure of pressure in inches. A decrease in pressure allows the mercury to drop, thus reducing the height of the column. This is interpreted in terms of inches of mercury.

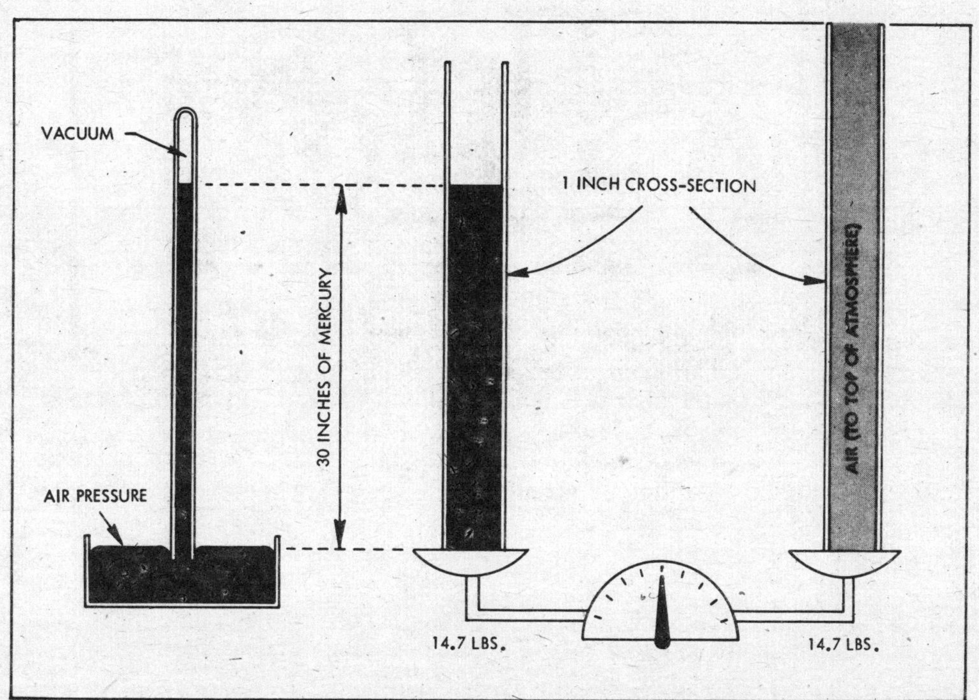

The mercurial barometer showing air pressure balancing a column of mercury. At the right a column of mercury 30 inches high and one square inch across section weighs approximately 14.7 pounds – the same as a column of air one square inch cross section extending to the top of the atmosphere.

FIGURE 1-2

9. ANEROID BAROMETER

An aneroid barometer is a partially evacuated cell which is sensitive to pressure changes. This cell is linked to an indicator hand which indicates pressure on a graduated scale. The instrument is smaller, more compact, and much more portable than the mercurial barometer, but generally less accurate and more likely to get out of adjustment over a period of time. When used for official observations it must be checked against a mercurial barometer at least once a week.

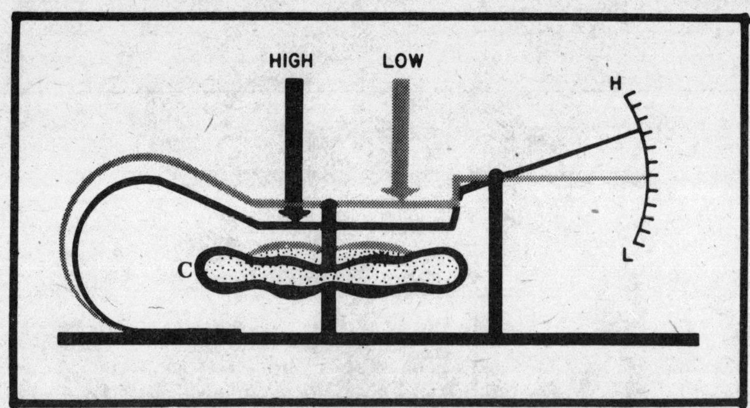

The aneroid barometer. The aneroid barometer in which the partially evacuated cell (C) expands and contracts with changes in atmospheric pressure. Movements are magnified through a linkage system moving an indicator hand across a graduated scale.

FIGURE 1-3

10. CONVERSION TO SEA LEVEL PRESSURE

If all weather stations were at the same elevation, barometer readings would give a correct record of distribution for atmospheric pressure when entered on the weather map. However, pressure decreases with height at the rate of approximately 1 inch of mercury per thousand feet in the lower few thousand feet of the atmosphere. (This rate of decrease is greater in colder air.) Since reporting stations have a wide range of elevations, barometer readings must be converted to a common level referred to as "sea level" to present meaningful data on weather reports and maps.

11. CONVERSION TO MILLIBARS

The barometer reading, after conversion to the equivalent sea level pressure, is translated into MILLIBARS for use on weather charts. By comparing pressures at different stations it is possible to determine many symptoms indicating the trend of weather conditions.

12. ALTIMETER

An altimeter is a form of aneroid barometer which measures the difference in pressure between a given altitude and sea level calibrated in feet. An altimeter reading is most accurate with respect to true altitude when it is on or near the airport from which the altimeter setting was obtained. When set at the local altimeter setting an accurate altimeter will read field elevation when it is on the surface.

13.-15. RESERVED

SECTION 3
TEMPERATURE

16. TEMPERATURE DISTRIBUTION

Two temperature scales are commonly used in communicating weather information - Fahrenheit (F) and Celsius (C)(Centigrade). The freezing point of water is 32° on the Fahrenheit scale (32°F) and zero on the Celsius scale (0°C), and the boiling point of water is 212°F and 100°C at sea level.

17. LAPSE RATE

Temperature normally decreases with increasing altitude in the lower 30 to 40 thousand feet of the atmosphere. This decrease in temperature with an increase in height is defined as lapse rate. A standard lapse rate is approximately 2°C per thousand feet.

18. INVERSION

Inversion is an abnormal increase of the temperature of the atmosphere with height. The inversion layer is usually characterized by haze and smooth air. The inversion layer bends radar waves causing abnormal radar coverage.

19. ISOTHERMAL LAYER

An isothermal layer is a layer in which temperature does not change with height.

20.-22. RESERVED

SECTION 4
STANDARD ATMOSPHERE

23. STANDARD ATMOSPHERE

A. Several values assigned to the atmosphere have been mentioned, but in order to measure a change from the normal, we have to establish a standard. Conditions throughout the world for all latitudes and all seasons have been averaged, to arrive at a specific surface temperature, surface pressure, and rate of change of temperature and pressure with height for given layers within the atmosphere.

B. The following is a partial list of values assigned to the STANDARD ATMOSPHERE and is sufficient for our study.

(1) A surface temperature of 59°F (15°C) at sea level.

(2) A surface pressure of 29.92 inches of mercury (1013.2 millibars, 14.7 pounds per square inch) at sea level.

(3) A lapse rate (decrease of temperature with height) in the troposphere of approximately 2°C per thousand feet.

(4) A tropopause of approximately 36,000 feet.

(5) A temperature at the tropopause of -55°C.

24.-26. RESERVED

SECTION 5
CIRCULATION

27. BASIC CIRCULATION

The atmosphere tends to maintain an equal pressure over the entire earth just as the ocean tends to maintain a constant level. Whenever the equilibrium is disturbed, air begins to flow from areas of higher pressure to areas of lower pressure.

28. CAUSES OF ATMOSPHERIC CIRCULATION

A. The factor that upsets the normal equilibrium is the uneven heating of the earth. At the equator, the earth receives more heat than in areas to the north and south. This heat is transferred to the atmosphere, warming the air and causing it to expand and rise. Thus an area of low pressure is produced at the equator, and the heavier, cooler air from the north and south moves along the earth's surface toward the equator to equalize the pressure. This air in turn becomes warm and rises, thereby, establishing a constant circulation that might consist of two circular paths, the air rising at the equator, traveling aloft toward the poles, and returning along the earth's surface to the equator.

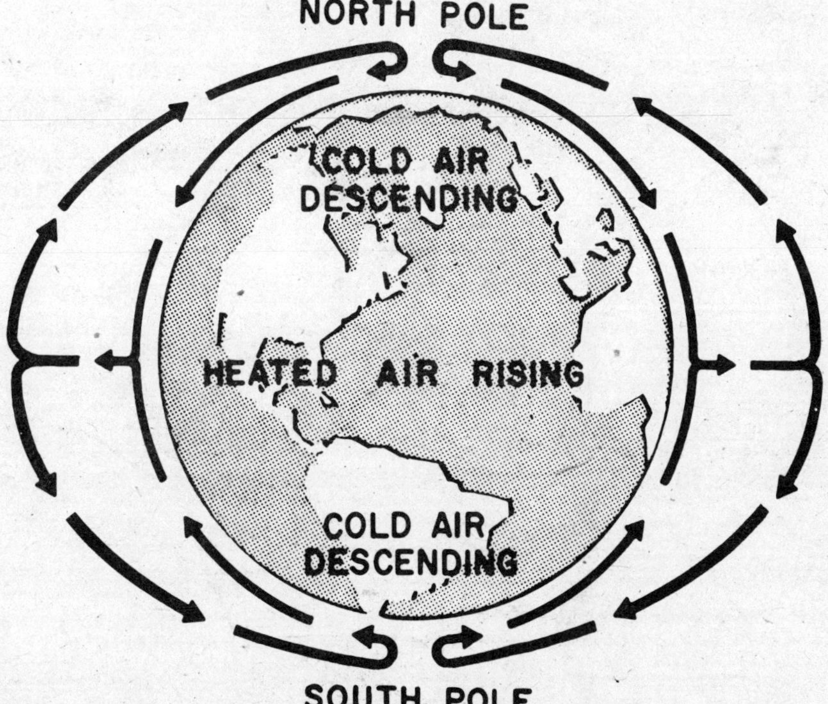

Circulation as it would be on a non-rotating globe. Intense heating at the Equator lowers the density. More dense air at the poles flows toward the Equator forcing the less dense air upward where aloft it flows toward the poles.

FIGURE 1-4

B. This theoretical pattern of circulation, however, is greatly modified by many forces, a very important one being the rotation of the earth. In the Northern Hemisphere, this rotation causes air to flow to the right of its normal path. In the Southern Hemisphere, air flows to the left of its normal path. This action caused by the earth's rotation is called the Coriolis force. For simplicity our discussion is limited to the motion of air in the Northern Hemisphere.

C. As the air rises and moves northward from the equator, it is deflected toward the east, and by the time it has traveled about a third of the distance to the pole it is no longer moving northward, but eastward. This causes the air to accumulate in a belt at about latitude 30°, creating an area of high pressure. Some of this air is then forced down to the earth's surface, where part flows southward, returning to the equator, and part flows northward along the surface. A portion of the air aloft continues its journey northward, being cooled en route, and finally settles down near the pole, where it begins a return trip toward the equator. Before it moves very far southward, it comes into conflict with the warmer surface air flowing northward from latitude 30°. The warmer air moves up over a wedge of the colder air, and continues northward, producing an accumulation of air in the upper latitudes.

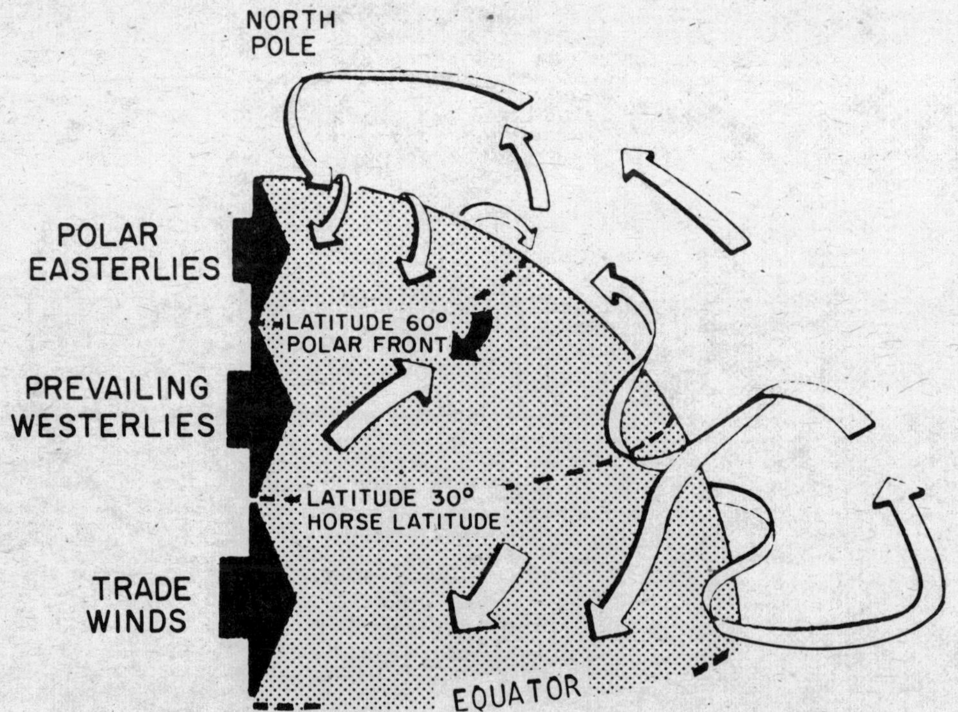

The mean general circulation. The Coriolis force deflects high-level southerly winds from the equator into westerlies at about 30° latitude. It deflects low-level northerly winds from the poles into a belt of easterlies near 60° latitude. Between the two is a giant mixing zone in which the air completes its migration between the equator and poles.

FIGURE 1-5

D. Additional complications in the general circulation of the air are brought about by the irregular distribution of oceans and continents; the relative effectiveness of different surfaces in transferring heat to the atmosphere; the daily variation in temperature; the seasonal changes, and many other factors. The general flow of weather in the United States is from Northwest to Southeast.

29. LOWS

Regions of low pressure develop where air lies over land or water surfaces that are warmer than the surrounding areas. Semipermanent lows form over the desert southwest during the summer months.

30. HIGHS

Regions of high pressure develop where air lies over surfaces that are cooler than the surrounding area, and where air en route from the equator to the poles is forced to descend.

31. WIND PATTERNS

Wind flows from high pressure to low pressure. In the Northern Hemisphere wind is deflected to the right of its course by the earth's rotation. Air moving outward from a "high" flows in a clockwise spiral around the "high" center, and air moving toward a low flows in a counter clockwise spiral around the "low" center.

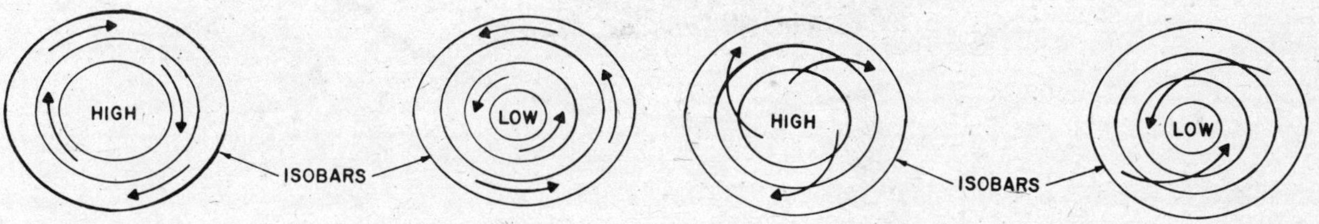

Flow of air around a high and low pressure area in the Northern Hemisphere above the friction layer.

Flow of air around a high and low pressure area in the Northern Hemisphere at the surface.

FIGURE 1-6

32. ISOBARS

The pressure at each station is recorded on the weather map and lines called isobars are drawn to connect the points of equal pressure. Many of these lines make complete circles and surround areas marked H (high) or L (low). Isobars are quite similar to contour lines appearing on aeronautical charts. However, instead of indicating the altitude of terrain and the steepness of slopes, isobars indicate the amount of pressure and steepness of pressure gradients. If the gradient (slope) is steep, the isobars will be close together, and the wind will be strong. If the gradient is gradual, the isobars will be far apart, and the wind gentle. Isobars furnish valuable information about winds aloft. Close to the earth, wind direction is modified by the contours over which it passes, and wind speed is reduced by friction with the surface. At levels two or three thousand feet above the surface however, the speed is greater and the direction is usually parallel to the isobars.

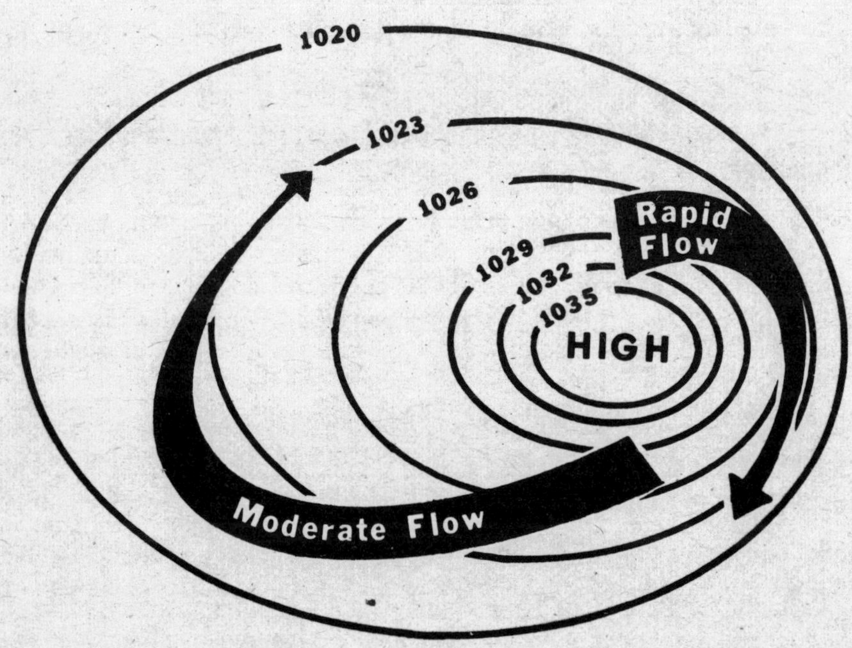

FIGURE 1-7

33. CONVECTION CURRENTS

A. When two adjacent bodies of air are heated unequally, the warmer air expands and becomes lighter or less dense than the surrounding cool air. The more dense air is drawn to the ground by its greater gravitational force and lifts or forces the warm air upward.

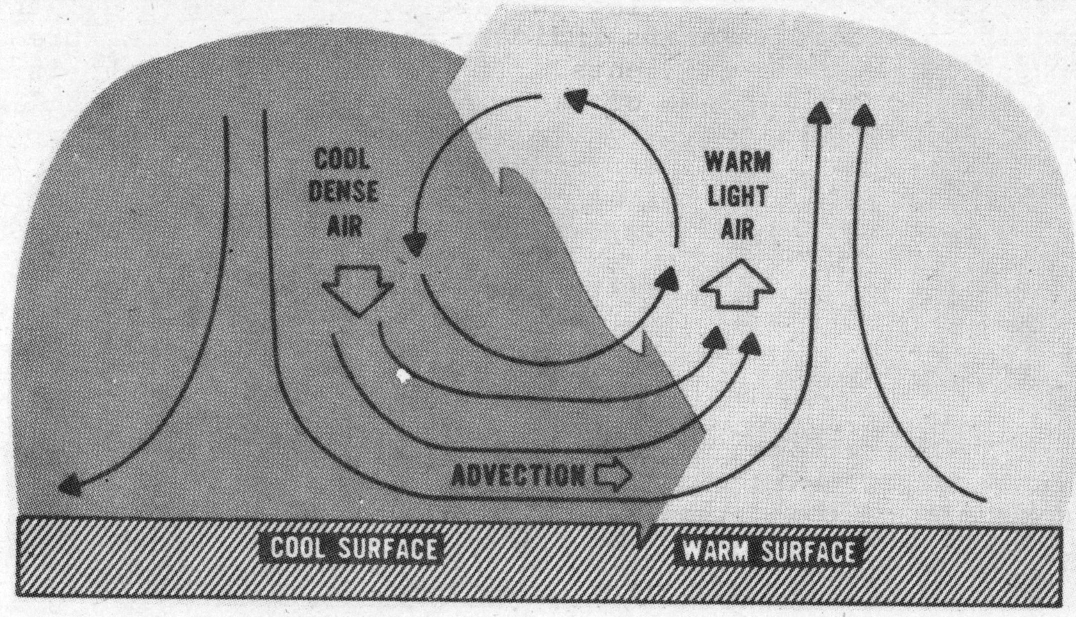

Convection current resulting from uneven heating of the atmosphere by contrasting surface temperatures. Cold air sinks forcing warm air upward. The horizontal flow in a convective current is commonly called *advection.*

FIGURE 1-8

B. These convection currents cause small-scale wind systems superimposed on the larger-scale circulation. These local systems may influence local weather and be small enough to affect only one airport or large enough to affect an area of several thousand square miles, but do not include large migratory lows and highs.

34. JET STREAM

The jet stream is a narrow, high speed, meandering river of wind moving at high altitude around the earth in wave-like patterns, imbedded in the normal wind flow aloft, often in several discontinuous segments. Wind speeds in the jet stream range from 100 to 150 knots, and in rare cases 200 to 250 knots. A well developed jet stream normally varies from 1000 to 3000 miles in length, 100 to 400 miles in width, and 3000 to 7000 feet in thickness.

35.-37. RESERVED

SECTION 6
AIR MASSES

38. GENERAL

A. The various air masses assimilate the temperature and moisture characteristics of the areas in which they originate - the coldness of polar regions, the heat of the tropics, the moisture of oceans, the dryness of continents.

B. As they move away from their source regions and pass over land and sea, air masses are constantly being modified through heating or cooling from below, lifting or subsiding, absorbing or loosing moisture. In general, however, they retain some of their original characteristics and can be recognized and identified.

39. MOVEMENT OF AIR MASSES

Since the general motion of the atmosphere in the United States is toward the east, the polar and arctic air masses generally move toward the southeast and the tropical and equatorial air masses move toward the northeast. The speed varies according to the season and the type of air mass, but it generally averages from 500 to 700 miles a day. Cold air masses move somewhat more rapidly than warm.

40.-45. RESERVED

SECTION 7
CLOUDS

46. GENERAL

Cloud types are classified by their method of formation, composition, and the altitude at which they are found.

47. CLOUD TYPES

A. CUMULUS - Clouds formed by vertical currents in unstable air are cumulus, meaning accumulation or heap; they are characterized by their billowy appearance.

Cumulus of fair weather (Cu). Cumulus clouds form in convective currents and are characterized by relatively flat bases and dome-shaped tops. Fair weather cumulus do not show extensive *towers* or vertical development and do not produce precipitation. A cumulus may, however, be the early stage in the development of towering cumulus or cumulonimbus. More often, fair weather cumulus indicates a relatively shallow layer of instability.

FIGURE 1-9

B. STRATIFORM - Stratiform clouds are formed when an entire layer of stable air is lifted. They are characterized by their stratified or layered appearance.

Stratus (St). Stratus is a low, uniform sheet-like cloud. It usually has a relatively low base. When stratus is associated with fog, the combination can become quite troublesome for visual flying.

FIGURE 1-10

48. CLOUD TYPE SUBCLASSIFICATIONS

A. NIMBO-NIMBUS - The prefix Nimbo- or suffix -nimbus means rain cloud. Thus, stratified clouds from which rain is falling are "nimbostratus;" a heavy and swelling cumulus type cloud which produces precipitation is a "cumulonimbus."

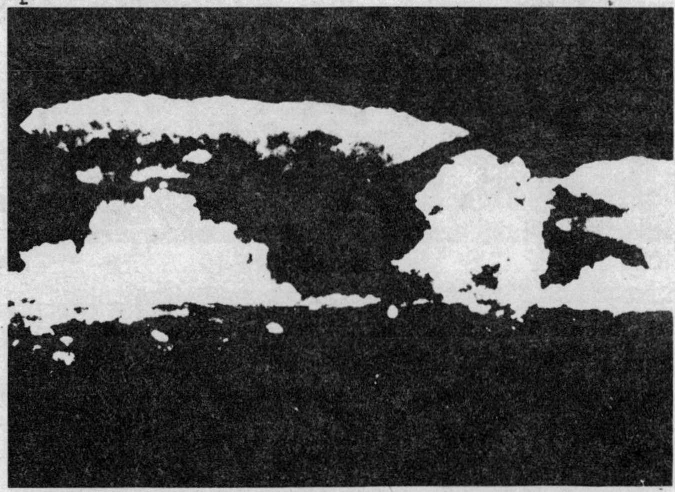

Cumulonimbus (CB). This is the anvil portion of a CB. The anvil is largely composed of ice crystals. The CB or thunderstorm contains most types of aviation weather hazards; particularly turbulence, icing, and hail.

FIGURE 1-11

Nimbostratus are gray or dark massive cloud layers diffused by more or less continuous rain, snow or ice pellets; precipitation usually reaches the ground.

FIGURE 1-12

B. FRACTUS - Clouds broken into fragments are often identified by adding the suffix fractus; for example, fragmentary cumulus are cumulusfractus.

49. CLOUD FAMILIES

A. LOW CLOUDS - Stratus and stratocumulus clouds are in the low clouds group. The bases of these clouds range from near the surface to about 6500 feet. Low clouds are almost entirely water but the water may be supercooled at sub-freezing temperature. They can contain snow and ice particles.

Stratocumulus (Sc). Stratocumulus bases have globular masses or rolls unlike the flat, sometimes indefinite, base of stratus. This cloud often forms from stratus as the stratus is breaking up or from the spreading out of cumulus clouds.

FIGURE 1-13

B. MIDDLE CLOUDS - Middle clouds are the altostratus, altocumulus, altocumulus castellanus, and nimbostratus clouds. The height of the bases of these clouds ranges from about 6500 feet to 23,000 feet. These clouds are primarily water; however, much of the water may be supercooled, and the clouds can contain some ice crystals.

Altocumulus (Ac). Altocumulus are composed of white or gray colored roll like elements or bands. The individual elements are larger and darker than in cirrocumulus

FIGURE 1-14

Altocumulus castellanus (ACCAS). Altocumulus castellanus are middle level convective clouds, and possibly they should be classified as clouds with extensive vertical development. They are characterized by their billowing tops and comparatively high bases.

FIGURE 1-15

Standing lenticular altocumulus (ACSL). Standing lenticular clouds are formed on the crests of waves created by barriers in the wind flow. The clouds show little movement hence the name *standing*. Wind, however, can be quite strong blowing through the cloud. They are characterized by their smooth, polished edges. At high levels similar clouds, standing lenticular cirrocumulus (CCSL), also may form on wave crests. CCSL are ice crystal clouds and generally are whiter than ACSL.

FIGURE 1-16

Altostratus (As). Altostratus is a bluish veil or layer of clouds having a fibrous appearance. The outline of the sun may show dimly as through frosted glass. It often merges gradually into cirrostratus. As with cirrostratus, altostratus often is part of a cloud shield associated with a front.

FIGURE 1-17

C. HIGH CLOUDS - High clouds are cirroform and include cirrus, cirrocumulus, and cirrostratus. The height of the bases of these clouds range from about 16,500 to 45,000 feet. Cirroform are composed primarily of ice crystals.

Cirrus (Ci). Cirrus are thin, feather-like clouds composed entirely of ice crystals. A special kind of currus, cirrus densus, originates from the anvils of cumulonimbus (See Fig. 5-39). These clouds are called false cirrus because they are more dense than other cirrus.

FIGURE 1-18

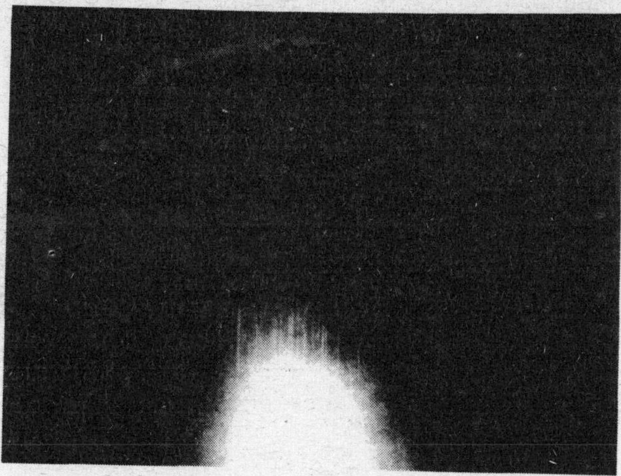

Cirrostratus (Cs) with *halo*. Cirrostratus are thin, whitish cloud layers appearing like a sheet or veil. They are diffuse sometimes partially striated or fibrous. Due to their ice crystal makeup, these clouds are associated with halos – large, luminous circles or arcs of circles surrounding the sun or moon. The layer frequently is the edge of a frontal cloud shield as will be discussed with *fronts and weather*.

FIGURE 1-19

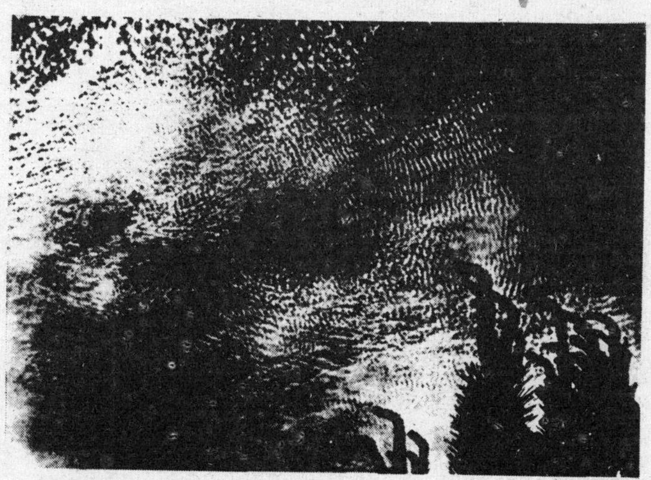

Cirrocumulus (Cc). Cirrocumulus are thin clouds, the individual elements of which appear as small white flakes or patches of cotton, usually showing brilliant and glittering quality suggestive of ice crystals.

FIGURE 1-20

D. CLOUDS WITH EXTENSIVE VERTICAL DEVELOPMENT - The vertically developed clouds are called cumulus and cumulonimbus. The height of their bases ranges from as low as 1500 feet to a bit more than 10,000 feet. Tops in fully developed cumulonimbus clouds may exceed 50,000 feet. Clouds with extensive vertical development are positive indications of unstable air.

Towering cumulus (TCU). Towering cumulus signifies a relatively deep layer of unstable air. Their bases are flat and usually appear darker than the bases of fair weather cumulus. They show considerable vertical development and have billowing cauliflower tops. Showers can result from these clouds.

FIGURE 1-21

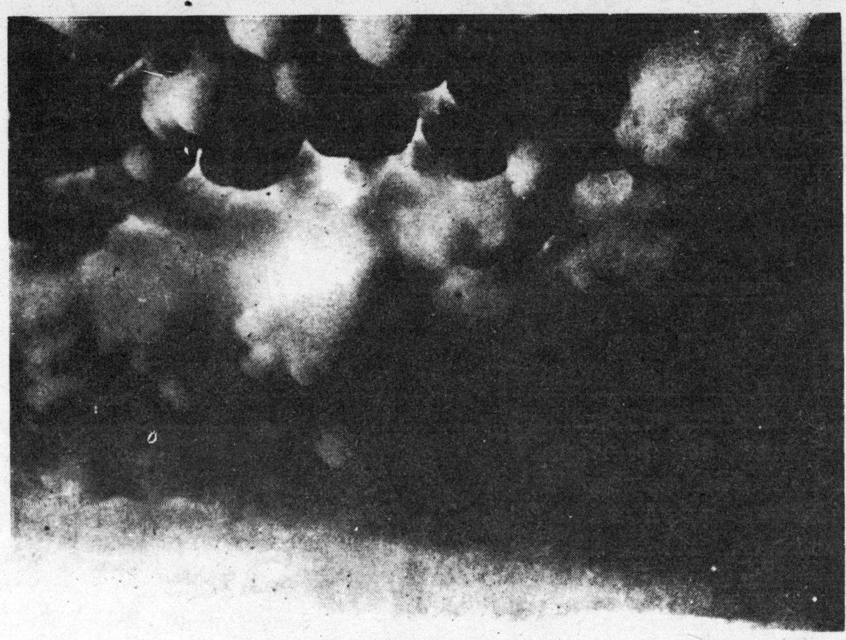

Cumulonimbus Mamma (CBMAM). This characteristic cloud results from violent up and down currents and is often associated with severe weather. It indicates probable severe or greater turbulence.

FIGURE 1-22

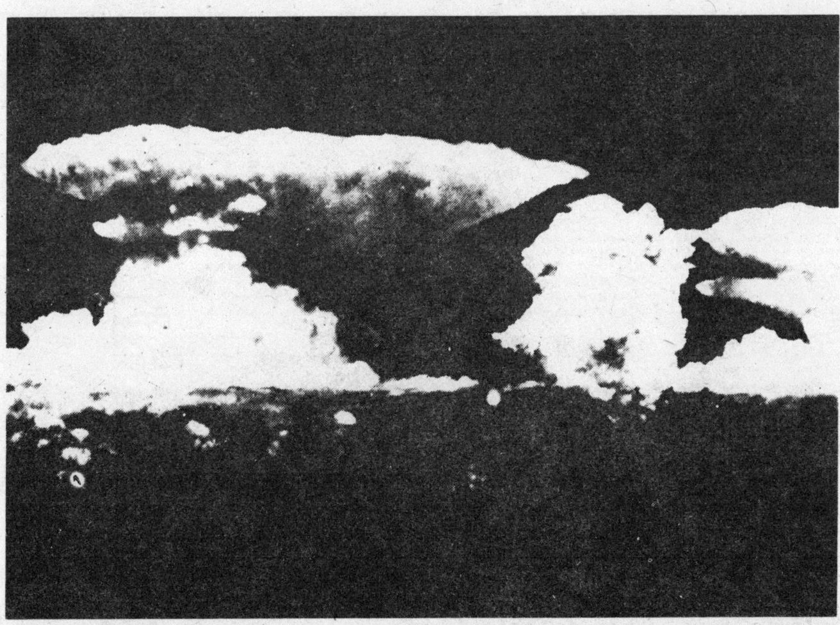

Cumulonimbus (CB). This is the anvil portion of a CB. The anvil is largely composed of ice crystals. The CB or thunderstorm contains most types of aviation weather hazards; particularly turbulence, icing, and hail.

FIGURE 1-23

50.-56. RESERVED

SECTION 8
FRONTS

57. GENERAL

A. When two different air masses meet, they normally do not mix (unless their temperatures, pressures, and relative humidities are very similar). Instead, a boundary is created called a frontal zone or "front." The colder air mass projects under the warmer air mass in the form of a wedge. If the boundary is not moving, this condition is termed a "stationary front."

B. Usually the boundary moves along the earth's surface, and as one air mass withdraws from a given area, it is replaced by another. This action creates a moving front. If warmer air is replacing the colder air, the front is called "warm"; if colder air is replacing the warmer air, the front is called "cold." Since fronts normally lie between two areas of differing pressures, wind shifts occur in both types, but are usually more pronounced in cold fronts.

58. WARM FRONTS

A. When a warm front moves forward, the warm air slides over the wedge of colder air ahead of it.

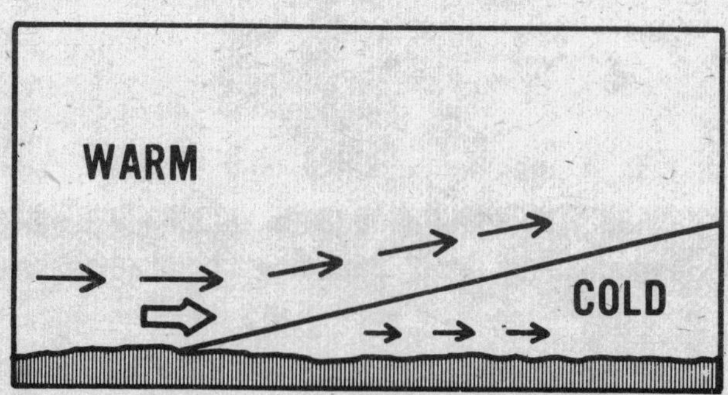

Cross section of a warm front. The slope of a warm front generally is more gradual than the slope of a cold front. Movement of a warm front shown by the open arrow is slower than the wind in the warm air represented by solid arrows. The warm air gradually erodes the cold air.

FIGURE 1-24

B. Warm air usually has higher humidity. As this warm air is lifted, its temperature is lowered. As the lifting process continues, condensation occurs, low nimbostratus and stratus clouds form and drizzle and rain develop. The rain falls through the colder air below, increasing its moisture content so that it also becomes saturated. Any reduction of temperature in the colder air (air forced to rise up sloping terrain), which might be caused by upslope motion or cooling of the ground after sunset, may result in extensive fog. As stable warm air progresses up the slope, with constantly falling temperature, clouds appear at increasing heights in the form of altostratus and cirrostratus.

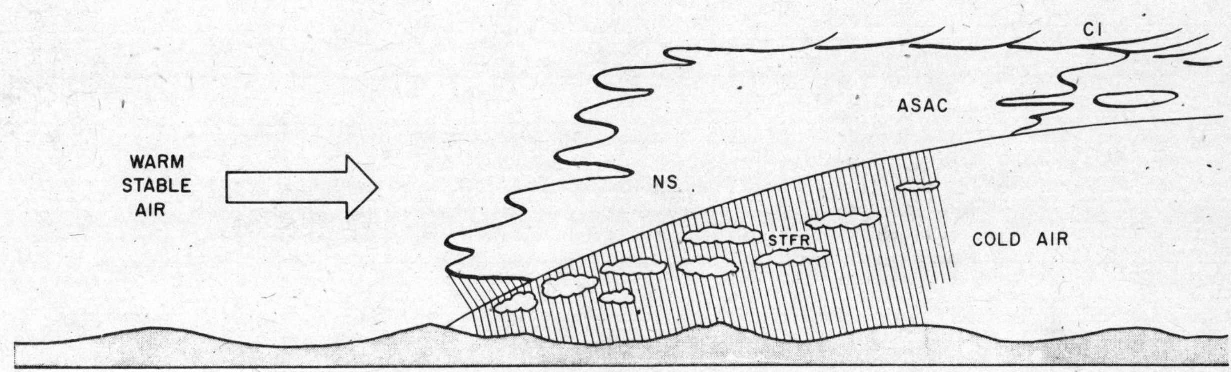

A warm front with overriding warm, moist, stable air.

FIGURE 1-25

C. If the warm air is unstable, cumulus clouds (CU), cumulonimbus clouds (CB) and altocumulus (AC) will form and frequently produce thunderstorms.

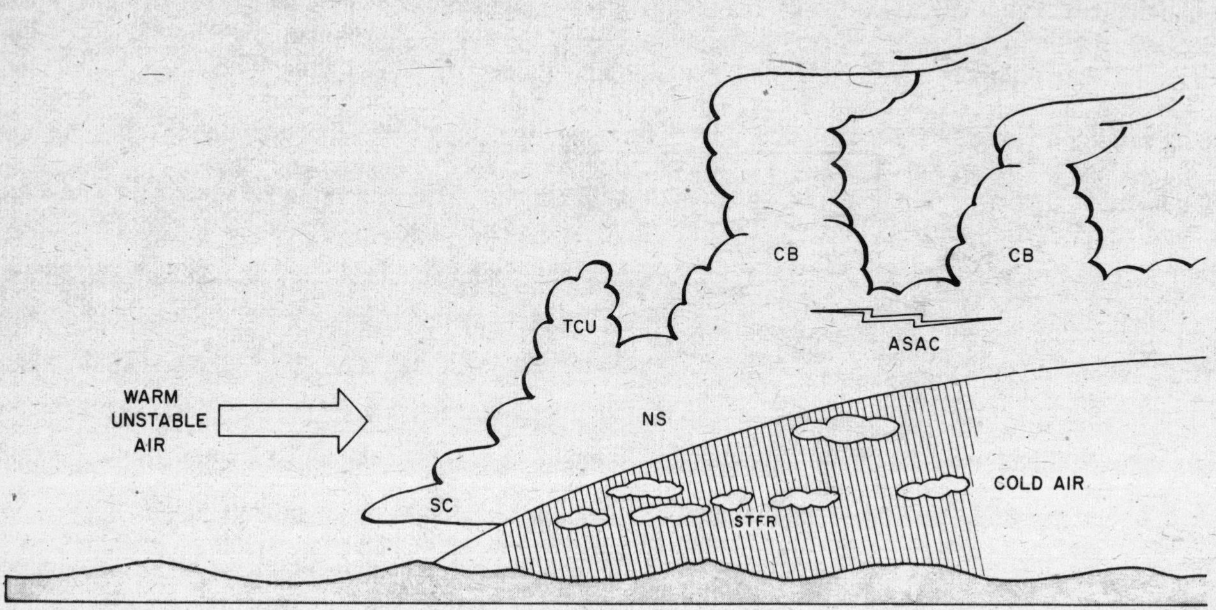

A warm front with warm, moist, unstable air overriding cold stable air. Lifting along the shallow front is more gradual than along the cold front. Instability showers and thunderstorms are spread out above the frontal surface convective storms may be imbedded in a thick deck of stratiform clouds. Stratus fractus forms in the precipitation due to evaporation of water from the warm rain drops and subsequent condensation in the cold air.

FIGURE 1-26

D. Finally, the air is forced up near the stratosphere, and in the freezing temperatures at that level, the condensation appears as thin wisps of cirrus clouds (CI). The upslope movement is very gradual, rising about 1000 feet every 20 miles. Cirrus clouds may form at an altitude of approximately 25,000 feet and 500 miles in advance of the point on the ground which marks the position of the front.

59. COLD FRONTS

A. When a cold front moves forward, it slides under the warmer air and tosses it aloft. This causes sudden cooling of the warm air and forms clouds. The type of clouds depends on the stability of the warm air.

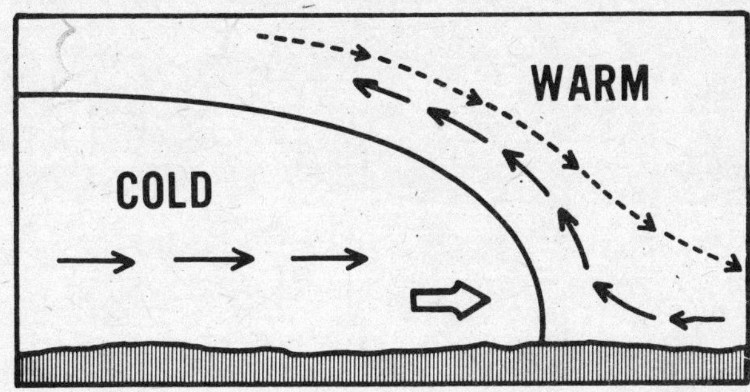

Cross section of a cold front. The frontal slope is steep near the leading edge as cold air replaces the warm air. The open arrow shows movement of the front. Warm air may descend over the front as indicated by the dashed arrows; but more commonly, the cold air forces warm air upward over the frontal surface as shown by the solid arrows.

FIGURE 1-27

B. In fast moving cold fronts, friction retards the front near the ground, which brings about a steeper frontal surface. This steep frontal surface results in a narrower band of weather concentrated along the forward edge of the front. If the warm air is stable, an overcast sky may occur for some distance behind the front, accompanied by general rain.

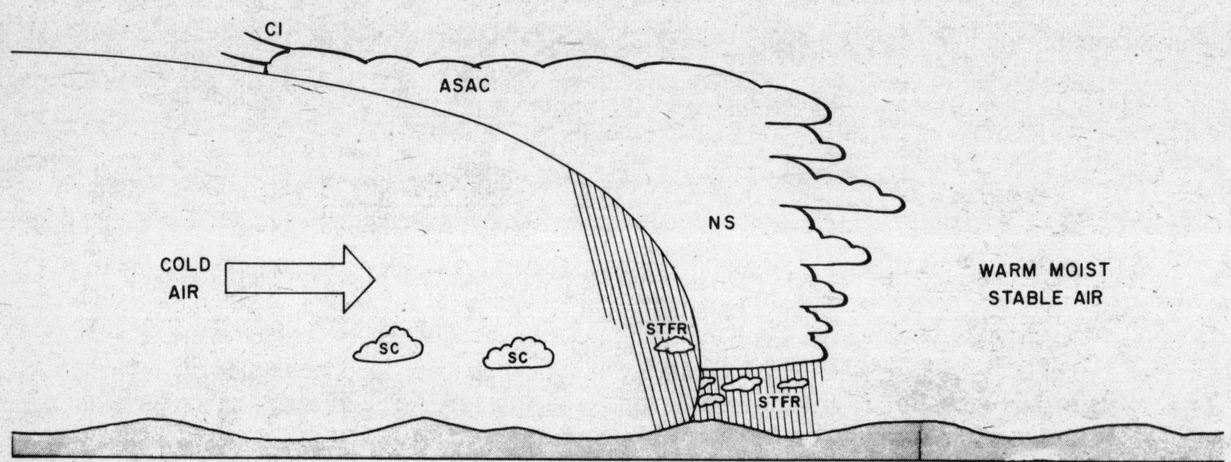

A cold front underrunning warm, moist, stable air. Stable stratified clouds form above the front much as above the warm front in Fig. 1-26 except that the slope is steeper and the clouds not as widespread. The cold air is stable except where surface heating has created a very shallow convective layer. Clouds forming in this cold air are stratocumulus. Comparing this figure with the warm front in Fig. 1-26, you will note that cloudiness associated with the warm front appears *before* surface passage of the front; widespread cloudiness with the cold front occurs *after* surface frontal passage.

FIGURE 1-28

C. If the warm air is unstable, scattered thunderstorms and showers may form in it. In some cases, an almost continuous line of thunderstorms may form along the front or ahead of it. These lines of thunderstorms, "squall lines," contain some of the most turbulent weather experienced by pilots.

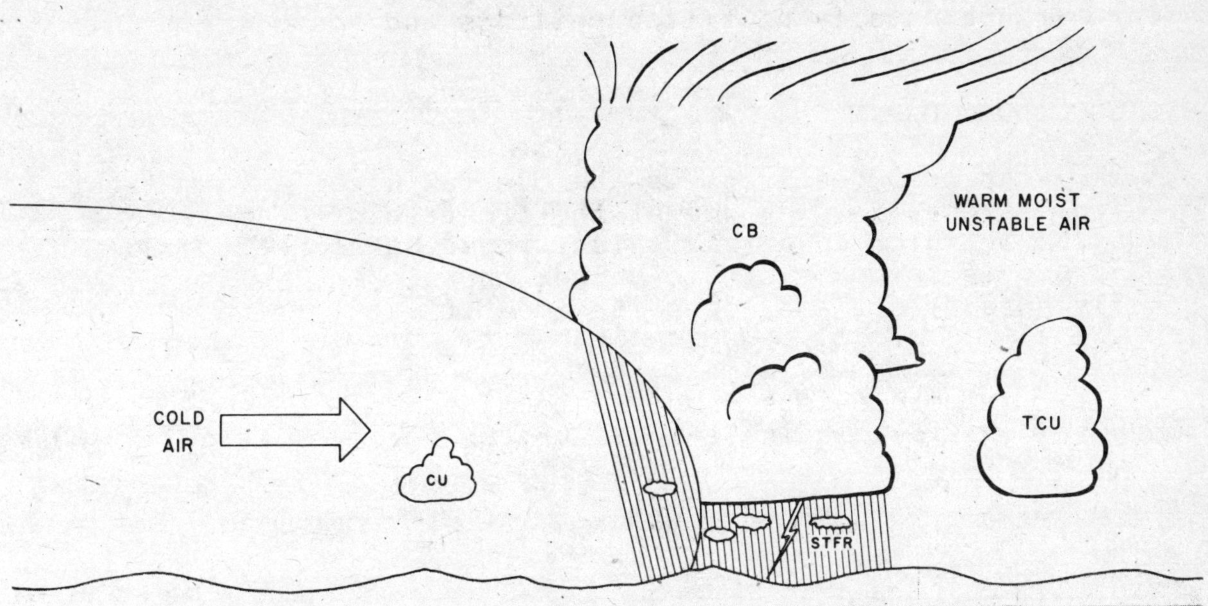

A cold front with slightly unstable cold air underrunning warm, moist, unstable air. Abrupt lifting at the surface frontal position releases the instability into a line of thunderstorms. Fair weather cumulus develop in the slightly unstable cold air. Cumulus also may develop ahead of the front due to surface heating in the warm air.

FIGURE 1-29

D. Behind the fast moving cold front there is usually rapid clearing, with gusty and turbulent surface winds, and colder temperatures. The slope of a cold front is much steeper than that of a warm front and the progress is generally more rapid. Usually it moves at a rate of 20 to 35 miles per hour, although, in extreme cases cold fronts have been known to move at 60 miles per hour. Weather activity is more violent and usually takes place directly at the front instead of in advance of the front. However, in late afternoons during the warm season, a squall line will frequently develop as much as 50 to 200 miles in advance of the actual cold front. Whereas warm front dangers lie in low ceilings and visibilities, cold front dangers lie chiefly in sudden storms, high, gusty, shifting surface winds and turbulence.

E. Cold fronts move in rapidly, make a complete change in the weather within the space of a few hours, and pass on. The squall line is ordinarily quite narrow--50 to 100 miles in width--but is likely to extend for hundreds of miles in length. Altostratus clouds sometimes form slightly ahead of the front, but these are seldom more than 100 miles in advance. After the front has passed, the weather clears rapidly and we have cooler, drier air and usually unlimited ceilings and visibilities.

60. OCCLUDED FRONT

A. An occluded front is the overtaking of a warm front by a cold front, forcing one of the fronts aloft. This is a condition in which an air mass is trapped between two colder air masses and is forced aloft to higher and higher levels until it finally spreads out and loses its identity.

B. Meteorologists subdivide occlusions into two types, depending on the relative temperature of the overtaking air mass.

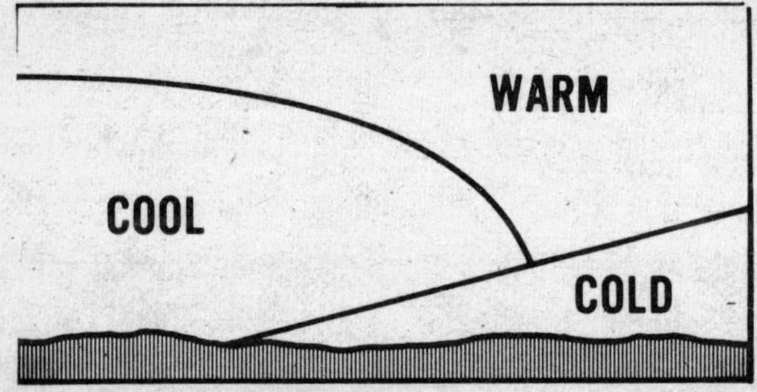

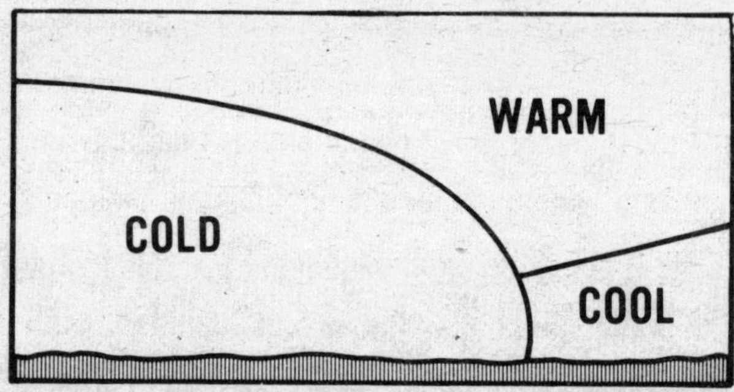

Cross section of a warm front occlusion, air under the cold front is not as cold as air ahead of the warm front; and when the cold front overtakes the warm front, the less cold air rides over the colder air. Thus in a warm front occlusion, comparatively warm air replaces cold air at the surface.

Cross section of a cold front occlusion. In the cold front occlusion, the coldest air is under the cold front. When it overtakes the warm front, it lifts the warm front aloft; and cold air replaces comparatively warm air at the surface.

FIGURE 1-30

C. The weather in any occlusion is a combination of warm front and cold front conditions. As the occlusion approaches, the usual warm front indications prevail--lowering ceilings, lowering visibilities and precipitation. Generally, the warm front weather is then followed almost immediately by the cold front type, with squalls, turbulence and thunderstorms, followed by rapidly clearing weather.

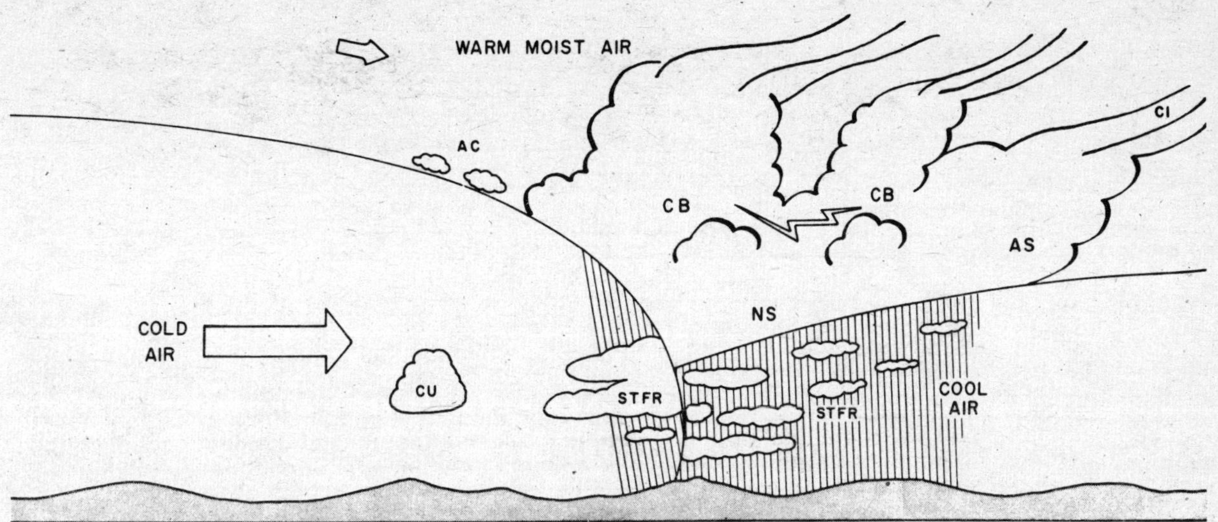

A cold front occlusion. Note that cold air replaces cool air at the surface forcing the *warm front* aloft. Cold air is moderately stable; cool air, stable; and warm air, unstable.

FIGURE 1-31

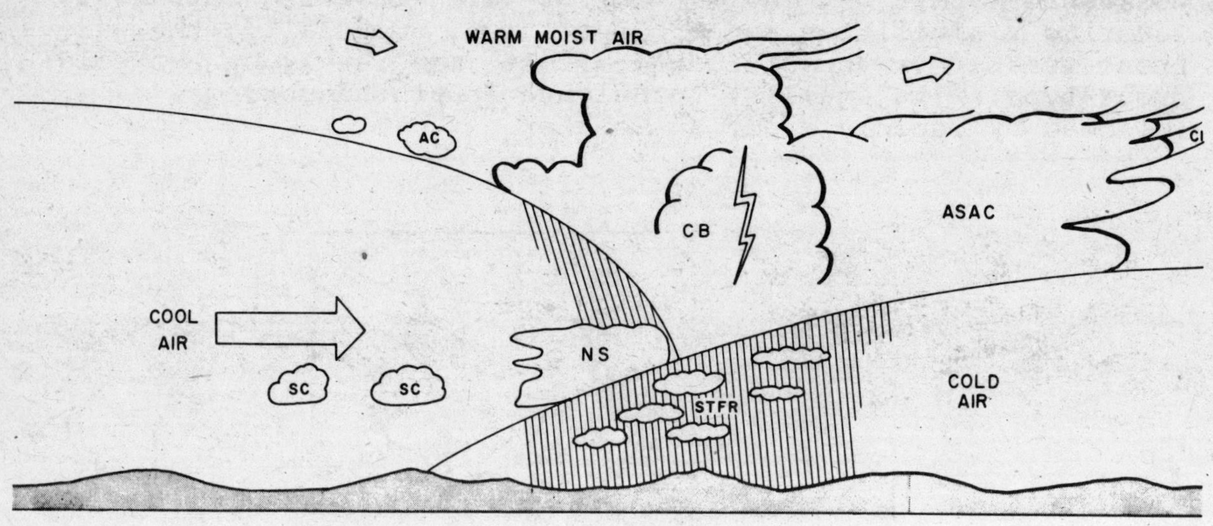

A warm front occlusion. Here cool air is overriding cold air forcing the *cold front* aloft. The cool air is stable; cold air, stable; and warm air, unstable. Cloudiness has features described in preceding figures. Maximum convective cloudiness is along the cold front aloft; stratified clouds with possible imbedded thunderstorms develop above the warm front; stratocumulus form in the stable cool air; and stratus fractus form in the cold air due to warm rain falling through the cold air.

FIGURE 1-32

61. STATIONARY FRONT

As its name implies, the stationary front does not move. The slope of a stationary front generally is gradual, although it may be steep if density change across the front is small or if wind distribution is favorable.

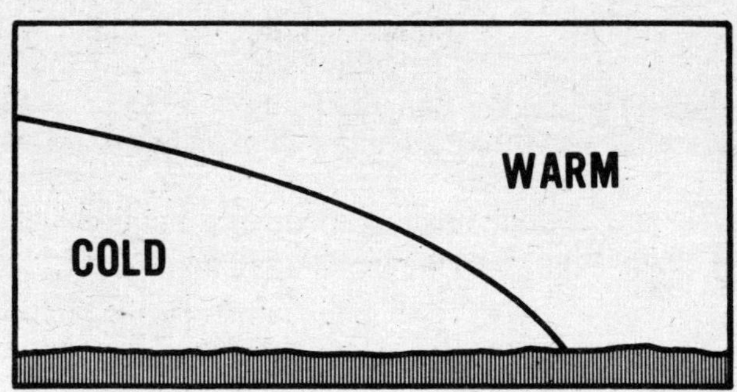

Cross section of a stationary front. The front has little or no movement and winds are nearly parallel to the front both in the warm and cold air. Slope of the front may vary considerably depending on wind and density differences across the front.

FIGURE 1-33

62.-64. RESERVED

CHAPTER 2
WEATHER HAZARDS

65. GENERAL

One responsibility of the air traffic specialist is to assist pilots in avoiding weather hazards. To aid you in providing this service, a review of the primary hazards of weather to aviation is covered in this section. It includes: restrictions to visibility, aircraft icing, turbulence, thunderstorms, high density altitude, and potential hazardous weather reports. Hazardous weather reports and forecasts include: AIRMETs, SIGMETs, hurricane advisories, severe weather outlook narratives, severe weather watch bulletins, and special flight forecasts. These will all be covered in more detail later in this publication.

SECTION 1
RESTRICTIONS TO VISIBILITY

66. VISIBILITY

A. There are three types of visibility which affect aviation. They are: horizontal surface visibility; air to air, or flight visibility; and air to ground, or slant visibility.

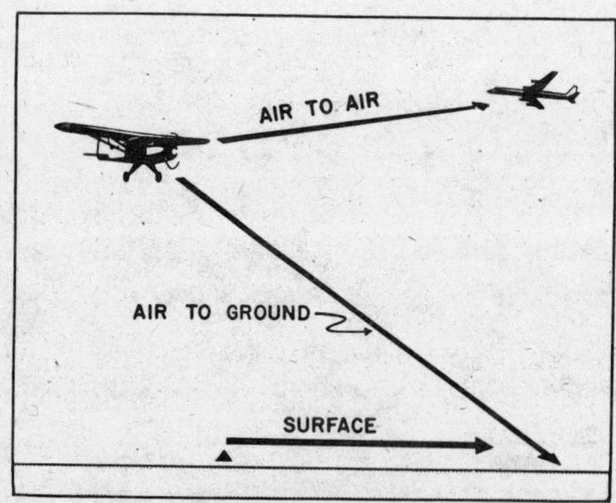

Types of visibility in aviation: air to air, air to ground, and horizontal surface. Only the latter can be routinely observed and reported. Reports of air to air and air to ground visibility are from pilots in flight.

FIGURE 2-1

B. The type and intensity of restrictions to visibility near the ground depends largely upon stability of the air. Stable air, which resists vertical motion, will not disperse restrictions to visibility. On the other hand, unstable air produces vertical currents which tend to dissipate fog and to spread haze and smoke both vertically and horizontally. Precipitation in stable air is persistent and continuous, while precipitation in unstable air is spotty. Thus, we can say, stable air will have a characteristic of poor visibility and unstable air, good visibility.

C. As the earth and lower layers of air warm during the day, air that was stable during the early morning hours may become unstable. For this reason visibility usually improves as temperatures rise. If cloud layers aloft prevent the sun's heat from reaching the ground, visibility improvement is usually slow.

67. FOG

A. Fog is a cloud with its base at the earth's surface. Fog forms by an atmospheric process that effects surface air in one or both of the following ways:

(1) Cooling the air to its dew point or to saturation by:

(a) The ground being cooled by nighttime loss of heat, which subsequently cools the air contacting it.

(b) The movement of moist air over cold ground.

(c) Moving air being cooled as it is forced to rise up sloping terrain.

(2) Raising the dew point to that of the air temperature. Normally this happens when the evaporation of warm rain adds water vapor to the air. This air is then cooled by surrounding cold air.

B. The conditions favorable to fog formation are: light winds of 10 knots or less, and a small temperature-dew point spread.

68. STRATUS CLOUDS

At times when conditions are favorable for fog, a very low cloud layer may form. This is especially true over flat terrain when surface winds exceed 15 knots. These fog-like clouds form in stable air and often exist together with fog. In this case there is no real line of distinction between the fog and stratus. One merges gradually into the other, and the ceiling reported by the weather observer is the vertical visibility from the surface into the fog.

69. HAZE AND SMOKE

Haze is a concentration of dust or salt particles within a stable layer of the atmosphere that occasionally may extend from the surface to 15,000 feet. Haze layers often have definite tops above which air to air visibility is good. However, air to ground visibility from above a haze layer is poor, especially on a slant. Smoke restricts visibility in a manner similar to haze. Smoke sometimes is concentrated in layers aloft with good visibility beneath the smoke. Haze and smoke will normally be a more severe restriction to visibility when a temperature inversion exists.

70. BLOWING SNOW, DUST, AND SAND

Strong surface winds and vertical currents in unstable air carry aloft loose materials from the surface such as dust, sand, or snow. These conditions can reduce surface visibility to near zero over extensive areas. Under favorable conditions dust can be carried aloft to 15,000 feet and restrict slant, flight, and surface visibility. Sand and snow seldom are carried aloft beyond a few hundred feet.

71. PRECIPITATION

Snow, drizzle, and rain are the most common forms of precipitation causing restrictions to visibility. Of these, snow is usually the most effective in reducing visibility. Heavy snow frequently reduces surface and slant visibility to near zero. Rain rarely reduces surface visibility to below one mile and has a tendency to wash dust, smoke, and even fog particles out of the air. Conversely, drizzle often accompanies fog, haze, and smoke, resulting in lower visibility than rain.

Precipitation on the windshield of an aircraft sharply reduces the pilot's vision, and if it freezes he may have NO forward visibility.

72.-74. RESERVED

SECTION 2
ICING

75. GENERAL

Aircraft icing can render an aircraft unable to maintain sustained flight by altering its aerodynamics and increasing its weight, or by choking the engine induction system.

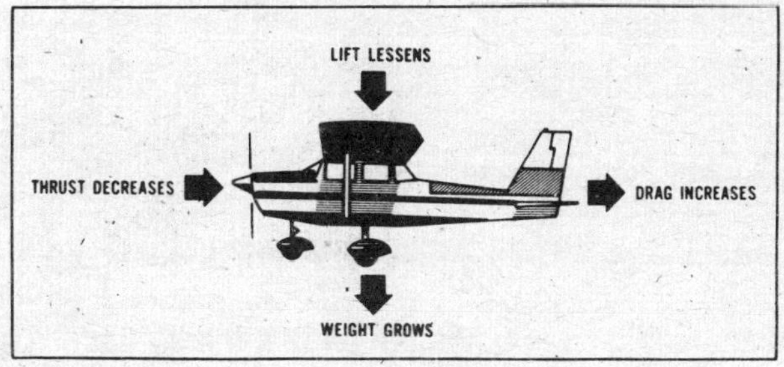

Icing is a cumulative hazard. Note how thrust, lift, drag, and weight change.

FIGURE 2-2

76. STRUCTURAL ICING

Shape, size, speed, and angle of attack of the airfoil each affect rate of ice accumulation. Some aircraft tolerate more ice than others, but ice hampers all aircraft to a significant degree. Although ice may form on any exposed surface of the plane, ice on the airfoils has the greatest effect on flight characteristics. Two conditions are necessary for substantial ice accumulation on aircraft: (1) the aircraft must by flying through visible water such as rain or cloud droplets, and

(2) the temperature of the water or of the plane must be 0°C or colder. Supercooled water is in an unnatural state; when an aircraft strikes a supercooled drop, part of the drop freezes. The speed with which it freezes governs the type of ice formed. The types of ice are clear (glaze), rime and mixed.

77. CLEAR ICE

A. Clear ice is a transparent ice with a glassy surface, identical to the glaze which forms on trees and other objects during a freezing rain. It is formed by the relatively slow freezing of large, supercooled water droplets. Ice is smooth and stremalined when deposited from large supercooled cloud droplets or raindrops without solid precipitation. Ice tends to take the shape of the surface on which it freezes, but builds out against the airflow and becomes blunt nosed with a gradual tapering toward the training edges.

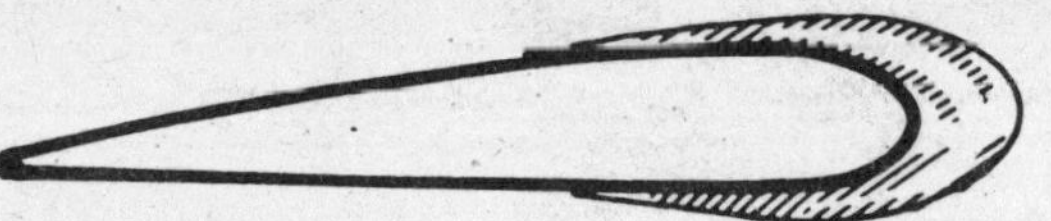

CLEAR: SMOOTH AND GLASSY

Clear ice can appear in seconds and accumulates rapidly. Pilots have the greatest difficulty in removing clear ice.

FIGURE 2-3

B. Clear ice is the most serious of the various forms of ice because of its rapid accumulation. It adheres firmly to the aircraft and is very difficult to remove.

C. Conditions most favorable for clear ice formation are high water content, large droplet size, temperature only slightly below freezing, high airspeed, and thin airfoils. It is encountered most frequently in cumuliform clouds and freezing rain or drizzle.

78. RIME ICE

A. Rime ice is a milky, opaque, and granular deposit of ice with a rough surface.

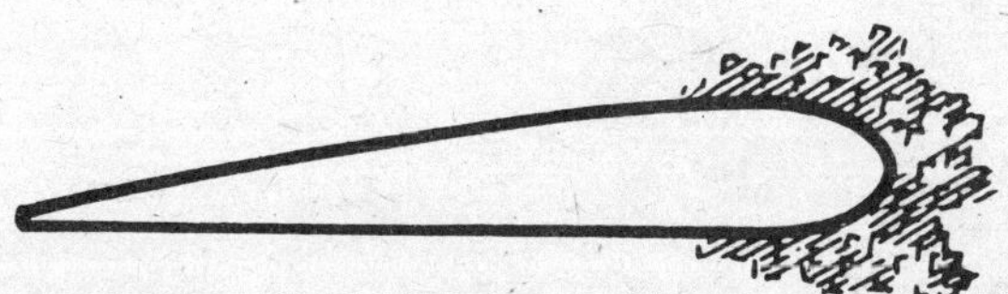

FIGURE 2-4

B. Rime ice is formed by the instantaneous freezing of small supercooled water droplets upon contact with exposed aircraft surfaces. This instantaneous freezing traps a large amount of air, giving the ice its opaqueness and making it very brittle. Rime ice usually forms on leading edges and protrudes forward into the air stream. It has little tendency to take the shape of the airfoil. Fast-freezing rime ice is most likely to accumulate between -10°C and -20°C. Rime ice is most frequently encountered in stratiform clouds, and is also common in cumuliform clouds at temperatures below -10°C.

C. The primary danger from rime ice is the distortion of air flow over the airfoil, since it seldom builds rapidly. It is comparatively easy to remove by conventional deicing methods.

79. MIXED ICE

Rime and clear ice frequently occur together containing the most dangerous characteristics of both types. If liquid drops are mixed with snow, ice pellets or small hail, it becomes rough, irregular and whitish.

80. FROST

A. Frost is a light, feathery crystalline ice structure of snowlike character. It is the same substance that forms on your car windshield when the temperature drops below freezing and moisture is in the air.

B. Thin metal airfoils are especially vulnerable surfaces on which frost will form. Frost does not change the basic aerodynamic shape of the wing, but its roughness spoils the smooth flow of air over the aircraft's control surfaces. This causes early air flow separation over the affected airfoil resulting in a loss of lift. A heavy coat of hard frost will cause a 5% to 10% increase in the stall speed of the aircraft.

81. ICING INTENSITY

By mutual agreement and for standardization, the FAA, the National Weather Service (NWS), and the military aviation services have classified aircraft icing into four intensities.

ICING INTENSITIES

AIRFRAME ICING REPORTING TABLE

Intensity	Ice Accumulation	Pilot Report
Trace	Ice becomes perceptible. Rate of accumulation slightly greater than rate of sublimation. It is not hazardous even though deicing/anti-icing equipment is not utilized, unless encountered for an extended period of time – over one hour.	A/C Ident., Location, Time (GMT), Intensity of Type*, Altitude/FL, Aircraft Type, IAS
Light	The rate of accumulation may create a problem if flight is prolonged in this environment (over one hour). Occasional use of deicing/anti-icing equipment removes/prevents accumulation. It does not present a problem if the deicing/anti-icing equipment is used.	Example:
Moderate	The rate of accumulation is such that even short encounters become potentially hazardous and use of deicing/anti-icing equipment or diversion is necessary.	Holding at Westminister VOR, 1232Z
Severe	The rate of accumulation is such that deicing/anti-icing equipment fails to reduce or control the hazard. Immediate diversion is necessary.	Light Rime Icing, Altitude six thousand, Jetstar IAS 200 kts

* Rime Ice: Rough, milky, opaque ice formed by the instantaneous freezing of small supercooled water droplets.

Clear Ice: A glossy, clear or translucent ice formed by the relatively slow freezing of large supercooled water droplets.

FIGURE 2-5

82. GROUND ICING

Water is blown by propellers or splashed by the wheels of the airplane as it taxis through pools of water or mud. When temperatures are below freezing, ice may form in wheel wells, brake mechanisms, flap hinges, etc., and prevent proper aircraft operation.

83. INDUCTION SYSTEM ICING

Induction system icing is sometimes called "carburetor icing" and is caused by the vaporization of fuel, combined with the expansion of air as it passes through the carburetor, causing a sudden cooling of the mixture. The temperature of the air passing through the carburetor may drop as much as 60°F within a fraction of a second. Water vapor in the air is "squeezed out" by this cooling, and if the temperature in the carburetor reaches 32°F or below, the moisture will be deposited as frost or ice inside the carburetor passages. Even a slight accumulation of carburetor ice will reduce power and may lead to complete engine failure, if it is allowed to continue to build.

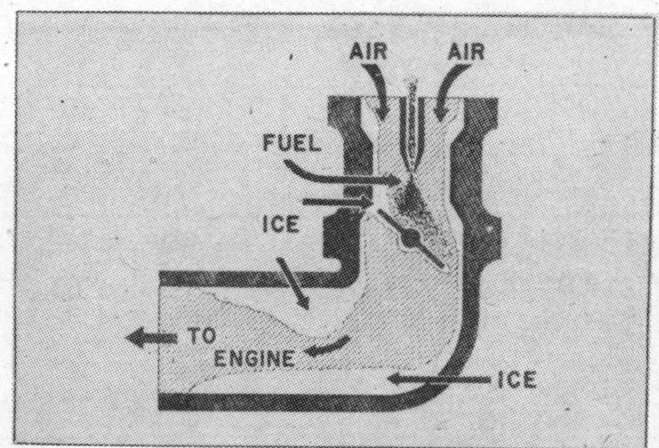

Carburetor icing, a form of induction system icing. This type icing occurs under a wide range of atmospheric conditions. More accidents result from carbureeor icing than from any other kind.

FIGURE 2-6

84. CONDITIONS FAVORABLE FOR CARBURETOR ICING

Carburetor icing may form under conditions in which structural ice could not possibly form. If the relative humidity of the outside air being drawn into the carburetor is high, ice can form inside the carburetor in cloudless skies and with the temperature well above freezing. It is most serious when the temperature and the dew point approach 68°F. It can form with outside temperatures are as low as 14°F but normally does not form when the outside temperatures are below freezing.

85. ICING AND CLOUD TYPES

A. Thick, extensive stratified clouds that produce continuous rain usually have an abundance of liquid water because of the relatively large drop size and number. Such cloud systems in winter may cover thousands of square miles and present very serious icing conditions. The heaviest icing usually will be found at or slightly above the freezing level. In layer type clouds, continuous icing conditions are rarely found to be deeper than 5000 feet above the freezing level, and usually are two to three thousand feet thick.

B. Cumuliform clouds contain vertical currents which are favorable for the formation and support of many large water drops. When an aircraft enters the heavy water concentrations found in cumuliform clouds, and temperatures are freezing or colder, the water freezes quickly to form a solid sheet of clear ice. On rare occasions icing has been encountered in thunderstorm clouds at altitudes of 30,000 to 40,000 feet where the free air temperature was colder than minus 40°C.

86. ICING AND FRONTS

A. A condition favorable for rapid accumulation of clear ice is freezing rain below a frontal surface. It may occur with either a warm front or cold front. The icing can be severe because of the large amount of supercooled water.

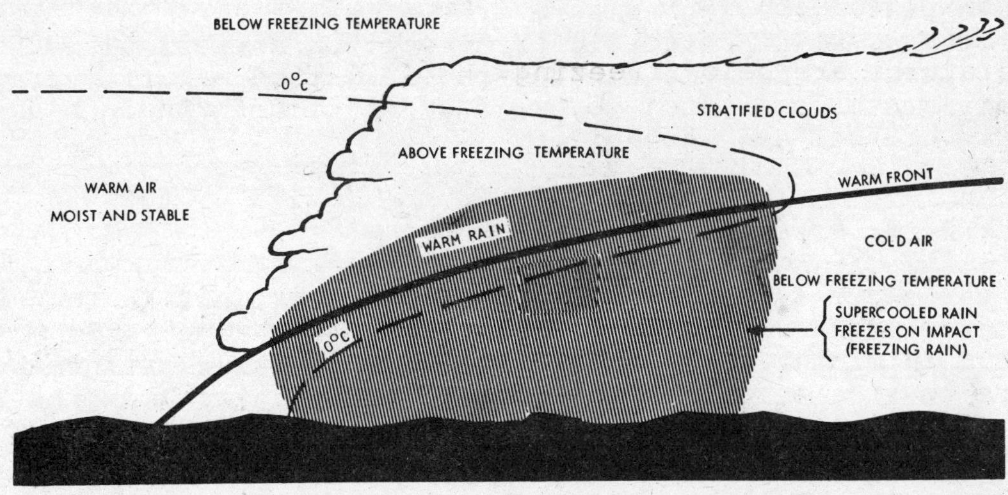

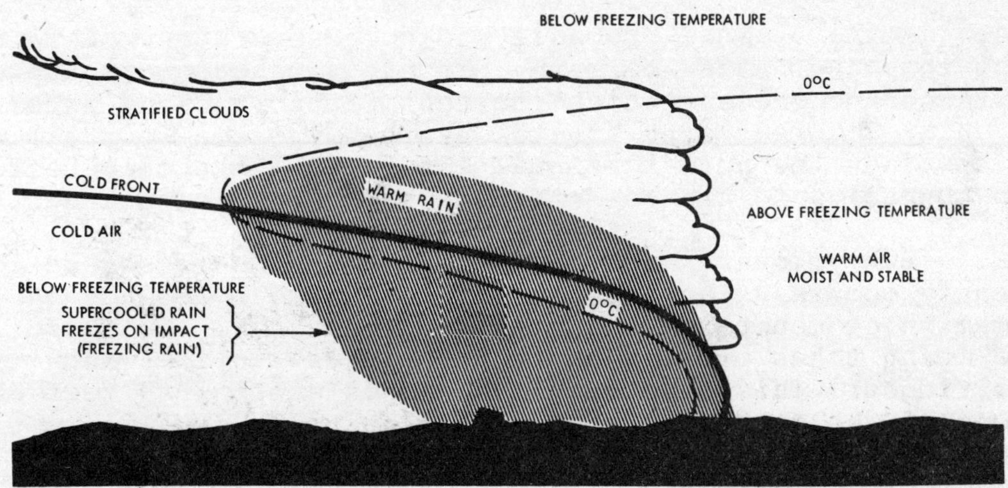

Freezing rain with a warm front (top) and a cold front. Rain forms at temperatures warmer than freezing and falls through cold air with temperatures below freezing. Note the 0°C isotherm. The rain becomes supercooled and freezes on impact.

FIGURE 2-7

B. Icing can also become severe in cumulonimbus clouds along a surface cold front or above a warm front.

87. ICING IN AIR MASSES

Icing is most likely in air masses that are (1) very moist, and (2) have below freezing temperatures after being lifted by some means such as sloping terrain or convection as well as by a front. Icing conditions encountered in lifted maritime tropical cold air masses are often severe because of both their high moisture content and instability.

88. SEASONAL EFFECTS

Icing may occur during any season of the year, but in temperate climates which cover most of the United States, icing is more frequent in winter. The freezing level is nearer the ground in winter, leaving a smaller low-level layer of airspace free of icing conditions. Storm activity also is more frequent, and the resulting cloud systems are more extensive.

89. EFFECT OF MOUNTAINS

A. Icing is more probable and more severe in mountainous regions than over other terrain. Mountain ranges cause upward air motions and these vertical currents support large water drops. The movement of a frontal system across a mountain range often combines the normal frontal lift with the upslope effect of the mountains to create extremely hazardous icing zones.

B. Every mountainous region has areas where severe icing frequency occurs. The location of these areas depends on the orientation of mountain ranges to the wind flow. The most severe icing takes place above the crest and to the windward side of the ridges. This zone usually extends about 5000 feet above the tops of the mountains; but when clouds are cumuliform the zone may extend much higher.

90. ICING AND AIR TRAFFIC SERVICE

Icing occurs when cloud structure and vertical temperature distributions are favorable. Forecasting of specific icing conditions is difficult; reliable information is dependent to a great extent upon the availability of pilot reports. By piecing together reports of locations and severity of icing, you can frequently get a more comprehensive picture of icing potential.

91.-93. RESERVED

SECTION 3
TURBULENCE

94. GENERAL

A. Turbulence effect on aircraft ranges all the way from a few annoying bumps to severe jolts which are capable of producing structural damage. Since turbulence is associated with many different weather situations, a knowledge of its causes and the behavior of irregular air movements is helpful in understanding the effects of this disturbed air.

B. The atmosphere is considered turbulent when irregular whirls or eddies of air effect aircraft so that a series of abrupt jolts or bumps are felt. A large range of eddy sizes exists, but those causing turbulence are about the same size as the aircraft and usually occur in an irregular sequence. The reaction to the turbulence varies not only with the intensity of the eddies but also with aircraft characteristics such as flight speed, size, wing loading, and aircraft altitude.

95. INTENSITY OF TURBULENCE

A. Classification of turbulence intensity is a difficult problem for pilots and forecasters. The pilot's judgment of turbulence severity may be influenced by the length of time his plane is subjected to turbulence, the pilot's experience and the type of aircraft.

B. In order to provide a standard for reporting and describing turbulence, the FAA has classified turbulence into four intensities according to its effect on aircraft and occupants.

TURBULENCE REPORTING CRITERIA TABLE

INTENSITY	AIRCRAFT REACTION	REACTION INSIDE AIRCRAFT	REPORTING TERM-DEFINITION
Light	Turbulence that momentarily causes slight, erratic changes in altitude and/or attitude (pitch, roll, yaw). Report as **Light Turbulence**;* or Turbulence that causes slight, rapid and somewhat rhythmic bumpiness without appreciable changes in altitude or attitude. Report as **Light Chop**.	Occupants may feel a slight strain against seat belts or shoulder straps. Unsecured objects may be displaced slightly. Food service may be conducted and little or no difficulty is encountered in walking.	Occasional – Less than 1/3 of the time. Intermittent – 1/3 to 2/3. Continuous – More than 2/3.
Moderate	Turbulence that is similar to Light Turbulence but of greater intensity. Changes in altitude and/or attitude occur but the aircraft remains in positive control at all times. It usually causes variations in indicated airspeed. Report as **Moderate Turbulence**;* or Turbulence that is similar to Light Chop but of greater intensity. It causes rapid bumps or jolts without appreciable changes in aircraft altitude or attitude. Report as **Moderate Chop**.	Occupants feel definite strains against seat belts or shoulder straps. Unsecured objects are dislodged. Food service and walking are difficult.	**NOTE** 1. Pilots should report location(s), time (GMT), intensity, whether in or near clouds, altitude, type of aircraft and, when applicable, duration of turbulence. 2. Duration may be based on time between two locations or over a single location. All locations should be readily identifiable. EXAMPLES: a. Over Omaha, 1232Z, Moderate Turbulence, in cloud, Flight Level 310, B707. b. From 50 miles south of Albuquerque to 30 miles north of Phoenix, 1210Z to 1250Z, occasional Moderate Chop, Flight Level 330, DC8.
Severe	Turbulence that causes large, abrupt changes in altitude and/or attitude. It usually causes large variations in indicated airspeed. Aircraft may be momentarily out of control. Report as **Severe Turbulence**. *	Occupants are forced violently against seat belts or shoulder straps. Unsecured objects are tossed about. Food service and walking are impossible.	
Extreme	Turbulence in which the aircraft is violently tossed about and is practically impossible to control. It may cause structural damage. Report as **Extreme Turbulence**.*		

* High level turbulence (normally above 15,000 feet ASL) not associated with cumuliform cloudiness, including thunderstorms, should be reported as CAT (clear air turbulence) preceded by the appropriate intensity, or light or moderate chop.

SC/AMS Meeting 7/67

FIGURE 2-8

96. TYPES OF TURBULENCE

Turbulence is divided into four general types based on the meteorological and physical properties responsible for its existence. These types are convective, mechanical, wind shear, and high-level clear air turbulence. Although the principal cause of clear air turbulence is wind shear, it is given a special category because of its significance for jet aircraft.

97. CONVECTIVE TURBULENCE

A. As discussed in Weather Causes, convection results from uneven heating of the earth's surface causing currents of variable strength. The following illustrations show how a normal glide may be distorted by nearby changes in the type of earth surface.

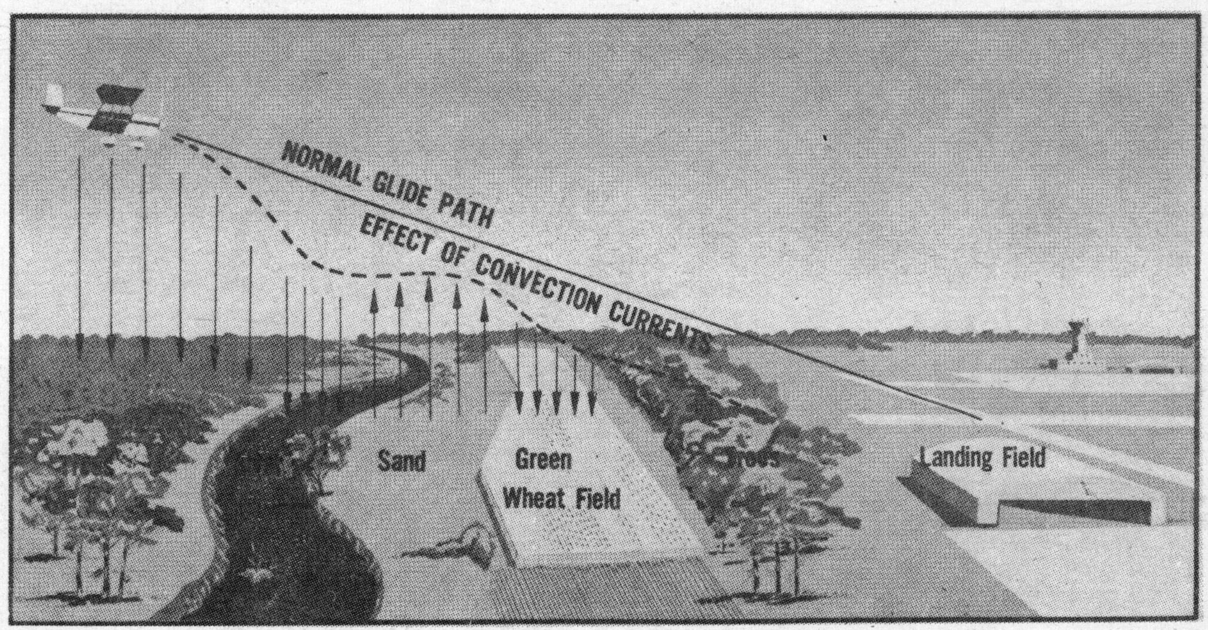

Predominantly downward currents allow the aircraft to fall below the normal glide path causing it to undershoot the touchdown point.

FIGURE 2-9

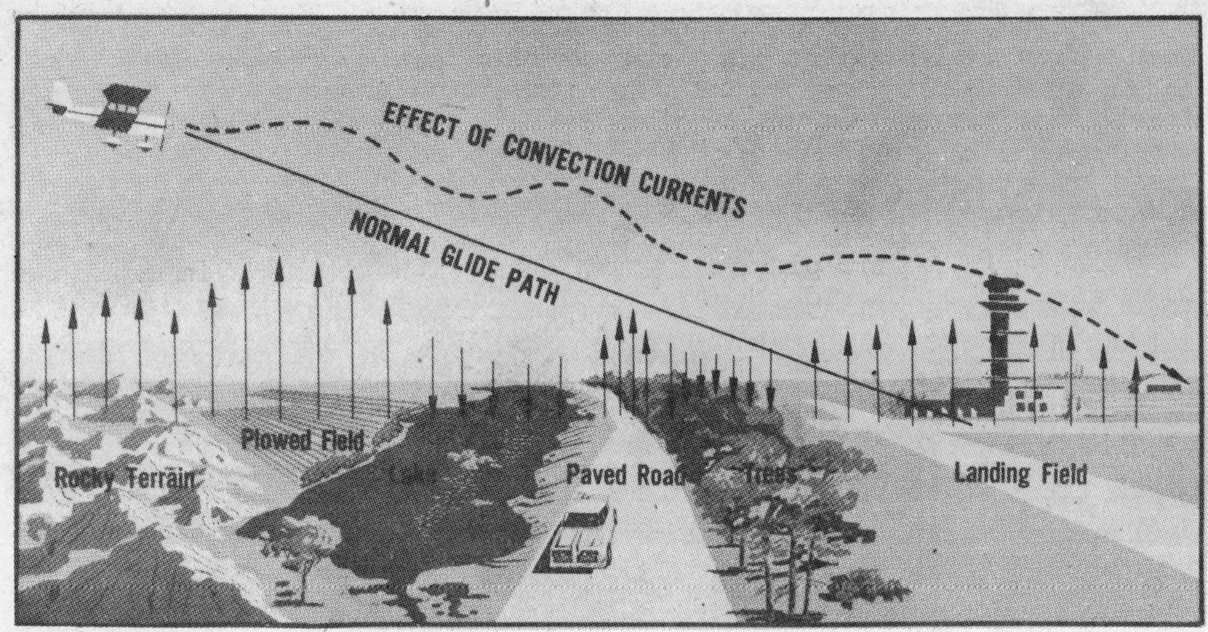

Predominantly upward currents force the aircraft above the normal glide path resulting in overshooting the touchdown point.

FIGURE 2-10

B. Thermal turbulence is common during sunny afternoons. As the air is heated, bubbles of warm air are forced to rise in convective currents. Upward moving air continues to accelerate until it reaches a level where the temperature of the rising air is cooled to that of the surrounding air.

Cumulus clouds are signs of convective currents. Aircraft flying below the tops of cumulus clouds encounter turbulent air. Above the tops smooth flight is possible if convection does not extend above the cloud tops.

FIGURE 2-11

C. It is important to note that both up and down drafts develop. Turbulence is more severe when the updrafts and downdrafts are closely spaced. Even if the air is very dry with no clouds, convective turbulence may be present.

98. MECHANICAL TURBULENCE

A. An object placed in any moving air current impedes the flow causing the wind to go around the object changing its direction of flow.

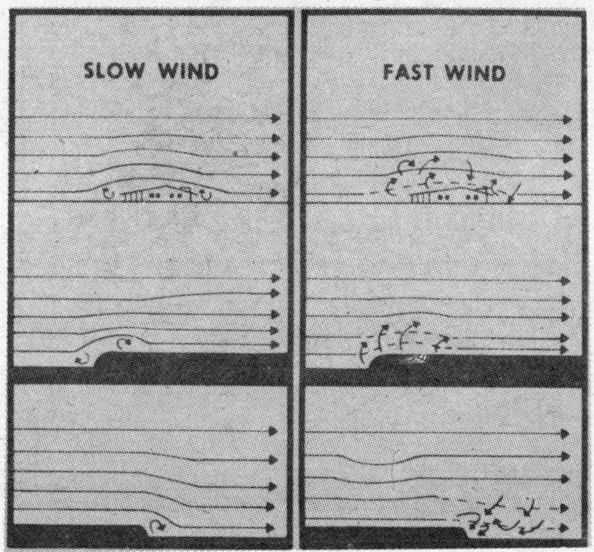

Obstructions to wind flow cause irregular eddies along and downwind from the obstruction. The degree of turbulence depends on the size and shape of the obstruction, the speed of the wind, and the stability of the air.

FIGURE 2-12

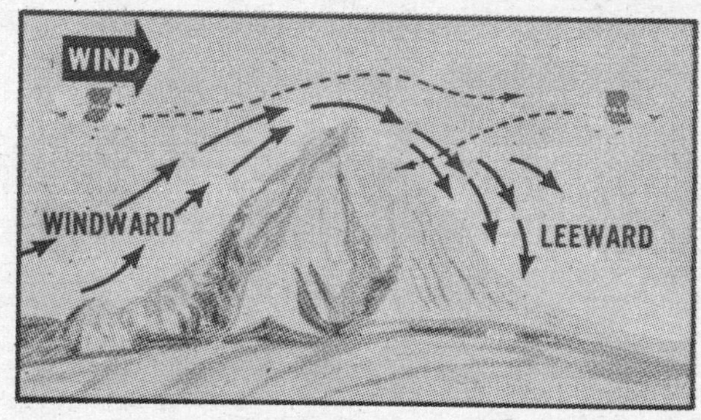

Mechanical turbulence in mountains. Air flowing through mountainous terrain is forced upward on the windward side and spills downward over the leeward side. The degree of turbulence induced by mountains depends upon the shape and size of the mountains, the direction and speed of the wind, and the stability of the air.

FIGURE 2-13

B. As the current closes in behind the object in returning to its original flow, eddy currents develop leeward of the obstruction. These eddies create mechanical turbulence. If the object were removed and no other influences on the flow were present, the wind would flow smoothly and undisturbed. Mechanical turbulence is caused by obstructions in the path of the wind and not by any meteorological causes in the air mass itself. Some objects which are conducive to this type of turbulence are mountains, hills, buildings, and moving aircraft.

99. LOW-LEVEL MECHANICAL TURBULENCE

The variability of wind near the ground is an extremely important consideration during takeoff and landing for the pilots of light aircraft.

Obstructions at an airport may induce turbulence in the takeoff, landing, and taxi areas. Each air traffic specialist should become very familiar with areas where obstructions cause turbulence at his airport of concern and with meteorological conditions that produce turbulence.

FIGURE 2-14

100 HIGH-LEVEL MECHANICAL TURBULENCE

A. A much disturbed condition occurs when wind blows over large mountain ridges. The wind blowing up the windward slope is usually relatively smooth if the air is stable. On the leeward side, the wind spills rapidly down the slope. This sets up strong down drafts and causes the air to be very turbulent.

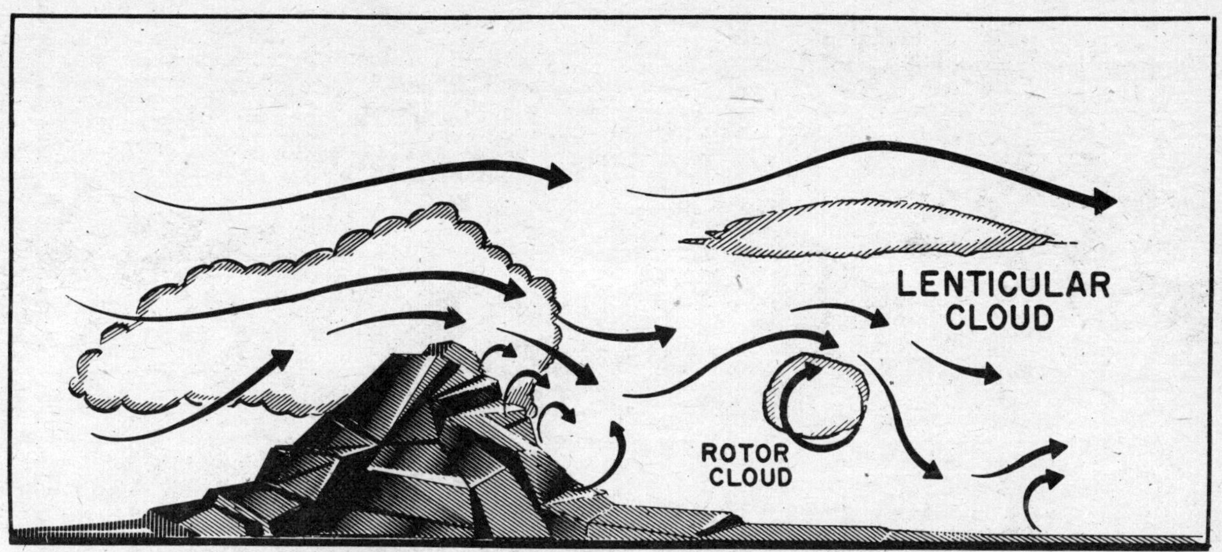

When air is forced over mountains and the air has ample water vapor, characteristic clouds can form. The most characteristic clouds are those that surround the mountain top and the lenticular and rotor clouds downwind. Lenticular (standing wave) and rotor clouds are signs of *severe* turbulent conditions; however, severe turbulence can exist even when these characteristic clouds are absent.

FIGURE 2-15

B. When winds in excess of about 50 knots blow approximately perpendicular to a high mountain range, the resulting turbulence may be extreme. Areas of steady updrafts and downdrafts can extend many times higher than the elevation of the mountain peaks. Under these conditions, large waves tend to form on the lee side of the mountains and sometimes extend upward to beyond the tropopause.

C. In horizontal dimensions, these waves sometimes extend as far as 100 miles downstream from the mountain range. These are referred to as standing waves or mountain waves, and are characterized by standing lenticular altocumulus, and/or rotor clouds when sufficient moisture is available.

Photographs of standing wave clouds. They are named standing because they have very little movement, but the wind flowing through the clouds can be extremely strong.

FIGURE 2-16

D. Reports of turbulence in these waves may range from none to extreme, but most pilots encounter moderate to severe turbulence. The most dangerous characteristic of the standing wave is the magnitude of the sustained updraft and downdraft.

101. WAKE TURBULENCE

Every airplane generates a wake while in flight. This disturbance is a pair of counter rotating vortices trailing from the wing tips. The strength of the vortex is governed primarily by the weight, speed, and shape of the wing of the generating aircraft.

FIGURE 2-17

102. WIND SHEAR

Wind shear turbulence is caused by a change in wind speed and/or wind direction in a short distance, resulting in a "tearing" or "shearing" effect. Wind shear can exist in a horizontal or vertical plane at any altitude. The degree of turbulence increases as the amount of wind shear increases.

103. SHEAR WITH TEMPERATURE INVERSION

A. A narrow zone of wind shear, with its accompanying turbulence, is often encountered when climbing or descending through a temperature inversion. The wind speed and/or direction sometimes changes very abruptly with altitude in this zone.

B. Wind shear that is associated with a strong temperature inversion near the ground presents a particular hazard to aircraft immediately after takeoff or on final approach. In a typical case, nighttime radiational cooling forms a layer of cold air near the ground. The cold air, only a few hundred feet thick, may be underneath a moving layer of warmer air. Because of the wind speed difference between the moving warm air and the still cold air, a narrow zone of wind shear develops along the boundary. The degree of turbulence will vary with the speed of the warm air since the cold air is calm.

Wind shear turbulence located in a zone between relatively calm wind within an inversion and relatively strong wind above the top of the inversion. This condition is most common at night.

FIGURE 2-18

104. SHEAR TURBULENCE WITH FRONTS

A. Because winds on either side of a front have different speed and direction, a shear zone exists along the boundary of these winds.

B. This shear can produce hazardous turbulence in the terminal area for aircraft conducting approaches and landings. The accompanying frontal windshift at the airport also intensifies the local traffic problem since the flow of traffic may also have to be changed. The air ahead of a fast moving cold front often is forced upward by convergence of strong low-level winds. This results in gradually increasing low level turbulence as the front approaches the terminal.

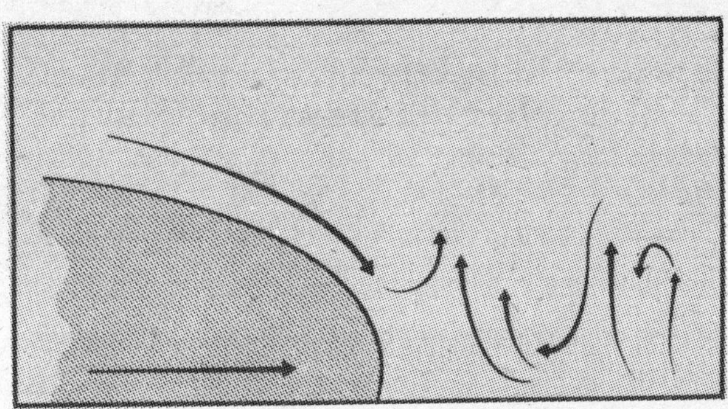

Turbulence ahead of a fast moving cold front. The rapid movement of the approaching cold air mass stirs the air up into snarling eddies ahead of the front. The frontal zone is another favorite location for wind shear turbulence.

FIGURE 2-19

105. CLEAR AIR TURBULENCE

The term, clear air turbulence (CAT), generally is reserved for high level wind shear turbulence and most frequently occurs in the vicinity of the jet stream. This turbulence may be sufficiently intense to cause serious stresses on the aircraft and physical discomfort to its passengers.

106. CHARACTERISTICS OF CAT

High-level clear air turbulence is very patchy and transitory in nature. The dimensions of these turbulent patches are quite variable and thought to be on the order of 2000 feet in depth, 20 miles in width, and 50 or more miles in length. The patches elongate in the direction of the wind. The exact position of these individual cells is difficult, if not impossible to locate. Determining location of individual cells is largely dependent on pilot reports; however, the meteorologist can forecast general areas where this phenomenon is likely to occur.

107. CAT BY SEASONS

There are from three to four times more CAT occurrences during winter than summer. The most frequent mean sea level altitude of jet stream CAT encounters is 30,000 feet in winter and 34,000 feet in summer.

108. - 112. RESERVED

SECTION 4
THUNDERSTORMS

113. GENERAL

The thunderstorm (cumulonimbus cloud) is always accompanied by lightning and thunder. Thunderstorms are particularly dangerous for pilots because they are almost always accompanied by strong gusts of wind, severe turbulence and icing. Heavy rain showers normally accompany the thunderstorm and hail is not uncommon. The air traffic controller frequently must relay thunderstorm information to a pilot and occasionally must advise a pilot on thunderstorm avoidance. To provide the controller with the necessary background to serve pilots flying in or near thunderstorms, this section describes the structure, general categories, and hazards of thunderstorms.

114. FORMATION

A. For thunderstorms to form, air must have sufficient water vapor, be unstable, and initially undergo forced lifting. Surface heating, converging winds, sloping terrain, a front, or any combination of these can force the necessary initial updraft.

B. Expansional cooling in the upward moving air results in condensation and formation of a cumulus cloud. Condensation releases latent heat which partially offsets further expansional cooling. If a saturated updraft becomes warmer than the surrounding air, its buoyancy is increased causing the updraft to accelerate. As more water vapor is drawn into the cloud and condenses, the cloud builds upward into towering cumulus and finally a thunderstorm (cumulonimbus).

C. When air is moist and unstable, thunderstorms may be caused by daytime heating of the ground, low pressure areas, upslope winds, or fronts. Even dry air masses coming in contact with moist air (a dry line or dew-point front) can trigger thunderstorms. Once started, thunderstorms generally move with the upper winds and may travel a considerable distance from their source. Thunderstorms caused by a front can move well ahead of the front as a squall line. Thunderstorms formed over mountains often drift many miles out over adjoining flatlands.

115. LIFE-CYCLE

All thunderstorm cells progress through three stages called the life-cycle. These stages are (1) cumulus, (2) mature, and (3) dissipating. The difference between a severe and a less severe thunderstorm is the mechanism of the mature stage.

116. CUMULUS STAGE

Although most cumulus clouds do not become thunderstorms, the initial state of a thunderstorm is always a cumulus cloud. The main feature of the cumulus or building state is the predominant updraft which may extend from the earth's surface to several thousand feet above the visible cloud top. During the early period of this stage, cloud droplets are very small but grow into raindrops as the cloud builds upward.

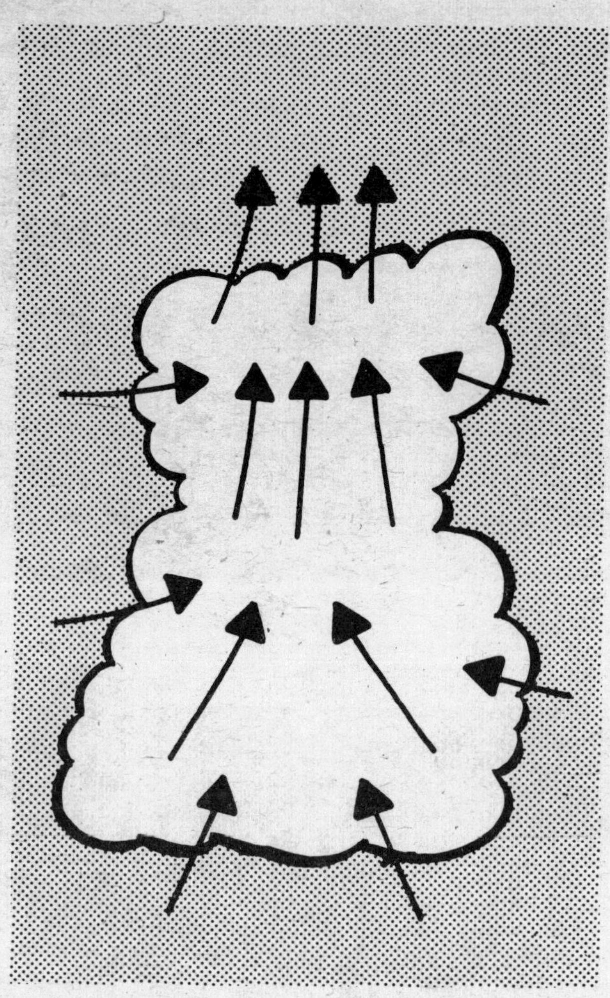

Cumulus stage of a thunderstorm cell showing all upward vertical currents or updrafts.

FIGURE 2-20

117. MATURE STAGE

A. The mature stage begins when drops are ejected from the updraft or they become so large that the updraft can no longer support them and they begin to fall. This occurs roughly 10-15 minutes after the cloud has built upward beyond the freezing level.

B. As the raindrops fall, they drag air with them. This is a major factor in the formation of downdrafts which characterize a thunderstorm in the mature stage.

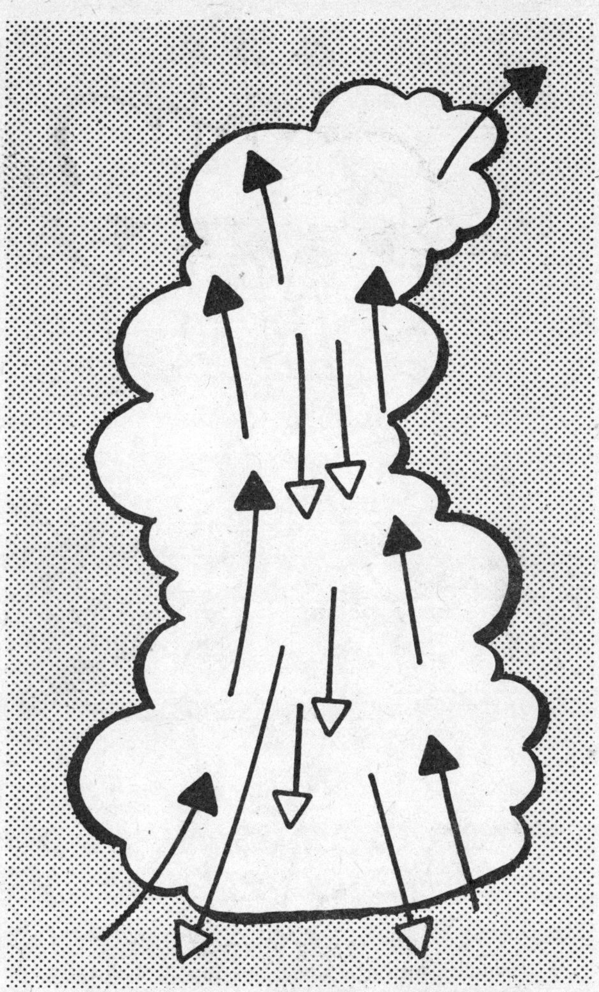

Mature stage of a limited state thunderstorm cell. Downdrafts are penetrating updrafts destroying them. The mature stage has the greatest vertical shears and is the most turbulent stage in the life cycle of any thunderstorm.

FIGURE 2-21

C. The air being dragged downward by the falling rain is cooler than its surroundings, and the drag accelerates downward motion. Throughout the mature stage, downdrafts continue to develop, and they coexist with updrafts.

118. DISSIPATING STAGE

The dissipating stage begins when downdrafts predominate. When the updraft is too weak to support the raindrops, precipitation falls through the updraft. If the updraft is strong enough to prevent precipitation from falling through it, the precipitation may fall immediately outside the upward current. In either event, the effect of the falling precipitation decreases buoyancy; and along with the frictional drag, it slows on the updraft and finally reverses the flow to a downdraft. The downdraft and precipitation cool the lower portion of the storm cloud and the surface over which it lies. It cuts off the inflow of water vapor (the thunderstorm cell runs out of energy), and the storm dissipates. When all rain and hail have fallen from the cloud, the dissipating stage is complete.

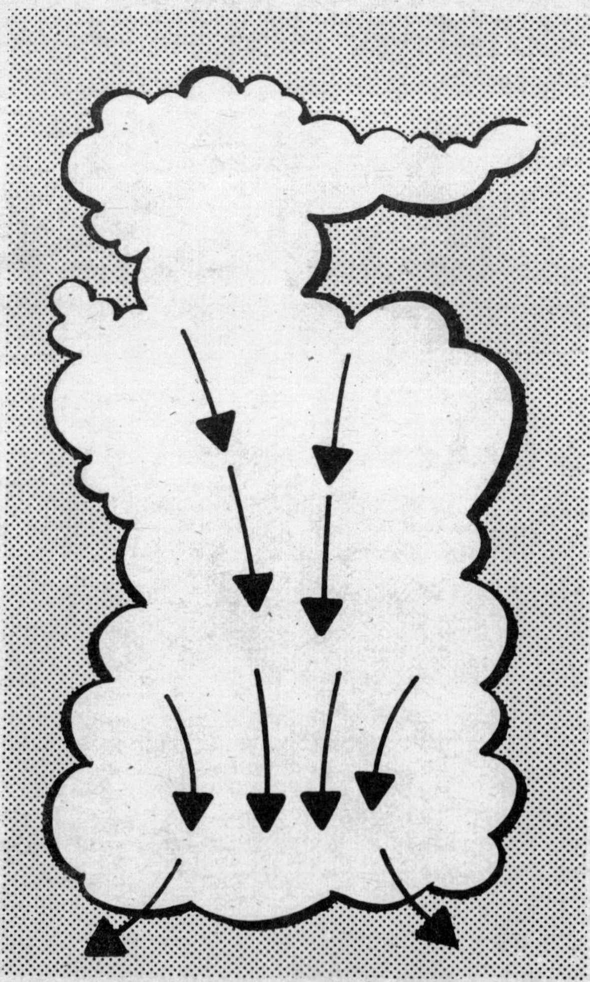

Dissipating stage of a thunderstorm cell. Vertical currents are all downdrafts; buoyancy has ended and precipitation formation has ceased.

FIGURE 2-22

119. GENERAL CATEGORIES

Structure, while in the mature stage, has an important bearing on the duration and potential severity of a storm and leads to classification of thunderstorms into two general categories--(1) the limited state thunderstorm generally referred to as an air mass thunderstorm, and (2) steady state thunderstorms which often form into squall lines.

120. LIMITED STATE THUNDERSTORMS

Limited state airmass thunderstorms are usually caused by daytime heating. They usually progress rapidly through the mature state. An airmass thunderstorm usually has a life-cycle of about 20 minutes to 1 1/2 hours. A group of scattered thunderstorms may consist of many cells in various stages and persist for several hours. Individual cells can produce icing, severe turbulence, and hail.

121. STEADY STATE THUNDERSTORMS

Steady state thunderstorm cells are the most severe type of thunderstorm and often produce extreme turbulence and large hail. They are usually in lines and are associated with a weather system such as a front or low pressure trough either at the surface or aloft. The life of an individual cell may be considerably longer than that of an airmass thunderstorm cell. A line of severe storms, often consisting of many individual cells may, in extreme cases, last as long as 24 hours and move as far as 1000 miles. The thunderstorms continue in this steady state until the entire system weakens.

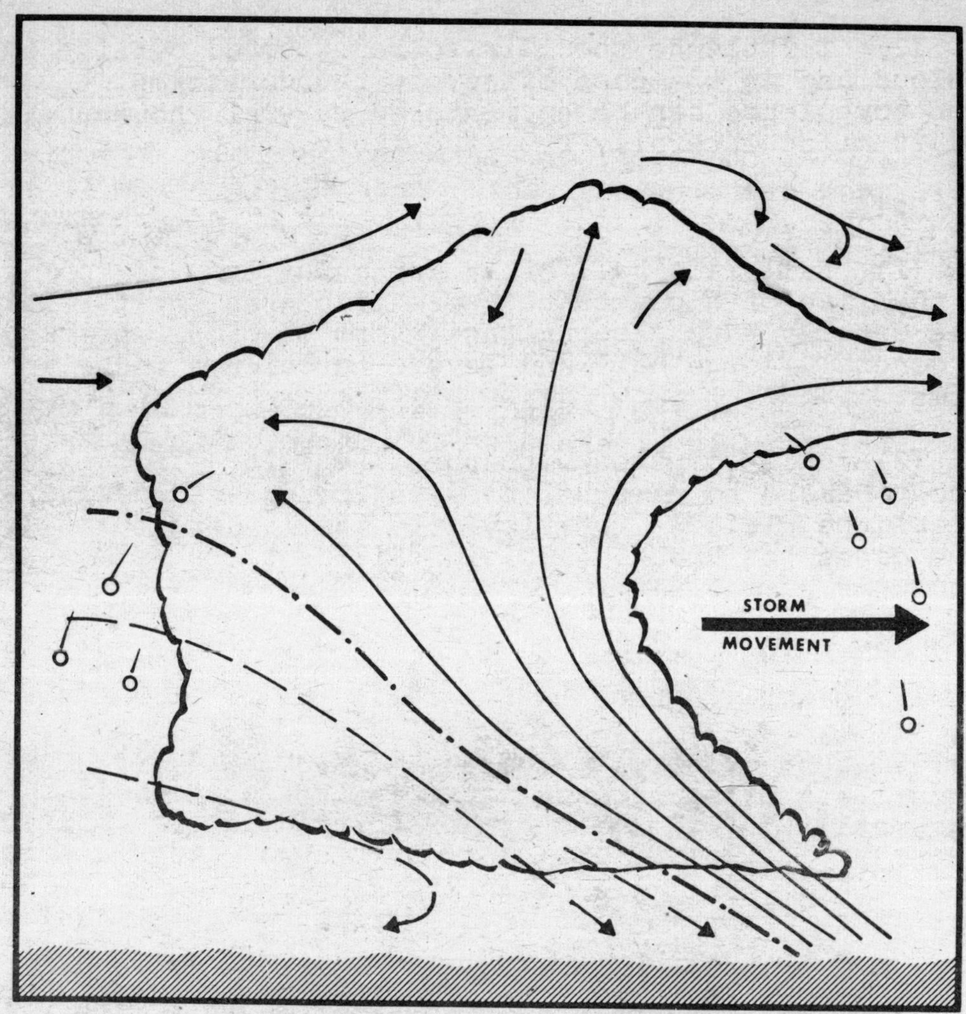

Schematic of the mature stage of a steady state thunderstorm cell showing a sloping updraft with the downdraft and precipitation outside the updraft not impeding it. The steady state mature cell may continue for many hours and deliver the most violent thunderstorm turbulence.

FIGURE 2-23

122. THUNDERSTORM HAZARDS

A. Turbulence -

(1) All thunderstorms are turbulent, and some are potentially destructive to aircraft. Almost any thunderstorm has the potential to produce "severe" turbulence and some may produce turbulence classified as "extreme."

(2) Turbulence should also be expected outside the visible cloud and in the case of severe thunderstorms, severe to extreme turbulence can be encountered several thousand feet above and 20 miles laterally from the storm.

B. Hail -

(1) Hail is a ball or an irregular lump of ice, ranging from the size of a pea to the size of a grapefruit. Large hailstones usually have alternating layers of clear and cloudy ice. In general, large hail and severe turbulence occur in the same storms.

(2) Hail competes with turbulence for first place as the greatest hazard to aircraft produced by the thunderstorm. Hail batters the airfoils, particularly the leading edges, and in extreme cases has knocked out windshields.

Hail damage to aircraft.

FIGURE 2-24

(3) Frequently hail is carried aloft and tossed out the top or side of the cloud by updrafts and may be encountered in clear air several miles from the thunderstorm. Most thunderstorms have hail in the interior of the cumulonimbus cloud. In a large percentage of the cases, the hail melts before reaching the ground, but this does not lessen its danger to the pilot who encounters it aloft.

C. Lightning - The electricity generated by a thunderstorm is rarely a great hazard to aircraft from the standpoint of airframe, but its hazards include:

(1) Temporary blindness during hours of darkness.

(2) Damage to navigational and electronic equipment.

(3) Punctures in the aircraft skin from direct lightning strikes.

D. Icing - Clear ice accumulation in thunderstorms above the freezing level can be so rapid that an aircraft may become incapable of maintaining level flight.

E. Precepitation - Low ceiling and visibility - A thunderstorm contains considerable quantities of liquid water, but this moisture is not necessarily falling to the earth as rain. Water drops are carried aloft by the updrafts, or may be suspended in them resulting in near zero visibility within a thunderstorm. When rain showers reach the earth, they usually are heavy enough to cause low ceilings and poor visibility. In addition, dust between the cloud base and the ground cause an additional decrease in visibility.

F. Effect on altimeters - Pressure usually falls rapidly with the approach of a thunderstorm. It rises sharply with the onset of the first gust and the arrival of the cold downdraft and heavy rain showers. The pressure then falls back to the original pressure as the rain ends and the storm moves on. This cycle of pressure change may occur in 15 minutes. Altitude indicated on an altimeter during the heavy rain may be in error by over a hundred feet a few minutes after the rain stops.

G. Surface winds -

(1) The horizontal spreading out of the downdrafts beneath a thunderstorm causes a rapid change in wind direction and speed (low-level wind shear) in the vicinity of the storm. The gusty, shifting winds are usually hazardous to landing aircraft.

Cross section of a thunderstorm showing location of surface wind gusts, roll cloud, and other turbulent areas relative to the movement of the storm. Surface gusts and rotor motion can be extremely hazardous to aircraft landing, taking off, and flying at low altitude.

FIGURE 2-25

(2) Usually the first gust accompanied by low-level wind shear precedes the arrival of the roll cloud and onset of rain as a thunderstorm approaches. Frequently, surface winds stir up considerable dust and debris as it plows along so that one can see it approaching. The strength of the first gust frequently is the strongest wind observed at the surface during a thunderstorm and may approach 100 knots in extreme cases. The roll cloud is not always present, but it is found most frequently on the leading edges of fast moving fronts or squall lines and represents an extremely turbulent condition.

H. Tornadoes -

(1) Tornadoes occur only with the most violent thunderstorms. They are circular whirlwinds of air, cloud, and debris that usually range in diameter from 100 feet to a half mile. Pressure is extremely low in the center of the whirlpool and winds probably are up to 200 knots. Tornadoes appear as funnel-shaped clouds from the base of thunderstorms and usually move at a speed of 25 to 50 knots.

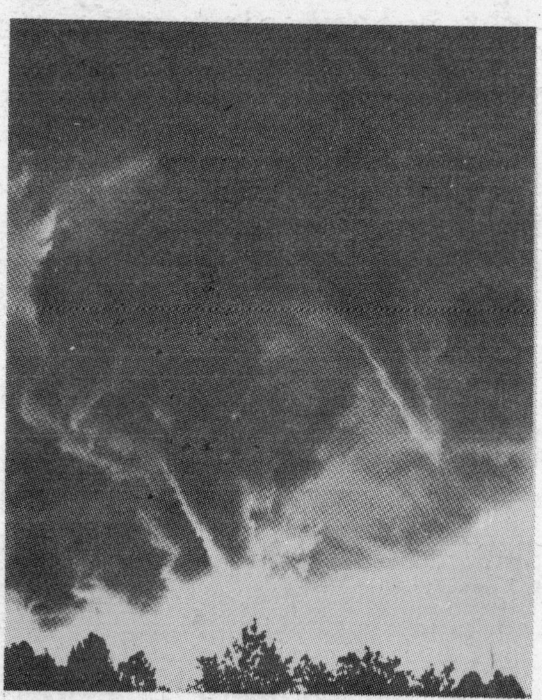

FIGURE 2-26

(2) Technically, they must touch the ground to be called tornadoes. When they occur over water, they are called waterspouts. When the characteristic whirling clouds extend downward from the parent cloud but do not reach the surface, they are called funnel clouds.

(3) Frequently, cumulonimbus mamma clouds occur in connection with violent thunderstorms and tornadoes. This type cloud is noted in the remarks section of surface aviation observations as CBMAM (Figure 1-22). Tornadoes occur with isolated thunderstorms at times, but more frequently with cold fronts and squall lines.

I. Squall lines -

(1) A non-frontal, narrow band of active thunderstorms. Often it develops a few hundred miles ahead of a cold front in moist, unstable air, but may develop in unstable air far removed from any front. The line may be several hundred miles long and may vary in width up to 50 miles.

(2) The squall line often contains severe steady state thunderstorms and presents the single most intense hazard to IFR flight in heavy aircraft. A squall line usually forms quickly and moves rapidly. It generally completes its life cycle within 24 hours with maximum intensity during late afternoon or early night.

123.-125. RESERVED

SECTION 5
DENSITY ALTITUDE

126. GENERAL

A. Density altitude is pressure altitude corrected for temperature variations. It is not used as a height reference, but as an index to tell us how well the aircraft will take off or climb.

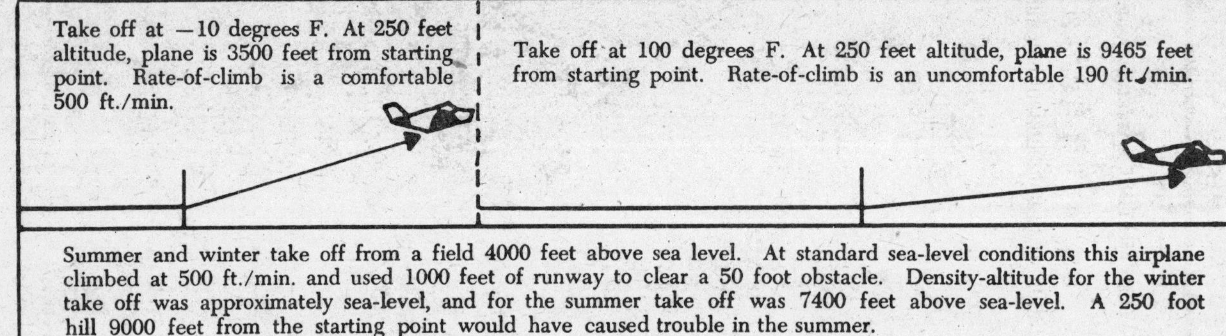

Take off at —10 degrees F. At 250 feet altitude, plane is 3500 feet from starting point. Rate-of-climb is a comfortable 500 ft./min.
Take off at 100 degrees F. At 250 feet altitude, plane is 9465 feet from starting point. Rate-of-climb is an uncomfortable 190 ft./min.
Summer and winter take off from a field 4000 feet above sea level. At standard sea-level conditions this airplane climbed at 500 ft./min. and used 1000 feet of runway to clear a 50 foot obstacle. Density-altitude for the winter take off was approximately sea-level, and for the summer take off was 7400 feet above sea-level. A 250 foot hill 9000 feet from the starting point would have caused trouble in the summer.

Effects of density altitude on take off and climb from a 4,000-foot airport.

FIGURE 2-27

B. High density altitude, or light air, affects three parts of the aircraft performance:

(1) The engine develops less power.

(2) The propeller develops less thrust.

(3) The wings develop less lift.

127. KOCH CHART

This chart gives the pilot and controller information about altitude-temperature effects on airplane performance. The chart indicates typical representative values for personal type airplanes. Use of the chart is explained in the instructions within the chart. It is of value to the controller in showing the relationship between temperature and take off distance.

THE KOCH CHART FOR ALTITUDE AND TEMPERATURE EFFECTS

TO FIND THE EFFECT OF ALTITUDE AND TEMPERATURE
CONNECT THE TEMPERATURE AND AIRPORT ALTITUDE BY A STRAIGHT LINE.

READ THE INCREASE IN TAKE-OFF DISTANCE AND THE DECREASE IN RATE OF CLIMB FROM STANDARD SEA LEVEL VALUES HERE

AIRPORT TEMPERATURE - DEGREES FAHRENHEIT
120
110
100
90
80
70
60
50
40
30
20
10
0
−10
−20
−30
−40

PERCENT DECREASE IN RATE OF CLIMB
90
80
70
60
40
20
0

ADD THIS PERCENTAGE TO NORMAL TAKE-OFF DISTANCE
260
200
140
100
60
40
20
0

AIRPORT PRESSURE ALTITUDE - THOUSANDS OF FEET
(READ YOUR ALTIMETER SET TO 29.92 INCHES)
16
14
12
10
8
6
4
2
0
−2

EXAMPLE: The diagonal line shows that 230% must be added for a temperature of 100° and a pressure altitude of 6,000 feet. Therefore, if standard temperature sea level take-off distance, in order to climb to 50 feet, normally requires 1,000 feet of runway, it would become 3,300 feet under the conditions shown. In addition, the rate of climb would be decreased 76%. Also, if normal sea level rate of climb is 500 feet per minute, it would become 120 feet per minute.

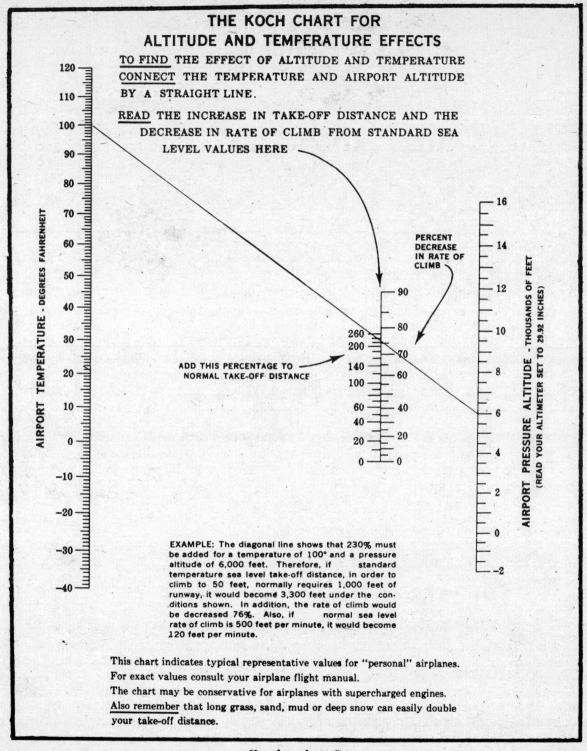

This chart indicates typical representative values for "personal" airplanes.
For exact values consult your airplane flight manual.
The chart may be conservative for airplanes with supercharged engines.
Also remember that long grass, sand, mud or deep snow can easily double your take-off distance.

Koch chart.

FIGURE 2-28

128.-130. RESERVED

CHAPTER 3
AVIATION REPORTS

SECTION 1
SURFACE AVIATION WEATHER REPORTS

131. GENERAL

A. Weather observations are measurements and estimates of existing weather conditions. A recorded observation becomes a weather report. Observations are made from vantage points at the surface, aloft, and from outer space. These reports are the basis of all weather analysis and forecasts. You will routinely use these observations in providing air traffic services.

B. Surface aviation weather reports are the backbone of the aviation weather service. You need not know all the details of taking and recording observations but you must be able to decode reports and accurately communicate significant weather information to pilots.

C. Most aviation weather observations are scheduled every hour on the hour and identified as an hourly collection. However, significant changes are reported as they occur when they affect the safety of flight.

132. SURFACE OBSERVATION TYPES

A. Record observations are scheduled observations taken on the hour and contain all pertinent elements normally observed by the reporting station.

B. Special observations are unscheduled observations taken to report significant changes in weather and at any time such a change occurs. The special may contain all or part of the elements of a record observation.

C. Local observations are taken to support local operational needs and when aircraft accidents occur. They are only disseminated locally and do not contain all the elements of a record observation.

133. HEADING OF AN HOURLY COLLECTION

Type and observation time of each report must be identified. A scheduled hourly collection has a heading for this purpose at the beginning of the collection.

HEADING OF AN HOURLY COLLECTION

SA21 051100

CODED	MEANING
SA	Hourly surface aviation collection
21	Area Circuit (8021)
051100	6-digit date-time group in Greenwich Mean Time. The first two digits are day of the month (5th) and the last four digits are observation time (1100)

FIGURE 3-1

134. HEADING HOURLY SUPPLEMENTAL REPORTS

A. Hourly supplemental reports are transmitted in a collection as teletypewriter time becomes available. In this collection the reports are listed by state in proximity to the area circuit. The reporting stations are listed alphabetically within the state.

HEADING OF A SUPPLEMENTAL REPORT COLLECTION

TEXAS Ø615Ø3
ABI
ALI
AMA

Coded	
TEXAS	State for the reporting stations that will follow.
Ø615Ø3	Date-time group - 6th day of the month collection sent at 15Ø3 GMT.
ABI ALI AMA	Reporting stations listed alphabetically.

FIGURE 3-2

B. An individual special, delayed, or corrected report is identified in the body of the report.

135. ELEMENTS OF THE SURFACE AVIATION WEATHER REPORT

To conserve teletypewriter time and space, aviation weather reports are coded in a prescribed format of symbols and contractions. If one element of this format is missing, it is shown by a blank. The controller must memorize and learn to interpret these symbols and contractions.

OKC	SP	M24 OVC	21/2	S-BS	21Ø/	3Ø/27	3618G22/	Ø11/	VSBY W1]
a	b	c	d	e	f	g	h	i	j

Legend		Paragraph Reference
a.	Station designator	136
b.	Type of report	137
c.	Sky and ceiling	138
d.	Visibility	139-141
e.	Weather and/or obstruction to vision	142
f.	Sea level pressure	143
g.	Temperature and dewpoint	144
h.	Wind direction, speed, and character	145 & 146
i.	Altimeter setting	147
j.	Remarks	148

FIGURE 3-3

136. STATION DESIGNATOR

OKC SP M24 OVC 21/2S-BS 21Ø/3Ø/27/3618G22/Ø11/VSBY W11/2

The station designator in the U.S. is a three letter group identifying the station which makes the observation. An attempt is made to assign designators that suggest the name of the observing station. OKC-Oklahoma City, HOU-Houston, SEA-Seattle, CLE-Cleveland, DEN-Denver, DAL-Dallas, SFO-San Francisco, ATL-Atlanta, etc. The FAA Location Identifiers Handbook contains a complete listing.

137. TYPE OF REPORT

OKC SP M24 OVC 21/2S-BS 21Ø/3Ø/27/3618G22/Ø11/VSBY W11/2

The letters "SP" as shown here mean a scheduled observation with significant weather change since the previous observation, otherwise this entry is omitted in a scheduled collection. In a non-scheduled observation the letters "SP" would be followed by a 4-digit time group in Greenwich Mean Time. SP 1710 -- The four digits are the observation time (1710GMT). You will note that in a scheduled observation that a time group is omitted.

138. SKY AND CEILING

OKC SP M24 OVC 21/2S-BS 21Ø/3Ø/27/3618G22/Ø11/VSBY W11/2

A. The purpose of the SKY condition explanation is to give the user as much information as possible about clouds and obscuring phenomena. All layers of clouds and obscuring phenomena visible from the ground are reported. The amount of sky coverage of a layer is reported by a contraction of the first four contractions illustrated and defined in the following table. When at least half of this layer aloft is transparent, the layer is classified as thin. This thin layer is indicated by prefixing a minus sign to the sky cover contraction.

SUMMARY OF SKY COVER CONTRACTIONS

CONTRACTION	MEANING	SPOKEN
CLR	Clear. (Less than 0.1 sky cover.)	CLEAR
SCT	Scattered layer aloft. (0.1 through 0.5 sky cover.)	SCATTERED
BKN	Broken layer aloft. (0.6 through 0.9 sky cover.)	BROKEN
OVC	Overcast layer aloft. (More than 0.9 sky cover.)	OVERCAST
X	Surface based obscuration. (All of sky is hidden by surface based phenomena.	SKY OBSCURED
-X	Surface based partial obscuration. (0.1 or more, but not all, of sky is hidden by surface based phenomena.	SKY PARTIALLY OBSCURED
-SCT	Thin scattered. At least 1/2 of the sky cover aloft is transparent at and below the level of the layer aloft.	THIN SCATTERED
-BKN	Thin broken.	THIN BROKEN
-OVC	Thin overcast.	THIN OVERCAST

FIGURE 3-4

B. The height of each layer's base is indicated by prefixing a figure or figures to the sky cover contraction. All heights are in hundreds of feet above ground level (AGL); 1 represents a height of 100 feet; 24, a height of 2400 feet; and 100, a height of 10,000 feet; etc. All layers are reported in ascending order. For example:

20 SCT 50 SCT

represents a layer of scattered clouds at two thousand feet and another scattered layer at five thousand feet.

C. An observer cannot see an entire layer when part of that layer is hidden from view by lower clouds. A method of summation is used to circumvent this difficulty. For any given layer aloft the amount of coverage is determined by adding the unconcealed amounts at that level and the amounts at all levels below it. For example: a sky with 3/10 coverage at 2000 feet plus 3/10 additional coverage at 5000 feet plus another 4/10 coverage at 10,000 feet would have the following sky cover amount for each layer (refer to figure 3-4):

2000 feet; 3/10 or SCT
5000 feet; 3/10+3/10=6/10 or BKN
10,000 feet; 3/10+3/10+4/10 = 10/10 or OVC

D. The complete sky cover report would appear as 20SCT E50BKN 100OVC. Significance of the letter "E" preceding the 50BKN layer will be explained in the Ceiling section. For multiple layers the symbol given in figure 3-4 represents a summation of sky coverage at and below each layer. Experience has shown that sky condition reported in terms of scattered, broken, or overcast is not always appropriate. The sky may be obscured by surface based phenomena other than clouds (such as fog, precipitation, dust, smoke, or haze), and to report these as clouds would be misleading. The letter "X" indicates a sky that is totally obscured by surface based phenomena.

CEILING DESIGNATORS

CODED	MEANING	SPOKEN
M	Measured. Determined by instruments such as ceilometer or ceiling light cloud detection radar or by the unobscured portion of a landmark protruding into ceiling layer.	MEASURED CEILING
E	Estimated. Determined by any method, but height may be too uncertain to be classified as "M".	ESTIMATED CEILING
W	Indefinite. Vertical visibility into a surface based obscuring phenomena. Regardless of method of determination, vertical visibility is classified as an indefinite ceiling.	INDEFINITE CEILING

FIGURE 3-5

E. Thus, the ceiling is described by (1) a ceiling designator, (2) a height, and (3) a sky cover contraction.

Ceiling examples:

M24 OVC	Spoken as MEASURED CEILING TWO THOUSAND FOUR HUNDRED OVERCAST.
W5 X	Spoken as INDEFINITE CEILING FIVE HUNDRED SKY OBSCURED.
M5 OVC	Spoken as MEASURED CEILING FIVE HUNDRED OVERCAST.
E17 BKN	Spoken as ESTIMATED CEILING ONE THOUSAND SEVEN HUNDRED BROKEN.
M20V BKN	Spoken as MEASURED CEILING TWO THOUSAND VARIABLE BROKEN.

F. In the last ceiling example, the "V" following the height value indicates a variable ceiling, a condition in which the height rapidly increases and decreases while the observation is being taken. The reported height represents an average of all observed values. The range of the variation will be shown in the remarks section, element j in figure 3-3 for example CIG 18V23 spoken: CEILING ONE THOUSAND EIGHT HUNDRED VARIABLE TO TWO THOUSAND THREE HUNDRED.

139. VISIBILITY

OKC SP M24 OVC <u>21/2</u>S-BS 21Ø/3Ø/27/3618G22/Ø11/VSBY W11/2

A. Visibility is the greatest horizontal distance at which a prominant object can be seen and identified and is reported in <u>statute</u> miles and fractions. Prevailing visibility is the greatest visibility prevalent throughout one-half or more of the horizon not necessarily continuous. Prevailing visibility is recorded in the body of the report.

B. When visibility in any direction varies significantly from prevailing visibility, the differing visibility is reported in remarks. For example, VSB W11/2 is spoken VISIBILITY WEST ONE AND ONE HALF.

C. When prevailing visibility varies as the observation is made, the letter "V" is added to the visibility value. An example is "3/4V" spoken VISIBILITY THREE QUARTERS VARIABLE. In such cases the range of variation is shown in the remarks section as: VSBY 1/2V1 and spoken as VISIBILITY VARIABLE BETWEEN ONE HALF AND ONE.

D. At an airport with an operational control tower, control tower personnel normally make visibility observations when visibility is less than 4 miles. If the control tower visibility is more representative for aircraft operations, it becomes the prevailing visibility in the body of the report; and surface visibility appears in remarks, i.e., SFC VSBY 2. If surface visibility is more representative, it is the prevailing visibility; and tower visibility if considered significant appears in remarks, i.e., TWR VSBY 8.

140. RUNWAY VISIBILITY

Runway visibility is the visibility from a particular location along an identified runway, usually determined by an instrument used to measure this visibility called a transmissometer. It is recorded in miles and fractions, and appears in the remarks section prefaced by "VV."

141. RUNWAY VISUAL RANGE

Runway visual range is the maximum horizontal distance down a specified instrument runway at which a pilot can see and identify high intensity runway lights. It is recorded in hundreds of feet and normally read from a meter located in the control tower. Runway visual range "VR" readings in the remarks section consist of the extremes during the 10-minute period prior to the observation separated by the letter "V". R18VR20V30 - is decoded "RUNWAY ONE EIGHT VISUAL RANGE VARIABLE FROM TWO THOUSAND TO THREE THOUSAND." RUNWAY VISIBILITY and RUNWAY VISUAL RANGE information from the remarks section are not issued as approach information but may be relayed as advisory information.

142. WEATHER AND OBSTRUCTIONS TO VISION

```
OKC SP M24 ØVC 21/2S-BS 21Ø/3Ø/27/3618G22/Ø11
                    A B
```

A. Weather -

(1) "Weather" in this element refers only to those items listed in the following table, rather than to the more general meaning of all atmospheric phenomena.

WEATHER SYMBOLS AND MEANINGS

CODED	SPOKEN	CODED	SPOKEN
TORNADO FUNNEL CLOUD WATERSPOUT	TORNADO FUNNEL CLOUD WATERSPOUT	ZL	FREEZING DRIZZLE
		A	HAIL
T	THUNDERSTORM	IP	ICE PELLETS
T+	SEVERE THUNDER-STORM	IPW	ICE PELLET SHOWER
		S	SNOW
R	RAIN	SW	SNOW SHOWER
RW	RAIN SHOWER	SP	SNOW PELLETS
L	DRIZZLE	SG	SNOW GRAINS
ZR	FREEZING RAIN	IC	ICE CRYSTALS

FIGURE 3-6

(2) Weather is always reported when observed regardless of the extent to which it restricts visibility and includes all forms of precipitation, plus thunderstorms, tornadoes, funnel clouds, and waterspouts. Intensity of precipitation, with the exception of hail (A) or ice crystals (IC), is shown by the following symbols:

PRECIPITATION INTENSITY* SYMBOLS

CODED	MEANING	SPOKEN
-	light	LIGHT
(none)	moderate	(not spoken)
+	heavy	HEAVY

*Intensity symbols are not appended to hail or ice crystals.

FIGURE 3-7

(3) Maximum diameter of hailstones is reported in remarks.

B. Obstructions to vision - These are particles suspended in the atmosphere or lifted by wind from the surface. To be reported as an obstruction to vision, these particles must restrict visibility to 6 miles or less.

OBSTRUCTION TO VISION SYMBOLS AND MEANINGS

CODED	SPOKEN
BD	BLOWING DUST
BN	BLOWING SAND
BS	BLOWING SNOW
BY	BLOWING SPRAY
D	DUST
F	FOG
GF	GROUND FOG
H	HAZE
IF	ICE FOG
K	SMOKE

FIGURE 3-8

EXAMPLES OF CODED REPORTS
AND CORRESPONDING PHRASEOLOGIES

CODED	SPOKEN
20 SCT E30 BKN 280 BKN 4GFK	TWO THOUSAND SCATTERED; ESTIMATED CEILING THREE THOUSAND BROKEN; TWO EIGHT THOUSAND BROKEN; VISIBILITY FOUR; GROUND FOG, SMOKE.
M12 BKN 50 BKN 12	MEASURED CEILING ONE THOUSAND TWO HUNDRED BROKEN; FIVE THOUSAND BROKEN; VISIBILITY, ONE TWO.
-X M5 OVC 3/4F	SKY PARTIALLY OBSCURED; MEASURED CEILING FIVE HUNDRED OVERCAST; VISIBILITY, THREE QUARTERS, FOG.
5SCT E10 OVC 2VR-S-F	FIVE HUNDRED SCATTERED; ESTIMATED CEILING ONE THOUSAND OVERCAST, VISIBILITY TWO, VARIABLE; LIGHT RAIN, LIGHT SNOW, FOG.
2-BKN M8 BKN 30 OVC 4RIP	TWO HUNDRED THIN BROKEN;MEASURED CEILING EIGHT HUNDRED BROKEN; THREE THOUSAND OVERCAST; VISIBILITY FOUR; RAIN, ICE PELLETS.
CLR 3 BNBD	CLEAR; VISIBILITY THREE; BLOWING SAND, BLOWING DUST.
W0 X 0F	INDEFINITE CEILING ZERO SKY OBSCURED; VISIBILITY ZERO; FOG.
10 -OVC E300 OVC 7	ONE THOUSAND THIN OVERCAST; ESTIMATED CEILING THREE ZERO THOUSAND OVERCAST; VISIBILITY SEVEN.

FIGURE 3-9

143. SEA LEVEL PRESSURE

OKC SP M24 OVC 21/2S-BS 21Ø/3Ø/27/3618G22/Ø11/VSBY W11/2

Sea level pressure is reported in millibars and used mainly by meteorologists. They should not be broadcast to pilots. If you receive a request for a setting in millibars, do not use this reading but forward the request to the Weather Service or a Flight Service Station for conversion.

144. TEMPERATURE AND DEW POINT

OKC SP M24 OVC 21/2S-BS 21Ø/3Ø/27/3618G22/Ø11/VSBY W11/2

Temperature and dew point are in whole degrees fahrenheit. The first entry is temperature and the second dew point. The difference between temperature and dew point indicates the amount of water vapor in the air. A small spread, usually 3 degrees or less, indicates a strong possibility of fog formation. Some examples of Temperature/Dew Point--how they are coded and how they would be spoken:

Coded	Spoken
30/27	TEMPERATURE THREE ZERO DEW POINT TWO SEVEN
104/72	TEMPERATURE ONE ZERO FOUR DEW POINT SEVEN TWO
-3/-7	TEMPERATURE MINUS THREE DEW POINT MINUS SEVEN

145. WIND

OKC SP M24 OVC 21/2S-BS 21Ø/3Ø/27/3618G22/Ø11/VSBY W11/2

A. Coding includes direction, speed, and character of the wind. Direction and speed are always reported. Character is reported only as wind variability requires. If either wind direction or speed is estimated, the letter "E" precedes the wind group.

B. Direction - The direction from which the wind blows determines the wind direction. A north wind means the wind is blowing from true north. Wind direction is reported to the nearest ten degrees starting at true north and moving clockwise through east to west with true north reported at 360 degrees. Two digits are transmitted omitting the final zero; i.e., 01 represents 010 degrees; 10,100 degrees; 28, 280 degrees; etc. A calm wind is reported as a direction of 00.

C. Speed - Wind speed is given in knots. The speed reported is actually the average speed for a period of time, usually one minute. If the wind is calm, the speed is reported as 00.

D. Character -

(1) Character of wind is the variability of speed in gusts or squalls. A gust is a variability in speed of 10 knots or more occurring over brief intervals. It is reported by suffixing a "G" to the speed followed by peak speed in gusts. If the wind is from 270 degrees and of 18 knots but ranges from 12-25 knots, it would be reported as 2718G25.

(2) A squall is a sudden increase in wind by 15 knots or more to a peak of at least 20 knots lasting for a minimum of one minute. It is reported by suffixing a "Q" to the speed followed by peak speed squalls. An average wind speed of 20 knots with peak gusts to 35 knots in squalls would be coded "20Q35."

146. TRANSMITTING SURFACE WIND

A. Wind directions shown in teletypewriter weather reports are referenced to true north, but a magnetic direction has more meaning to a pilot landing or departing since headings and runway directions are in magnetic degrees. Keeping the previous information in mind the rules for transmitting surface wind to pilots are:

(1) State wind direction from locations other than your own station with reference to true north, as obtained from weather reports.

(2) State local wind direction with reference to magnetic north, as obtained from the direct reading wind instrument in the tower.

(3) State all winds in ten-degree increments, always expressing direction in three digits.

B. Below are some examples of winds for stations other than your own and the phraseologies used in transmitting them to the pilot.

CODED	SPOKEN
3618G22	WIND THREE SIX ZERO AT ONE EIGHT, PEAK GUSTS TWO TWO.
0000	WIND CALM.
0415	WIND ZERO FOUR ZERO AT ONE FIVE.
3330Q55	WIND THREE THREE ZERO AT THREE ZERO, PEAK GUSTS IN SQUALLS FIVE FIVE.
E1815	WIND ONE EIGHT ZERO ESTIMATED ONE FIVE.
E1814G25	WIND ONE EIGHT ZERO ESTIMATED ONE FOUR, PEAK GUSTS TWO FIVE.

FIGURE 3-10

147. ALTIMETER SETTING

OKC SP M24 OVC 21/2S-BS 21Ø/3Ø/27/3618G22/Ø11/VSBY W11/2

A. The altimeter setting is a presuure measurement in inches of mercury reported to the nearest hundredth. In order to save teletypewriter space and time, only the last three digits are recorded and the decimal point omitted. An altimeter setting of 29.92 inches of mercury would appear as 992. Normal sea level pressure ranges from 28.00 inches of mercury to 31.00 inches. Thus, a 2 or 3 is prefixed to bring the value as close as possible to 30.00 inches.

B. In radio transmission of the altimeter setting, all four digits are spoken, but the decimal point is not. An altimeter setting shown in a teletypewriter report as 011 would be spoken as ALTIMETER THREE ZERO ONE ONE. The letter "E" preceding the altimeter setting indicates the observing station used an altimeter setting indicator that had not been compared with a mercury barometer or another altimeter setting indicator. Example E994, would be spoken ESTIMATED ALTIMETER TWO NINER NINER FOUR.

148. REMARKS

OKC SP M24 OVC 21/2S-BS 21Ø/3Ø/27/3618G22/Ø11/VSBY W11/2

A. The remarks section is utilized to give additional information that may be beneficial to pilots, air traffic specialists, and meteorologists. The remarks include weather information not covered in the body of the report and qualifying information to the main items of the sequence report. Following are some items that might appear in the remarks section.

(1) Obscuring Phenomena:

CODED	MEANING
D5	Dust obscuring 5/10 of the sky.
S7	Snow obscuring 7/10 of the sky.
BS3	Blowing snow obscuring 3/10 of the sky.
FK4	Fog and smoke obscuring 4/10 of the sky.
K20SCT	Scattered smoke aloft based at 2000 feet above the surface.
THIN FOG NW	Thin fog northwest (from reporting station).

(2) Wind Shifts:

WSHFT 30 means: Wind shifted at 30 minutes past the hour.

(3) Heights of Bases and Tops of Sky Cover Layers:

The heights of the bases of layers not visible at the station and the tops of any layers of clouds or obscuring phenomena may be reported. These remarks originate from pilots. Heights are above MSL.

BKN 50	Tops broken layer 5000 feet (MSL).
OVC 30/60 OVC	Top lower overcast 3000 feet (MSL), base of higher overcast 6000 feet (MSL).

(4) Sky and Ceiling

FEW CU	Few cumulus clouds
HIR CLDS VSB	Higher clouds visible (above overcast)
BRKHIC	Breaks in higher overcast
BINOVC	Breaks in overcast
BRKS N	Breaks north
BKN V OVC	Broken layer variable to overcast
CIG 14V19	Ceiling variable between 1400 feet and 1900 feet
30 SCT V BKN	Scattered layer at 3000 feet variable to broken
SC BANK NW	Stratocumulus cloud bank northwest
TCU W	Towering cumulus clouds west
CB N MOVG E	Cumulonimbus north moving east
CBMAM OVHD-W	Cumulonimbus mamma overhead to west
ACCAS ALQDS	Altocumulus castellanus all quadrants
ACSL SW-NW	Standing lenticular altocumulus southwest to northwest
ROTOR CLDS NW	Rotor clouds northwest
VIRGA E-SE	Virga (precipitation not reaching the ground) east through southeast
CONTRAILS N 420 MSL	Condensation trails north at 42,000 feet MSL
CLDS TPG MTNS SW	Clouds topping mountains southwest
RDGS OBSCD W-N	Ridges obscured west through north
CUFRA W APCHG STN	Cumulus fractus clouds west approaching station
LWR CLDS NE	Lower clouds northeast

(5) Visibility (statute miles)

VSBY S1W1/4	Visibility south 1, west 1/4
VSBY W11/2	Visibility west 1 1/2
VSBY 1V3	Visibility variable between 1 and 3
TWR VSBY 3/4	Tower visibility 3/4
SFC VSBY 1/2	Surface visibility 1/2

(6) Weather and Obstructions to Vision:

TB26 W FQT LTGCG W	Thunderstorm west, began 26 minutes after the hour. Frequent lightning cloud to ground west
RB30	Rain began 30 minutes after the hour
SB15E40	Snow began 15, ended 40 minutes after the hour
UNCONFIRMED TORNADO 15 W OKC MOVG NE2000	Unconfirmed tornado 15 (nautical miles) west of Oklahoma City, moving northeast, sighted at 2000 GMT
TB13 OVHD MOVG E	Thunderstorm overhead, moving east, began 13 minutes after the hour
OCNL DSNT LTG NW	Occasional distant lightning northwest
AB35E55 HLSTO 2	Hail began 35 ended 55, hailstones 2 inches in diameter
INTMT R-	Intermittent light rain
OCNL RW	Occasional moderate rain shower
WET SNW	Wet snow
SNOINCR 5	Snow increased 5 inches during past hour
R-OCNLY R+	Light rain occasionally heavy rain
RWU	Rain showers of unknown intensity
F DSIPTG	Fog dissipating
K DRFTG OVR FLD	Smoke drifting over field

KOCTY	Smoke over city
SHLW GFDEP 4	Shallow ground fog 4 feet deep
DUST DEVILS NW	Dust devils northwest
PATCH GF S	Patch ground fog south

(7) Pressure:

PRESRR	Pressure rising rapidly
PRESFR	Pressure falling rapidly
LOWEST PRES 631 1745	Lowest pressure 963.1 millibars at 1745GMT
PRES UNSTDY	Pressure unsteady
PRJMP 8/1012/18	Pressure jump (sudden increase) .08 inches began 1012 GMT, ended 1018 GMT

This is not a complete list, just a representative example of some of the entries you might find in the remarks section.

149.-151. RESERVED

SECTION 2
PILOT WEATHER REPORTS (PIREPS)

152. GENERAL

A. Pilots often report weather conditions in flight not observed by any other means. These observations contribute significantly to the safe and efficient flow of air traffic. You are obligated to solicit pilot weather reports and transmit them into the NAWS.

B. Pilot weather reports (PIREPs) are reports of weather observed while in flight. PIREPs are the only means of precisely determining various weather conditions such as cloud tops, icing and turbulence. Controllers will receive these pilot weather reports directly from pilots and by teletypewriter.

153. PIREP FORMAT

A pilot weather report follows a prescribed order of entering elements in a coded format. Altitudes are shown in hundreds of feet above sea level. Distances are recorded in nautical miles except visibility which is always stated in statute miles. The same symbols used in surface reports are used for cloud cover, weather and obstructions to vision. Cloud types, if reported, are in international cloud abbreviations (CB, AC, AS, etc.). Most weather conditions are noted by contractions, however, extremely hazardous or destructive weather conditions are spelled out (such as a TORNADO). The letter "U" indicates some unknown value such as "RWU" for rain showers intensity unknown.

154. PIREP TELETYPE FORMAT (FAA Form 7110-2)

A. Order and content of an individual PIREP as it appears on the teletype circuit:

(1) Originating station designator.

(2) UA followed by location of phenomena, time, and flight level.

(3) Type aircraft (Reported in all PIREPs - if not known shown "UKN".

(4) Flight condition. (SK - Sky Cover, TA - Temperature-Celsuis, WV - Wind-Direction, TB - Turbulence-Intensity, IC - Icing-Intensity, RM - Remarks).

EXAMPLE:

DDC UA/OV DDC 360050 1240 FL100 /TP DC3 /TB MDT

Dodge City PIREP 1240 GMT fifty north of Dodge City moderate turbulence at 10,000 reported by a DC3.

155. OBTAINING PIREPS

A. When receiving or requesting PIREPs from a pilot obtain all necessary information for relay to FSS specialists for dissemination. Obtain from the pilot a minimum of:

(1) Location and altitude of aircraft.

(2) Condition and extent of condition being reported.

(3) Type of aircraft.

B. Include the time (GMT) that the pilot weather report was received. When relaying a PIREP containing turbulence information; do not interpret the pilot's description, but pass the report exactly as given by the pilot. FSS may change for computer format but will place pilots description in remarks: e.g. "rougher than a corn cob".

156. SOLICITING PIREP

Request weather reports from pilots when requested by an FSS, WSFO or WSO or when one or more of the following conditions exist or are forecast for the area:

(1) Ceilings at or below 5000 feet.

(2) Visibility (surface or aloft) at or less than 5 miles.

(3) Thunderstorms and related phenomena.

(4) Turbulence, especially clear air turbulence, of moderate degree or greater.

(5) Icing of moderate degree or greater.

(6) Wind shear

157. RELAYING PIREP INFORMATION

Relay significant PIREP information to other aircraft and to appropriate air traffic facilities providing En Route Flight Advisory Service, as soon as possible, and advise aircraft entering your control sector/area on initial contact of any significant weather that may affect their route of flight. PIREPs pertaining to cloud base/tops are to be relayed to the FSS serving the departure airport of the reporting aircraft.

Relay significant and routine PIREP information to FSS, WSO, WSFO, appropriate military units and team supervisor/area supervisor/assistant chief as appropriate.

158. RESERVED.

CHAPTER 4
AVIATION WEATHER FORECASTS

159. GENERAL

Control facilities cannot plan workload on existing weather only; they must also rely on expected weather forecasts. National Weather Service forecasters prepare several types of forecasts specifically to serve aviation. To assist the controllers in reading and interpreting these forecasts, this section explains the format and decoding of the following types of aviation weather forecasts:

A. Terminal Forecasts (FT).

B. Area Forecasts (FA).

C. SIGMET (WS) & AIRMET (WA).

D. Hazardous Weather Reports.

E. Winds and Temperatures Aloft Forecast (FD).

SECTION 1
TERMINAL FORECAST (FT)

160. GENERAL

A terminal forecast is for a specific location. Terminal forecasts are issued three times daily by WSFOs, and are valid for a period of 24 hours. The first 18 hours are forecast and the last 6 hours a categorical outlook. Each new forecast supercedes preceding issuance, and amendments are issued as needed. All forecasts will be reviewed regularly at 4-hourly intervals, and most amendments will be issued at these times. An FT will not be issued for a terminal unless an observation taken within the past hour is available.

161. FT FORMAT

The format for all terminal forecasts is identical, and contains the following elements:

A. Heading.

B. Station identifier.

C. Valid period.

D. Sky condition.

E. Visibility.

F. Weather and obstructions to vision.

G. Wind.

H. Times of expected changes.

I. Remarks.

J. Outlook.

EXAMPLE:

FTØ2Ø94Ø
DAL Ø21Ø1Ø 8Ø SCT. 15Z O 1812. 19Z 5ØSCT 1914. Ø1Z CLR 171Ø.Ø4Z VFR.

162. FT HEADING

Terminal forecasts are transmitted as a collection. The collection is always headed by the initials FT followed by a six number group indicating date and time in GMT. This is the time the collection is issued. Example - FT Ø6Ø94Ø would mean the information that follows are terminal forecasts and the issuing time is the sixth day of the month at zero nine four zero GMT.

163. FT STATION IDENTIFIER

The station identifier is a three letter group as set forth in the FAA location identifiers handbook, for the location where the forecast is made.

164. FT VALID PERIOD

The valid period is indicated by a six digit number showing date and valid time period in GMT. The four digit valid period shows the hour only. Example - OKC Ø62222 would mean this terminal forecast is for Oklahoma City and is valid on the sixth day of the month from two two zero zero until two two zero zero on the seventh day of the month.

165. FT SKY CONDITION

Forecast sky cover is in coded symbols and heights in ascending order of height just as they are in Surface Aviation (SA) reports. A forecast ceiling layer is always identified by the letter "C" preceding the height of that layer. The "C" is also used for forecasting vertical visibility into a surface based obscuration. Example: C5X means CEILING FIVE HUNDRED SKY OBSCURED.

166. FT VISIBILITY

When visibility is expected to be 6 miles or less, it is entered in miles and/or fractions. When visibility is expected to be more than 6 miles, it is omitted. Weather and obstructions to vision are entered when expected to occur but otherwise omitted.

167. FT WEATHER AND OBSTRUCTIONS TO VISION

The weather and obstructions to vision are entered and read identically as they are in SA reports. When none are entered make no mention of them when reading the forecast.

168. FT WIND

When wind is expected to be 10 knots or more, wind is encoded in a four-digit group; the first two are direction in 10's of degrees and the second two are speed in knots. If less than 10 knots are expected it will be omitted. When wind is expected to be gusty, the speed is followed by the letter "G." Expected peak speed in knots follows the "G." Example: 2015G30 means WIND TWO ZERO ZERO AT ONE FIVE PEAK GUSTS THREE ZERO.

169. TIMES OF EXPECTED CHANGES TO FTS

Weather conditions will not always be constant throughout a forecast period. The initial conditions in the forecast are valid at the beginning of the valid period and continue valid until the first time designated in the forecast. If a time group is not entered, the conditions are expected to remain constant throughout the forecast period. When a change is forecast, a period follows the preceding conditions before the time entry. A time entry may be either two or four digits followed by a "Z" to indicate time either in hours or in minutes GMT.

Example: CLR. 11z CLR 2GF means:
CLEAR, VISIBILITY MORE THAN SIX, WIND LESS THAN TEN, BECOMING BY ELEVEN HUNDRED GREENWICH, CLEAR, VISIBILITY TWO, GROUND FOG, WIND LESS THAN TEN.

170. FT REMARKS

Remarks may be inserted in addition to the coded format to amplify the forecast; i.e., to indicate brief fluctuations, gradual changes, or causes of the changes. Example: 2ØSCT OCNLY C2ØBKN means TWO THOUSAND SCATTERED OCCASIONALLY CEILING TWO THOUSAND BROKEN.

Example: PTCHY GND FOG ARND DABRK means:
PATCHY GROUND FOG AROUND DAYBREAK.

171. FT OUTLOOK

The last 6 hours is a categorical outlook; these categories are:

LIFR - Ceiling less than 500 and/or visibility less than 1.
IFR - Ceiling less than 1000 and/or visibility less than 3.
MVFR - Ceiling 1000-3000 and/or visibility 3-5.
VFR - Ceiling greater than 3000 and visibility greater than 5.

State the cause of LIFR, IFR, and MVFR conditions in the categorical outlook. If the category is due only to ceiling, this is shown by the contraction "CIG." If it is due only to visibility, standard Weather and Obstructions to Vision symbols will be used. If it is due to both ceiling and visibility use both the contraction "CIG" and contractions from the standard Weather and Obstruction to Vision table. If wind and/or gusts 25 knots are expected during the outlook period this will be indicated by the word "WIND."

Following are examples of scheduled, delayed, amended, and corrected FT's:
FT Ø2Ø940
ABI Ø21Ø1Ø CLR. 16Z CLR 1815. 19Z 5Ø SCT 25Ø SCT 1915G25 Ø1ZCLR 171Ø. Ø4Z VFR...
SJT Ø21Ø1Ø 3Ø SCT 8Ø SCT. 15Z CLR 1914. Ø4Z VFR...

FT DLAD until first observation of day is received:
BGM FT RTD 1Ø12Ø5 C8 OVC 3R-F ETC.

Amended FT example:
LAN FT AMD 1 24161Ø 16ØØZ C12 BKN 7 2315 BKN V SCT. Ø5Z MVFR...

Example of corrected FT:
SAV FT COR 222222 5ØSCT 25ØSCT 3415. 17Z VFR...

172-173. Reserved.

SECTION 2
AREA FORECAST (FA)

174. GENERAL

Area Forecasts (FA) describe cloud, weather, and icing conditions anticipated within a prescribed geographical area for a 18-hour period with an additional 12-hour catagorical outlook. All times are GMT to whole hours (two digits), e.g., 13Z. FA's are issued twice daily at 124ØZ and ØØ4ØZ and amendments to the FA are now issued as needed.

175. FA FORMAT

The format for all Area Forecasts is identical and contains the following elements:

A. Heading.

B. Forecast area.

C. Height statement.

D. Synopsis.

E. Significant clouds, weather, and outlook.

F. Icing and freezing level.

Example of heading and forecast area in an Area Forecast:

MKC FA Ø2124Ø
13Z FRI - Ø7Z SAT
OTLK Ø7Z SAT - 19Z SAT

COLO WYO KANS NEB SDAK AND N DAK

176. FA HEADING

The heading identifies the type of forecast (FA), the forecast office, the scheduled filing date and time in six digits, the valid period of the forecast, i.e., the first 18-hour period, and the 12-hour Outlook period. All time is in GMT. The heading in the previous example means: KANSAS CITY FORECAST OFFICE FILED THE AREA FORECAST ON THE SECOND DAY OF THE MONTH AT 1240 GMT, THE VALID TIME FOR THE FORECAST IS 1300Z FRIDAY UNTIL 0700Z SATURDAY, AND THE OUTLOOK FROM 0700Z SATURDAY UNTIL 1900Z SATURDAY.

177. FA FORECAST AREA

The forecast area identifies the geographical area covered by the forecast. The forecast area for the above example is Colorado, Wyoming, Kansas, Nebraska, South Dakota and North Dakota.

178. FA HEIGHT STATEMENT

The height statement, "HGTS ASL UNLESS NOTED," alerts the user that height values quoted in the forecast refer to mean sea level (MSL) unless otherwise indicated by the text.

179. FA SYNOPSIS

The synopsis is a brief summary describing the locations and movements of significant fronts, pressure systems, and circulation patterns. It may also refer to significant moisture and stability conditions and is identified in the forecast by "SYNOPSIS" spelled out or the contraction "SYNS."

180. Reserved.

181. FA SIGNIFICANT CLOUDS AND WEATHER AND OUTLOOK

Significant clouds and weather are identified in the body of the forecast by: SIGCLD AND WX with the outlook for each area identified by the abbreviation OTLK. The Significant Clouds and Weather and Outlook section does not describe clouds in detail, but in general terms. It describes the expected amount and height of cloud cover, cloud tops, surface visibility, weather and obstructions to vision, and surface winds.

182. FA CLOUD COVER.

The expected cloud coverage of individual layers is indicated, rather than the summation of the layers, as used in surface aviation observations and terminal forecasts. The following contractions are used:

Contraction	Definition
CLR	Sky Clear
SCT	Scattered
BKN	Broken
OVC	Overcast
OBSC	Obscured, Obscure or obscuring
PTLY OBSC	Partly Obscured
THN	Thin
VRBL	Variable
CIG	Ceiling
INDEF	Indefinite

183. FA CLOUD HEIGHTS

Cloud heights are in hundreds of feet with reference to MSL unless otherwise stated. Example: 1ØØ SCT AGL means ten thousand scattered above ground level. The contraction "CIG" means ceiling. Ceiling by definition is above ground level. Heights less than one thousand feet AGL are stated as ceilings below one thousand feet (CIG BLO 10).

184. FA CLOUD TOPS

The height of cloud tops is stated for cloud layers with bases 20,000 feet MSL or lower. Cloud tops are in hundreds of feet normally identified by "TOPS". Example: CIG BLO 10 OVC TOPS 3Ø means ceiling below one thousand overcast (AGL) with tops at three thousand feet MSL. 12Ø BKN 16Ø means broken clouds 12,000 feet MSL, tops 16,000 feet MSL.

185. VISIBILITY

Surface visibility of more than 6 statute miles is ommitted from the forecast. When visibilities are forecast to be 6 statute miles or less, weather and obstructions to vision are included.

186. FA WEATHER AND OBSTRUCTIONS TO VISION

These are in contractions (i.e., SNW, DRZL) when included with a plain language statement. The symbolic form (S, L, etc.) with a plus or minus sign as appropriate is used in a symbolic group, such as C8 OVC S5-.

187. FA SURFACE WINDS

These are in symbolic form for any area of expected sustained speeds of 25 knots or more. Directions refer to true north, and speeds are in knots. The contraction "SFC WND" precedes the direction and speed group. Gusty surface winds in plain language or abbreviated text are denoted by the term "GUSTY" or GUSTS TO..." or when in symbolic group, by the form "25G," "25G40," or "30G65."

188. FA ICING

A. The icing section, identified by the contraction "ICG," includes a statement of expected icing conditions and the height of the freezing level. Contractions such as CLR, RIME, or MXD indicate types of icing. Sometimes contractions such as ICGIC (icing in clouds), ICGIP (icing in precipitation) and ICGICIP (icing in clouds and in precipitation) appear in combination with icing type and intensity. The forecast of the freezing level is always shown in the icing section.
Example: MDT CLR ICGICIP means - Moderate clear icing in clouds and in precipitation.

B. Qualifying terms such as probable, likely, and locally are used when these add to the value of the forecast such as:

MXD ICGIC LKLY.

189. Reserved.

190. FA OUTLOOK

The outlook is appended to each subsection of Significant Clouds and Weather and is identified by the contraction "OTLK." It contains a catagorical statement of the catagory of weather to be expected in the 12-hour period immediately following the first 18-hours of the forecast. These catagories are:

LIFR - Ceiling less than 500 and/or visibility less than 1.
IFR - Ceiling less than 1000 and/or visibility less than 3.
MVFR - Ceiling 1000-3000 and/or visibility 3-5.
VFR - Ceiling greater than 3000 and visibility more than 5.
State the cause of LIFR, IFR, and MVFR conditions in the categorical outlook.

191. FA EXAMPLE

The following are examples of FA's and amended FA's:

```
MIA FA 2ØØØ4Ø
Ø1Z FRI - 19Z FRI
OTLK 19Z FRI - Ø7Z SAT

FLA E OF 85 DEGS GA AND CSTL WTRS

HGTS ASL UNLESS NOTED

SYNOPSIS...HI PRES RDG NCAR CST EWD OVR ATLC WL RMN.  E TO SE FLO
CONTG OVR FLA AND GA.  CDFNT CNTRL TEX/ERN OKLA MOVG EWD SLOLY.

SIGCLDS AND WX...

NRN AND CNTRL GA.
4Ø SCTD VRBL BKN LYRD TO 14Ø.  AFT Ø7Z OCNL CIGS BLO 1Ø VSBYS BLO
5HK.  CONDS IMPVG BY 15Z TO CIGS ABV 15 VSBY 5 HK.  OTLK.  VFR.

E CST SECS CNTRL/SRN FLA AND ADJ CSTL WTRS.
GENLY 25 SCTD VRBL BKN TOPS 1ØØ-12Ø.  SCTD SHWRS OVR WTRS DRFTG
WWD OCNLY MOVG ONSHR CSTL AREAS WITH CONDS LCLY CIG 25 BKN 2 RW
TOPS 18Ø.  OTLK.  VFR.

SRN GA AND RMNDR FLA AND ADJ WTRS.
NO SIGCLD AND WX.  OTLK.  VFR.

ICG... LCL MDT IN TCU/RW.  FRZG LVL 11Ø N GA TO 14Ø S FLA.
```

```
SLC FA AMD 281Ø3ØZ
11Z - 19Z THU

SYNS AMD.
CDFNT RWL-MFL TO DVLPG LO LAS-ELY AREA.  NRN PTN OF FNT WILL BCM
STNRY AS LO DVLPS SRN NEV 19Z

ICG AMD.
MDT LCLY SVR ICGICIP NEV WRN UTAH 7Ø-16Ø.  FRZL LWRG TO SFC AFT 16Z
```

192-194. Reserved.

SECTION 3
AIRMETS AND SIGMETS

195. AIRMET

AIRMETs contain information on weather conditions which are not adequately covered in other forecasts and are potentially hazardous to small aircraft or to the relatively inexperienced pilots. Conditions requiring AIRMETs include:

A. Moderate icing.

B. Moderate turbulence over an extensive area.

C. Extensive areas of visibility less than three miles and/or ceilings less than 1000 feet.

D. Sustained winds of 30 knots or more within 2000 feet of the surface.

196. AIRMET HEADING

The heading identifies the issuing station, the type of forecast (WA), the weather system, the filing date and time, and the valid period (up to 6+ hours) of the forecast. Example: MKC WA 191512
191540-192100

This means Kansas City issued an AIRMET advisory on the nineteenth day of the month at one five one two GMT and will be valid on the nineteenth day of the month from one five four zero until two one zero zero GMT.

If the AIRMET advises of continued low ceiling and/or visibility or continued moderate turbulence in mountainous area it is identified as "WAC", and is valid until cancelled.

Note: Alfa refers to a series of inflight weather advisories relating to the same continuous phenomena, Bravo another series, etc.

197. AIRMET TEXT

The text of the message identifies which advisory is being transmitted, and the advisory per se. The advisories are in contractions and symbols. Cloud heights are MSL unless otherwise stated. The message is as brief as possible, consistent with clarity. The area for which the AIRMET is valid is stated with respect to distances from weather reporting stations, geographical features such as mountain ranges, or readily understood geographical areas such as the Texas Panhandle or upper Michigan.

An AIRMET area is confined to the forecast office area of responsibility. Example: AIRMET ALFA 1. RAIN AND FOG WITH CIGS LWRG TO BLO 1 THSD FT AND VSBY BLO 2 MI OVER CAROLINAS EAST OF MTNS BY Ø9ØØZ SPRDG OVER VA SOUTH OF RICHMOND ROANOKE LINE BY 12Z.

198. SIGMET

SIGMET's contain forecast weather particularly significant to the safety of all aircraft. Conditions requiring SIGMET's include:

A. Tornadoes.

B. Lines of thunderstorms (squall lines).

C. Embedded thunderstorms.

D. Hail 3/4 inch in diameter or more.

E. Severe and extreme turbulence.

F. Severe icing.

G. Widespread dust storms or sandstorms lowering visibilities to less than 3 miles.

199. SIGMET HEADING

A. The heading identifies the issuing station, the type of forecast (WS), the filing date and time, and the valid period (up to 4+ hours) of the forecast:
Example: MIA WS 090230
090230-090700

B. This means Miami issued a SIGMET advisory on the ninth day of the month at zero two three zero GMT and it will be valid between the ninth day of the month at zero two three zero and the ninth day of the month at zero seven zero zero GMT.

200. SIGMET TEXT

The text of the message identifies which advisory is being transmitted, and the advisory itself. The advisory is in contractions and symbols. Cloud heights are MSL unless otherwise stated. The message is as brief as possible. The valid area is stated with respect to distances from weather reporting stations, geographical areas such as the Texas Panhandle or upper Michigan or

NOTE: In AIRMET and SIGMET, following the number is a flight precaution (FLT PRCTN); example on following page.

geographical features such as mountain ranges. A SIGMET area is confined to the forecast office area of responsibility.

EXAMPLE: SIGMET BRAVO 7. ROCKY MTN AREA COLO AND SRN WYO. STANDING WVS E OF RDGS CAUSING EXTNSV AREAS OF STG UP AND DOWN DRAFTS AND LCLY SVR TURBC TO 18Ø.

201. HURRICANE ADVISORIES (WH)

When a hurricane threatens, complete information normally does not appear on teletype circuits. To alert aviation to the existance of the storm, the responsible forcast office issues an abbreviated hurricane advisory for teletype distribution. This advisory gives location of the storm and its expected movement. It contains information on maximum winds in and near the center, but does not issue details of associated weather. Other forecasts contain specifics on ceilings, visibility, weather and hazards.

202. SEVERE WEATHER OUTLOOK NARRATIVE (AC)

The Severe Local Storms (SELS) forecast unit of the National Severe Storms Forecast Center at Kansas City, Missouri issues the severe weather outlook narrative. It is distributed routinely on teletype at 0900Z and 1500Z with amended and unscheduled outlooks as needed. It describes in plain language the prospects of both severe and other thunderstorms during the following 24 hours. The outlook alerts aviation interests so they can plan their operations.

203. SEVERE WEATHER WATCH BULLETIN (WW)

The severe weather watch bulletin is a detailed description of expected severe weather which will meet the following criteria: A. Severe thunderstorms: (1) Damaging wind - sustained or gusty surface wind of 50 knots or more,and/or (2) Hail 3/4 inch or more in diameter; B. TORNADO - The Severe Storms Forecast Center issues a watch at any time the location, time, and severity of the weather become evident, WWs are unscheduled.

204. SPECIAL FLIGHT FORECASTS

Upon request, the forecast offices issue special flight forecasts or outlooks for pilots flying nonroutine missions over domestic areas. This service is provided if scheduled forecasts are insufficient to meet the special need. Types of flights which may require special forecasts are hospital flights; rescue flights; experimental flights; photographic missions; test flights;

record attempts; flights carrying radioactive cargo; and mass flights such as air tour, air races, and fly-aways from special events. If a specialist determines that a special flight forecast is needed, he should forward all the information to his forecast office.

205.-208. RESERVED

SECTION 4
WINDS AND TEMPERATURES ALOFT FORECAST (FD)

209. GENERAL

Winds are forecast for nine levels (MSL) and temperature for all levels above the 3000 foot level that are more than 2500 feet above the surface. The forecast levels are: 3000-6000-9000-12,000-18,000-24,000-30,000-34,000 and 39,000. FDs are issued four times daily. The forecast period covered by one forecast may overlap a period covered by the preceding forecast.

210. FD HEADING

The heading identifies the forecast (FD) followed by the initials US (indicating United States) and a number between one and four that identifies the order of the issuance; KWBC, the international identifier for the issuing station (Washington, D.C.), a six number group indicating date and time of issuance. The second line communicates the observation time of the data on which the forecast is based. The third line indicates the valid time of the forecast; the "for use" period of the forecast and the statement "TEMPS NEG ABV 24ØØØ." The fourth line lists the forecast levels in feet MSL.

211. FD FORECAST SEQUENCE

Winds aloft are forecast for approximately 100 stations within the conterminous United States. These stations are broken down to groups of 40 to 60 on a geographical and usage basis and transmitted on a teletype circuit. The stations on your FD are sequenced alphabetically and are based on your geographical area. Some circuits include Canadian stations forecasts.

212. FD DIRECTION, SPEED AND TEMPERATURE

A. Wind speed and direction are forecast for the first standard level that is at least 1500 feet above the ground, and temperature for the first standard level above 3000 feet that is at least 2500 feet above the ground. Forecasts are in either four or six digit groups. A four digit group is wind direction and speed only. A six digit group includes forecast temperature in degrees Celsius (C). The first two digits are direction in tens of degrees and the next two are speed in knots; i.e., 275Ø means 270° at 50 knots. When forecast speed is 100 to 199 knots, 50 is added to the direction code and 100 subtracted from the speed, i.e., decode 775Ø as 270° at 150 knots. Speeds in excess of 200 knots are coded as 199 knots. When forecast speed is less than 5 knots, the group is coded 99ØØ and reads as "LIGHT AND VARIABLE."

B. The last two digits in a six digit group are temperature. Temperatures for levels from 6000 through 24,000 are prefixed by a plus or minus sign. Above 24,000, temperature is always negative and the minus sign is omitted.

EXAMPLE:

FDUS3 KWBC 1ØØ945
DATA BASED ON 1ØØØØØZ

VALID 11ØØØØZ FOR USE 21ØØ-Ø3ØØZ. TEMPS NEG ABV 24ØØØ

FT	3ØØØ	6ØØØ	9ØØØ	12ØØØ	18ØØØ	24ØØØ	3ØØØØ	34ØØØ
ABI		1929+18	1932+13	2Ø3Ø+Ø5	2131-11	2248-22	226836	228Ø45
ABQ			99ØØ+Ø3	211Ø-Ø5	2Ø28-19	2141-29	216143	217849
ALS				1712-Ø5	1825-19	2Ø36-3Ø	215643	21745Ø
AMA		19Ø5	1917+1Ø	1925+Ø3	2Ø44-14	2158-25	217539	219348
ATL	12Ø6	16Ø7+14	99ØØ+Ø9	99ØØ+Ø3	Ø111-1Ø	3517-22	342538	342947
BHM	17Ø6	1712+14	17Ø8+Ø9	99ØØ+Ø4	34Ø7-Ø9	3315-22	332537	323Ø47
BLD	3511	3614+Ø7	Ø325-Ø1	Ø227-Ø5	3637-16	3657-28	357942	348148
BNA	161Ø	1913+14	1912+Ø9	2Ø11+Ø4	23Ø7-Ø9	281Ø-22	311738	312247
BOI		99ØØ+Ø7	99ØØ-ØØ	3511-Ø6	3523-16	3528-28	343444	343752
BRO	1621	172Ø+2Ø	1919+15	2119+Ø8	2423-Ø6	243Ø-18	243933	244543
CRP	162Ø	1824+2Ø	1923+14	2Ø21+Ø8	2323-Ø7	2434-19	244733	245543
DAL	163Ø	1834+19	1932+13	1929+Ø6	2Ø26-Ø9	2237-21	235136	246Ø45
DEN			99ØØ-Ø6	15Ø6-Ø6	1921-19	2Ø34-3Ø	215343	216751
DRT	1515	1819+21	212Ø+13	2222+Ø6	2332-Ø9	2349-2Ø	236934	237844
DSM	2124	2223+12	2226+Ø7	2231+Ø1	2143-11	2251-24	23614Ø	236247
ELP		28Ø5	2616+Ø7	253Ø-Ø1	2449-14	2364-26	22814Ø	228748
GCK		Ø2Ø9+11	1915+Ø6	1926+ØØ	2Ø45-15	2159-26	21754Ø	218848
GJT			Ø4Ø9-Ø8	Ø8Ø8-Ø9	Ø714-21	Ø611-32	99ØØ45	23Ø751
HLC		351Ø+Ø7	2Ø11+Ø4	2Ø23-Ø1	2Ø46-15	216Ø-26	21764Ø	218448

*39,000 level omitted from this example.

APPENDIX C
ATC RADAR FOR WEATHER OBSERVATION *

PURPOSE. The purpose of this air traffic training manual entitled "ATC Radar for Weather Observation ETM 7-0-2" is to provide specialists supplementary study material to support the training requirements of the National Air Traffic Training Program. It has been prepared in coordination with the Weather Service Coordinator and Training Consultant at the FAA Academy.

*This FAA training material is not required information for the Air Traffic Control Employment Examination but is considered useful and important to air traffic control work.

INTRODUCTION

Although the Air Traffic Control Specialist need not have the knowledge of the experienced weather radar specialist, the recognition of echo returns which indicate severe weather is essential for the provision of more efficient air traffic control service.

At specified training times the air traffic specialist reviews weather information which includes weather radar reports (RAREPs). In order to make operational use of these reports, the controller must know what weather radar detects. Additionally, he must be aware of the limitations of ATC radar as a weather detection tool. Prior to reading this manual, a review of the Weather for Controllers, ETM 7-0-1, is recommended.

This manual is for Air Traffic Control Specialists who have a basic knowledge of radar. It does not attempt to reteach the fundamentals of radar. However, radar specifically designed for weather surveillance, its background and presentation will be presented and compared with ATC radars.

This reference manual is designed to provide specialists with:

(1) Methods of determining weather location and intensity presented on ATC radars.

(2) An understanding of weather radar reports (RAREPs) and their use.

(3) An understanding of the basic functions of radar types.

To achieve this purpose the manual contains information concerning:

(1) The characteristics of frontal systems and how to identify them.

(2) How controllers can determine weather intensities by manipulation of gain controls. Caution. Exercise care when using this procedure. The gain controls should not be manipulated to the point that target identification is lost.

(3) The severe storm detecting ability of weather surveillance radar and air traffic control radar.

A list of references is included in the appendix for controllers wishing to delve deeper into the study of weather surveillance radar.

ATC RADAR FOR WEATHER OBSERVATION

THE DETECTION OF SEVERE WEATHER BY RADAR

It is not difficult to understand how radar detects aircraft. As long as the aircraft size exceeds the operating wave length of the radar we can expect a reflection of radar energy. However, when the target is small in relation to the wave length, the problem of detection is more complex. This is the case when radar attempts to detect a raindrop or group of raindrops.

Since the mathematical equations for determining how radar detects precipitation are relatively complex, this discussion will be in general terms. We know that the radar signal reflected by water drops and ice particles are displayed on the radar scope. The size and number of drops as well as the distance of the drops from the antenna affects the strength of the echo.

Water particles return almost five times as much signal as ice particles of the same size. Hence, rain is more easily detected than snow but, occasionally large, wet snowflakes will give a strong return. Hailstones usually have a thin film of water on their surface and, consequently reflect as water particles of the same size. Because hailstones usually are larger than raindrops, thunderstorms with hail generally return stronger signals than those with rain.

"The strength of a signal reflected by precipitation is related to the number and size of water drops. Drop size has more influence on signal strength than the number of drops. Dry hail and snow return a much weaker signal than water drops of comparable size, but when covered with films of water, they reflect as water drops. Any storm sufficiently intense to produce hail will return a strong echo. However, hail below the freezing strata level produces the strongest weather echoes because of the large water-covered surfaces. Hail is one of the worst hazards of thunderstorms and generally very intense echoes are associated with thunderstorms. It is important to remember that the more intense the echo, the more severe the storm."

WEATHER RADAR NETWORK

The weather radar network is made up of selected ARTCCs, military, and Weather Service Offices throughout the contiguous U.S. At an ARTCC the weather report is a composite of the various sites that make up the facility's area of surveillance. At each selected military site the radar in use is a CPS-9 or other type. The Navy uses the WSR-57 under a different designator. The principle set of the Weather Service is the WSR-57 supplemented by the WSR-1 and WSR-3.

The most effective storm detection radar in use today is the Weather Service's WSR-57. This radar has a range of 250 nautical miles and is strategically placed for surveillance of most of the contiguous U.S. east of the Rocky Mountains. It is this area where severe storms are most frequent. For a detailed overview of the weather radar network in the contiguous U.S. see Figure 1.

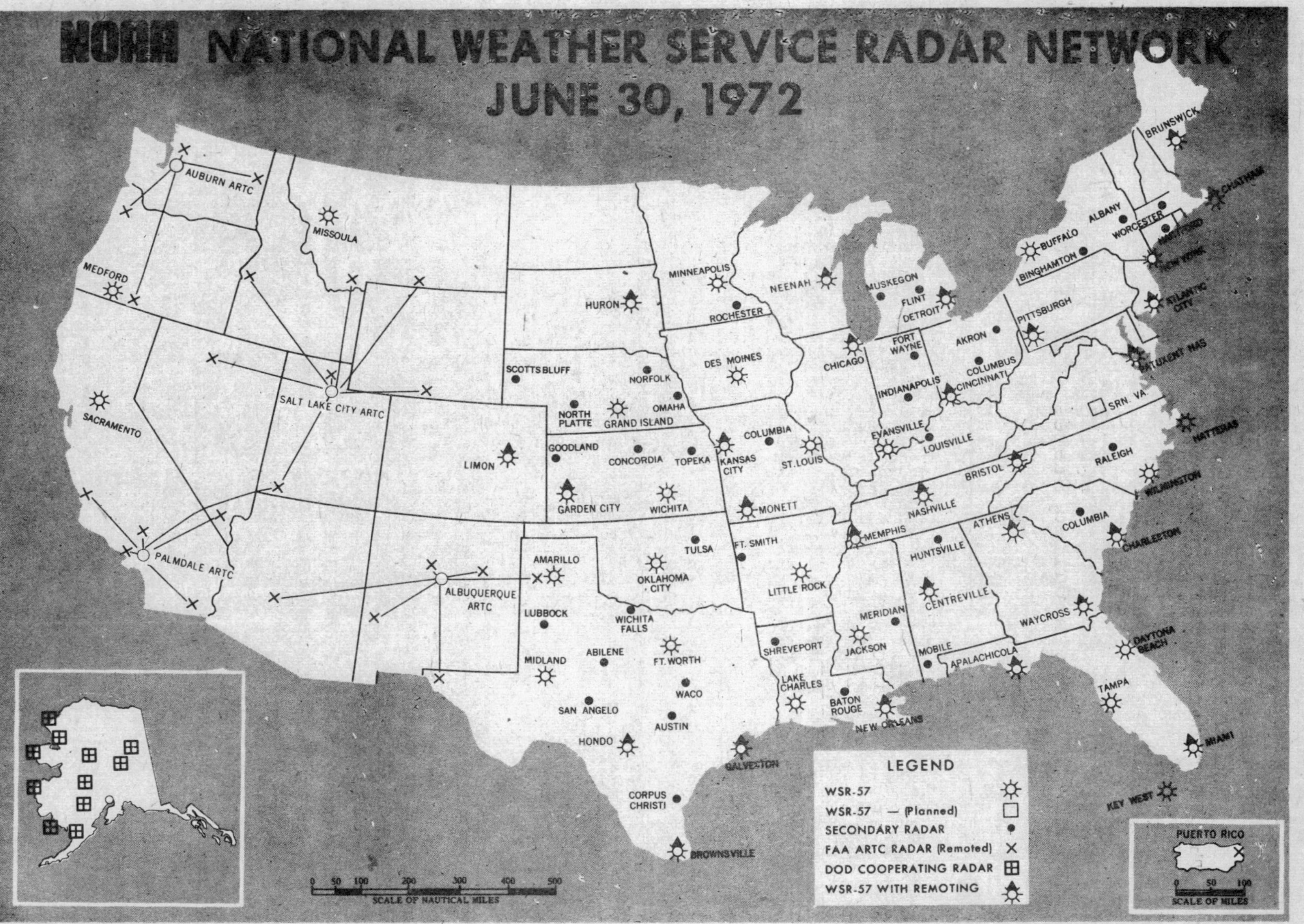

Figure 1. Weather radar stations in the contiguous U.S.

The Weather Service codes radar reports and distributes them via Service A. The Weather Service's Radar Analysis and Development Unit has divided the contiguous U.S. into five geographical areas. The SB radar summary which air traffic facilities receive reflects the grouping of radar echoes within these areas. When extensive radar echoes overlap in two adjacent areas, those two areas are grouped into one large appropriate area. For example, echoes in the northeast and southeast areas would be grouped under the Eastern United States (ERN US) heading.

WEATHER SYSTEMS

Complete precipitation fields associated with massive weather systems are usually too large to be detected and displayed by a single radar. Experience has shown, however, that we can infer much about the weather system from the radar display. The different types of weather systems have characteristic radar "signatures" and by observing the variation in these signatures with time and distance as shown by radar, we can make valid conclusions about their size, intensity, and movement. By continual scanning of a large area, the observer quickly detects changes in precipitation intensity, coverage, and movement that might take several hours to detect from a nonradar observation network.

TYPES OF STORMS

Winter Cyclones

Cyclonic storms are those rotating about a moving center of low atmospheric pressure. In the northern and central parts of the U.S., these storms often exhibit a large, almost solid, mass of stratiform echo that shows some vertical development within about 150 miles of the low pressure center. In some cases the echo mass breaks into showers along the cold front and cuts off rather abruptly in the cold air mass. The high-level cirrostratus and snow virga often seen far out ahead of an advancing winter cyclone are frequently detected by radar, and elevated echoes may be first to appear on the scope as a winter storm approaches. Storms over southern states seldom exhibit the "standard" winter cyclone pattern. Figures 2 through 4 are PPI presentations rather typical of early phases of the approach of a winter cyclone.

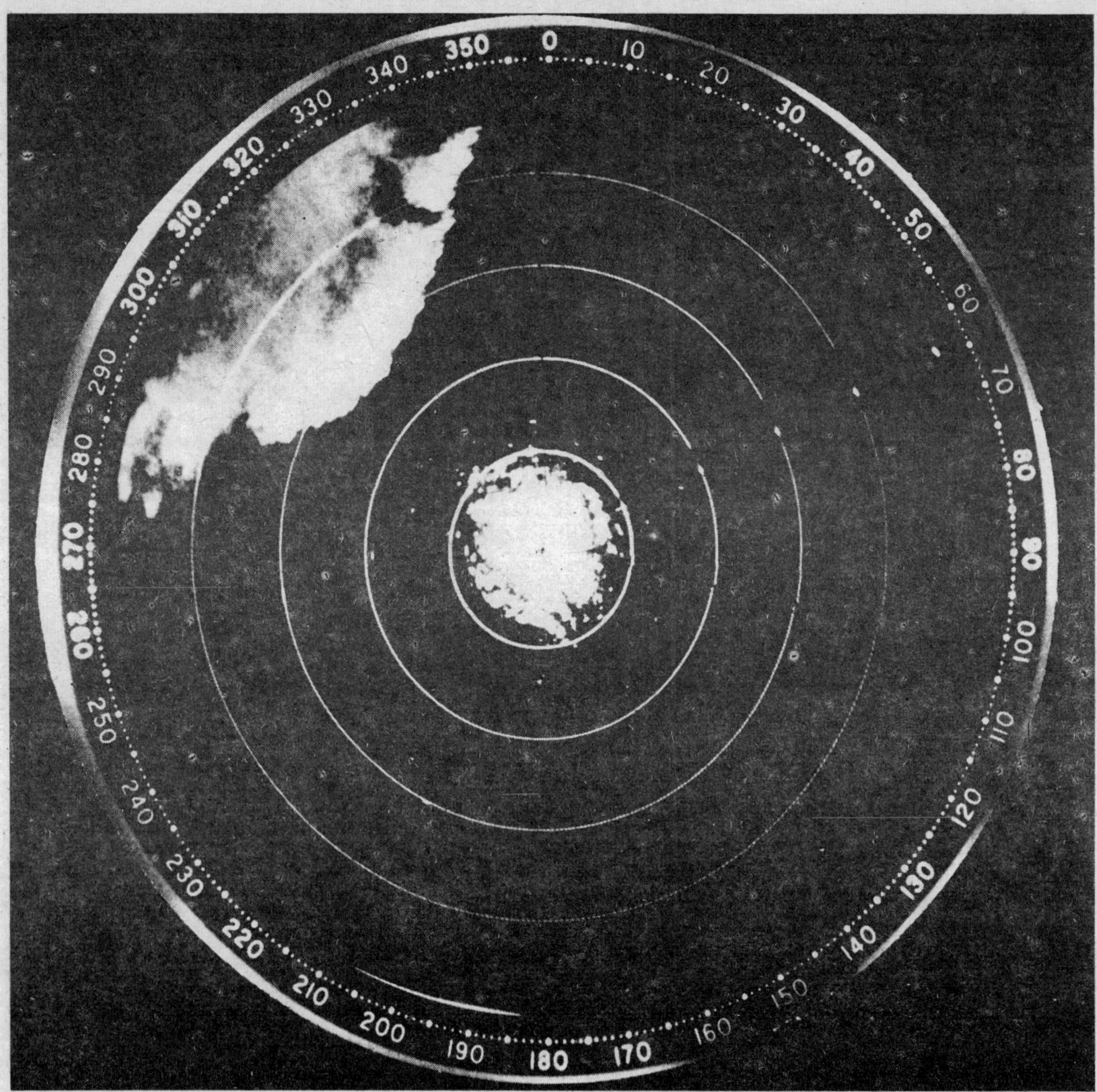

Figure 2. Typical PPI appearance of echoes from convective type rainfall. Note the irregular but generally sharply defined edges of the precipitation. Range marks are 20 NM.

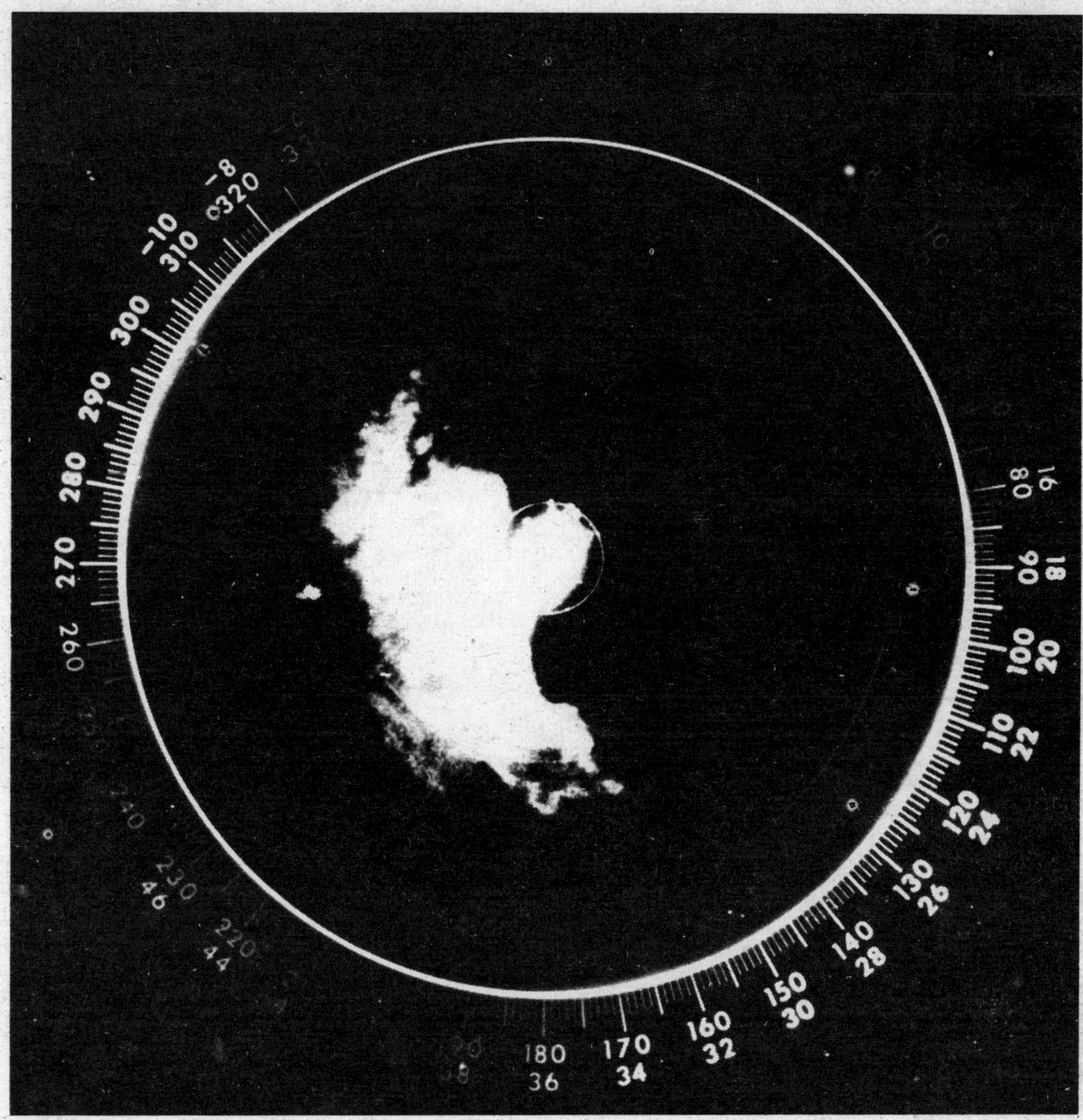

Figure 3. Typical PPI appearance of echoes from stratiform type rainfall. Note the maximum range of precipitation detection is roughly a semicircle. This may indicate that the area of rainfall is low level and extends to greater aerial coverage than shown.

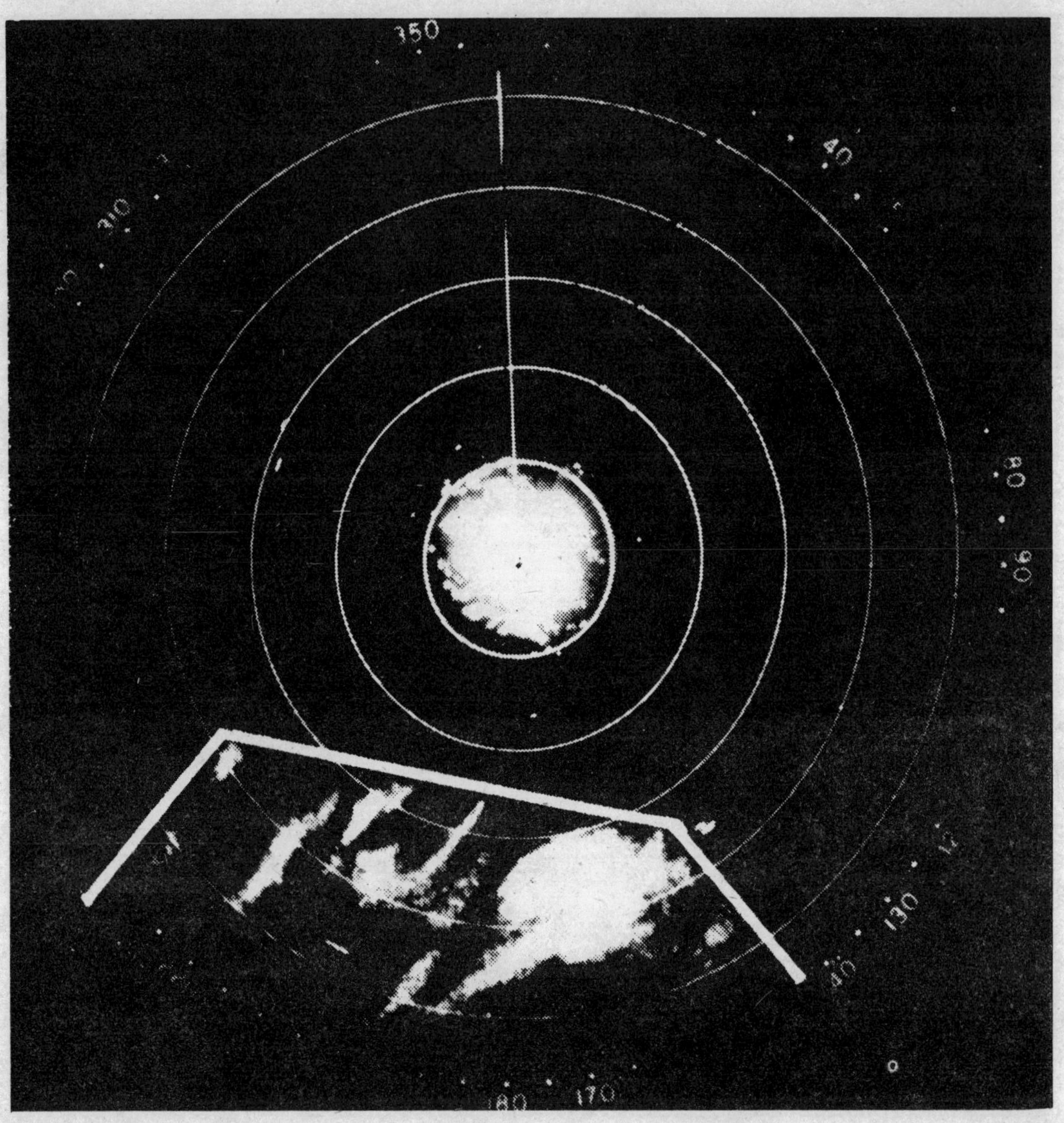

Figure 4. Typical PPI appearance of echoes from snow. Since reflectivity of snow is low, it may not be detected at great ranges. The area of falling snow is probably larger than shown on the scope. Range marks are 20 NM.

SUMMER CYCLONES

The echoes associated with the summer storms are normally convective and cellular in nature. Since the cyclonic system is usually far too large to be viewed by a single radar, any single radar will generally display a field of scattered to broken echoes with a random, or at least difficult to recognize, pattern. Exceptions will be echo lines associated with fronts and squall lines and large, fairly solid, echo areas close to the center of northern sides of well-organized summer cyclone systems. Movement of echoes associated with summer cyclones is usually relatively easy to measure because of their cellular nature, but care should be used in using this cell movement to infer cyclone motion. Very often a single radar cannot see enough of the echo field to identify field motion.

HURRICANES

Hurricanes are the most spectacular of the large scale echo patterns. A well-developed storm is recognizable even when the center of the storm is a great distance from the radar and, when the center gets close enough that the wall cloud is detected, the hurricane is usually unmistakable (Figure 5). Hurricanes are detected and tracked by satellites, and occasionally by ships and island reporting stations. When hurricane echoes first appear, they are not easily recognized as a hurricane. However, they usually can be associated with the storm because of its known existence and location. These outer bands often contain squalls of greater severity than normally associated with tropical thunderstorms. By international agreement, tropical cyclones have been classified:

(1) Tropical depression - winds up to 34 knots.
(2) Tropical storm - winds of 35 to 64 knots.
(3) Hurricane or typhoon - winds of 65 knots or higher.

The eye of a well-developed hurricane is a very important feature, and its movement occasionally can be tracked by radar. It is necessary to be cautious in attempting to predict motion from such observations, since experience has shown that the eye does not advance at a steady pace, but rather has variations in both speed and direction. Eye paths have been noted to zigzag, loop, stall, and even appear discontinuous, with the eye apparently collapsing and reforming at another location. The resultant track has short term variations about the mean track of the hurricane, and these variations could be very misleading if used to estimate the position of the storm. The position and movement of a hurricane center, as stated by hurricane advisories and bulletins, result from the analysis of data from several sources and represent the best information available.

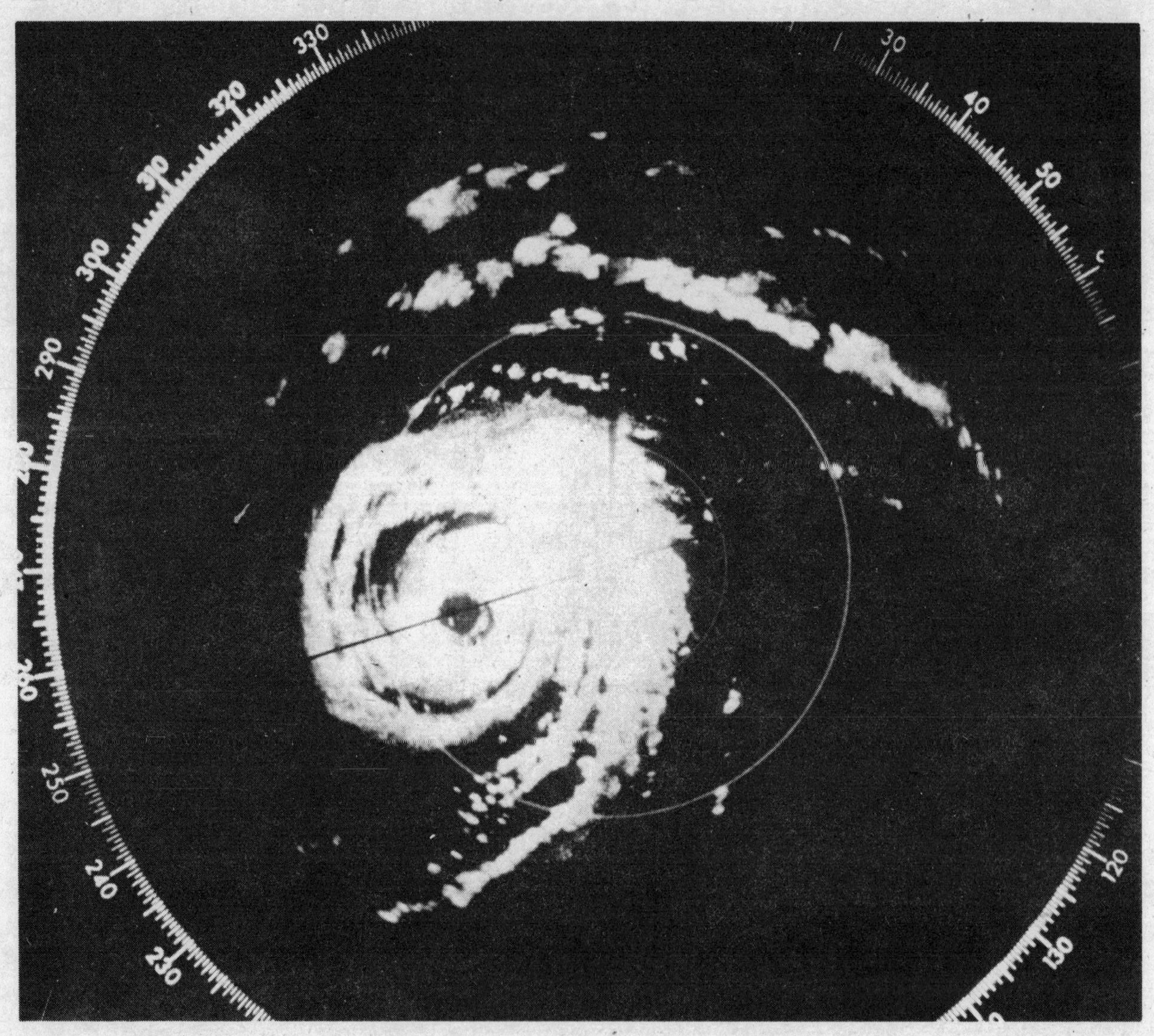

Figure 5. Typical hurricane echo.

Fronts

Precipitation associated with a front does not always indicate the position of the front as placed on weather maps, nor does it follow any set pattern. The wide-spread overrunning often occurring with a warm front produces a large smooth echo resembling somewhat the approach of a winter cyclone. As the front approaches, the base of echoes initially at high level gradually reaches the ground. Radar is particularly useful in locating the thunderstorms occasionally embedded in warm front weather. As radar controllers, we should be alert to cores of high reflectivity in otherwise large formless echoes.

The echoes associated with cold frontal showers and thunderstorms are cellular in nature, and not always arranged in a line along the front. Often when a line forms, it will not coincide with the surface position of the front, but the motion of any such line can often be associated with motion of the front. Radar is particularly useful in following the movement of precipitation associated with a cold front, and in quickly detecting changes in precipitation patterns. The early detection of developing thunderstorms along a front, or developing squall lines out ahead of the front, can add important minutes or even hours to a warning service.

Squall Lines

A squall line consists of a line of convective cells that can on occasion produce squalls, hail, or tornadoes. Squall lines range in length from less than 100 miles to several hundred miles and in width from less than five miles to about 50 miles. The large scale motion of a squall line is fairly conservative. However, close inspection of echoes usually will show that internal movement is irregular because of growth and decay of individual cells in the line. Sometimes the formation of new cells is dramatic, with almost simultaneous appearance of many cells in a completely new line near the old one. Although there may be great variation in the appearance, intensity, and even position of a squall line, tracking a line by radar over several hours shows that the activity remains in an instability zone that has a fairly constant size and motion. Squall lines exist because of unusual instability, and therefore the chance of the occurrence of severe weather increases tremendously in a squall line complex. Individual cells of high reflectivity or with unusual height, motion, or longevity should be considered probable generators of hazardous conditions. Aircraft are particularly vulnerable to the extreme instability in and near squall lines. You, as a radar controller, should plan vectors to avoid all parts of a line giving the aircraft a wide margin of safety.

When a squall line is on the scope it should be monitored continuously for indications of severe weather. A rather large scale development on a squall line that sometimes indicates severe weather is a wave, it resembles the early stages of a wave along a frontal surface. This is called Line Echo Wave Pattern (LEWP) and is reported in the RAREP.

Severe Local Storms

Because FAA radar views all points in its area of surveillance, it can be adjusted to provide information on storms that might otherwise be easily missed and it can provide information on size, shape, and changes in storms, that can seldom be determined from the visual observation network.

By observing a radar scope we can usually determine not only the places where precipitation is occurring at any given time, but also the movement and intensity of the precipitation and the characteristics of the weather system. One important factor in interpreting echo movement is continual monitoring. Observing an instantaneous display is much like viewing one frame of a movie film. You may be able to identify the characters, provided their faces are not turned from the camera, but you find it difficult to determine its movement or action.

Weather Service radar uses circuits designed to determine echo intensity. Since ATC radar presently is not equipped with these circuits, the controller must determine intensity by step gain reduction. He can determine to some extent the most intense echoes by using circular polarization. When CP is engaged, remaining echoes generally are the most intense. As radar controllers we must get echo heights from PIREPs, RAREPs or by contacting the radar meteorologist. However, we can determine many characteristics of the echo pattern directly from the control scope. Whenever areas of suspected thunderstorms appear on the scope, we should become immediately acquainted with the echoes in the above described manner so that any changes are quickly noted. In general, the more intense the storm as measured by reflectivity, the greater the chance of severe weather. Local severe storms sometimes present "signatures" by which they can be identified. It should be well understood that although certain echo patterns have been identified in connection with severe weather, they are by no means infallible indicators.

Local severe storms have been noted in every season of the year, with single thunderstorms as well as with squall lines, and with nearly stationary thunderstorms as well as with rapidly moving ones. However, storms associated with intense squall lines or with a line echo wave pattern, or having extreme height or rapid speed, are particularly suspect. Rapidly moving thunderstorms are usually associated with sharp wind shifts and relatively high gusts at the surface; echoes with high reflectivity usually contain heavy rain and possible hail. Severe weather has been observed on several occasions near the junction of two thunderstorms. This junction is most common when one or both of the storms move quite rapidly. When two storms approach one another, the wind shear that results can be severe due not only to the difference in their movements, but due to the differing wind components in and near each storm. Time-lapse film indicates that within many intense thunderstorms, circulation rotates about a vertical axis.

TORNADOES

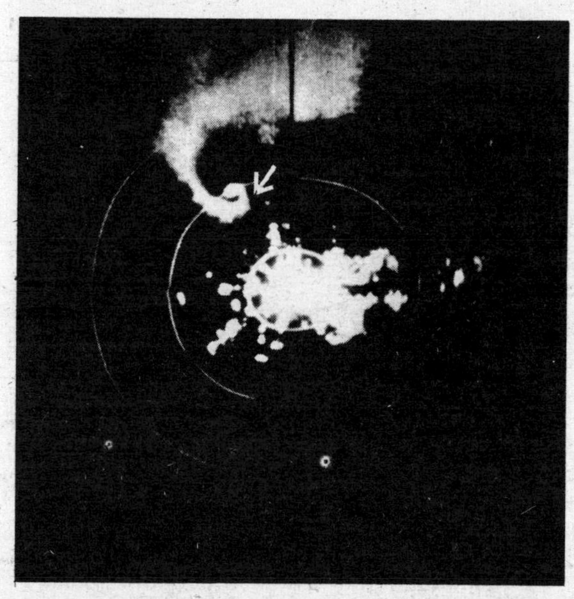

Figure 6.

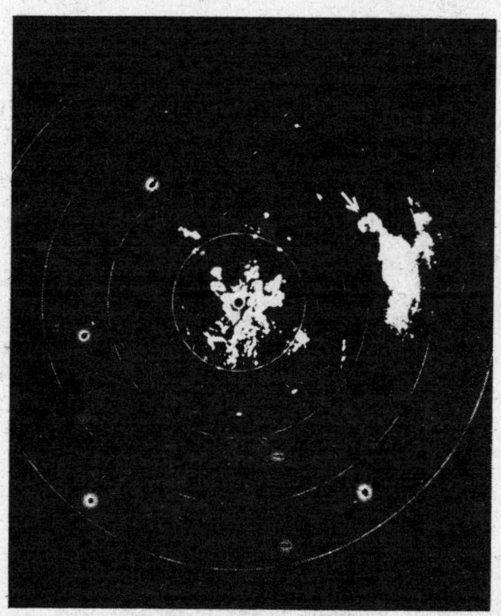

Figure 6A.

Tornadoes are often associated with storms of high reflectivity, and in some cases the tornado (Figure 6 and 6A) itself may be highly reflective. The associated hook that has been observed on the radar is found in the trailing half of the storm echo. Often, the hook is masked in the large echo displayed on radar. Due to the CP and MTI on the ARSR radar the weaker echo around the hook may not be detected and an echo of a hook extending from the main echo body is displayed. Hooks have been observed to swirl from the parent cloud. The circle ascribed by the main part of the hook is usually from 4 to 12 miles in diameter.

The surface position of the tornado is usually near the small end of the hook. Although hooks appear sometimes where there is no visual evidence of a tornado at the surface, their association with tornadoes is certainly strong enough to warrant immediate warnings when one is definitely identified on the scope. Always keep in mind that the absence of a hook echo does not preclude the presence of a tornado. The tornado hook echo has rarely been detected by radars with wide vertical beams, such as the ARSR series and can scarcely be distinguished at ranges much beyond 50 miles even with narrow beam radars. Hailstones are highly reflective and will generally produce an intense echo. This can appear as a hard core within a thunderstorm's echo, or may extend as one or more "fingers" protruding from the edge of a thunderstorm echo. These fingers may be evident at full gain. Thunderstorms that produce hail are particularly violent, with intense updrafts and tops that usually penetrate the tropopause.

As discussed previously, stratiform precipitation presents a featureless echo, usually relatively large, that changes intensity and shape rather slowly and is not associated with violent weather. One difficulty in dealing with large apparently stratiform echoes, is the possibility of overlooking embedded cells of high reflectivity that indicate heavy rainfall, and may indicate localized convective activity particularly dangerous to aircraft because it is unexpected and hidden. Embedded thunderstorms generally are less severe than cold frontal or squall line storms. Turbulence is seldom extreme, but icing can be quite heavy since strong updrafts can suspend huge quantities of supercooled water.

CONVECTIVE AND STRATIFORM PRECIPITATION ECHOES

Convective storms are not clearly separated into classes of severity but form a continuum from light showers to intense thunderstorms which produce hail and tornadoes. For convenience, however, we have by arbitrary choice of boundaries separated them into classes for aviation use. Classes are:

(1) Shower - precipation from cumuliform clouds without lightning and thunder.

(2) Thunderstorm - precipitation from cumulonimbus clouds with lightning and thunder, surface gusts less than 50 knots, turbulence no greater than severe, and hail (if any) less than 3/4 inch in diameter.

(3) Severe Thunderstorm - thunderstorm with extreme turbulence, surface gusts 50 knots or greater, and/or hail 3/4 inch or more in diameter.

Radar can help in two ways, the appearance of certain storm echo features can serve to focus the attention of the controller to a particular area, at a particular time, in which the thunderstorms of greater than ordinary intensity are probably taking place. This may signify nothing more than a reasonable expectation of small hail or moderate wind gusts. On the other hand, it may provide a warning of the impending development of a severe thunderstorm in the suspect echo or in one of its neighbors, which will attain maturity during the following hour or two. As radar controllers using radar for meteorology purposes we should recognize the possibility for development of severe storms when we observe any of the following conditions:

(1) Echoes are in a line with a wave pattern.

(2) Echoes are noticeably converging.

(3) Echo speeds exceed 30 knots.

(4) Echo edges are sharply indented or scallop-shaped.

SUMMARY

As radar controllers, we should learn how to distinguish between echoes from convective and stratiform precipitation. With convective precipitation the echoes are cellular and display a tendency to form into linear groups. Convective echo intensities were qualitatively observed to be greater, in general, than the intensities of stratiform echoes, as indicated by echo brightness on the radar indicator.

CLASSIFICATION OF ECHOES

Contractions are used in radar summaries received in Air Traffic facilities on Service A to indicate the echo systems being reported. The following table lists the contractions used for each echo system together with its definition.

Characteristics of Echoes

Echo System	Definition	Contraction
Isolated echo	Independent convective echo	CELL
Widely scattered area	Related or similar echoes covering less than 1/10 of the reported area	AREA WDLY ⦶
Scattered area	Related or similar echoes covering 1/10 to 5/10 of the reported area	AREA ⦶
Broken area	Related or similar echoes in a pattern that covers 6/10 or more of the reported area but contains breaks or corridors	AREA ⦷
Solid area	Contiguous echoes covering, usually, more than 9/10 of the reported area	AREA ⊕
Line of widely scattered echoes	Related echoes in an extended pattern covering less than 1/10 of the reported line	LN WDLY ⦶
Line of scattered echoes	Related echoes in an extended pattern covering 1/10 to 5/10 of the reported line	LN ⦶
Broken line of echoes	Related echoes in an extended pattern that covers 6/10 or more of the reported line but contains breaks or corridors	LN ⦷
Solid line of echoes	Contiguous echoes in an extended pattern covering, usually, more than 9/10 of the reported line	LN ⊕
Spiral band area (broken or scattered)	Echoes associated with tropical storms, hurricanes, or typhoons and systematically arranged in curved lines. This grouping may include a wall cloud	SPRL BAND AREA (⦷ or ⦶)
Stratified elevated echo	Precipitation aloft	LYR (O, ⦷, OR ⊕)

Echo System	Definition	Contraction
Fine line	Narrow nonprecipitation echo pattern associated with a meteorological discontinuity such as the cold air outflow in advance of a squall line or the leading edge of a sea breeze	FINE LN

An area may have breaks and still be classified as "solid" if coverage is more than nine-tenths. A line will be classified as "solid" if echoes are contiguous throughout the line even if the rectangle describing the line is not entirely covered. The terms describing tenths coverage for echoes are the same as those used to describe tenths cloud cover in Service A weather reports, except "solid" is used in lieu of "overcast."

Echoes are classified also by precipitation type, intensity, and tendency. Classification as to type is strictly the responsibility of the radar meteorologist. Usually echoes are described as "light rain," "thunderstorms with very heavy rain showers," or some other word description.

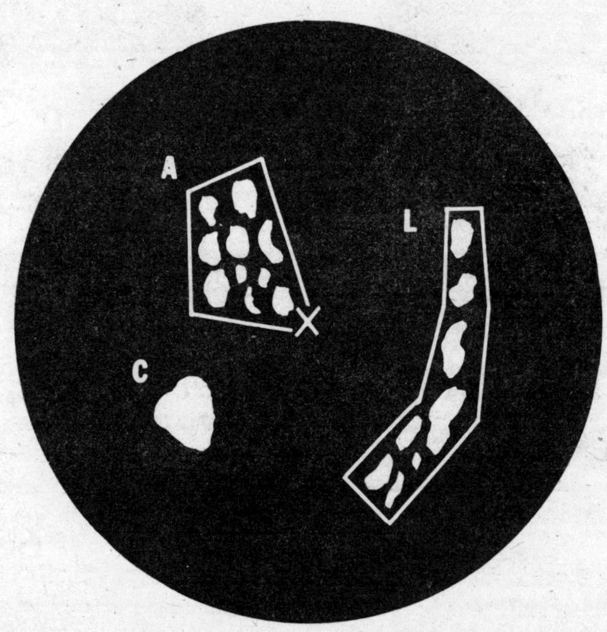

Figure 7. Photo showing three configurations: A cell (C), an area (A) and a line (L).

If echoes are grouped as shown in Figure 7, their character readily can be identified. Three configurations used in describing character are a cell, an area, and a line. A cell, labeled C, is a single echo isolated from other echoes or clearly distinguishable from surrounding echoes. An area, labeled A, is a group of similar echoes which appear to be associated. A line, labeled L, is any group which is more or less in a line, either straight, curved, or irregular. To be classified as a line, the line must be at least 20 miles long and must be at least five times as long as it is wide.

In Figure 8, the scope photograph shows two types of precipitation echoes. At the top of the scope note that the echo edges are sharp and very bright. At the bottom of the scope are the type most frequently associated with snow or light rain. Note that the edges are fuzzy and echoes are not as bright as the shower and thunderstorm echoes.

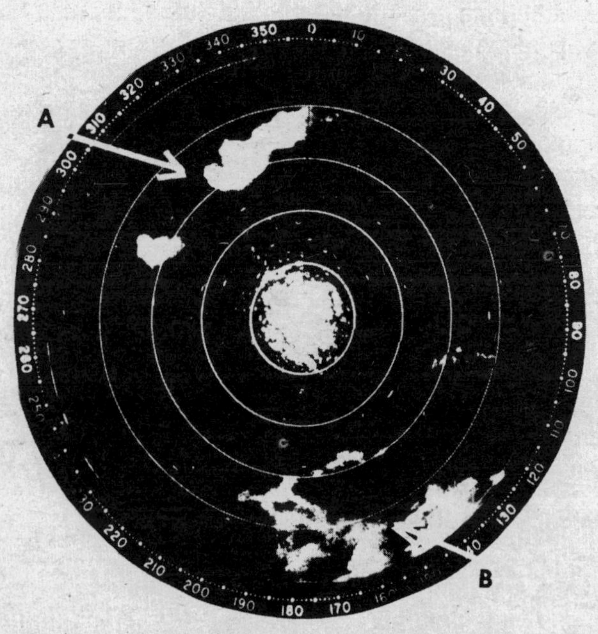

Figure 8. Scope photograph showing two types of precipitation echoes: (A) showers and (B) continuous.

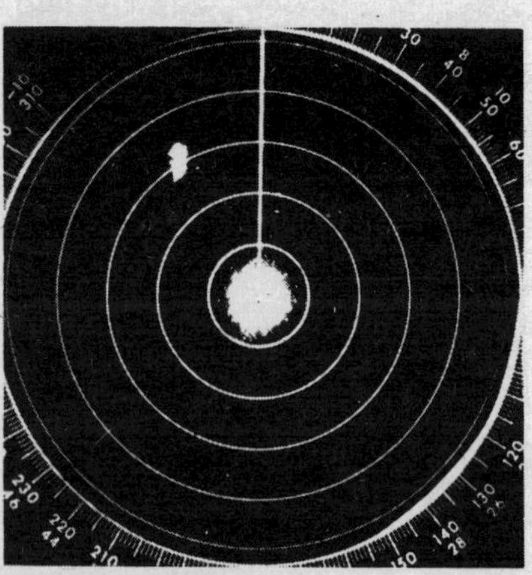

Figure 9. Scope photograph of isolated cell.

In Figure 8, you could, by step reduction of gain, determine which of the cells is the most intense. At the first step of reduction, the echo represented by "B" disappears. When further reduction of the gain is made, just an outline of the two echoes at "A" remains with an isolated cell within the outline showing at 328°, as represented in Figure 9. When you check the area weather reports, the only significant weather reported in the area of surveillance is a cell of heavy rain showers centered at 328° 60 miles, and 12 miles in diameter. This report coincides with the echo displayed. On the basis of this display and report, you should permit deviation by radar equipped aircraft and suggest vectors for other aircraft around this area. You are now current on the weather in your area of surveillance. By keeping a close check on the echoes of the two figures, you remain current.

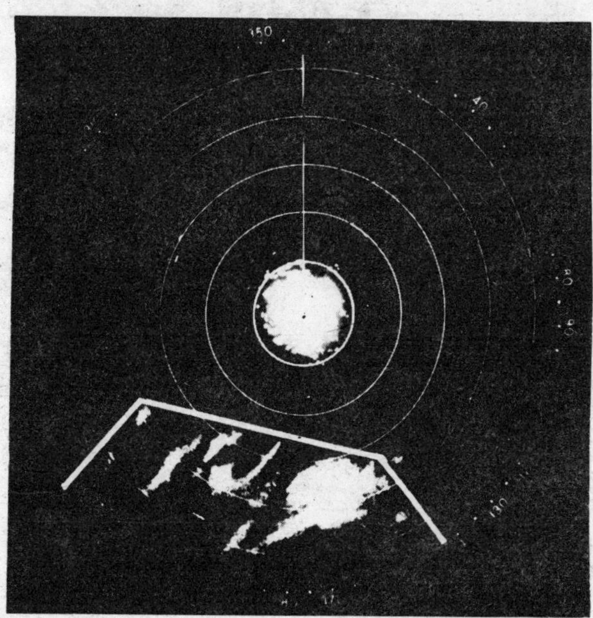

Figure 10. Scope photograph of broken area of echoes from precipitation falling from stratiform clouds. (NSSL photo)

Broken Area

The scope photograph, Figure 10, shows an area of broken echoes from precipitation falling from stratiform clouds. Note that more than half of the area is covered. More than likely you, as the radar controller, will identify these as continuous precipitation of some type. With such a scope pattern it is important that you solicit PIREP's and refer to teletypewriter weather reports to determine visibility and the extent of cloud cover. IFR flights most likely could proceed through this area of echoes, but do not jump to conclusions. Check your area forecasts and inflight weather advisories. Icing and/or turbulence could be a problem. This storm was reported as heavy snow 60 to 100 miles south of Norman, Oklahoma, and photographed from the NSSL WSR-57.

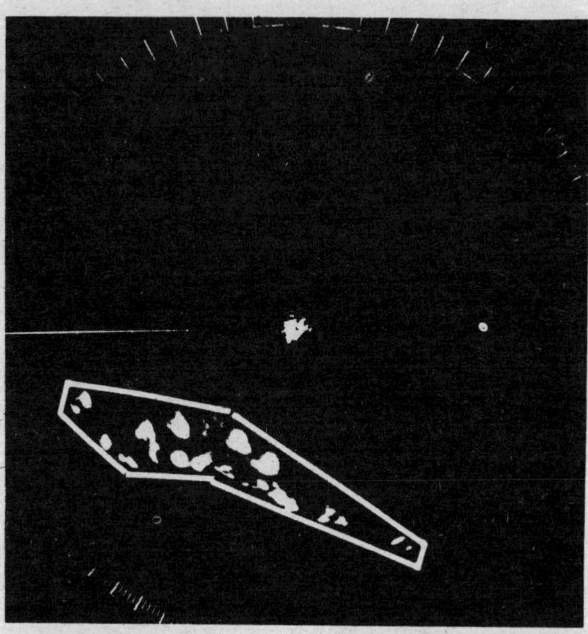

Figure 11. Scope photograph of a scattered line of echoes from precipitation out of convective clouds.

Scattered Line

Figure 11 is a scope photograph of a line of scattered echoes from precipitation out of convective clouds. Note that less than half the area is covered. These echoes usually are associated with turbulence. This is especially true when they form a line such as this. Again, information from teletypewriter weather reports helps to determine the local severity of associated weather. From a display such as this, you would be wise to suggest to the VFR flight that it avoid this area unless it can clear all cells by at least 20 miles; in other words, the gap between echoes is at least 40 miles wide. Advice to an IFR flight would depend on the indicated severity in current forecasts, inflight weather advisories, RAREPs, and observed changes of echo intensity on the control scope. Severe to extreme turbulence and hail have been encountered as far as 20 miles from the edge of very strong echoes.

You should issue pertinent information on radar observed weather, permit weather deviations to aircraft equipped with weather radar, and suggest radar navigational assistance to aircraft without weather radar as your workload permits. Weather information should be issued by stating its azimuth and distance from the aircraft (in terms of the 12-hour clock) or a fix. Suggest a vector or alternative route to avoid such areas. (Unless actual reports are received, do not use the word "turbulence" in describing a condition with weather echoes.) A direct measuring system has not been devised capable of identifying turbulence or its intensity. The measurement of turbulence is subjective in nature, dependent upon observer judgment and experience.

Figure 12. Scope photograph of scattered area of showers or thunderstorm echoes.

Scattered Area

Figure 12 shows an area of scattered showers or thunderstorm echoes. Again you can obtain local conditions from the teletypewriter reports. Since the turbulence is associated with convective areas, you should advise the aircraft affected of the weather formation. If workload permits or the pilot requests, vector the aircraft clear of the area.

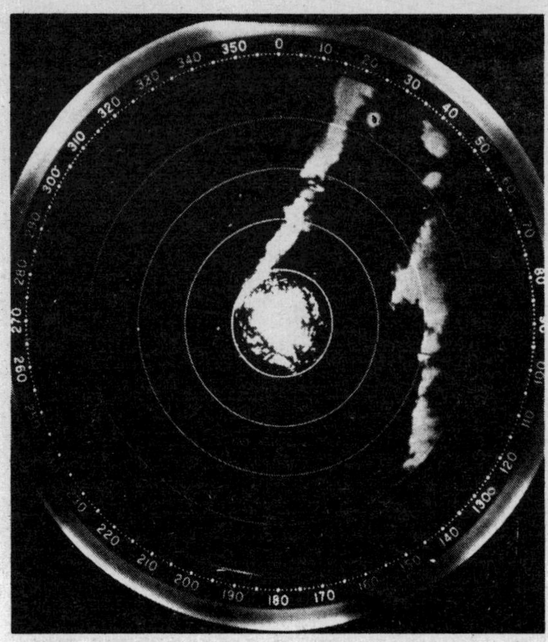

Figure 13. Scope photograph of two solid lines of echoes. The line to the west is echoes from an active cold front while the one to the east is echoes from a squall line. (NSSL photo)

Solid Line

The solid line of echoes usually is the type associated with the most severe flying weather. Severe squall lines and very active cold fronts produce this kind of echo. Figure 13 shows two lines. The one to the east is a squall line preceding a cold front marked by the line to the west. You can see that both lines are quite extensive. Northern extremities of the lines appear to be broken but central and southern portions would be classified as solid. Of course, a solid line does not always mean severe weather. Consult forecasts carefully. Whenever severe weather occurs with a solid line of echoes, no pilot should attempt to fly through it.

SUMMARY

Generally, echo systems are classified into three divisions - cells, lines and areas. A cell is a single echo. Lines and areas are further defined by the amount of cloud cover within the reported geographic area.

AIR TRAFFIC SPECIALIST WEATHER OBSERVATIONS AND REPORTING

The ultimate in operation is to have a radar meteorologist on duty at all facilities to determine weather intensity and location, and to disseminate the weather data. The radar meteorologist would relay pertinent weather information to those facilities (not equipped with remoted radar) within the area of surveillance. However, at present the cost prohibits this desired goal. The alternative is--become familiar with weather conditions in your area prior to assuming control duties as stated in the Air Traffic Control Handbooks. In addition, determine if your radar system is operating on linear or circular polarization. (Solicit and check RAREPs, outline in grease pencil significant echoes on your display, and orient this information to other pertinent positions.) When you are observing weather echoes you should note:

(1) Direction of movement

(2) Speed

(3) If masses are joining

(4) If new formations are observed

(5) Location of new formations

(6) Dissipating areas

(7) When an area is clear

STEP REDUCTION OF VIDEO GAIN CONTROL

Caution. Exercise care when using this procedure. The gain controls should not be manipulated to the point that target identification is lost.

We have observed on our bright display equipment that the intensity of an echo varies, that is, the outer edge of the echo is the least intense and the intensity normally increases toward the center of the target. The least intense echo that can be detected and displayed is called the threshold of detection. If we draw a line around this threshold of detection we have isolated an area of echo power that has the same value. This line is called an iso-echo contour.

By setting the video gain control at its maximum level and outlining, with grease pencil, the threshold of detection of weather echoes, we can establish an iso-echo contour of the weather system. To determine the most intense areas within the weather system hold the video gain on decrease for one revolution of the sweep (about 10 sec.) and again draw a line around the threshold to establish a second iso-echo contour. This process can be repeated until the gain control is decreased to the point where no signal is received. The most intense portion of the weather system normally will be that portion that will be received with the least amount of gain.

Ideally, the contouring of a weather system should be done with the radar on linear polarization and the MTI off. We know that the controller does not always have control of the polarization selection. However, MTI can be turned off, or the gate may be reduced for a short period until you have completed the contouring of the weather system. Keep in mind if your set is utilizing circular polarization, the "punch through" displayed is probably the moderate to severe portion of the weather and less intense areas surround this "punch through."

Once you have contoured the weather echoes on your position you should update this information about every 25 minutes noting the seven items listed under weather observations and reporting.

As previously stated, generally, the stronger the signal the more intense rainfall is and the higher that particular cell may be. Since the radar controller does not have height information he should secure pilot reports of the area in question.

Storm movement can be satisfactorily charted on FAA radar by contouring the echo at predetermined time intervals. Measure the distance of travel in the time elapsed and compute speed.

SUMMARY

"Do's" and "Don'ts" of scope interpretation:

"Do"

Familiarize yourself with the ground return patterns of your radar systems.

Always make certain that permanent echoes are in proper orientation to the NAVAID or feature.

Determine configuration (Cell, line or area) directly from your scope.

determine coverage (widely scattered, scattered, etc.) directly from your scope.

Use pilot reports to determine height and intensity wherever possible.

Determine past movements of echoes and group of echoes by observing the scope presentation.

Notify the associated radar meteorologist immediately if a hook shaped echo appears on your scope. Difference in radar site location may prohibit one radar from detecting a hook echo.

When tracking weather echoes on radar, use all available teletypewriter weather reports to assist you in arriving at a determination.

<u>"Don't"</u>

Do not misinterpret ground clutter as precipitation echoes.

Do not determine type of precipitation (rain, thunderstorms, etc.) without using all available reports.

Do not assume the echo pattern to be the entire cloud pattern; compare with sequence reports, weather depiction chart (if available), and forecasts.

Do not use past movements as forecast movement. Forecast movement can be obtained from forecasts (in Airmets, Sigmets, FAs, etc.).

Do not classify a hook echo as a tornado until cleared by a radar meteorologist if a tornado is reported by a pilot.

Do not reduce gain controls to the point that target identification is lost.

WEATHER SURVEILLANCE RADAR

During World War II radar operators soon discovered that radar could "see" water drops nearly as well as ground and airborne targets. Precipitation echoes interfered with the intended use of the radar and, generally, operators regarded them as "clutter." Meteorologists were quick to use this "clutter" as a means of weather detection.

After the war some radars were modified to improve weather detection capability. Some early modifications were the Weather Surveillance Radar One (WSR-1) and the Weather Surveillance Radar Three (WSR-3). In 1947 the Weather Service began installation of these converted military radars. The primary installation areas were those sections of the nation most frequently subjected to tornado activity. The WSR-1 and the WSR-3 were used during the interim period (1949-1959) until the WSR-57 became available. The WSR-57 was specifically designed for weather detection and has become the workhorse of the

National Weather Service since its adoption in 1959. Weather Service radars are being systematically placed so that their respective areas of observational coverage will interlock. The goal, of course, is to have the entire nation under weather radar surveillance. Ultimately, radar weather information could be digitized and interfaced directly on the plan view display of the controller.

Echo patterns presented on a radar scope depend not only on characteristics of the targets, but also on the capabilities and characteristics of the radar.

Weather radar is used primarily for detecting and tracking severe storms such as thunderstorms, tornadoes, and hurricanes. Therefore, Weather Service and military weather radar equipment is designed with a wave length that gives the best return signal from water droplets and other precipitation particles. As a comparison, air traffic control radar employs a wave length that minimizes the echoes from small water drops.

The WSR-57 has two circuits that are not included in FAA Radar:

(1) Contouring--this circuit employs a process showing the intensity steps of an echo.

(2) Attenuation--with predetermined steps, cuts the return echo so that only the more intense portion of the return is displayed.

In addition to these circuits the radar meteorologist has the capability of stopping the antenna at any desired azimuth, reversing, and/or changing the tilt of the antenna.

Following is a list of the general types of radars used by the FAA and the Weather Service together with a general indication of their operating characteristics and range.

Type	Operating Frequency Band	Operating Wave Length	Maximum Range
ASR	3000 MHz	10 cm	60 NM
ARSR	1300 MHz	23 cm	200 NM
PAR	10,000 MHz	3 cm	10 NM
ASDE	24,000 MHz	1.25 cm	3 NM
WSR-57	2700-2900 MHz	10.35-11.1 cm	250 NM
WSR-1	2840 MHz	10.5 cm	150 NM
WSR-3	2840 MHz	10.5 cm	180 NM

This list indicates that the FAA has designed their radar systems in such a manner that the radar type with the longest range requirements operates in the lower frequency or longer wavelength band. One of the factors influencing this decision was to minimize precipitation targets.

COMPARISON BETWEEN THE ASR, ARSR & THE WSR-57

Until 1964 the potential of the ARSR as a weather observing tool was unknown. During that year the national Severe Storms Laboratory (NSSL) located in Norman, Oklahoma, made a study comparing the ASR-4, the ARSR-1D, and the Weather Service's WSR-57.

The conclusions of this study indicate that the weather detection capabilities of the ARSR and WSR-57 are very similar to a range of 150 NM providing the anti-clutter (C.P. and MTI) circuits of the ARSR are not used. This is remarkable considering the ARSR was specifically designed for air traffic control. The operation of the ARSR in the L-band normally would make it less sensitive to weather than the S-band WSR-57. However, the very high power output of the ARSR series overcomes this deficiency and makes the ARSR series a potentially good weather detector for the purpose of air traffic control.

Probing details of storm formations with the ARSR is less reliable than with the WSR-57. This is due to the WSR-57's pencil beam radiation pattern compared to the larger fan shaped pattern of the ARSR series. MTI and CP circuitry on the ARSR decrease its sensitivity to weather echoes considerably. The suppression of weather targets in relation to aircraft targets when utilizing anti-clutter circuits is drastic. Circular polarization suppresses weather targets about 50 percent and MTI suppresses weather targets approximately 55 percent. When MTI and CP are used in combination weather targets are suppressed about 80 percent. Few useable weather returns are available when the anti-clutter circuits are used in combination. This is understandable as the anti-clutter circuits were specifically designed to reduce clutter from weather so that aircraft echoes could be received and observed.

The ASR-4 does not detect light precipitation and has marginal capability for the detection of moderate precipitations. It can detect strong thunderstorms. The ASR-4, therefore, is unsuited for monitoring the intensification of moderate storms.

Meteorologists measure radar echo intensities on a graduated scale of five intensities ranging from very heavy to very light. The ARSR series, without the use of anti-clutter circuitry, can be used for severe reports accurate to within one intensity class.

The five photographs in Figure 14 compare weather echoes as seen on the WSR-57 and the ARSR-1D. These photographs were made during the comparative study of weather detection capabilities of the two radars using the weather radar from the National Severe Storms Laboratory at Norman, Oklahoma, and the Control Radar from the FAA Academy located on Will Rogers World Airport, Oklahoma City, Oklahoma. The distance between the two points is approximately 12 miles. Range markers on both scopes are spaced 20 miles apart. Integrated contouring circuits were used on both radars. The contouring circuit is similar to the iso-echo except that these contouring circuits show five intensities of precipitation instead of the single hard cores as displayed with the iso-echo. The contouring circuit is not a feature of the operational control radar and, therefore, weather echoes shown here on the control radar present much greater weather detail than the controller will see on the job.

Photographs A and E are of the WSR-57 taken about 6 minutes apart. The other three are from the ARSR taken during the intervening 6 minutes with the scope in different configurations. Photograph B is normal video. Comparison with Photograph A shows that in this configuration the ARSR has excellent weather detection capabilities comparable to the WSR-57. Photograph C was taken with the amplitron off and CP disengaged. Here much of the detail of the weaker echoes is lost; however, the heavy precipitation still shows up essentially as in Photograph A. Photograph D was taken with both the amplitron and CP engaged. Here still more of the weather detail is lost. This is the configuation most frequently used in actual control operations except for the integrated contour. Without the contouring circuit, the presentation here would be little more than a smudge although the echoes shown would represent areas of heaviest precipitation. Especially significant is that the echo about 55 miles northeast of the scope center disappears completely.

SUMMARY

The ARSR compares favorably with the WSR-57 as a weather detection tool if the anti-clutter circuits of the ARSR are inhibited. When the anti-clutter circuitry (MTI and CP) is in use, weather returns are suppressed to the point that any "punch-through" received would be of questionable use. CP engaged and MTI inhibited presents the most intense areas of the storm system.

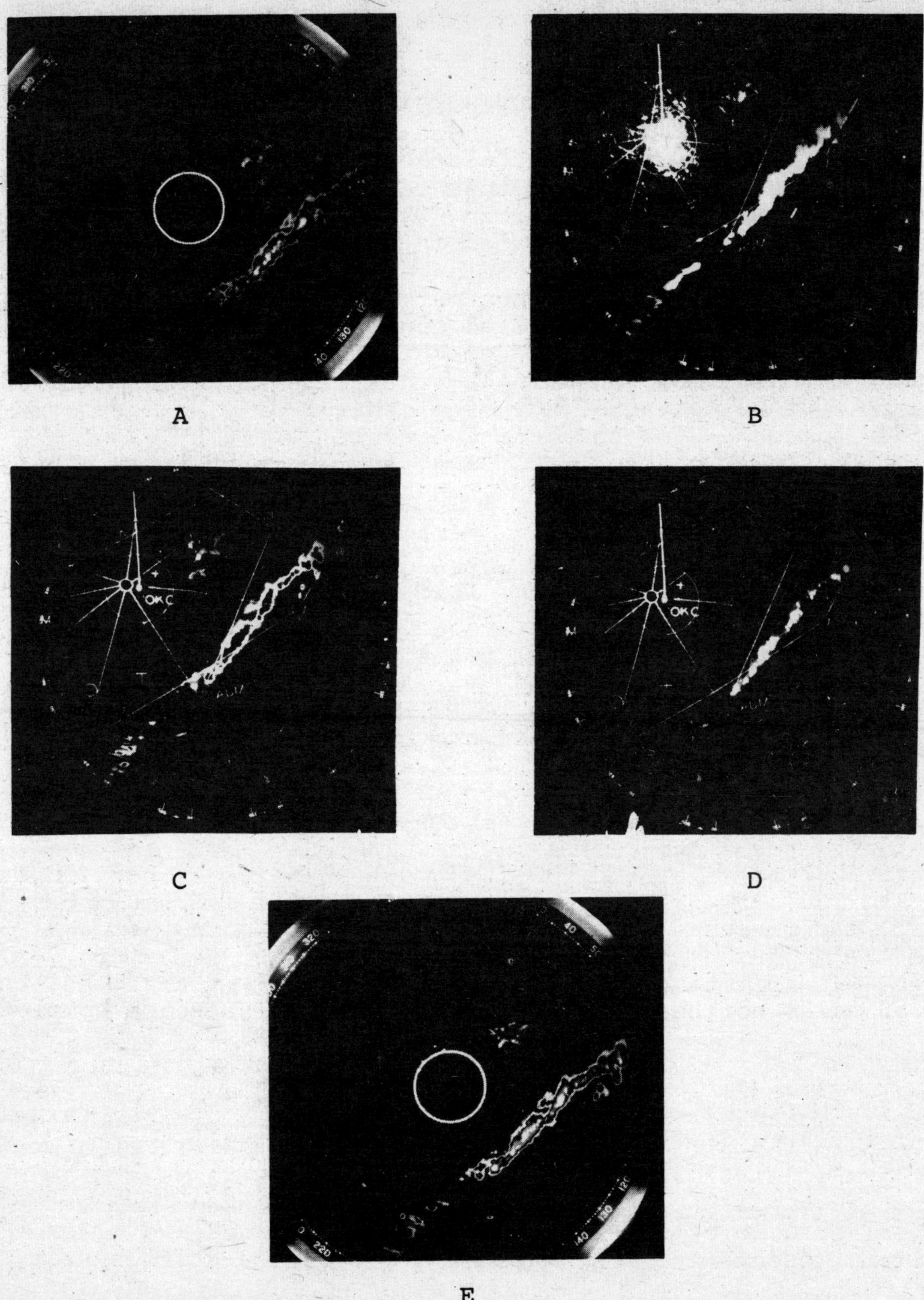

Figure 14. National Severe Storms Laboratory Photographs.

REFERENCES

1. Weather Detection by ARSR-1D, ASR-4, and WSR-57 Radars Technical Memorandum No. 1, NSSL, March 1965

2. A Study of Radar Meteorological Findings Related to Radar Weather Detection and Air Traffic Control, Report No. RD-66-65, NAFEC, October 1966

3. Introduction to Weather Radar, U.S. Department of Commerce, April 1969

4. Weather for Controllers (ETM 7-0-1), Department of Transportation, FAA Academy, May 1971

5. Radar Observes the Weather, Louis J. Battan Doubleday and Company, 1962